INDUSTRIAL PSYCHOLOGY AND ORGANISATIONAL BEHAVIOUR

DR. GIRISHBALA MOHANTY
Professor of Psychology
Former Member,
Orissa Staff Selection Commission, Cuttack
Formerly Director,
Higher Education, Orissa

KALYANI PUBLISHERS
LUDHIANA • NEW DELHI • NOIDA (U.P.) • HYDERABAD
CHENNAI • KOLKATA • CUTTACK • GUWAHATI • COCHIN

KALYANI PUBLISHERS

Head Office

B-1/1292, Rajinder Nagar, **Ludhiana**-141 008 • Ph : 0161-2760031

Administration Office

4779/23, Ansari Road, **Daryaganj,** New Delhi-110 002
Ph : 011-23271469, 23274393, 23278688

Works

B-16, Sector-8, **NOIDA** (U.P.)

Branches

1, Mahalakshmi Street, T. Nagar, **Chennai**-600 017 • Ph : 044-24344684
110/111, Bharatia Towers, Badambadi, **Cuttack**-753 009 (Orissa) • Ph : 0671-2311391
3-5-1108, Narayanaguda, **Hyderabad**-500 029 • Ph : 040-24750368
10/2B, Ramanath Mazumdar Street, **Kolkata**-700 009 • Ph : 033-22416024
Arunalaya, 1st Floor, Saraswati Road, Pan Bazar, **Guwahati**-781 001 • Ph : 0361-2731274
Koratti Parambil House, Convent Road, **Cochin**-682035 • Ph : 0484-2367189

O-25746 05

Reprinted, 2018

First Edition, 1997
Reprinted, 1999, 2001, 2004, 2006
Second Revised and Enlarged Edition 2010
Reprinted, 2014
978-81-272-6004-0

PRINTED IN INDIA
At Kalyani Printings, B-15, Sector 8, NOIDA
and published by Mrs. Usha Raj Kumar for
Kalyani Publishers, New Delhi-110 002

Dedicated
to
the sacred memory of
My Parents

Acknowledgements

I acknowledge my indebtness to Houghton Mifflin Company, U.S.A., Publishers of *Industrial Psychology,* N.R.F. Maier (1965) and Prentice Hall of India Private Limited, New Delhi, Publisher of *Industrial Psychology* by J. Tiffin and E.J. McCormick (1971) for their permission to use certain figures and few brief quotations from the above books. I am also grateful to Harper and Row Publishers, U.S.A., Publishers of the book *Industrial Pschology Its Theoretical and Social Foundations* written by M.L. Blum and James C. Naylor (1968) to which reference has been made in the book and from which some quotations have been used. I am indebted to all investigators and authors to whom I have referred in the text.

My thanks are due to M.C. Mohanty, P.C. Maharana, T. Tripathy, R.K. Ransingh who helped in the preparation of the final manuscript. Lastly, I express my appreciation to my sons Dr. Aaron Mohanty and Dr. Atanu Mohanty for their constant inspiration and encouragement to complete the book.

GIRISHBALA MOHANTY

Foreword

Industrial Psychology is a subject which is of signal importance to a country which is on the path of rapid socio-economic development. Without creation of wealth no programme of development can be successful. Creation of wealth largely involves work in an organised setup. Experience of functioning of industries in the West over many years has brought into the foreground the importance of the human factor in work. Today anyone concerned with economic progress as well as welfare of people cannot afford to ignore this factor. It is equally important both for the sake of efficiency and for the welfare of the individual. Therefore, it is gratifying that Dr. (Prof.) Girishbala Mohanty has prepared a textbook of industrial psychological in which she has comprehensively dealt with the human aspect of work especially in the industrial setup. It is also very gratifying to note that she has not only covered almost all the important topics which come within the purview of industrial psychology but has put in a separate chapter on the growth of development of industrial psychology in India. Though this chapter is a short one, it is hoped that it would stimulate the readers to put the subject in the proper socio-cultural perspective of their country so that the teaching would be more meaningful and relevant. Further, the book deals with the newer lines of a development of this subject, namely organisational behaviour.

The book has a very wide and comprehensive coverage. It is lucid in style and covers the syllabus of industrial psychology that is common in most of the universities in this country. I have no doubt that not only the teachers and students of industrial psychology would find this book to be valuable but all persons concerned with various aspects of industry will discern may things of vital interest in it.

Durganand Sinha
Director
A.N.S. Institute of Social Studies
Patna
December 6, 1982

Preface to the Second Revised Edition

Keeping in view the present courses of studies of various Indian Universities, autonomous colleges and need of the students of engineering colleges of India the book Industrial Psychology and Organisational Behaviour has been revised.

In the present revised edition four more chapters namely Stress in Organisations and its Effect on Performance, Mental Health of Organisational Employees, Career Planning and Career Counselling and Effective Communication and Organisational Success have also been added to the existing chapters. Also more recent studies and facts have been added to the existing chapters.

My efforts would be worth doing if the revised edition of this book will be useful as a text book for the students of psychology, business management, engineering and various industrial organisations. It is hoped that the revised edition will also be helpful as a source book to candidates preparing for various civil services and other careers including persons occupying leadership and executive positions in various organisations and industries. The book has been written in a lucid style and particularly in the Indian context which would probably be helpful to persons interested in area of industrial psychology and organisational behaviour.

GIRISHBALA MOHANTY
Mohanty House, Friends Colony
Cuttack

Preface to the First Edition

More often than not readers wonder, why prefaces are ever written. It is also unknown if they are ever read by every reader. Victor Hugo, in his preface to his outstanding book 'Crom Well' has mentioned that one really inspects the cellar of the house after visiting its salons, or examines the roofs of a tree after eating its fruit. Though the readers of this title will judge it in view of its contents, style and lucidity and not by the preface offered by the author, a preface is however, necessary as it indicates in a comprehensive manner the contents and purpose of the book.

In view of the need of a simple, lucid book on Industrial Psychology and Organisational Behaviour in the Indian context, the book has been prepared. Further, the rapid changes in the field of industrial and organisational psychology during the last three decades also inspired me to write this book. Scientific knowledge of human behaviour in industries and organisations has also become essential in the modern era. Rapid changes in the problems and approaches of industrial psychology started with the classic Hawthorne studies. The findings of these illuminating studies changed the scope of industrial psychology from machine to man, *i.e.*, studying man in relation to work. The approach thus become more worker oriented than work oriented. The socio-psychological conditions of the workers received increased attention. The emphasis was thus placed on developing and establishing certain underlying behavioural principles for the greater understanding of man's behaviour in the work situation.

With this background the book reflects the basic principles, theories and problems of industrial psychology and organisational behaviour and their applications. Twentynine chapters have been included in this book keeping in view the syllabi of industrial and organisational psychology of undergraduate and postgraduate students of different universities of India. Emphasis on the organisational and social context of human work has been put in chapters like psychology in organisations, industrial incentives, employee-employer relationship, leadership and executive qualities, attitude, industrial conflict and frustration industrial absenteeism and labour turn over, decision-making and mental health. The fact that more than fifty per cent of the contents of the book have been devoted to social foundations of industrial psychology suggests the need for more employee oriented rather than work oriented research in modern industries and organisations.

Analysing the conditions of Indian employees in relation to work and work place the author has indicated the growing need for better employee-employer relationship. Prevalent dehumanised conditions of Indian workers can be improved by improvement in the socio-psychological and work climates of various organisations of different categories. This has been hinted in most of the chapters.

A survey of researches in industrial psychology in India before and after independence has been made in chapter three of the book. A special feature of this book is the critical analysis of the recent status of industrial psychology in India and the trend of researches in the area. The increasing interest in research on various areas of industrial psychology in India and the trend of reseaches in the area have been demonstrated by indicating the rapid rise in the number of studies conducted between 1970 and 1980. A full chapter has also been devoted to important Indian studies on industrial psychology and organisational behaviour published during 1991-92.

Separate chapters have also been devoted to scientific management, individual differences. Hawthorne Studies, Testing in Industry, Job Analysis, Vocational selection and placement and Human Engineering. In chapter 23 road accidents in India and the personality of safe and unsafe drivers have been discussed. In almost all chapters reference to available Indian studies has been made with an attempt to include the latest available findings in the field.

It is therefore hoped that this title Industrial Psychology and Organisational Behaviour will serve the needs of the students and teachers as a text book and as a hand book respectively. It will also be useful as a text book for the students of business management, industrial organisations, personnel psychology and other related disciplines. It can also be helpful to managements and persons occupying executive and leadership positions in different organisations as a source book. It is thus hoped that persons concerned with different aspects of organisations and industries will find this book most helpful particularly in the Indian context.

1997

GIRISHBALA MOHANTY

Contents

Introduction

Emergence of Industrial Organisational Psychology

After the industrial revolution and as a result of expansion of various industrial setups in different parts of the world, industrial and organisational psychology emerged as a very significant branch of applied psychology. Particularly the concern of the employers for the welfare of their employees brought tremendous changes in the welfare policies of public sector and private sector undertakings. To add to this, the findings of the famous Hawthorne studies indicated glaringly that the psychological climate of the work situation, attitude of the employers towards the employees, employee-employer relationship and the cooperation and understanding among the employees and employers are of paramount importance not only for higher production but also for avoiding and preventing all sorts of tensions, misunderstandings and communication gap between the worker and the boss. The significant and illuminating findings of the Hawthorne studies conducted over 12 years not only changed the production oriented attitudes of the employers to worker oriented attitude but there was also a sincere feeling that the approach to deal with the workers should change from economic to social. They clearly understood that worker oriented attitude is always conducive for better production than work oriented attitude.

The managements of various industries and organisations also realised that financial benefits and higher salary will not necessarily yield higher output without having considerations for proper human relations and sympathetic treatment towards the employees. Man is not a machine, but is a living being of flesh and blood having the capacity to feel the insult, having the emotions and sentiments to enjoy and obey as well as to revolt and assert. He has the desire and love for power, prestige and recognition. Mere money without good behaviour may not extract from them higher production as money is only a means and not the end.

With these realizations by the management and the desire to establish friendly relationship between the employees and the employers, the need for the emergence of a specific brand of psychology called the Industrial and organisational psychology arose. Inspite of the machines and mechanical devices used in various modern industries, man-power is necessary to deal with the machines. Thus to find out the various psychological and personal problems of the men and women at work in various industrial and organisational setups the need for the development of industrial and organisational psychology was felt. Even around 1945, engineers and psychologists worked together to solve the varied problems related to man and machine. Gradually industrial psychology became more interested in the social aspects of the working man which were avoided at the initial stage. The social foundations of industrial psychology were stressed by the upcoming psychologists in view of the growing importance of attitude, employee-employer relationship, job satisfaction, non-financial incentives and problem of supervision and leadership etc. It was also strongly felt that the problem of mental health of the workers engaged in industries and organisations should get special attention in addition to the above factors. Thus, after the initial emergence of industrial and organisational psychology as a separate branch of psychology, subsequently the trend changed from economic to social aspects. Optimum emphasis was put on human beings and their needs, demands and overall welfare measures. With more and more findings coming to picture various empirical researches were conducted inside the industries and organisations as well as in the workshops and laboratories under natural and controlled conditions respectively. Due attention was focussed on human and social problems related to work, work space and job requirements etc. Problems related to the prestige and recognition of merit of the workers, good behaviour, cooperation from the management, supervision and leadership, group dynamics and group interaction, in group and out group feeling, conflict and tension due to the communication gap between the worker and management and a host of other related problems were tried to be solved through the appointment of industrial psychologists and personnel managers.

Thus the study of men at work by psychologists and personnel managers brought a new chapter in the history of industrial and organisational psychology. However in the early part of the 1960s organisational psychology began to enter the field of industrial psychology, and since then it has occupied a major position in concerning itself with the problems of men working in various organisations. Currently the various companies and industries engage psychologists and personnel officers to act as a bridge between the employees and the employers relating to the problems of both the parties. It has become a basic necessity. Industrial and organisational psychologists also are doing great job in the area of advertising and consumer psychology. They apply their psychological knowledge to the world of advertisement and consumer psychology. They use various tactics in advertisement to allure the common man. They also help in marketing research survey and public opinion research. Besides the emergence of industrial and organisational psychology was actually necessary to deal with the problems of salaries and wages job analysis, rating of employees, selection and training of new employees, dealing of employee problems, transfer, promotions and termination of employees, industrial hygiene and morale of the workers and a host of other related factors.

Thus the industrial and organisational psychologist has to tackle any problem relating to human beings. It has been noticed that he has to be concerned with more than 150 specific kinds of problems. The consultants attached to various industries, companies and organisations, who are basically industrial psychologists help in the conduction of psychological tests, recruitment and employee evaluation. They prepare testing programmes for various new recruits or already existing employees to improve training programmes for management personnel, supervisors high, middle and low level managers, and try to reform various techniques and principles in human relations organised in 1921 by a group of psychologists. The Psychological Corporation of U.S.A. is the oldest and largest firm for personnel and market research, professional examination and experimental laboratory. Some other consulting firms also specialise in constructing various materials and developing several advices based on empirical research related to behavioural science for various government and non-government organisations and industries. Tests are also developed for schools, colleges and for recruitment of defense personnel including police and intelligence bureau. The American Institute of Research and Behavioural Sciences carries diverse types of research programmes in education, organisational behaviour, training, human engineering etc. Several centres conduct research in marketing products and consumer psychology, and advertisement keeping an eye on the psychology of the consumer and making the job of the executives more interesting. Finally the industrial and organisational psychology has also helped in inter disciplinary research combining the efforts of psychologists, anthropologists, sociologists, economists, political scientists under one umbrella. Their combined efforts have made successful contributions to the phenomena of group dynamics relating to the formation, change or dissolution of the group. Inter group relations and tensions, communication problems, ingroup-outgroup relationship and their effects on group productions in various organisational set ups are also being studied through interdisciplinary research.

Though in 1901 Scott, a prominent psychologist discussed the important application of psychological principles to the field of advertisement in 1903, he published a book on the theory of advertising. This is the first dealing with the application of psychology to the field of business. Subsequently Scott extended psychology to other areas of business. Scott's contributions to the industrial and organisational psychology are so numerous that it is difficult to recall them in detail here. However Munsterberg became famous with his title "Psychology and Industrial Efficiency" published in 1913 and was somehow credited as the first industrial psychologists applying psychology to business. It is said that psychology and Industrial efficiency served as a model for the development of industrial psychology. Scott and some other psychologists founded the first psychological consulting firm in 1919 to solve their personnel problems in industry. Subsequently, other big firms were established. Thus the emergence as well as the importance of the need of studying the psychology of the employees working in industries ane organisations were actively felt.

1

The Nature, Scope and Problems of Industrial Psychology

THE CONCEPT OF INDUSTRIAL PSYCHOLOGY—NATURE AND DEFINITION

Industrial psychology, as an important branch of applied psychology makes a scientific study of the behaviour of the employees engaged in industrial organisations. Their behaviour is studied with special reference to production and efficiency. Industrial psychology further studies the problems and adjustment pattern of workers in field and laboratory situations. According to Tiffin and McCormick (1971), "Industrial psychology is concerned with the study of human behaviour in those aspects of life that are related to production, distribution and use of goods and services of our civilisation". In short, industrial psychology applies various techniques, theories and principles of psychology to study the multifarious problems of employees working in industries and organisations. In the words of Blum (1949), "Industrial psychology is simply the application or extension of psychological facts and principles to the problems concerning human relations in business and industry".

Harrell (1964) has defined industrial psychology as a complicated study of a number of things, but it is always primarily the study of people as individuals or in groups in the work situation. Harrell has therefore emphasised the importance of studying the worker as an individual in the work situation.

Blum and Naylor (1968) state that industrial psychology draws upon the facts, generalisations and principles of psychology. It uses the methods of psychology to study the industrial and organisational setups. Though industrial psychology applies the techniques of psychology to the industrial situation and the problems confronting it, it nevertheless modifies such procedures, and formulates new procedures and techniques to face and solve the conditions found on the job rather than in the laboratory. Industrial psychology also believes that scientific conditions must be objective and based upon facts gathered as a consequence of defined procedures.

HISTORICAL DEVELOPMENT

During the First and Second World Wars, when various industrial organisations and plants faced a number of problems related to production, efficiency and individual employees, the help and advice of industrial psychologists was in great demand. At this stage, industrial psychology received a special status, although it began in America in 1901, and in England soon after.

Observations and empirical studies indicate that the field of industrial psychology progressed rapidly from the first quarter of the twentieth century. The first book, namely, *The Psychology of Industrial Efficiency*, dealing with various problems of industry and the analysis of such problems from the psychological point of view, was written by Hugo Munsterberg in 1913. During the war years, the Fatigue Research Board was organised in Great Britain to discover the problems connected with hours of work, conditions of work, problems associated with fatigue and boredom, accident and safety and many other related matters. The problem of advertising and selling also drew the attention of industrial psychology, and soon after it expanded into researches around personnel selection, training and vocational guidance.

However, after the First World War, active interest was shown in industrial psychology, applied to human problems in industry. Thus, by 1925, social psychology of industry entered into the arena of industrial psychology and hence, group behaviour in organisations, theories of motivation, importance of communication, interpersonal relationship and allied areas were investigated.

The classic studies, started in 1927 by the famous Hawthorne group, which included Roethlisberger, Diskson, Whitehead and Homans with Professor Elton Mayo as the guiding star, contributed to the development of industrial psychology in a major way. The Hawthorne experiments which continued for over 12 years brought to light many significant findings. These findings ultimately changed the trend and approach of industrial psychology from economic to social, from the work-oriented attitude to a worker-oriented attitude.

During the Second World War, the applied psychology research unit of the Medical Research Council of Great Britain carried out several researches and investigations to solve many industrial and organisational problems.

Around 1945, engineering psychology, otherwise known as human engineering, became a part of industrial psychology, when engineers and psychologists joined hands to solve the man-machine problem. Engineering psychology further increased its scope by studying human factors in the man-machine system.

With the changing status of industrial psychology from economic to social, the optimum emphasis was put on human beings who are mainly responsible for the production and distribution of goods. This change from the economic foundations to the social foundations could be possible due to the improved method of research work and because of the change in the outline of various human problems in industry. For instance, during the latter part of 1940 and in the 1950s, considerable attention was focussed on various human relations and social problems of industry, such as problems of supervision, group dynamics and group interaction, leadership and leadership training, employees' attitude, morale and job satisfaction and above all, the communication process.

In the beginning of the 1960s organisational psychology began to enter the area of industrial psychology and as such, special emphasis was given to the organisational inputs in the industrial situation. Currently, organisational psychology is concerned with the psychology of the employees, with special emphasis on man, work and production.

Gilmer (1971) has therefore rightly remarked, "While early industrial psychology was concerned with men and organisations, the present developments centre around multidisciplinary approaches to problems."

The psychologists who have made valuable contributions to the development of industrial psychology are Walter, Dill and Scott. To them we owe the beginning of industrial psychology in America. Similarly, Bingham, Moore, Strong, Munsterberg, Williams and Mayo, and few others have made brilliant and stimulating contributions to industrial psychology through their valuable researches and written books on the various problems of industry. Engineers like Taylor and Gilbreth have contributed to the development of the efficiency of workers and the economic development of industrial psychology. Scientific management and the time and motion study principles developed by them are still very much accepted and practised by modern organisations, of course, with some modifications. Subsequently Viteles (1932) and Ferguson (1962-63) proved to be very useful in popularising the various concepts and problems of industrial psychology through their valuable publications. Consulting firms and organisations have also played their respective roles in the development of industrial psychology. Journals, books and various professional organisations have also contributed significantly in enlarging the boundaries of industrial and organisational psychology.

The industrial psychology division of the American Psychological Association was established in 1945 and gave professional recognition to industrial psychology. Since then industrial psychology has gained ground and prospered speedily. After the Second World War, it spread over Europe, parts of Africa and Asia.

Though industrial psychology was a neglected branch of applied psychology in India, after the Second World War and particularly after Independence, it got special recognition from Indian psychologists. An eminent industrial and organisational psychologist of India, Professor Durganand Sinha (1971) has made a valuable survey of the important topics of research in industrial psychology in India.

With the establishment of various university centres and institutes in India, research in industrial psychology has been accelerated after 1950. The Institute of Management at Ahmedabad, the Institute of Psychological Researches, Patna, the Ahmedabad Textile Industries Research Association, the Sree Ram Centre for Industrial Relation, the South Indian Textile Research Association, the Indian Institute of Science, Bangalore, and the department of Applied Psychology, Calcutta, have stimulated a number of valuable and original research in industrial psychology. Indian industrial and organisational psychologists like Ganguly, Bose, Sinha, Kakar, Chatterjee and Mohanty, etc., have enriched the field of industrial psychology in India despite several handicaps and lack of facilities for research.

In 1970, the division of industrial psychology was renamed as the division of industrial and organisational psychology. Meltzer (1960-1969) has given a valuable account of the more recent history of industrial and organisational psychology.

As Gilmer (1971) points out, Mccollom, Wickert, Miname and Berrien, while studying the development of industrial psychology throughout the world, have found its importance in America, Western Europe, and Japan. In Russia, until 1960, industrial psychology remained a neglected branch of applied psychology.

Berton (1972) has made an important survey of the major topics of research in industrial psychology in Japan. His survey report indicated that environmental and mass media effects, human factors, personnel selection, communication, group dynamics, sensory interaction and perceptual judgement and the organic approach to human behaviour are the main areas of investigation.

Analysing the present status of industrial psychology in Columbia, Sutter (1971) remarks that, although the need of industrial psychologists and research in industrial psychology is very strong, the opportunities for doing so are scanty. Hence, very little research has been conducted in industrial psychology in Columbia. Moreover, many Columbia business managers and directors are aware of the urgency of industrial psychologists in industrial organisations. Fortunately, interest in this area is growing.

FIELD AND SCOPE

It has been rightly remarked by Viteles (1932) that the principles of scientific management developed by Taylor and his pupils greatly influenced the growth and development of industrial psychology in two directions. Firstly, it guided the type of investigations conducted by the industrial psychologists and secondly, it established firmly the economic objectives of industrial psychology.

A bulletin issued by the National Institute of Industrial Psychology of Great Britain gives the following as the scope of industrial psychology stated by Viteles (1932) :

1. Study of the requirements of occupations and the elaboration and application of suitable tests so as to secure (*a*) the scientific selection of workers, and (*b*) more reliable guidance for children when choosing their life's work.
2. Investigation of the best methods of applying human energy with regard to (*a*) the elimination of unnecessary movements, (*b*) advantageous distribution of rest periods, and (*c*) the reduction of monotony and increase of interest, etc.
3. Realisation of conditions (*a*) in regard to lighting, ventilation, etc. which lead to maximal health, comfort and well-being of the worker, and (*b*) in regard to methods of payment, labour representation, etc. which lead to the best relations between management and labour.
4. Training of workers with reference to psychological principles involved in learning and habit formation among the beginners, the training of foremen, etc.
5. Study of the factors influencing the sale of products, *e.g.* advertising, designing etc.

Viteles holds the view that while making a comparison of the scope of industrial psychology already referred to with that of principles of scientific management, the degree to which psychologists have accepted Taylor's contribution to industrial psychology is clearly evident. Though later psychologists have accepted Taylor's efficiency principle on the whole, they are also critical about the over-emphasis of Taylorism on efficiency and output. They hold that "industrial efficiency may be achieved without the sacrifice of individual welfare" (Viteles, 1932).

With the change in the economic orientation of man to the social and psychological arena, the welfare and happiness as well as the comfort of the workers have been given top priority. Any attitude which neglects the welfare of the individual employees has been criticised by the modern psychologists.

Recently, the human problems associated with industry have undergone tremendous changes. The technological advancement and the problem arising out of it has also brought a significant change in the field and scope of industrial psychology. Though industrial psychology started with the problem of advertisement and selling, it rapidly expanded into a full-fledged branch of applied psychology, keeping itself busy with various problems relating to human behaviour in industry. More recently, the current trend towards automation has brought about major additions and alterations in the nature and organisation of human work.

In the opinion of Tiffin and Mccormick (1971), "the application of psychology to problems of industry generally cover the following area :

1. Personnel psychology, which is concerned with such matters as the selection, placement and training of personnel and related matters.
2. Social industrial psychology, which is concerned with the behaviour of people within the organisations and in groups, the design of man-machine systems and other equipment, facilities, work environment and the job in consideration of human capabilities and limitations.
3. Consumer psychology, which is concerned with the behaviour of people when they are serving in their role of consumers in our economy".

In other words, industrial psychology today is primarily concerned with problems of organisation, communication process, employee-employer relationship, supervisor, leadership and the method of supervision, incentives both financial and non-financial, selection, placement and evaluation of employees, problems of individual differences, special environment and working conditions, problems of accident and safety and fatigue, monotony and boredom. Human engineering, industrial conflict and frustration, psychological stress, absenteeism and labour turnover, job and work analysis, attitude, job satisfaction and morale, consumer and advertisement psychology market research, mental health of workers career selection and career counseling socio-psychological environment of employees in public and private sector etc. also come within its purview. It is, therefore, obvious that the systems and principles of modern industrial psychology are mostly developed with the purpose of studying the human problems in industry.

Though, by the first half of the twentieth century, the field of industrial psychology centred around the above problems, more recently, there has been a further change in the emphasis on different problems of industrial and organizational employees. For the last three decades especially, more emphasis is being given on industrial organisational psychology with special relation to work and production, managerial training, executive behaviour and human engineering mental health and stress and organisational.

In short, industrial psychology today deal with a wide range of human problems involved in the production and distribution of goods for the use of mankind.

AIMS AND OBJECTIVES

Improvement of efficiency and output in industry and organisations is no doubt one of the chief objectives of industrial and organisational psychology. In every organisation where goods are manufactured, increased production with low expenditure has been the important consideration in determining the destiny of the plant or organisation. One has to accept the fact that Bertan industry or an organisation it has largely largely accepted psychology as an aid which can improve production with less expenditure and good mental and physical health.

Viteles (1932) opines that "the acceptance of psychology in industry represents that the machine is insufficient in itself to meet the demands of industry and industrial civilisation. It is recognised that perfect as they may be, machines can only be used to advantage by properly selected and adequately trained men conversant with methods for most efficiently employing the energy at their disposal and willing to do so." He further adds that ingenuity and inventiveness in perfecting machines must be supplemented by a complete utilisation of human energy, human ability and human motives to the human and social problems of employees in industry and in bringing solution to it.

The basic aim of an industrial psychologist is, therefore to help the worker to produce the maximum with minimum cost, minimum effort and maximum comfort.

While giving importance to more production, he also keeps in view the fact that the worker is basically a human being with an ego and a sense of self-respect. He is also aware of the fact that every worker is basically a human being first, with a personality which has the desire for power, prestige and recognition, and that he is a worker afterwards. The modern industrial psychologists have criticised those industrialists who consider the employee as a worker first and human being next afterwards. With this changing outlook towards employees the industrial psychologist has realised that money may be a basic necessity for the employee to maintain his livelihood, but it is never the end. It is only a means to achieve the end and under no circumstances should so much of emphasis and importance be given to money alone.

Maier (1970) has therefore rightly commented, "The aim of industrial psychology is not primarily to obtain greater output, but to give the worker greater ease at his work. Ease does not mean physical ease but also mental ease". This has been extended to organisations also.

Industrial psychology also aims to discover the best possible human conditions in work, the choice of the best vocations according to the ability and aptitude of the individuals, the selection of the most suitable workers, the most effective way of avoiding fatigue, monotony and boredom and the best possible incentive plans. It also aims to discover the cause and remedy of irritation, discontentment and unrest, suitable methods of training the labourers, supervisors and executives and methods of allocating the needless efforts and the strain due to ill-considered arrangement of machines, etc. Industrial psychology is also concerned with the construction of tests, questionnaires and rating scales and other types of instruments, the administration and scoring of tests and questionnaires, interviewing individuals for collection of data, evaluation of employees, planning researches, surveys and studies. Its aim is also to study the psychological climate of the work situation and the human side of management which would counteract and over emphaise the economic aspect of Taylor and Gilbreth. Industrial psychology also attempts to train people to use safety devices, to develop consciousness in using preventive measures, to avoid accidents and to motivate the workers to give the best in them for the benefit of both the employees and the employers.

While giving his views on the aims of industrial psychology Blum (1949) has commented, "Industrial psychology offers a dynamic solution to the perplexing problems which confront our industrial society and economic system. It is a means of encouraging and promoting democracy in industry and thereby enhancing the satisfaction of the employers and the employees".

Emphasising the tremendous importance of the employee as a social human being with the capacity to feel and experience and having the need for love, security and sympathy, Blum has further remarked, "The aim of industrial psychology should be the satisfaction of man, not of any man to the advantage of others. Men must be free to express their feelings, to reach goals, produce and develop as secure individuals." To add to this Mace (1948) has stated: "A new chapter in the history of industrial psychology opened when the scientists began to enquire what was implied by the sociability of man in the work situation. The facts of informal organisation and its impact upon the motivation of the individuals then came as a blinding revelation. Industrial psychology ceased to be a minor branch of applied physiology of industrial engineering and became a major branch of social psychology".

Jamieson (1974) has discussed three current trends in the industrial and organisational psychology :

(*i*) The continuing trend towards more social orientation,

(*ii*) A trend towards more theory development, and

(*iii*) Changes in graduate education.

He has further noted the multidisciplinary scores of the mainly opportunistic nature of industrial organisational psychology with the lack of professional identity among industrial psychologists. It is suggested that the progressive trend towards "social orientation" in industrial organisational psychology may create slight feelings of nostalgia among psychologists raised in a differential tradition. It has also been apprehended that the trends in graduate education may raise certain problems to alarm psychologists who are interested in the long term validity of the field.

MAJOR PROBLEMS

Modern industries face a wide variety of problems such as the situational, the social and the personal. Unfortunately, each and every person is not capable of performing each and every job efficiently because of individual difference in ability and capacity, interest and aptitude. Besides, for the efficient operation and control of machines competent persons having not only the ability but also the interest and the aptitude for such jobs are to be selected. Usually, the problem arises in selecting competent and qualified persons for each job and in finding suitable work for each employee.

Though such problems change from time to time, the major problems which an industrial psychologist faces in an industry are associated with work, units of production, training, motivation, incentives, employee-employer relationship and selection and placement of workers. The problem of attitude, morale, and job satisfaction, industrial unrest such as strikes and lockouts, and sometimes violence, absenteeism and labour turnover, supervision and evaluation of employees along with the problems of organisation, equipment design, are also some of the major problems faced by the industrial psychologist.

But with the shift from the economic foundations to the social foundations of industrial psychology the problems of industrial psychology has also changed. An industrial psychologist today is mainly concerned with the psychological problems of industry.

According to Maier (1970) the lack of personal contact between employee and employer makes it impossible for one to know the other closely and intimately. The absence of direct contact leads to absence of first hand knowledge of each other. As a result the social distance and gap in communication between both the parties become wider and confidence in each other wanes.

It is an accepted fact that the attitude, morale and employee-employer relationship influence the way in which the worker will work, the units which he will produce, and finally, how he will cooperate with the management. Therefore, industrial psychology has devoted itself to solving these problems leading to industrial unrest and tension.

The problem of job analysis should also be attended to, as the abilities necessary for each job should be found out and the person best suited for each job selected. After a careful and judicious selection and by teaching and training men for jobs, the worker's adjustment to his work improves and his satisfaction with job as well as efficiency increases. This substantially improves out put level and job satisfaction.

The problem of fatigue, monotony and boredom needs the special attention of psychologists. How to do more work with the same amount of energy is an industrial problem which should be solved by psychologists and men with a scientific knowledge of the subject.

The problem of accident has a strong psychological aspect. Some may have more accidents despite all situational and mechanical precautions. The problem can be solved by developing safety habits and making proper placement of men on the basis of psychological test scores. These are psychological tools for accident prevention. The problems of factory environment such as illumination, ventilation and noise, etc. need study by the industrial psychologists along with suitable suggestions to improve the conditions of the factory environment. These are conditions to which the workers react and they definitely influence his degree of fatigue, boredom, attitude, motive and, above all, the level of production.

Besides, problems of absenteeism and labour turnover, industrial tension and unrest, etc. are of major importance which should be attended by psychologists.

The role of organisational structure in labour management relations has created fresh problems for modern organisational psychologists. With the rapid technological changes, organisations and industries are also changing their structure, value system, aims and objectives and quite obviously employees resist to such changes, thus creating problems for the management.

However, with the intimate contact and active cooperation between the industrialists and industrial psychologists, the multifarious problems of industry with special reference to labour management problems can be better solved through essential and meaningful research.

ROLE OF A PSYCHOLOGIST IN INDUSTRIES AND ORGANISATIONS

Due to the rapid technological changes in different parts of the world, division of labour and automation of work, work has become mechanical, uninteresting and monotonous. Technological changes have also led to conflict between man and machine, man and management and intellectual and emotional factors. Such problems along with the resistance of the workers to change have multiplied the functions of a psychologist in industrial organisations. He is, on the whole, interested in an effective utilisation of human resources. Today, psychologists not only work in industrial and other organisational settings, but also in civil service commissions, rural and community development schemes, military organisations, etc. They also work as consultants in various public and private sectors.

Currently, the industrial and organisational psychologist has shifted his attention and interest from the physical environment of a work situation to the scientific and clinical studies of people who work in this environment. He is greatly interested in the study of supervision and leadership types, employee-employer relationship and change of attitude of the workers. From various field and laboratory investigations, a psychologist has been able to accept the fact that the participative, cooperative and democratic human relations approach is more conducive to efficiency and all-round improvement of the employees and employers.

A psychologist has also to play an important role in planning tile structure of an organisation so that the needs of the employees can be satisfied in a more suitable way. The psychologist also works in collaboration with engineers when the engineers face various problems. While designing machines, tile engineers seek tile advice of the psychologists in order to be aware of the abilities and limitations of individual workers.

However, the most important function of a psychologist is to deal with the frustration, conflict, stresses and strains of the workers caused by the industry variables and organisational structure. It is true that hard work is not so dangerous or harmful for the worker as the stresses, strains mental tensions and frustrations of life. Under these circumstances, the industrial or organisational psychologist has a tremendous responsibility. He helps the workers as well as the executives to uncover many of their repressed and suppressed feelings, thereby helping them to see their own problems and solve them judiciously. They work as a mirror and show proper guidance to solve their varied problems whether personal or job related.

In the beginning, the management and industrialists were utilising the services of the psychologists in the construction and administration of various psychological tests. But now the testing work is being covered by other people while psychologists are engaged in giving advice and counsel to the industrial relations and personnel department. A modern psychologist also renders his services by working as a mediator between the management and the labour union to contract negotiations. Research in consumer and advertisement psychology is another important function of the modern industrial psychologist. Not only are his services needed for planning the design of a study or the investigation of morale, but he also gives training to supervisors and executives, a fact which has drawn the attention of every management in a major way.

Thus the modern industrial or organisational psychologist has to deal with innumerable problems relating to human behaviour within the industry or organisation. For these reasons at present, psychologists are so much in demand that they are employed in almost all industries and organisations on a permanent basis.

Realising the important and diverse role a psychologist has to play in an industry or an organisation, Gilmer (1971) has remarked, "From personnel selection to training, from supervision to job evaluation, from career planning to labour relations, the industrial psychologist moves in a wide and ever varying scene".

QUESTIONS

1. Discuss the practical importance of studying industrial and organizational psychology.
2. Define industrial psychology. Discuss its nature and scope.
3. What is meant by industrial psychology ? What are its main aims and objectives ?
4. Critically examine the historical development of industrial psychology.
5. "Industrial psychology is simply an application or extension of psychological facts and principles to the problems concerning human relations in business and industry". Critically examine the above statement, citing suitable empirical studies.

REFERENCES

Bertin, Morton A. *A Review of Some Psychological Researches in Japan,* Arlington, Va, U.S. Deptt. of Navy, No. ONR, 32, 1972, p. 22.

Blum, M.L. and Naylor, J.C. *Industrial Psychology: Its Theoretical and Social Foundations,* Harper and Row, 1968.

Ferguson, L.W. *The Heritage of Industrial Psychology*, Hart Ford, Conn, Finley Press, 1963.

Gilmer, Bvon Haller, *Industrial and Organisational Psychology,* McGraw Hill, Kogakusha Ltd., 1971.

Harrell, T.W. *Industrial Psychology*, New York, 1964.

Jamieson, Bruce D. Current Trends in Industrial Organisational Psychology, *New Zealand Psychologist,* 1974, Vol. 3, pp. 28-36.

Male, C.A. *Satisfaction to Work Occupational Psychology.* 1948.

Maier, W.R.F. *Psychology in Industry,* Oxford & IBH Publishing Co. Pvt. Ltd., New Delhi, 1970.

Mccollom, L.N. Psychologists in Industry, in the United Kingdom and West Germany, *American Psychologist,* 1960, Vol. 15, pp. 58-64.

Meltzer, *A scope and References of Industrial Psychology,* 1960-1969, Personnel Psychology.

ICSSR, New Delhi, *A Survey of Research in Psychology,* Popular Prakashan, 1932.

Sutter, Christien and Morales, Manuel. Present States of Industrial Psychology in Colombia, *International J. of Psychology*, 1971, Vol. 6 (4), pp. 323327.

Mccormick, E.J. *Industrial Psychology*, Prentice-Hall of India Private Limited, New Delhi, 1971.

Viteles, M.S. *Industrial Psychology*, Norton, 1932.

2

Psychology in Organisations

A review of the historical development of Industrial psychology after the industrial revolution in particular, indicates that following the Second World War and with the classic findings of the Hawthorne studies, industrial psychologists shifted their interest from the production and working environment to social interaction and human behaviour in industry. Thus, with the changing status of industrial psychology from the economic to the social field, from machine to man, experimental social psychology and clinical and engineering psychology joined hands to help the personnel psychologist; the line supervisor or the training director to solve many problems facing the industry. Moreover, with the growth and development of various organisations throughout the world, psychologists extended the scope of industrial psychology to the study of organisations. In the early stage the psychologies were interested only in industry, but subsequently then took care of organisations also.

While psychologists were thus getting interested in the social and clinical aspects of human behaviour in various plants and organisational set-ups, there was an urgent need for the classical industrial psychologists and human relation psychologists to work in collaboration with each other, to solve varied industrial and organisational problems relating to man and production. This contributed to the development of organisational psychology throughout the world. With the publication of *The Organisational Man* by White (1956), especially, the role played by various business organisations in human life has been recognised.

Thus Mills (1953) rightly comments, "Organisation is now being studied from the point of view of its effects, not only on behaviour within the organisation, but also in the way it determines community life and social and cultural values" (quoted in Gilmer, 1971).

CONCEPT

As already mentioned, organisational psychology is a comparatively new area in which various disciplines like psychology, management, sociology, mathematics and economics have been involved. The field of organisational psychology is so vast that it not only studies the behaviour of the individuals within the organisation, but also the manners in which it determines our social and cultural values including community life.

The direct and face-to-face relationship between different numbers of the organisation belonging to different status creates a member of socio-psychological problems. To solve such problems, current organisational psychologists have been particularly interested in the study of leadership, supervisory relationships, human relations and communications.

WHAT IS MEANT BY AN ORGANISATION ?

An organisation is contributed by so many disciplines that it has become quite difficult to define an organisation, keeping in view its essential characteristics. So far as the definition of an organisation is concerned, the different disciplines like sociology, psychology, mathematics and economics do not take a common stand on the subject.

However, in spite of the differences of opinion, two essential characteristics of an organisation can be mentioned. Briefly, each and every orgainsation must have a structure and purpose. On the basis of these two basic characteristics, organisations may be classified into various types, such as industrial organisations, social organisations, political and religious organisations, commercial and business organisations, religious and cultural organisations, etc.

According to Bakke (1959) every organisation should have the following specific characteristics such as the name of the organisation, the functions of the organisation; its main purpose and goal, for the realisation of which every member of the organisation makes some significant contribution, the distinct and specific principles of and policies of the organisation, the mutual rights and duties of the members of the organisation and lastly, the significance and ideals of tile orgnisation. Bakke concludes, "It is essential that the organisation as a whole means a few things definite, that the name of the organisation calls to mind unique, indentifying features. This image and its content is labelled as the organisational charter".

In short, every organisation has its own special characteristics which are unique in their own way, and different from other organisations.

IMPORTANCE

Realising the tremendous importance of organisations in human life, Leavitt (1961) holds that it is high time one considered changing the name of industrial psychology to organisational psychology. Explaining the nature of organisational psychology, Leavitt (1961) comments, "Organisational psychology occupies itself with the study of organisations and the organisational process. It is as much descriptive as normative, as much more basic as applied, as much interested in developing theories of organisational behaviour as ways improving organisational practice".

PURPOSE OF STUDYING

As already indicated, the field of organisational psychology is remarkably vast and it is allied to the human relations psychology. It also deals, to some extent, with experimental psychology and empirical sociology. Its boundary also touches economics and mathematics, operation research and computer science. It covers the human problems in governmental, semi-governmental and private organisations.

Keeping in view the vast area of organisational psychology, the industrial organisational psychologists study leadership and supervision relations, human relations and communications, the problem of decision making and mental health. Organisational psychology not only studies the men at work, but also the professor in the college, the doctor in the hospital, the executive in organisation, the worker while laying bricks, handling iron or loading cement. It also studies the psychological functions of the skilled, semi-skilled and unskilled workers while on job. It studies their leaders. Organisational psychology is also interested in studying the changing values of the society.

Though both classical industrial psychologists and organisational psychologists work together, the purpose of the latter is different from the former in that it gives major emphasis in understanding organisations and bringing improvement in them though it studies human behaviour in all sectors, special emphasis is given to the study of people in industrial situations.

Organisational psychology, in particular, is interested in the study of the psychological climate of the work situation. In other words, it refers to the personality of the supervisor or boss, whether he is democratic or authoritative, aggressive or submissive, passive or dominant, formal" or informal, friendly or impersonal, According to Gilmer (1967), "The personality of a company in many respects is a compositive of varied ways of behaving with the people within it". The importance of the supervisor has already been highlighted in the Hawthorne findings. It also studies the human side of management, and the behaviour of the first line supervisor towards the labourers and employees of the lower rank, their interpersonal relationships, etc. It studies the relationship between the labour and the management, their problems and frustrations, tensions and conflicts, gaps in communication, etc. It also makes attempts to solve many of their personal problems and brings improvement in them by bridging the gap in communication. Organisational psychology tries to study consumer psychology to determine the workers' needs, preferences and habits and advises the management to gear up production accordingly. The problem of the motivation of workers also comes under the study of organisational psychology. Analysing the basic needs of the employees, it tries to motivate them in the right direction. Realising the seriousness of the problem of accident in industrial organisations in particular, it tries to develop various techniques for the prevention of accidents, and to train people to use safety devices and to develop safety consciousness.

Application of various psychological tests for the judicious and scientific selection of employees, including supervisors and executives, and the training of the technicians and personnel, are the important duties of an organisational psychologist. An organisational psychologist also tries to reduce absenteeism and labour turnover rates in industries and organisations. He is also interested in improving and maintaining the internal health of the worker, giving counsel and guidance whenever necessary. Thus, organisational psychology studies human behaviour in all sectors with special emphasis on industry. In short, it is, more or less, an outcome of the contribution of classical industrial psychologists and human relations psychologists.

Kolb, Robin and Mcintyre (1974) in their recent book on organisational psychology, *i.e. An Experimental Approach,* have communicated the general psychological principles and skills to be applied to social and organisational situations. The book considers international preception, communication, leadership, inter-group relations, organisational structures and personal growth and career development.

Analysing the role of a psychologist in modern organisations, Saleh and McNeil (1973) have discussed the multifarious roles that psychologists usually play in the organisations. They have suggested that in carrying out the role of a psychologist in an organisation, individual difference may be important determining variable. They conclude that the psychologist must have a wide educational and experimental background in order to deal with the varied and complex problems of modern organisations.

ORGANISATIONAL STRUCTURE

The way in which an organisation is structured or organised is called the organisational structure. Every organisation has a formal structure. But the structure varies from organisation to organisation depending upon their specific characteristics. These factors are, however, interrelated. The success of an organisation, to a considerable extent, depends upon the organisational structure. The organisation should be structured in such a way that the members of the organisation are able to work efficiently.

Leavitt (1964) perceives an organisation as having the following characteristics :

1. The pyramidal shape which increases interpersonal competitiveness.
2. The hierarchical distribution of authority with a tendency to increase dependency.
3. The idea of individual responsibility with the hope that a complicated and big task can be cut down to individual size and pieces.
4. Large size with consequent difficulty of communication.

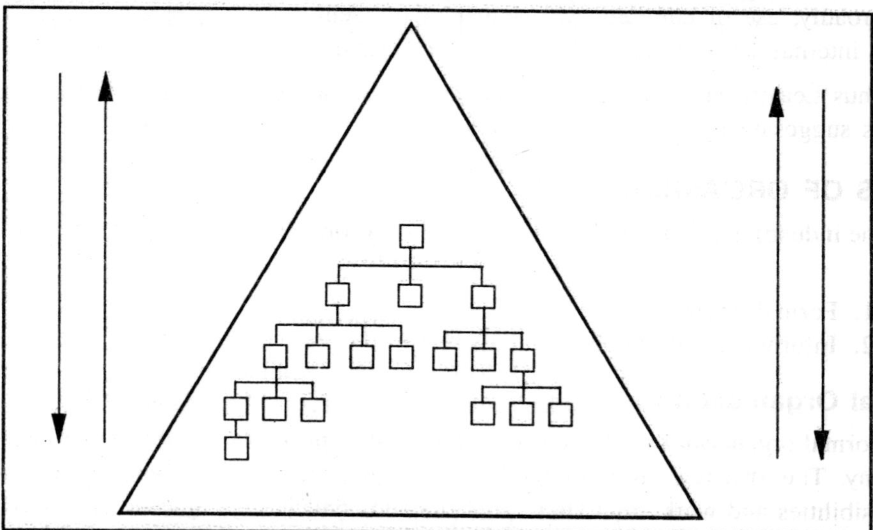

Fig. 2.1. The organisational pyramid.

The pyramidal type of structure is shown in the figure above. The pyramidal shape represents an organisation which traditionally assumes that the only important linkage in an organisation lies between superiors and subordinates.

Each box presented in the organisation chart refers to an organisational position. Blum and Naylor (1968) hold that these organisational positions are connected by organisational linkages. The linkage pattern between the units provides the structure to the entire organisation system.

The connecting links between the units are assumed to represent the relationships that exist between the superiors and subordinates. If no direct link is shown between the units, then no direct relationship is assumed to exist between them. In the opinion of Sayles and Strauss (1966), the pyramid type linkage assumes the following kinds of relationships between units :

1. Nearly all the contracts take the form of orders going down and reports of results going up the pyramid.
2. Each subordinate must receive instructions and orders from only one boss.
3. Important decisions are only made at the top of the pyramid.
4. Each superior has only a limited "span of control" that is, he supervises only a limited number of individuals.
5. An individual at any level (except at the top and bottom) has contact only with his boss above him and his subordinate below him.

Recent findings point out that the horizontal linkage may be of remarkable importance in the successful operation of an organisation, especially when the concept of team work emerges.

Leavitt (1964) holds the view that each of these characteristics carries a potential for intensifying the conflict and frustration of individuals and for increasing psychological pressures in the managers. He has suggested some organisational changes which can reduce some of the psychological problems created by organisations. Some of them are the recent trend in industry for decentralisation or division of work, separation of staff from line to distribute responsibilities more broadly, use of committees, opening of horizental communications, and providing some type of internal sense organ for detecting organisational conflict and troubles as they develop.

Thus Leavitt has given greater emphasis to the solution of psychological problems by the changes suggested by him in organisations.

TYPES OF ORGANISATIONS

From the industrial and organisational point of view, organisations may be divided into two major types :

1. Formal organisation
2. Informal organisation.

Formal Organisation

Formal organisations are usually guided by the specific rules and regulations framed by the company. The structure of a formal organisation is just like a pyramid. Division of duties, responsibilities and work are done to pre-arranged conditions. The structure and functions of the group is also determined according to these prescribed rules and regulations. The pyramidal structure of an organisation is just like a triangle, where the director of the company has got the highest position, the foreman or the supervisor gets the middle position and the workers get the lowest position in the pyramid. Hence, in formal organisations, three distinct categories of senior and subordinate employees are found. The problem of fatigue, monotony and boredom, incentive and other allied problems kill a lot of the time of the management in an organisation where there is strong competition. Formal organisations also give greater attention to the wage incentive system than to labour management problems.

Informal Organisation

In informal organisations there is no rigid rule and regulation like a club, a dramatic cultural association or a play group. The importance of informal organisations first came to light with the findings of the bank wiring observation room experiments of the famous Hawthorne studies. Roethlisberger and Dickson (1943) observed that due to the importance of informal organisations, workers intentionally restricted output. Needless to say, in every industry there is a formal organisation. Informal organisations, however, also develop within the group. They determine and regulate the functions and activities of its members.

Interest in the study of informal organisations has increased considerably of late. Research findings indicate that an informal organisation determines the level of production and extent of efficiency of its individual members. It is the informal organisation which determines the nature of attitude, morale, job satisfaction and finally, the level of production of the workers. Studies also suggest that those who go against the rules, regulations and guidelines of the informal organisation to which they belong, are isolated from the social group. This separation brings psychological dissatisfaction and insecurity among them. Those who belong to the informal organisation are known as the members of the 'in' group and those who go against the decision of the group are identified as members of the 'out' group.

Commenting on the formation of informal organisations, Barnard has held that so many small groups taken together constitute a big group or organisation. As the size of these small groups increases in course of time, their problems also increase. Since it is not possible to look after the needs and desires of all the members of such a big organisation, some develop the tendency to form small informal groups of their own with a particular goal in view. This goal may or may not have similarity with the purpose and aim of the management. Thus like the formal organisation the informal organisation has also some goal which every member of the group to tries to achieve. An informal organisation is move personalized than a formal organisation.

In informal organisations all members are united in a feeling of togetherness and loyalty. Each member of the group has a definite attitude towards the other members of the group. If the members of the group feel that the interest of its group and the interest of organisation are not identical, they at no cost, agree to support the management's interest. On the contrary, they engage themselves in such activities which oppose the interest and aim of the employer and management.

It is to be accepted that informal organisations have tremendous significance in regulating and controlling the moral and social activities of its individual members. The development of attitudes, values, thought processes, action tendencies, expectations, norms and goals of individual members also depend upon the informal organisaions :

By and large, the informal group determines, regulates and restricts the behaviour of the individual employees working in various plants and organisations.

RECENT STUDIES ON ORGANISATIONAL BEHAVIOUR

Hinrichs (1970) has reviewed the research literature in industrial and organisational psychology (with the exception of selection research between 1967 and 1969). The research has been divided into the following three areas :

(*a*) Job content and contextual factors consisting of the work environment, including task characteristics, the occupational role, leadership, communications and the reward system.

(*b*) Individual characteristics of ability, personality, motivation; needs, goals, expectancies and job attitudes.

(*c*) Specific personnel management topics related to industrial training, employment and minority groups, assessment, turnover, safety and accidents, labour relations, research methods and techniques. It is concluded that although significant progress has been observed towards the development and testing of theory, more longitudinal research designs, standardisation of research designs and instruments are necessary.

Analysing the specific studies conducted on organisational industrial psychology, it is found that Shartle (1964) Dunteman (1966), Vroom (1966) Findikonand and Sells (1966), Triandis (1967), Aiken and Haje (1968), O'Brien and Owens (1969), Bailey (1969), Burke (1970), Singh and Kiran (1971), Porter (1972), and Sinha (1973) have made significant contributions to the field of organisational psychology.

Shartle's study on three different types of organisations like a business firm, the military service and public high school, shows that in terms of values, similarities and differences exist among the three types of organisations. Shartle's work can be considered as a brilliant approach to gain further insight into the basic patterns of organisational behaviour. It has also stimulated valuable research in the area of organisational psychology.

Another valuable investigation undertaken by Dunteman (1966) is worth mentioning. Indus study he tried to find out some of the relationships among 84 different variables relating to different organisational characteristics, management qualities, incentive systems, characteristics of workers, personnel performance and organisational functions. The correlations among the 84 variables were factor analysed and 14 dimensions of organisational attributes and behaviours were isolated and interpreted. The 14 dimensions are size of organisation, economic growth, tardiness versus family responsibility, pay skill level, personnel tenure, ownership and concern for organisational interests, work force reduction and job mechanisation, technical personnel and control versus protection against human liabilities, minority group composition, improvement of working condition, retail sales personnel and authority-conflict behaviours, community and employee support versus work output restriction, employee selectivity, and allocation to labour versus product development.

Palmer (1961) conducted a similar study on 188 manufacturing firms in a southern metropolitan area taking 35 different organisational variables. He identified the following eight different organisational dimensions :

1. Retirement welfare
2. Cooperation with survey
3. Size of work force
4. Thrift benefits

5. Cost of sickness versus use of machinery
6. Job aversion
7. Insurance benefits
8. Product theft versus discount on products.

Analysing the studies of Shartle, Dunteman and Palmer, Blum and Naylor have noted the major differences between Shartle and the Dunteman-Palmer study. According to them, "Shartle's point of view has the implicit assumption that organisations are best studied through the kinds of behaviours or policies that the organisation exhibits (acts) and how "good" or "bad" they are. It is an evaluative, judgemental approach which in a sense, says that you must take society (that is people) into account in studying organisations". The Dunteman Palmer approach simply groups organisations on the basis of a number of more or less physical attributes. While both methods no doubt contribute to our knowledge of organisations, the approach of Shartle would some how seem to be the more psychologically richer of the two methods.

Studies of Dunteman-Palmer type have been criticised by Vroom (1966). He calls these studies "static correlational studies" and hints at an alternative method named "dynamic correlation studies" which gives an idea about the correlations between changes in organisational variables overtime, "radler than in simply looking at absolute values at one specific moment in time".

Research on international organisations has become very meagre. Triandis (1967) has reported a preliminary study on the interpersonal aspects of organisational relationship in Greek and American organisations. These findings indicated that interpersonal stereo-types were markedly influenced by the amount of contact between organisational members.

Aiken and Hage (1968) have studied the relationship between organisational interdependence and internal organisational behaviour for health and welfare organisations. The results revealed that the organisations with varied joint programmes have more active internal communication channels and somewhat more decentralised decision-making structures. No relationship was observed between the number of joint progranmtes and the degree of formalisation. It is held that organisations become more complex and innovative with increase in the division of labour.

Meyer (1968) conducted a study on the automation and bureaucratic structure. The findings suggested that the consultant's role and horizontal channels of communication are institutionalised in automated organisations. In this study, implications for classical organisational and human relations theories have been discussed.

Chatterjee (1972) studied the relationship between group cohesiveness and organisational factors organised in section units as primary work groups and completed questionnaires dealing with attitudes towards these groups. An index of group cohesiveness (defined as satisfaction with one's work group) was calculated and compared with organisational factors such as productivity, size of work group, length of service and satisfaction with managers. The data indicated that group cohesiveness was positively related to length of service in organisation, satisfaction with supervision, satisfaction with management and productivity, but negatively related to the size of the work group. The results suggest that the group cohesiveness may be a significant factor in effective management.

In a study on "organisational psychology, problems and prospects for the future", Schein (1973) has discussed the content, area and application of organisational psychology. This includes :

(*a*) Integration Of the process models of how organisations are arranged for task performace.

(*b*) Integration of non-human information systems with human processes in organisations.

(*c*) Concern for the total human being, and not only his productivity, eorale and potential.

(*d*) Development of the organisation's team-work, internal communication and interpersonal relationship.

The application of these principles to non-profit sector growth (education, urban and health systems) and to international growth are noted. An increase in mutual confidence between organisational professionals and psychologists is urged as a basis for changing theory into practice.

Sinha (1973) has contributed significantly to organisational psychology by a valuable study on the organisational climate and the problems of management in India. In this study, he has discussed the public and private sectors of Indian economy which have produced totally different climates of management. The findings of this study indicate that the private sector, evolving a family type organisations combined with bureaucracy has produced a task-oriented, exacting and personalised management. On the contrary, the public sector, an outcome of the extension of the government structure incorporation, the present political forces and participant management has led to a friendly, but unproductive bureaucracy.

In another investigation Lawer, Hall and Oldhum (1974) made an attempt to examine the contention that organisational structure and process are related to the organisational climate which is ultimately related to organisational performance and job satisfaction of employees. The findings of the questionnaire study, indicated that several organisational process variables were significantly related to the climate of organisation as perceived by scientists. The perceived that climate in turn was significantly related to measures of organisational performance and job satisfaction.

DECENTRALISATION OF ORGANISATIONS

With the rapid growth and expansion of various plants and organisations, the inevitable problem of centralisation or decentralisation arises.

According to Blum and Naylor (1968), decentralisation refers to the procedure of cutting up an organisation into more self-sufficient and independent units and then locating these units at different places. Thus, the total organisation is divided into different divisions and subdivisions or branches, and each branch is allotted some specific responsibilities and duties. For example, the advertisement, marketing, administrative and distribution divisions of a film production company may be separated and located at different places.

Advantages

Those who support decentralisation of big firms argue that decentralisation enhances efficiency by developing a desire to grow on its own, and develops a competitive spirit. It is also viewed that due to decentralisation, there is better division of labour and specialisation in work which ultimately reduces the expenditure of energy and cost of production. Efficiency can be increased by dividing the responsibilities.

Decentralisation may also increase job satisfaction in Certain cases, especially where the need for self-actualisation is fulfilled by doing something responsible and useful.

Disadvantages

When the corporation or organisation either in the public or private sector is divided and sub-divided into different units, communication, contact, and interpersonal relationship may be difficult.

Because of autonomy, there may be the feeling of separation or isolation among the employees and workers. Because of decentralisation the employees do not usually get the opportunity to come in contact with the management and executive. Consequently, they may have the feeling that their problems and difficulties are not attended to. According to Blum and Naylor (1968), decentralisation in some cases may lead to duplication of effort and unnecessary competition between sub-units. There is also the possibility that lack of proper communication may lead to unnecessary misunderstanding between the sub-units. Some are also of the opinion that the morale of the employees may be affected because of decentralisation, as it may be hard for an individual employee to get any real 'we' feeling necessary for the fulfilment of the aims and objectives of tile organisation. But researches are scanty in this area and such views have not been supported by experimental findings. Since the problem of decentralisation is of paramount importance owing to the growth of organisations, it is high time additional importance be given to scientifically based investigations on the various problems of decentralisation.

QUESTIONS

1. Critically examine the concept of organisational psychology.
2. What is meant by an organisation ? Evaluate the importance of organisational psychology in modern life.
3. What are the main purposes of studying behaviour in organisations ?
4. What do you understand by organisational structure ? How does a pyramidal shape of organisation represent ? Illustrate your answer with recent findings.
5. Make a critical analysis of different types of organisations.
6. Examine the recent findings on organisational behaviour.
7. What do you understand by decentralisation of organisations ? What are the main advantages and disadvantages of decentralisation ?

REFERENCES

Aiken, Michael and Hage, Jerald. Organisational Interdependence and Intra-organisational Structure, *American Social Review*, 1968, 33 (6), pp. 912-930.

Bailey, Gerald. A Study of the Effect of Staff Line Role and Organisational Climate Upon Task Estimates, *Dissertation Abstracts International*, 1969, 30, pp. 1-13.

Bakke, W.E. *Concept of Social Organisation* in M. Haire, *Modern Organisation Theory*, Wiley, New York, 1951.

Blum, M.L. and Naylor, J.C. Industrial Psychology : *Its Theoretical and Social Foundations*, Harper and Row, 1968.

Chattrejee, Amitav. The Organisational Variables of Group Cohesiveness, *Indian Journal of Psychology and Education*, 1972, Vols. 2, 3, pp. 43-52.

Dunteman, G.H. Organisational Conditions and Behaviour in 234 Industrial Manufacturing Organisations, Journal of Applied Psychology, 1966, 50, pp. 300-305.

Gilmer, B. von, Haller. *Industrial and Organisational Psychology,* McGraw Hill Koga Kusha Ltd., 1971.

Ganguli, H.C. *Structure and process of Organisations*, Bombay, Asia Publishing House, 1964.

Hinrichs, John, R. Psychology of men at work, *American Review of Psychology,* 1970, 21, pp. 519-554.

Jamieson, Bruce, D. Current trends in industrial organisational psychology. *New Zealand Psychologists,* 1974, 3, pp. 28-36.

Klob, D. David, A. Rubin, Irrin and Mclntyr, James M. *Organisational Psychology—An Experimental Approach,* (2nd ed.), Englewood Cliffs, N.J., Prentice-Hall, 1974.

Lawer, E.E., Hall, D.T. and Oldhum, Geg. R. Organisational Climate-Relationship to Organisational Structure, Process and performance, *Organisational Behr and Hum.* Pert., 1974, 11 (1), pp. 139-155.

Palmer, G.J. Jr. Incentive conditions and behaviour in 188 industrial manufacturing organisations, *Technical Report*, No. 3, 1961.

Roethlisberger, F.J. and Dickson, W.J. *Management and the Worker*, Harvard University Press, Cambridge, Mass, 1943.

Sehein, Edgar H. Organisational Psychology-Problems and Prospects for the Future, *Training and Development Journal*, 1973 (March), 27 (3), pp. 43-49.

3

Growth and Development of Industrial Psychology in India

INTRODUCTION

In any branch of applied science, progress in research depends upon the scope and facilities available, demand for its services, competency for conducting research, and suitable application of the facts and findings for the welfare of human society.

As an important branch of applied psychology, industrial psychology came into prominence in the first quarter of the twentieth century. Industrialists and managements at last began to realise the need of psychologists for the solution of innumerable problems of industry, starting from rate cutting to strikes and lockouts. Although it is not possible to wipe out completely the day-to-day problems of industry, nobody can deny that industrial psychology can be of immense help in reducing and solving the urgent problems of industry and in producing results for the benefit of the society at large.

DEVELOPMENT OF INDUSTRIAL PSYCHOLOGY IN INDIA BEFORE INDEPENDENCE

Keeping in view, the development of industrial psychology in the west after the industrial revolution, it would be worthwhile to review the progress of industrial psychology in India in spite of the innumerable hindrances and obstacles. In fact, before Independence, research on industrial psychology has been so negligible that only 25 studies were conducted in different areas of industrial psychology. Interestingly, a major portion of these studies have been conducted by economists. In India, psychologists entered the field of industry rather late probably because of the inadequate progress of the subject in the home country. Hence research in this field has been very meagre.

However, with the establishment of psychology as a subject in different colleges and university centres of India, interest and curiosity for research in industrial psychology developed considerably. But it is a fact that most of these researches have been conducted in academic centres to fulfil the curiosity or need of the persons of the educational institutions. Therefore, basically, the findings of such studies have not served much practical purpose. The type of academically oriented research developed as most industrial organisations did not realise the tremendous need in industry to solve the problems related to production, attitude, morale, labour-management and employee employer relationship, accident and safety, incentive and job satisfaction etc. Thus, by and large, industrial psychology remained a rather neglected and retarded branch of Psychology in India until 1947.

DEVELOPMENT OF INDUSTRIAL PSYCHOLOGY IN INDIA AFTER INDEPENDENCE

Fortunately, the situation has improved substantially during the last 35-40 years or so. The realisation of the fact that the research in industrial psychology leads to considerable increase in the efficiency of industrial workers, solution of employee-employer problems, the awareness on the part of the employer and management that the psychologist can be an asset to improve industrial management led to a number of researches in the field itself.

In the twentieth century, management and industrial psychologists tried to give more importance to humanitarian relationship which is conducive to increase production and congenial atmosphere in the factory. They felt that a worker oriental attitude is more desirable than a work-oriented attitude. Thus, emphasis was put on better interpersonal relationship in the factory. Keeping pace with the social foundations of industrial psychology, the problem of employee-employer relationship also got primary attention.

Making a survey of the studies conducted during the last 50 years (up to 1969) in the field of industry in India, it is noted that out of 533 studies, only 25, *i.e.*, 4 per cent of the studies were conducted during the pre-Independence era, whereas approximately 96 per cent of the studies were conducted since Independence (Table 3.1). From this survey, it is evident that research in the sphere of industrial psychology in India is a recent phenomenon and has been greatly neglected before Independence.

An analysis of the studies conducted in different sub-fields of industrial psychology indicates that the number of studies under different sub-fields differ substantially in quantity. It also seems that the favourite areas of research for Indian industrial psychologists have been performance and job satisfaction, management and organisation. Engineering psychology, advertising and consumer psychology have been thoroughly neglected.

A further analysis of the nature of these studies suggest that out of a total of 533 researches about 145 (*i.e.*, 28.7 per cent) were theoretical and non-empirical in character.

Before 1947, most of the studies were limited to some prominent textile, jute and tea industries of the country. Out of the 25 studies conducted; task and work analysis (6), performance and job satisfaction (5) and selection and placement (4) seem to have received more attention than other areas of industrial psychology.

TABLE 3.1
Number of studies in different sub-fields before and after Independence

Serial No.	*Subfields*	*Up to 1947*	*1948-69*	*Total*
(*i*)	Vocational choice and guidance	1	36	37
(*ii*)	Selection and placement	4	63	67
(*iii*)	Training	0	11	11
(*iv*)	Task and work analysis	6	24	30
(*v*)	Performance and job satisfaction	5	139	144
(*vi*)	Management and organisation	0	128	128
(*vii*)	Special environment	0	27	27
(*viii*)	Advertising and consumer psychology	0	3	3
(*ix*)	Engineering psychology	0	14	14
(*x*)	Driving and safety	1	23	24
(*xi*)	Survey and general studies	8	40	48
	Total	25	508	533

Source : A Survey of Research in *Psychology,* 1972, page 177.

After Independence, however, with the rapid growth of industries in India, researches in other areas were also accelerated. Not only did the quantity and quality of researches increase but the researches have also become more systematic, showing initiative and inventiveness. Besides, because of greater interest in most of the major areas of industrial psychology, almost all the sub-fields have been touched. To be more specific, in the areas of vocational choice and guidance, selection and placement, training, work performance and job satisfaction, absenteeism and turnover, work environment, accident, management and organisation, fatigue, monotony and human engineering, researches have been conducted in a more systematic and scientific way.

Of course, it cannot be denied that some of these investigations have certain flaws. Defects have been noticed in the sampling technique, methodology and equipment used to conduct the study. Besides the overlapping of studies in certain cases, relatively more studies have been conducted in areas like management and organisation, attitude, performance and job satisfaction, selection and placement, while other areas have been neglected.

After the Second World War, the same trend in research has been observed both in India and abroad. This is so probably because of the special significance attached to the interpersonal relationship between the worker and the management and the human values and social foundations of industrial psychology.

A comparison of the studies on industrial psychology conducted in India and the West would further reveal that although these findings do not corroborate each other, yet it has been widely agreed that the successful qualities of a supervisor, and congenial employee-employer relationship are of paramount importance, not only for more production, but also for the maintenance of discipline in the industry.

With the establishment of the institute of management at Ahmedabad, a number of valuable researches have been conducted in the area of group and organisation. Such studies have in fact, tremendous significance for Indian industries and needless to say, more researches are definitely necessary in this area.

A few studies have also been conducted in India on the causes of selecting specific vocations. UNESCO has encouraged the studies conducted in India on the effect of socio-cultural factors in the efficiency of employees and the importance of adjustment in industry, the findings of which are quite encouraging. Some industrial psychologists have made an attempt to standardise imported psychological tests in India for the purpose of their application to Indian industrial workers. But in practice they have not been fully successful in their effort.

A few studies conducted on work environment, accident, fatigue, boredom and monotony and engineering psychology seem to be mostly designed on the pattern of Western studies.

Of course, a number of valuable studies have been conducted on absenteeism and labour turnover in some light industrial organisations of India. Some of these studies have reflected on the specific causes of absenteeism and turnover among the Indian workers. Remedies have also been suggested by the investigators. In a few studies however, different and confusing findings have been obtained and hence more systematic research is necessary on absenteeism and labour in Indian industries and organisations.

A survey of Indian researches also suggests that studies on industrial motivation and incentives have been neglected. However, currently some psychologists are conducting research on Mclelland's *Generation of Achievement Motivation*. This will definitely provide tremendous impetus for further research on motivation in industry.

The organisational difference in public and private sectors and their impact upon the psychology of industrial workers which were mostly neglected before 1970 have however, now attracted the attention of psychologists. A number of studies have been conducted on leadership qualities, executive training and employee-employer relationships.

A detailed analysis of the development of industrial psychology in India suggests that by and large most of the investigators have followed the Western pattern in studying Indian industrial problems. They have mostly depended upon the test materials, questionnaires, and the equipments developed by the psychologists of the west. Except for a few studies most lack the originality of the investigator. It would not be an exaggeration to mention that many studies are mere repetitions of the Western studies. Also Indian investigators have used the survey technique in certain researches where its use was not desirable.

Since the problems of Indian employees and employers, labour and management are different from those of their counter-parts in the Western countries, researches should be designed, tests constructed and studies conducted according to the needs and problems of Indian industries. Recently however, keeping in view the problems of Indian industries, some psychologists have taken up necessary steps to conduct researches in India and have expressed their originality and inventiveness.

It is a fact that to study most of the problems by the survey technique is far from desirable. But in such cases the investigators have practically shown no interest or inventiveness in exploring new techniques of study, besides the survey technique. In this connection, Lambat (1963) has opined that for the purpose of studying Indian workers there is a lot of difficulty and danger in applying the questionnaire and survey method. Finally, while studying attitude, morale, neuroticism and other personality traits as well as job satisfaction and motivation of Indian industrial employees, questionnaires and other measures of study used have been framed according to the Western model. As a result, such studies have not been able to measure what they intended to measure.

Thus, the industrial psychologists interested in studying the human and situational problems of Indian industries should construct tests and questionnaires suitable to measure their problems. They ought to show initiative, originality, speciality, and inventiveness in the construction of tests and questionnaires meant for the Indian industrial workers. However, one notes that currently many Indian psychologists have shown tremendous interest in constructing and standardising test material and questionnaires keeping in view the problems and needs of Indian workers.

Another major limitation of Indian industrial psychological studies is that in many cases the studies have been conducted to fulfil the academic interest of the investigators. As a consequence, the findings of such investigators have not been very helpful in solving the problems of Indian industries. The gap in communication and lack of intimate contact between the academic psychologists and the management being the main cause of this drawback, it is desirable that there should be constant communication and contact between both the parties to solve the problems and fulfil the necessities of industrial organisations.

PRESENT TREND OF RESEARCH ON INDUSTRIAL PSYCHOLOGY IN INDIA

With the establishment of the Ahmedabad Textile Industries Research Association, The Sree Ram Centre for Industrial Relations, The South Indian Textile Research Association, The Indian Institute of Science, Bangalore and The Tata Institute of Social Sciences, Bombay, more meaningful researches are now being conducted. Various Indian Institutes of Technology are also conducting valuable researches on organisational behaviour.

In this connection, the work of Ganguli (1964) on structure and process of organisations, Chatterjee (1972) on the organisational variables of group cohesiveness, Kakar on the Authority Patterns and subordinate behaviour in Indian organisations (1971) and Personality and Authority in Work (1947) are valuable contributions to the research literature on organisational behaviour in India.

Other notable studies are the studies by Ghosh and Manerikar (1974) on the personality factors of Indian managers, and by Negandhi and Prasad on comparative management studies on employee-employer relationships and incentives have also indicated a slight upward trend during the last two decades.

A number of studies on job satisfaction have been conducted by Indian industrial psychologists between 1970 and 1980. The studies conducted by Rao and Ganguli (1971), Rao and Rao (1973), Kalanidhi (1973), Rao (1973) and Mohanty (1980) have thrown some light on the different variables of the job satisfaction of Indian employees. Heizberg's two-factor theory has also been tested in some of these studies.

SUGGESTIONS FOR FURTHER RESEARCH ON INDUSTRIAL PSYCHOLOGY IN INDIA

The current trend in research on industrial and organisational psychology in India thus indicates greater attention being focussed on the study of the employee-supervisor relationship, organisational structure and organisational behaviour, leadership qualities and executive training methods. The need of the time infact demands more and more research in these areas to solve the pressing problems of Indian industries and organisations. Improvement of the employee employer relationship and dehumanised conditions of the Indian workers can be possible by further research and suggestions based on the research findings.

Research on the structure of Indian organisations, in particular, should be undertaken and suggestions should be offered in the light of the research findings for more congenial relationship between the employees and the employers. Investigations on the frustration, conflict and level of aspiration of the Indian employees (which have so far been neglected) should be conducted on a large scale, in heavy, medium and light industries and in various private and government organisations with a view to bring an improvement in the psychological climate of the organisations.

QUESTIONS

1. Give a brief outline of the development of industrial psychology in India before Independence.
2. Make a comparative study of the studies conducted on industrial psychology before Independence and up to 1969.
3. Make a critical analysis of the major limitations of the studies conducted in Indian industries and organisations.
4. Give a brief outline of the current trends in industrial psychology in India. What are the chief handicaps that a psychologist has to face while conducting research in Indian industries ?
5. Discuss briefly some recent Indian research on organisational psychology and human resource management.

REFERENCES

Boaz, M.Z. *Papers on Industrial Psychology*, Harper and Row, 1968.

I.C.S.S.R, New Delhi. *A Survey of Research in Psychology*, Popular Prakashan, Bombay, 1972.

Sinha, D. *Studies on Industrial Psychology*, Sri Ram Mehara and Co. Publishers, Hospital Road, Agra, 1973.

4

Scientific Management

ROLE OF SCIENTIFIC MANAGEMENT IN INDUSTRY

The advancement of efficiency in industry is one of the chief objectives of industrial psychology. In every enterprise where goods are produced, increased production at a lower cost has been the chief consideration in guiding the destinies of the enterprise. In spite of the early recognition of this by Dubin and others, it remained for an American engineer, F.W. Taylor, to take the first definite step in the rationalisation of human work towards the end of the nineteenth century. Taylor has, since then, become the pioneer of the movement which has spread throughout the entire world under the name of "Taylorism".

The factor of the rationalisation of the human methods of work got careful attention from Taylor (1947). From the beginning of the industrial revolution attention had been devoted only to the perfection of the machine. In the development of his systems, Taylor (1947) started with two assumptions, the first being that, "what the workers want from their employers beyond anything else, is high wage and what the employers want from their work-men is low labour cost of manufacture".

The second assumption is that no system or scheme of management should be considered, which does not, in the long run, give satisfaction to both employer and employee, which does not make it apparent that their best interests are mutual and which does not bring about such thorough and hearty cooperation that they can pull together instead of apart.

While discussing the role of scientific management, one has to consider the part played by the economic, social and psychological factors.

Taylor (1947) observed two important factors in industry, workers want high wage and employers want 'low labour cost and more production. In order to solve these two problems,

Taylor developed four fundamental principles upon which scientific management is based and which are said to be his major contribution to industrial psychology.

PRINCIPLES

1. The development of a science for each element of man's work to replace the old rule of thumb method.
2. The selection of the best worker for each particular task, followed by a programme for training the workmen, to replace the practice of allowing the worker to select his own task and train himself as best as he could.
3. The development of a spirit of hearty cooperation between the workers and the management in carrying on their activities in accordance with the principles of developed science.
4. The division of work is almost shared equally between the management and the workers, each department taking over the work for which it is better fitted, as a substitute for the conditions in which almost all the work and the greater part of the responsibility was thrown on men.

In other words, the four principles of Taylor can be summarised as follows :

1. The one best method of doing work.
2. The one best worker selected for the work.
3. The one best method for incentive.
4. The one best method for employment.

These four practices can again be explained in the following ways :

1. The scientific method which is easy, less costly and time-saving must be found out for each type of work by avoiding the unscientific method of doing work. Application of force and power must be removed.
2. Each person has got some aptitude, *i.e.*, special capacity and interest for a particular work, Hence, by applying various aptitude tests the special qualities and interests of the worker can be traced out. He should, then, be allowed to join in a job in the line of his choice, or he should be given training accordingly. A person who is a neurotic or is liable to commit accidents should not be given, say, the job of a taxi driver, otherwise he will be involved in accidents. Thus, careful selection of the workers should be made before they join the job. The worker must be mentally and physically fit for the job. Otherwise, it will lead to a tremendous amount of loss and wastage of energy and national property. Besides selection, training is essential. The worker must be well trained. Proper training will lead to more production with less expenditure of energy.
3. There must be cooperation among the management and workers. Such reinforcement will motivate the workers to work more sincerely. Healthy cooperation between both the parties will lead to prosperity in the country.
4. In the factory, according to Taylor, the responsibility must be divided between the employee and the employer. If the worker is given all the responsibilities, he is over-burdened. So the management should come forward to reduce the responsibility of the workers.

These four principles are important contributions of Taylor and are related to the time and motion study. According to Taylor, there must always be a best procedure of doing any type of work. Secondly, the workers selected for the work must be trained and 'suitable for the particular work. Thirdly, proper wage incentive plans should be introduced to improve production and last but not least, the employee employer relationship must be congenial. These four principles of Taylor have been well demonstrated in a classic experiment conducted by the Bethlehem Steel Company while selecting and training men to handle pig iron.

EXPERIMENTS CONDUCTED FOR THE APPLICATION OF PRINCIPLES OF SCIENTIFIC MANAGEMENT

Seventy-five workers with average capacity in handling pig iron were employed in the job under the guidance of a very good foreman who himself was an excellent pig iron handler. After carefully observing the methods of work and studying the number of voluntary pauses etc., Taylor reached the conclusion that a first class pig iron handler ought to handle between 47 and 48 tonnes per day instead of 12½ tonnes. However, in a gang of 75 pig iron handlers only working about one men in eight was found physically capable of at this rate.

The selection of specially competent men, according to Taylor represents one, of the fundamental responsibilities of scientific management. The increment of nearly 35 tonnes is due to the application of the four principles of scientific management propounded by Taylor and known as the 4B's of Taylor or the Four Best Methods of Taylor.

A Dutchman was selected as the subject for the application of these principles. He was given necessary instructions at different times such as—"now pick, now walk, now sit, now rest etc". He followed all these instructions strictly and by the end of the working hour, the production was 47½ tonnes.

In this very experiment, the average production increased more than three times and earning of the workers also increased accordingly. Similarly, in another experiment, F.B. Gilbreth (1885), an engineer and a student of Taylor, observed the workers in brick laying. Through his minute study of the motions to be made by the brick layer in laying bricks, under standard conditions, he reduced the movements from 18 motions per brick to 5 and in some cases 2 motions per brick. Thus adopting the principles of scientific management. Gilbreth reduced the unnecessary movements and instead of 120 bricks, the average worker could lay 350 bricks per hour.

This experiment indicates the importance of scientific management in industry. Thus Taylor's principles of scientific management have helped in more production and also in an increase in the earning capacity of the worker.

Besides the four principles, there are some other aspects of scientific management. To ensure the most satisfactory conditions for increased production, Taylor recommended a number of procedures which have been an essential part of the scientific management programme.

Some of these principles stated by Viteles (1932) are the following :

1. A time study with the implements and methods for properly studying it.
2. Functional or divided foremanship.
3. The standardisation of all tool and implements used in trades and also of the movements and activities of workers for class of work.

4. The establishment of a planning room department.
5. The exception principle in management, *i.e.*, more wage for extra work.
6. The use of slide rules and similar time saving implements.
7. Instruction cards for the workmen, which must always be strictly followed, so that a worker would not be pressed by the employer to work more.
8. The task idea in management accompanied by a large bonus for the successful performance of the task.
9. The differential rate among the trained and untrained workers.
10. Mnemonic systems of classifying manufactured products as well as implements used in manufacturing, *i.e.*, the system of classifying the production.
11. The routine system.
12. The modern cost system.

IMPROVING THE OUTPUT OF BALL BEARING INSPECTORS

According to Viteles, the work of Thompson in improving the quantity of the output of ball bearing inspectors is cited by Taylor (1947) as another example of the possibilities of scientific management in making more effective use of the energy employed by the workers in their daily tasks.

Thus, Thompson conducted this experiment to make more effective use of the energy of the worker instead of wasting it in unnecessary movements. Improvement in the method of work, rest pauses and proper selection led to the following improvements :

1. Thirty-five girls were able to do the work done previously by 120 girls, and the accuracy of the work at the higher speed was greater than at the former low speed.
2. Wages increased by 80 per cent to 100 per cent more.
3. Workers got more rest and recreation.
4. Workers got better care from the management.
5. The hourse of work were shortened from 10½ hours to 8½ hours per day, with a holiday on Saturdays.
6. Each worker was made to feel that she was the object of special care and interest on the part of the management.

CRITICAL ANALYSES OF THE PRINCIPLES

Taylor (1947) gave a momentum to the development and growth of industrial psychology for high production. His principles of scientific management have no doubt helped in more production and less expenditure of energy. Industrial psychology has profited not only from the foundation of the techniques of scientific management, but from the demonstration by Taylor that industry can expect a definite return from an investigation and analysis of human behaviour. Industrial psychology has taken on the obligation of scientific management for the efficiency of the industrial workers, and in this way, has contributed to the further development of industrial civilisation. It is partly because Taylor showed that return or benefit to both the management and the worker could be increased through the study of the human elements. Thus, early psychologists were granted an opportunity by industry to conduct investigations designed to increase human effectiveness in industry.

It has been rightly remarked by Viteles (1932) that the principles of scientific management have vastly influenced the growth and development of industrial psychology by determining the scope of industrial psychology and by establishing clearly its economic objectives.

An overall comparison of the scope of industrial psychology indicated in the bulletin issued by the National Institute of Industrial Psychology of Great Britain (see introductory chapter) with that of the principles of scientific management, shows the degree to which psychologists have accepted Taylor's contribution to industrial psychology. However, in spite of these contributions of Taylor, his principles of scientific management have been criticised on certain grounds. Undoubtedly, later psychologists based their principles on the foundation laid by Taylor, but it is also true that the structure of their principle differs greatly from Taylor's plans and principles. Though Taylor's efficiency principle has been accepted, by and large, later psychologists have been critical about the over-emphasis of Taylorism on efficiency and output. What they hold is that "industrial efficiency may be achieved without the sacrifice of individual welfare" (Viteles 1932).

With the change in the economic orientation of man to the social and the psychological plane, the tendency and overall attitude to neglect the welfare, happiness and comfort of individual workers for more production has not been favourably accepted by modern psychologists.

Taylor rejected the human factor in industry. He did not consider the health, prestige, safety and above all, the ego and the total personality of the worker as a human being. He was guided by the economic philosophy of the time and hence it was not so much of Taylor's fault as possibly the attitude of society at that time, which was responsible for his philosophy. The material philosophy at the time did not consider that human beings worked with their rational minds. It considered men as machines. Titus Taylor's emphasis was more on the economic aspect than on the psychology of the workers.

However, this being the most glaring shortcoming of Taylor's system, he was severely criticised by the latter day socially oriented industrial psychologists for his over-emphasis on money and other financial incentives.

In fact they held that the application of the principles of scientific management would not bring more production after a certain limit. It was further held that higher wage only works as a means and not as the end.

It has also been felt that the essentially limited procedure of Taylor's system must be supplemented by more careful study of other resources of human proficiency and by a more exhaustive consideration of other tasks of human satisfaction. Studies must also be made on the cause of human adjustment and maladjustment in industry, if extended, productivity is to be obtained.

This solicitude for the individual worker has been fostered by the changing social philosophy and the growing insistence that individual welfare be made the central objective of social activities.

However, in spite of its defects, scientific management is definitely a classic system in its own way and is largely accepted by the industry because of the scientific basis of the principles.

QUESTIONS

1. What is understood by scientific managements? Discuss its contributions to the development of industrial psychology.
2. Examine the important principles of scientific management.
3. Critically analyse the importance of scientific management in improving output.
4. With suitable experimental studies discuss the economic implication of Taylorism.
5. Why were Taylor's principles of scientific management criticised by the twentieth century industrial psychologists ? In this connection give a brief outline of limitations of Taylor's principles.
6. Write notes on
   (*a*) One best method of doing work.
   (*b*) Four B's of Taylor.
   (*c*) Experiment on pig iron.

REFERENCES

Blum, M.L. and Taylor, J.C. *Industrial Psychology : Its Theoretical and Social Foundation*, Harper and Row Publishers, 1968.

Gilbreth, F.B. *Motion Study*, Princeton, N.J., van Nostrand, 1911.

Gilbreth, F.B. and Gilbreth, LM. *Applied Motion Study*, Macmillan, New York, 1917.

Taylor, F. W. *Principles of Scientific Management*, Harper and Row, New York, 1947.

Viteles, M.S. *Industrial Psychology*, Norton, 1932.

5

Time and Motion Study

IMPORTANCE

The main motive of the industrial psychologist is to increase the efficiency of the workers. Different methods have been used to increase the efficiency of the employees and the time and motion study is a definite attempt in that direction.

The idea of the time and motion study was first put forward by Taylor (1911) and later developed into a highly organised system of time and motion study by Mr and Mrs Gilbreth (1911), Taylor remarked, "each job should carefully be sub-divided into its elementary operations and each of these should receive the most thorough time study". The time and motion study principles are definite contributions of Gilbreths to the study of job design. The elimination of unnecessary movements, retention of shortest and economical movements, simplification of work patterns and assigning different work to different people formulate the basic principles of the time and motion study.

NATURE AND CHARACTERISTICS

What is meant by the motion study ? Associated with the time study is the motion study of a job. It is the procedure of analysing a job into component operators so that the job can be completed in a minimum time, with least effort and least expenditure of energy. It is the process of eliminating the unnecessary movements and improving the necessary ones.

After examining the different elements of work, the work is organised in such a way that it becomes smoother, easier and simpler. In short, the motion analysis is only finding out the short cuts. The operation of the skilled workers is photographed by movie cameras and then the simple and correct movement of each job is determined, once it is found out it can be used to train new workers in an efficient manner.

Farmer (1923) states that the motion analysis breaks the various movements by reassembling them, removing the unnecessary movements and improving the necessary ones.

Gilbreth (1911) has described the motion study as a philosophy of work in as much as it looks for the causes and effectiveness in work. As a method and as a technique the time and motion study shows how best to perform an activity.

In its heyday, the time and motion study represented something more than just a job analysis procedure. It represented a particular philosophy of how to study men at work with a clearcut objective of improving work proficiency by utilising the time and motion methodology. In time studies the emphasis is on determining the standard time required to complete a task. In motion studies, the methods, motions and movements of the worker are analysed.

In the time study, the time taken for different operations by efficient workers may be noted and how much time is taken for a particular task can also be noted. A standard time fur each job can be found out. Thus the time and motion study increases production without increasing the expenditure of human energy.

The jobs are selected, modified and reorganised in a desirable manner. The study tries to make the work easier and more effective by eliminating unnecessary, painful, troublesome and fatiguing movements. An attempt has also made to make the operations smooth and rhythmic. Hence the attempt of the time and motion study is fundamentally different from the 'speed up' attempt in which production is increased by increasing human energy. This is the experience which all gathered during the last World War.

It is quite true that men differ in abilities. But it is equally true that there are some similarities among men. From this it necessarily follows that there are certain natural ways of doing things due to a similar make-up. The unusual methods of doing work are always costly, time consuming and require extra effort and energy. But the more natural ways consume less energy and increase production.

The approach of time and motion study is to fit jobs to men rather than men to jobs. It pleads for the change in the design and operation of machines to suit human abilities and purpose. So it supports the aim of human engineering.

One of the functions of the time and motion study is to determine the most efficient way to do a job. One should be guided from the very beginning to do a particular work following the best procedure. For every work there is one inferior and one superior style of performing it, and the aim of the time and motion study is to acquire the superior style.

The time and motion study lays down a standard method and a standard time in which the work is to be done. Gilbreth holds the standardised method to be superior and the best way of doing work. In the time and motion study a job is split up, and on the basis of efficiency and capacity different portions of the job are assigned to different people. The time and motion study thus advocates division of labour and does not ignore individual difference.

In fact, 25 per cent to 50 per cent of the manual work done in many factories is unnecessary. The time and motion study reduces the unnecessary movements. Practice and efficiency increase when these unnecessary movements are reduced.

In, thus connection, Taylor (1947) remarked, "we see our forests vanishing, our soil being carried by floors into the sea, our water power going to waste, but our large wastage of human efforts are less visible, less tangible and are but vaguely appreciated".

Engaged as a foreman in a steel factory, Taylor did not find any correlation between energy expenditure and output. He held that in order to find out a better method of production with less expenditure of energy all the methods and implements should be analysed together with accurate time and motion study.

USE OF THERBLIGS IN TIME AND MOTION STUDY

Gilbreth and Gilbreth (1911) have given major importance, to the breakdown of a task into its basic elements of motion, elimination of unnecessary movements and combination of efficient and necessary movements into a standard method of work. This is called the best way of doing a work.

This analysis and breakdown of a task into basic elements of motion has been called 'THERBLIGS' by Frank Gilbreth.

After analysing any job, it is found that it involves a number of therbligs (basic elements of motion). But all these therbligs are not necessary for completing a job. Thus, the unhecessary motions or therbligs are eliminated and the necessary therbligs are indentified and put into practice. For instance, for preparing a cup of coffee certain basic elements of motion are necessary, such as putting milk into the kettle, lighting the stove, bringing coffee powder, sugar, spoon, coffee pot and coffee mug etc. A lot of unnecessary movements are required to prepare a cup of coffee if things required for this purpose are not in proper place and proper order. By analysing this job into therbligs unnecessary therbligs may be avoided and the necessary ones accepted for quick preparation of coffee.

As pointed out by Viteles (1932), the best combination of efficient movements or the one best way of doing work, according to the Gilbreths, is determined from the comparison of the constituent elements or therbligs of a task as performed by expert operatives. Each of these therbligs is given a name and a symbol and entered in the following chart (Fig. 5.1) :

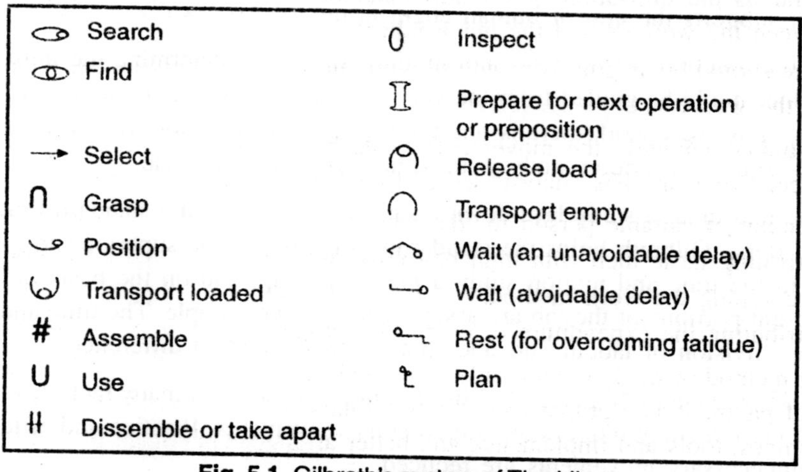

Fig. 5.1. Gilbreth's system of Therblig.

These therbligs indicate the elements or motion and their time vertically and the portions of the body involved horizontally. As Viteles (1932) points out, by this a simultaneous motion cycle chart is produced which is a graphical representation of the bodily parts involved in the motion made by each element and the relative and actual time consumed by each element of motion.

According to Viteles "where timings for therbligs differ, that which is the shortest is selected, its characteristic determined and the movement combined with others selected in the same way into a single series of movements constituting the standard method of doing work. The sum of the times of these constituent elements plus a percentage of unavoidable delays, plus a percentage to allow for average workers determine the standard time for the task."

In other words, in the time and motion study therbligs suggest that an operation in question is analysed into different components, and after observing the operation of other workers completing the job in minimum time, the quickest, most economical and best movements are collected and coordinated into one best way of doing the work. This one best way is afterwards applied to every worker. Thus it is the most effective combination of movements made by a detailed and careful job analysis. This job analysis requires quite a lot of preliminary preparation such as preparation of a process chart on which every movement is recorded in order of sequence.

In spite of the difficulties, it is an extremely helpful and timesaving technique of preparing standard methods of work. Wage rates can also be easily fixed according to this technique. This is definitely one of the important contributions of Gilbredt to modern organisations which are always anxious to perform more work in less time, with less cost and less expenditure of energy.

PRINCIPLES

According to Taylor, for effective production, not only are certain incentives required, but the following methods are also to be followed :

(*a*) The old rule of thumb method must be replaced by a scientific study of each element of man's work.

(*b*) Workers must be selected and trained.

(*c*) As far as the utilisation of scientific methods is concerned, there must cooperation between the workers and the management.

(*d*) There should be an equal division of work and responsibility between the management and the workers.

Taylor studied minutely the movements made by the workers in raising pig iron in the Bethlehem Steel Company. His analysis led to four basic changes in method.

1. Selection of suitable person for the job.
2. Motivating these men with high pay provided they would learn the new way.
3. Stereotyping the work method.
4. Distributing the expenditure of energy by proper distribution of rest periods.

A better method of work was not only suggested by Taylor, but he also discovered the piece rate method of payment as a proper and effective financial incentive. He also advocated the use of better machines, tools and implements, and better arrangements of all these four for efficient production.

The system of the time and motion study devised by Gilbreths (1911) as pointed out by Blum and Naylor (1968) includes nine principles. They are : 1. individualisation, 2. functionalisation, 3. measurement, 4. analysis and synthesis, 5. standardisation, 6. records and programmes, 7. teaching, 8. incentives, and 9. welfare.

By following these principles the Gilbreths could show to the world that production could be increased significantly without increasing the cost of production and the energy consumed for production.

EXPERIMENTAL WORK

The use of proper workers, a proper selection of men and more efficient work habits lowered the cost of production from 70 per cent to 31 per cent per tonne, while production per man rose by 37 per cent. Thus the pay increased by 63 per cent.

Gilbreth (1911) made a minute study of the motions involved in brick laying. He found that in the whole process of brick laying among 18 movements, 5 movements were only necessary. In his study he prearranged the tools and machines in a particular manner and asked the workers to work using both the hands, which in turn resulted in time saving and high production. Output increased from 120 to 350 bricks per man hour.

Thus, the engineers drew the conclusion that faulty procedure of doing work should be eliminated.

Tiffin and Rogers (1941) studied the work of inspectors in tinplate factories. Thompson analysed the job in a ball bearing factory. He found that the job of 120 inspectors could be done by 35 inspectors. It is, however, also true that due to this labour saving device the security of the workers was strained.

In a study Vernon (1924) applied the piece rate method of payment to increase efficiency. But this did not work, so he applied time and motion study and found that efficiency increased to a great extent.

Stakhanov applied the procedures of the time and motion study in a coal mine in Russia. He organised the pattern of work in such a way that the job of one might not interfere with the others. After following the techniques of the time and motion study he found out that production rose from 7 tonnes to 70 tonnes, and afterwards from 70 to 102 tonnes. Wages also increased considerably. Soon it became an industrial movement, and spread all over Russia and came to be known as Stakhanovism.

The present author (1980) has very successfully applied some of the principles of the time and motion study in the kitchen and in other domestic work. She has noted with the utmost satisfaction that because of previous planning, elimination of unnecessary movements and unscientific postures, good house keeping, arranging thing in proper order the application of scientific and systematic methodology while doing work and specialisation in work, the time taken to prepare food in the kitchen was reduced by 50 to 60 per cent. Proper organisation of work is vary essential for getting the best out of time and motion study.

PSYCHOLOGICAL IMPLICATIONS AND SHORTCOMINGS

It is Important to emphasise that the time and motion studies need not be unfair. They can be useful in promoting the aims of both management and labour, provided they are carried out correctly and are not misapplied. Hence, when they lead to increased efficiency they result in some gains to the worker as well as to the management. But in circumstances where the workers are not satisfied with the introduction of the time and motion study, they do not produce greater efficiency. Its introduction merely produces greater dissatisfaction and insecurity as well as anxiety in the minds of the workers. Consequently, they resist.

There are three major forms of resistance to the time and motion study :

1. Objection to change

The serious implications of this resistance to change and newness must be recognised. The time and motion study offers point to the fact that something new is needed in the job. It is a fact that the introduction of a new method may lead to improvement, but when it is being introduced, the possibility of improvement still remains as a question mark. The worker may accept it or reject it, not because it is a better way of doing the job, but because it is a way which in novel for the workers and they normally don't change. This authors advice supervising the construction of her building (2006-2009) which continued for about three years tried to apply time and motion study techniques on the unskilled and semi-skilled workers. She asked the labours while they were carrying some they to a place to also carry something on their return. For example they were carrying some bricks to first floor when the came back keeping the bricks to carry the unused garbages kept on the first floor to the ground floor, they refused them revoled and most of them did not agree garbages.

2. Intrusion as an outsider

Practically every worker does his job in a certain way and has got reasons for doing it that way. But after the introduction of new principles of doing work by an outsider (whom tile workers consider as a member of the out group), the workers resent the new ways of doing work. In fact, it cannot be said that they dislike the new methods of doing work They merely resent the intrusion of an outsider. The very feeling that an outsider is imposing on them certain principles of doing work is not accepted favourably by most of the workers. So by and large, they resist the new methods even if these methods are quite scientific and economical.

3. Increased feeling of insecurity

The third resistance to the time and motion study is the increased feeling of insecurity which is partly psychological and partly economic. The time and motion study aims at increased production and lower wage rates. Insecurity increases and the workers often apprehend that they will be dismissed from their job. Thus, they try their best to find out reasons why the new method will not work.

The present author has made an interesting observation (1978) about the resistance to the time and motion study principles by the skilled, semi-skilled and unskilled male and female workers engaged in the construction of a building. The construction work continued for over a period of two years. The author, who was supervising the construction of the building, made an attempt to apply some of the principles of the time and motion study like avoiding unnecessary movements and unscientific postures. Accordingly, she asked the workers to follow her instructions while working. Though a few workers followed some of the instructions which brought about a significant rise in output, most of the workers resisted directly or indirectly and grumbled. When the author wanted to know the cause of such resistance, not as the owner of the building but as a psychologist engaged in research work, many of them stated that this would consume extra energy as a result of which they would be ill, which was of course, a wrong impression. Some of them, however, remarked that if two workers could do the work of three it might lead to retrenchment of workers and insecurity in job. Thus, they wanted to slow the pace of work so that they would be engaged for a longer period.

The labour union resents the time and motion economy. It holds the view that the time and motion analysis considers man as a machine and the analysis wants to make them mechanical throughout the day. The analyst must, however, understand that money is not the only incentive for which people work. It should be realised that higher wages work as a means but not the end. Material philosophy would not bring more production after a certain limit. The workers also object to the fact that their work is being studied without their knowledge and permission. Hence, they are not very cooperative.

Tolman (1938) described the application of the study as having an atomistic concept of behaviour because the time and motion study is based on the fallacious assumption that each movement of a total complete task can be considered as a separate independent unit. The time and motion study holds that these movements can be arranged and rearranged without affecting the character of each independent movement. Thus, the analyst takes a behaviouristic approach. The Gestaltists objected to this and pointed out that the summation of different elements is not the same thing as the total task itself. Hence, we find that any change in the elementary movement will cause a necessary change in the character of other movements.

Ghiselli and Brown (1955) did one study on key pressing and found that elimination of some unnecessary movements reduced the time taken to perform the task.

However, some other studies have been carried out where it was noted that the time could not be reduced by eliminating unnecessary movements. This indicates that elimination of some movements may reduce the time taken in some tasks, while the principles may not work in some other tasks.

Barness and Munde (1963) did another experiment where the subjects were asked to sort pins into the holes. In putting the pins, three elementary movements are necessary. They are : 1. carrying, 2. positioning, and 3. sorting. According to the time and motion study each of these three elementary movements will take the same time. This is a fallacious assumption.

Again Barness (1963) points out that the time and motion economy assumes a high degree of consistency in the human body which is not really true. The time taken for performing a task differs not only from person to person but also from time to time.

Another criticism has been made from the Gestalt point of view. The Gestaltist pointed out that the totality of the task may be affected by the performance of each one of these elementary movements. The work consists of something which is more than the mere collection of parts. When the whole task is divided, the essential quality of the whole work is destroyed from this point of view some have advocated that the time and motion study is not a desirable attempt.

It is argued that the time and motion study ignores, individual difference and with the few observations made by the time and motion study, we should not fix the standard time for jobs. This objection has been greatly supported by Barness. He found a lot of variations in different types of work and therefore found it extremely difficult to fix standard time for any set of work.

Psychologically and physiologically, we cannot ignore the point of individual difference and connot force all the workers to follow the best methods of doing a job. It is not necessary that every worker should follow the same pattern even if he suffers from handicaps.

Moreover, the standard time and the best method of work have been based on the observation of the performance of a few most efficient workers. Above all standard method suggested by the time and motion study analysis may not be the best method for all workers. According to Jenkins, it is better to have a best method for each worker. In other words, the individual should not adopt to a method, the method, on the other hand, should be designed to suit the individual which ultimately supports human engineering.

The time and motion study suggests fewer bodily movements more geometrically performed for less consumption of energy. It assumes that the smaller the area of the body involved in the work situation, the less the amount of fatigue the individual experiences.

Moore (1962) has objected strongly to this theory. According to Moore, the movement of an area is not complete without the movement of fingers and hence the gross movement of the body musculature involves less amount of fatigue. The standard time fixed up by the time and motion study is sometimes unusually high and the analyst arbitrarily fixes the standard time with minimum scientific accuracy.

Another objection is that the time and motion study ignores the social setting on the job. In the time and motion analysis recognition and competition among workers and appreciation of one's performance have been ignored. These factors usually determine the individual's behaviour and efficiency, and hence any analysis that ignores the importance of such psycho-social factors and takes into account only the physical determinants, fails to diagnose the most important motivating force. Due to these factors, the time and motion study, despite its great value, has lost much of its charm.

The time and motion study implies a division of labour. Each portion of the job becomes mechanised and it leads to monotony and boredom and the workers loose interest in job.

The piece-rate of payment emphasises material incentives, but it neglects the health and psychological limitations of the workers. The workers try to produce the maximum at the cost of their health. The after-effects of such hard work are undesirable and in this sense the time and motion study is not entirely different from the speed-up attempt. Employees misuse the procedure of the time and motion study by always insisting on more production.

A good perspective on the happenings in the field of the time and motion study since the early 1900s is gained from F.W. Schumard's *A Primer of Time and Motion Study*. Schumard listed 24 inherent and acquired qualities such as honesty, imagination and sympathy etc., of the time study men.

Mogensen (1932) has much more practical and valuable approach, *i.e.*, the education of the foreman and the employees which will encourage their becoming motion minded. Sometimes, average workers lack enthusiasm without proper training on the time and motion study.

Mogensen (1932) encouraged motion-mindedness in a plant by showing motion pictures of work done without and with the help of the time motion studies in other plants.

He then trained the foreman and executives in some of the specificity or the time and motion study which produced effective result. It is again the job of the executive to convince the workers that they would not be subjected to dismissal. Mogensen's approach could overcome the three serious difficulties in the time and motion studies.

1. It avoids both the resistance to an outsider initiating change and the insecurity producing factors.
2. In encourages an acceptance to change since the workers themselves participate in contributions to the change.
3. The foremen and the employees become involved in many of the intricacies of the study. They construct process charts and make suggestions as to how to achieve greater efficiency.

Gomberg directed the management engineering departments to pursue two objectives :

1. To assist in improving the manufacturing techniques and the operating methods of all branches of the industry with which workers' earnings are intimatly bound.
2. To serve as a central information agency.
   (*a*) To determine the level of fair price rates.
   (*b*) To record the production system and manufacturing techniques under which these rates are paid.
   (*c*) To assist in training shop members and committees in distinguishing the bad time study practices from the good time study practices in the determination of rates.

Advantages

In spite of the limitations of the time and motion study it has definitely certain advantages and hence has stood the test of time.

The chief advantages are as follows :

1. It tries to find out the most satisfying method of doing the work and on this basis it provides a line of training to workers by making the work simple and mechanised.
2. It avoids the old rule of thumb method which takes more time and energy and puts the output at a lower level.
3. The aim of the study is the well-being of the workers, employees and the nation at large. So it is a means to an end and not the end in itself. But it is a tool which can be misused. Contrary to Taylor's principles, however, the Gilbreths emphasised that the details of the work situation should be adjusted to the individual. Under no circum stances should the individual be pressurised to adjust with the pattern of the job. This line of thought of the Gilbreths has been very much appreciated by the modern psychologists. In their writings the Gilbreths (1916, 1917) also gave a lot of emphasis and importance to the individual, in contrast to Taylor, who was only concerned with high production and economic benefit, neglecting the human side of the work.

The success of the time and motion study depends on the ability and the tact of the time and motion study engineers. The engineers should have the knowledge of human behaviour in order to understand, predict and control it. In short, the success of the time and motion study engineers lies in their tact and skill.

To conclude, intelligently applied time and motion study is an excellent instrument, but like any other instrument, it may become an end in itself in which case it is useless or even pernicious. Mechanically used, it loses all humanity as workers are considered appendages to the machine.

Eysenck thus rightly remarks "it is not only with the time and motion study but with the new discoveries that its misapplication proves fatal even for the innocent theory".

QUESTIONS

1. What do you understand by the time and motion study ? How is it related to scientific management ?
2. Discuss the nature, characteristics and principles of the time and motion study.
3. Critically examine some of the classic experiments conducted in industry to justify the application of the time and motion study for improving efficiency and output.
4. Make a critical analysis of the psychological implications of the time and motion study.
5. What are the limitations of the time and motion study? How can they be avoided ?

REFERENCES

Barness, R.M. *Motibn and Time Study*, 5th ed., New York, John Wiley and Sons Inc.

Blum, M.L. and Naylor, J.C. *Industrial Psychology: Its Theoretical and Social Foundations*, Harper and Row Publishers, 1968.

Ghiselli, E. and Brown, C. *Personnel and Industrial Psychology*, 2nd ed., McGraw Hill, New York, 1955.

Gilbreth, F.B. *Motion Study*, Princeton, N.J, van Nostrand, 1911.

Gilbreth, F.B. *Brick Lying System*, Clark Publishing Co., New York, 1911.

Gilbreth, F.B. and Gilbreth, L.M. *Applied Motion Study*, Macmillan, New York, 1917.

Maier, N.R.F. *Psychology in Industry*, Oxford and IBH Publishing Co. Pvt. Ltd., New Delhi, 1970.

Mogensen, A.H. *Common Sense Applied to Motion and Time Studies*, McGraw Hill, New York, 1932.

Moore, J.M. *Plant Layout and Design*, MacMillan, New York, 1962.

Mohanty, Girishbala. An Observational Study on Resistance to the Time and Motion Study Principles, 1978.

Mohanty, Girishbala. Application of Time and Motion Study Principles in Kitchen, 1980.

Taylor, F. W. *Principles of Scientific Management*, Harper and Row. New York.

Tiffin, J. and Rogers, H.B. *The Selection and Training of Inspectors*, Viteles, M.S. *Industrial Psychology*, Norton, 1932.

6

Individual Differences

CONCEPT

The concept of individual difference was brought to light in a scientific manner for the first time by Sir Francis Galton (1869). Galton was not a psychologist and his interest in psychology was largely incidental. However, the variation within the human beings in physical and mental traits drew his attention to the subject of individual difference which had great importance in psychology. Galton devised test for revealing differences in individual capacity and statistical methods for analysing data.

Subsequently, Cattell did some valuable research to find out the significance of difference in the activity of various people. It is true that individuals are born with some common characteristics. It is equally true that every individual has a personality unique in itself. In fact, certain significant qualities in his personality differentiate him from other human beings. This is possible because of the role of heredity and environment. Keeping the environment constant, the difference in two personalities is due to the influence of heredity.

IMPORTANCE OF INDIVIDUAL DIFFERENCES IN INDUSTRY AND ORGANISATIONS

The recent trend in industrial psychology which emphasises the role of individual workers in industry and their personality differences has further elevated its status in industrial and organisational psychology. Industrialists do realise that improper placement and poor employee-employer relations and usually if not always, the result of unsuitable selection. Keeping in view the glaring truth that people do differ in their abilities and capacities, temperament and interest, industrial orgainisations have put special emphasis on the concept of individual differences. Evidences indicate that all workers cannot be suitable for all type of jobs. For instance, a very good taxi driver may not be a good foreman as there in difference in the job qualities required for these two types of jobs. Similarly, an efficient and competent mechanic may not be suitable for the job of an executive. Since there is difference in temperament and interest, in attitude and outlook, in traits and characteristics different people should be appointed in different types of jobs on the basis of scientific and judicious selection. Unless the problem· of individual difference is considered, different persons for different jobs cannot be selected.

Various studies on individual differences justify that there is difference among people in I.Q. : in sensory motor coordination, in sensitivity, in balance, in steadiness of motor control, in strength, in grasping capacity, in perceptual capacity, in reasoning and thinking capacity, in the capacity for learning and retaining, in honesty and emotionality, in various aptitudes and interests, in likes and dislikes, in social adjustment and in the capacity to solve various problems of life. Knowledge of such· differences obtained by careful selection procedures will also to aid on the psychologists to impart further training and guidance in bringing the best out of the employees.

Thus, it has been seen that whenever individuals come into close proximity it is inevitable that certain differences among them would be recognised. Even in the selection of workers in the factory, variation in the capacity of the applicants is observed. It has also been observed that some people are more temperamentally suited for a job in comparison to other competitors. Equipped with the same facilities, similar training and similar equipment and working under similar physical conditions, some can produce more than others. For example, because of the difference in intelligence, grasping and remembering capacity, two students may have remarkably different results in the examination even though they are provided with equal facilities and even if, they study equal hours per day.

Differences in sensory motor tests, perceptual traits, age and sex also make difference that have tremendous influence on industry and organisational set-ups.

Difference in physique, such as height and weight have importance in the selection of men for certain types of industrial work. Similarly, difference in posture, poise and movements, coordination of hand, fingers and feet are important in many jobs such as, that of sewing machine operators etc.

T.A.T. and Rorschoch tests of personality can also be made use of industry by trained psychologists to assess the personality of individual workers.

There is this common belief that older persons (above 35-40 years age) cannot learn and imbibe so well and there is an age restriction in respect of certain jobs. But studies indicate that abilities of older workers are comparable to the younger ones in speed tasks which involve neither precision nor complex mental process. Of course, it is true that the older groups do not perform so well in abstract and complex tasks. It is also held by some that older people are rigid and stubborn. This does not hold true of all older people. Only those who have been seriously frustrated might be rigid and stubborn.

FACTORS

Studies in different weaving industries indicate the extent of individual difference in productive capacity. Not only does individual difference play an important role in production, but also in the prevention of accident, in the development of training programmes, in avoiding fatigue and monotony, in job satisfaction etc. An accident-prone personality is more liable to commit accidents under similar circumstances than a person who is not accident-prone. In such a situation, an accident-prone person may be given a job which provides less scope for accidents.

Individual differences due to sex has brought about a lot of discrimination in industry. Difference due to sex occurs because of the cultural influence and physiological differences. Women are also kept out of certain jobs because of prejudice. But during the Second World War it was found that women could do many jobs effectively which were previously denied to them. As studies show, men and women are similar in mental abilities and I.Q. Women are even better in memory work and in jobs involving details. But the difference due to sex cannot be ruled out entirely.

Individual differences in performance traits are of greater importance in industry. Performance traits consist of physical, intellectual and non-intellectual characteristics. Individual differences in various performance traits have been tested and measured in both laboratory and field situations.

So far as special aptitudes are concerned, mechanical and clerical aptitudes are referred to most often in industry. Mechanical aptitude mainly deals with ability to deal in space relationships. It is important in visualising how objects can be taken apart and put together again. It is essentially necessary for repairing machines. Reasoning is also important in mechanical aptitude. Manual dexterity and finger dexterity are necessary in some day-to-day routine jobs. But they are independent of mechanical aptitude.

Clerical aptitude is made up of the verbal, numerical and perceptual speed factors. In the jobs of executives and salesmen interest traits and non-intellectual personality traits are important.

Emotional and personality difficulties lead to a lot of trouble in industry. It is often the cause of absenteeism, labour turnover, conflict, accident and fatigue. But not much work was being done in industry about personality and emotional tests except a few studies on personality and non-intellectual factors related to operational success in sales and executive position.

To bring satisfaction in job and industrial success for an employee, interest in work is necessary. Whether a person has got interest in a job or not can be known by giving interest tests for various jobs. In fact, separate interest scales have been developed for separate jobs.

NATURE

The nature of individual difference can be explained by the help of a normal distribution curve. The different traits of personality are distributed normally in the population in the fashion of the normal distribution curve. To determine individual differences, when any trait of personality of a sample is being measured, such as for example, the ability to memorise, half of the population who are near average in memory would score in the middle range. Scores above and below the middle range become less and less as they occur less frequently in the population. Therefore the lines become progressively shorter towards the two extremes. A theoretical normal distribution curve for individual difference which represents, difference in work performance of a hypothetical groups of workers in a job, is shown in figure 6.1.

The distribution curve describes the way in which a particular ability is distributed in a population and this has important significance for the management to consider. Therefore, under no circumstances, can differences be overlooked.

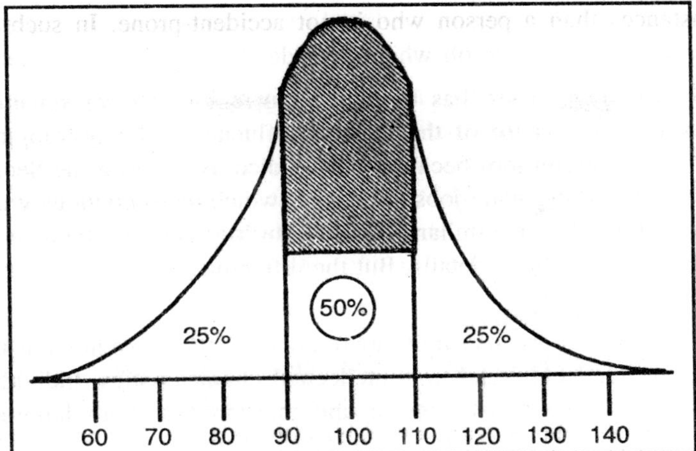

Fig. 6.1. Normal distribution curve

According to Maier (1970), "The first step in meeting the problem of individual differences in ability is to recognise them and accept the differences as facts. To expect the same from each person can at best lead to a condition in which the slowest man sets the pace for all". A normal distribution curve hence gives the supervisor an idea about the type of workers working in his group. But some variations in the spread of scores in a normal probability curve may occur as it is not always possible to get a normal distribution of a particular trait. When this occurs, it is evident that it is the score of a deviant or special group of people or some other factor operating to influence the measurement of ability.

According to Maier (1970), "The spread of a distribution curve is greater for complex than for simple abilites. When the range is great, it is particulary important to encourage the superior individuals to remain with the company, since their ability is an important factor in the total population. The inferior workers either should be transferred to a simple type of operation where the distribution is less widely spread and where varying degrees of ability show minor differences in production, or be placed in occupations very different from those in which they are at a disadvantage."

It is evident from the findings of the study conducted by Paterson and Darley (1936), that it is a mistake to choose employees on the basis of length of experience. Practice and experience do not lead to the equalisation of productive ability. Experience can develop the inner capacities and potentialities, but only to a certain limit, after which it will depend on the inner capacity. Generally the most proficient persons will improve very quickly to reach the highest level.

CAUSES

Psychologists have long been interested in determining the causes of individual differences among people. Keeping in view the importance of individual differences in industry and organisations, it seems neccessary to analyse how individuals differ, why they differ and how such differences are significant in daily life. Whether a person is born industrious, liberal or conservative, or is made so, can be understood by analysing the causes of individual differences. Whether the poor performance of a person after a particular training, is due to lack of capacity to receive the training or because he has not developed the interest for such training can be determined by going through the causes of individual difference.

The causes of individual differences are mainly divided into hereditary and environmental. However, the relative importance of heredity and environment in the development of individual differences has become a controversial issue. The supporters of heredity uphold it as the sole determinant of individual differences, while the advocates of environment claim that opportunity, training and environmental factors are the prime determinants of individual differences. Galton describes this controversy as one between nature and nature.

CONTRIBUTIONS OF HEREDITY

According to Pintner (1931), "The potency of environment is not merely so great as is commonly supposed. A child's abilities are determined by his ancestors and all that the environment can do is to give the opportunity for the development of his potentialities". Pintner further adds that an environment-cannot creat new powers and abilities. Pintner finally concludes that, "All that we can claim is that our calculations agree perfectly with· the hypothesis that intelligence is inherited in the same way as physical characteristics are inherited". Thus according to him, heredity is more important than environment in explaining the causes of individual differences.

Several experimental findings also emphasis the importance of heredity in individual differences. Pearson (1904) found a remarkable resemblance among members of the same family in colour of hair, height, colour of eyes, ratio of width and length of head and in physical traits which are more or less unaffected by environmental influences. He also noted that the effect of heredity upon mental characteristics is the same as upon physical characteristics.

Comparing the educational and psychological test scores obtained by 18 pairs of siblings of 19 to 32 years of age Starch (1917) found that, "the resemblance of siblings is apparently no greater in those mental traits which are directly affected by school work than in those which are not so affected. This seems to indicate that mental similarities of children to the same parents are due primary to hereditary factors rather than to similarity of environment, since the resemblance is so greater in those traits which are more directly affected by environment".

Thorndike (1928) found the resemblance in intelligence of unselected siblings to be slightly greater than what was found by Pearson. May and Hart Shorne (1928) also support the contributions of heredity to the development of mental trait like deception. They conclude, "it seems as likely that deception is biologically conditioned as it does that intelligence is biologically conditioned".

Several twin studies by Muller (1925), Koch (1928) and New man (1929) also support the contributions of heredity to the development of mental traits.

Gilbert and his associates emphasise the contribution of heredity to individual differences on the basis of different types of investigations.

CONTRIBUTION OF ENVIRONMENT

In order to demonstrate the effect of changed environment upon mental traits some investigations have been carried out. Two investigations conducted by the Chicago university group headed by Freeman (1925), and the Stanford university group headed by Burks (1928) are worth mentioning. Both the investigations employed somewhat different methods, though the purpose was identical, *i.e.,* to study the influence of home environment upon the development of the mental traits of children. Freeman agrees with Burks' views that heredity is a force in the determination of mental ability by the side of which all forces are dwarfed in comparison. Both the studies agree on the influence of heredity in shaping mental ability. Both the groups show a general agreement on the role of environment in the development of intelligence. But the Chicago group seems to give greater emphasis to environment than to heredity.

Watson (1930), a staunch behaviourist, comments, "Give me a dozen of healthy infants ...... well formed and my own specified world to bring them up in and I will garantee to take anyone at random and train him to become any type of specialist. I might select-doctor, lawyer, artist, merchant-chief and yes, even beggarman and thief, regardless of his talents, penchants, tendencies, abilities, vocations and race of ancestors". In these lines Watson has strongly emphasised the importance of environment in individual differences.

Analysing the extreme views of the supportors of heredity and of environment, it is observed that an exclusive emphasis on heredity or on environment is unscientific. If an individual's abilities, efficiency and traits of personality have been exclusively influenced by heredity, environmental training and learning, would have no meaning whatsoever. Similarly, if training and education is considered as the sole factor influencing personality differences, then favourable environmental opportunities are everything and potentialities and gifted qualities have no implications for personality development.

Those upholding one point of view have decreased the importance of the other point of view or even neglected it completely. Such extreme views are not accepted by modem psychologists. It seems· more reasonable to say that both nature and nurture, heredity and environment have important roles to play in the development of individual differences. But their relative importance differs in the development of various traits of personality. Heredity is more important in determining the physical traits like height and weight, colour and texture of hair, body strength etc., although to some extent the effect of environment on these traits cannot be ruled out.

Similarly, environment has the upper hand in the development of personality traits like sociability, amiability, honesty, dominance submission, introversion-extroversion interests and several other social desirable-undesirable traits. As far as the mental activities are concerned, there are sufficient evidences to believe that hereditary factors determine the potential level of development (limit) which an individual can achieve at the maximum. Within the limit or ceiling, the environmental factors vastly influence the level of development that really occurs. Thus neither nature nor nurture alone can explain the differences among individuals in mental traits.

It can be finally concluded that for the development of various personality traits hereditary and environment variables interact and heredity imposes the relevant ceiling on the level of knowledge or skill which one can achieve. Environment as a general force makes definite contributions to individual variability, having its effect upon what is gifted by heredity.

Thus, variation among individuals is a function of the interaction of hereditary and environment factors and the effect of one may be insignificant without the other.

Besides these two important variables, there are şome other factors also contributing to individual differences. They are sex, nationality and race etc. Though these factors are different aspects of heredity and environment, they are important enough for separate consideration.

EFFECT OF TRAINING

Training programmes are urgently required for new employees for the development of several skills required for a particular job in question. To maintain the present skill and also to develop new skills training and orientation is necessary even for experienced employees.

According to Tiffin and McCormick (1971), training may have three possible effects upon individual differences (*i*) training may increase the differences, (*ii*) it may decrease them, (*iii*) or it may leave them unaffected. Evidences show that training decreases individual differences when the task is a simple one, *i.e.*, a task where the average worker shows little improvement after a short period of practice. Evidences also suggest that training increases the extent of individual differences as far as performance in a given job is concerned. The employees who are more alike during the earlier stage of training period vary significantly in the later stages.

On the basis of several observations and experimental findings Tiffin and McCormick (1971) have given the following tentative conclusion about the effect of training, on individual differences; "Training tends to increase individual differences with the increase in the complexity of the task".

However, in spite of the training, the effect of individual differences on production cannot be ruled out. Differences in performance will continue during the course of training and training can never bring all trainees to an identical level of proficiency. In spite of the limited effect of training, proper selection of personnel is necessary for a job, for the very reason that it can select individuals who are less variable, better in job performance and finally, fit for the job requirements.

APPRAISAL OR EVALUATION OF EMPLOYEES

It has already been discussed that different types of traits bring about differences among people. Therefore, it seems necessary to evaluate the difference among individuals in organisations and industries. The success of a person in a job can only be determined by applying various evaluation techniques. Such evaluation can also bring to light the existing differences between the superior and the inferior workers. Moreover, by knowing the traits of the superior and inferior workers it can be determined whether specific traits are present in varying degrees in high producing workers. A scientific knowledge of the desirable characteristics of various jobs would greatly help the selection and placement of workers.

Therefore, from the point of view of the management and the employees, it is desirable to evaluate the differences between individuals. Promotions and transfers should also be based on the evaluation of individual workers. Besides, in order to improve the performance of employees through training it is necessary to measure proficiency first. Finally for determining the effectiveness of the existing methods of personnel selection, evaluation of employees is also essential.

METHODS OF EVALUATING EMPLOYEES

Rating Method

There are certain jobs, where the quality of work is more important than in others. In such cases, quantitative methods of measurement may not be very effective. For instance, the success of a policeman or a teacher cannot be measured objectively, but subjective methods like human judgement can measure it.

By the rating method, the individual's ability is judged in terms of its relation to the abilities of his co-workers. The merit of the employee or his value to the company is measured besides his production. The scoring is usually based on a five point scale.

According to Maier (1970), "Rating is a technique by means of which we evaluate members of a group by comparing them with one another". In this, the immediate supervisor may be asked to grade the workers on the basis of their contribution to the job and their degree of proficiency. For this purpose he observes the men while working and makes comparisons among them, taking the average worker of the group as the standard.

Limitations of the Rating Scale

1. Rating is made purely on the basis of human judgement which is likely to the coloured with subjectivism and bias.
2. The supervisor has to give his rating, judging several job dimensions and qualities necessary for the job. This is really a difficult job. For successful rating, skilled raters are required.
3. The importance of production is over-shadowed by the qualities of the rater. Although certain traits are necessary to maintain an interpersonal relationship, on no account should it be forgotton that high production is the real aim and should not be overlooked.
4. Different rating standards are used by different raters. Consequently, the rating loses its real implications. However, by giving training to the raters and defining the standards some of the defects to rating method can be avoided.

For the successful operation of the rating technique, the executives at Gimbels have recommended two elements.

1. Highly competent personnel analysts, it other words, skilled and proficient raters are required. Hence raters should be trained and the purpose of rating should be defined to them in clear terms.
2. Strong line support including the full backing of top management is essential. The personnel analyst should be very competent to give correct, objective and unbiased ratings and judgement. The senior officials and executives above the cadre of supervisor, including the top management, should not interfere in the work of the evaluators.

Field Review Technique

Field review is used to refine the merit rating method. To avoid the defects and limitations of the rating method, attempts have been made to evaluate the employees through the field review. In this technique, the proficiency of the employees is evaluated with the combined cooperation of a member of the personnel department and the foreman or supervisor.

Evaluation is made through interviews in the plant or organisation where the employee is employed. During the interview the personnel representative talks freely with the employees, asking questions on employee performance. Out of this discussion he tries to find out the characteristics, abilities and performance of the subordinate workers. After the interview with the workers has been completed, the personnel representative studies and reviews his notes prepared on each employee and drafts a tentative summary rating. Then he checks it with the supervisor who makes additions and alterations. After discussion with the supervisor, the final rating is drawn up. The supervisor is responsible for the rating but the details required for its preparation are handled by fully trained representatives of the personnel selection department.

Field review has several advantages.

1. Supervisors prefer oral evaluations rather than the more conventional ratings like written evaluations.
2. Management becomes better acquainted with the performance and development of each employee and the results of ratings are prepared by trained hands regularly reviewed and effectively used.

Critical Incident Technique

The critical technique advanced by Flangan (1954) is one of the newly developed methods leading to greater objectivity in employee evaluation. It is simply a procedure to collect relevant data about employee performance. It was developed because of the criticism of many merit rating plans for the highly subjective nature of the traits measured. This critical incident technique is, however, based on more refined and objective criteria.

In this technique, a large number of day-to-day incidents regarding the workers, such as quarrelling with fellow workers, calmness during emergency situations, willingness to work overtime during peak periods, unwilling to accept additional training and responsibility are recorded and analysed. This analysis helps to determine which qualities are significantly connected with success on the job and which qualities are found in the performance of poor and unsuccessful employees.

On the basis of these observations and evaluations, a scientifically constructed rating scale may be developed which contains factual elements important to success on the job. Such incidents may be recorded by the supervisors and foremen as they take place, so that they can appraise themselves of the relative merits of their workmen more objectively.

The critical observation record and analysis of incidents provide standards for the rater's judgements. It also supplies many observations of behaviour upon which various raters can agree. It also helps to reduce the tinge of personal bias present in the rating method.

In a study Flanagan and Burns (1955) developed 16 critical job requirements for hourly employees of the Delco Remy Plant. With the help of forms the time taken by the foremen for recording their observations was only five minutes per day. This indicates that in a very short time a lot of information can be obtained about the workers.

According to Maier (1970), "A major advantage of this method is that the behaviour record of a man is more complete and does not depend on recall which may be incomplete and subject to moods. It is claimed that the record of the critical incidents also can serve as a basis for employee counselling because 'specifics' rather than general evaluative judgements are involved. However, unless the suppervisor is skilled in discussing such matters with an employee, such detailed reports might be seen as spying".

Thus, the limitations of this technique are some prominent sources of error in observation, like relying upon memory, having complex aims, incapability to know what is important of these errors can be avoided.

IMPLICATIONS FOR INDUSTRIAL PSYCHOLOGY

Common observation and results of various investigations indicate that the success or failure of a worker in his job mainly depends upon the selection procedure, as native and acquired abilities can be changed very little. Therefore, refined selection procedures should be followed before appointing workers to different jobs.

While considering transfer and promotion to a job requiring change in duty, an analysis of individual capacity is necessary. The extent of individual adjustment is also determined by individual capacity.

Since practice improves performance, systematically organised training programmes can be developed, keeping in view the difference in the ability and capacity of different persons.

After being aware of the limitations of workers, conditions of work can be changed accordingly so that they can utilise their capacities to the maximum extent.

QUESTIONS

1. What is meant by individuals differences ? Discuss the importance of individuals differences in industry.
2. Critically examine the role of heredity and environment in individuals differences.
3. Evaluate the causes of individual differences and discuss the merits and defects of each cause.
4. Make a critical analysis of the techniques used to evalate industrial employees.

REFERENCES

Blum, M.L. *Industrial Policy and Its Social Foundations*, Harper and Row Publishers, 1956.

Flanagan, J.C. The Critical Incident Technique, *Psychol. Bull.*, 1954, p. 51, pp. 327-358.

Flanagan, J.C. and Bums, R.K. *The Employee Performance Record-*A New *Apprasial Development Tool*, Harvard Business Review, 1955, p. 33, pp. 95-102.

Maier, N.R.F. *Psychology ill Industry*, Oxford and IBH Publishing Co., 1970.

Pinter, R. *Intelligence Testing*, New York, 1931, p. 507.

Starch, D. The Similarity of Brothers and Sisters in Mental Traits, *Psychol. Review*, 24, 1917, pp. 235-38.

Tiffin, J. and McCormick, E.J. *Industrial Psychology*, 5th edn., Prentice-Hall of India Private Limited, New Delhi, 1971.

Waston, J.B. Behaviourism, New York, Norton and Co., 1930.

Viteles, M.S. *Industrial Psychology*, Norton, 1932.

7

Hawthorne Studies

HISTORICAL BACKGROUND

The history of industrial psychology indicates that the materialistic and economic philosophy of the time centered the discussion of efficient production around the question of material incentives.

In fact, in the nineteenth century, emphasis was mainly given on the amount of production. The importance of scientific management and the time and motion study are glaring examples to illustrate the view.

In the twentieth century, it was slowly but gradually realised that production did not improve in spite of high wages. There were, however, a few idealists who held that people do not always work for money alone. They suspected the operation of certain non-material factors which perhaps motivated the workers to work.

Thus the industrial psychologist, according to Blum (1956), "tried for other means by which the workers can be bribed to work, some of which are excellent ideas, others merely an insult to intelligence."

While this question hunted the minds of many psychologists, industrial and social, in the years 1924-27, there was regular disturbance in the Hawthorne works of the Western Electric Company, necessitating a thorough investigation of the relationship between production and various factors of efficiency.

Hence, a number of studies were conducted by Professor Elton Mayo, Professor of industrial research at Harvard University and the guiding star of the studies. To be more exact, the Hawthorne studies started in 1927.

The Hawthorne studies are divided into five major parts. Each part is an outgrowth of the preceding one. In many respects, each study follows the other logically.

The five studies are as follows :

1. Experiments on illumination.
2. Relay assembly test room experiment. (*a*) Second Relay Assembly Test Room (*b*) Mica Splitting Test Room.
3. Mass interviewing ptogramme.
4. Bank wiring observation room.
5. Personnel counseling.

EXPERIMENTS ON ILLUMINATION

In the first stage, psychologists wanted to find out the relationship between workers and management and optional illuminations for higher efficiency.

In the controlled and experimental conditions all factors remained constant except illuminations. Various levels of average illumination varied from time to time.

The illuminations experiment assumes that the production would be minimum under the best lighting conditions. To verify these assumptions, the workers were given three different jobs :

1. Inspection of small parts.
2. Assemblies of relays.
3. Windings coils.

Production in each of these jobs was measured under four carefully controlled conditions which varied from low to high intensity of illumination. They wanted to find out the relationship between efficiency and illumination.

Among the inspectors, production went up without any relation to the illumination. In the case of the assemblers, production continued to increase throughout the experiment. However, the increase was not related to improvement in the amount of illumination.

Among the coil winders, production tended to increase with increasing illumination. But production did not decrease when illumination was decreased. Thus, by and large, it was noted that production increased invariably with and without the increment of illumination.

In the words of experimenters, "the study brought out very forcibly the necessity for controlling or eliminating the various additional factors which affected production output in either the same or opposing directions to that which we can ascribe to illumination" (Snow, 1927).

In the last study two groups of coil winders were subjects with similar experience and capacity. The experimental group first worked under an illumination of 24 foot candles which was later doubled and tripled. The controlled group worked throughout the experiment,' under an illumination of about 24 foot candles. To eliminate any competitive factor, the two groups were kept in different places. The results again were discouraging. The production of the experimental group increased significantly, but so did the control group.

Another more precise experiment was set entirely with artificial light. The control group worked under a constant intensity of 10 foot candles. The test group began with 10 foot candles but the intensity was reduced by one foot candle per period, until they were working under only 3 foot candles. However, the results were no more conclusive. Both groups increased their efficiency slightly. Finally, two girls volunteered to work under conditions equivalent to ordinary moonlight. But the girls were just as efficient under moonlight conditions and reported no eye strain and less fatigue when working under bright light.

The last study leads to the conclusion that an entirely new approach to the problem was necessary. The coil winding girls were asked to comment on different intensities of light. The light bulbs were changed. But the same intensity was kept. In the last part of the experiment, the illumination was decreased. The girls commented favourably on the increased illumination, but they felt the same when the light remained constant.

From these five experiments relating to the increase and decrease in illumination, it was finally noted that the production of the workers increased invariably with and without the increment of illumination.

The confusing results obtained from these five studies led to the apprehension of the operation of some non-material factors. This result led to the second study *i.e.,* Relay assembly test room study.

RELAY ASSEMBLY TEST ROOM EXPERIMENT

In this experiment, more refined techniques were followed. An effort was made to test the hypothesis that production would be higher under an improved incentive system and under a shorter work week with rest and lunch periods. The task was to assemble small telephone relays, "because it is simple and highly repetitive and requires no machinery and permits an accurate measure of production" (Blum and Naylor, 1968).

Two experienced workers were invited to participate and they selected the other subjects in the experiment.

This experiment had 13 test periods. Period 1 was to get an accurate measure of each girl's production under typical work conditions. Period 2 attempted to determine the effects of a change in work place upon production. Period 3 introduced a change in the method of payment. In period 4, two rest pauses of 5 minutes each were introduced. In period 5, these rest periods were increased to 10 minutes. Period 6 had six rest pauses of 5 minutes each. In period 7, the rest pauses were given and free mid-morning lunch was added. Period 8 was similar to period 7, but the working day was shorter by half an hour. Period 9 was the same as period 8, but the working day was shortened by another half hour. Period 10 was similar to period 7. In period 11, the group went on a five day work per week. Period 12 was the same period 3. Period 13 was exactly a repetition of period 7 and 10 except that the operators provided the morning lunch.

The variation in conditions produced extremely interesting results. Each test period had higher production than the preceding one. Thus with the change in each factor, production went up compared to the preceding period, even if sometimes they were given no facilities. Moreover the spontaneous remarks, free conversation and behaviour of the workers revealed a thorough change in the social atmosphere of the group.

SECOND RELAY ASSEMBLY TEST ROOM

The original relay assembly test group had a change of environment as well as of payments whereas the second relay assembly group had only a change of payments. Five experienced operators were put on a payment basis similar to that of the original group, but were kept in the factory. This group increased production almost by 12 per cent and it continued at this level. But when the group went back to the original method of payment, there was a drop.

MICA SPLITTING TEST ROOM

The primary purpose of this investigation was to study the effects of the change in payment in the test room. Five operators participated in the experiment. Two were selected at random and these two selected the other three. Their production increased by an average of 15 per cent in 14 months. In the relay assembly test room· production rose to 30 per cent. Thus 15 per cent raise in production is the maximum that can be attributed to change in financial incentives the remainder must be attributable to other factors.

This experiment continued for five years. The situation and atmosphere of the testing room was very normal and similar to the factory, and the psychologists in charge of observation worked as supervisor as well as an observer. Throughout the experiment the supervisor tried to keep a healthy relation with workers, such as listening to their complaints and grievances, giving them free advice and information, and being friendly and intimate with them.

From the findings of this study it was noted that the attitude between the workers and supervisors was very congenial. The morale of the group was high. Solidarity and loyalty in the group was marked, and production improved. Thus, it was felt that production improved primarily because of the change in the attitude of the workers in the positive direction. In spite of the several unfavourable conditions it was found that output was the highest ever recorded *i.e.*, 30,000 relays a week.

MASS INTERVIEWING PROGRAMME

This investigation was designed to study the existing relationship between the employees and supervisors. It emphasised the study of human relation or of attitudes concerning human relations more than the study of the environmental factors.

Another outstanding aspect of this study was its flexibility. The programme was expanded and the method of conducting interviews underwent drastic changes as the factors became known. The interview procedure was changed from the direct to the indirect method as direct questions inhibited the spontaneous expression of the men's real conviction.

The main aim of the study was to know the attitude and morale of the workers towards the company. By interviewing the supervisor, they could get someone to whom they could speak of their personal and emotional problems and there was some evidence of the development of informal relationships in various groups because of this.

A major finding of this programme was that complaints are often symptoms of difficulties rather than indications of the causes of difficulties. In other words, the employee's complaints often indicated a personal difficulty rather than difficulty in the immediate environment. The employee might complain of his pay because in the work set up, the supervisor liked his rival more than him. The complaints generally involved an employee's social position in the group in which he worked. The interviews concluded that, wages, hours of work and working conditions are carriers of social values. For thus, they could not be considered separate from their social significance to the employee. The position and significance assigned to these factors varied according to the employee's social position in the group, the group's attitude towards the specific item and his relations with people outside the job.

In this study the workers were interviewed and during the course of interview they could get a chance to talk about their personal problems. This study collected a large number of data regarding the attitude and opinion of the employees. The study further suggests that a good supervisor is one of the fundamental factors leading to efficient production.

BANK WIRING OBSERVATION ROOM

How do the social values of the workers influence satisfaction and productivity on the job ? This problem led to the bank wiring observation study. It was designed to obtain more exact information on the nature and influence of the informal organisation within the company. The interview resulted in several immediate benefits. The reaction of the employees was generally favourable to the management, because they thought that the management was not neglecting their opinions and feelings. The results were also helpful in improving the company's supervisory training course. Finally, the list of complaints about specific environmental conditions led to investigations and constructive changes by the management.

It was clearly evident from the interviews that social organisation is of vital importance to the employees within the company. The purpose of the study was to discover what this social organisation and how it operated. Fourteen operators were assigned to a separate room where they wired banks and did repetitive manual work.

The observer in the experiment played the role of a disinterested but aloof spectator. He strictly followed the rule, did not try to prove his authority or argue, and finally did not violate the confidence of the employees. The observer remained within the group for more than six months, noting the formal organisation of the supervisor. and the employees, the informal grouping of the men and the interrelatedness between the two types of organisations.

From the experience of the observer it was noted that the wage incentive system did not motivate the workers as much as it was thought to be. There was actually no relation between measured aptitude for the work and productivity. Whether the workers resistance to the incentive system was in their best economic interest is doubtful. There was, however, no question that they did not restrict production and that the restriction was a result of well organised group activity. By interviewing each worker individually, it was noted that the workers were keen to keep the rate of production constant because of the apprehension of being retrenched. The worker's position in his group seemed more important to him. He would not endanger that position by violating the standards of the group in order to make more money. To the workers, interpersonal relationship was more important than the wage incentive plan. This was by and large, the conclusion drawn from this study.

PERSONNEL COUNSELLING

This is the final and last study. According to Bulm (1956), "This study may be regarded as the culmination of the experimenter's effort to bring the idea of interpersonal relationship between the workers and boss".

The counselling programme developed after the bank wiring observation experiment. It had two-fold purpose.

1. A non-authoritative interview to find out the problems of the workers and to know their attitude towards their work and their supervisor.
2. To improve the method of communication within the company, in view of the ample evidence indicating that it was lacking in certain situations especially when the social organisation conflicted with managerial organisation.

With this purpose, the decision was made that personnel men would be assigned to the departments and would be free to talk to the employees. The programme, led to the improvement in the following three fields :

1. Personnel adjustment.
2. Supervisor employee relationship.
3. Employee management relation.

Employees showed, freedom from anxiety and other forms of behaviour that might be diagnosed as psychoneurosis. Less emotion and understanding is required on the part of the supervisor so that policies could be formulated which would result in less friction between management and worker. This could also be possible through personnel counselling programme.

IMPLICATIONS OF HAWTHORNE STUDIES

By and large, it can be said that the Hawthorne studies are the most expensive and influential studies of human behaviour ever conducted in industry.

The Hawthorne studies, for the first time established the importance of the possibilities that the apparent benefits of the physical changes are not due to changes as such. It may accidentally have some favourable effect upon social behaviour.

According to Blum and Naylor (1968), "The Hawthorne studies are significant because they represent an honest and concerted effort to understand employees instead of approaching the problem from the managerial point of view of increasing 'efficiency' on an economic level.

"Moreover, they are interesting because they are a type of experiment which is rarely performed in industry. They do not try to define a response or the result· of the introduction of change, they recognise that it is a result of the specific change, plus the employee's attitudes, his social situation on the job and his previous attitudes as determined by his personal history and background".

CRITICISM

In spite of the important significance of the findings of the Hawthorne studies, some have been quite critical of it and have pointed out a few limitations of these studies.

It is held by some that the importance of supervisors in the Hawthorne studies come out because of the 'touchy' attitude of the women employees. This point was illustrated by the significant difference in the results of the relay assembly test room and bank wiring observation room, where one group was female and the other group was male. General observation and evidences from different sources as well as the personal experience of the present author who is an employee, and also a woman, suggest that women regard supervisors as more important in comparison to their male counterparts. Also, they are usually more tolerant both at home and in the work situation. Normally the pay packet is not so important to them in comparison to men, because in our society men are taken for granted to be the bread earners. Of course, sometimes women work out of sheer necessity but often they look upon their jobs as a temporary stopgap arrangement until marriage or child birth. They are often more moved and influenced by an understanding and sympathetic boss than by a good salary. So the effect of sex difference may be a possible variable influencing the results of the relay assembly test room experiment. But accepting the fact that women employees add greater importance on the behaviour of the supervisor than the male employees, it is also true that the supervisor's behaviour influences employees irrespective of sex, though the difference may be in degree. This view gets ample support from several research findings in the area of supervision and leadership.

CONCLUSION

After nearly 30 years of investigation it was found that there is something more important than hours of work and physical conditions of work, something which increases output without being affected by the physical conditions of work. This conclusion brought a change in outlook as it was realised that (1) The factory is a world by itself and the working environment consists of physical, social and personality factors. (2) The importance of supervisor. in industry was realised from these studies. A supervisor is obviously the first and last link with whom the workers come in immediate contact. (3) It was realised that the psycho-social aspect is more important than the material one, and that the personal lives of the workers cannot be separated from their factory life.

Lastly, it was also observed that social relationship among the workers has its repercussion upon their attitude and efficiency.

According to Blum and Naylor (1968), "The significance of the Hawthorne studies can be understood not only in relation to their findings, but also because they are an outstanding example of research that was not steered to predetermined conclusions and because they raised questions that otherwise might not have been asked".

On the whole, the Hawthorne studies show the weakness of financial incentives and the necessity of a new and scientific approach to the study of motivation, with special reference to interpersonal relationships between the employees and the employers.

The Hawthorne studies may not be the ideal one. They may not be the receptacle of perfection. They have, infact, several limitations which have already been discussed. But no one can deny the fact that the Hawthorne studies are the pivot and the centre around which all the problems of industrial psychology move. Needless to say, the Hawthorne experiments are classics in industrial psychology and the findings of these studies have provided tremendous impetus for research. Therefore, it has been rightly pointed out by Blum and Naylor (1968) : the Hawthorne studies can be considered as the coming of age of industrial psychology just as Munsterberg's work might be considered its birth.

QUESTIONS

1. Briefly describe the experiments on illumination conducted at the Hawthorne works of the Western Electric Company and critically examine the merits and defects of each study.
2. Why and how the Hawthorne studies came into existence ? Describe the important limitations of the Hawthorne studies.

3. "Hawthorne experiments are classic experiments and interesting models. They represent the most significant research programmes undertaken to show the enormous complexity of the problem of production in relation of efficiency". Examine the above statement in the light of studies conducted in the Hawthorne works of the Western Electric Company.
4. "The significance of the Hawthorne studies can be understood not only in relation to their findings but also because they are an outstanding example of research that was not steered to predetermined conclusions, and because they raised questions that otherwise might not have been asked", Elucidate.
5. The Hawthorne experiments have given importance to the social and personal needs of the worker. Justify the above statement.
6. Analyse the contributions of the Hawthorne studies to the present status of industrial psychology and give a critical evaluation of these studies.

REFERENCES

Blum, M.L. *Industrial Psychology and Its Social Foundations*, Harper and Row Publishers, 1956.

Blum, M.L. and Naylor, J.C. *Industrial Psychology: Its Theoretical and Social Foundations*, Harper and Row Publishers, 1968.

Mayo, E. *The Human Problems of an Industrial Civilisation.* Macmillan, New York, 1933.

Roethilisberger, F.J. *Management and Morale,* Harvard University Press, Cambridge, Mass, 1943.

Roethlisberger, F.J. and Dickson, W.J. *Management and the Worker*, Harvard University Press, Cambridge, Mass, 1943.

Snow, C.E. A discussion of the relation illuminating intensity to production efficiany, *Technical Engineering News,* 1972.

8

Testing in Industry and Organisations

SIGNIFICANCE OF PSYCHOLGICAL TESTS IN INDUSTRIES AND ORGANISATIONS

The recognition of the significance of individual differences in industry has increased the application of psychological tests in industry, particularly for the selection, placement and training of workers.

Prior to 1910, Hugo Munsterberg used psychological tests while doing research in the Boston Elevated Railway Company. Since then, and especially during the last two world wars, the application of psychological tests in industries and organisations have increased steadily. Now-a-days, for the selection, placement, promotion and transfer of employees applications of psychological tests have become a common practice. Organisation and managements, infact, do realise the importance of testing in industry particularly for the selection of employees for different type of jobs.

Today, in almost all competitive examinations various types of paper pencil tests are being used for the selection of individuals for different services.

In 1972, Murphy conducted an investigation on the extent of which psychological testing was being employed by police agencies on their personnel. Only 80 out of 203 replying agencies indicated the use of psychological examinations in personnel selection. A review of testing methods used, indicated that there was a significant increase in the number of agencies using personality and intelligence tests, along with various other paper pencil tests and interview techniques.

Psychological tests are mostly used to assess the intelligence and personality of the applicants for selection and posting. Psychological tests also facilitate successful training of workers and executives. However, it cannot be said that tests are the only means of selection. Along with tests, informations obtained by application blanks and interviews aid in better selection.

DEFINITION

According to Anastasi (1961), "Psychological tests are essentially objective and standardised measure of a sample of behaviour". Cronbach (1960) holds that, "A test may be defined as a systematic procedure for comparing the behaviour of two or more persons".

Thus, while Anastasi has opined that a test is an objective and standardised measure of the behaviour of a sample, Cronbach points out the need of tests for the comparison of the personality or behaviour of two or more persons.

Psychological tests have three major purposes :

(*i*) To test the personality of individuals which may aim at diagnosis.

(*ii*) To predict behaviour, *i.e.*, prediction on the probable way one is going to behave.

(*iii*) To conduct research.

APPROACHES OF PSYCHOLOGICAL TESTING

The history of psychological testing indicates three distinct approaches.

1. Psychometric Approach

It started in the first two decades of the twentieth century and derived inspiration from Galton. The major work of his approach is the study of intelligence, psycho-motor skill etc. to assess certain traits in the population.

2. Clinical Approach

The clinical approach is interested in finding out the standing of particular mind. Here the interest of the psychologist is not to assess a certain capacity in a population, .but to find out the interaction between different traits.

3. Research Approach

The research approach is used in psychological tests controlling certain variables. In group experiments control and variable groups are taken and they are matched according to their abilities and personality patterns.

CHARACTERISTICS

A psychological test is a sample of an aspect of an individual's behaviour and performance. It is assumed that the sample measured is sufficient to predict the most usual or typical functioning of the individual. Merely assembling a batch of questions does not produce a psychological test. A test may best be defined as measuring a standardised sample of human behaviour. As such, it must meet certain basic requirements.

1. The sample of behaviour should be both large and, representative enough of the class of which behaviour going to be measured, to allow one to generalise and predict from the test results.
2. By requiring the test to be standardised, a series of questions or tasks should be uniformly administered whenever the subjects are given the test.
3. Finally, all psychological tests must have the prerequisite characteristics of validity, reliability and norms. The two permanent requirements for any predictor are validity and reliability.

VALIDITY

The most important characteristic of psychological testing is validity. When the test actually measures what it intends to measure it is, said to be valid. The procedure to determine the validity of a test is to compare the test with performance on the job. A valid test that measures a specific ability must differentiate between the more able and the less able. If it is unable to do this, it is invalid and does not measure the ability in question. A valid test in industry in other words must differentiate 'between poor and good workers. Tests must be developed or used experimentaly in order to obtain a measure of their validity, but tests should never be used as a basis for employee selection unless their validity has been established.

Broadly speaking, three types of validity have been mentioned in literature :

1. Logical validity,
2. Empirical validity,
3. Factorial validity.

Logical Validity

A test consists of many items or tasks and these tests are tests of capacities like intelligence, aptitude, etc. When the items of the test are examined to find out whether they are relevant to the concept, its logical validity is determined. In logical validity the logical analysis of an item incorporated in the task is examined.

Empirical Validity

In empirical validity the relation between the subject's performance in one situation with his performance in another situation is examined. For instance, the test of the students success in the college examination when it has a relation with his intellectual standing in other situations, is said to have empirical validity. In empirical validity, therefore, the subject's performance in certain tests situations is correlated with certain criteria. For instance, intelligence test scores and scholastic achievements are related. Sometimes tests of performance are correlated with sales record. Personality scores and the rating of the student's qualities by his teachers are also related. The relationship between intelligence test scores and class performance marks are also examined.

One limitation of this type of validity is that unless the choice of external criterion has been widely tested, one can not conclude whether the test is valid or not. Various other psychological variables and internal conditions of the subject might have influenced his performance. Therefore, one has to be very careful in the selection of criteria. Again, the test scores have to be correlated with previously established test scores. For example, if one scores 120 in the Standard Binet Test, and 115 in another test of intelligence, it can be concluded that there is a high correlation between these two tests. Similarly, if the relationship between the symbol digit test score and Rotter's level of aspiration board test score is significant, it can be taken for granted that the two tests have a good correlation.

Factorial Validity

A test having factorial validity is a pure measure of certain capacity. It measures a number of statistical concepts. It may test various capacities, but it should be free from the influence of other variables.

Blum and Naylor (1968) have held the view that the specific kind of validity that a test involves depends upon the specific aim of the user in any situation. On the basis of the aim of the user, according to them, the validity of a test can be of the following types.

1. Predictive Validity

It is otherwise known as follow-up activity, where the user attempts to predict the future performance of the employees on some other variable or criterion. It is said to be the most important type of validity in the selection of employees.

2. Concurrent Validity

The main purpose here is to estimate the present performance of employees on some criterion measure from scores on the predictor. Here the present and not the future status of the people is predicted.

Blum and Naylor (1968) assume that the high concurrent validity of a test does not assure high predictive validity. However, it is often found, that in industries, concurrent validity is used as a substitute for predictive validity. This is highly' unfortunate. Generalising concurrent validity to a predictive validity situation is therefore undesirable and should be avoided in industries at any cost.

3. Content Validity

When the content of a test is the representative of a class of situations, the test is said to have content validity. Content validity cannot be quantitatively measured. However, content validity is greatly used in achievement test. An examination in the school or test of achievement will be said to have content validity if it has adequately represented the various items of the course. For example, if a question paper on general psychology only contains questions on learning and perception it cannot be said to have content validity.

4. Construct Validity

The construct validity of text indicates the possession of some characteristics which are presumed to be reflected in the test performance. In other words, a test having construct validity must reflect some traits of the individual in his performance. If not, it is held that the test lacks construct validity. Blun and Naylor (1968) hold the view that construct validity is not much used in industry. It is used more in theoretical rather than pragmatic situations.

5. Synthetic Validity

According to Blun and Naylor (1968), "One might consider synthetic validity to be assumed predictive validity". A test which has shown high predictive validity in certain situations like selecting foremen for a plant can be used in selecting foremen in other plants only when there is similarity in the nature of the job of the foremen in both the plants. Blum and Naylor therefore hold the view that synthetic validity should only be substituted for predictive validity with the full awareness of its possible limitations.

6. Face Validity

A test is said to have face validity when it appears to measure the qualities required for a particular job in question. If the test or prediction instrument does not seem to have much relationship with the job for which one is appearing in the test, the test is said not to have face validity. For example, for the job of a taxi-driver when a language aptitude test is given or an arithmetical ability test is administered, it may be concluded that the test lacks face validity.

RELIABILITY

The second important characteristic of a psychological test is reliability. A reliable test brings similar results in retesting. But when a particular test gives a high score to an individual at one time and a low score at another time it cannot be used for prediciting the usual performance and hence would be said to be unreliable.

The actual process by which one can assess the reliability of a test depends upon many factors. The three techniques for obtaining reliability are : (1) Repeated measures on the same people with the same test or instruments, (2) Measurement on the same people with two equivalent forms of the measuring instrument, and (3) Separation of the measuring device into two or more equivalent part scores.

If all the measuring instruments and measuring methods were error-free then we would always obtain the true scores of people, and the correlation between the two measurements on the same group of people would always be +1.00 or perfect reliability. Unfortunately, such error-free measurement is never completely available, since a wide variety of things contribute to performance at any particular moment.

1. Test-retest Method

One method to evaluate stability consists of measuring the individual's performance twice with the same instrument. The resulting reliability measures the stability of the true score over time.

2. Parallel Test Method

Blum and Naylor (1968) point out that two forms of tests should be as identical as possible except that specific item or questions on each form would represent a similar sample of items chosen. One form may be administered immediately after the other, or they may be administered at intervals. This kind of reliability measures the stability of the test. But the problem here is that it is often difficult to construct alternate forms of measuring devices or tests. Therefore, psychologists have tried for additional methods of assuming reliability besides the two methods already mentioned.

3. Subdivided Test Method

This method measures the internal consistency of a test. It is the most extensively used method of measuring reliability, as it requires only one which is administered only once. In this method the test is divided into two halves, one half consisting of the odd numbered items and the other half consisting of the even numbered items. The correlation between the two halves of the test provides an idea about the reliability of the test.

However, this method has certain drawbacks in the case of speed tests like simple clerical tests where the alternate half procedure gives a spuriously high positive correlation.

4. Kuder-Richardson Method

The Kuder-Richardson method measures the internal consistency reliability. Here, each item is considered as a subtest, so that instead of dividing the test into two halves, the test is divided into N subtests when N implies the total number of items in the test.

CLASSIFICATION

(Refer to the "Vocational Guidance and Selection" Chapter)

ADVANTAGES AND LIMITATIONS OF TESTING IN INDUSTRY AND ORGANISATIONS

Advantages

Psychological tests are considerably more objective and scientific, easier to administer and more economical in measuring the capacities and abilities of an individual in comparison to other method of selection like the application blank, questionnaires and interview techniques etc.

The results of psychological. tests can be statistically analysed. Psychological tests are subjected to less bias and prejudice of the .tester in comparison to other methods of selection. The cost of tests are not high and in very short period plenty of information can be obtained.

Testing can be used to improve the selection process; promotion and transfer principles. The cost of hiring and training inexperienced and incapable people can be reduced by using reliable and valid tests. According to Blum and Naylor (1968), "Psychological testing can reduce the costs of hiring people who will be successful for its goal in measuring aptitude and predicting ultimate success among inexperienced applicants".

After reviewing a large number of studies, Ghiselli (1952) points out that it is not safe to presume that tests which predict trainability best, also predict job proficiency equally well. However, a well standardised test can predict the accuracy and speed of performance. The performance of an individual can be compared with the performance of the group when norms are made available.

Finally, psychological tests are also useful for promotion and transfer or training, for discovering accident liability and inefficiency or failure in a job.

Limitations

Empirical evidences indicate that many other factors like job satisfaction and morale, attitude etc., may be related to the level of performance besides ability. In spite of possessing the necessary abilities, a person may not show proficiency in a job for a number of factor which are more or less interrelated. Infact, most of the psychological tests only measure specific abilities and the other contributing factors to success and failure in job are not assessed.

To measure an ability accurately, a test must be reliable and valid and it should measure what it intends to measure. But the validity and reliability of certain psychological tests can be questioned.

There are some culture free tests which can be used universally without any modifications whatsoever. But certain tests constructed for one culture, are sometimes applied in another culture without any modification, even though such tests are not culture-free. Such tests should be standardised before administration. It is often found that tests constructed and standardised in the

Western culture are administered on the Indian sample without being modified. As a result, such tests fail to measure tile abilities and capacities of an individual. Of course, many present day psychologists of India are constructing their own tests for Indian industrial personnel or are modifying and standardising Western tests for Indian use.

Finally, one of the important drawbacks of psychological testing is that the testers often do not have adequate training for administering tests. The competency of the tester, his personality and relationship with the industry are also overlooked more often than not. As a result the purpose of using tests in industry is not fulfilled.

However, in spite of the various drawbacks of psychological tests, the most of industrial organisations and plants have benefitted by the use of psychological tests in the selection and placement of employees.

QUESTIONS

1. Give a brief outline of various psychological tests applied on industrial workers.
2. Discuss the importance of psychological tests in industry.
3. Write notes on :
   (*i*) Reliability and validity of tests.
   (*ii*) Test-restest method.
   (*iii*) Subdivided test method.

REFERENCES

Anastasi, Anne. *Psychological Testing*, 2nd ed., McMillan, New York, 1961.

Blum, M.L. and Naylor, J.C. *Industrial Psychology : Its Theoretical and Social Foundations*, Haper and Row Publishers, 1968.

Brown, C.W. and Ghiselli, E.F. The relationship between the predictive power of aptitude tests for trainability and for job proficiency. *Jn. of Applied Psychology*, 1952, 36, pp. 370-377.

Cronbach, L.J. *Essentials of Psychological Testing*, Harper and Row, New York, 1960.

Murphy, Joseph J. Current Practices in the Use of Psychological Testing by Police Agencies. *Jn of Criminal Law Crimnology & Police Science*, 1972, Vol. 63.

Tiffin, J. and McCormick, E.J. *Industrial Psychology*, 5th Ed., Prentice Hall of India Private Limited, New Delhi, 1971.

9

Job Analysis

PRACTICAL IMPROTANCE

Every job has certain specific and unique requirements and every individual's personality consists of certain specific traits and characteristics. Thus, each and every worker is not suitable for each and every job, and conversely, each and every work cannot be successfully performed by any and every employee. The individual who fulfils the specific requirements of a job is the best and fittest person for that job. If he is appointed in such a job, production not only increases qualitatively and quantitatively, but also the worker has job satisfaction, is happy in his job and creates no problems for self and the management. Thus, for the overall betterment of the industrial organisation, evaluation and analysis of each and every job into different components, an accurate and minute study of such components is extremely essential.

Job analysis has tremendous practical importance in modern industries and organisations. For proper and judicious vocational selection and guidance, its role is of tremendous importance. Moreover, in order to avoid square pegs in round holes job analysis is also necessary. Thus, to avoid unnecessary wastage of man power, energy and national property industry has to take the help of job analysis.

USES OF JOB ANALYSIS

Lawshe and Satter (1944) have pointed out four primary uses of job analysis :

1. The derivation of training content.
2. The setting up of personnel specifications.
3. The improvement of job efficiency.
4. The establishment of wage structures.

On the basis of a survey of 401 articles on the literature of job analysis Zerga (1943) holds that there are mostly 20 specific uses of job analysis.

1. Job grading and classification.
2. Wage setting and standardisation.
3. Provision for hiring specifications.
4. Clarification of job duties and responsibilities.
5. Transfer and promotions.
6. Adjustment of grievances.
7. Establishment of a common understanding between various levels of workers and management.
8. Defining and outlining promotional steps.
9. Investigating accidents.
10. Indication of faulty work procedures or duplication of effort.
11. Maintaining, operating and adjusting machinery.
12. Time and motion studies.
13. Defining limits of authority.
14. Indicating cases of individual merit.
15. Indicating causes of personal failure.
16. Education and training.
17. Facilitating job placement.
18. Studies of health and fatigue.
19. Scientific guidance.
20. Determining jobs suitable for occupational therapy.

A careful analysis of these uses of job analysis suggests the tremendous importance of job analysis. As already pointed out, improvement of production and efficiency, reduction of conflict in small and big organisations depend to a certain extent on job analysis. For example, if the different components of the job are distributed to different workers, and if there are clear cut statements of specific requirements for the various jobs, there will not be any opportunity for quarrel and difference of opinion as to who will do which part of the job. Secondly, the work can be completed with ease and discipline.

The information provided by job analysis can serve many other purposes. It provides directly the specific information required for individual jobs and group jobs. Job analysis also gives information about personnel, administration, work design, administrative controls etc.

Tiffin and McCormick (1971) have given the following uses of job analysis information as shown in Table 9.1.

According to Blun, "In many respects, a job analysis is a vital part of working efficiency besides promoting smooth working relationship among the employees. In can be regarded as the foundation upon which a system of efficency is built."

TABLE 9.1

Personnel Administration	Uses of Job Analysis		
	Work Design	Administrative Control	Other Uses
Personnel recruitment	Engineering design	Organisational planning	Planning educational curricula
Selection and placement	Work method Job design	Man power planning and control	Vocational counseling
Training and personnel development			
Performance measurement and rating			
Wage and salary administration			
Labour relations			

Without job analysis, endeavours to increase efficiency, to undertake training programmes and erase labour management problems, will not be very effective. In fact, before applying psychological tests on applicants for a particular job, and before appointing workers in various jobs it is essential that a job analysis should be made.

The form used by the United States Employment Service to obtain data for a job analysis is the following :

JOB ANALYSIS SCHEDULE

1. Job title .... 2. Number ....
3. Number employed .... 4. Establishment No.....................................
5. Alternate titles.............. .... 6. Date ....
No. of sheets ....
7. Dictionary title and code ....
8. Industry .... 9. Branch ....
10. Department .... 11. Work performed.......................................

Viteles has suggested a different job analysis form known as Guide of Job Analysis (1932) with the 11 items given below :

1. Indentification of the job
2. Number employed
3. Statement of duties
4. Machines used
5. Analysis of operations
6. Conditions of work
7. Pay and non financial incentives
8. Relation to other allied jobs (place in the organisation)
9. Opportunities for transfer and promotion

10. Time and nature of training
11. Personal requirements
    (*a*) General (*e.g.*, age, marital status)
    (*b*) Physical
    (*c*) Educational
    (*d*) Previous experience
    (*e*) General and special abilities
    (*f*) Temperamental and character requirements.

Shartle (1952) has prepared a form of job analysis which includes the following divisions :

1. Job name or title
2. Classification title
3. Industry, plant, department, division, section
4. Number employed
5. Hires, quits, job absences
6. Work performed
7. Supervision given and received
8. Levels of difficulty
    (*a*) Responsibility
    (*b*) Knowledge
    (*c*) Initiative
    (*d*) Mental alertness
    (*e*) Judgement
    (*f*) Dexterity
    (*g*) Accuracy
    (*h*) Experience and education required
    (*i*) Other factors
9. Pay rate
10. Hours and shifts
11. Output standards
12. Job combination or breakdown
13. Job relationship
14. Machines, tools equipments, material used
15. Working conditions
16. Social environment
17. Physical demands
18. Worker characteristics
19. Previous experience required
20. Training required
    (*a*) General level
    (*b*) Vocational training
    (*c*) Technical training
    (*d*) On the job training
21. Selection methods.

An overall comparison of these three schedules indicates overlapping or repetition. Of course, the specific items to be included in job analysis schedules would obviously vary from plant to plant according to its needs and necessities. In other words, it will depend on which aspect of job analysis is considered most important.

JOB ANALYSIS PROCEDURES

As described by Tiffin and McCormick (1971) there are many variants of job analysis procedures that have been used.

Among them, usually there are two main aspects of job analysis procedures used to obtain data for a job analysis :

1. Method of obtaining job information.
2. Nature of job information.

Method of Obtaining Job Information

***(a)* Observation.** Here the analyst observes the workers while they are performing their job in the plant. Using normal observation procedure the observer collects data on job description right on the job. This method is more effectively applicable to short cycle than long cycle jobs, or to those jobs that differ considerably from time to time. Observation is a slow and costly method and the bias of the observer may influence the analysis of the job.

***(b)* Interview.** The analyst, usually outside the actual job situation, interviews the representatives of the workers or the individual workers and asks questions to get the necessary information about the job. At times, he might interview formen, supervisors or experts who are quite experienced in the job in question.

Though this technique is very time consuming and costly it gives a definite and full picture of the job in question. (Refer to interview technique under "Selection" Chapter)

***(c)* Questionnaire.** This method is applied to obtain information about the job through a well-prepared questionnaire. The questionnaires are either delivered to the workers personally or by post. The employee is instructed to provide data about the job and about himself by answering the questions and filling up the questionnaire. Workers, supervisors and executives who are familiar with the job supply information about the job in view.

It is a suitable method for those who can write easily and express themselves clearly. But low-level employees who are not sufficiently educated and lack the facility for self-expression usually cannot provide correct information about the job by this method. The job incumbents may also answer the questions quite carelessly and without interest if the questionnaire is mailed to them. Moreover, coding and analysis of data by the questionnaire method consumes a lot of time and is also a labourious process. (Refer to questionnaire method under "Selection" Chapter.)

***(d)* Work Diaries.** It is otherwise known as the self-recoding method. By this technique, the job incumbents are normally required to record their daily activities in a diary. In this diary the job activities are recorded over a period of time, may be for several months or years, and it gives a comprehensive and intergrated picture of the job. The chief advantage of this method is that systematic and orderly information about the job can be obtained without much labour and expenditure. But a lot of time of the job incumbent is consumed in daily recording. However, it is specially useful for high level jobs such as executives, management or scientific positions. Dubin and Spray (1964), Hinrichs (1964) and Home and Lupton (1965) have used this procedure recently for job analysis.

But, if recording forms are not systematic it may consume a lot of time of the workers to record the information and of the analyst to find out the job characteristics.

(e) Moving Picture Films. Used to advantage by Taylor and Gilbreth for the scientific analysis of work and application of scientific management principles to job, this method of job analysis records the work in progress. It is different from the observation method in that here permanent record of the performance of the job is made. Furthermore, there is less chance for bias and subjectivism of the observer to influence the information. This trend may be found to a considerable extend in the observation method.

(f) Use of Source Material. Under some special situations valuable information can be obtained directly from various sources. For example, maintenance records of the plant may be used as a source of information about the frequency of repair activities. This information gives an idea about the quality and manufacturing defects of the machines. Technical publications about the mechanical equipments prepared by the manufacturer can be highly useful for developing training programmes for the employees and operators.

Nature of Job Information

The general nature of job information obtained by job analysis procedures will depend upon the purpose in mind. Certain types of job information can be obtained by one of the methods discussed below.

(a) Essay Description Technique. Tiffin and McCormick (1971) hold the view that certain types of job information can be obtained by the essay description technique. This technique provides information about the job in the form of an essay description. It also supplies other information such as the listing of equipments and materials used, description of working conditions etc. It also gives indications of the personal characteristics which are considered necessary in the selection of individual for the job. The information is put in the form of an essay description of a job.

Observation and interview techniques are usually used for getting the easy description.

(b) Job Check List and Questionnaires. Job check lists and questionnaires consist of listing of job activities and other job characteristics such as working conditions, job activities of different categories of employees etc. With the analysis of job, information is given about each item.

In the case of the check list, the individual has to mention whether or not the items apply to the job. Further details can also be obtained about the job if there is a provision for getting such information in the questionnaire. The job activity questionnaire developed by Kay and Meyer (1962) for use in a study of the activities of production men serves a good example.

(c) Activity Analysis. Otherwise referred to as 'task analysis', it makes a list of job activities. This technique of job information has two distinct characteristics.

(i) It makes an orderly and systematic list of job activities in the same order as found in the job.

(ii) It includes job activities in detail.

With the variation of need or purpose, different procedures are used in activity analysis.

By the observation or interview method activity analysis information can be obtained for existing jobs that are still in the design stage. At present this method is being used quite extensively in the prediction of jobs and development of various training programmes.

(d) **Motion and Time Study.** An analysis of job activities is made by the motion and time study developed by Gilbreth. Essential and elemental motions of a particular job are indentified in the motion study and unnecessary motions are eliminated for developing scientific and economic methods of performing a job. After the motion analysis, the time spent for completing each element of the job is fixed and the standard time for the total operation is determined. For the purpose of job analysis by motion and time study, usually observation and photographic methods are used. (Refer to the "time and motion study" chapter for the details.)

(e) **Critical Incidents Technique**. Flanagan (1954) has developed the Critical Incidents Technique, which he holds, integrates the problem of job definition, selection, classification and the development of criteria measures. It provides for the listing or checking of job behaviours that are considered to be critical to job performance. These job behaviours may be positive or negative, depending upon their desirability or undesirability.

He also holds the view that critical incidents technique makes it possible to conduct research on the criterion problem on a sound and rational basis. Through direct observation by participants and supervisors, this method establishes the critical requirements. A critical requirement is a requirement which is critical in the sense that it has been responsible for outstandingly effective or definitely unsatisfactory performance of an important part of the job. Information about critical incidents is obtained by the observation, interview and questionnaire methods.

Until 1963 people were more concerned with performance, appraisal, selection and training. Smith and Kendall's (1963) paper on critical incident technique elevated the use of the technique by incorporating it with their behaviourally anchored scale. This definitely brought a significant turning point. Further, the technique is extending its usefulness in other areas such as team building activities, conflict resolution and studies of the quality of life. The dream of Flangan in 1954 is thus tending towards reality. The technique is also being used in many organisations by professional experts but there is very little published research about these issues. Ansari and Baumgartel (1981) remark that the use of this technique has become institutionalised and hence research interest has waned.

The investigators are hopeful about the technique to be further developed for the prediction and assessment of managerial success. The extended use of critical incidents method may help to identify the behaviour critical for successful and unsuccessful executives taking in to account the newer contigency approaches to the understanding of organisational behaviour (Ansari, 1979a).

Besides these methods of job analysis, Blum and Naylor (1968) have suggested some additional methods of job analysis like the check list method, the observation method, the interview method, the group interview method, the technical conference method, the work participation method etc.

Check List Method

In this method, from a detailed list of possible task statements, the worker checks the tasks he performs. Dunnette and Krichner (1949), Dunnette and England (1957) and the United States Department of Labour have developed various check lists of job activities.

Check lists are quite easy for the job incumbent to give his reply. The collection of information through check lists is less time consuming and less expensive. The data can be collected from large groups and it is also economical to calculate.

However, the preparation of the check list is quie time consuming and it requires a lot of preliminary work and experience to gather appropriate task statements. Moreover, as viewed by Blum and Naylor, they do not give an integrated picture of the job in question.

Observation-Interview Method

It is an integration of observation and interview technique. The analyst observes the worker on the job situation as well as asks him questions to collect relevant information about the job.

Though it is a good method as it tries to get information by two different techniques and to integrate them, it is slow, time consuming and costly. It may also disturb the normal operation of the workers by distracting their attention as the data is collected on the job.

Group Interview Method

By this method a number of employees working in a particular job are interviewed simultaneously. After discussions with the interviewees, the interviewer integrates and coordinates the views and opinions of different employees into a single job description.

One advantage of this method is that it saves a great deal of time in comparison to the individual interview method. However, integrating and coordinating the views of different interviewees is quite a hard job and requires considerable ability, training and experience.

Technical Conference Method

This is categorically different from the other techniques of job analysis, as here, technical personnel and experts are engaged in gathering information about the job, rather than the job incumbents as traditionally used in other techniques. Foremen and supervisors who have considerable knowledge of the job being analysed are appointed as experts to collect the relevant information about the job. These experts hold discussions with the job analyst and accordingly try to list all the characteristics of the job.

One limitation of this method is that since experts do not perform the task themselves, they usually do not have enough practical experience on the job in question to give adequate job information. Their judgement and views on the job characteristics may be a reflection of their background experience only.

Work Participation Method

In this method the job analyst, instead of depending upon the job incumbents or experts for job analysis information, depends upon his own estimates and judgement by engaging himself actively on the job. He actually performs the job himself and gets direct information about the characteristics of the job in question.

Blum and Naylor (1968) opine that this is not only a time consuming and costly method, but also requires the analyst to have sufficient training specially in complex jobs. However, for simple jobs it has proved to be useful and beneficial.

In addition to these techniques, force choice technique and rating system have also been used to assess supervision ability.

Forced Choice Techniques

Ghiselli (1954) has found that the forced choice techniques can give satisfactory predictions of supervisory ability. Thus view confirms that the report given by Radom (1950) who found this technique to be useful in picking better foremen at Standard Oil of New. Jersey.

Rating System

The rating system has also its advantages which should not be overlooked. Of course the reliability and validity of the rating system should be checked and it must qualify itself to measure what it intends to measure.

Conclusion

It has been noticed that the job evaluation system, critical incidents and forced choice have been the favourite means of psychologists to obtain objectivity. In spite of the objectivity and advantages to these methods the rating system should also be taken into consideration for the purpose of job analysis.

According to Habbe (1951), job evaluation is also necessary for promotion, increase of salary and for the solution of other personal problems. It is observed that currently forced choice and critical incidents techniques are being introduced in industries though the importance of conventional rating methods cannot be ruled out.

The primary interest of a psychologist in job analysis is the main aspect or individual aspect of the job. Viteles's (1932) job psychograph and the occupational ability pattern devised by the Employment Stabilisation Research Institute of the University of Minnesota are two main contributions in this regard. Though they have only historical importance as they are not very much used today, they are definitely classic contributions.

Job Psychograph

It consists of a complete statement of the personnel requirements for a job. A job psychograph involves and analysis and specification of special abilities necessary for success, in a particular job.' It is an analysis in terms of the abilities required to do the job.

In job psychograph a list of traits from different areas is presented and each trait is rated on a five point scale in accordance with its degree of importance for a particular job in question by a person familiar with the job. The rater, by putting across mark in space 1, 2, 3, 4, 5, indicates that he regards a specific trait as negligible, barely significant, of great importance or of utmost importance.

In Table 9.2, the job psychograph of a machine operator is shown.

TABLE 9.2

	1	*2*	*3*	*4*	*5*	*Remarks*
1. Energy		x				
2. Rate of discharge				x		
3. Endurance		x				
4. Control		x				
5. Coordination				x		
6. Quick decision					x	
7. Initiative		x				
8. Concentration			x			
9. Distribution of attention			x			
10. Persistence			x			
11. Alertness		x				
12. Associability			x			
13. Visual discrimination				x		
14. Auditory discrimination	x					
15. Tactual discrimination	x					
16. Kinesthetic discrimination			x			
17. Space perception				x		
18. Form perception		x				
19. Accuracy			x			
20. Visual memory		x				
21. Auditory memory	x					
22. Kinesthetic memory	x					
23. Understanding		x				
24. Understanding (Quickness)			x			
25. Observation			x			
26. Planfulness		x				
27. Intelligence			x			
28. Judgement	x					
29. Logical analysis	x					

Key: 1. Negligible 2. Barely significant 3. Significant
4. Of great importance 5. Of utmost importance.

TABLE 9.2(a)
A job psychograph of a driver employed in the Orissa Road Transport Services for the last 20 years

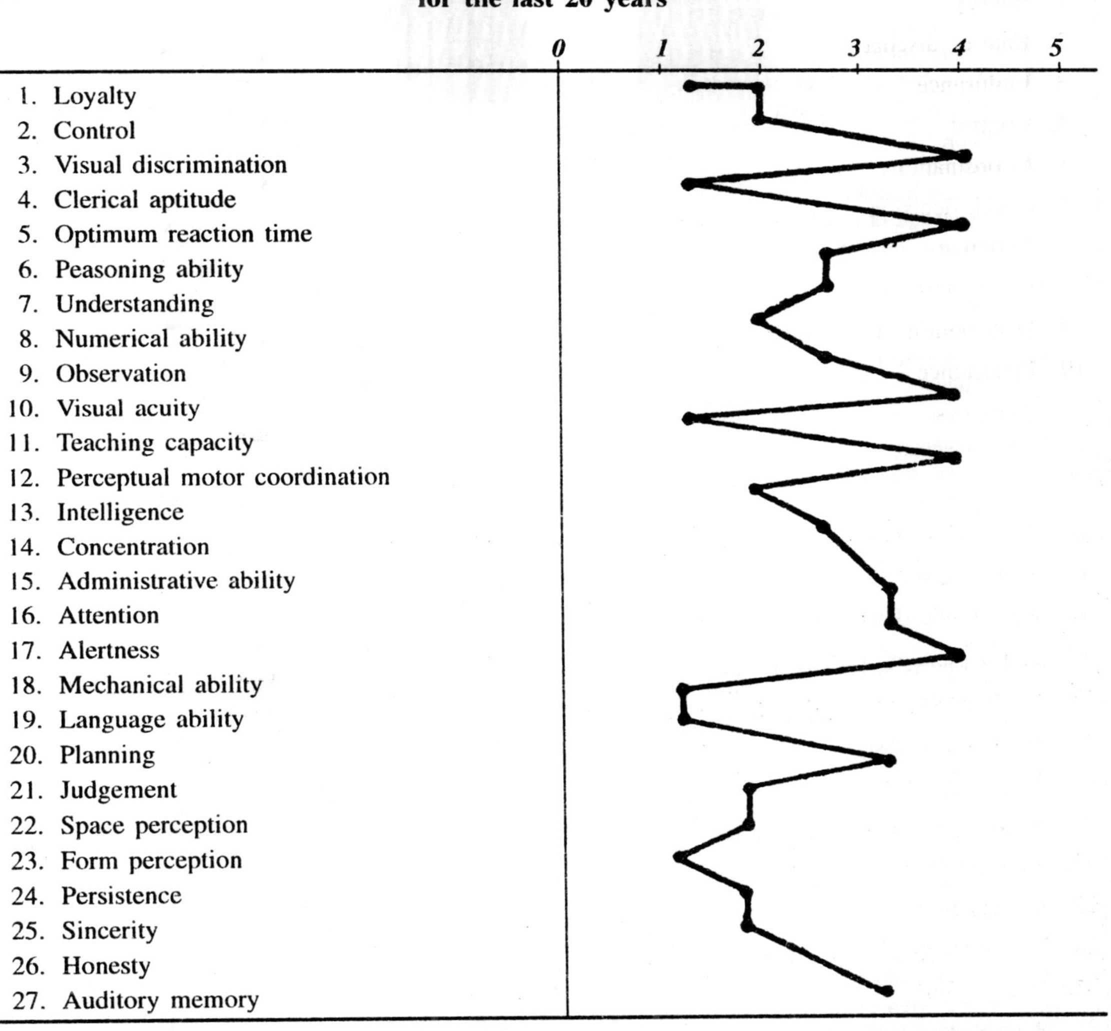

Key : 1. Negligible 2. Barely significant 3. Significant
4. Of great importance 5. Of utmost importance.

Based on the Study "Job Psychograph in Job Analysis", Mohanty, G.B. (1981).

COMPOSITE JOB PSYCHOGRAPH

When a group (If persons familiar with the job make a psychograph, a composite job psychograph is prepared in terms of the average rating which each trait in question received. According to Maier (1970), "A group psychograph largely eliminates non representative ratings such as those influenced by prejudice and halo effects. By connecting the ratings of the various traits with a line, a psychograph is formed.

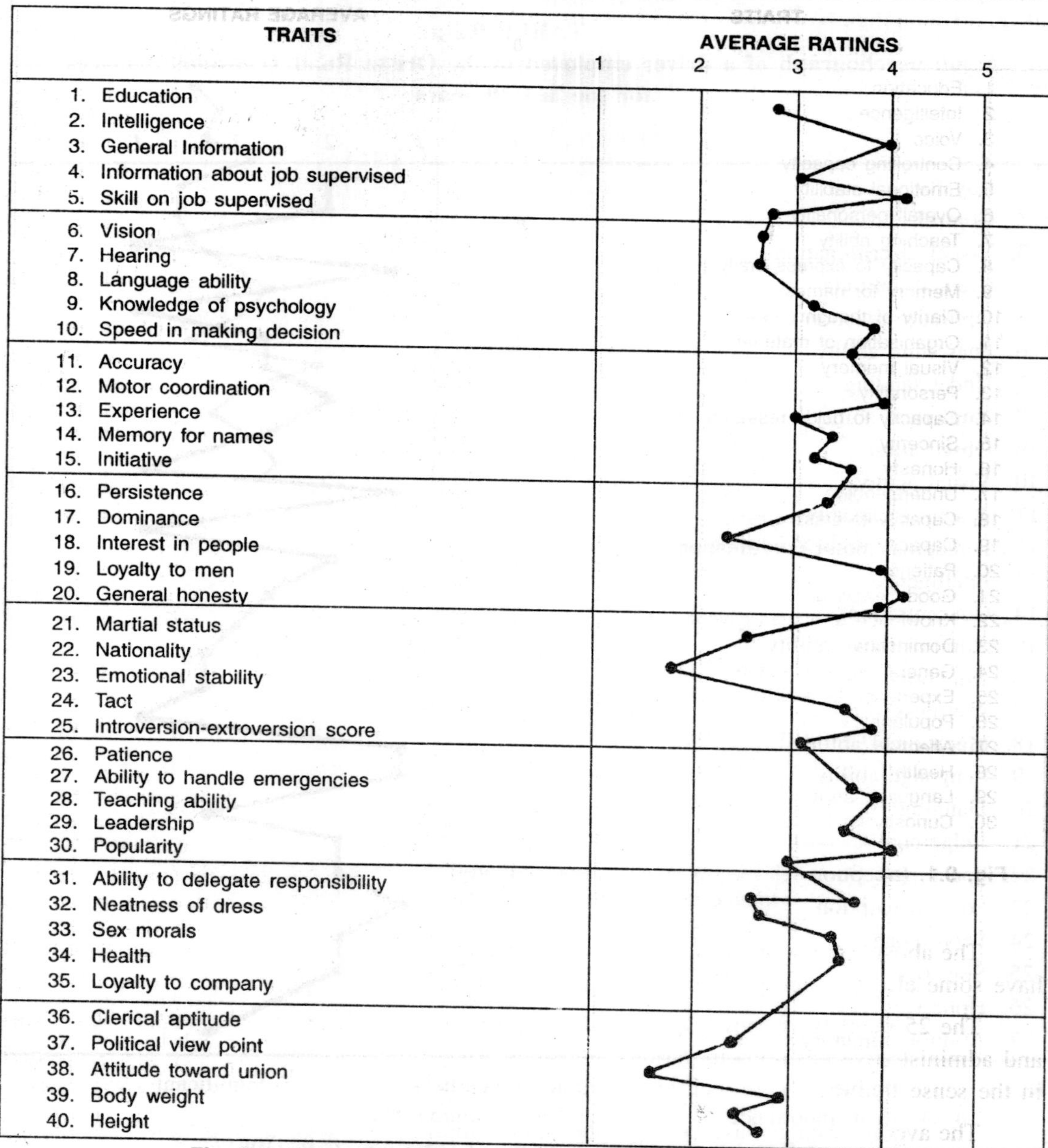

Fig. 9.1. Composite job psychograph of occupation of Foremen (Adapted from Mairer, N.R.F., page 259, 3rd Ed.)

A composite job psychograph of the occupation of foremen is given in Figure 9.1. This figure shows the composite rating for a list of 40 traits which might have a bearing on performance on the job of foremen.

Muhanty (1981) prepared this composite job psychograph taking the average rating on a group of 33 female college teachers (Age 37-45 years; having teaching experience 15 years and more) of the Orissa Educational Service.

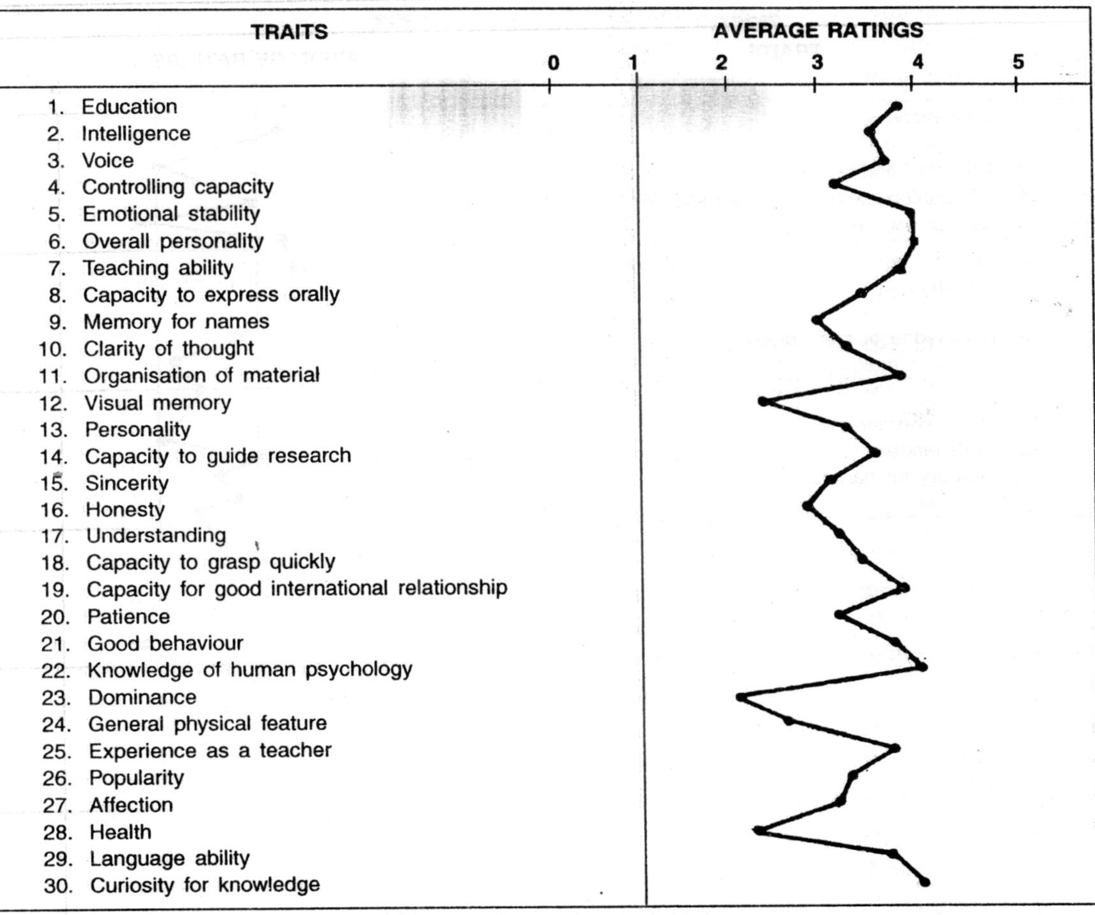

Fig. 9.1. (a). Compositive Job Psychograph prepared on the average rating of a group of 33 female college teachers of Orissa, (teaching job).

The above job psychograph presents the composite rating for a list of 30 traits which might have some effect on the performance of college teachers.

The 25 raters were mostly qualified engineering graduates holding responsible supervisory and administrative positions in various industries. They are considered qualified and competent in the sense that they were well aware of the duties of a foreman from first hand experience.

The average ratings have been graphed which indicates the relative importance of the traits at a glance.

LIMITATIONS OF JOB PSYCHOGRAPH

Blum has pointed out the following limitations of job psychograph.

1. Each trait listed requires specific definition.
2. The person doing the rating should be trained in the understanding and knowledge of the specific traits.

3. Up to now psychologists have not been able to develop to their full satisfaction the valid measures of many of the traits listed, such as proficiency, alertness and initiative, to name a few.

In spite of the difficulties, the job psychograph has its merits and is also used in industry.

In the job psychograph there is an important implication for vocational guidance and selection. A person who has applied for a specific job can be rated as having certain traits and this profile can be matched with the profile containing the traits and qualities required for a specific job. When there is a lot of similarity between these two profiles, the person can be selected for that job.

Occupational Ability Pattern

As pointed out by Blum and Naylor (1968), Paterson, Dvorak etc., associated with the Employment Stabilisation Research Institute of the University of Minnesota, devised the Occupational Ability Pattern. This occupational ability pattern assumed that abilities on a job can be measured by a representative sampling of psychological tests. With this point in view, they gave a group of tests to a number of individuals who were quite successful in specific occupations and obtained scores and profiles of the most typical test performances of people on the job.

The occupational ability pattern, therefore, attempts to avoid trait specifications suggested by Viteles (1932). It also tries to avoid evaluation and subjective opinions even though they are obtained from experiments. The psychological tests try to sample the abilities and aptitudes of the individuals on a wide range and include tests like verbal intelligence, finger dexterity, spatial relations and eye hand coordination etc.

Another important merit of this technique is that there is a more obvious relationship between this technique and vocational guidance and selection than there was with the job psychograph by Viteles.

A person can be given a battery of tests and on the basis of the scores obtained in these tests a job profile can be prepared. This profile can be compared with the profile usually found in various other occupations.

Then the worker can be selected for a job, the profile of which has the maximum resemblance with the job profile of the individual.

CRITICAL ANALYSIS OF JOB ANALYSIS PROCEDURE

"Job analysis has been characterised as a sort of hand-maiden, serving in various ways a variety of needs and all the while floundering in a morass of semantic confusion".

This view of A.M. Kershmer (1955) points to the basic problems of job analysis in characterising job activities and other job-related information in definite and objective terms. The limitations of job analysis are especially observed in the essay types of descriptions where the same activity can be described in different ways. According to Tiffin and McCormick (1971), "If the same activity occurs in two positions and if it is described somewhat differently in both position descriptions, it may be difficult to determine whether the two positions are or are not alike in this respect".

In order to make the job information scientific and systematic, then it is necessary that the same job element or characteristic be identified or qualified in essentially the same manner, regardless of the job in which it occurs. But in traditional, descriptive job analysis procedure we have not been able to do this as yet.

However, more recently, same significant and valuable contributions have been made to overcome these shortcomings, especially by the development of check lists and rating scales.

QUESTIONS

1. What is job analysis ? Critically examine the practical implication of job analysis in industry.
2. Describe in detail the uses and applications of job analysis in industrial organisations.
3. Analyse the various methods used to obtain data and information for analysis.
4. What is a job analysis schedule ? Critically examine Viteles' job analysis schedule.
5. Compare some of the important job analysis schedules and point out the merits and defects of each schedule.
6. What is understood by the job analysis procedure ? Make a critical evaluation of the main aspects of job analysis procedures.
7. What is a job psychograph ? Describe a job psychograph and point out its limitations.
8. Write notes on the following :
   (*a*) Uses of job analysis.
   (*b*) Composite job psychograph.
   (*c*) Occupational ability pattern.
   (*d*) Technical conference method.
   (*e*) Critical incident technique.

REFERENCES

Ansari, M.A. and Baumgartel, H. The Critical Incident Technique : Description of Current Uses; *J. Soc. Econ. Studies,* 1981 ix(2).

Blum, M.L. *Industrial Psychology and Its Social Foundations*, Harper and Row Publishers, New Delhi, 1956.

Blum, M.L. and Naylor, J.C. *Industrial Psychology and Its Social Foundations*, Harper and Row, 1968.

Dunnette, M.D. and Kirchner, W.K. A check list for differentiating different kinds of sales jobs, *Personnel Psychol.* 12, 1959, pp. 421-430.

Flanagan, J.C. The critical incident technique, *Psychological Bulletin*, 54, 1944, pp. 327-358.

Ghiselli, E.E. The forced choice technique in self-description, *Personnel Psychology*, 7, 1954, pp. 201-208.

Habbe, S. *Appraisal of job performance studies in personnel policy*, National Industrial Conference Board, New York, 1951.

Kay, E. and Meyer, H.H. The development of a job activity questionnaire for production foremen, *Personnel Psychology*, 15, 1962, pp. 411-418.

Maier, N.R.F., Otis, J.N. and Smith, K.R. Psychology in industry, *Job Psychograph in Job Analysis Occupation,* 1934, pp. 12, 10, 47-56.

Mohanty, G.B. Job Psychograph in Job Analysis (1981).

Shartle, C.L. *Occupational Information, Its Development and Operation*, 3rd ed., Englewood Cliffs.

Tiffen, J. and McCormick, E.J. *Industrial Psychology,* Prentice Hall India Private Ltd. New Delhi 1971.

Viteles, M.S. *Industrial Psychology*, Norton, 1932.

10

Vocational Selection and Placement

IMPORTANCE OF SELECTION AND PLACEMENT IN INDUSTRY

According to Viteles (1932), "Fitting the worker to the job represents the first and most important step in promoting individual efficiency and adjustment in industry". Fitting the workers to the job here mainly refers to vocational selection.

It is said that : Getting a job is not nearly so important as getting the right job; getting a man is not nearly so important to the company as getting the right man. A mistake on the part of either is bound to be costly.

Improper and careless selection and misplacement of the worker is one of the most important drawbacks of modern industrial organisations which leads to tremendous wastage of human power and national wealth. In fact, if a worker is not fit for a job, he is not interested in it. He may not appreciate his co-workers. Besides, constant irritation, carelessness in work, lack of desire to specialise in the job and inattentiveness due to boredom lead to further loss, not only to the management, but also to the employees. This is turn leads to low production, high rate of accident and fatigue. Failure as a good worker leads to the development of inferiority complex, frustration and hence makes the worker maladjusted in his professional as well as personal life. Therefore, the selection of workers before placement is essential.

Poor selection paves tile way for inefficiency, wastage, loss of time, complaints and ultimate discharge. Absenteeism and turnover also increases due to bad selection. In actual practice selection and placement often merge into a single process. Placement specifically deals with the problem : "which man should be put in which job ?"

Hence, selection should be scientific, objective and based on tests and interviews.

SELECTION

According to Blum and Naylor (1968), "Selection involves picking for hire a subset of workers from the total set (population) of workers available. Efficient selection is therefore a nonrandom process, in so far as those selected have been chosen on the assumption that they are more apt to make better employees than those who have been rejected. The task of the industrial psychologist is to make certain that the assumption is indeed a valid one as a result of using objective and scientific procedures and instruments rather than subjective and biased judgement".

The existence of individual differences provide the basis for the selection and the placement process. Every worker, irrespective of training and occupation, will differ considerably in terms of their relative work efficiency and performance. Hull (Blum and Naylor 1968) reported some ratio of efficiency between the least efficient and most efficient workers in different occupations. He found that in the case of spoon polishers, the best worker was over five times as efficient as the poorest worker.

METHODS OF SELECTION

The method of selection is usually divided into two parts :

(*i*) Unscientific method of selection.

(*ii*) Scientific method of selection.

Unscientific Method of Selection

(*a*) Physiognomy. Physical features, such as the shape of the face, colour, testure of hair, different parts of the body etc. sometimes influence in the selection of workers.

(*b*) Graphology. Selection is made on the basis of hand writing. For example, there was a belief that writing of small letters indicate miserliness, self-centredness, paying attention to minute detail and writing large letters indicated that the person is highly imaginative, amibitious and proud. Heavy lines in writing supposed to indicate strength of will, light pressure in writing indicated emotional depression, moodiness and vertical writing suggested self-control. A slant to right indicated emotional susceptibility and impulsiveness, and slant towards left meant concealment.

But the results of various studies on graphology do not corroborate each other.

Selection of employees on the basis of astrology is equally unscientific.

Scientific Method of Selection

(*a*) Photograph. Those jobs which demand frequent contact with people such as sales officers, insurance agents, advertisement agents, medical agents should have employees having no facial defects. But judging mental abilities and qualities only from a photograph without interviews and tests is just like tossing a coin.

(*b*) Letter of Application. The letter of application is a good basis of prediction about the job success of the individual which gives sufficient information about the applicant. The amount of information required in such applications may vary from name, age, address, to a lengthy document covering the personal history and biodata of the individual such as previous education, work history, previous illness and private life.

Though it is not always desirable to rely entirely on this procedure of selection yet much preliminary information, is obtained, about the applicant which may be useful for a final selection.

(c) Application Blanks. An application blank is prepared from the application form. For different jobs different application blanks are prepared and given to the applicants before the interview to fill up the necessary requirements. It is more specific compared to the application forms.

Application blanks usually have two functions.

1. They provide useful information about the employee according to the requirements of the company, such as the age, sex, number of dependants, social security etc.
2. Application blanks provide information about job applicants which the personnel officer considers necessary to the hiring process. Thus, it can be held that the application blank is a highly structured interview in which the questions have been formulated and standardised in advance.

The application blank mainly requires the personal history of the applicant.

According to Blum and Naylor (1968), "used properly as all aid to selection, the application blank can be, and sometimes is, one of the better selection devices at the disposal of the personnel technician".

They further say, "one advantage of the application blank over the interview and tests of personality and interest is that response bias does not usually play a great role. Even if a person did tend to bias his answers on the application on matters to which he felt some concern about giving an honest answer, in many cases such data is subject to rather easy verification from other sources.... Certainly a person's previous work history should provide some sort of clue to the probability of successful performance on the job under consideration". Moreover, case history and personal data also gives some indication about the personality traits of the individual which may have some bearing on the eventual job adjustment.

References and Recommendations

Documentary evidences in favour of satisfactory performance in the past are provided by references and recommendations from the previous employer.

A letter of recommendation or reference, while giving clue about the conduct, morals, ability and skills of the applicant is more often than not inaccurate and misleading because of :

(i) Lack of knowledge about the applicant.

(ii) Lack of sufficient ability to assess the applicant.

(iii) Lack of the ability to communicate the impressions of the applicant through a letter of recommendation.

(iv) Lastly, the reluctance on the part of the employer to throw light on the unfavourable aspects of those he is asked to recommend is the most serious of all the defects of letter of recommendation. Such reluctance may possibly arise mostly out of a tendency to be kind and sympathetic to the previous employee and hence intentionally the previous employer may give good recommendations so that he can get a job in future.

Besides the above predictors, Stern and Gordon (1961) have used successfully the recruit's ability to follow simple instructions as the predictor.

Peer rating has been successfully applied by Weitz (1958) to select supervisors.

An overall review of all the predictors of job success indicates that, by and large, personal history data and tests are perhaps the most useful predictors. The other predictors in spite of their bias and limitations have significant role to play in the process of selection.

INTERVIEW

Interview techniques are extensively used for the selection of employees in any and every job. This is a very popular and traditional technique of selection. By this technique, the interviewer gets an idea about the overall personality of the interviewee. It is definitely a good source of obtaining information about the person seeking a job.

Blum and Naylor (1968) suggest that interviews used in industry differ according to the following objectives :

(*i*) To evaluate the candidate for purposes of hiring, promotion or transfer, interviews conducted are generally referred to as, "selection and placement interviews". This type of interview is very often used in different organisations and plants for the selection of different categories of employees.

(*ii*) To obtain information from the interviewee concerning his attitudes about his job, the company etc., which are called "attitude interviews". This is necessary to determine whether the candidate is really interested in the job and whether his attitude is pro- or anti-job.

(*iii*) To help the employee with any personal or on the job problem which might be harmful to his performance both on and off the job. These interviews are known as, "counselling interviews". Interviews conducted with these objectives particularly help those who have some situational or personal problems which are likely to influence his efficiency and adjustment.

(*iv*) To evaluate the interviewee for his ability to perform under a particular set of different circumstances. These interviews are often called "assessment or stress interviews". Here the interviewer intentionally and purposefully creates stressful and anxiety-provoking situations with the hope of assessing a person's ability to perform under such conditions. The present author in the capacity of a member of several interview boards has successfully applied some of the techniques of the stress interview while selecting lecturers, executives, school teachers, jailors, welfare officers and family planning officers etc. Such interviews were made popular for the first time during the Second World War. More information about atress interviews can be obtained by referring to the book, *Assessment of Man* (1945).

Currently, industries are using this type of interview more and more as in this age of stress and strain, employees are likely to face stressful situations off and on the job.

The usefulness of the stress interview technique has been observed by the present author. She has been able to judge the personality, characteristics and capacity to adjust to stressful circumstances of the interviewees. While a number of interviewees reacted with anger, hostility and depression to various remarks and anxiety provoking verbal stimuli, some reacted in a very calm and composed manner without being disturbed or emotionally upset.

Use of Situation Tests in Interviews

Besides the techniques just mentioned, situation tests can also be used in interviews with the aim of studying the reactions of the interviewee in a specific situation.

The present author applied this technique while conducting interviews for the selection of candidates for different types of posts. For instance, while interviewing candidates for the post of lecturer in psychology, in a number of cases the author asked the candidates to give a lecture on, "What is the present status of psychology" or "What is psychology", assuming the board to be the intermediate psychology students. The results have been quite encouraging in the sense that some candidates with brilliant academic careers were not able to express their views orally. A few others could not give clear and basic concepts. A few seemed to be unaware of the fact that they were facing the students of an introductory psychology class.

What the author gathered from such experiences is that many applicants who were otherwise academically quite successful could not perform well in the situational tests. The view that a good scholar need not necessarily be always a successful teacher has been substantiated by the author's observation and experience gathered from several interview situations Though the artificial nature of the situation is a limitation, it has been noted that some have been able to communicate very successfully while others were quite clumsy and confused in their expression.

The situation test is definitely a good method to assess the candidate on the job'.

SELECTION INTERVIEW

There is rarely any person who is selected for any job, be it the job of a hotel boy, an executive, an air hostess or a managing director without being interviewed. Various surveys further indicate that the use of selection interview is almost universal. Spriegel and James (1958) report data from a 1930 surveys of 336 firms and a 1957 survey of 852 firms.

In the former survey 93 per cent of the firms reported using interviews as a part of their selection process while in the later survey this increased to 99 per cent.

The length of selection interviews varies with the type of position, number of applicants, importance attached to the interview as a selection device, nature of job and the personality of the interviewer. But as experience shows, unfortunately many selection interviews are conducted by untrained hands. However, a generalisation can not be made between the length of the interview and interview value.

The interview technique has not received great attention concerning its reliability and validity in spite of its wide application in employment situations. It has not also been fully known whether the length of an interview has any effect on the validity and reliability of the interview (Mayfield, 1964). The basic purpose of an interviewer is : (*i*) to gather as much data as he can, which is relevant to the selection decision, and (*ii*) to evaluate the data available and decide to select or reject the applicant.

The data collected during an interview depends upon the personality of the interviewer, his degree of training, his biases and prejudices, and the position he is attempting to fill up. Hence, through the use of a highly structured interview session, data can be collected very systematically in which a planned series of questions, prepared in advance are presented to the applicant. Highly structured interviews are also called "patterned interviews".

On the contrary, when one intends to explore only the applicant's qualifications, the interview can be of the unstructured (open end) type, where questions are neither prepared in advance nor planned. Questions are asked 'on the spot' which are likely to produce critical information. Commenting on the job of an interviewer, Blum and Naylor view, "His job is one of attemping to collect, combine and weigh the interview data in such a fashion that he comes up with a prediction of how successful the applicant may be, should he be hired. The degree to which he can successfully predict eventual job success is his validity."

CHARACTERISTICS OF SELECTED INTERVIEWS

The interview is a verbal and visual interaction between the interviewer and the interviewee. So the language and appearance of the interviewee provide important clues to the interviewer. The basic structure of an interview being conversational, it is the task of the interviewer to use this conversation tool to elicit as much relevant information as possible. Hence, the conversational skill of the interviewer can be an important variable in the success of any interview.

The behaviour of the interviewer also has a significant effect on the performance of the interviewee. The clues supplied by the interviewer serve as a kind of feedback or reinforcement to the applicant. Studies by Verplank (1955) and Green Spoon (1955) support this view.

Besides, individual interviews, group interviews or situation tests are used now-a-days. How far an interview is accurate and supplies accurate information through the interview method is a possible question. The tinge of bias and subjectivism cannot also be ruled out in interviews. To avoid this, the interview data can be checked with the data obtained from the past employment through the previous employer, and the job duty in previous work.

It can, therefore, be concluded that as bias, prejudice and impressions are the main drawbacks of the interview method it lacks reliability and validity. Hence, the interview needs to be subjected to more empirical research and until this is accomplished there will be many unanswered questions concerning not only its validity, but also the best interview technique to be used.

Finally, it can be opined that the interview alone should not be the only method of selection. The interview may be used as a supplementary method to other methods of selection.

PSYCHOLOGICAL TESTS

Tests standardised and constructed in a scientific manner and applied for selection of employees are reliable and valid.

Different types of tests are applied to the applicants, keeping in view the capabilities and abilities required for different jobs.

Just assembling a batch of question does not produce a psychological test. A test may be defined as measuring a standardised sample of human behaviour.

The following psychological tests are usually applied in industry for selection of employees depending upon the requirement of the job for which the selection is being made :

Type of Behaviour Measurement

The most frequently used psychological tests are based on the type of behaviour that the test proposes to measure, such as intelligence test, personality tests, interest tests, vision tests, mechanical tests, verbal tests etc. Indicating the importance of intelligence tests, G. W. Woodworth said, "Intelligence Tests can be applied in a service organisation in such a way as to multiply the chances of successful selection".

Achievement and Aptitude Tests

The achievement tests measure a person's potential in a given area while the aptitude tests measure a person's current skill or ability at the moment of testing. However, the same test can be considered both an achievement test and an aptitude test, depending upon its use.

Paper Pencil Tests and Performance Tests

In paper-pencil tests the condidate simply receives a test paper or a printed booklet containing the test questions and he records his responses in a written manner on the provided answer sheet.

Those tests which do not require a written response but involve some of active manipulation like handling pegs or blocks or assembling mechanical objects, are known as performance tests.

Speed and Power Tests

Here the task is to complete as many items as possible in a short time. When the test performance is based primarily upon the speed with which one works, the test is called a speed test. A power test is one where the items are difficult and the person is given as much time as required to complete the test. In such tests a person's score is based mainly upon his ability to answer the questions correctly and the time factor is not important.

For the selection of the workers in industry the following tests are applied, keeping in view the job requirements.

Special Aptitude Tests

Different types of aptitude tests are applied for different jobs. For example, the Telford and Moss Test for the selection of policemen, consists of testing the observation, memory, comprehension and judgement power of the applicant.

Trade Tests

The trade test is an achievement test for mechanical workers.

General Ability Test

The mechanical ability test, the motor coordination test, the fine visual discrimination test, the various paper pencil tests, the Minnesota Paper Form Board Test, the finger dexterity test, the knot and bolt test, the test requiring judgement of size, form and position, the strength test, the auditory test, the reaction time test, and personality test, are used to select workers for different jobs.

In spite of the wide application of psychological tests in industry for tile selection of employees, it is to be kept in mind that the tests which are applied should be standardised and should have reliability and validity. Testing in industry has value only when the tests are used correctly and cautiously.

Beside these, there are also a few factors which need careful consideration before the selection of the workers. They are as follows :

1. Physical characteristics, such as, height, weight, visual activity, etc.
2. Individual and personal characteristic such as, marital status, number of children, age, sex, past lifc, and case history etc.
3. Competency—This refers to the potentiality and capacity possessed by the individual.
4. Proficiency—It refers to the knowledge of the individual information and experience proposed by the individual. Proficiency is measured after training is given.

Temperament and Character

Here certain personality tests are considered such as punctuality, honesty, truthfulness, social adaptability, emotional stability etc. For example, a cashier is to be honest, a foreman sociable and an executive emotionally stable.

Interest

A liking or dislike for the job, acceptance or rejection of the situation can be detected much ahead by giving interest tests. A person might be proficient and competent, but if he has no interest in work, his efficiency will go down. Woodworth says, "Interest is important for job satisfaction and job efficiency".

Creativity

While selecting executives, scientists, personnel and other high level officials, tests of creativity should be applied to measure their creative ability. The criteria used in Taylor's study (1961) measure creativity in general. By using aptitude and attitudinal test scores Jones (1964) have made an attempt to predict the creativity of industrial scientists.

QUESTIONS

1. Evaluate the defects of the interview technique in the selection of industrial workers. Can the defects of the interview technique be controlled ?
2. Discuss in detail the importance of psychological tests in the selection of industrial employees.
3. Critically analyse the merits and limitations of various psychological tests used in industry for the selection of workers.
4. Write notes on :
   (*a*) Application blank. (*b*) Psychological tests.
   (*c*) Unscientific methods of selection.

REFERENCES

Blum, M.L. and Naylor, J.C. *Industrial Psychology and Its Social Foundations,* Hwper and Row, 1968.

Jones, F.E. Predictor variables for creativity in industrial science, *Jn. of Applied Psychology,* 48, 1964, pp. 34-136.

OSS Assessment Staff. *Assessment of Man,* Rinehart, New York, 1948.

Stern, F. and Gordon, L.V. Ability to follow instructions as a predictor of success in recruit training, *Jn.· of Applied Psychology,* 1961, p. 45.

Taylor, C.W., Smith, W.R., Ghiselin, B. and Ellison, R. *Exploration in the Measurement and Prediction of Contributions of One Sample of Scientists,* A-SD-TR 61-96, Lack Land Air Force Base, Texas, April, 1961.

11
Training the Worker

NECESSITY

In modern industrial organisations training is an essential part of the programme. Every worker requires training for a job. Training is a process that improves skills and abilities related to performance. The aim of training is to establish certain habits which are necessary for the performance of a job. Effective training programme leads to increased production, reduced labour turnover, less absenteeism and greater employee satisfaction.

Earlier, training was only confined to teach the man to learn the mechanism of operating a machine. But now it has extended to all jobs and occupations with special emphasis on the training of supervisors and executives.

Training should be given to all employees starting from labourers and factory workers to executives. It should also be imparted to inexperienced workers who are new to the company. Traning can also be imparted by means of refresher courses.

The National Institute of Industrial Psychology conducted a number of experiments to determine the importance of training to increase efficiency. An investigation of about ten different jobs led to the conclusion that the trained group produced 10 to 40 per cent more output than the untrained one.

Vanvyck gives the following habits which every worker should acquire through training.

HABITS AND WORKS CULTURES TO BE DEVELOPED THROUGH TRAINING

1. Cleanliness.
2. Adequate personal appearance.
3. Getting along with others.

4. Following orders and directions.
5. Promptness.
6. Keeping busy.
7. Persistence.
8. Checking and correcting work.
9. Accuracy in work.
10. Speed in performing work.
11. Neatness in work.
12. Cooperation with others.
13. Accepting criticism as a means for self-improvement.
14. Proper conduct on the job.
15. Orderliness and a systematic approach.
16. Proper care of tools and equipments.
17. Safety and health precautions.
18. Efficient methods of working.
19. Economy in the use of materials and supplies.

It would be erroneous to conclude that these habits were not there earlier. But training is only an adaptation of previous habits and personal charactcristics to certain new situations. These qualities become more prominent and significant when their presence is required. But how far one can develop such habits out of training depends upon the training given by home and school in the first five to seven years of life. If previous training is in the proper direction, it will be easier to acquire the skill. Of course different types of special skills are required for different types of jobs and hence the training and the training period necessarily vary in different jobs. Special training necessary for different types of jobs are also given.

The length of the training period depends upon the nature of the skill to be acquired, the type of training technique that is used, and the learning and acquiring capacity of the employee. It also depends upon the interest with which the worker takes the training. In spite of the individual differences, if certain common methods of training are followed, the time taken to complete the training will vary slightly with different people.

The length of the training period, however, can be reduced by careful selection, proper planning of the instruction programme and care in the selection and training of instructors.

TYPES

Tiffin and McCormick (1971) have classified training into the following seven categories.

1. Orientation training to acquaint new employees with the company.
2. On the job training.
3. Apprentices training.
4. Off the job training (Off the job training is carried out in a stimulated job situation with equipments and facilities similar to that used on the job. But here the emphasis is not on production as such, but strictly on training. Such types of training centres are known as vestibule schools.)

5. Technical training.
6. Supervisory training.
7. Other training.

Training can also be classified on the following basis :

1. Purpose of training experiences.
2. Location of training experiences.
3. Trainee characteristics.
4. Techniques used.

AREAS

Today management training and team training are considered as the two most important areas of training.

Management training is otherwise known as executive training or leadership training. Most executive training situations may be classified into : (*a*) Human relations training, (*b*) Decision training.

Human Relations Training

Modern industrial psychologists and managements accept beyond doubt that interpersonal relationship between the employees and the employer is an important aspect of the managerial decision process. So training is given to improve the human relationship between the workers and the management. Training in human relations skill can be given by stimulated situations and group discussions.

Stimulated Situations. Any situation which is set up to stimulate the technical aspects of a decisions-making job can be used as a device in human relations. Role playing and in basket techniques are the two such methods of training devices.

Harris and Fleishman Study. This investigation was designed to measure the effect of a human relations supervisory training programme, in terms of the attitudes and behaviour of the trainees afte- they had returned from the actual work situation. Supervisory behaviour was evaluated in terms of two critieria of performance measured by a questionnaire. One group received human relations training while the other group did not. No significant differences were found in the mean scores made by either group before and after training period. Also, the effect of the refresher course upon supervisory behaviour did not bring any effect as studied by Harris and Fleishman.

Decision Training

The cream of managerial position is decision-making. Executives, managers and leaders exist basically to make decisions. To be a good leader or a good executive one must be concerned with developing his decision-making skills.

The decision-making skill depends upon technical and interpersonal knowledge.

Kinkade and Kidd Study. This study was designed as a method of training for a complex decision-making task. In the task of an air traffic controller, a very demanding and stressful decision-making task was to be learnt. Since air traffic controllers continuously direct pilots into their approaches, it is a continuous management role. Kinkade and Kidd (1962) designed a game which embodied many kinds of decisions required for an air traffic controller, at least in an abstract sense. One group of trainees was given six hours of practice on the game before going into training on the air traffic control task. The other group went directly into air traffic without any practice. The effect of the training on the game showed that the amount of delay and the number of errors committed were reduced by this technique.

According to Blum and Naylor (1968), "This study is an excellent example of the effectiveness a game can have in learning the technical aspects of a complex management task".

By and large, technical knowledge can be imparted to the executive by means of : (*a*) on the job training, (*b*) stimulated training, (*c*) class room instruction.

METHODS

Now the distinct training methods may be examined. It is to be kept in view that certain training methods may be used to teach both the technical and human relation aspects of management. In such methods training is usually conducted by experienced operators, foreman or specially appointed instructors. Production starts as soon as training begins.

In Basket Training

For both the human relations and the technical aspects of a managerial position in basket training has many appealing features. One of its main advantages is that quantitative indices of performance are possible with this technique which is not available with most other methods.

Lecture Method

Lectures are given relating to various problems which have to be faced in industry. But it is a superficial method and the majority of the trainees acquire nothing by this method.

Case Method

A general discussion is made regarding the skills that the trainees have to learn. This method is slightly better than the previous method having a close acquaintance with the training situation. But the problem of training is half solved because it does not give the trainee scope to handle the actual situation.

Role Playing Technique

The technique of role playing differs from the in basket method in that a number of individuals are assigned roles to play and instructed to work out a solution to the given problem. Here, in face, the trainees are confronted with the actual situation and are requested to deal with the situation according to the instructions given.

Thus, according to Blum and Naylor, "Role playing permits practising human relations skills in the relative safety of a labouratory environment. Role playing is not acting. Persons are asked to play the roles they have been assigned by putting themselves into these hypothetical situations. This permits the interaction between players to be representative of their own personalities. The roles and problems are structured only to facilitate the kinds of inter-personal relationship that are to be studied". (Refer to Training of Supervisors for details)

Management Games

Business games are a recent phenomenon in executive training. As viewed by Blum and Naylor, business games have been popular and practical with the tremendous growth in computer technology. According to Carter (1965), "in typical games the designer makes assumptions regarding the influence on the business enterprise of such factors as price of the products, costs and capabilities of production, advertising and selling costs and effects of plant and equipment and dividend rates".

The players are usually formed into groups of four or five without any organisational structure being defined. Teams often complete with each other, each team representing a business attempting to maximise its goals in a competitive market.

At the begining of the play each team is given identical consolidated reports of profit and loss statement of the financial condition, plant capacity etc. The players are allowed to spend funds for the expansion of the plant research and development, advertising, market research and similar items. The result of such expenditure is not normally known to the players, but has been programmed into the enterprise model used in playing the game. At the end of each time period a computer calculates the results of a period's operations and appropriate reports are furnished for each team. On the basis of these reports and the records made by the players of their actions, they go further to plan and execute their operations of the next time period and so on, until five to ten years operations have been completed. At the end of a play, a criticism of the play and the decision made is conducted with a discussion of factors which might have improved the player's performance. Business games are mainly used for the teaching of modem management marketing principles as opposed to human relations skills.

Sensitivity Training

An unstructured group of people with a common interest in human relations is the essence of the sensitivity training method. This approach to training has developed from the training methods advanced by the National training laboratory in group development and from certain schools of group psychotherapy and non-directive counselling.

Counselling

Tannenbaunm, Weschler and Massarik (1961) hold the view that while the characteristics of the sensitivity training process vary somewhat, the educational methods used is primarily training oriented. Trainees are permitted a maximum amount of leeway of action, and their interaction subsequently provides the subject for discussion and analysis. During the training experience, it is the process (the how) rather than the content (the what) that receives most attention. Trainees are encouraged to deal with their feelings about themselves and about others and to explore the impact they have given each other. Thus, they examine feelings, expressions, gestures and subtle behaviour which in every day life often are taken for granted.

"Sensitivity training is still experimental, as carried out in university workshops, group development laboratories and plant settings. No formula or cook book for conducting this type of training has been nor it is likely to developed. In general, however, some essential elements have emerged".

The essential elements are the following according to Blum and Naylor (1968) :

1. Sensitivity training is process-oriented rather than content oriented.
2. The training is unstructured in terms of method and content.
3. Frustration appears essential to the success of training.
4. The training is optional in small groups.
5. The atmosphere must be permissive.

TEAM TRAINING

A team refers to a group of individuals who work together towards a common goal. When two team members have different goals or objectives, the performance of the team is likely to be poor. With the increased frequency of team tasks in recent days, the importance of team training with the larger training complex has also increased. It is believed that any task requiring a group of individuals for its successful completion can be done more efficiently through team training. However, very little research has been done in this area to draw any definite and clear-cut conclusions.

Horrocks, Krug and Heermann (1960) found individual training superior, while some other studies found individual unit training most efficient (Glasen, Klaus and Egerman, 1962). As suggested by Blum and Naylor (1968), it can however be concluded, that the effectiveness of the two approaches to training seemed to be a function of the type of task for which one was trying to develop skill. Evidence was given especially in favour of the Naylor hypotheses which suggested that part or whole training depended upon job complexity and task organisation.

The view that group training is more efficient for tasks of high organisation, and individual training for tasks of low organisation, needs further investigation.

Effect of Feedback in Team Training

Indicating the powerful effect of feedback on team training, Rosenberg and Hull (1958) hold the view that the way in which feedback is handled in the team situation may often be the key to the actual communication structure of the team. However, there is some difficulty regarding the application of feedback in team training. Under team feedback conditions, an individual team member gets very little direct information about his own performance and hence it may be difficult for team members to learn under team feedback conditions.

Rosenberg and Hull (1958) have found individual performance to be tremendously affected by the kind of knowledge of result team members are given. They further noted that under conditions of team feedback, the team members seemed to develop compensatory behaviour. That is, if one team member was an "over responder", the other team member would become an "under responder".

It is more or less true that the average worker is never trained for his job. But it is now time that business organisations, big or small, recognise their responsibility and create training departments on a larger scale than has been done in the past. In fact, now all business departments are giving more attention to training and orientation programmes.

QUESTIONS

1. What is understood by industrial training ? Describe the importance of training industrial workers.

2. Describe the different types of training used in industry.

3. Discuss in brief the different areas of training.
4. Critically examine the importance of the lecture method, the case method and the role playing method in training workers.
5. Write notes on :
   (*a*) Sensitivity training
   (*b*) Team training
   (*c*) Management games
   (*d*) Effect of feedback in team training.

REFERENCES

Blum, M.L. and Naylor, J.C. *Industrial Psychology : Its Theoretical and Social Foundations*, Harper and Row Publishers, 1968.

Harris, E.F. and Fleishman, E.A. Human relations training and the stability of leadership patterns, *Journal of Applied Psychology*, 39, 1955, pp. 20-25.

Kinkade, R.G. and Kidd, J.S. The use of an operational game as a method of task familiarisation, *Journal of Applied Psychology*, 1962, 46, pp. 1-5.

Maier, N.R.F. *Principles of Human Relations*, Wiley, New York, .1952.

Maier, N.R.F. *Psychology in Industry*, Oxford & IBH Publishing Co. Pvt. Ltd., New Delhi, 1970.

Tannenbaum, L.R., Weschler, I.R. and Massarik, F. *Leadership and Organisation : A Behavioural Science Approach,* Mc-Graw Hill, New York, 1961.

Tiffin, J. and McCormick, E.J. Industrial Psychology, 5th ed., Prentice Hall of India Private Limited, New Delhi, 1971.

Smith, M. C. and Pears, M. A. Conventional research vs. discovery training methods in the preparation of immigrant bus conductors, *Jn. Of Cross Cultural Psychology*, 1972, December, Vol. 3(4), pp. 407-412.

12

Industrial Incentives

IMPORTANCE OF INCENTIVES IN INDUSTRY

Incentives in industry deal with a topic coming under the psychology of motivation. Incentives, in short, refer to the 'why' of human behaviour. According to Blum (1956), the term incentive is used for a spurring force, that is introduced as a means of achieving goal.

It has been observed from the findings of the Hawthorne studies and other experiments, that in spite of physical fitness for the work and capacity, some factors act as a hindrance to arrest the effort and cooperation of the workers. This is why a particular worker restricts output intentionally even if he has got the capacity to produce more. Some time back it was observed that in spite of giving high wages and following the principles of scientific management, production did not improve satisfactorily. Psychologists therefore tried to find out what were the basic incentives which could motivate the workers to produce more.

The incentives can be divided into two parts.

1. Financial
2. Non-financial.

Realists say that financial incentive or money is the only incentive for which people work. Idealists, on the other hand, hold that work is very natural for man in spite of reward or punishment. But the additional work which man does is due to a force or reinforcement other than money. This is called the non-financial incentive.

There are also some semi-economic incentives dealing, not directly with increased money, but are indirectly related to financial incentive such as free education, free medicine, free housing and transport facilities etc.

FINANCIAL INCENTIVE

Ever since the time of Taylor, emphasis was given on financial incentives to increase the efficiency and output of the workers. Experimental studies also indicate increased production with the introduction of wage incentive plans. This was probably because of the economic philosophy of the time. Lawer (1965) holds the view that salary is indeed important. Pay is an unique incentive, one that is able to satisfy almost all levels of needs. While such incentives cover mainly wages there are also various fringe benefits that enter the picture, such as overtime pay, bonuses, insurance plans, group insurance plans, profit sharing plans, stock ownership plans, provident fund plans and pension plans etc.

Types of Wage Incentive Systems

Time Rate System of Payment. When payment is made according to the time spent for a particular work, it is called the time rate. For example, when an employee is paid a fixed rate per week without considering the units or amount produced, and only on the basis of the time of work done, it is called payment on the time rate basis. But this method fails to recognise the concept of individual differences. The superior worker is not encouraged to produce more beyond a certain level. According to Maier (1970), the daily wage method fails to reinforce the employees to produce the maximum.

Piece Rate Method of Payment. This method is otherwise known as pay in terms of production. When payment is made according to the units and amount produced it is called the piece rate or straight piece rate method of payment. Contrary to the time rate system of payment, this method emphasises individual differences and encourages the superior workers for more production. More efficient and competent workers are rewarded by this method. A study by Wyatt (1934) suggests that production increased by 30 per cent with the introduction of the piece rate system. To add to this, the workers considered piece rate as the best method of pay.

Piece rate is beneficial when the speed of work depends upon the will, ability and capacity of the workers. But this method does not encourage older workers. Security in job may be affected, though it is a matter of individual responsibility. Another limitation of this method is that signs of fatigue, irritability and stress may be noticed in the workers. Lastly, in the piece rate method, the quality of work may be affected.

Multiple Piece Rate. This was introduced by Merrick. Here three parallel piece rate systems are introduced for different units of production. For instance, for the lower to middle there is one type of wage, for the middle to high another type of payment and for the high to higher there is still another type of wage. The speciality of Merricks multiple piece rate is that it guarantees minimum piece rate for low producers and beginners. Here a standard is fixed with the help of the time and motion study.

Differential Piece Rate. In this case also, the standard rate of production is fixed. A man who reaches the fixed standard is paid at a particular rate and if this standard exceeds by 10 or 20 units he is paid at a higher rate according to the decision of the management. Of course, after a certain unit the rate of pay does not increase. Thus, for the same work two types of rates exist. If the standard units fixed is 100, and if a man reaches the standard, he is paid at a fixed rate and if it exceeds by 10, he is paid at higher rate.

Profit Sharing Plans

This system of payment has been extensively used in American industries from 1974 onwards. There are three types of profit sharing plans.

1. Workers get a share in the net profit of the company with a particular length of service. Sometimes distribution is made on the basis of employees' earnings and savings etc.
2. Payment of a share of the profit is made after deducting the necessary cost and requirements of the company.
3. The same percentage of the profit is paid to the worker which is also obtained by a stock holder.

Besides these plants, there are also some other financial incentives such as group incentive plans. In this case supplementary payment is made to the particular department or section for increased production beyond a standard.

Saving Plans and Provident Funds

Though a lot of wage incentive plans have been established, saving plans also help in getting some amount of profit in the form of incentives. There are also pension and gratuity etc.

Factors Responsible for the Effective Application of Wage Incentive Plans

By and large, it can be said that there are different types of wage incentive plans. The most important problem, however, is to see under which plan a given incentive is to be applied. This depends entirely upon the nature of the worker, the nature of his work and his socio economic standard.

Any incentive plan which leaves out the above three conditions will be only half-true psychologically.

1. Nature of Work. When the work is interesting, the time rate gives the best result, *i.e.*, workers can devote time to work irrespective of the high quality of things. But in mass production the quality of work suffers.

If the work is, however, uninteresting, repetitive and monotonous, output can be maintained at a high level by the piece rate method of payment. In such a case, interest is no longer in the work, but in earning. The worker overcomes the burden of the uninteresting nature of the work due to this incentive.

2. Nature of the Worker. Whether money and other financial incentives are important or not depends on the age, sex and the socio-economic status of the worker. In such cases, an employee who is planning to marry considers earning as an important factor. Here, the time rate will not help him much. A young worker may need extra money for his family and for himself and so he may be interested in the piece rate system. But an older man who is about to retire may not like the piece rate method of payment.

3. Socio-economic Status of the Worker. If the worker belongs to the poor socio-economic status, he may need more money to maintain his family. Under such circumstances, the piece rate system would work more effectively.

However, during years of depression the piece rate was found to be extremely unpopular. Observation also indicated that production was not increasing in spite of the piece rate system of payment. The prime reason for this was insecurity. In such circumstances people are not usually interested in pay or money but in security. Therefore, of late, unions have become very suspicious of the piece rate system of payment and in quite a number of cases it has not operated successfully.

According to Lytle (1938), different wage incentive plans are to be used under different conditions. He briefly describes the plans and their following uses :

1. Day rate plan with production records and promotions for unstandardised work, permanent or temporary. It is simple and can be used. The management should eliminate unsupported time payment wherever and whenever possible.
2. Multiple time plan with high bonus steps for upgrading employees formerly on day rates, and also for group applications: It is strong at task points and simple at all points. It must be more carefully managed than a more elaborate plan.
3. High piece rate plan with or without a minimum guarantee and with time basis for computation: For repetitive work, not involving expensive machine rates, it is the simplest and most sound of all plants. Equalisation requires care as task per unit of time may not be evident.
4. Merrick's multiple piece rate for upgrading inefficient employees formerly on low piece rate: It is flexible, strong and relatively simple for what it can do.
5. Ganlt task and bonus plan: For machine jobs liable to delay and where machine rates are high it provides security and strength.
6. Halsey (50-50) constant sharing plan with time guarantee : For guessed at standards it gives a high wage on time rates through intermediate production efficiencies. Task or rate inaccuracy is less serious.
7. Halsey (40-60) constant sharing without time guarantee up to 70 to 75 per cent of high task: It compromises for low efficiency. It is simple to understand.
8. Bendaux point plan: For strongly centralised management and for widely diversified operations, it gets results through its production control rather than through improved operation and high wage rates. It involves a lot of figuring.
9. Berth variable sharing plan-up to day wage only : For beginners and unskilled workers, it gives a high wage for low production efficiencies without any guarantee.
10. Emerson empiric scale plan: between 70 and 100 per cent task only: For gradual transition from day work plan to high piece rate plan. It avoids the abrupt step and may be justified in some cases. The empiric principle is only used within the above limits and outside of these other plans are preferable.

Marrow (1937) made a survey to show up to what extent the wage incentive plans are being used in industry. He published the results in an article, "How 133 plants looks at the wage incentive system". 45.86 per cent of these plants were using straight piece rate and individual bonus, 34.6 per cent, were using group bonus plan, 6.8 per cent were using a measured day work plan and 54 per cent reported increased use of incentive plans.

Criticism and Conclusion

The piece rate system is often cursed, as extra work leads to extra expenditure of energy and added fatigue. Health suffers due to extra labour and for this costly food and medicines are required.

When there is a speed-up, the security of the worker is affected. There is a voluntary restriction of output and rate cutting because of the suspicion of being retrenched.

Rate cutting or scaling done of payment is done to the differential payment system. Factory owners suggest the original rate to be unfair and hence rationalise it. In 99 per cent of the cases, workers have not liked the differential rate of payment since the rate is cut down.

Lastly, for many workers, piece rate is a danger signal. Layoff sets in the factory and working hours decrease. Ultimately, unemployment is caused and everybody suffers.

For these reasons the piece rate system has been restricted by many labour unions.

Financial incentives have only a limited play. Generally speaking, financial incentive in the shape of the piece rate system causes danger to labour. Firstly, labourers feel that if they produce more and earn more, the commodity will be overproduced and layoff and unemployment will be caused.

Some studies have been conducted in this area to determine the importance of incentives. Jones and Jeffrey (1964) made a study to evaluate preferences among electrical workers for alternate forms of job compensation. They considered each of four different compensation dimensions.

1. Hourly wage vs. monthly wage.
2. Merit incentive vs. no merit incentive.
3. Piece work incentive vs. no piece work incentive.
4. Regular pay rate vs. high pay rate.

It was found for the non-union workers, the weekly wage, the merit incentive, the piece work incentive and the higher wage were all significantly preferred. With union workers, the no merit incentive choice was significantly preferred as was the piece rate and the higher piece rate.

Interestingly enough, it was noted that the union members were willing to take jobs with no merit incentive and regular pay in preference to jobs having merit incentive and high pay. This suggests that the union as an orgainisation provides the workers with some form of group protection and security which is worth a sacrifice in actual money units.

In a recent study, Nealey (1964) found that, in general, the workers preferred the hospital insurance option and the union shop and were quite unimpressed with the enticement of 37½ hour week. He found that as one grows older, there is tremendous increase on preference for the pension plan. Additional vocation was preferred by younger workers in comparison to the workers of older age groups.

According to Blum (1956), "Ever since Taylor's time the experts have been connecting one wage incentive system after another until now there are literally hundreds of such systems". One of the most comprehensive reviews of wage incentive plans is that offered by Carles W. Lytle who believes that such plans are important in any cost production problem According to him incentive payments have two advantages such as :

1. an increase in production per unit, and
2. an increase in employee earnings.

He believes that the advantages of a properly selected, well installed and ably managed payment plan accrue annually to employees and employers. Of course, Lytle does not say that these advantages "accrue mutually and fairly" for they do not.

As Mark Spade says (quoted in Maier, 1970) in his most illuminating book *How to Run a Bassoon Factory* "Wage incentive systems are a means of paying employees more, but not so much".

NON-FINANCIAL INCENTIVES

Need of Non-financial Incentives

In spite of the emphasis of the time and motion engineers on the financial incentives to motivate the workers since the ninteenth century, and in spite of the wide use of the wage incentive plan, it is a hard fact that financial incentives worked only as a means and not as an end. It is to be kept in mind that there are many factors, other than money and wage, which induce the workers to work efficiently and produce more, factors which bring pride and interest in work.

The results of the Hawthorne studies and many other investigations in industry suggest that there are many other factors besides money which induce the workers to work efficiently. It is true, that money alone does not work to motivate the workers to produce the maximum.

In spite of the application of Taylorism and the time and motion study, when production did not improve as expected, the industrial psychologists were puzzled and suspected the operation of some other factors besides money for motivating the workers. They realised that even though the financial incentives have a limited play, they have been overdone and overplayed.

Referring to the rabble hypothesis Centres, Richards and Cantril have opined that, "The assumption that employees only respond to money has been called the rabble hypothesis because workers are treated as a group of unorganised rabble, insensitive to the social motives of approval and self-respect".

In fact, when the psychologists had to pass through such a transitional period, there were only a few idealists who stuck to the theory that people do not always work for money and money alone.

As a natural consequence of the Hawthorne studies, management and industrialists began to realise slowly that employees are people, and that they behave in human ways. Though they act like machine they are capable of experiencing emotions of love and hatred, sorrow and disappointment, of holding attitudes and developing interests. They are quite conscious of prestige and self-respect like any other person in the world. In the eyes of the efficiency engineers, man was looked upon as an unwilling ass who has a reward hung before his eyes as well as the fear of punishment. Strangely enough, the ass and carrot view of man proved to be futile, fruitless and an insult to man's intelligence. In fact, workers did not react positively to the magic of financial incentive to the extent Merrick, Gnats and Emerson believed.

According to J.A.C. Brown (1956) "Trying to satisfy people with material gifts is, in the long run, like trying to fill a bottomless pit". In 1947-48, during the fuel crisis in England, people were surprised to note that coalminers were not producing more in spite of higher wages.

The chief inspector of factories in 1947-48 in England remarked that in the sphere of the industrial revolution, a kind of radical change has taken place. Since the time of First World War, people had thought of the environment factors as important. But after the Second World War, physical factors including the significance of the individual and his interrelationship in his environment have become important. Thus there are certain intangible incentives operating all the while in the determination of human motive.

In spite of high wages, perhaps, due to a gap in communication between the workers and the management, the workers may look towards the management with grave suspicion. The ultimate result of this is voluntary restriction of output which is one of the paramount causes of the failure of financial incentives.

In the words of Blum (1956) "Some people believe that money is the only incentive in industry and many believe that it is the most important incentive. This false premise and oversimplification has caused many of the best laid incentive plans to fail".

Blum further holds that the bank-wiring observation room experiment in the Hawthorne plant showed clearly that restricted rather than unlimited production characterises the workers. Blum again opines, "not only has the financial incentive plan been overdone but in many cases the financial incentive has not operated as an incentive".

In the opinion of Harrel (1964) "High pay is effective in many situations in attracting persons to new jobs but it is less effective in holding them on jobs. The results of a study conducted by Stockford and Kunze (1950) indicated, " .... the value of wages is relative and not absolute". Even with the same salary the employees may have favourable or unfavourable sentiments towards the company.

Types of Non-financial Incentives along with Studies

The field and laboratory studies conducted by management, efficiency engineers and psychologists began to reveal many clearcut information regarding the non-financial incentives. The need that the workers have for security, independence, social status, self-expression, prestige, advancement and promotion, job satisfaction, attitude and supervisory relationship, knowledge of result, cooperation and competition, praise and blame and many such related factors are the non-financial incentives which motivate the workers to work efficiently.

The field and laboratory studies conducted in this area signify the importance of non-financial incentives in industry. The findings especially of the Hathorne studies have been the torch bearers and stimulants for further studies in this area. These non-financial incentives are aspects of environment which will be discussed later.

Attitude

The importance of attitude as a non-financial incentive came as a natural consequences of the Hawthorne studies. Matheson (1931) conducted a study to find out why, despite all the methods of payment, expected production was not obtained. Thus Mathewson worked as a participant observer in a factory and found that voluntary restriction of output was practised on a large scale. This was because of dislike, suspicion and grievances towards the management. This study of Mathewson thus brought out the importance of attitude as a non-financial incentive, something which the Hawthorne studies had indicated. To refer to Blum (1956), additional money has not meant as much to the employee as the employer assumed it to be."

The present author (1980) did not find the significant effect of employees' attitude on production. She carried out an investigation on 120 semi-skilled and 200 unskilled workers employed in some small scale industries of Orissa to examine the relationship between the attitude of the employees towards work, the work situation, management and the production level.

Though results indicated a positive relationship, the relationship was not significant enough to draw any clearcut relationship between overall attitude and productivity. Interestingly, it was found that in most cases, the employees expressed a favourable attitude. It is apprehended that most likely, the workers hesitated in disclosing their real attitude for fear of being punished, transferred or retrenched.

This study, however, supports Stogdill's (1959) view that the degree of satisfaction in job may not necessarily be related to job performance.

To measure the attitude of the workers towards the management, the impressionistic method, questionnaires, surveys and interview techniques have been used. Attitude is also measured by giving questionnaires to those workers who have just left the job or are about to leave the job. In the interview technique a sample survey is preferred for cost, trouble and time considerations. But the sample should be properly selected to avoid errors. A fairly good measurement of attitude can be made by this method. But these methods may not be suitable in India. Rallis wanted to know which method is suitable for India. In India, peculiarly, an average villager wants to please the visitor while answering to questions. So highly structured techniques are most applicable to Indian workers.

When there is a gap in communication between the workers and the management, attitude becomes unfavourable. Sometimes when the management ignores the hope ambitions and feelings of the workers misunderstanding crops up. Thus the danger of misunderstanding is rooted in as one is not always aware of these attitudes. Of course, various assessment methods are there to bridge this gap between workers and management.

Supervisory Relationship

According to Blum (1956), in the mind of the employee a minimum of five drives are likely to operate on the job. They are advancement, hours of work, salary, security and supervisory relationship.

A study conducted by Blum and Russ (1942) attempted to determine the relative importance of these five incentives. Following the paired comparison method, data was collected from a group of 181 men and 105 women gainfully employed in occupations ranging from unskilled manual labour to all professions.

The findings of this study indicated that salary is not always considered important by the workers. Advancement and security were the first two incentives. Further analysis showed that both men and women agreed on the relative importance of various incentives. Men considered advancement and salary as more important. For women, however, the supervisor was more important than men. Further analysis showed that married women attached greater importance to the supervisor than married men. The attitude towards salary is unaffected by marriage, a finding similar to that reported by Cole (1940). The married men care least about the number of hours worked, and the married women care most about it. No difference is observed, however, between single men and women.

Advancement and Security

The significance of advancement as an incentive decreased with age for both sexes and security became more important with age. But advancement and security were considered more important than salary.

Jurgerson (1947) found that job preferences were affected more by the extent of education than by most other variables. As education increased, advancement became more important and security less. According to his findings, wages, hours and working conditions are not so important as is generally thought and the type of work is more important than is ordinarily stated.

Kornhouser and Sharp (1932) made a study in the Kimberley Clark Corporation on 300 women workers, but found, surprisingly, that the relationship between good attitude and high efficiency did not operate.

This study on the other hand, brought the importance of supervisory relationship as one of the non-financial incentives. Keeping all other conditions constant except one, in two departments, only the supervisors were changed. In one department 29 per cent had a favourable attitude while in the other 71 per cent had a favourable attitude. Thus, they pointed out that the significance of difference was related to the difference in supervisors.

Wyatt made a study on 328 factory operators in England. In this study, opportunity for advancement and steady work got the first and second preference. This also indicates the importance of advancement as a non-financial incentive.

Watson, Fosdick, Goodwin and Seidman took eight incentives, both financial, and both the employees and the employers were asked to mark these incentives in order of preference. The incentives ranked in order of preference by the employees are as follows :

1. Credit for work done.
2. Interesting work.
3. Fair pay.
4. Understanding and appreciation.
5. Counselling on personal problems.
6. Promotion policy.
7. Good physical condition.
8. Security.

The employers on the other hand ranked incentives in the following way :

1. Good physical condition.
2. Fair pay.
3. Credit for work done.
4. Counselling on personal problems.
5. Security.
6. Understanding and appreciation.
7. Promotion policy.
8. Interesting work.

A comparison between these two rankings indicates that though money has not been given the first preference by both the groups, yet employers have given more emphasis on financial incentives, preferring good physical condition and fair pay as the first two incentives.

The findings of this study suggests that there is a gap in communication between the workers and the management.

Stagner (1950) reports a study conducted upon 7000 employees of a nation-wide corporation. Stagner concludes on the basis of the findings, "that neither executives and workers are concerned about pay as such, except when economically pinched. At other times, they prefer ego satisfaction, such as prestige, power, recognition, security and treatment as an individual."

An overall analysis of these studies indicates that although different methods were used and the studies included different complexities, and sampling, the results tend to be more similar than dissimilar. The findings substantiate the view that salary is not the most important factor on a job, nor does it operate as the all-powerful incentive. Thus the wage is not the sole consideration of doing work.

The present author (1976) conducted an investigation on 210 skilled and semi-skilled male workers and 102 male and female unskilled workers of Cuttack city in Orissa, engaged in the construction work of private buildings. The workers were given six incentives to rank in order of preference. Illiterate workers were personally interviewed by the author and their preferences were recorded. The six incentives were: interesting work, high pay, credit for work done, less working hours, good behaviour and security in job.

These results indicated that in the ease of male workers high pay, less working hours and good behaviour of the supervisor got first three positions and interesting work got the last position. Security in job got the fourth preference. However, in the case of female workers less working hours, high pay and good behaviour of the supervisor got the first three rankings respectively, and security in job got the last ranking. Credit for work done got the fourth preference.

TABLE 12.1

Mean ranking of incentives of male and female workers

Sex			*Male*		*Female*
N	*N*	*Skilled*	*Semi killed*	*Unskild*	*Unskilled*
Incentives	*272*	*100*	*110*	*62*	*N-40*
	Ranking	*Position*		*Ranking*	*Position*
1. Less working hours	4.33	(2)		5.45	(1)
2. Good behaviour of the employer	3.54	(3)		3.87	(3)
3. High wage	4.93	(1)		4.00	(2)
4. Interesting work	2.78	(5)		1.95	(5)
5. Security in job	3.52	(4)		1.25	(6)
6. Credit for work done	2.76	(6)		3.56	(4)

A comparison of the rankings by the skilled, semi-skilled and unskilled workers further indicated that skilled and semi-skilled workers gave higher preference to interesting work and credit for work done, respectively, in comparison to the unskilled labourers.

The findings of this study are in many respects different from the findings of similar studies conducted in the West.

TABLE 12.2

Mean ranking of incentives of skilled, semiskilled and unskilled workers

Sl. No.	*Types of Incentive*	*Mean Ranking Skilled Male*	*Semi skilled*	*Unskilled Male*	*Unskilled Female*
	N	*100*	*110*	*62*	*40*
		Ranking	*Ranking*	*Ranking*	*Ranking*
1.	Less working hours	3.90	4.25	4.85	5.45
2.	Good behaviour of the employer	3.50	3.28	3.85	3.87
3.	High wage	4.20	4.75	5.76	4.00
4.	Interesting work	3.40	3.00	1.95	1.95
5.	Security in job	3.75	3.15	3.65	1.25
6.	Credit for work done	3.65	3.10	2.14	3.56

In India, the financial position of the workers is not favourable in comparison to their counterparts abroad, where the studies mentioned earlier have been conducted. Hence, Indian workers have obviously given more importance to money than to any other single factor.

Dudycha-Naylor (1966) conducted a study on college students (who mostly had never held a regular job) to examine what job characteristics were of primary importance to them. The subjects gave the following rank order of job traits.

1. Pay.
2. Opportunity for growth and advancement.
3. Security.
4. Fellow employees.
5. Working conditions.
6. Supervisor-employees relations.

It is surprising as well as interesting to note the high value given to pay by this group.

The survey research centre of the University of Michigan (1948) has conducted some studies on the relationship between productivity, supervisor and employee morale and it has been concluded that, people are more effectively motivated when they are given some degree of freedom in the way in which they do their work than when every action is prescribed in advance. They do better when some degree of decision making about their job is possible than when all decisions are made for them. They respond more adequately when they are treated as personalities rather than as cogs in a machine. In short, if the ego motivation of self determination, of self expression, of a sense of personal worth can be tapped, the individual can be more effectively energised. The use of external sanctions, of pressuring for production may work to some degree, but not to the extent that the more internalised motives do. When the individual comes to identify himself with his job and with the work of his group, human resources are much fully utilised in the production process.

Therefore, as noted by Viteles (1953), the relationship between the worker and the first line industrial supervisor is of tremendous importance in determining the attitude, morale and efficiency of the workers than any other single factor.

Supervision

It occupies an indispensable position in the structure of industrial psychology. It is said that the supervisor is the pivot around which the wheels of industrial psychology move. One major role of the supervisor in the non-financial incentive is to set the kind of production for the employees to decide the target of work. The supervisor must himself possess a realistic level of aspiration among the employees to fulfil the above purpse.

Elliot Smith (1928), commenting on the importance of a supervisor as a nonfinancial incentive has rightly made the following comment : "A company pays the same for the labour whether it is managed well or not, but what it gets from its labour depends much upon whether the employees work with a will. This in turn depends largely upon the skill of the junior executives in dealing with human nature."

Job Satisfaction

It is an important nonfinancial incentive, in the sense, that lack of job satisfaction will make the work unpleasant and would lead to lack of interest in the job. As a result, efficiency may be affected. On the other hand, job satisfaction will lead to a sustained interest in the job and may motivate the workers to produce more. (Refer to the Job satisfaction Chapter.)

Praise and Reproof

Praise acts as a more positive incentive than reproof for individuals of all ages, as it is a form of ego satisfaction. Of course, praise works as a better incentive for poor workers and low producers while blame motivates the successful and able workers more effectively. However, day-to-day observations in various industries and organisations do indicate that more often than not, blame and reproof more than praise are practised to motivate the workers, especially when one fails to achieve the expected standard. Several empirical studies have been conducted to demonstrate the effect of praise and reproof on the quality and quantity of work, Moore (1939) found that praise increased work in 87.5 per cent of the college students and the work was poor only in the case of 0.5 per cent of the students. But various degrees of disapproval of work performed led to 11.9 and 66.5 per cent of subject to do better, while poorer results occurred in 10.7 to 65.1 per cent of the cases. This cleary suggests that praise for work done has definitely a more facilitating effect than disapproval (of any type) of the past performance. One cannot deny the fact that the ego or self of any individual is insulted and hurt by blame, scolding, reproof and punishment. Disapproval and insult in public particularly, injures the ego and brings down the prestige of an individual. Blame and disapproval expressed in private is definitely more beneficial in this respect.

Knowledge of Result and Experience of Progress

Field and laboratory studies conducted in the area of learning indicate that knowledge of previous performance motivates the workers to work efficiently and produce more. In a particular study, inspectors who learnt the element in an incidental manner did not do as well as the inspectors who were told about their errors and defects and who then made conscious efforts to facilitate their progress.

A day-to-day analysis of the experimental results on incidental and intentional learning and knowledge of results conducted by the undergraduate and postgraduate psychology students, also support these findings.

It is generally held that without the experience of progress, competition would be ineffective and knowledge of result would be limited, as every worker wants to know whether he is progressing or not. Usually, new employees experience the progress relatively better than old employees, who have already reached the level of profinciency and have very little to improve.

Cooperation and Competition

It has been found that results are better under cooperation and competition. Carnegie made a study of this problem. The units of production of the morning shift workers were written on a board, so that the evening shift workers could see it. It was noted that this knowledge brought about a competition among the other workers to produce more.

Individuals usually compete with one another to achieve the reward when it is limited. People also compete to get mental satisfaction and social status. The person who succeeds in the competition may gain status or may experience need achievement besides financial benefits. In sharp contrast to this, the looser experiences failure and loss of status. Thus a competitive situation creates satisfaction or a deprivation feeling. In some studies the positive effect of competition on performance has been noticed. But several other investigations question the favourable effects of competition on production. Deutsch (1949) did observe that greater production was possible when a group of students were encouraged to work cooperatively on problem solving tasks, than was obtained by those encouraged to work under a competitive atmosphere.

A similar study was conducted by Goldman and Hammond (1961) to examine the findings of Deutsch just mentioned. The results supported the previous findings in that, non-competitive as compared competitive conditions increased attentiveness and involvement for both groups and individuals. But when they worked in groups rather than individually, indication of significant improvement in the quality of solutions under both competitive and non-competitive conditions were obtained. Thus, the effect of group on performance was more evident than mere competition.

Marquis, Guetzkow and Heyns (1951) found that cooperative groups completed more items than the competitive groups. The study reported by Coch, French (1948) and Marrow (1948) indicated increased production of the group that participated as compared to group that competed.

The importance of success and failure on competition has also been observed in a few studies. Some of these studies indicate that constant failure reduces motivation and repeated success fails to hold motivation. However further investigations are necessary to confirm this view.

In any case, competition should be healthy and free from rivalry to create motivation and facilitate production. Emphasising the importance of cooperation, Harrell (1964) remarks : "Participation is a key incentive. It is more likely to take place under conditions of successful leadership and team spirit".

Level of Aspiration and Nature of the Goal

The goals of the employee and the employer must be more or less akin. Optimum efficinency is achieved when goals are identical and are coordinated. The goal is to be perceived as short-term and long-term. Short-term goals are more likely to succeed when they reinforce and lead to satisfaction of long-term goal as well. If short-term goals, have no relationship with long-term goals, they may not be very effective.

Professor Mace (1952), conducted an experiment on (1) Near goal and distant goal, and (2) Fixed goal and flexible goal.

The poorest performance came from the group having no fixed goal. Mace thus finally concluded that the standard is effective only when it is a reasonable goal, that is the kind of goal which the worker can reasonably aspire to and can achieve on reach. It ceases- to be effective when the goal is too high. Thus Mace viewed that performance could be more effective when the goal setting is adjusted according to the level of ability and the skill of the worker.

According to Blum, when management and employees clearly state their goal, deal openly and honestly with the employees and try to ascertain their goals, the employees and employers can work together. Each will give a little, but in return each will be likely to gain more.

Goal oriented behaviour is always effective as a strong non-financial incentive. The workers' level of aspiration is also effective as a strong non-financial incentive.

The level of aspiration of the employees functions as a regulator of success or failure and obviously protects the ego from frustration. It also keeps the goal above his achievement. If the level of aspiration of the employee is low, and if he underestimates his abilities and performances, he will not be motivated to go ahead. Maier (1970) holds the view that under conditions of normal and healthy functioning, a person never achieves this goal as it always moves ahead when it is approached. In other words, the aspiration level should remain above the performance level for higher efficiency. In developing countries like India, especially, the level of aspiration should always be set above the performance score.

The present author (1977) conducted a study on the level of aspiration behaviour of some employed and unemployed youths of Orissa. An anaylsis of the findings indicated that respondents employed permanently in different organisations indicated lower goal discrepancy score, had

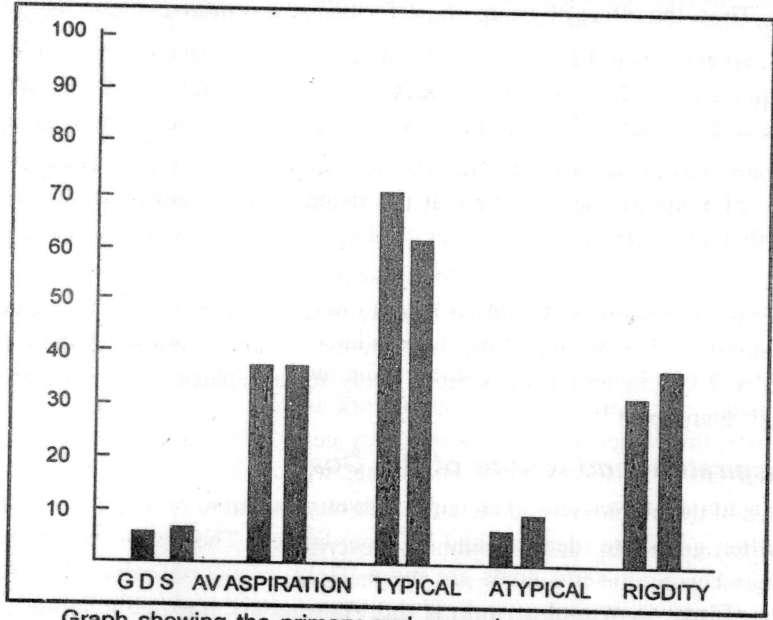

Graph showing the primary and secondary measures of level of aspiration of employed and unemployed youths.

more typical shifts and were less rigid in their level of aspiration. In contrast, the unemployed graduates scored significantly higher goal discrepancy score, showed less typical shifts and more rigidity. The following figure represents these results.

Such statistical differences in the primary and secondary measures of the level of aspiration behaviour of these two groups clearly suggest that employment gives security and has a satisfying effect. This feeling of satisfaction acts as a positive reinforcement to motivate the workers to keep their aspirations reasonably ahead of their performance. On the contrary, unemployment creates frustration and insecurity among individuals and so they are quite erratic in their level of aspiration (which fluctuates from high to low) without keeping in view their previous performance.

However, taking the average aspiration alone into consideration, none of the comparable groups indicated a significant difference. This suggests that unemplyment did not lower the aspiration of the unemployed workers, but they could not adjust their aspiration to their achievement, leading to significantly higher G.D. score, more rigidity and less typical shifts. This is most likely due to frustration and insecurity. Moreover, evidences indicate that persons with greater failure and anxiety show larger variations in their level of aspiration than persons with lesser anxieties. Such erratic and unhealthy level of aspiration behaviour (as found in the study of the author) of the unemployeds is not desirable for the growth and development of India.

This study finally implies that employment not only gives economic security but it also acts as a non-financial incentive by giving social security, prestige, power and recognition. It brings a sense of confidence and improves aspiration and performance.

Emphasising the importance of the level of aspiration in industry Mairer (1970) comments :

"A person who is adjusted to his work has the proper balance between ability and level of aspiration. It is important that production supervisors and men assigned to industrial training aid their trainees in finding their proper levels of aspiration. Men should not expect too much improvement in themselves, but they should always expect enough. In all acquisition of skill, effort tends to fall off when the aspiration level is not advanced".

Besides, the non-financial incentives just mentioned, security, status, need for power and recognition are considered as essential non-financial incentives. Blum (1956) thus views the mastery of the job and pride in successful accomplishments as the real reasons why men work and work hard. This applies to all jobs that are recongnised as jobs, regardless of where they stand in the social hierarchy.

The studies conducted in the field of industry and elsewhere, do suggest that financial incentive does not play an overwhelming role in a man's working life. Prestige, social acceptance, pride in work, self-expression and the many related social drives are equally or even more meaningful. Thus Williams has rightly opined, "The motives for working cannot be assigned only to economical needs, for men may continue to work even though they have no need for material goods." Obviously, this is because the rewards they get from the work are social, such as respect and admiration from their fellow men. For some, work becomes an avenue for securing ego satisfaction by gaining power and exercising it over others.

Seven Shifts, edited by Jack Common, describes the life and work of seven ordinary Englishmen. It indicates that money is not the most important incentive to a worker. A worker does not separate his living from his working life. He is a human being, embodying many motives and conflicts and his behaviour is as unpredictable on the job as it is in life.

As Jack Hilton puts it, We get the satisfaction that we have really done something; something that a machine has not done, something that has called for patience, ingenuity and skill than a four minutes job.

INDIAN STUDIES ON INCENTIVES

Some studies have been conducted in India on worker's motivation, level of aspiration and incentives. The results obtained by Bose (1958). are as follows :

1. Satisfaction and dissatisfaction with wage does not always go with high and low productivity respectively.
2. Working conditions and welfare measures create a good attitude but do not decrease productivity efforts necessarily.
3. Higher productivity will go with job satisfaction only if job satisfaction creates interest in work.
4. Cohesiveness and pride in group contribute to efficiency.
5. Close correspondence between the level of expectations of the management, supervisors and workers help to maintain high production standard.

The study by Ganguly (1954) reveals that the three mostly highly ranked incentives are (*a*) adequate earning, (*b*) job security, and (*c*) opportunity for promotion. He concluded that, unlike the western investigation where pay is often marked lower in the hierarchy of incentives, income and security of service are the most important incentives for the Indian worker. The exact nature of the work done, the amount of responsibility given to the workmen, appreciation of the work by others were the items of relatively low incentive value. In this study, the nature of supervisor, ranked fifth while in Western investigations it usually occupies first position. The incentive value of such items like medical and health insurance, housing, subsidised canteen and other fringe benefits was difficult to assess. This study supports the findings of the study by Mohanty (1976) on the incentive of a group of skilled, semi-skilled and unskilled workers.

Ganguly (1956) further studied the relative importance of different incentives for the supervisory staff in a government railway workshop. The results indicated that incentives were more or less the same as in the case of workers. A comparison of supervisors of different levels showed that a supervisor in the higher posts tended to put greater stress on his having more authority and power over the affairs of his group.

Bhatt (1962) conducted three investigations and found that, of the nine possible incentives, choice of work, advancement and co-workers were preferred in the order mentioned Wages had fourth position. Benefits, condition of work and the supervisor got the fifth position, and next came security, hours of work and holidays. Findings of this type definitely yield confusing results. The variation in the opinion of the workers regarding the importance of incentives may depend upon the local conditions prevailing in the plant, as well as the general situation regarding the earning and other facilities available to them.

The study conducted by Chowdhry and others (1952a) on the textile workers of Ahmedabad seems to be a more fruitful investigation with clear-cut results. In this study the group non-technique was used. The workers were given the knowledge concerning breaks and damages as well as the quantity of work done by the working group within a period of time. As a result, the average efficiency of the workers was found to increase considerably and damages were also reduced significantly. Such a trend was consistently observed in different mills. In the control group of workers, there was only a slight improvement. This study cleary indicates how experimental manipulation of a social variable can provide a strong incentive for enhancing the efficiency of employees.

DECLINING WORK MOTIVATION IN INDIA

Currently it is being widely found and believed that the Indian workers show increasing organisational inefficiency, low morale and low productivity. There are very few plants in India which have not gone through strikes, lockouts and labour problem. The general consensus is that this state of affairs is found both in public and private secter enterprises. In a Seminar a senior level executive commented that what is happening publicly in the public sector is also happening privately in the private sector. It is also commonly felt that there is an overall lack of proper work ethic in the Indian Society. It is believed by many experts in this area that the Indian organisations lacked proper work motivation among employees at all levels of the organisation. This has led to probably improper utilisation of resources. Further they view that worker alienation pervades Indian Society resulting in passivity and indifference towards the attainment of work objectives.

Kanungo and Mishra (1986) state that a participant from a public sector organisation suggested that low work motivation among Indian employees is because they do not value work as intrinsically satisfying. Unless they believe that goodness of work and industry is their moral responsibility, work motivation in organisations is not going to improve. Organisational culture lacks in such organisations.

A private sector executive was of opinion that non participative and authoritarian style of management is the essential cause of low work motivation. He suggested that organisations must involve its employees in the decision-making process by adopting the participative style of management. Another Manager was of the view that low employee motivation results from repetitive and boring jobs. Jobs should be redesingned in such a way that employees get intrinsic job satisfaction.

The above are the views of some executives based on their personal experiences. But diagnosis of low work motivation needs a systematic and comprehensive approach towards the study of the behaviour of the employees. In order to enter into the roof of low work motivation one has to specify the behavioural problems through adequate and specific diagnosis research. Each behavioural problem then needs unique solution in a very specific and particular manner which may be different from the other. It may be a preventive measure or a therapeutic one.

Kanungo and Mishra suggest a shift in the employer's present orientation towards its employees. Providing incentives to employees should be viewed as a source of investment. Organisations must give priority to activities such as man power, planning, recruitment, training, rewarding and developing its employees through continuing education etc. Money spent on employees should therefore be considered as a source of investment to get the return in terms of high production, high morale, positive attitude, loyalty, dedication to work and organisational commitment.

The investigators view that an orgnisation in which the management does not consider human resources as an investment does very little to ensure adequate returns in the form of high work motivation and morale. They have suggested that to improve work motivation executives and management should (*a*) give up the piece meal personal approach in favour of a more systematic behavioural approach, (*b*) develop an orientation for discovering 'specifics' of problems and solutions related to work motivation issues, and (*c*) develop an investment rather than cost attitude towards management of human resources. Unless the specific behavioural problems are analysed, indentified and defined, their solutions cannot be foreseen. For effective human resources management, various stages of organisational process like man power planning, recruitment, induction and training, job maintenance; performance improvements and employees development should be systematically analysed. Under staffing or over staffing sometimes also lead to low work motivation and productivity.

By judicious selection suitable persons should be recruited who can best meet the requirements of the many problems as well can be identified job at the recruitment stage. The must competent person for the job should be recruited. Improper job analysis, personal bias in selection and biased personal reference, arbitrary selection without proper testing and planned interview are major factors responsible for injudicious recruitment. In the absence of proper job description, the recruiter and the applicants fail to know what is required of them. Without explicit behaviour criteria, the selection of candidates often depends on the arbitrary subjective interpretations of the criteria by the recruiter. When the recruited candidate discovers his inability to fulfil the requirements of the job his work motivation is lowered and consequently productivity suffers.

Very often counter productive informal norms existing within the Organisation are followed by new entrants resulting in low work motivation. In the absence of formal orientation employees develop their own expectations from observation of informal norms governing attendance behaviour. If they find that many employees come late or leave early, they are likely to behave in the same way.

Similarly in the areas of job maintenance, performance improvement and employee development, lack of job clarity, role ambiguity, and role conflicts form major sources of work motivation. Defective reward and punishment systems within the organisation can also lead to poor motivation and low productivity. When high performance goes unrewarded, motivation to work also decreases. Perceived inequality in task assignment and reward allocation may also lead to poor work motivation.

It is viewed that the behavioural symptoms of tardiness, slowness of work etc. of the Indian workers are partly the results of early conditioning and socialisation process and partly due to their present perceptions of the need satisfying potential of the job.

Kanungo and Mishra hold "Indian workers have developed a family centred work ethic. Most of them believe that work is necessary and good primarily for maintaining one's family. Duties are generally performed in the family context, but the same sense of duty does not prevail at work place".

The authoritarian practices in the family produce a strong sense of dependence. The reward systems within Indian Social institutions tend to promote helplessness and external orienation. Family and religious traditionalism of the Indian Culture has created a time perspective that has an emphasis on the past rather than on the present. Time is often considered in an abstract philosophical way as being eternal, ever present but never passing. So delays in actions and slow-lessness is easily tolerated as normal. Punctuality, sense of time, dead line are meaningless. Delays are accepted very normally. Persons are recruited for jobs not on the basis of their job competency but on the basis of demands and pressure from different quarters. In addition to the above factors lack of proper task objective and job perception also lead to low work motivation.

Finally the investigators have concluded that "Organisationally dysfunctional behaviour among Indian employees is so pervasive that like the black money crippling Indian Economic system, black mailing at work (through deliberate inefficiency and apathy) is destroying the moral fabric or *Dharma* and *Karma* ethic of the Indian society". The Indian organisations today are giving more and more importance to strong organisational culture to reduce organisationally dysfunction behaviour.

Kanungo and Mishra have suggested the following "ten commandments" for Indian Management to improve work motivation of employees.

I. If the management is earnest about harnessing human resource effectively, it ought to be guided by the dictum : Labour is an investment.

II. The management must undertake systematic manpower planning and evolve recruitment criteria and procedures based on behaviour or skill anchored job analysis.

III. Having recruited people for different tasks, the management should take positive steps to socialise the employees within the organisation. This could be formally done through short duration in-house orientation programmes to familiarise the employees with task requirements and expected job behaviour.

IV. In-house training programmes should also emphasise retaining of employees to counter some of the early socialisation influences. For instance, employees should be trained to get over the feelings of helplessness on the job. The 'chalega' syndrome (mediocrity) that is so common while performing one's job should be discouraged by promoting task-achievement orientation training.

V. Supervisors should be trained to develop institutional leadership. They should be encouraged to practice control and, influence for task-goal rather than personal-goal accomplishment. Through such behaviour they can act as role models for other employees to follow.

VI. Organisations need to analyse their reward system in terms of :
What are the rewards ? and How are these administered in reality ?

(*a*) The various rewards should be classified under the following categories :
Individual rewards (merit, pay, wage, etc).
Group rewards (group incentive schemes).
Organisation wide reward (profits sharing).
Extra-organisational reward in the environment (place of posting, housing, transport, schooling for employees' children, etc.).

(*b*) The management should attempt to make these rewards contingent on specific forms of desirable employee behaviour such as punctuality, regular job attendance, customer service, etc.

(*c*) The management must know which rewards are more valued by various categories of employees.

(*d*) The management must strive towards maintaining internal equality in reward allocation on the basis of job analysis and evaluation (grade classification) and external equality on the basis of wage surveys and cost of living adjustments.

(*e*) The employees, as far as possible, should get concrete and visible rewards immediately following desirable behaviour.

(*f*) The organisation must provide feedback to its employees regarding the reward system as a whole.

VII. The management must develop job standards for different categories of jobs based on job analysis and set up appropriate performance appraisal system necessary for effective reward allocation and job training programmes.

VIII. The management should clarify to its employees the job expectations and use of goal setting, time targeting, reporting system, etc. to realise its expectations. Role clarity on the job is essential for minimising responsibility diffusion among job incumbents at various levels.

IX. The management should develop mechanisms to constantly monitor and evaluate the impact of various actions with respect to the above on the performance of its employees. Necessary changes whenever implemented should be communicated to all employees affected by them.

X. Any organisational change or intervention contemplated should be data based.

QUESTIONS

1. What is meant by incentives in industry ? Discuss the importance of financial incentives in industry.
2. Distinguish between financial and non-financial incentives. Which incentive, according to you, is more important for increasing efficiency of industrial workers ? Give reasons for your answer.
3. Describe in detail the piece-rate and time-rate method of payment. Why and when is the piece-rate method of payment more effective ?
4. Describe in detail the different kinds of financial incentives.
5. The major difficulties with financial incentives have been the fact that additional money has not meant as much to the employee as the employer assumes it to be. With reference to the above, discuss the importance of non-financial incentives in industry.
6. Review the significant contributions of Indian and Western studies conducted on incentives and make a comparative analysis of the findings.

REFERENCES

Blum, M.L. *Industrial Psychology and Its Social Foundations*, Harper and Row, 1956.

Blum, M. and Russ, J. A study of employee attitudes towards various incentives, Personnel 19, 1942, pp. 438-444.

Blum, M.L. and Nayler, J.C. *Industrial Psychology : Its Theoretical and Social Foundations, Harper* and Row, 1968.

Brown, J.A.C. *The Social Psychology of Industry*, Pelican book series, 1956.

Cole, R.J. A survey of employee attitudes, *public Opinion Quarterly*, 1940.

Deutsch, M. An experimental study of the effects of cooperation and competition upon group process, *Human Relations*, 2, 1949, pp. 199-232.

Goldman, M. and Hammord, L.K. Competition and non-competition and its relation to individual and group productivity, *Sociometry*, 1961, p, 24.

Kanungo, R.N. and Mishra, Sasi. Declining work motivation in India : Indian Management, 1985.

Lytle, C.W. *Wage Incentive Methods*, Rev. Edition, Ronald, New York, 1938.

Marrow, A.J. Goal tensions and recall, *J. Gen. Psychol.*, 1938, p. 19.

Mace, C.A. Incentives, some experimental studies, *Industrial Health Research Board*, 1952.

Marrow, A.J. and French, J.R.P. Changing stereotype in industry, *J. Soc. Issues*, 1945.

Mohanty, G.B. *A study of Attitude of Skilled, Semiskilled and Unskilled Workers of Orissa Towards Incentives*, 1976.

Mohanty, G.B. Level of aspiration of employed and unemployed educated youths, *U.G.C. Project Report*, presented in the 64th session of Indian Science Congress, 1977, Abstract of paper published in part III of the *Proceedings of the 64th Session, Indian Science Congress*, 1977.

Nealey, S.M. Determining worker preferences among employee benefit programmes, *Jn. of Applied Psychology*, 48 (1) 1964, pp. 7·12.

I.C.S.S.R., New Delhi. *A Survey of Research in Psychology*, Popular Prakasan, Bombay, 1972.

Stock Ford, L.O. and Kunze, K. *Psychology and the Paycheck Personnel*, 27, 1950, pp. 129-143.

Tiffm, J. and McCormick, E.J. *Industrial Psychology*, Prestice-Hall of India Pvt. Ltd. New Delhi, 1971.

Viteles, M.S. *Industrial Psychology*, Norton, 1932.

Viteles, M.S. *Motivatian and Morale in Industry*, Norton, 1953.

Vroom, V.H. *Work and Motivation*, New York, Wiley, 1964.

13

Employee-Employer Relationship, Supervision and Leadership

PROBLEM OF EMPLOYEE-EMPLOYER RELATIONSHIP

The problem of the employee-employer relationship, supervision and leadership in industry is not of recent origin. Since it circumscribes every organisation, institution and office, beginning from a forman to a managing director, its importance is recognised every where.

In each and every type of organisations it is found that the function and qualities of a supervisor is linked with attitude, morale, job satisfaction, industrial disputes and ultimately production. Due to the growth of new social values the concept of leadership and the role of a leader etc. have changed. Maier (1970) has therefore remarked "The supervisor becomes the pivot around which many things revolve. The type of personal contact which he builds can obviously make and break morale".

The supervisor of a fabricating plant recently remarked that his headaches were not with the problem of production, but with the problem of supervision.

Bass (1960), a great contributor of quality research on leadership, in his outstanding book *Leadership*, *Psychology* and *Organisation Behaviour* has defined leadership as the observed effort of one member to change another member's behaviour by altering the motivation of the members, or by changing their habits.

Thus, according to Maier (1970); the effectiveness of a leader is determined by whether there is any change in the observed behaviour of the followers. This change is induced by changing motivation and by initiating structure into the work situation.

Today the part played by leadership in industrial relations is gaining increasing recognition. According to Blum and Naylor (1968), "Just as society looks for a leader to define its purpose and lead it forward, so both management and labour have been concerned in the selection and development of men who can successfully attack the many perplexing problems that confront them. The psychological aspects of effective leadership and of the training of leaders deserve serious thought.

The valuable studies as well as the pregnant illustrations in industry, indicate that the supervisor who mostly determines the employee-employer relationship is the centre and the crux around which the varied problems of industrial psychology move.

The problem of the employee-employer relationship came into focus when, during the application of the principles of scientific management, it was found that production did not improve as expected, in spite of high wages and the introduction of all sorts of financial incentives.

Professor Elton Mayo, the guiding star of the Hawthorne studies, conducted several investigations in the Western Electric Company (1927) for about 13 years. Among several other classic and important findings the role of the first line supervisor came into prominence.

The twentieth century industrial psychologists have noted from research findings and day to day observations, that the relationship between the worker and the supervisor or the employee and the employer is the most important and fundamental human relationship in industries and organisations.

The studies at the Western Electric Company were perhaps the first to point out the difficulties of communication in a large industrial plant.

Besides, the Hawthorne studies, Kornhauser, Sartin and many others support this view. As noted by Putnam, this relationship is so important that it exerts its maximum influence on production and efficiency, keeping behind all other financial and non-financial incentives. It would not be an exaggeratior to say that a good employer is the most important non-financial incentive for an employee. Employees may come and go; but if the supervisor is tolerant, co-operative, well-behaved, sympathetic and a patient listener, and by and large human, then the attitude, morale and job satisfaction of the employees will never be other than good.

A supervisor, who is basically the leader of the group, is the torch bearer, the guiding star who gives proper guidance to the employees and directs them in and around their work.

LEADERSHIP TYPES

For the purpose of management, the leadership can be classified into three levels :

1. Top management or the big boss.
2. Middle management or the boss.
3. Front line management or the foreman and supervisors.

These three types of leaders operate at different levels and have different responsibilities and duties. But all the three categories come across the problem of how to deal with the employees and lead them. Therefore, it is essentially to be kept in view to always keep contact with people. An effective and successful leader is one who always tries to keep close contact with the workers or the employees. Blum and Naylor (1968) hold the view that leadership is not an one way affair.

It involves interaction of the leader and the group. From this standpoint, the first-line supervisor is considered as the leader or the supervisor for all practical purposes, as he is the only person with whom the workers come in immediate contact.

Barnard (1938) says that the job of an executive is responsible for devising a system of communication which will allow the organisation to function smoothly. Since the executive is always concerned with securing services form individuals, he must show a strong willingness to co-operate with people According to Blum and Naylor (1968), "The executives formulate the general purpose of the organisation and they must indoctrinate their subordinates with these general purposes, so that the organisation will function in a unified manner".

Studies made in the West, especially by the Michigan University group, on the importance and pattern of effective supervision with regard to productivity and morale, have reinforced a lot of work in India.

Bose (1955) studied the importance of supervision on productivity in an aircraft factory. High productivity was associated with employee centred supervision, general rather than close supervision and skill in supervising the group as a whole, Ganguli (1956) conducted investigations on the worker perception of supervisors and an analysis of their roles in the government railway workshop at Kharagpur. The findings were approximately the same as those found in the Western studies.

According to Sequeira (1962) "the conclusions regarding the effective supervisory practices are less ambiguous and less relative. The main factor here seems to be the level of the supervisor in the hierarchy. At the first line level, factors like the supply of tools, materials, training of men etc. are important. At a higher level, general supervision is more important. The less concrete points relating to attitudes and loyalties of supervisors are more elusive and subject to controversies".

Bhatt and Pathak (1962) have analysed the functions of the supervisory staff and the characteristics essential for their seccess as perceived by a group of supervisors themselves. Yoga (1963) studied the problems of the first line supervisor in a number of engineering and textile industries and found that :

(*i*) A large number of supervisory functions were common to different types of industries.

(*ii*) The pattern of supervisory authority varied with industrial units, though there was a common pattern in each type of industry.

(*iii*) The supervisory pattern in engineering, textile and processing industries showed significant differences and in general supervisors had a minor role with regard to costs and recruitment functions. Interesting differences between supervisors in the textile and engineering industries were observed.

These studies, on the whole, have corroborated the findings made in the West and have indicated a number of interesting differences with regard to the pattern of an effective supervisor.

QUALITIES OF A SUCCESSFUL SUPERVISOR/LEADER

Since congenial relationship between the employee and the employer depends essentially upon the supervisor, it is absolutely essential for the supervisor to possess certain qualities to be successful. An employer must maintain close contact with the workers. His most important problem is how to deal with men, how to lead them, guide them and above all, direct them. Of course it cannot be denied that the employee-employer relationship is not an unilateral affair. It involves interaction of the leader and the group. It deals with a bilateral relationship. The problem has terrific importance not only in industry but in every front.

It is quite difficult to give the various criteria of a successful leader as there is a variety of ways of defining the success of a leader. However, one essential criterion of determining good leadership is whether or not his men follow his orders without question.

The behavioural approach states that the best way to study and to define leadership is in terms of what leaders do, rather than in terms of what leaders are. So it is concerned more with the leader's behaviour than with the leader's traits.

Research in the field of leadership characteristics indicates that the qualities of a successful supervisor is behavioural or situational. It is related to the interactions of the leader and the group.

A supervisor is not born but made, and the good qualities of a supervisor depend mostly upon the environment. It also depends upon the situation at hand. It cannot be denied that a person who is a successful leader in an autocratic group, may not be so in democratic group. Therefore, so far as the personality factors are concerned, there is a wide variation regarding the qualities of a successful supervisor/ leader.

Following Dr. May Smith (1952) it can be said that a leader must have intelligence, good judgement, insight and imagination, a sense of humour, a sense of justice and, above all, a well balanced personality.

According to Puckey, a leader should be able to coordinate and he should have the power to reflect the progress of the group.

The National Industrial Conference Board has classified the qualifications necessary for potential supervisors under three headings.

1. Health and Age : The supervisor should be of sound health, between the age of 25-45 years.
2. Technical Knowledge: It is absolutely essential to guide, direct and control the workers.
3. Personality Traits of the supervisor : So far as this quality is concerned, psychologists do not meet at a general point, but vary widely.

But one cannot deny that the overall personality of an individual is greatly responsible for determining leadership. For instance, in India, besides other factors, the overall personality of Mahatma Gandhi, Pandit Jawaharlal Nehru, Sri Jaya Prakash Narayan, Netajee Subhash Chandra Bose, Sri Atal Behari Bajpaee and Mrs. Indira Gandhi has attracted many followers and they are all glowing examples of leaders possessing a great attraction for the people. History will record their leadership qualities for all times to come.

According to the Industrial Conference Board the ability to analyse and gather new information, the ability to learn, industriousness, resourcefulness and persistency in attacking work problems, willingness to accept criticism, emotional stability and a sense of humour, the ability to inspire confidence, respect for others' capacity for decision and ability to express oneself orally are some of the important qualities necessary for a successful leader.

Craig and Charters, on the other hand, have emphasised forcefulness, ability to command and respect, personal interest in employees, ability to praise and blame effectively and self-confidence as necessary characteristics of a successful leader.

Gibb (1922) has given a list of seven aspects of leadership behaviour. They include performing professional and technical speciality, knowing subordinates and showing consideration for them, getting channels of communications open, accepting personal responsibility and setting an example, initiating and directing action, training men as a team and making decisions. Kretch and Crutchfield (1948) have suggested about 11 qualities of a good leader. They include the qualities of a planner, an executive, and gate keeper, a mediator, an expert, a lawmaker, a father figure etc.

According to Blum and Naylor (1968), a successful leader is he "whose men respect him, whose men follow his orders without question, whose men like him, whose work group has high morale and who looks out for his men". In short, the leader must act as an ideal for the follower. He should also be capable of fulfilling the needs of the followers. Otherwise, he will lose the confidence of people and be an utter failure as a leader. A number of researches and meaningful studies have also been conducted in the area of leadership.

STUDIES ON LEADERSHIP

Michigan Leadership Studies

Likert, Katz, Maccoby Kahn and Seashore at the Survey Research Centre of the Institute for Social Research, Michigan University, have conducted studies on leadership behaviour. The initial study done by Katz, Maccoby and Morse (1950) is now something of a classic and illustrates the early Michigan approach to leadership. The results indicated that supervisors in charge of high producing sections were found to be employee centred in terms of their attitude and supervisors in charge of low producing sections were found to be production centred in their orientation.

The study conducted by Lawshe and Nagle (1953) indicates the influence of the supervisor on the performance of the group. These studies clearly suggest that the attitude of supervisors, appeared to be related to the productivity of the work group. Lewin, Lippit and White (1939) conducted a number of studies on leadership behaviour using experimental procedures. They studied the behaviour of children of 10 to 11 years by giving them training in authoritarian, democratic and 'laissez faire' leadership. In other words, each group was exposed to each of the three kinds of leadership. The results indicated that there was more ego involvement and 'we' feeling in the democratic atmosphere than in the authoritarian, atmosphere. The authoritarian group shared either a sense of apathy or aggression. But aggressiveness was very low under the democratic group which suggests that the conduct of the group is a function of its structure. It was also noted that some boys preferred the autocratic to the democratic order, perhaps because of their home background. This interesting finding is supported by Peaks' study (1954).

Kipnis and Cosentino (1969) in a follow-up study tried to examine the use of leadership powers in industry. The results indicated that both situational and personal factors such as the number of employees supervised, years of experience as a supervisor and the nature of the problems presented by the subordinates influence the supervisor's choice of corrective power.

In a study on leadership beliefs of 1339 Australian Managers (1970), it was noted that they showed beliefs similar to those of Managers in England and U.S.A. They differed from the managers of other cultural groups. In common with all managers, they did not believe that the average individual has got capacity and initiative for leadership. But they accepted the democratic participative method of leadership.

Meade (1967) demonstrates that both morale and productivity were higher under authoritarian leadership. The important factor here is that the leader's effectiveness is related to the satisfaction of the follower's needs.

England and Lee (1975) investigated the relationship between managerial values and managerial success in the United States, Japan, India and Australia. Cross-validated results showed that value patterns were significantly predictive of managerial success and could be used as a basis for selection and placement decisions. Results further indicated that managers from the four countries were more or less uniform in terms of the personal values that were related to success. More successful managers had dynamic, pragmatic and achievement oriented values. But the less successful managers had static and passive values.

Ansari, Baumgartel and Sullivsan conducted a study named "The Personal Orientation Organizational Climate Fit and Managerial Success" (1982) to test the hypotheses that the interaction of fit between personal work orientations and organizational climate makes a significant contribution to the variance in career success among managers. Precisely, the present study was conducted to determine the factors associated with managerial success.

Ghiselli and his associates in a number of studies have explored the relationship between the need system and managerial success. Ghiselli (1968) has reported that those successful middle managers were likely to have less desire for security and high financial reward than those who were unsuccessful. Ghiselli and Johnson (1970) noted that for managers in tall organizations, there was little relationship between the degree of need satisfaction and success, while in flat organizations a positive relationship existed between the degree of need satisfaction and success. Siegel and Ghiselli (1971) also found a positive relationship between pay and measures of managerial talent for young managers. England and Weber (1972) found that successful managers favoured pragmatic, dynamic and achievement oriented values while the unsuccessful ones preferred more static and passive values. Moreover, value patterns were found to be significantly predictive of managerial success and could be used for selection and placement decisions (England and Lee, 1974; Watson and Williams, 1977).

In a review of hundreds of studies (1919-1964), Ghiselli (1966) found that proficiency in executive roles was most efficiently predicted by tests of intellectual ability, perceptual accuracy, and to some extent personality. According to Korman (1968) objective personality inventories and leadership ability tests have' generally not shown predictive validity with the possible exception of a projective test of management motivation developed by Miner (1968) and the well documented leaderless group discussion technique. Dubno (1968) using MMPI observed that successful managers possess personality characteristics that are relatively free from encroachment and neurotic reactions to stress situations.

Henry (1949) reported that the T.A.T. themes of successful business managers contain a crystallization of high drive and achievement desire, strong mobility drive, willing acceptance of authority relationship and ability to organize unstructured situations and to see that the implications for their organization. The thematic analysis also revealed that successful executives possessed the trait of decisiveness, sense of selfhood, aggressiveness, fear of failure, reality orientation, indentification with superiors and a detachment from parents. In a review of eleven studies with projective tests Kinslinger (1966). Observed that in nine of the reported studies certain indications and signs distinguished between the more successful and less successful managers. Fiedler and Mahar (1979) on the basis of 12 studies postulate that the effectiveness of a leader also depends upon the appropriate match between two major factors motivational structure and situational control.

Indian Studies

Some natable studies have been conducted in India on the image of the employees about their supervisors.

Kakar's study (1971) on authority in social relations in India indicated that the image of the supervisor in all; cases was that of an autocrat. There was not a single case in his study in which a supervisor had been described to be permissive and relatively equal.

Ganguli (1964) conducted a study on leadership behaviour in an engineering factory, which revealed that the prevailing pattern ranged midway between the bureaucratic (impersonal) and the autocratic (assertive) supervisor.

In an useful investigation on management practices in different countries Nagandhi and Prasad (1971) brought to light the leadership styles, that is the manner in which individuals occupying similar positions make use of power of authority in their office. The investigators conducted studies in 17 Indian owned companies. The results showed that only three perceived their leaders as democratic, nine as authoritarian and five as bureaucratic. They found that usually the superiors hold the subordinates in low esteem and low trust.

Kumar and Singh (1976) have pointed out' 'The preponderance of the authoritarian style is supported further by existence of many more layers of hierarchy (8-10) in the Indian organisations as compared with U.S. subordinates in India (5-7). This difference in the orgnisational structure affects the authority's need for delegation of powers to their subordinates". They hold that in India the bureaurcatic organisations, due to emphasis on objectivity, impersonality and heirarchical authority suit the Indian managers as they embody standards which they would like to apply to others.

Ghosh and Manerikar (1974), in a study entitled "In search of Personality Characteristics of Indian Managers", have found that Indian managers have greater similarities than differences in different functional areas.

The hypothesis that Indian managers in functional areas would have personality characteristics similar to the Indian general managers was partly supported by the results. Dominance, casualness, sensitivity, realism, adaptability, practicality, confidence, conservatism and group independence, were the common personality characteristic which emerged.

Chattopadhaya (1983) in his paper "Motivation and Leadership Styles in Indian Enterprises" has attempted to describe interesting linkages between motivation and leadership while discussing the complexities of the Indian Social System of which any institution or organisation is only a minute part. The author throws light on the emergence of the power motive in Indian enterprises. The author has linked the emergence of power motive to two hypotheses (*a*) child rearing practices are at the base of omnipotent and impotent ambivalence in the child, (*b*) Senior Managers striving for power damper the enthusiasm, in the Junior Managers, etc.

There is a general feeling that Indian employees fell demotivated in their work situation and to bring improvement in work motivation it is necessary to develop new leadership styles.

Leadership according to Chattopadhaya consists of ably differentiating between what is inside a system and what is outside of it, with the idea of regulating appropriate transactions between the two. An appropriate transaction between the two can lead to products that are' superior in quantity and quality. It is viewed that motivation, leadership and management are interlinked processes. In order to ably manage the institutional boundaries, the acknowledged leader must be aware of his inner world that determines his own motivation and behaviour. His followers are likely to feel motivated to perform tasks to a great extent. Thus the author suggests that for a person to a have leadership and managerial skill of an order that will create a situation where his followers are likely to feel motivated to engage with their institutional tasks, that person must have a high degree of awareness of his *inner world.* The inner world of the human being consists of both the memories and the store house of forgotton experiences or the unconscious. Awareness of one's inner world should be such that a person can utilise both pleasant and painful experiences of the past as resources in the present as well as acknowledge one's limitations which minimise the probability of making mistakes or pushing oneself to destruction.

Chattopadhaya further is of opinion that the practice in most regions of India is a kind that hinders the growth of a mature personality. In some situation the Indian child is allowed to feel that he is so important that everything will be done for him ... In some other situation he finds himself facing insurmountable barriers of do's and don'ts that make him feel altogether important in terms of his need satisfaction. He is infantalised and his behaviour reflects it. The Indian personality grows on this foundation. Thus, the grown up Indian faced with a difficult anxiety producing situation tries to achieve either omnipotence or behaves as if he is impotent. Precisely, he either seeks to consolidate so much power that hopefully he can influence his environment, so that everyone there will respond to his demands; tries to seek out some one on whom he can completely depend, some one who can in an omnipotent fashion guide him to success. The author speculates in this context that this power motivation stems from the inability to provide leadership *i.e.*, differentiating between what is inside a system and what is outside. Thus, management becomes a precess of veiled feudal mode of getting people to work for the most powerful in any institution.

Kapoor, Ansari and Shukla (1986) have conducted a study on *Upward Influence Tactics as a Function of Locus of Control and Organisational Context*. The study based on a social psychological contingency perspectvie was designed to test the hypotheses that the interaction between locus of control and superior's leadership behaviour and the goals of influence attempt makes a significant contribution to the variance in upward influence tactics.

An organisation is constituted of both superiors and subordinates, both of whom can influence each others attempt. For the proper and effective functioning of the organisation a kind of harmony and sound relation between the two are needed.

Results of this study indicated that the main effects of locus of control and organisational context on upward influence tactics were significant and consistent. This supports the findings of previous studies by Ansari and Kapoor (1986), Ansari and Rehna (1986) and Chengand (1983).

A study has been conducted on "*Executive Success as a Function of leadership' Style Organisational Climate Fit*" by Ansari and Rub. to test the hypotheses that interaction or fit between personal work styles and organisational climate makes a significant contribution to the variance in career success among executives.

In a number of earlier studies attempts have been made to correlate executive success with biographical data (Ansari 1981), need structure (Ghiselli) 1968a, 1968b, Ghiselli and Johnson (1970), values (England and Lee 1974) Watson and Williams (1977), life style (Ansari 1981) and intelligence and personality (Ansari 1982), Ghiselli (1966), Henry (1949), Kinslinger (1966), Kultz (1949). But most of these studies do not explain more than a small amount of variance in career success. Furthermore, most of the studies on this area have tried to focus either on personality or situations ignoring the importance of the interaction between the two.

The present research assume that for each individual there are environment the characteristics of his or her personal style and orientation, leading to better performance, satisfaction and very little stress. It proposes to investigate the salience of three relevent and appropriate matched pairs, authoritarianism, nurturant task and participative dimensions of individual and environment in predicting career success. Thus, the expectation is that how successful an executive is in his or her professional careers or a function of the extent to which the climate of work environment is congenial with his or her motivational predispositions.

The findings indicate strong support for the contingency proposition regarding the importance of the significant contribution of person environment interactions to career success. The study thus provides significant evidence that the Indian executives in middle position thrive best, in the sense of salary progress, in organisational environments congenial to their own motivational orientations towards nurturance and task dimensions.

Ansari, Kapoor and Rehana in their study entitled "Social Power in Indian Organization" have attempted to find out the answer to two questions (*i*) what do the organisational members mean when they speak of power, (*ii*) what are the common power strategies being adopted in Indian organisations.

The findings indicate that almost every member of the organisation thinks that he knows a lot about what power is and how to judge who has it and who has not. Organisational members have definite ideas about what power is, and their ideas are not very different from those of the experts. However, power does not mean the same thing to every one as data in this study indicated. While in the present study 59 per cent of the respondents viewed power as authority and position, in a similar observation made in the U.S. Organizations (1980) the respondents talked of power as synonymous with position and formal authority, or ability or potentiality to influence others.

In the present study it was found that supervisory and lower levels of management rely more on the strong means of influence such as sanctions, persuasion and treat while the top managers use most often more softer means of influence like personalised relationship, manipulation and maintaining alliance with others. However, evidence from the United States, England and

Australia indicate that Managers from these countries by and large use reason most frequently and sanctions least frequently (Kipnis *et al.*, 1983). This difference is explained by the fact Indian organisations are in some ways unique and their uniqueness has significant implications to organisational behaviour including power relationship (Sinha, 1982). According to Kakar (1978) an Indian is born with a readymade rule book for social relationship, his social roles are arranged in hierarchical order *i.e.* of superior subordinate relationship. Obviously he neither feels comfortable working at equal levels, nor he believes in maintaining partnership in group. This is the reason why in India sanctions work best and friendliness in not encouraged in Indian organisations. Thus Shina (1980) reasonably claimed that the task-oriented, (with a blend or nurturance orientation,) discipline minded, leadership with personalised approach is more condusive to the Indian organisations. The investigators have however suggested that before generalising the above conclusion additional efforts should be made to investigate the individual characteristics and the characteristics of the overall organisation (*e.g.* norms, climate, structure) which are likely to have an effect on the relative effectiveness on various methods of influence.

Ansari (1986) has conducted an empirical study to determine the need for Nurturant task leaders in India. It is commonly believed by some managements that the basic difference between a successful and an unsuccessful organisation lies in its leadership. Evidences indicated that many failure in organisations are caused by poor, leadership.

Empirical data have demonstrated that Indian students score higher than the students in other countries on authoritarianism (F) scale. In a further study Canadian students were found to exhibit less authoritarianism than Indian students. With the above back ground Meade (1967) has hypothesised that authoritarian leadership would be a good bet to promote organisational productivity in the Indian set up. Thus he replicated the study conducted by Lewin, Lippitt and White on a group of North Indian 10-11 years school children. He concluded that "work done under authoritarian leadership was a higher quality than that done under democratic leadership. That the morale of the Ss working under authoritarian leaders was higher than that in democratic leadership was indicated by the lower rate of absenteeism, the greater number wishing to continue in the authoritarian conditions, and the number of persons expressing a preference for the authoritarian leader". These findings obtained with Ss in India were the opposite of Lewin, Lippitt and White who used American Ss. Thus Meade and others have concluded that Indian culture by and large is authoritarian and Indians foster excessive dependency in their children.

This author (2009) has made several investigations and observations on different domestic employees and worker engaged in construction work for the 30-35 years and has come to the conclusion that in most cases democratic uper leadership and democratic attitude in work situation has failed on the contrary authoritarians behaviour has proved fruitful comptroller the work situation and extracting the best from them. This author has personally observed that her democratic behaviour to most of the domestic helpers has failed miserably and as they consider it probably a weakness and take advantage of the situation with domestic dealings they try to neglect their work remain absent often show disobedience and cheating behaviour. But with authoritarian behaviour the same person improve in their performance and show good work culture. But this did not happen in all cases, but in most cases. So I agree with the findings of pleade and associates. In society the child rearing practices are mostly one of authoritarian than demotic unlike the western culture. Probably for this reason authoritarian leadership in more successful in Indian work situation than democratic ones. However currently a mixture or democratic and authoriate work culture is more condesive to good performance rigid authorities behaviour is more tolerable as people in India with their change in attitude because of globalization and cross cultural influency. Hence keeping in mind the humanitarian and human source factors the employee or immediate supervisor should be flexible and too much authoritarian or too much democratic leadership is utilize the type of leadership as per the need generous for Indian workers and Indian organisation.

However, Sinha and Sinha (1974) have expressed doubt about the appropriateness of the authoritarian (F) style in Indian culture. They on the other hand have identified certain socio cultural values like preference for rest and relaxation without being tired, dependence proneness, lack of commitment, showing off personalised relationships and lack of team orientation some of which of course seem to share the rubric of authoritarianism. Given the presence of such values Sinha wondered whether a task oriented, discipline minded, tough leadership with a personalised approach would be more successful in the Indian setting. Such a leadership style was named "nurturant task" (NT).

The findings of the present study supports the NT styles of leadership in Indian organisations. The NT style is perceived as distinctly different from the other styles although it has a positive overlap with the caring and friendly style and inverse correlation with F & B climates. The NT style positively affects several indications of organisational effectiveness, while the F style of F climate negatively affects the factors of efficiency and satisfaction.

This study has therefore provided sufficient evidence on the usefulness of the NT model.

Chattopadhyay and Lawrence (1985) consulting with several public sector enterprises have attempted to throw light on the private nature of public sector enterprises in India. They have attempted to find out an answer to an urgent issue "why public enterprises are not so cost effective and productive as the sponsoring governments would want the citizen as tax payer to believe".

The authors point out that the top management believed that all problems lay at the door of their subordinates Chattopadhyay (1975, 1980, 1980a, 1982) has made research on the dependency in Indian culture. In his opinion "both due to certain historical processes and various aspects of child rearing practices in India, there is a strong belief in the unconscious of the Indian that either he must have enough power to invade their people's boundary or he must allow more powerful people to invade his boundary. This results in pre-occupation with power or sycophancy or apathy, depending on the perceived power of the individual in his or her dominant or more important systems". Under these circumstances, if in the current situation they feel very powerful, they act as omnipotent parents; if the current situation gives them a sense of powerlessness, they may nurse the frustration by becoming apathetic or run almost berserk through acting out infantile temper tantrum as a response to one's rage.

There was (the author views) a strong feeling that the public sector is created primarily for giving employment opportunity to people. There is a myth that all public sector managers by and large are inferior in terms of skill and capability compared to private sector managers (Ganjee, 1985). But it is a fact that many public sector managers are more skilled and capable than numerous managers of very big business houses.

Thirdly, it is pointed out that in the public sector Ministers and Secretaries for obvious political reasons always meddle with not only policies but also with operations of the enterprises in that sector.

It is held by the investigators that for various reasons the public sector managers hold a sense of shame and guilt that lead to their making public sector matters more private than the private sector.

Ansari (1984) in his paper on "Psychodynamics of a successful executive" has attempted to answer the question what makes an executive successful ? What are the factors associated with career success. He conducted an indepth interview on 150 middle level male Executive representing three business concerns in Northern India. A statistical comparison of successful and unsuccessful business executives (successful and unsuccessful in terms of their background variables, critical decisions of life and their interpersonal relationships with people around job. Several other studies show that successful executives have perceived spatial mobility, reliably more than their unsuccessful counterparts. Wives of successful executives are found to be better educated and in better employment positions. Further it has been found that most of the successful executives (63.46%) decided their career themselves because of their interest and aptitude. The critical decision of life play a significant role in career success. The successful executives are also more independent than the unsuccessful ones. The feeling of psychological success has been found to be related with career progression.

It was also expected that successful and unsuccessful executives would differ significantly in terms of their dealings with their coworker.

The following major conclusions were drawn from the present study regarding the qualities of a successful executive. A successful executive is better educated, and professionally brained, first or second in birth order, has experienced a great deal of spatial mobility, has an educated and employed wife and has a fairly past socioeconomic background. A successful executive decides his academic and professional careers himself. Because he is responsible for his own career, he feels that his present career meets his expectations and gets a sort of psychological success. A successful executive maintains cordial relationship with his coworkers. He receives good support from his superiors. He prefers to solve the personal problems of the subordinates and even takes personal care of them. Successful executives are more interaction oriented than the unsuccessful executives *i.e.* they maintain high informal relationship with their subordinates on the job. Precisely, they maintain better social relationship with their subordinates. They take care to please their superiors. They distribute their time in different ways performing different functions and roles than do the unsuccessfuls (Broks, 1955). They feel that the responsibility of an executive to be a successful and effective leader is to help others and create the understanding of the teaching learning process combined with self-understanding (Cantor, 1986).

Ansari and Kapoor conducted a study on organisational context and upward influence tactics :

The study examined immediate superior's leadership styles and the goals of influence attempts on subordinate's use of power strategies. Sixty nine engineering undergraduates participated in role playing situations and were assigned to superiors with particular leadership style as well as given influence attempt goals. Major findings were that (*a*) influence strategies used by subordinates varied as a function of goals sought from superiors, (*b*) influence strategies used by subordinates were significantly affected by the superiors leadership styles, and (*c*) only one significant interaction between the leadership behaviour and influence attempt goals *i.e.* on blocking strategy, was noted.

A global analysis of the various Western and Indian studies on leadership, Supervisor and managerial qualities suggests that though certain common qualities and personality characteristics are essentially required for the success of a leader or employer, yet, the effectiveness of a leader depends by and large upon the satisfaction of the follower's need.

The qualities of a successful leader also varies with the variation in the situation and also depends to a great extent on the spirit of the time.

Fredgold therefore remarks that certain good qualities do not even exist in the most successful leaders of the industry. History adds concrete evidence to this. Some of the successful leaders of history have been neurotic, epileptic, paranoid, insane and humourless. Ford was an obsessional neurotic and Hitler and Napolean were paranoids. But history has remembered them as successful leaders of the world. This was perhaps because their defects matched with the existing situations. Hearst, Ford, Carnegie, Morgan, etc., in the words of Brown, were by no means either paragons of virtue or normalcy.

However, that does not mean that good qualities are not essential. A successful leader should be reasonably intelligent, well balanced and sensitive to the feelings of the group. Besides bossing and giving orders he should also be capable of taking news from his own environment. Eventually, a good supervisor must have deep insight and understanding into the hearts of the workers. Developing these qualities a modern supervisor is expected to help others in older to help himself. He must not only be capable but must also be in close touch with the people who work under him.

In addition to the qualities described a supervisor must be able to recognise a problem when it exists, decide what additional information is needed, realise what is desirable and then make a decision. He must translate into action the principles of good human relations, strike a balance between consideration and the demands of the time and adopt rapidly to technological and social dangers. He must be more a patient listener than a big talker. Gap in communication should be bridged and cemented at any cost. Communication should be regarded as a two way process in which employees and employers have equal opportunity to convey their feelings and their action of each other. No suspicion should exist in the minds of either party. Flexibility of attitude, understanding, sympathy and tolerance on the part of the employer is also necessary.

An employee-oriented attitude rather than a production-oriented attitude is more conductive to good employee-employer relationship. Supervisors are expected to take a personal interest in their employees, to be more understanding, to punish them less often when mistakes are made and to groom them for promotion by teaching them new skills. It is true that personal relationship is the key to successful employee employer relationship.

It has also been observed from the Michigan leadership studies that supervisors in charge of high producing groups have a more employee-centred attitude, while supervisors in charge of low producing groups have a more work-centred attitude. Low producing supervisors are mostly management-identified, while high producing supervisors are employee-identified. Studies by

Kornhouser show that department production differs with the difference in employee-employer relationships.

Listening to the employees point of view gives the employers emotional relief; and has a tonic effect on them. The employees thus get a chance to express themselves fully and clean their minds from burdensome thoughts. Studies by Kornhouser and Sharp corroborate the Hawthorne studies in demonstrating the role of the supervisor.

According to Kupuswamy (1961), "A successful leader is he who gives the full credit to the followers and takes the full blame on himself for any failures of the group action. This is how, he can succeed in keeping the whole group as a team".

FUNCTIONS OF A SUPERVISOR

According to Tiffin, the foreman today is something like a statesman whose personality and behaviour towards the workers determines to a great extent on the rate of production. In other words, he acts as a helper as well as commander.

In tracing the history of the supervisor, one can say that a long time back a supervisor was all powerful, he was the monarch of all hierarchies. He was only interested in hiring and firing the workers, and was always considered right while the workers were always considered wrong.

A few years back the supervisor had to do a lot of work and he had tremendous responsibilities. He was in charge of :

1. Wage,
2. Rate of work,
3. Controlling the quality of work,
4. Method of work,
5. Training the worker,
6. Maintenance of machinery, and
7. Problems of discipline.

These being his main functions, he was called a "Jack of all trades, but a master of none". At that time no consideration was given to the executive ability of the supervisors, perhaps because it was not needed then.

But with the development of scientific management and the growth of new social values drastic changes have taken place in the role of a supervisor. He is no more a dictator. He has become democratic and his self-centred attitude has changed. Due to modern industrial development the supervisor has become a controversial figure in industry. His responsibility has increased effectively. Houser and Kornhouser have pointed out that various relations in industry depend upon the changing role of the supervisor. He is the representative of the management to the workers. Since the average workers come in direct contact with him, his role or position is very important.

Today, many of the old functions of the supervisor have been taken away, such as the hiring of the workers, discipline, lay-off and strikes. These functions have been taken over by the personal department.

Fixing the rate of payment has been taken up by the job evaluation department. Quality control is given to a specialised technical department. The rate or method of work has been put in charge of the time and motion analysis department, maintenance, repair and training departments, respectively.

In spite of the fact that these duties have been taken away from him, still the supervisor's responsibilities have become more grave and his duties more important. He has to know a little of law, as everyday he is faced with the problem of making decisions about transfers, recruitment and promotion, etc. The various factory acts, wage acts and contracts are handled by him. Quick decisions are to be taken because of the urgency of the work. The various legal requirements are to be interpreted in different ways, depending upon the situation concerned. Disputes are increasing due to the formation of various labour unions. So the supervisor or the leader has to know a bit of law also. Previously, the supervisor was always right and the worker always wrong. But today with the change in the status of the employees and spirit of time both are partly wrong and partly right. The supervisor has to tackle both the boss and the worker. With a high degree of social skill in a peculiar situation he has to handle various conflicting orders. Today, the method of dealing with the employees has changed from an autocratic stance to a democratic one. Understanding has become more important than bossing around. If the supervisor is not careful about his dealings he may breed discontentment among the workers. He is the pivot around which problems revolve.

To quote Brown (1958), "The supervisor is the conductor of an orchestra rather than a one-man band and he realises that his job is to coordinate the willing work of his employees".

On the psychological plane, the supervisor-cum-employer has terrific role to play. The employer works as a father-figure and the employees depend upon him for emotional security, self-realisation and release of tensions. The supervisor should, therefore, have the ability to take the workers into confidence. There should not be any sudden or immediate change without the knowledge of the workers. The employees should be in a position to predict what is expected of him, so that in turn the actions of his supervisors will be predictable. Instead of rigid and strict discipline, consistent and mild discipline by the employer should be encouraged. Observations and experiences show that leaders and top boss of various organisations and institutions who are in the habit of expressing their dislikeness and disapproval towards their employees in the public, are proved to be worst leaders. Such persons fail to understand that each individual has an ego and insult or resentment is definitely repulsive and doubly hurts the individual when such negative remarks are expressed in the public.

Therefore, disapproval and resentment towards the employees, whenever absolutely necessary, should be expressed in person though praise could be made in public.

TYPES OF SUPERVISORS

Bradford and Lippitt (1946) have referred to four types of supervisors.

1. The hard boiled autocrat.
2. The benevolent autocrat.
3. The *laissez faire* supervisor.
4. The democrat.

The Hard Boiled Autocrat

The hard boiled autocrat constantly checks production, gives orders and expects immediate acceptance. He is mostly a rigid disciplinarian and believes that praise will spoil the workers' efficiency. He is very much status conscious and does not trust the employees' initiative. Under such circumstances, the workers criticise the leader at his back which can obviously be called 'back-biting'. Because of such behaviour the group feels that he is insecure, tense, aggressive and egocentric. But the Indian employees usually show an uncritical reaction to authority. According to Kakar (1971) the autocratic authority is the ideal image of the Indian employees.

The Benevolent Autocrat

A benevolent autocrat dominates all employees. When the employee fails to meet the standards it makes him feel hurt, angry and surprised. In such a group, the employees depend upon the leader for all decisions and demonstrate a slow regression to more aubmission, dependency and inability to accept responsibility.

The *Laissez-faire* Supervisor. This type of leader often busies himself in paper work and hence stays away from the employees. Such a leader has no goal and is indecisive. Such a group has the tendency to find scapegoats, is unstable and has low output.

The *laissez-faire* group lacks direction and in such a directionless group, frustration, failure and insecurity are typical.

The Democrat

The democratic supervisor shares group decisions and devotes time for planning. He is quite decisive. He has a lot of confidence and security. According to Lippitt and Bradford, democratic leaders encourage employees to function in a democratic framework.

According to Blake and Mouton (1964) the two major dimensions of the managerial grid is concern for production and concern for people. This leads to five types of managers.

1. Exacting Task Master. The exacting task master is. concerned with production and very little with human relations. The supervisor-subordinate relationship is one of authority and obedience. More emphasis is given on selection and less on training. It is always necessary that from the beginning the right man should be selected rather than training be given to the wrong man.

2. Worker-Oriented Manager. The second type of manager is highly concerned with human values and relatively less concerned with production, or at least, not immediately concerned with it. He is a humanist in the sense that he helps the workers in their difficulties, patiently listens to their complaints and grievances and becomes an aid in solving their problems. Instead of forcing the employees, he gently persuades them to follow certain guidelines or principles. He is not bossy, but is an understanding employer.

3. Passive Manager. This type of manager is neither concerned with production nor With people. He only works formally as a manager by maintaining tile *status quo*. Somehow he wants to manage and survive. He has minimum involvement with the organisation.

4. Complete Manager. The fourth type of manager is neither concerned about the people nor concerned about production. The basis of this manager is to promote the conditions that integrate creativity, high productivity and high morale through concerted team action. Therefore he is viewed as a complete manager who relies on mutual understanding. He also believes in the acceptance of organisational goals. In the solution of any problem of the organisation or in the achievement of a goal he seeks the participation of the his staff members. A complete manager encourages communication between the managers and staff in two ways. He believes that the communication must not be unilateral, but bilateral.

5. Individual-Organisational Centred Manager. This type of manager puts emphasis in bringing optimum coordination between the qualities and attitudes of the individual worker and the requirements of the organisation. Thus, he tries maintain a balance between the needs of the workers and the requirements of the organisation. He believes that the system of work should be designed and planned in such a manner that both the employees and the management can achieve the best. He also tries to select workers in such a way that the qualities of the applicant fulfil the job requirement.

SELECTION OF SUPERVISORS

In the past, supervisors were usually selected on the basis of the production record. This was not a desirable system. According to Gray (1952), "The supervisor may understand how to control the machine, but not how to control his men. Much of the time of the experts in industry is spent repairing damage to human feelings by their supervisors who do not know how to deal with their men. While the supervisor is the master craftsman with material, he is a novice with the personnel". In other words, the supervisor takes care of the machine elements but leaves the human elements untouched. Hence the selection of the supervisors should be made from the humanitarian standpoint. In fact, the production record is not as important for a successful supervisor as the right attitude and the right practice of this attitude.

According to Blum and Naylor (1968), psychological tests have been successful in the selection of many different types of employees, but to date they have not been of any great help in the selection of potential executives.

A job analysis of the qualities of a supervisor are necessary for the selection of a supervisor. A job analysis, however, has not yet been made with the result that it is quite difficult to select a supervisor.

According to Kretch and Crutchfield (1948), merely having potentiality is not enough. The supervisor must know how to behave and deal with the workers. He must also know how to apply his potentiality in the right direction.

As already indicated, supervisors may be selected on the basis of tests and interviews. The right method of selecting supervisors, however, has not yet been developed.

As suggested by Blum and Naylor (1968), by applying various psychological tests, psychologists can, by and large, effectively describe a person's characteristics such as his intelligence level, ambition level, maturity level, interests and abilities, using these variables and their probable inter-relations as a basis. Psychologists can offer descriptive evidence that will enable the management to decide whether it wants such a person for a specific executive position. If the criterion is known, the psychologists can do the matching. But for most of the executive positions the criterion is usually not clearly defined, or it varies from company to company.

TRAINING OF SUPERVISORS AND EXECUTIVES

Since supervisors are made and not born, the qualities of a supervisor are situational and behavioural. Therefore, the successful qualities of a supervisor can be developed through proper training.

With the realisation of this fact, the need for training administrators has been recognised and put into practice. But it should also be recognised that training should also be imparted to people working under different organisations, starting from a first line supervisor to a minister. It should not be taken for granted that one who has been elected as leader by the people, has got all the leadership qualities and therefore does not require any training or orientation.

A lot of inefficiency can be avoided if training is given at all levels. A study on leadership training by Bevlas (1942) indicated that the period of a three weeks training helped the poor leaders to become good and successful leaders.

In order to have the right attitude and a sharp insight into the heart of the workers, training is very essential. The findings of the Hawthorne studies and Houser have further enhanced the need of supervisor training and have given tremendous impetus to open training centres in industry. Psychologists have therefore begun to develop a number of methods to train supervisors.

They are :

1. Lecture method or class room method.
2. Conference or case method or discussion method.
3. Role playing technique.
4. Employee problem approach.

Lecture Method

To start with, the potential supervisors are selected on the basis of tests. They are then given various lectures by experts on problems like cost of material, incentive, cooperation, recognition of ideas, discipline and on the do's and don'ts of a supervisor.

At the end of the course it is taken for granted that supervisors are trained. The lecture method is said to be quite economical and less time consuming as it gives several informations in a very short period. However, a good lecture facilitates learning and influences attitude more than mere passive reading. Good lectures also help in understanding and in selective learning.

But no lecture serves the purpose of helping people to develop associations. Moreover, it is a very superficial method as by this the majority of people do not gain much. The gain is very little as it only touches the surface. By listening to the lectures, making associations and understanding them becomes quite difficult. Again practising theories in the practical day-to-day field is far different from theoretical lectures.

Maier (1970) holds the view that not much research has been carried out by this method of training. He says that lectures are of little value in changing attitudes, developing job skill or training in human relationship skills. Lectures may also be boring. Even in the case of perfect lecture there may be difficulty in holding the attention and concentration of the trainees. People of above average intelligence usually gain more from lectures than people of average and below average intelligence as lectures convey ideas and concepts which cannot be easily grasped by all.

The Conference or Discussion Method

Being dissatisfied with the dry and superficial method of lecturing, psychologists next attempted to train supervisors by the discussion and conference method.

A series of topics of problems of the industry are thrown to the group for discussion in the conference or discussion group. Topics may relate to any problem of the industry starting from wages to accidents. The various members take part in the discussion and' give a number of suggestions. At last a solution is arrived at.

But this is also a superficial method since knowledge becomes theoretical somehow or other the right solution is rarely arrived at. In all practical cases the right solution may not be arrived at all.

Besides, members taking part in the discussion should be of a proper level of intelligence to take part in such a discussion.

Role Playing Technique

This is one of the most important and extensively used techniques to train leaders in various types of training programmes which are called 'reality practice' or the 'problem approach'.

A realistic day-to-day problem of the Industry is presented and the trainees are put either in superior or subordinate positions to provide them the opportunity of experiencing, approaching and viewing the problems from different positions. Then they instructed to act and bring about a solution. For example, a group of supervisors who are being trained in effective leadership are presented with the problem of the employer being 'gheraoed' by the employees. One of the trainees is asked to play the role of an employee and another to take the role of an employer. Now the two persons plan the handling of the problems and they act out the situation before the group. After the role playing is over, the group discusses the problem, considering the mistakes made by the two foremen. The performance is then repeated by two other men who play the two roles to see if they can avoid the mistakes committed by the previous two trainees. There is also a group discussion and the members try to determine which solution was better.

Blum and Nalyor (1968) opine that in a variation of this technique one man takes the role of the employee who has broken the rule and is confronted by three different foremen, none of whom knows the approach used by the other two. The group then decides which is the best way to handle the situation or what particular aspect of each technique would contribute most to the solution. The three foremen are asked to repeat their performances, modifying them according. to the suggestion of the group.

Advantages. Training of this type encourages learning at a very meaningful level. The person in charge of the training has a passive role though it is quite important too. What is more important is that the leader must encourage active participation.

Bradford and Lippitt's study on the training of supervisors in a business organisation shows certain advantages of the role-playing technique. By assuming the roles of supervisors and employees the trainees could see the problems involved from a new angle and improve their leadership qualities. Because of the role playing technique each party gets a chance to get an insight into the attitudes and behaviour of the other party.

According to French (1946), in training foremen to handle interpersonal relations, role-playing has a number of distinct advantages over the conventional methods of lectures, discussion, conferences and reading. Blum and Nalyor opine that role playing provides an excellent bridge between discussions of inter-personal relations and their actual handling. It presents test situations to determine how well a trainee can handle various problems and makes the leader sensitive to different methods and styles of leadership.

Tannenbaum, Kallejian and Weschler (1954) indicate three· limitations of the conventional training programme.

1. The trainee is removed from the social setting in which he customarily performs.
2. Imparting human relations information may have little or no effect including changes in behaviour.
3. The carryover from the training to the work situation may be negligible.

To minimise these limitations, they propose that a trainee group be vertically structured, *i.e.* include different levels of management as in the work situation and that the training emphasises the development of the trainee's sensitivity to himself, to others and to the ways in which people react. They regard the functions of the trainer as creating situations conducive to learning by developing interpersonal skills in the group members. Tannenbaum, Weschler and Massarik (1961) have supported the use of the 'T' group strategy for training executives.

Planty (1952) has described a training programme which includes fourteen aspects. It is also felt that the combination of many techniques leads to better training results than following a single technique only.

1. Review of economic conditions,
2. Multiple management,
3. Role playing,
4. Case studies,
5. Specialised conference,
6. Harvard advanced management course,
7. Wharton school of finance,
8. Reading,
9. Conference leadership,
10. Public speaking,
11. In-plant conference,
12. Psychiatric group study,
13. Out of plant conference, and
14. Short courses, Seminars, school and college programmes.

Van Ark describes the General Foods Corporation progranmme including job rotation, understanding outside courses, internal informal training individual counselling and staff meeting participation.

According to Worthy (1953) the following four points would be conducive to a successful development programme.

1. System and organisation.
2. Measurements focussed on the man and on performance.
3. Programme being based on the principle of morality and fair deal.
4. Wholehearted understanding and support of the top management.

In cooperation with the National Industrial Conference Board, Habbe (1950) conducted a study on nine companies offering training progranmmes for executive development. He summarised the following twenty techniques found in use.

Almost always used

1. Merit or performance reviews.
2. Visits to other companies.
3. Attendance of technical meetings and management conferences.
4. Distribution of reading lists and management bulletins.
5. Group meetings.

Often used

6. Job rotation.
7. Advanced management courses at Harvard and elsewhere.
8. Consultants.
9. Committee assignments.
10. Executive inventions.
11. Job descriptions.

Sometimes used

12. Special trainee positions.
13. Multiple management plans.
14. Management cabinets.
15. Under study or assistant to positions.
16. Community leadership.
17. Health and fitness programmes.
18. Individual counselling.
19. Assignment to training or scales department.
20. Sponsor plan.

Situational Testing

This is a new method of selecting potential supervisors by presenting a problem situation in fornt of the executive, which he is likely to face in future. In the situational testing the reaction of the trainee is observed on the spot. It also studies how he handles the workers who obstruct them, how he reacts to frustration and whether he is able to get the job done. All this is observed bit by bit and recorded.

Inbasket Training

It is a modification of the situational testing technique. It has particularly proved useful in management training programmes. It also shown some advantages as a selection device.

Krishna (1974) conducted a study on democratic participation in decision-making by employees in an American Corporation.

He found that the majority of executives believed in traditional managerial prerogatives and did not favour allowing employees direct input to the decision-making process.

It is viewed by some eminent researchers working in the area of executive training that attitudes do change over the training period, but the question remains as to what happens when the executive goes back to his job. In this connection, Fleishman (1950b) has remarked "It casts grave doubts as to whether any type of human relations training is really worth the time and effort put to it".

Later on, he conducted another study to examine what happens to the attitude and behaviour of a supervisor who has received human relations training and who is then thrust back to his original work environment.

The findings of the study are as follows :

1. The effect of training may or may not result in a clear initial change of altitude or behaviour.
2. Even if training does have an effect it may be only temporary.
3. The behaviour of a supervisor seems to be primarily related to the behaviour of his own immediate supervisor. If his supervisor is, considerate he will also be considerate.

Blum and Naylor (1968) state, " Leadership training cannot be considered in isolation from the social environment in which the foreman in foreman as a result of this training may be difficult if the work situation remains constant. In other words, certain aspect of the foreman's environment may have to be effective in modifying his behaviour".

According to Blum and Naylor a perfect executive would be a person who has no work to do himself because his subordinates do it for him. He assigns the work and sees that it is done perfectly.

Do's and Don'ts to Improve Employee-employer Relationship

To sum up the discussion on employee-employer relationship, it can be reasonably opined that the following are some of the do's and don'ts which an employer should follow to improve the employee employer relationship.

Do's

1. Delegation of authority
2. Fair treatment to all
3. Availability to all employees
4. Discussoin of the employee problems
5. Recongnition of merit
6. Expressing appreciation in the public
7. Patience and understanding

Don'ts

A first line supervisor must avoid the following :

1. Dependence upon supervisor
2. Lack of technical knowledge
3. Interference with the work of the employees
4. Favouritism, partiality and discrimination
5. Expressing resentment and blame in the public

6. Pettiness and jealousy
7. Conflicting orders
8. Superfluous orders
9. Impulsiveness and sudden emotional outbursts.

INDIAN STUDIES ON LEADERSHIP TRAINING

In India, psychological work on leadership training has not been reported in large numbers, though currently many organisations have given special attention to leadership and executive training. Training facilities for both skilled and semiskilled operators as well as for supervisory personnel have been started in many industries. The problem of training has received special stimulus and enlightenment through the efforts of the National Productivity Council, various management institues and other management organisations set up in recent years.

Chowdhry and Trivedi (1958) report four cases of training in a textile mill in Ahmedabad. Daboo (1961) reports on evaluation of T.W.I. (Training within industry) programme in TISCO.

Currently, with the increased emphasis on leadership training in India, it is expected that more and more research work on leadership and executive training will be conducted.

EFFECTIVE PARTICIPATION OF WORKERS IN MANAGEMENT

A recent case study of eight leading public and private sector enterprises conducted by experts from Sri Ram Centre for Industrial Relations and Human Resources indicates that effective participation of workers in management considerably improves the achievement of targets. It also handles problems facing the management, improves efficiency and obviously level of production. The name of the study is "In search of Participation".

It was a multidisciplinary study conducted by a group experts from different disciplines like Psychology, Economics and Sociology which indicated that workers participation contributed significantly not only improving production but also in maintaining cordial relationship between the workers and management. It also increased mutual trust and satisfaction. These participations of the workers were mostly studied at departmental and shop level organisations. However, it is expected to be true for all types of works and all types of workers. It has been seen that when medium or lower level employees are allowed to take part in discussion regarding the issues and problems relating to the organization, they feel encouraged and most enthusiastic. They have a feeling that the management is considering them as a part and parcel of the organisation and taking their views. These boost the morale of the workers.

The above study named "In search of participation" emphasizes the role of top level management as a very vital determinant of success in any scheme encouraging employee's participation. Workers participation in the affairs of management of the organisation or industry should be a continuance process. Regularly and frequently there should be meetings and conferences consisting of small groups or one section, where the employees should be allowed to share about different problems and solution relating to the organization where they work. The management must believe from the heart of their heart about the fovourable effect of worker participation. Not only participation is essential but also whenever some acceptable and good suggestions are in the offing, the management should also implement them. It is seen in some cases management allows the employees to participate just for the sake of participation (a kind of eye wash), and so throw the suggestions to the cold storage without implementing them. This is not fair and definitely not in the interest of the management. Once or a couple of times if the employees come to know about this tactis of the management they loose confidence in them, become suspicious and start revolting first silently and then of course openly in various outbursts.

The participative forums must be institutionalized by the management. The above study was funded by the Fried rich Ebert Foundation. The companies selected for study did not give total decision making powers to the participatory group or authorities.

Findings of the above study indicate that the participation in order to succeed for a long term basis should coordinate and integrate it with all other programmes and policies of the company. This requires for an overall organizational climate helpful to the working of a participative system. It was observed that it was only possible in the departmental level and the shop floor level in which the representatives of the workers were involved in the participation and decision making process.

This study also highlighted the importance of involvement of trade unions in the participation process. Now a days every industry or organisation has a trade union or sub trade union attached to the central trade union of a distinct for a particular organization. These trade unions as it is seen are very very powerful today and if they or their representatives are not involved in the decision making process they create all sorts of problems and complicate the whole situation for the management. They even do not allow any body to work. So instead of sidelining the unions, the management must take themselves in to confidence and seek their suggestions and cooperation for the successful implementation of the participative system. In this connection one should not forget the problems that Nano car project faced in West Bengal and Tata and Posco authorities faced in Orissa. The problem went to such an extent that Nano car project was shifted from West Bengal or Gujarat. Secondly both direct and indirect participation and formal and informal participation are necessary for successful decision making as they are mutually exclusive. This has been proved by various other investigations conducted in companies where participation has succeeded. They have utilized both direct and indirect as well as formal and informal participation of their employees in the management system. There must be a similarity in the goal of the management and the employees though the means or practices used to achieve the good may be different. On the bases of several observations and findings in the area various managements have realized that many employees have tremendous useful ideas in their minds which can be best utilized through their participation in decision making. Provision of material benefits to the employees including ensuring their prestige, dignity and ego identity in the work place is essential for a successful employee participation in the decision making process.

In certain companies managements are found to share informations about the company even in day to day matters. Manufacturing managers as the head of the plants who undertake periodical presentation in the nature of intimate talks have obtained excellent support from the employees in solving the various problems of the organization.

This study further indicates that direct participation is desirable and can be introduced through quality circles and the suggestion box schemes, where suggestions are called for to put in the box. However, indirect participation with the representatives of the workers or their unions is equally effective. Formal and informal participatory forms like direct and indirect participation are not mutually exclusive. Now a days various banks in India are requesting the customers to participated in discussions relating to the bank's activities, and also ask for suggestions for improvement in customer's service.

In organisations where participation has been successful, both these forums have been introduced and practiced. Particularly in shop floor and welfare related issues workers and union representatives prossess a much greater knowledge as this study shows. In view of this, several managements implement their decision regarding shop floors to be influenced and benefitted by participatory meetings.

Worker's participation should however be implemented in a healthy and unbiased manner. They should not only be healthy, they should also appear to be healthy. Unless workers and trade unions see a fairness and biasless management practices, they will not get themselves involved. They most have to develop a faith in the system. The attitude should always be welfare of the employees or welfare friendly along with the welfare of the management also, so that the aim of the participation forum can be achieved by both the sides.

All these findings and observations go to show that worker participation in the decision making process is essential and hence those who have not introduced the system should introduce it. There should be a democratic trend than an autocratic one in worker participation system. Instead of imposing everything on the middle level and lower level employees, the management and authorities at the higher level should also develop the attitude to involve them in the decision making process through various processes, one of which is participation process.

SEXUAL HARASSMENT OF EMPLOYEES

With globally changed attitude towards women going to work outside, reservation for women in different jobs, and increasing eligibility of women for various professional, technical, civil and IT jobs, more and more women are joining full time jobs in various industries and organisations through out the world. But discrimination in work for women has been a big problem. One of the major issues that working women are now facing in various organizations is the rise in the incident of eve teasing and sexual harassment which is most serious of all the problems of working women. Through the problem of sexual harassment is an old issue, its effects can be new. Women today are highly educated, well qualified, perform brilliantly, have an ego identity, confidence and in many cases perform more efficiently than their male counterparts. They are more aware of their rights, duties and dignity. They refuse to accept any insult to their modesty and dignity.

Issues of sexual harassment of various women employees by their supervisors are serious and frequently reported in media and it is increasing day by day rapidly. So the human resource and welfare deptt. of every organisation big or small must make sure that policies that exist in this regard are very severe and stringent like in some western countries. That would send a message to every one in a serious way. Early finalization of case and exemplary punishment are the two most important steps to reduce sexual harassment of women. Moreover, women students should also be made aware of these rising incidents so that they can be cautious. Such issues are not easy to report and a sexual harassment suit can also affect the reputation of the organization. Long years of good reputation earned through tremendous efforts and professional service can be lost in minutes due to such accusations from women employees. Thus it is obvious that sexual harassment has very dangerous consequences on the organisation as well as on individual workers.

Situation under which sexual harassment can occur in the organisation are many. The sexual harasser can be a coworker, a boss, a client or any other employee. Sexual harassment may be of many types. It may be direct or indirect through a vulgar remark or comment passed, a vulgar letter written, or any kind of offensive behaviours. This may be done directly or by another person through the instigation of the male culprit.

Sexual harassment is not always done by the opposite sex or outsiders, it is also sometimes done by the employees or employers. Ragging very often found in colleges and High schools may also be applied to new comers in an organisation as a type of sexual harassment like (if it is serious in nature) nacked dancing and other perverted sexual behaviour where the modesty of the person is affected either by a person of the same sex or opposite sex. When things go out of hand or control ragging is also called sexual harassment.

The effects of sexual harassment also varies as it depends upon kind and degree of harassment experienced and the time period over which it has been experienced. It can be either annoyance, irritation or any severe type of repurcassion which may have drastic effect on their life. Due to sexual harassment amount and quality of work may deteriorate, the person may remain absent frequently to avoid the harassment or in worst case he or she may leave the job or take legal action by going to the police or court of law. In addition to these reactions, when the matter licks, humiliation, gossips and back biting may also follow. The victim inspite of her innocence can not stop foul mouths. Because of these reactions from people, the victim gets unwanted experiences and negative feelings. If it continues regularly for a period of time, the victim may be in depression or may break-down which may have very bad effect on the course of her life. She may leave the job, sit and brood at home or at best go to a psychiatrist for counselling. In worst cases, she may commit suicide.

Action taken by the organisations

In view of these negative effects of sexual harassment on the organisation its employees, the victim and the society at large, many organizations today have started recognising it and taking serious view on the issue.

Consequently, they have started taking precautions. Though human nature cannot be fully predicted as it may be situational, but precautions are to be taken. An environment should be created which is not too casual and not condusive to sexual harassment. A little bit of discipline like proper dress code, using minimum make up, avoidance of too much of informal relationships and personal talks may prevent these unwanted incidents. It is a fact that a lot of sexual harassment occur on the spur of the moment. So enough percautions should be taken. Since prevention is better than cure women should not wear alluring semi nacked dresses where half of their body or portions of private parts are seen. They should use simple dignified dress and simple make up while coming to the work place.

There should also be strict rules for offensive behaviour like suspension, termination, wage or salary cut, suspension of monthly salary, warning, censure or entry into their ACR (Annual character record). They may even be asked to go on compulsory leaves depending upon the degree of their illegal act. Precautions and preventions are to be taken to over come these problems. Most important prevention is passing the right message to all who are involved. Besides, when employees join an industry or organisation their biodata and previous records should be carefully checked and they should be informed about the company's view on sexual harassments. Characterless persons, persons without integrity and morality should not be allowed to join. It possible the previous employer or employers of the candidate should be consulted to know his or her past records. It must be enquired if the person is single or married or a divorcee. So all personality factors and past-occurances are to be properly checked before giving green signal to a person.

Men and women employees should be instructed (particularly women employees) to follow a dress code which is very very important in preventing sexual harassment. A man or woman may have the right or independence to dress up according to his or her choice, but that should not go against one's culture, tradition and ethics. The dress and make up must be simple and dignified. In my view women as far as practicable should not be appointed as private secretary, personal Assistant or confidential Assistants etc. to the various male heads or who have the provision of a P.A. as quite a number of sexual harassments are done at this level, because of the nature of work. In Indian organization as far as practicable women should not be given night shift or late night duties as in nights there is enough scope for such harassment. Strict laws should also be framed and exemplary punishments should be enforced to prevent sexual harassment.

QUESTIONS

1. Give a brief outline about the importance of suitable employee-employer relationship in industry.
2. What is the need for better understanding between the employees and the employers ? In thas context describe the importance of attitude in influencing the employee-employer relationship.
3. How can better understanding and good relationship between the employees and the employers be established ? Support your answer with experimental findings.
4. Describe the adverse effects of strikes, lockouts and union movements opon production. What setps can you take as an industrial psychologists for reducing strikes, lockouts and union movements and promote better understanding among the employees and employers ?
5. Describe the qualities of a successful supervisor.
6. Critically examine the various techniques used to train leaders and supervisors in industry.
7. Critically examine the need of effective participation of workers in management.
8. Describe about sexual harassment of employees and how to prevent it.

REFERENCES

Ansari, M.A., Baumgartel, H. and Sullivan, S. The Personal Orientation Organisational Climate fit and Managerial Success, *Human Relations*, Vol. 35, No. 12, 1982.

Ansari, M.A. and Rub, M. Executive Success as a Function of Leadership Style Oranisgational Climate Fit, *Managerial Psychology*, Vol. 3, No. 1, 1982.

Blum, M.L. and Naylor, J.C. *Industrial Psychology: Its Theoretical and Social Foundations*, Harper and Row, 1968.

Bradford, L.P. and Lippitt, R. Role Playing in Supervisor Training Personnel, 22, 1946, pp. 358-369.

Chottopadhaya, G.P. Motivation and Leadership Styles, *Indian Enterprises Management Psychology*, Vol. 4, Nos. 1 & 2, 1983.

Clark, Alfred W. and Mccabe, Sue. Leadership beliefs of Australian managers, *Jn. of Applied Psychology*, 54, 1970.

England, George W. and Lee, Raymond. The relationship between managerial success in the United States, Japan, India and Australia, *Jn. of Applied Psychol.*, Vol. 59, 1975, pp. 411-419.

Ganguli, H.C. *Structure and Process of Organisations*, Bombay, Asia Publishing House, 1964.

Gilmer, B., Von Haller, *Industrial and Organisational Psychology*, McGraw-Hill-Koga Kusha Ltd., 1971.

Ghosh, P.K. and Manerikar, V.V. In search of personality Characters of Indian managers. *Indian Jn. of Applied Psychology*, Vol. II (1), 1974, pp. 1-6.

Gray, J.S. *Psychology in Industry*. McGraw-Hill Book Company Inc., New York, Toronto, London.

Kapoor, A., Ansari, M.A. and Shukla, R. Upward influence tactics as a function of locus of control and organizational context, *Psychological Studies*, Vol. 31, No. 2, 1986.

Katz, N. Maccoby and Morse, N.C. *Productivity, Supervision and Morale in Office Situation.* Survey Research Centre, Institute of Social Research, Univ. of Michigan, 1950.

Kakar, S. Authority patterns and subordinate behaviour in Indian Organisations, in K. Chowdhury and S. Kakar (ed.), *Understanding Organisational Behaviour*, New Delhi, Tata McGraw-Hill, 1971.

Kipnis, David and Cosentio, Joseph. Leadership Powers in Industry, *Jn. of Applied Psychology*. 53 (6), 1969, pp. 460-466.

Kretch, D. and Crutchfield, R.S. *Theory and Problems of Social Psychology*. Tata McGraw-Hill Publication Company Limited, 1948.

Krishna, Rama. Democratic participation in decision-making by employees, American Corporation, *Academy of Management Journal.* Vol. 17, (2), 1974 pp. 339-347.

Maier, N.R.F., Solemn, A.R. and Maier, A.A. *Supervisor and Executive Developments—A Manual of Role Playing*. New York, 1970.

Marrow, A.J., Frech, J.R.P. and Maier, N.R.F. Changing stero-types in industry, *J. Soc. issues*. 1945.

McNair, M.P. *The Case Method of the Harvard School of Business,* New York, McGraw-Hill, 1954.

Meade, R.D. An Experimental study of leadership in India, *Jn. of Psychology*, 72, 1967.

Mohanty, G.B. *Employee-Employer Relationship*. U.G.C. Guest lecture Series, 1978.

Mohanty (2009). A comparison of democratic and autheritarian leadership in domestic and instruction workers (unpub.)

Negandhi, R. and Prasad, B.S. *Comparative Management,* New York, Appleton Century Crofts, 1971.

Tiffin, J. and McCormic, E.J. *Industrial Psychology*. 5th ed., Prentice-Hill of India Private Limited, 1971.

14

Attitude

NEED AND IMPORTANCE OF STUDYING ATTITUDE IN INDUSTRY

Taylor, the efficiency engineer of the nineteenth century could not tolerate the idea of human labour being wasted. He held that large wastage of human efforts are less visible, less tangible and only vaguely appreciated. But Taylor perhaps forgot to note that behind the large wastage of human efforts and power, to a great extent, lies the attitude of the workers towards the management. It was the findings of the Hawthorne experiments which brought into focus the importance of attitude and morale in industry. Nobody can also deny the fact that to a large extent interpersonal relations are determined by the attitudes people hold. Favourable attitude tends to produce more co-operation and dissimilar attitudes produce more friction among individuals. Hence there is an urgent necessity to study the attitude of the employees and the employers to get a complete and accurate picture of the employee-employers relationship.

By attitude is generally meant the beliefs, actions, tendencies, and the positive or the negative feeling of the individual towards objects, ideas and people. Attitudes are reflected by the opinions and views that one holds.

Looking back to the Hawthorne studies (1927) it is in the bank wiring observation room experiment that the workers complained about wages, supervisors, hours of work, the physical environment; dust and coal etc. So a general dissatisfaction was found among the workers, along with real and imagined grievances. Though they were complaining about the manifest content of the problem. the significant aspect of it was the latent content, which in turn referred to the attitude of the workers towards the management. Many of the reasons for these unfavourable attitudes are unconscious.

Good attitude towards the supervisor in the relay assembly test room increased the rate of production. It was further found that many of these attitudes had no real basis. They were learned predispositions having a strong irrational component based on emotion and not on reasons. Various defence mechanisms, especially rationalisation were applied to support their attitudes.

If the attitude of the workers towards the management is unfavourable, various welfare measures undertaken by the management are not warmly welcomed. There is voluntary restriction of output due to such unfavourable attitude. They feel that the management is unnecessarily playing tricks with them. This is an imagined grievance due to prejudice and an unfavourable attitude towards the management. Most of these attitudes are coloured with emotion and are not the result of intelligent comprehension. They are more egoistic and emotional in character.

CONSEQUENCES OF UNFAVOURABLE ATTITUDE

The consequences of unfavourable attitude towards the management may be diverse :

1. Direct and indirect grievances and strikes.
2. Rate of sickness and absenteeism increases.
3. High labour turnover.
4. Rate of accident increases.
5. Rate of production decreases.

It is therefore necessary to study the determinants of the attitudes of the employees and the employers. Not only should the attitude of the employees towards the employers be favourable, but the employer should also have sound and positive attitudes towards the employee. The employer may, on the one hand, believe that his employees are interested only in salary and are not concerned with his (employer's) problems. An employee, on the other hand, may believe that his employer is only interested in profits and that he treats him with less consideration and care, than he does his machine. As Blunt and Naylor (1968) comment :

"An employer with an unfavourable attitude towards his employee, is no more likely to understand his employees than an employee with an unfavourable attitude towards his employer is likely to understand his own employer." Thus gap in communication leads to such misunderstanding. Under such circumstances better mutual understanding of attitudes and congenial interpersonal relationship will enable one to predict behaviour with more accuracy. It may also avoid conflict by bringing about changes in attitudes in a favourable direction.

ATTITUDE STUDIES

A number of field and laboratory studies have been conducted to find out the relationship between employee's attitude and the level of production. As already pointed out, the importance of attitude came into light as a natural consequence of the Hawthorne studies.

The Hawthorne studies clearly indicated that because of the friendly behaviour and the employee-centred attitude of the supervisor, the attitude of the workers changed in the positive direction. The rate of absenteeism decreased and eventually production improved. The findings of this study stimulated Mathewson (1931) to investigate, why, in spite of high wages, employees did not reach the expected level of production. Mathewson noted with great interest, that due to unfavourable attitude, dislike, suspicion and grievances towards the supervisor and the management at large, there was intentional and voluntary restriction of output otherwise known as 'rate cutting'.

As pointed out by Gilmer (1971), in the review of 26 studies, it was noted that in 14 of these studies workers with positive job attitudes showed higher productivity than those with negative job attitudes. In three studies, workers with a positive attitude had less production records. In nine studies no relationship was found. Such conflicting findings may be due to the nature of the job, method of research and the environment of the worker.

Heizberg and his associates (1951) found, that in 21 out of 24 studies, the workers with positive job attitudes had less turnover and absenteeism than those with negative job attitudes. Two studies did not show any effect and one study showed that workers with favourable attitude had more turnover.

Conducting an investigation on a telephone company employees, Wickert (1951) observed that those who were less involved with their jobs and had no chance to make decisions, left the job.

The present author conducted an investigation (1980) to examine the relationship between the employees' attitude and productivity. The results indicated a low positive but insignificant relationship between the overall attitude of the workers towards work, supervisor, management and their production. In an observation made for three years between 2006-2009, the present author further tried to study the relationship between leadership type, and attitude and productivity." The observation was made on zero skilled semi-skilled and unskilled construction workers spreedly for a period of 3 years. The author was the immediate supervisor of the construction work of work residential building and a nurshing home. Finalings of the observation indicated that good attitude and behaviour of th. immediate supervisor immediate payment of dues of the workers and honesty did to highly improve production level.

The difference in the results of the Hawthorne studies, Mathewson and the present author may be due do several uncontrolled variables. Besides, attitude may be one of the factors of increased output, but it is not necessarily the only factor. Besides, the subjects of the author's investigation might not have expressed their real attitude out of fear.

However, in spite of such conflicting findings, it is justifiable to hold that the findings of Roethlisberger and Dickson (1939) brought into recognition the importance of attitude in the work situation. It may not always influence production, but it definitely influences the morale and job satisfaction of the employees, A favourable attitude reduces tension and conflict in the work situation. The Hawthorne studies also clearly indicated that the attitudes of the employees are important determinants of industrial relations which not only influence the performance of the individual alone, but also of the group.

The importance of attitude has stimulated various organisations to develop training programnes for the supervisors. Supervisors are trained to be more tolerant, understanding and considerate. They are expected to give counselling to needy workers and to expand the medical department to give psychiatric help to the employees whenever the occasion arises.

Since attitudes lie at the root of all industrial and organisational problems, steps should be taken to improve the attitude of employees towards the employers and *vice versa*.

For the improvement of attitude, measurement of attitude in industry is essential. If the attitude of the workers can be known before hand, strikes and various other similar reactions of the workers can be controlled, Secondly, by knowing their attitude various welfare measure and policies can be introduced. Even the cause of general dissatisfaction can be known by attitude measurement. When one party is not aware of the attitude of other, misunderstanding is rooted and gap in communication is observed. Hence, to bridge the gap between the workers and the management, assessment of the workers attitude is important.

MEASUREMENT

For the measurement of attitude in industry several methods are used. Blum and Naylor (1968) have described the following six methods of attitude measurement.

1. Impressionistic Method

It is one of the common and widely used methods to measure attitude in industry. It is entirely qualitative, nonstatistical and based upon observation of behaviour and attitudes. Experts visit a factory for a few days and for a few hours each day. They also ask questions from the workers and then give a report to the management regarding the attitude of the workers. In this method there is no personal interview and the experts have no idea about the previous attitude of the workers. Therefore, it is not accurate and cannot be relied upon. Thus is so especially when the management wants to change the policy of the company on the basis of the results obtained by this method.

This is a method whereby attitude measures attitude. As the very source of data is highly subjective, since it does not have any scientific basis, it is the least desirable of all the six methods. Of course, this method can be used as a preliminary to other methods or when a very rapid spot survey is to be made.

By the impressionistic method, industrial towns, factory sites, work conditions and employee morale are often measured. But there is some sort of distortion and over generalisation in this method. Blum and Naylor (1968) hold the view that rigid and exacting techniques for measuring attitudes are therefore necessary. These deficiencies have been supplied by the other five techniques.

2. Closed or Guided Interview

In this technique, the investigator has got a number of questions relating to various aspects of the worker's life with reference to the company. Each question is to be answered in one or two words. Therefore, it is called closed end or structured. The answer is limited. There is no ambiguity in the answers. Sometimes the attitude of the sample group is studied. The group acts as a representative of all the workers of the factory.

The samples should, therefore, be properly chosen to avoid errors and bias. The interviewer must not give the personal views of his life. He should encourage the workers, be sympathetic, but should not suggest anything. All the subjects must be asked the same standard questions and then a complete report of all the answers should be compiled. But this method is expensive and time consuming. Further, in India, this method may not be fruitful.

Stagner, Rich, Britten and others (1941) listed 34 questions which were of the type to be answered by a 'yes' or a 'no'. This was a closed type of interview where the attitude of a group of machine tool workers was studied by interviewing them at their house.

Kornhauser (1952) and Heron (1954) also conducted attitude measurement studies using the guided interview technique.

3. Unguided Interview

Otherwise known as the nondirective interview this method was first promoted by Karl Roger (1942) as a form of psychotherapy. Prior to Roger, of course, the Hawthorne experiments highlighted many aspects of this technique by using them in their studies and thus made it prominent. But Roger for the first time gave it a separate status.

Certain rules and specifications are observed in the unguided interview. It is characterised by the free nature of the discussions and by the fact that it is the person interviewed who really defines its limits.

In this technique informal conversation goes on between the workers and the interviewer. The aim of the interviewer is to make the workers talk in a particular area. By giving a push or stimulus to the workers, the conversation is carried on. The nature of the interview is totally free and no specific question is asked to the workers. In this technique the interviewer is more interested in the emotional expression of the interviewees. Therefore, importance is not given to the manifest content, but to the latent content. The Personal Counselling Programme of the Hawthorne experiments refers to this method.

For the success of this method a trained interviewer is necessary. This is also costly and time consuming. It is also sometimes difficult to analyse the contents of the unguided interview as the type of data collected by this method is on several occasions outside the scope of industrial psychology.

Taking into account these difficulties most industries take the help of questionnaires and scales to measure attitude in industries and organisations. However, even after collecting the data by the questionnaire method, interviews can be conducted on the sample to verify the data obtained and also to gather extra information about their attitude.

In spite of the limitations of this technique if properly used and rightly interpreted, it gets at the right attitude of the workers. Rallis is of opinion that this method can work more successfully because it helps in getting over the initial suspicion of the worker thus creating a rapport between the counseller and the client.

4. Questionnaire Technique

It has a lot of similarity with the guided interview technique, The study of Stagner, Rich and Britten (1941) was of this type. The interviewer distributes the questionnaire by hand or through post and obtains the result. Here there is no direct contact between the interviewer and the workers. In an interview, there is scope to observe the feelings of the interviewee and the manner of his answering the questions which the questionnaire technique lacks. On the contrary, the questionnaire technique is less costly, less time consuming and without much difficulty enough data can be collected in a short duration. Therefore, the questionnaire technique has been used as a mass production technique, both in social and industrial psychology. The bias of the interviewer is an important disadvantage in the interviewing technique. But the personal factor of bias in data collection is eliminated by the questionnaire technique. This method also does not require much experience on the part of the person to collect data. However, it lacks the spontancity and naturalness of a well conducted interview. In the questionnaire technique the 's' cannot be forced to give all the replies as can be done in the case of interviews.

The percentage of questionnaires returned after being filled up is generally 25 per cent to 30 per cent. This happens especially in India because of the questionnaire sophistication. A level of psychological set-up or training is required to fill up the questionnaire. Questionnaires also lack reliability and validity. The sample obtained may be psychologically different from the population.

The form of the questionnaire is very important. Item analysis is required to frame the questionnaires. Questionnaires should be understood properly because they are mailed. A pilot study is essentially important before making the questionnaire ready for a final study.

Kolstad's (1938) study, designed to measure the attitude of the workers by questionnaire techniques can serve as a fine example to demonstrate how questionnaires are applied in industry. In this questionnaire centred around certain specific factors in the job and morale, ten questions were used to cover the various aspects of the morale of the workers.

1. Promotion policy of the company and attitude towards it.
2. Help available from the factory manager.
3. Whether workers are encouraged to give new ideas and thoughts. This was found to be associated very closely with morale.
4. Whether the grievances of the workers arc attended to or not.
5. Increase in pay when deserved.
6. Invitation to offer suggestions when plans are being made.
7. Freedom to seek advice when there is a problem in the factory.
8. Whether the workers are satisfied or not when any change in the method of work or machinery is made.
9. Information concerning plans and results.
10. The future plan and policy of the factory also influences the attitude and morale of the workers.

On the basis of data obtained, Kolstad found out morale score for the group. A new type of questionnaire technique has been found out by Kerr (1948). Appropriate questions are asked. Each question has five answers and the worker has to tear the appropriate arrow-head at the end of the answer.

5. Attitude Scales

Thrustone, Likert, Doob, Cantril, Blank, Day and Guttman, etc. have had a lot to say on the subject of scales of attitude measurement.

There are thousands of scales for attitude measurement. The construction of attitude scales in industry actually refers to the construction of Thurstone or Likert scales to measure the various aspects of the environment.

In an attitude scale, a series of statements are made. The employee checks one of the statements and thus the attitude of the workers is found out quantitatively. In the case of the questionnaire, questions are used rather than statements and numerical weights are not given here. In the case of a scale for each reply, a scale value is worked out previously. In the case of the Likert scale, the scale ranges from most to least and in the Thurstone scale the answers are of the 'yes', 'no' and 'don't know' type. Here the purpose of the survey must be explained to the workers and they should be assured that neither of their views will be exposed to the management nor would it affect their service.

The advantage of the scale method is that it can be easily quantified and numerical value be attached to it.

Uhrbrock (1934) constructed an attitude scale and applied it to 4430 employees working in industry, to measure their attitude towards their company. As reported by Blum and Naylor (1968) in this study of Uhrbrock statements expressing a favourable attitude towards the company were checked by more than twice as many workers as checked the unfavourable statements. It was noted from the findings that foreman had more favourable attitudes than factory workers, and this was true more of women than of men. To add to this the employees who had worked in the company for more than six years were slightly more favourably inclined than those with a shorter period of service.

Thus, Uhrbrock finds a difference in attitude between males and females, whereas Kolstad does not find the same. This may probably be due to different samples, different levels of employment and other similar uncontrolled variables.

6. Indirect Method

Weschler and Bernberg (1950) describe it as the indirect method. It is a kind of projective approach to attitude measurement.

This method is intended to provide more free rein of expression. As held by Blum and Naylor the objective is to explore the deeper levels rather than to deal only with the manifest verbal content. Many techniques like word association, sentence completion or picture and story theme completion etc. are used in this method.

The indirect method of measuring attitude is the newest development. It is used when the subject is not able to express his views accurately or when he hesitates to express himself. This technique gives a scope for freedom of expression and spontaneous flow of feelings. But precautions in the use of the data and refinement in the technique is necessary to make it a successful method of attitude measurement. Analysis of the data by untrained hands has dangerous implications.

Fresen (1949) has developed an incomplete sentence blank which is an attempt to standardise the indirect technique of measuring the attitude of the employees. The Evans and Laseau (1950) research known as "My Job Contest" is an illustration of research using the indirect method of attitude measurement.

Gilmer (1971) has mentioned several methods of getting information about employer attitudes. Among these methods, some have been discussed in detail earlier.

1. Formal Communication Channels. In this method the foremen and supervisors evaluate the feelings and views of the workers and finally report it to the executives and other superior officers. But in many instances the information proves to be unreliable and biased and sometimes false ideas are added. Bellows (1963) reports that many foremen do not even know how to deal with their men. So it is just not possible for them to effectively analyse and interpret the feelings of the workers. Besides, most of the workers do not have direct contact with the management. The management has, therefore, to depend on the foremen and supervisors for information regarding employees' attitude. Since the interpretations are sometimes biased and inaccurate, in such situations objective analysis and accurate measurement of the workers' feelings becomes impossible.

2. Grapevine channels. The information regarding the attitude of employees is changed in the process while being carried to the management. This is equivalent to how rumours spread in which process the original incident becomes extremely distorted with the help of several additions and subtractions. Thus, Gilmer (1971) comments 'More dangerous still are the attitudes communicated by the grapevine for they reflect only the extremes. With this structure the attitudes of the majority of the workers never get impartially expressed.

3. Behaviour Manifestations. By this method the attitude of the workers is assessed from their behaviour and reactions. Restriction of output, slow down, excessive absenteeism and turnover, leaving the job early and lack of interest in work indicate the real attitude of an employee. Here attitude is manifested in the behaviour of the employee.

4. Interviewing Techniques. It is a traditional method of attitude measurement. Besides open end and closed end interviews here are also counselling interviews and exit interviews to reveal the attitude of the employees.

5. Questionnaire Techniques. Under the questionnaire technique various types of attitude scales have been prepared to know the attitude of the workers. (Refer to questionnaire technique discussed earlier.

INDUSTRIAL STUDIES ON ATTITUDE MEASUREMENT

Studies conducted on employer attitudes are very few. A report by Fosdick (1939) published in the 1939 *Personnel Journal* clearly showed that employees and employers have different attitudes on industrial morale. The results indicated that while credit for work done got the first ranking by the employees, it got the last but one ranking by the employers. Similarly, job security got the last ranking by the employees while it got second position by the employers. This finding indicates that there is gap in communication and misunderstanding between both the parties.

Cherington and Bergen (1941) conducted a stimulated research on the attitudes of 51 senior executives in a large company. As pointed out by Blum and Naylor (1968) the findings show that more than 50 per cent of the executives were not satisfied with their salary and more than two thirds expressed dissatisfaction over the promotion policy. Moreover, the executives under study expressed firmly the need for a clearcut organisational plan and for more effective coordination of the various executives. The respondents wanted more intensive executive training and information of the company's plans and programmes, business conditions and development of labour relations.

In this study the employees' and employers' attitude differed significantly in the ranking of 10 selected personnel practices which, like the previous study, indicated a room for misunderstanding.

TECHNIQUES USED TO IMPROVE ATTITUDE, IN INDUSTRY

Attitude surveys only treat the symptom and not the causes. In the words of Maier (1970) "Attitude surveys reveal only that something is wrong in the work place; they don't reveal what it is."

In addition to conducting the work on altitude measurement in industries and various organsational set-ups, the Survey Research Centre at the university of Michigan has attempted to improve attitudes.

The development of congenial relationship between the employees and the employers has been advised. Several studies particularly by Katz, Maccoby and Morse (1950) indicate the relationship between productivity and the attitude of the supervisor towards the workers rather than productivity and the attitude of the employees as earlier held. Of course a good attitude of the Supervisors will obviously influence the attitude of the employees towards the supervisor in the favourable direction and it would be justified to expect, normally, a positive relationship between the attitude of the employees towards the employers and *vice versa*.

Studies also indicated that employee-oriented supervisors get work done more quickly and easily than production-oriented supervisors. Therefore, care should be taken to improve the attitude of both the employees and the employers towards each other as well as towards the management.

Maier (1970) has suggested that : (*i*) by influencing the experience of the group membership that is, by making the employees feel that they are members of the group and belong to the group, (*ii*) by using the role playing technique (refer to Training of Supervisors), (*iii*), by the use of listening skill, that is, by being a patient and understanding listener of the complaints and grievances of the employees, by allowing him to express his feelings freely without any inhibition, and, (*iv*) by using discussion skills such as well-conducted group discussions attitude can be changed.

Well conducted discussions in group clarify many doubts, misunderstandings etc. The sense of belonging to a group and identification with the group also develops spontaneously in group discussions. Marrow's and French's study (1945) indicate how management personnel changed their hostile and unfavourable attitude towards older women employees after supervisors participated in a group discussion.

A study conducted by Levine and Butler (1961) also suggests that the discussion method is superior to the lecture method in significantly reducing biases.

Good Behaviour of Immediate Supervisor

The immediate or first line supervisor is usually responsible for the formulation of many attitudes of the subordinate employees, because emotional experiences, which are greatly responsible for the development of such attitude are gathered from their interaction with the immediate supervisor. The findings of the Hawthorne studies and several other investigations in the field of industrial psychology including the observations of Mohanty (2009) strongly support this view. Hence, if the immediate supervisor deals with the workers on humanitarian grounds the attitude of the employees will undoubtedly change from an unfavourable to a favourable direction.

Persuasion

Many use the persuasion method to change attitudes. They describe the points which they favour to the employees in such a way that their point of view appears to be more favourable than the others. They then try to make the employees accept the point which they favour. Suggestible employees are more easily persuaded by this method than those who are less suggestible.

Though persuasion should not be used as a technique as it puts pressure upon the employees, it is a fact that some attitude changes occur due to this method.

QUESTIONS

1. Examine the need and importance of studying attitude in industy. What are the consequences of unfavourable attitude towards the management ?
2. Discuss the various methods used for measuring attitude in industry.
3. What is understood by attitude scale ? Critically examine the advantages and disadvantages of various attitude scales.
4. Give some important industrial studies on attitude measurement.
5. Critically examine the techniques used to improve attitude in industry.

REFERENCES

ICSSR, New Delhi. *A Survey of Research in Psychology*, Popular Prakashan, Bombay, 1972.

Blum, M.L. and Naylor, J.C. *Industrial Psychology: Its Theoretical and Social Foundations*, Harper and Row, 1968.

Boaz, M.Z. Papers on Industrial Psychology, Harper and Row, 1968.

Cherington, P.T. and Bergen, H.B. What do bosses think ? Advanced Management, 1941, pp. 66-69.

Fosdick, S.J. Your employer wants you to know him, Personnel Journal, 1939, 17, 357.

Gilmer, B., von Haller. *Industrial and Organisational Psychology*, McGraw Hill, Koga Kusha Ltd., 1971.

Mohanty, G.B. *Relationship between Employees. Attitude and Productivity.* 1980.

Mohanty, G.B. *Relationship between leadership, type attitude and productivity unpublished (2009).*

Maier, N.R.F. *Psychology in Industry*, Oxford and IBH Publishing Co. Pvt. Ltd., New Delhi, 1970.

Roethlisberger, F.J. and Dickson, W.J. *Management of the Worker*, Cambridge, Mass, Harvard University Press, 1939.

Stagner, R.J. Rich and Britten, R.H. Job attitude-defence workers; *Personnel Journal*, 1941, 20, pp. 90-97.

Uhrbrock, R.S. Attitudes of 4430 employees, *Jn. of Social Psychology*, 1934-35, pp. 365-377.

15

Industrial Morale

INTRODUCTION

A human being is a member of a team. The factory is a world by itself and the workers lead a social life in the factory. Therfore, the worker rarely functions as an isolated individual and it is in fact impossible to deny the existence of the social structure in any company.

Blum (1956) says, "to do so is to refuse to face reality, men and women lead a social life in the job and they make friends and enemies, they exchange confidences, meet socially after working hours, talk together and so on. In short, consciously or unconsciously they form groups. These groups at last become the basic core of morale formation".

In the Hawthorne studies also, the existence and formation of social groups within the factory has been observed.

Thus, today the emphasis of industrial psychology has shifted from the studies of isolated individuals and physical environment to the studies of motivation and morale in group. The problem of morale has drawn the attention of many psychologists in industry today. The zeal, vigour and enthusiansm that is found in the work of a group is never found in a single-minded work, perhaps because of the absence of morale. Similarly the difference between the organisation or group that cooperates and unites and the one that does not is surely due to the difference in morale and cohesiveness.

A.L. Kress states, "When we talk about morale, we have these problems in peace time as in war time. We are dealing here the way they regard their jobs, their supervisor, the company; its working group and everything that goes to make the background of the individual's place in the organisational scheme."

To begin with, morale is a group phenomena, *i.e.* it functions at the level at which the group functions. Thus, when we speak of mar ale, we refer to the operation of the group. The way in which the group thinks feels, and acts. "The importance of morale is observed in a number of individuals doing something in a team. Blum holds the view that morale is a by-product of the group and is generated by the group.

Definition

Allport has defined national morale as an individual's attitude in a group endeavour. According to Maier (1970) this statement implies that both personal and social features are involved in the mental condition which recall morale. The importance of morale in team work, in community action, in group behaviour, in class in trade union, in management association, in military and army etc. is observed. In fact, most of the studies on morale come from the military and industry.

According to Blum and Naylor (1968) "Industrial morale may be defined as the possession of a feeling on the part of the employee of being accepted and blonging to a group of employees through adherence to common goals and confidence in the desirability of these goals." This comprehensive definition refers to what morale is as well as hints at the determinants of morale.

A detailed analysis of this definition indicates that it consists of three different aspects:

1. Feeling accepted by one's own group.
2. Showing common goals with the group in which one works.
3. Having confidence and faith in the desirability of these goals.

Thus, morale develops a 'we' feeling among the workers. It also develops a sense of belonging to the group.

CHARACTERISTIC

People become aware of morale when something goes wrong in industry. For no obvious reasons production goes down or workers complain too much and the attitude becomes unfavourable. Under all these circumstances, one usually remarks that the morale of the factory or the group is shattered.

According to Guin (1958) morale is defined as :

1. The absence of conflict.
2. It is a feeling of happieness.
3. It is a good personal adjustment.
4. It is ego involvement in one's job.
5. Morale is group cohesiveness.
6. Morale is a combination of job related attitudes.
7. Morale is defined as the individual's acceptance of the goals of the group.

Analysing the above characteristics of morale, Guien (1958) defines morale as "the extent to which an individual's needs are satisfied, and the extent to which the individual perceives that satisfaction as stemming from his total job situation." In this definition the group reaction aspect of morale is overlooked.

According to Guien, "High morale under this concept would be reflected by little aggressiveness or frustration-instigated conflict, by a reasonably euphoric work force, by fairly well adjust employees who can become quite ego involved in their work, by many favourable attitudes and by the cohesiveness which comes from finding personal need satisfaction within the group." Guien also gives five different attributes which he feels are essential for an adequate concept of morale.

1. It must recognise the dynamic complexity of morale.
2. It must treat morale as basically an attribute of the individual.
3. It most recognise that morale exists with reference to the job situation.
4. It must recognise the role of motivation to morale.
5. It must be applicable to employees at any job level.

According to Stagner (1958) morale must always be defined in terms of individual group relationships. The state of an individual's morale is gauged from the morale of his specific working group and company. High morale exists when the individual perceives himself as a member of the group and intentionally seeks to achieve the goals of the group because they are important to him.

Morale includes personal and social features as well, with the group goal as the cementing agency which keeps the morale of the group intact. In industrial situations, morale will be high if the common goal is realised through others' co-operation. It is thus important to find out what could be the goals in industry to serve as common goal. The goal must be specific, desirable and attainable. Every individual of the group must be aware of his contribution to the group endeavour. Maier (1970) states "Poor morale is generally and is more often than not characterised by an attitude of apathy and resignation. Either interest in the goal is absent or the obstacles between the individual and the goal are regarded as insurmountable". Thus, the attitude towards the employee forms one important aspect of Industrial morale.

MORALE AND JOB SATISFACTION

There is sometimes a confusion between morale and job satisfaction. Smith recently used the term 'job satisfaction for' morale. But according to Blum, although morale is related to job satisfaction, morale and job satisfaction are different and morale is not same as job satisfaction.

Blum and Naylor (1968) hold the view that there is no justification for using the two terms interchangeably. Job satisfaction is the result of various attitudes the individual holds towards his job, related factors and life in general. On the contrary, industrial morale is a composite expression of the attitudes of various individuals employed by a company. Secondly, morale is a group phenomenon while job satisfaction is an individual phenomenon. Industrial morale is never as average of the individual attitude. For example, a company's morale may be low even though many employees enjoy considerable job satisfaction Certain individuals who are dissatisfied with their job may lower the overall morale.

However, though no one can deny that job satisfaction is an essential determinant of high morale, it would be erroneous to consider the two as similar and identical.

DETERMINANTS

From the findings of several investigations in the field of industry and elsewhere, certain factors have emerged as being conducive to good morale. The more important of these are attitude, type of supervision, method of supervision, sacrifice, participation in group activity, tolerance and freedom within the group, confidence in leaders, etc.

Blum (1956) has mentioned the following four most important determinants of morale :

1. Feeling of solidarity, indentification and belonging.
2. Experience of progress towards the goal.
3. Need for a goal.
4. Tolerance and freedom.

By and large, the determinants of morale can be divided into two parts:

1. Situational determinants.
2. Determinants outside the work situation.

Attitude

As a natural consequence of the Hawthorne studies, the importance of attitude came to the limelight. A favourable attitude of the workers towards the management as in the case of the relay assembly test will never create conflict between the workers and the management. But if the attitude is unfavourable, a slight disturbance will create all sorts of complications, being an indicator of low morale. Allport has therefore emphasised the importance of attitude in morale.

Type of Supervisor, Foreman and Method of Supervision

It has been suggested that the supervisor can make or break morale. The supervisor is the first and the last link with whom the workers come in immediate contact and hence his behaviour and dealings determine the morale of the group. The supervisor is not only the centre of parental identification and a father substitute; he is also a good and sympathetic friend. This, it has been said "the make and break of morale, the type of contact, the direction of attitude and the amount of production depends upon the behaviour of the supervisor."

The fact that the level of morale differs greatly from one factory, company to another, indicates that employee morale is closely associated with the attitude of the first line supervisor towards its employees. This view has been supported by the findings of a survey based on interviews with employees in war plants.

Lewin (1942) conducted a classic experiment on children and found that autoratic and democratic leaders lead to different types of group formation.

Jenkins (1947) made a study using the method of group dynamics in two groups and found that the type of leadership determines the morale of the group. Further studies by Lewin, Lester, Coch and Bevlas support the view that the type of supervisor determines morale. It is, therefore, suggested that a worker-centred attitude is more conductive to good morale than a work-centred attitude.

Thus Maier (1970) concludes, "The supervisor is the pivot around 'I which many things revolve. The type of personal contact which he builds obviously makes or breaks morale.... The possibilities however of raising morale would appear unlimited if management and unions would see to it that those representing them in closest contact with the workers possessed real human understanding."

Maier further adds "When employees say their boss makes them feel cheap and treats them like children, they are describing a kind of personal treatment that injures their pride and self esteem."

Friendly Criticism and Correction

Criticism and blame pointed against the workers should have real justification. The suspicious supervisor who always finds faults with the workers and blames them lowers their morale.

Besides this, a suitable wage incentive system, sanitary facilities, lighting and ventilation, the experience of the worker with the management, whether he takes care of him or exploits him, the security and status of the worker determine morale inside the factory.

Feeling of Solidarity, Indentification and Belonging

When the members are united and indentify with the group it allows the individual to produce his best in attending the group objective. Maier and Wright have demonstrated that a couple of strong friends among children are less affected by a frustrating situation than the pair who are not friends. The workers hence should have a feeling that their efforts are not fruitless but indispensable.

Tolerance and Freedom

If each member of the group is allowed and encouraged to participate in achieving the common goal the worker feels that his efforts are important and significant in achieving the final goal. Hence he becomes cooperative.

Congeniality, group spirit and friendship within the department should be encouraged. Further more, any condition which lowers a man's dignity should be discouraged and free participation in group effort should be favoured.

Advancement and promotion, periodic praise, reward etc. are important stimulating factors in determining morale.

Feeling of Mutual Sacrifice

According to Maier (1970) "People will tolerate deprivation and hardship if all are subjected to the same conditions." When there is a sense of sharing the difficulties morale goes up. No question of privilege or favouritism should be there. When some are given special privileges others of the group are demoralised.

A number of studies at the time of the War showed that people can tolerate deprivation and hardship if it is felt that everybody is subjected to it. To quote an interesting case in a London slauthter house, six girls worked in a small room which was dimly lit, with cold floors covered with animals' intestines, water and blood. However, in these nasty surroundings the six girls worked happily and cheerfully because they believed that they were a happy working group, doing a skilled job under the control and care of a supervisor who praised them judiciously. In this department individuals had come and gone, but morale had never been other than good.

Workers in industry often feel that they are not fairly treated by the management and, of course, the frequency of this feeling varies from company to company and factory to factory. Maier holds the view that when the employer explains to the employees the necessity of taking certain actions, of adopting certain policies or of insisting on a high degree of accuracy, the number of such complaints decreases. The level of morale is upheld if the group really understands why certain things are done or why certain changes are made.

Therfore, it is generally conceded that sacrifice need not be a frustrating factor if deprivation is fairly and uniformly distributed.

Blum and Naylor (1968) have given four important determinants of morale :

1. Group cohesiveness or a feeling of togetherness.
2. Need for a goal.
3. Observable progress towards the goal.
4. Meaningful tasks necessary for the achievement of the goal.

Group Cohesiveness

In a normal work situation employees rarely work as totally isolated individuals. The workers always form a group or a number of sub-groups with or without the knowledge pf the management. The ideal situation for highest morale is to have a single group consisting of all the employees and the employer. It is very unfortunate that the importance of group formation is overlooked or neglected very often in industry and organisations. It is the reaction of the group to the change introduced by management which is most important for determining the level of morale. If the group accepts the steps taken by the management for improving morale it is alright, but if the group suspects the change it becomes dangerous for morale.

The feeling of togetherness or group co-operation is extremely important. The adoption of a democratic group structure by the management is also conducive to good morale. Elaborating this point, Blum and Naylor (1968) have opined "Men and women lead a social life in the job. They make. friends and enemies. They exchange confidences, meet socially after working hours, eat together and do favours for one another. In short, consiously or unconsciously they groups. These groups can be the basic core of morale formation, if the management will only recognise this and if it can tunnel this energy into the proper channels of cooperation."

Goals

It is viewed by dynamic psychologists that the group goal is the cemeting agency which keeps the group cohesive. Morale is high when the group goal is well defined, well understood, fully accepted and looked upon as attainable and desirable.

Maier adds that as far as possible there should not be an essential conflict regarding the final goal. A cricket team having high morale may differ as to how to play match, but would never differ in winning the match.

Thus, if the group has a goal to achieve, group cooperation is easily promoted. The advancement, security, increased earning and individual and group welfare can all be goals, provided management encourages them and the employee is convinced that they are real and attainable.

Sub-goals and near goals are important determinants of morale. Mace compared the state of learning when the goal is fixed and not fixed. Goals adjusted according to the skill of the worker and near goals have a better effect on morale.

Experience of Progress Towards the Goal

The progress towards the goal must be experienced and observed by the group. The group spirit remains at a high level if the group is conscious of the progress made towards the goal. Thus knowledge of result motivates the workers and determines the level of morale.

The following study by Marrow (1942) in his own plant supports the progress towards the goal as an important determinant of morale. One group of power machine operators was told the level of production which they would have to reach within 14 weeks. Another group was told the final goal, but was also given weekly goals. Findings indicated that the second group had better performance than the first group. Blum therefore holds that the goal keeps the work sustained.

Meaningful Tasks

The individuals in the group must have specific meaningful tasks to perform. Each individual worker must clearly understand his contribution to the attainment of the group goal. If the production is merely to the advantage of the employer and does not help the employee in any definite way the goal is likely to be regarded as the management's 'and not the workers'.

The worker should also be properly informed about the setting of a goal and should get proper share from the benefit only then can the goal be very strong.

STUDIES CONDUCTED ON ATTITUDE AND MORALE ON INDIAN INDUSTRIAL ORGANISATIONS

The industrial psychology division of the Labour Institute analysed the attitude and morale of three units of a large chemical process undertaking. Jones, Ganguli and Sequeria (1964) noted that the older unit was lower in the level of satisfaction with regard to factors of the work situation. Maule and Ganguly (1964) have studied the attitudes of officers towards changes in the management practices.

Ganguly (1958) tried to re-orient the attitude of 238 foundry workers through lectures and discussions and compared their post orientation attitudes towards the supervisor, the national government and the job with that prevailling before it. The training programme produced a significant improvement in the participants mental disposition and relationship with various personnel. No such improvement was noticed in the controlled group.

Sinha and Sarma (1973) found the length of union membership to be associated with a lower score on job satisfaction in the attitude scale. Such studies have pointed to the role of the union in creating hostile feelings of the workers towards the working condition and the management.

Mohanty's (2009) observation or a large number of skilled, semiskilled and un-skilled employees for 3 years found that when a group having good relationship with each other work together (good intrapersonal relationship and have a common group goal the quality and quantity of production is high.

MEASUREMENT

Morale can be measured by following the same method that measures the formation of groups and sub-groups. This technique is called the sociometry method devised by Moreno (1943).

Jenkins (1947) has modified Moreno's technique and has named it as the "nominating technique". He has used it most successfully in studying the morale in the navy.

In this technique, every member of the group is asked to name the person in the group whom he considers the best worker, or the best supervisor. Each individual is represented on a diagram by a circle; an arrow is drawn from it to the circle representing the person he names. The person who is selected by the largest number of people in the group is called the "leader". If this individuals is also the boss he is both the formal and the informer leader. But if the formal leader does not receive many 'votes', it is obvious that he is the leader for the sake of appearances, and that the informal leader is the real leader in the group. This person is known as the star.

In fact there may be more than one star in a group. Those persons who are never selected are called isolates and if such persons are dropped out of the group, the structure or morale of the group would not change.

According to Blum and Naylor (1968) a triangle occurs when X chooses Y, who in turn chooses Z. This is the beginning of a sub-group and may be enlarged into a clique.

Figures 15.1, 15.2 and 15.3 are simple sociograms that illustrate some of the various types of group structures.

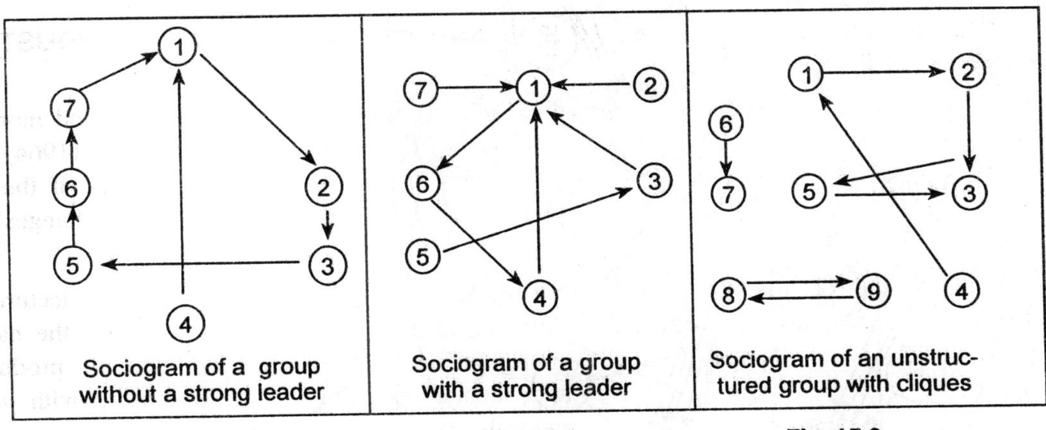

Sociogram of a group without a strong leader

Fig. 15.1

Sociogram of a group with a strong leader

Fig. 15.2

Sociogram of an unstructured group with cliques

Fig. 15.3

Actually sociograms may become very complicated. Figure 15.4 shows a complex sociogram made by Jenkins in his work with a Navy squadron.

In the opinion of Blum and Naylor (1968) "the study of sociograms is valuable. It can furnish leads as to clique formation and the extent to which they may act as disruptive influences in the organisation". Suspicious observations can be substantiated by this technique.

Work teams selected sociometrically can increase production. Blum and Naylor (1968) opine, "Thus principle of having workers assign themselves to pairs on work location rather than have management superimpose rigid rules is not idle folly. It is of the essence in building morale. More of it should be applied to industry, since workers often work in teams."

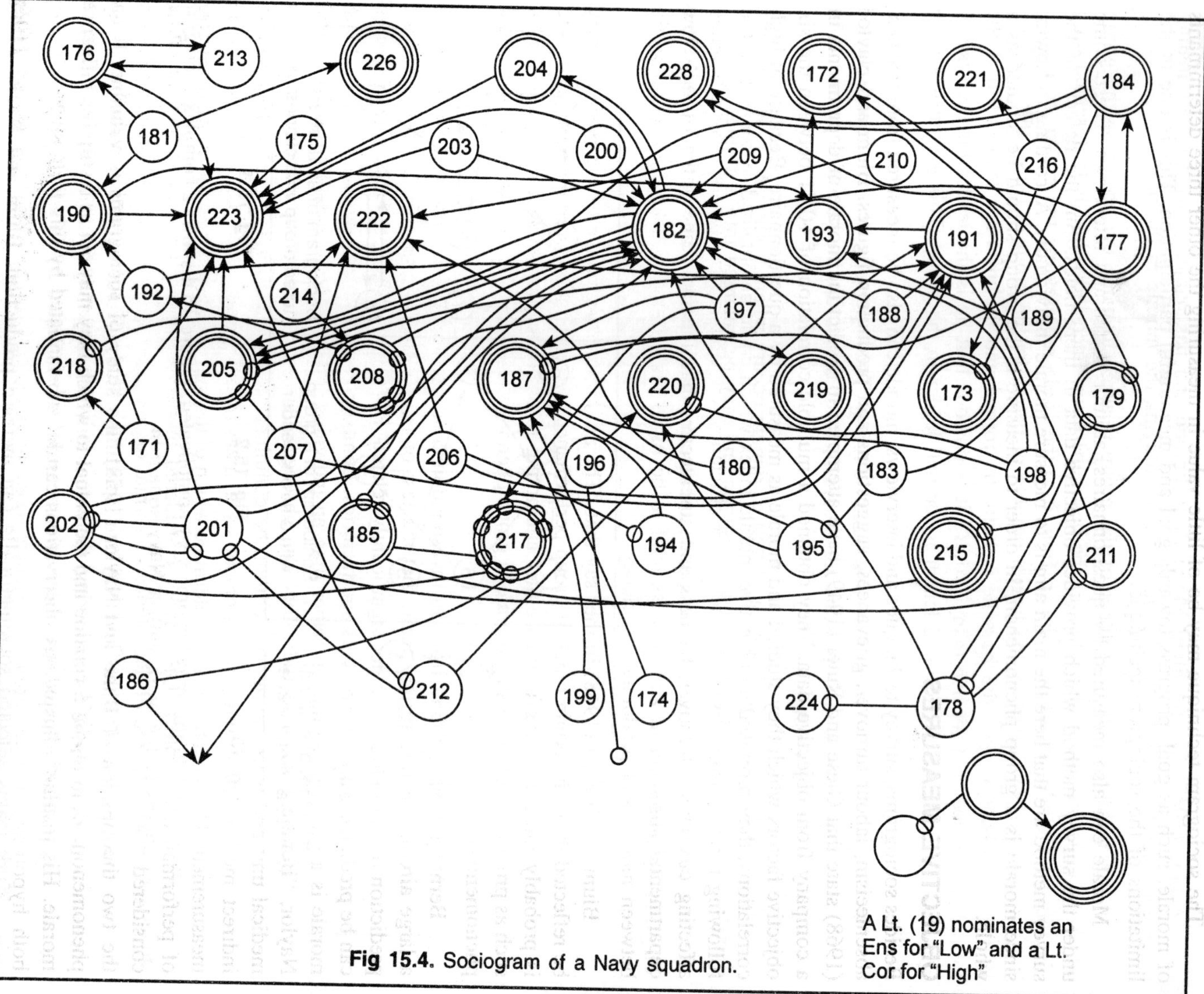

Fig 15.4. Sociogram of a Navy squadron.

The sociogram technique may be of little value in measuring the other three determinants of morale, such as goal, progress towards goal and meaningful participation. This is one of the limitations of the sociogram technique.

Morale can also measured by questionnaires, attitude scales and interviews. These come under the survey method which provides objective data in there fields. But the defects of the survey method are that here the main aim is to measure morale individually. According to Lewin, since morale is a group phenomenon, in order to measure it the group should be studied as a whole.

OBJECTIVE MEASURES

Besides sociograms, survey techniques and interviews, morale can also be measured from strickes, absenteeism, labour turnover, grievanees, suggestions and production figures. Blum and Naylor (1968) state that Giese and Ruter (1949) have attempted to predict the morale of departments in a company from objective data. They obtained a multiple correlation of +0.71 between the six objective factors which they studied and morale as measured by a questionnaire. Because of high correlations; they proposed an objective morale index which could be obtained by measuring the following factors: productive efficiency, error efficiency not affecting customers, error efficiency affecting customers, turnover, lateness and absenteeism. They found that when morale is low departmental absenteeism and lateness tend to be high. They found only a slight relationship between morale and productive efficiency.

Blum and Naylor (1968) further say that "The notion that the morale of a department may be reflected through certain types of group performance in combination is an interesting one and is probably more meaningful than either attempting to correlate morale with a single criterion such as production or confusing morale (a group phenomenon) with job satisfaction (an individual phenomenon)".

Bernberg (1952) found from an investigation conducted on 890 hourly paid employees in a large aircraft manufacturing plant, that the test of morale and the specific indicators for the prediction of individual s are not significantly related. But he however noted that tests of morale can be predicted from departments and factories. Bemberg's rusults hance emphasise the fact that morale is a group phenomenon rather than an individual phenomenon. According to Blum and Naylor, "Bemberg has five indicators *i.e.*, absences, tardiness, short time absence, trips to a medical unit and merit rating. In addition he combined these into a total indicator. He used an indirect method of attitude measurement as a measure of morale and also a direct attitude measurement. His objective was to determine which of the two morale theories was more predictive of performance indicators. One theory considered morale a group phenomenon and the other considered it as a degree of acceptance of formal organisation. Actually the difference between the two theories was Oil the level of hair splitting. Both were intended to measure group phenomenon. Both avoided considering individual attitude and job satisfaction as equivalent to morale. His results indicated that these two measures correlate to the extent of +0.77. Clearly both hypotheses predict group differences (*i.e.*, departmental differences) but not individual differences on performance variables.

While making a critical analyis of the objective indicators of morale Blum and Naylor (1968) have opined that they may be called the external indicators of morale and besides indicating low morale they may otherwise indicate ineffective leadership or inadequacies of training, selection or work standards.

Blum and Naylor further say, "the difficulty with these indicators is that they may be due only in part to morale. There is no certainly as to how much other factors enter the picture. For example, a strike may indicate not low morale, but a reflection of business conditions. Similarly, workers with low morale may not dare to stike because they feel much too defeated and beaten; in this instance the absence of a strike is due to low rather than high morale. Nor can absenteeism and labour turnover always be looked upon as indicators of low morale because conditions in labour market, the weather and other factors may induce such behaviour on the part of the worker".

METHODS OF INCREASING INDUSTRIAL MORALE

One of the pressing problems in industry today is to increase the morale of the workers. When it is suspected that the morale of a group has gone down anyone of the following four methods or all of them may be used to raise morale.

1. Expert approach.
2. Industrial spy approach.
3. Industrial counsellor approach.
4. Employee problem approach.

Some of these methods have been used much more extensively than others because of their importance. For example, the employee problem approach is more popular than the industrial spy approach which has now become a matter of historical interest.

Expert Approach

The expert approach is the most frequently used technique in industry. If things do not go well in a factory and the trouble persists in spite of the best effort of an industrialist, an expert is appointed for the time being to find out the core of the trouble. The important aspect of this approach is the use of an expert in making a spot survey. The expert comes, inspects the plant, looks at fans, washing basin and playground, discusses the other problems with important people, makes a spot survey and writes a report with some suggestions and advice to improve morale. For example, he may suggest any or all tile following items, like posters, speeches, slogans, parties, welfare associations etc.

As a result of this the manager takes necessary steps to improve the morale and the workers possibly feel that something, if not much, is being done for them. There is thus a temporary rise in morale for a short period. But after a few days again the trouble reappears, the reason being that this kind of analysis is purely superficial. When the trouble reappers, the company appoints another expert, shows him the report of the previous expert and informs him that things did not go as predicted. Under such circumstances, he provides some new methods to raise morale. Again, morale is slightly elevated for short time after which it becomes impossible to raise morale by this technique. Such temporary rise in morale is because of superficial analysis of the problem. It only throws light on some of the surface causes and many a times the real cause of the trouble is missed. The us, it only treats the symptoms and not the causes.

Of course, when any of the suggestions given by the experts promotes group co-operation, establishes goals, allows for observable progress towards goal and presents an opportunity for the employees to participate meaningfully and actively in their achievement, it can increase morale.

Thus, the expert approach, according to Blum and Naylor's observations has resulted in mixed success and failure though it is the most frequently used approach.

Industrial Spy Approach

An expert whose true identity is not known to the employees and who acts as a participant observer in disguise is appointed as the spy. The industrial spy is engaged in tracing out the real causes of the workers grievances which they hide because of fear retrenchment, or punishment. The spy works and makes friends with other workers, but secretly sends all informations to the management about the complaints and grievances of the employees. By gaining the confidence of the fellow workers and being intimate with them, he acquires a deep knowledge about the group and its complaints. He sends a confidential report to the management and eventually disappears. The management, in turn, takes necessary steps to improve the morale of the workers, may be by dismissing some union leaders or agitators on the recommendations of the spy.

One major disadvantage of this technique is that once tile workers suspect the spy, morale goes down instead of coming up. Secondly, sometimes there is tile probability of tile bias and prejudice of tile spy colouring his recommendations. Under such circumstances, the industrial spy approach becomes ineffective. However, not all industrial spies are biased or prejudiced. Some of them, in fact, are very objective and are genuinely interested in tile welfare and betterment of the employees.

In order to make this method a success, proper cautions should be taken by the spy in his dealings with the workers. Steps should also be taken to see that the employees do not have the justification or opportunity of suspecting the spy.

In spite of the limitations of the industrial spy approach, it serves an useful perpose of raising the morale of the employees when applied without any bias or prejudice or without the intention of worker hunting.

Industrial Counsellor Approach

The importance of an industrial counsellor has been revealed by the classic findings of the Hawthorne studies.

The Hawthorne studies indicated that the industrial counsellor is useful in increasing morale by improving relations and by acting as a mediator between the employee and the employer.

The employees are informed that the industrial counsellor is a representative of the personal department and has been deputed by the management to talk with them. It has been noted from various experimental findings and observations that the employees voluntarily speak out their personal and professinal problems to the counsellor. Thus the counsellor talks with the workers, listens to their complaints and grievances and gives suggestions. As a result, the gap in communication is bridged, the spirit of the workers goes up and there is a stop to the personal conflicts and problems of the workers. The findings of the Hawthorne studies clearly support this view. When the counsellor is called for, the workers at least feel that something if not everything, is done fore them and that their grievances are being attended to.

The interview between the two parties fosters understanding and communication. It not only improves the supervisor-employee management relations, it has also been valuable and effective in improving the personal adjustment of the individual workers by giving them the scope to channelise and express their emotional blocks. Hence it has also a therapeutic value. This has been supported by a study conducted by the National Research Council cited in "Fatigue of Workers" (Blum and Naylor 1968) where the typical method of personal counselling has been used.

The industrial counsellor can promote group cooperation and help and direct the person see the goal, his progress towards it and the meaning of his work in relation to achieving it. In brief, the industrial counsellor acts as a mirror on which the varied problems of the workers are reflected.

But the difficulty with this method is that is does not go much beyond that. It does not go deep to treat the real causes of low morale.

Thus Blum and Naylor (1968) hold the view that "It may merely be a substitute for the employees a self expression rather than the expression itself".

Employee Problem Approach

The employee problem approach is said to be the most successful approach in increasing the morale of the workers. It is held to be the best among the four techniques, the most widely used and has the advantage of having a number of advantages over the other three.

The employee problem approach was originated by Kurt Lewin during the war years. One of the major advantages of this method is that it considers the group as a whole, while attempting to increase the morale of the employees. In this technique the group is directed to solve its own problems by the group discussion method. This approach is mostly a form of role playing where the foreman, the boss or a trained psychologist puts forth an urgent day-to-day problem to the employees, with some amount of guidance but very little interference. The workers are allowed to bring out tile solution on their own. This is only possible by group discussion. So group co-operation becomes an automatic by-product of this method which naturally increases industrial morale. When the supervisor or the boss throws the problem among the workers, the problem is analysed through various discussions and arguments. In the employee-problem approach, following a sensitivity training approach a group meeting is called and the problem is presented comprehensively by the leader of the discussion group who is trained in the art of conducting a democratic meeting. Finally, a solution or a goal is established. Thus workers not only see the progress they are making but also make active and meaningful participation in solving the problem. In this approach, all the determiners of morale are involved and increased morale is automatically achieved along with the solution of the specific problem. In the employee problem approach the types of problem that can be used are almost limitless and varied. Work hours, wage incentive systems, production increase, vacation schedules, overtime work as well as many irritations and discontentment, conflicts which arise form day-to-day can all be tackled by this technique.

In this technique the leader must encourage free and frank discussions. He must also be in a position to assure the group that the management will respect its final recommendations. It is important to note that no pressure should be put on the group to reach a decision and that the leader should handle the discussion in such a way that no one will get the impression that he is directing or imposing the group towards a certain decision.

As already pointed out, though this method is highly effective and beneficial in raising the morale of workers, it requires considerable skill and experience in conducting such a democratic meeting. Besides, the members of the discussion group should have a particular level of intelligence to take part in discussions. Of course, it does not necessarily mean that the success of this method depends upon the high intelligence of the discussion group. In fact, the method works equally well with people of average intelligence.

Blum and Naylor (1968) opine that "an extension of the employee problem approach naturally leads into the potent and meaningful concept of group dynamics in industry since a realistic study of human relations in industry demands study not only of individual-either employee or employer-but of the group or the groups that individuals form." Thus maximum attention should be given to solve the problems of individual workers in relation to the group, in a group situation and on the job, so that morale can be raised.

Blum and Naylor (1968) have therefore rightly commented : "Such awareness encourages the view that the solution of many industrial problems involving employees, supervisors and employers lies in a better understanding of the group dynamics involved".

QUESTIONS

1. Can morale be called an individual attitude in a group ? Discuss the characteristics of morale.
2. What is meant by industrial morale ? Is it different from attitude and job satisfaction ?
3. Critically analyse the important determinants of morale along with experimental studies.
4. What is the relationship between the type of leader and the morale of the group ? (1975).
5. Can morale be measured ? If so, discuss the different techniques used to measure morale in industry.
6. Briefly discuss the different methods used to raise the morale of the workers. Illustrate your answer with experimental studies.
7. Write notes on :
   (*a*) Morale and attitude.
   (*b*) Morale and job satisfaction.
   (*c*) Determinants of morale.
   (*d*) Measurement of morale.

REFERENCES

Bernberg, R.F. Socio-psychological factors in industrial morale : The prediction of specific indicators, *Journal of Social Psychology*, 1952, 36, pp. 73-82.

Blum, M.L. and Selltiz, C. The seminar as a method of in service training, *Jn of Educational Psychology*, 1946, 19, pp. 420-429.

Blum, M.L. and Naylor, J.C. *Industrial Psychology: Its Theoretical and Social Foundations, Harper International Edition,* Harper and Row Publishers, New York, 1968.

Fairchild, M. Skills and specialisation, Personality Journal, 9, 1930.

Giese, W.J and Ruter, H.W. *An Objective Analysis of Morale*. Gordon, O.J. A factor analysis of human needs and industrial morale, *Personnel Psychology*. 955, 8, pp. 1-18.

Guion, R.M. Industrial morale : The problems of terminology ? *Personnel , Psychology*, 1958, 11, pp. 59-61.

Hall, R. and Kolstad, A. *Morale on job* in Lewin, K. and Watson, G. (Ed.), *Civilian Morale*, Houghton, 1942.

Jenkins, J.G. The Nominating Technique : Its Uses and Limitations, Paper presented at Eastern Psychological Association meeting April, 1947.

Lewin, K. and Watson, G. (eds.) *Civilian Morale*, Houghton Mifflin, Boston, 1942.

Marrow, A.J. Cited in Lewin, K. and Watson, G. (eds.). Civilian Morale, Houghton Mifflin, Boston, 1942.

Mohanty G.B. Interpersonal relationship group, morale and productivity—An observation on 3000 skilled semiskilled and unskilled workers engaged in construction work in Orissa, 2009.

Moreno, J.L. *Foundations of Sociometry Monographs*, No. 4 Beacon Press, Boston, 1943.

Roethlisberger, F.J. *Management and Morale*. Harvard University Press, Cambridge, Mass, 1964.

Stagner, R. Motivational aspects of industrial morale, *Personnel Psychology*. 1958, 11 pp. 64-70.

Viteles, M.S. *Motivation and Morale ill Industry*, Norton, 1953.

16

Job Satisfaction

IMPORTANCE OF JOB SATISFACTION IN INDUSTRIAL ORGANISATIONS

It is an established fact that job satisfaction usually leads to qualitative and quantitative improvement in performance. Satisfaction in job induces motivation and interest in work. When work becomes interesting, the worker gets pleasure from work. More especially, the personal pleasure that the worker gets from a job of his choice gives him tremendous psychological satisfaction.

Every individual has certain needs and motives which he wants to fulfil. Any job which fulfils these needs and motives gives him satisfaction. It is probably the major aim of every worker to get maximum satisfaction from his job. Employers feel equally that pleasure in job enhances production and mental satisfaction. According to Tiffin and McCormick (1971) the satisfaction which people experience in their jobs is in large part the consequence of the extent of which the various aspects of their work situations tend to be relevant to their job related value systems. Thus, every individual has special abilities, aptitudes, inherited capacities, interests and aspirations. Those jobs which provide the worker a chance to fulfil his interests and aptitudes, give hint satisfaction and pleasure. Natural interest in jobs of his satisfaction motivates him for efficient and qualitative performance. Moreover, there are some situational factors responsible for job satisfaction. Some of the important causes of job satisfaction are wage incentive systems, the work environment, length of working hours, behaviour of the supervisor, security, scope fo promotion and recognition of merit. Besides proper evaluation of work, impartial behaviour and social relationship with co-workers etc. are also contributory factors.

MEANING AND DEFINITION OF JOB SATISFACTION

The term job satisfaction has been so often and so widely confused with attitude and morale, that it is quite difficult to give a satisfactory definition of job satisfaction. A review of several studies in the area of job satisfaction leads one to conclude that job satisfaction is any thing that anybody intends to measure when he thinks that he is measuring job satisfaction. There has been confusion both in the use of the term and in the factors that contribute to it. According to Blum and Naylor, "Some studies have dealt only with attitudes on some specific job factors, but have been called job satisfaction studies. Others have investigated other factors and have also been called job satisfaction research. Actually, not much study has been done on job satisfaction itself."

Job satisfaction is the result of various attitudes that the worker holds towards his job, towards related factors and towards life in general. It is a general attitude, an attitude which is the result of many specific attitudes in three major areas such as :

1. Situational factors or specific job factors.
2. Individual characteristics and traits.
3. Group and social relationship outside the job.

JOB SATISFACTION, ATTITUDE AND MORALE

The term job satisfaction is very often confused with attitude and morale. Although attitude, morale and job satisfaction are very much related and in many instances used interchangeably, they are not synonymous. Blum and Naylor view that an attitude through it may contribute to job satisfaction since the latter comprises a number of attitudes.

Similarly, job satisfaction is not the same as industrial morale although it may contribute to morale. Morale is a group phenomenon and job satisfaction is an individual feeling. Morale is generated by the group and it is a by-product of the group. Morale is defined by Blum (1949) as the possession of a feeling on the part of the employees of being accepted by and belonging to the group of employees through adherence to common goals and confidence in the desirability of these goals. Thus, job satisfaction may contribute to raise morale, but it is not the same as morale.

NECESSITY OF STUDYING JOB SATISFACTION

The findings of several investigations suggest that job satisfaction is positively correlated with high production. The results of a study by Katz and Haiman (1947) indicate that workers satisfied with their job produce more. Of course, some other studies also do indicate that not always and in all cases is high production due to job satisfaction. However, it cannot be denied that production is partly a function of job satisfaction.

Because of the specialisation of work in modern industries work lacks intrinsic interest and therefore the worker finds no incentive for work. In the words of Morgan, "Now work is so specialised, so devoid of intrinsic interest that the workman finds no incentive to work." Under these circumstances, to provide interest in work and make the job satisfactory and pleasant there is tremendous need for job satisfaction research. It is only front the data of scientific research that the management can know the factors contributing to job satisfaction and then only can necessary steps be taken to improve job satisfaction. Moreover, knowledge of the attitudes and factors leading to job satisfaction will provide scope for better selection procedure.

It is to be kept in view that job satisfaction is a personal and individual feeling. Thus Balchin has remarked "An effort should be made to give the average worker a job which is not merely a means of earning a living but which has in it all the ingredients of life itself." Job satisfaction not only increases efficiency, it also provides intrinsic motivation for work. Moreover, job satisfaction is also conducive to the all round development of the organisation because directly and indirectly it influences attitude, morale, absenteeism and production level.

Hence empirical research on job satisfaction in the field, with the aim to determine the contributory factors of job satisfaction and the measures to be taken to improve it should be conducted on a large scale.

CLASSIC STUDIES ON JOB SATISFACTION

Job satisfaction is the ultimate function of so many individual attitudes taken together. It is very complex, complicated and personal experience. A number of material and non-material factors contribute to job satisfaction and influence this very personal experience. Some of these variables play important roles while others play secondary roles in giving satisfaction in job. But it is quite difficult to determine the relative importance of the factors influencing job satisfaction as the importance varies with time and individuals.

Several useful and valuable studies have been conducted to throw light on the determinants of job satisfaction. The findings of these studies emphasise on specific factors like incentives, financial and non-financial, advancement and promotion, security, recognition of capabilities, good environment conditions, social relations in the job, age, sex, health, temperament, level of aspiration, socio-personal relationships, family life and relationship with co-worker etc.

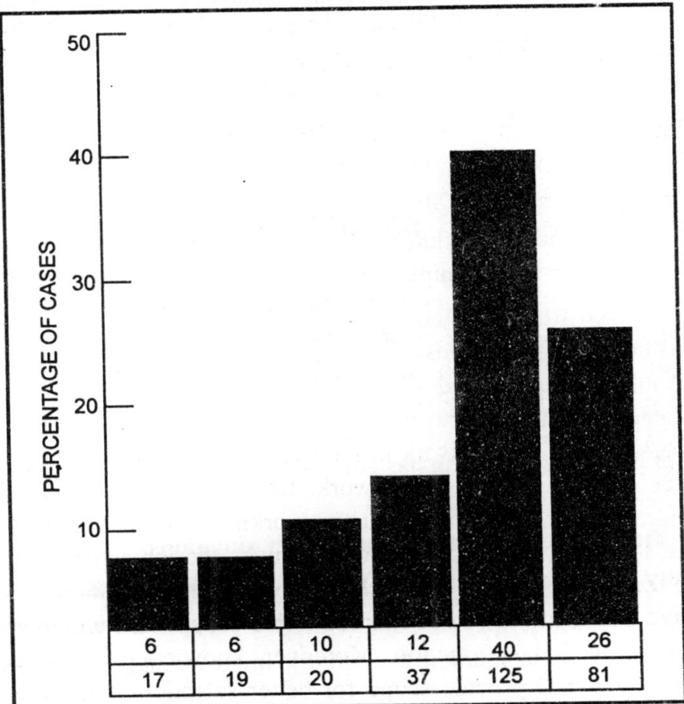

Fig. 16.1. Distribution of job satisfaction index, 309 employed adults. An index of 100 indicates extreme satisfaction, 400 indicates indifference.

Before going on to discuss in detail the determinants of job satisfaction an analysis of the findings of some important investigations on job satisfaction seems to be imperative as these studies have been able to trace the factors contributing to job satisfaction.

Hoppock (1934) conducted a classic study on 309 employees and found that 15 per cent of the workers expressed dissatisfaction in work. Hoppock's study indicates that the job satisfaction index vary with difference in profession.

Again in 1952 Robinson and Hoppock found that 18 per cent of the employees were dissatisfied. In the third part of the study 49 per cent of the workers indicated dissatisfaction in job. From this study it was further noted that untrained and unskilled workers get minimum job satisfaction while persons engaged in skilled and high jobs get maximum job satisfaction.

In the last and final point of the investigation Hoppock distributed attitude scales to 500 teachers from rural and unban communities in the Northern United States to make an estimate of job satisfaction. By combining these 4 attitude scales a measure of job satisfaction of the group was obtained.

The 100 most satisfied and the 100 least satisfied were asked nearly 200 questions. A comparison of the answers of these two extreme groups indicated the following differences between the highly satisfied and the least satisfied teachers.

1. The satisfied teachers showed fewer indications of emotional maladjustment.
2. The satisfied teachers were found to be more religious.
3. The satisfied teachers had better human relationship with their colleagues and superiors.
4. The satisfied group was teaching in cities with over 10,000 population.
5. The satisfied teachers felt more successful.
6. Family influence and social status were more favourable among the satisfied.
7. The satisfied teachers selected their own vocations.
8. Monotony and fatigue were reported more frequently by the dissatisfied group.
9. On an average the satisfied group was 7.5 years older than the dissatisfied group.

To add to these differences, it is interesting to note that there was no significant difference in the average salaries of the two groups.

It was further proved from the findings of Hoppock that those who were satisfied in their vocation and job usually did not express dissatisfaction over minor incidents. Hoppock's study also points out that job satisfaction and vocational interest are not identical, because 84 per cent of the dissatisfied teachers said 'yes' to the question 'Is your work interesting ?'

On the basis of his study Hoppock has suggested the following six main components of job satisfaction :

1. The way the individual reacts to unpleasant situations.
2. The facility with which he adjusts himself to other persons.
3. His relative status in the social and economic group with which he identifies himself.
4. The nature of work in relation to abilities, interests and preparation of the worker.
5. Security.
6. Loyalty.

These are die genuine factor which contribute to job satisfaction in a major way. In fact job satisfaction is correlated with the emotional adjustment of the person and those who are emotionally unstable not only face difficulty adjusting themselves in social and personal life but also to the job and hence become dissatisfied with it. Thus, Blum and Naylor (1968) have remarked that "job satisfaction is an important generalised attitude in an individual, not a specific attitude about specific job factors."

Surveying several studies, Vroom (1964) has suggested the following seven dimensions of job satisfaction.

1. Attitude towards the company and company management.
2. Attitude towards promotional opportunities.
3. Attitude towards job content.
4. Attitude towards supervision.
5. Attitude towards financial rewards.
6. Attitude towards working conditions.
7. Attitude towards co-workers.

From the findings of 16 different studies conducted on more than 1,100 employees Herzberg, Mausen, Peterson and Cap well (1957) report the following factors ranked by the workers in terms of their importance. They are : (1) security, (2) interest, (3) opportunity for advancement, (4) appreciation from supervisor, company and management, (5) intrinsic aspects of job, (6) wages, (7) social aspects of job, (8) working conditions, (9) communication, (10) hours, (11) ease, and (12) benefits.

Thus, security has been given the top priority while ease and benefits from job have been given the lowest ranking.

Hulin and Smith (1964) have proved that the sex variable influences job satisfaction. They wanted to find out the effect of sex differences on job satisfaction. The results indicated that in three plants male workers had comparatively more job satisfaction than female workers. But in the fourth plant the difference was not significant. On the basis of many surveys Blauner (196 reports that in general about 13 per cent of the employees covered indicated that they are dissatisfied with their work.

Attempting to examine the relationship between job satisfaction and various aspects of job behaviour, Vroom (1964) has noted that there has been a negative relationship between job satisfaction and labour turnover and between job satisfaction and absenteeism. Trying to determine the relationship between job satisfaction and accident, Vroom found a negative relationship, while in another study no relationship was obtained.

Similarly, Brayfield and Crockett's (1958) review of researches suggest, no relationship between job satisfaction and job performance. This finding goes against the traditional idea that a satisfied worker is highly productive. Additional research on this problem is therefore extremely essential.

RECENT STUDIES ON JOB SATISFACTION

Dunnette and Hokel (1967) noted that the job content, job context or both jointly may be responsible for job satisfaction or job dissatisfaction. They further found that job dimensions su as achievement, responsibility and resignation are more important for both satisfaction and dissatisfaction than certain other job dimensions such as working conditions, company policies and practices and the feeling of security etc.

Blauner (quoted in Gilmen, 1971) points out from the findings of many studies that there is a high consistency in the results that most of the people in almost all organisations are moderately or highly satisfied with their jobs. He has concluded that percentage of dissatisfied workers is quite low.

Schuh (1967) states that it is a fact that people do very little career planning before searching for a job. Industry often fails to select workers judiciously and to provide a climate for job satisfaction. In some cases the personality factors play such a remarkable role in dissatisfaction that industry sometimes fails to inject the feelings of satisfaction in spite of various endeavours. Exit interviews reveal some real causes of job dissatisfaction, but many times the workers, being polite, do not give the real cause. For instance, in one study while the workers said that they were leaving for high pay, a follow up study indicate that they left the job because of poor supervision and the psychological factors related to the job attitude.

Blood (1969) administered measure of job satisfaction and work values on 114 student, airmen and 306 non-commissioned officers. The results indicated a consistent relationship between these two sets of variables. Evidence indicates that the job satisfaction variance is controlled by work values.

Ronan (1970) conducted a study on individual and situational variables relating to job satisfaction, taking 1310 managerial supervisory, 3641 salaried and 6212 hourly employees concerning job satisfaction and using 32 items from a questionnaire. By and large, little relationship was found between satisfaction and behaviours. But when such a relationship was observed, the link seemed to be direct supervision. The findings also revealed that behavioural measures depend on more than one factor. This suggests that the inter relationship are extremely complex.

The investigator has recommended that in future such type of analysis should concentrate on the study of individual rather than on situational variables. A study on job satisfaction variables among female clerical workers was conducted by Williamson and Karras (1970). Thirty-four female clerical workers ranked 10 job characteristics in order of importance for self, importance for the same sex and importance for the opposite sex. These 10 job characteristics included five motivators and five hygienes taken from Herzberg, Mausner and Snyderman (1959).

The results were compared with the findings of two similar studies conducted on college females. A comparison indicated a significant difference between the two groups. College females ranked motivators significantly higher for self than the female clerical workers. The investigators viewed that the general need for self actualisation of the college females and greater anticipation of opportunities for advancement, self expression, higher responsibilities and other motivators are possible factors underlying such difference. This study supports the findings of a similar study conducted by the present author in 1981 on a group of female L. D. assistants and female college teachers of Orissa.

Ash (1972) compared the job satisfaction differences among women of different ethnic groups. Taking 47 black, 112 white, and 63 Spanish surname female production and clerical employees in an electrical components company, he found the black women were more dissatisfied than whites. Spanish surname employees in the study were generally more satisfied than blacks and less satisfied than whites.

Bulak (1973) studied job satisfaction among a group of 173 building industry workers from 14 plants of Czechoslovakia.

Out of them 81 per cent considered their salary to be independent of their work and dependent on the consideration of their bosses.

A closer relation was found between work satisfaction and absenteeism than between work efficiency.

Absence caused by illness is also considered to be a function of work satisfaction. It is concluded that work satisfaction is a result of the contemporary function relation of a man to his needs.

In a study on job satisfaction in relation to job performance and occupational level Prvbi' (1973) found a low positive relationship between job satisfaction and job performance, which support the results of previous investigators. However, results do not show any relationship between the occupational level and job satisfaction, a finding which conflicts with the results of previous studies.

In a comparative study of cultural and situational determinants of job satisfaction amongst managers in South Africa with those m several countries in other parts of the world, Blunt (1973) compared managerial attitudes in South Africa with those in several countries in other parts of the world. These managers answered a questionnaire regarding 16 items relevant to five need categories. The findings indicated that these managers were more dissatisfied in almost every need than managers in other countries except in France and Italy where there was more dissatisfaction with social needs. In developing countries like India, Argentina and Chile, Managers seemed to be more dissatisfied with all needs except self-actualisation.

The author suggests that dissatisfaction among South African Managers with self and self-actualisation arises from its political and social factors.

Ronan *et al.* (1974) administered Kornhauser's questionnaire at three military installations. The results did not indicate any substantial relationship between mental health and job satisfaction which confirms the findings of the Survey Research Centre (1970). The investigator hypothesised that relationship between mental health and job satisfaction exists only in the lower-skill, routine work level.

Fossun (1974) investigated the effects of urban rural socialisation on job satisfaction and productivity. There was no statistical difference between urban and rural groups, in ability or performance tasks. Task and pay satisfaction was higher in the rural group.

Carell and Elbert (1974) administered a questionnaire including the Brafield and Rothes Index of Job satisfaction to 397 Mid-Western postal clerks. The results show (*a*) significant main effects for the factors of age, education and home environment, and (*b*) significant interactior between home environment and education, home environment and location, and home environme and job category.

Spillance (1973) studied the two factor theory of job satisfaction in relation to labo turnover. Ratings for satisfaction, intrinsic job factors, together with reasons for remaining with or leaving organisations were obtained from 80 middle managers who had recently resigned from their jobs for at least one year. No significant difference was obtained between two groups in the scores on job satisfaction.

These recent studies conducted on the various aspects and problems of job satisfaction have significantly contributed to the area of job satisfaction in industries and organisations. Many studies have also suggested various useful measures for improving the job satisfaction of the workers. The traditional belief that job satisfaction is positively correlated with the production level and work performance has been proved false by certain studies.

RESEARCHES ON JOB SATISFACTION IN INDIAN INDUSTRIES

A review of Indian studies, indicates that a maximum number of investigations have been taken up in the area of Job Satisfaction and Performance. This constitutes about 27 per cent of the total Indian studies on industrial psychology till 1971. Thus, this field seems to be a favourite area of research for the Indian industrial psychologists.

In India, research on job satisfaction started in 1958 with the work of Professor Durganand Sinha, an eminent industrial psychologist of India. He attempted to compare the job satisfaction of office and manual workers. Sinha and Singh (1961) and Sinha (1965) tried to establish a relationship between job satisfaction and absenteeism. Ganguly (1961) views that Indian workers give priority to salary as the important factor influencing job satisfaction. But analysing the views of Ganguly, it can be said that money may be an important financial incentive for Indian workers, but it may not be an equally important determinant of their job satisfaction. It should also be kept in view that though the determinants of motivation and job satisfaction are related variables, yet the causes of both are not the same.

Sinha and Sharma (1962) found a negative correlation between the union attitude and job satisfaction and a positive relationship between job satisfaction and general adjustment. The relationship between job satisfaction with different background factors has been analysed (Sinha and Nayar, 1965) and its relation with worker behaviours has been investigated.

The effect of age, education and salary on job satisfaction has been observed by Natraj and Hafeez (1965), while Prasad (1965) and Guha (1965) have obtained the importance of personality and personality factors. Pestonjee (1967) has focussed on some organisational variables influencing job satisfaction. Ghosh and Shukla (1967) have found that job conditions rather than personal factors influence job satisfaction.

In a job satisfaction study, using a multidimensional questionnaire, Ganguly (1976) has found that satisfaction with the factory as a whole and benefits obtained for it is one of the important components of morale.

Making a survey of the Indian studies on job satisfaction Ganguly (1964) has found that Indian workers are less satisfied with their jobs in comparison to their Western counterparts. Ganguly (1954c) has also tried to study job satisfaction as a function of union membership. In a study by Veeraraghvan (1960) it was observed that private sector transport workers showed greater satisfaction than the public sector workers and were more favourably disposed towards the management. In a study, Sitra (1964) tried to find out the relationship between the level of job satisfaction and productivity. The level of job satisfaction in high productivity units was found to be significantly higher than in low productivity units. It was only noticed that dissatisfaction with certain aspects of work tended to spread to other areas. Some attempts have been made by a few inland psychologists to determine the cause and significance of job satisfaction. But unfortunately the results obtained have not been able to provide generalised and clear-cut information about the importance of the causative factors of job satisfaction.

A study was conducted of 124 Indian engineers by Sarveswara Rao (1973) to test the validity and generality of the two-factor theory of job satisfaction. A job attitude questionnaire consisting of two unipolar satisfaction and dissatisfaction scales and an overall satisfaction scale was administered to the respondents. Analysis of data showed partial support to the two factor theory. Satisfaction and dissatisfaction were found to be independent feelings and motivators contributed to both satisfied and dissatisfied feelings. Motivators and hygienes were not mutually exclusive in the factor analysis sense.

Kalanidhi (1973) surveyed the job satisfaction, home problems and emotional adjustment of 195 female workers working in five industrial plants. The results suggested that security and income were the most important job factors. It was further noted that workers with personal, financial or family strain were poorly adjusted and had less job satisfaction.

The present author (1981) has conducted a study on the pattern of Williamson (1970) to measure and compare the job satisfaction variables of a group of female college teachers and a group of female office assistants of Orissa. In this study Heizberg's two factor theory was tested.

The findings confirmed Williamson's results in that college teachers gave higher ranking to motivators than to hygienes in comparison to female assistants who gave more emphasis on hygienes.

Result

It is interesting to note that the results of the two studies (conducted in two different cultures) showed a similar trend. This legitimately suggests that in spite of significant economic and socio-cultural differences, motivators work as genuine satisfiers for those who have a need for self-actualisation. The clerical job does not provide any scope for self-actualisation. Therefore, most probably, the female assistants have given importance to hygienes.

TABLE 16.1(a)

Mean Ranking of Motivators and Hygienes by College Teachers

Sl. No.	*Motivators*	*Mean Ranking*			*Sl. No.*	*Motivators*	*Mean Ranking*		
		Importance for self sex	*Importance for same sex*	*Importance for opp. sex*			*Importance for self sex*	*Importance for same sex*	*Importance for opp. sex*
1.	Achievement	8.20	7.90	8.25	1.	Company policy and administration	4.50	4.76	5.25
2.	Recognition	7.90	7.92	7.60	2.	Supervision Technical	5.20	5.10	4.76
3.	Work itself	7.56	6.98	7.75	3.	Salary	8.70	8.56	8.92
4.	Responsibility	9.50	8.36	7.62	4.	Supervisor	5.80	5.82	6.30
5.	Advancement	8.30	8.35	8.35	5.	Working hours	4.50	4.30	4.70

TABLE 16.1(b)
Mean Ranking of Motivators and Hygienes by Office Assistants

Sl. No.	Motivators	Mean Ranking: Importance for self sex	Importance for same sex	Importance for opp. sex	Sl. No.	Motivators	Mean Ranking: Importance for self sex	Importance for same sex	Importance for opp. sex
1.	Achievement	4.50	3.95	5.25	1.	Company policy and administration	8.50	8.30	4.20
2.	Recognition	4.70	3.76	4.10	2.	Supervision Technical	7.50	7.30	6.50
3.	Work itself	3.72	4.10	3.91	3.	Salary	8.60	8.70	8.80
4.	Responsibility	4.80	4.25	4.15	4.	Supervisor	6.30	6.70	4.50
5.	Advancement	5.20	5.15	4.95	5.	Working hours	7.40	6.90	7.50

Sarveswar Rao and Ganapathi Rao (1973) conducted a study to determine the factors contributing to job satisfaction and importance of industrial personnel. In order to investigate the two factor theory of job satisfaction advanced by Heizberg, a job attitude questionnaire was administered on a number of different categories of employees. The results indicated that both motivators and hygienes contributed to overall satisfaction.

Sarveswar Rao and Ganguly (1971) made an investigation in an electrical equipment manufacturing unit on the perceived need, satisfaction and importance of highly skilled and skilled personnel.

Results indicate that in determining employees' satisfaction the occupational level had an important role to play. Both motivators and hygienes contributed to the satisfaction and dissatisfaction of highly skilled and skilled personnel.

The findings of this study support the results of the study by S. Rao and G. Rao (1973).

It appears from the review of Indian studies on job-satisfaction that while personnel and personality factors have received greater attention, the situational and environmental causes of job satisfaction have not been carefully investigated.

An overall analysis of the Indian studies reveals that in spite of the fact that the maximum number of studies have been conducted on performance and job satisfaction, more clearcut and careful studies should be undertaken to determine the causes and contributors of job satisfaction. In addition to this, methods used to improve the job satisfaction level of Indian workers should be found out in greater detail for the very reason that research findings have already indicated that more Indian workers are dissatisfied in their job than their counterparts in the West.

Kanungo and Misra *et al.* have conducted a number of valuable studies jointly and independently which need mention here in view of their importance for the Indian industrial-organisational employees. The studies are : (1) relationship of job involvement to perceived importance and satisfaction of employee needs, (2) the motivational formulation of job and work involvement : A cross National Study, (3) job involvement and alienation progress, issues and prosperity (4) job involvement of intrinsically and extrinsically Indian managers :

1. Relationship of Job Involvement to Perceived Importance and Satisfaction of Employee's Needs

Kanungo, Mishra and Dayal (1975) view that the attitude of job involvement has been considered as very central to work motivation. But to explore the relationship between job involvement and patterns of perceived needs, and their satisfaction on the job very few studies have been conducted. However, no one can deny job involvement as a moderator variable influencing employee's perception of importance, strength, and satisfaction of his needs. Thus in the present study the investigators have tried to explore the relationship between the attitude of job involvement and patterns of perceived importance of the needs and their satisfaction on the job.

When an employee is involved with his job, the total job satisfaction is thought to as being central to his life or self concept. An involved worker expects his work intrinsically meaningful and rewarding, as he feels that his work provides him the opportunity for self-expression. On the contrary, an alienated employee does not consider his work intrinsically rewarding and meaningful. The job involvement attitude refers to the internalisation of values about the goodness of work or the influence of work in the worth of the person. It represents an employee's ego, involvement or commitment in his job. A person's commitment to his job is a by product of his background, personal experiences and is carried by him from job to job. It is therefore conceived as a more stable individual characteristic and more a function of the person than of the job (Lawler and Hall, 1970).

The attitude of job satisfaction on the other hand is determined by the degree of fulfilment of an employee's needs on the job due to the presence or absence of certain job factors or outcomes such as salary, independence etc. Thus, precisely, it can be said that while job involvement dimension varies from complete identification to lack of any relation with the job, the job satisfaction dimension varies from specific need fulfilment to need frustration on the job depending upon the attainment of the desired goals through job activity. Thus, an employee may be highly satisfied but not involved or highly involved but not satisfied. Though some have argued that job involvement is positively related to job satisfaction, it cannot be undoubtedly said that this relationship is a stable one. The investigators have suggested the relationship between the two to be minimal on the ground that job involvement being more of an individual difference type variable is dependent on past socialisation of the employee and job satisfaction being more of job or situational difference type variable is dependent on presence or absence of job factors.

Each employee has a cognitive value system with regard to what job factors he considers more important than others. One employee may feel extreme satisfaction in an organisation providing excellent fringe benefit plans as he is looking forward for the same in the job. But another employee may not find the fringe benefits quite satisfying as he attaches less importance to fringe benefits. Thus, it is viewed that the cognitive value system representing employee's perceived importance of job factors rather than the experimental system representing degree of satisfaction with various job factors (Rowe 1973) is influenced by the attitude of job involvement. His attitude of job involvement would influence what he expects from job and would thus determine the valence of various job factors for him. Differences in the job involvement attitude among the employees may influence them to perceive the same job from different perspectives. This may further direct them to emphasise different kinds of goal attainments in the job.

In the context of Maslow's (1954) need categories and their hierarchy, the present study is designed to explore the relationships of job involvement to experiment and cognitive systems operating within employees. The following six hypotheses were tested.

Hypothesis 1 : The job-involved employees will attach greater importance of those job factors or outcomes that tend to satisfy higher order needs like ego and self-actualisation needs than to those job factors that tend to satisfy lower order needs like physiological, safety, and social needs.

Hypothesis 2 : The reverse of hypothesis I will be true for the job alienated employees.

Hypothesis 3 : The job-involved and job-alienated employees will not differ either with respect to their levels of satisfaction or with respect to their need strength for the various job factors.

Further to test some of the implications of Maslow's (1954) theory of growth motivation in a cultural set up different from the one to which Maslow's theory is mostly applied, the following three additional hypotheses were formulated.

Hypothesis 4 : The employees will show greater dissatisfaction with job factors that satisfy lower order needs than higher order needs.

Hypothesis 5 : Consequently, the employees will show greater need strength for the lower than higher order needs.

Hypothesis 6 : The over-all job satisfaction of employees will depend more on the satisfaction of lower than higher order needs.

The present study was conducted in India, a developing country where for most of the workers the lower order needs are not adequately met. Hence it is expected that the employees in general will show a greater concern and dissatisfaction with the lower order needs in comparison to higher order needs. Consequently the strength of lower order needs should be higher for them than the strength of higher order needs which in case of many employees may perhaps be psychologically nonexistent. The above three additional hypotheses were formulated to examine this.

Data were collected from 141 employees belonging to two different industrial organisations located in the north western region of India. The sample included within each organisation the non-supervisory rank and file and supervisory lower and middle management personnel. Almost half of the sample were college graduates and the other half high school graduates mostly of lower and lower middle class income categories. The sample approximates very closely the typical educated individual workers in urban India.

The findings of the present study supported the view that employee's attitude of job involvement can act as a medicator variable and can influence employee's cognitive evaluation of the importance of various job factors. Job involvement attitude however does not influence the actual experience of satisfaction on the job or the employee's strength of various needs. "Need satisfaction and need strengths are very much a function of the job and its environment in which appropriate goals for need satisfaction may be present, or absent in varying degrees. Thus, high and low involved employees did not differ with respect to their need satisfaction and need strengths but did attach differential importance to job factors representing higher and lower order needs."

Since the respondents of the present study belonged to India which is a developing country, it was expected by the investigators that the lower order needs would be the most important force governing their behaviour. But surprisingly the results indicated that the respondents in their cognitive evaluation consider self actualisation on the job to be more important than social and physiological need satisfaction, which is contrary to the expectations. Further it was also observed that the over all job satisfaction of the respondents is more strongly related to higher order need satisfaction than to lower order need satisfaction. These results thus do not support hypotheses 4, 5 and 6 and question the validity and generalisability of Maslow's need hierarchy concept.

The authors conclude "The present results, however are consistent with the notion that various needs coexist within the employees with varying degree of strength and that the satisfaction and strength of these needs are a function of the Cue properties of the job and its environment".

In an observation on 2500 unskilled workers Mohanty (2009) noticed that unskilled workers with low socio economic status get better job satisfaction when their lower order needs like physiological and safety needs were fulfilled.

2. The Motivational Formulation of Job and Work Involvement : A Cross National Study

Involvement with job has been studied by Kanungo (1979) in two clearly distinguished contexts *i.e.* involvement with "specific jobs" and involvement with "work in general".

The present research was conducted with two main objectives (*i*) Examination of the empirical properties of Kanungo's new job and work involvement measure in two other nations besides Canada, *i.e.* Federal Republic of Germany and India. (*ii*) To test three hypotheses desired from the motivational formulation on samples of German and Indian employees and compare these results with those obtained in the Canadian study to check on the cross national generalisability of the formulation.

Kanungo concluded that job involvement is not necessarily a multidimensional constitute as conceived and measured by the new familiar Lodahi and Kejner (1965) and other scales (Blood 1969; Saleh and Hosek, 1976). In Kanungo's view (1982) an individual can show personal involvement in two distinctly differently contexts (*a*) involvement in a particular job and (*b*) involvement in work in general.

Gron and Kanungo (1980) and Mishra and Kalro (1981) have found evidence in support of the view that intrinsic need satisfaction may be a sufficient but not a necessary condition for job involvement. Kanungo (1982 b) has emphasised that work involvement is largely determined by socialisation that promotes work as central to a person's life.

Kanungo's (1982) Canadian study indicated that job satisfaction has a strong relationship with job involvement than with work involvement.

The authors felt the need to test the generality of the motivational formulation in different socio-technocultural settings and standardise the new majors of involvement.

The sample of this study consisted of 929 West Germans employed as managers, bureaucrats, and technocrats in middle to senior level positions in a wide variety of orgnisations of different size, representing public, Private and government enterprises and 276 middle and senior level executives and bureaucrats of India representing a wide variety of organisations in the public and private sectors.

The findings of this study provide standardised measures of job and work involvement in two culturally diverse countries. The study also supports the claim that the motivational formulation of involvement has pan cultural validity and generalisability. "In three different countries, Canada, FRG and India, hypotheses derived from the motivational formulation were consequently supported."

In conclusion the authors of the present investigation have remarked "The evidence presented in this paper puts the motivational approach to involvement on firm footing. As a guiding conceptual framework of future research, it can be used in various ways. For instance, using the new measures, comparative profile of job- and work-involved employees can be drawn across nations. This implies that there is a need to re-examine the profile of the job involved person reported by Rabinowitz and Hall (1977). Another important line of inquiry pertains to the relationship between job involvement and mental health. It is commonly believed that job involvement is positively related to mental health and job alienation is related to poor mental health. However, Kanungo (l982b) has reported significant negative relationship between a widely used composite index of mental health and job involvement as measured by the new scales. In contrast, he found a significant positive relationship between mental health and intrinsic orientation (which according to the present conceptualisation, is independent of and distinct from job involvement). More specifically, Kanungo found that individuals with high intrinsic orientation and low job involvement exhibited the highest level of mental health, whereas, individuals with low intrinsic (or high extrinsic) orientation and high job involvement (low alienation) exhibited the lowest level of mental health. These nonobvious findings (see comments by Srivastva and Cooperrider, 1983) pertaining to the relationships between mental health, intrinsic motivation, and job involvement raise important questions for exploration in the areas of occupational stress and workaholism.

3. Job Involvement and Alienation-Progress, Issues and Prospects

Mishra (1979) has attempted to review and evaluate relevant research on job involvement and alienation in the Indian context in the light of the conclusions drawn by Rabinowitz and Hall (1977) in the Western context.

Rabinowitz and Hall's work on job involvement has brought forward some important conclusions given below :

1. Job involvement is related to three classes of working variables : personal characteristic, situational characteristics, and work outcomes. The situational variables appear to have greater effect on the attitudes of low job-involved persons than on high-job-involved persons. Taken together, the tentative profile of the job-involved person which emerges is that he "is a believer in protestant ethic, is older, has internal (vs. external) locus of control, has strong growth needs, has a stimulating job (high autonomy, variety, task identity, and feedback), participates in decisions affecting him, is satisfied with the job, has a history of success, is less likely to leave the organization" (Robinowitz and Hall, 1977, p. 284).
2. Job involvement is fairly stable. Even major job redesign may not increase job involvement or major organisational stress may not decrease involvement.
3. Job involvement appears to be both a cause and an effect of job behaviour.

4. The data are more consistent with the "psychological identification with work" definition of job involvement than with "self-esteem affected by perceived level of performance".

Rao and Sheth on the other hand, have systematically reviewed in the Indian context the psychological and the sociological research with respect to the various correlates of work in the Indian context. These studies indicate that research on job involvement and work alienation in India is sketchy and rather diffused.

However, Rabinowitz and Hall (1977) have concluded that internality and involvement go hand in hand. In the opinion of Rabinowitz and Hall, the work involved individual is a believer in protestant ethic. Mishra in this connection views "I, however, doubt whether Hindus in reality identify with the work ethic ordained by the Gita." He has further quoted Sinha's (1978) view about work ethic. Work is not that valued in India. Given the opportunity, we would rather prefer to rest and relax. We have, what we call 'Aram' culture. Part of the reason is the cultural priority assigned to relationship rather than to the 'task' 'Karma' which should have meant 'work' usually reflects one's 'obligation' to others—superiors, subordinates, peers, etc." Dependence, personalished relationship, and loyalty are "manifestations of a cultural prescription that one should aspire to be closer and closer to the superior whose Kripa (and not the task accomplishment) will yield success on the job. The ethos pervades all walks of our life ranging from family to the way one relates to God".

Sharma (1974) measured alienation among automobile factory workers in Bombay. He found that nearly 60 per cent of the workers interviewed in 1971 wanted to return to their villages and choose another job if they could. The majority of the workers reported that they did not feel involved in their jobs. They also perceived the organisational culture as irrational and unjust in terms of managerial behaviour. It would not, however, be possible to generalise on the relationship between employee alienation and their place of upbringing on the basis of one study. It is commonly observed that once an individual lives long enough in the city, the nostaligia for the idyllic rural surroundings diminishes. One oftcn hears how keen the professional doctors, engineers, and bureaucrats are to return from the rural areas to the State capitals or New Delhi. The stated reasons are usually earthy : good schools for children's education, higher wages, opportunities for advancement, and other little comforts of modern living.

Rabinowitz and Hall (1972) have concluded that job involvement and participation in decision making are positively and significantly correlated. Though there is no direct evidence to support this conclusion in the Indian context "Bhatnagar (1977) tried to study the worker's desire for participation in a textile and a fertiliser factory with respect to six categories of decisions; decisions related to one's work, safety, technical decisions, personal decisions, welfare decisions, and managerial decisions. She found that workers were not so keen to participate in the first instance. She further found that workers desired decreasing amount of participation from first to last decisional category. Workers in technologically advanced fertiliser factory demanded greater participation than those in the textile factory with traditional technology. In the textile industry with its long history of established trade Unionism, workers desired greater union involvement in personal and welfare decisions than the workers in the fertiliser factory. With respect to managerial decisions, workers in both the factories were not interested.

Mishra views that many managements in India and else where believe that high costs, poor service and misconduct are some of the major consequences of alienation.

De's case studies on participative redesigning of work systems conducted in three of the largest Indian organisations (a heavy electrical engineering industry, a service industry, and another service industry run departmentally by the Government of India) seem to have been beneficial for the "organisations."

Empirical studies however have demonstrated that even major job redesigning does not increase job involvement (Lawer *et al.*, 1973) and major organisatioal stresses were not sufficient to decrease involvement (Hall and Mansfield 1971). Kanungo (1977) has proposed a motivational framework to study alienation and involvement which operationally defines the concept of work involvement as "a generalised congitive (or belief) state of psychological identification with work, in so far as work is perceived to have the potentiality to satisfy one's salient needs and expectations". Likewise, work alienation is defined as "a generalised congnitve (or belief) state of psychological separation from work, in so far as work is perceived to lack the potentiality for satisfying one's salient needs and expectations".

Indicating the need for further research on the problem of job involvement and alienation Mishra points out that both the psychological and sociological formulations with respect to job involvement and alienation regard that work situations lacking in opportunity for the satisfaction of self-esteem, achievement, autonomy, self control, and power needs to a decrease in job involvement and increase in work alienation. This is so, presumably because the 'dominant values of industrialsed western societies have been achievement and individualism and their surrounding social order fundamentally democratic and economically advanced.

Job involvement and alienation is related to the meanings one attaches to work. The meanings of work and its importance may vary as jobs vary and as cultures vary. Transky (1974) have suggested six different meanings of work based on a review of studies on the meaning and functions of work. They are (*a*) an intrinsically satisfying activity, (*b*) a status and prestige bestowing activity, (*c*) a morally correct activity, (*d*) a source of satisfying interpersonal experience, (*e*) an economic activity, a means of survival, and (*f*) a routine activity which keeps one occupied.

Many social scientists are of the view that providing autonomy and power to the employee is desirable for increasing job involvement. Psychological identification with work is also necessary for job involvement.

In conclusion Mishra views "It is necessary to examine the effects of a variety of factors (such as individual differences, difference in socialisation, salient need patterns at various stages and levels of working life, institutional setting and top management style) on job involvement in a given cultural context in order to have a vertical understanding of its nature and process. It is also important to consider the legal, political end economic factors as necessary inputs which may enable us to avoid adopting spurious solutions to the problem of work alienation.

Kanungo has conducted a further study on *Work Alienation and Quality of Work Life : A cross cultural perspective.*

The work alienation models developed in the industrialised Western societies reveal that the models have strong cultural bias. It has been doubted whether these models can be successfully applied in the third world countries. Therefore as an alternative model a pan-cultural formulation has been proposed in the present study.

The present paper has two main purposes : (*a*) Quality of working life is intimately correlated with the work alienation or work involvement phenomenon. (*b*) The dominant quality of working life model practiced in the industrialised western culture in quite inappropriate in the context of the developing third world countries since the conceptual frameworks developed in the Western world have strong cultural bias thus constraining applicability of the Western QWL models in the third world countries.

Suttle (1977) holds that improving the quality of working life leads to healthier, more satisfied and more productive employees and more efficient adaptive and profitable organisations. On the contrary, a deterioration in the quality of working life lead to more alienated and unproductive employees and less efficient and unproductive organisations.

The western model is not tenable in the third world countries due to two reasions : (1) Workers have a variety of needs some of which are primary, others secondary. The strength of the needs in any individual is determined by his past socialisation in a particular culture and is constantly modified by present job conditions. Because of the difference in cultural background and socialisation, people may develop different need saliency patterns. There may be individual difference in need saliency patterns. Job expectations and satisfaction therefore may vary under similar factory environment but different cultural set-ups. Therefore particular group of workers may be involved in jobs and get job satisfaction which provide them with the scope for control and autonomy, while the same factors may not provide involvement and satisfaction to another group of workers. It should hence be kept in mind that people differ with respect to what constitute the core of their self concepts.

Kanungo points out that the industrially developed societies of the west may make their citizens believe that all that counts in one's life is to have individual liberty and freedom. So they may give greater importance to freedom and control. Conversely, in the developing countries of the east, economic and social security often are considered more important to life than are freedom and control at the work place. Workman of the east therefore may find work very involving if it guarantees economic security even if there may not be freedom and control in their jobs. Kanungo remarks that in these societies people may value equality more than liberty as the guiding principle of working life. (2) The faulty assumption that protestant ethic type socialisation training is the only appropriate way of bringing about higher work involvement and consequent industrial development is the second reason for the non-tenability of the western model. According to the author any type of training through which individuals realise that centrality of work role in life can fulfil their salient needs, will increase work involvement. Western cultures value individualism and promote in its members greater saliency for autonomy and personal achievement needs. The protestant work ethic in such cultures trains people to believe that work can satisfy these salient needs and can provide opportunities for the expression of one's individuality and hence work should be valued as being good and central to one's life. On the contrary, considering the process of socialisation in many eastern and third world countries it can be seen that cultures in these countries promote in their members a sense of collectivism and saliency for social and security needs. People in such cultures develop belief in centrality of work not because work can promote personal achievement, but because work can fulfil the collective goals of brotherhood and sharing in life. The author further cites the case of Japan which provides another example of work ethic that can result from socialisation training of a non-protestant variety. The Japanese stresses a rigid and hierarchically arranged collective society. Members of each collectivity are expected to maintain absolute loyalty and obedience to authority and to the group in the fulfilment of their obligations. Nakane (1970) concludes that Japanese tend to attach more importance to the frame or organisation situation within which the individual operates, than to the attributes of personal characteristics of the individual. England and Lee (1974) concluded that "In view of this cultural background it is not surprising that more successful Japanese manager, place relatively greater emphasis upon loyalty, and relatively less emphasis upon 'me' than do managers in other countries.

As Aonuma (1981) remarks "The Japanese equivalent of the protestant ethic lies in the concept of sacrificing personal interest for organisational good. Out of this ethic grew a sense of purpose regarding work, a concept of work not as drudgery, but as a kind of sacred duty. Work fulfils this duty and thereby establishes a sense of purpose.

The investigator finally concludes that the soicialisation training in any given culture that emphasises the instrumentality of work roles in satisfying people's culturally determined salient needs is primarily responsible for the development of work involvement.

Involvement and alienation are opposite poles of the same phenomenon. The state of involvement or alienation results from the perceived potentials of the work, job and organisation to frustrate or satisfy individual's salient needs and experiences of outcomes be they intrinsic or extrinsic. The intensity of different intrinsic and extrinsic needs is determined by individuals past experiences with groups of which they were members and with job that they have held. These past experiences vary from country to country and culture to culture. Even in the same culture, job involvement may be very different between managers and unskilled labourers because of the differences in the need saliencies of the two groups to decrease work alienation and improve in quality of working life, culture based value differences should be taken into account.

4. Job Involvement of Intrinsically and Extrinsically Motivated Indian Managers to Each According to His Need

Mishra and Kalro (1981) in the above study have attempted to test the notion that the attitude of job involvement is a function of the degree of satisfaction with one's salient needs be they intrinsic or extrinsic.

Although Lawler and Hall (1970) found intrinsic motivation and job involvement to be factorially independent, they still hold "………other things being equal, more people will become involved in jobs that are lacking these characteristics." Kanungo has however operationally defined job involvement as a generalised cognitive state of psychological identification with work, in so far as work is perceived to be instrumental in satisfying one's salient needs and expectations. Kanungo holds that all behaviour including the behaviour in work situations springs from need states of the individual and is directed towards obtaining outcomes for the satisfaction of salient needs.

In the present investigation out of a sample of 215 Indian managers, data from 33 primarily intrinsically motivated and 43 primarily extrinsically motivated managers were analysed to test the following two hypotheses : (1) The attitude of job involvement will be positively correalated with the satisfaction of salient needs only, and (2) both intrinsically and extrinsically motivated Managers will be equally job involved provided their salient needs are met and more job involved than those whose salient needs are not met. Hypothesis 1 was supported. Due to meagre data only partial support for hypothesis 2 was obtained.

The result of this study support the view that the attitude or job involvement is a function of the level of satisfaction of one's salient needs, be they intrinsic or extrinsic. Job involvement was found to be positively and equally correlated with the satisfaction of salient needs both in IMS and EMS and not significantly correlated with satisfaction of non salient needs. For both groups of managers job involvement was higher for those whose salient needs were met as compared with those whose salient needs were not met.

The author speculates that while involvement in a particular job may be more influenced by the experimental system of the extent to which salient needs are met, involvement with work in general may be more influenced by the congnitive value system representing the employees work ethic and the degree of centrality of work for his identity sense of being. Mishra suggests that further research in Indian context is needed to develop specific measures of these two dimensions of involvement and test explicit hypotheses as to the nature of their causes and consequences.

5. Employee's Job Anxiety as Resultant of Job Involvement

Srivastav and Sinha (1983) conducted a study on employees' job anxiety as a resultant of their level of job involvement. 200 semiskilled employees of 23-44 years age group from the Mechanical section of the Diesel Locomotive Workshop, Varanasi (India) were randomly selected for the above study. TIleir professional experience ranged from 6 to 16 years.

The job involvement scale by Lodhal and Kenjer (1965) was employed on the sample to ascertain employees level of involvement in their job. On the basis of the scores obtained on this scale the employees were divided into three categories *i.e.* high, moderate and low job involvement groups. These three groups were then administered with the job anxiety scale (Srivastava and Sinha, 1974) to assess the extent of employee's anxiety pertaining to various dimensions of job life. This scale measures employee's anxiety regarding the following components of job and its environment : (*a*) Job security and safety, (*b*) recognition and fair evaluation, (*c*) human relations at work and communication, (*d*) reward and punishment, (*e*) self esteem and social status of the job, (*f*) future prospects, and (*g*) capacity to shoulder responsibility, job aptitude and proficiency.

Results indicated that the employee's job involvement plays a significant role in determining their degree of anxiety with regard to all aspects of the job except future prospects. Employees' job involvement was found to correlate positively with job anxiety componants except recognition and future prospects.

The findings therefore confirm the functional relationship between job involvement and job anxiety. It also indicates the job involvement and job anxiety go together which was also found by Bajaj (1978). In this connection Saleh (1971) observed that the job involved subjects manifest more anxiety and uneasiness than the extrinsically oriented subjects. In the light of their findings Srivastava and Sinha (1983) have further viewed that the highly job involved employees who are mentally preoccupied with their job, become over cautious and highly sensitive to every happening of their job life. Such tendencies of these employees make them anxious about various aspects of their job. The investigators held that the highly job involved employees who psychologically identify with their job and organisation and to whom the job becomes as essential part of life, are quite likely to be highly anxious about the steadiness of their job. Kulkarni (1976) also found that highly job involved employees perceived pay, security and autonomy at work as first three important job factors.

6. Work Alienation and the Quality of Work Life

Kanungo (1982) has conducted a study entitled Work Alienation and Quality of Work Life: He suggests that the quality of working life (QWL) is intimately related to the work alienation or work involvement phenomenon. Secondly, he also argues that the QWL model practiced in the western world is not applicable to the developing third world countries. The difference in cultural bias constraints the applicability of the western QWL models in the third world countries. The past socialisation training varies from culture to culture. Workers have a variety of needs and their strength varies from job to job depending upon the socialisation process and cultural background. The value attached to work also varies from culture to culture. In view of these individual differences the alienation and attachment to work varies. The investigator views that "people belonging to different cultures tend to develop different salient needs being influenced by different cultural and group norms. However, the socialisation training in any given culture that emphasises the instrumentality of work roles in satisfying peoples culturally determined salient needs is primarily responsible for the development of work involvement."

The motivational approach to alienation briefly outlined in the present paper suggests an alternative model. According to Kanungo the strategies based on the model may have better cross cultural applicability.

DETERMINANTS OF JOB SATISFACTION

A clearcut analysis of the Western and Indian studies on job satisfaction throws light on some determinants of job satisfaction which may broadly be divided into three main categories.

1. Personal factors.
2. Factors related to job.
3. Factors controlled by the management.

Personal Factors

Sex. The findings of several studies reveal that women in general have more job satisfaction than men. Morse's (1953) study indicates that while the percentage of dissatisfaction is 55 in males it was 35 in the case of females. Such difference may be explained by the fact that females have relatively lower aspiration and expectations than males (Mohanty (1973) and they have less economic burden. Hence they ordinarily become easily satisfied in their jobs compared to their male counterparts. This study is not supported by Hublin and Smith (1964) regarding the effect of sex difference in job satisfaction.

Age. As evident from the findings, of the study conducted by Morse (1953) workers of the higher age group have more job satisfaction than the younger workers. But other studies do suggest that there is very little relationship between age and job satisfaction (Sinha 1973).

Number of Dependants in the Family. It has been proved from the findings of Morse's investigation that there is a negative relationship between the number of dependents and job satisfaction. Thus, as the number of dependents in a family increase job satisfaction decreases and *vice versa*. Most probably, financial difficulty is the major cause of job dissatisfaction in such cases. Sinha (1973) however did not find the effect of family and dependants on job satisfaction. Hence without further research on this problem no definite view can be taken on the relationship between job satisfaction and the number of dependents in the family.

Length of Service. The findings of some investigators suggest that in the preliminary stage of service more job satisfaction is experienced. But when the employee reaches the age of 50-60 years, job satisfaction decreases gradually. After thus age, again tile tendency of rise in job satisfaction is observed. Sinha (1965) did not find significant difference between the job satisfaction of workers and shorter and longer years of service.

According to Hull and Kolstad (1942), tile level of morale usually reaches the maximum after 20 years of service in an organisation.

Intelligence. It is a common assumption that to perform a job satisfactorily intelligence is necessary. Therefore many have hypothesised that there exists a positive relationship between intelligence and job satisfaction. But several investigations have brought quite confusing findings According to Ahbroke, workers having high intelligence have demonstrated dissatisfaction in job. From the findings of Wyatt and Langdon it has been proved that most intelligent women workers in a chocolate factory experienced monotony and boredom very quickly which is an indicator of dissatisfaction in job. However, from the study of Kornhouser and Sharp (1932), no significant relationship is observed between attitude and intelligence. Thus further research is necessary for a generalised conclusion on the relationship between job satisfaction and intelligence.

Level of Aspiration. According to Morse (1953) when the aspiration and performance of the employees do not run parallel there is frustration which leads to dissatisfaction in job. Morse opines that the level of aspiration of the employees determines the degree of satisfaction experienced by them. According to him, the level of satisfaction is a combination of both level of aspiration and the amount of return from the environment. He has advanced the hypotheses that satisfaction basically depends upon what an individual wants from the world and what he gets in return. Satisfaction is reached when these two are in line and job dissatisfaction exists when the return from the environment is much less than the need level of the individual.

Personality. It is a major factor in influencing job satisfaction. But since it is difficult to measure the traits of personality scientifically not much research could be done on the problem. From a study conducted by Kornhauser and Sharp on women employees, it is noticed that out of 25 highly neurotic workers 16 were always dissatisfied in job while only 3 out of 25 normal workers expressed job dissatisfaction.

In another investigation by McMurray, conducted on women employees of a bank, it was noted that because of the presence of a neurotic tendency, they showed some amount of dissatisfaction in job. From other findings it is evident that neurotic tendency is one of the primary causes of job dissatisfaction. According to Fisher and Hanna (1931) "a large part of vocational maladjustment and industrial unrest are secondary to and but a reflection of emotiona adjustment."

It has been previously mentioned that satisfaction or dissatisfaction is a generalised tenden of the personality. There are some who are normally satisfied in their personal, social a professional life while there are others who are dissatisfied in every sphere of life. Thus, becomes a generalised nature of the individual to show satisfaction or dissatisfaction. Sinha (1965) found significant positive relationship between a worker's total adjustment and job satisfaction.

According to Weitz (1952), certain specific traits of the personality are responsible for causing general dissatisfaction. It has been further observed that those who are related by their co-workers as having maximum interpersonal desirability, are usually satisfied in their job. Hence the capacity to adjust with varied circumstances may be one of the causes of job satisfaction. Personality maladjustment, on the contrary, may be responsible for job dissatisfaction. Schaffer (1953) comments "Overall dissatisfaction will vary directly with the extent to which the needs of an individual which can be satisfied in a job are actually satisfied. The stronger the need, the more closely will job satisfaction depend on its fulfilment."

It is an accepted fact that adjustment is the key to satisfaction and happiness in life. The worker who is incapable of adjusting with his coworkers, supervisor, and finally with the management, has to face a lot of difficulties on the job. This naturally culminates in general feeling of dissatisfaction in job.

Fulfilment of Personal Needs. More's and Schaffer's research (1953) leads one to conclude that job satisfaction depends upon the fulfilment of personal needs. Schaffer found that a high correlation existed between the person's strongest needs and overall satisfaction. Among the strongest needs, creativity and challenge, mastery and achievement are important ones.

Education. A number of contradictory findings have been obtained regarding the relationship between educational levels and job satisfaction. The findings of Morse's study indicate that employees who could not pass middle school examinations had greater job satisfaction than more educated employees. But the findings of other studies have not supported this view. Hence further research is necessary to throw light on this determinant of job satisfaction.

Factors Related to Job

The results of several studies point out that the level of job satisfaction is determined to a great extent by variables related to the job itself. Dissatisfaction in a job caused by such factors has no relationship whatsoever with the individual factors discussed earlier.

Some of the factors of job satisfaction related to the job itself are given as follows :

Chance and Initiative to Establish Oneself in Job. From the research of Form (1946) it is evident that workers who get a chance to establish themselves in their vocation expressed less dissatisfaction in job than those who could not get such a chance. It has also been noticed that vocations having less social prestige and status bring dissatisfaction. Job satisfaction can be increased by increasing the importance and status of the job.

Nature of Job. The findings of Morse's study suggest that rotating jobs and jobs giving the scope for variety and change gave many workers more satisfaction than routine and mechanical jobs. According to the results to Hoppock's (1935) study there may be a 100 per cent difference in job satisfaction because of the difference in the nature and variety of work.

Skill of Work. Fairchild (1930) opines that skilled jobs bring a strong feeling of satisfaction in the worker. The nature of work, the status of the job and responsibility, etc., are influenced by the skill of the job. According to Fairchild, "Where skill exists to a considerable degree, it tends to become the first source of satisfaction to the workman". Satisfaction in conditions of work or in wages becomes predominant only where satisfaction in skill has materially decreased.

Size and Location of the Factory. It has been viewed that small organisations and factories increase the level of morale of the workers as the hope for promotion facility based on impartiality, justice and competency is better there. This has been suggested by the findings of Se..s and Riback. According to them opportunity for better interpersonal relationship is available in small factories. The scope for recognition, feeling of security and sense of cooperation etc. also increase in small plants.

Similarly, keeping other factors constant, factories situated in small towns give more satisfaction to 'the workers as they feel more secure and satisfied in small towns. Also, there is no difficulty in adjustment. On the contrary, in big cities the worker may feel neglected and lost.

However, no generalised statement can be made on this point without further research.

Factors Controlled by the Management

There are certain psychological determinants of job satisfaction which 'Can be improved by the management to increase the level of job satisfaction of industrial employees. Some of these important determinants are discussed below.

Salary. Research findings of Watson (1939), Seidman and Watson (1940), Mohanty (1981) have thrown light on the importance of salary as a determinant of job satisfaction. From these findings it is implied that salary is not an important cause of job satisfaction. In this connection Watson writes "Without in anyway denying the need of many workers for higher wages, it may be recognised that sometimes workers, vaguely dissatisfied with the way things are going, know no other way of meeting the situation. They ask for more pay or shorter hours, and perhaps they should have these, but if these demands are attained the relief would be only temporary. T underlying cause of dissatisfaction may be not in the pay envelope or the time clock, but in the work itself." It is in fact not the employees, but the employer and the management who consider pay to be the important cause of job satisfaction. This is definitely due to the gap in communication between the workers and the management. Of course the role of pay in job satisfaction cannot be denied, because besides helping one to live and exist money gives social status, prestige and a sense of security. Nevertheless, its role has been over emphasised by the management.

In Herzberg, Mauser, Peterson and Cap well's (1957) investigations, wages get the sixth ranking in a twelve point scale. According to the reports of Kornhauser's study (1940) the higher income group indicated greater personal satisfaction. According to this study, if the economic range is great, salary may become a significant factor but that with any occupational group or within a limited range it is a minor factor. Sinha (1965) found that the higher and the lower income groups tended to be satisfied and the middle group was least satisfied. The lower income group had the highest job satisfaction score. But critical ratios of difference were not significant for any of the comparisons. These investigations therefore do suggest that wages are not the most important determinants of job satisfaction as is usually thought.

Security. The findings of several researches indicate that security contributes highly to job satisfaction. Each and every employee in the organisation or industry wants himself to be fully secure in his job. Insecure jobs doubtless bring a definite feeling of dissatisfaction in work.

Security may be social, economical and psychological. A worker who gets security in all these areas gets maximum satisfaction from his job. According to Knutson (1952), a feeling of security or insecurity may tend to become generalised throughout the personality structure or they may be projected from one area of striving into others......... He further writes, "A person's feeling of security or insecurity within any area of striving involves his own subjective evaluation of his success, satisfaction and surety or confidence with respect to the carrying out of his purpose in past and present situations and group relationships, also his expectations, hopes, fears or uncertainties with respect to the carrying out of his purposes and aspiration, in future situations and group relationships. Feeling of security within any functional area vary on a continuum so that security, status within any area of striving or within any situation may be considered a matter of degree rather than a matter of absolute."

It has been observed that people having better education, a higher level of aspiration and self-confidence are not usually satisfied with their present jobs and hence are always in search for better jobs. So the importance of security in job decreases for them. The feeling of security or insecurity gradually becomes generalised and becomes a permanent trait of their personality.

Vocational Guidance. Lack of proper vocational guidance may lead to job dissatisfaction. A person who is not suitable for a job, in terms of his capabilities, aptitudes and interests, is not expected to be satisfied with his job. It is a fact that people who do not possess the necessary abilities and aptitude for a job, will not like to continue in such a job. Besides giving dissatisfaction in job, many problems arise in almost all organisations when vocational guidance is not given. But proper guidance about the selection of a vocation in accordance with the ability and interest of the person, gives greater satisfaction in job. Thus, a suitable worker for a work and suitable work for a worker are necessary contributors of job satisfaction.

Scope of Promotion. Lack of facility for promotion got the fifth position as a determinant f job dissatisfaction in a list of 9 factors in the study conducted by Watson and Seidman (1941). Usually when there is sufficient scope for promotion workers get job satisfaction. Blum (1959) has mentioned that for skilled workers, the scope for promotion plays a greater role in job satisfaction than unskilled workers. In another study it was noticed that promotion is more important for younger than older workers. When the management does not care to give promotion to the capable and efficient workers there is an increased feeling of frustration. The attitude becomes unfavourable towards the management which leads to job dissatisfaction.

Hence scope for promotion should be provided by every organisation to the deserving, qualified and competent employees, so as to elevate the feeling of satisfaction in the job.

Working Conditions. The importance of working conditions and factory environment cannot be ruled out totally in giving job satisfaction, though it may have a secondary role to play. Suitable working conditions improve the attitude and morale of the worker and contribute to the feeling of satisfaction in work. Watson and Seidman (1941) found that uncongenial working condition got third position in a list of nine causes of job dissatisfaction. Wherry (1954), Dabas (1958) and Harrison (1961) have found in their studies that attitude towards working conditions is one of the underlying causes of job satisfaction.

Relationship with Co-workers. Every worker genuinely wants to be accepted by his co-workers and desires congenial interpersonal relationship with them. Better personal and social relationships in the working group have always been a contributing factor towards the maintenance of high morale and a favourable attitude. If one has more friends and less foes in the working group, he is accepted by the group and has the sense of belonging, he has a better feeling of job satisfaction.

Responsibility. From the findings of a study Watson (1939) has found that the morale of the concerned workers increase when the jobs require responsibility. Hartman and Newcomb (1939) have found that unemployed people appreciated jobs with more responsibility. But since no specific study has been conducted on the relationship between responsibility and job satisfaction no generalised conclusions can be made on this point.

Supervision. The Hawthorne studies have already emphasised the role of the supervisor and successful supervision in determining the attitude, morale and level of job satisfaction of workers. In Herzberg, Mausner, Peterson and Capwell's (1957) investigations, supervision has got the eighth ranking next to wages.

Roethlisberger and Dickson have also found that with the change in supervisor, the attitude of workers in an organisation changed. When the attitude is favourable towards the methods of supervision and the dealings of the supervisor, sincerity and loyalty to the job also increase. Watson (1939) has emphasised the role of the supervisor while conducting a study on morale. Kornhouser and Sharp (1932) have obtained positive correlation between successful supervisors and job satisfaction. From the results of these studies the importance of supervisors in job satisfaction is evident.

Besides these contributors, researches on job satisfaction also point out the contributions of loyalty, facility for adjustment, the relative status of the worker in the social and economic group with which he indentifies himself, scope for creativity and achievement and social contact, interest in job etc. towards job satisfaction.

Emphasising the role of loyalty in job satisfaction, Blum and Naylor have commented that the feeling that the worker has for his firm or boss or both contributes to job satisfaction. Loyalty is a factor which leads people to sacrifice their own needs and purposes. It is the factor that prompts service beyond the line of study in relation to job requirements.

MEASUREMENT OF JOB SATISFACTION

An overall analysis of the problem of job satisfaction leads one to conclude that job satisfaction is a generalised attitude in three areas such as specific job factors, individual adjustment and group relationships. It is indeed a highly complex topic of industrial psychology and to measure job satisfaction the techniques of attitude measurement can be applied. Some have tired to measure job satisfaction through production, hyposthesising a positive relation between job satisfaction and production. But this assumption cannot be always true. Production cannot is all cases be the index of job satisfaction. Kahn (1960) in his project. "Job Satisfaction and Productivity" asserts that productivity and job satisfaction do not necessarily go together. Perhaps there are certain kinds of circumstances where job satisfaction is related to work performance but in other kinds of circumstances this is not the case. By and large, job satisfaction is a generlised character of the personality of the worker and may or may not be related to production.

In order to measure job satisfaction the general level of satisfaction of the worker in his day to day life should be measured first. As already pointed out, a person who is satisfied in other situations of life is usually satisfied with his job also.

In order to study job satisfaction scientifically and determine the factors influencing it, it is absolutely essential to first determine the general indices of job satisfaction.

The job satisfaction of a person can be measured by considering work factors or factors related to work and secondly by analysing the factors which give satisfaction in life as a whole.

CONCLUSION

Various wage incentive plans like pay, bonus, profit sharing plans, piece rate method of payment, multiple piece rate system etc. allow one to have a better standard of living and increased social status whereby the feeling of satisfaction may be augmented.

The results of studies conducted by Watson, Watson and Seidman further indicate that recognition, friendly associations, work fitted to vocational level and a variety of duties have more important roles to play in job satisfaction than the salary itself.

TABLE 16.2

Reasons	*Watson, Seidman and Watson's study*		
	Men	*Women*	*Young men*
Congenial work conditions and social status	21 per cent	38 per cent	28 per cent
Responsibility, initiative prestige	27	23	19
In line with vocational aspirations	15	13	29
Variety	15	12	12
Salary	13	6	4
Shorter hours	3	6	4

Further studies conducted on the same problem from a slightly different angle by Watson and Seidman (1941) and Seidman (1943) indicate that the nature of the work, congeniality of working conditions and social contacts are more conducive to work satisfaction than wages and working hours.

Thus, for the job satisfaction of industrial workers all these factors as well those discussed earlier should be taken into consideration.

THEORIES OF JOB SATISFACTION

To explain the causes of job satisfaction some theories have been advanced. These theories have attempted to explain their overall influence on the worker's behaviour and performance in general.

Maslow's Theory (1943)

According to Maslow's theory human needs can be classified into 5 different groups such as : (1) Physiological needs, (2) Safety needs, (3) Love needs, (4) Esteem needs, and (5) Self actualisation needs. Thus, it proceeds from very primary needs such as physiological and safety needs to a group of higher social needs like love needs, esteem needs and self-actualisation needs. In other words these five needs according to Maslow form a "hierarchy of needs" structure.

Referring to the influence of Malsow's 'hierarchy of needs' structure on job satisfaction, Blum and Naylor have pointed out" Jobs which are able to satisfy more of the Malsow needs would be jobs which would result in greater satisfaction on the part of the employee."

Vroom's Theory (1964)

Vroom has viewed that the strength of the force on the worker to remain on his job is the increasing function of the valence of his job. According to Vroom the attractiveness of a job depends upon this valence. Vroom's theory suggests that job satisfaction should be negatively correlated to absenteeism and employee turnover. This has been supported by several experimental findings. However, the positive relationship between job satisfaction and production which may follow from this has not been proved in many cases.

Stogdill's Theory (1959)

Several investigations on the relationship between job satisfaction and job performance indicate no definite relationship between the two. In other words, jobs satisfaction need not necessarily be the cause of job performance. Stogdill (1959) on tbe basis of bis researcbes bolds the view that the output of organisations are group integration, production and morale. When individual expectations are fulfilled, cohesivenesss and integration of the group occurs, but satisfaction may not necessarily be related to production. Actually it is production which depends upon the group structure. Production and morale can only be a function of job satisfaction when the conditions leading to high morale and production are more or less identical with those variables which lead to the fulfilment of worker expectations.

Thus Stogdill has made an attempt to prove that the common notion that production is a necessary outcome of job satisfaction is not always true. This view of Stogdill has been supported by the findings of Mohanty (1981). Production and job satisfaction mayor may not go together.

Herzberg's Theory

Herzberg, Mausner and Snyderman (1959) made a study to find out the cause of job satisfaction and dissatisfaction of engineers and accountants. Feelings of satisfaction or dissatisfaction about the job were collected from these subjects by the individual interview technique. They then tried to find out factors mentioned along with job satisfaction and the factors mentioned along with job dissatisfaction. They also made a study to find out if the factors described under the feeling of satisfaction and dissatisfaction were different. The findings suggested that factors related to high satisfaction (satisfiers) were different from varibles or conditions which were associated with circumstances leading to low satisfaction (dissatisfiers). Under high satisfaction, achievement, recognition, responsibility and advancement etc. were pointed out. These are called satisfiers which are related to the content of the work. Under dissatisfaction were factors dealing with supervision, salary, the company policy and working environment. These items are named as 'context factors' as they relate to the situation in which a person performs his work.

Thus, the investigators classified the work variable into two main categories known as satisfiers and dissatisfiers. Satisfiers are other wise known as motivators and are usually job content factors which lead to job satisfaction. Dissatisfiers are called job context or situational or hygiene factor, which are usually associated with job dissatisfaction.

The satisfiers do not dissatisfy and the dissatisfiers do not satisfy. These two general classes of variables are known as Herzberg's two factor theory. Herzberg held the view that the satisfiers give job satisfaction and the dissatisfies give job dissatisfaction. The need for self-actualisation is presented in every individual and whenever this need is fulfilled, the individual gets satisfaction in his job. For this, his work is of the highest significance to him because it helps him to fulfil the aspiration arid ambition of his life and finally it brings fulfilment of the self.

Criticism

According to Blum and Naylor (1968), "The major objection is that when a person is asked to tell about something good, he is apt to attribute the causes of these to his own accomplishments and achievements (content items); we all like to satisfy our need for esteem. Similarly, when someone is asked to tell about an unpleasant or dissatisfying work experience, he is more apt to blame others for this (context items) than he is to blame himself Many attribute Herzberg's findings to this simple tendency on the part of people."

Studies conducted to test the validity of Herzberg's two factor theory have brought contradictory results.

Myers (1964) Schwatz, Jenusaitis and Stark (1963), Friedlander and Walton (1964) and Lodah1 (1964) have more or less supported the two factor theory of Herzberg. In a study conducted on a manufacturing company Myers (1964) noted that satisfaction was related to intrinsic work factor and dissatisfaction to extrinsic factors. But in all these studies no relationship between attitude and performance was observed.

A further study by Friedlander (1964) partly supported the two factor theory.

On the other extreme Dunnette (1963), Ewen (1964), Friedlander (1963), Kornhauser (1965) and Wernimont (1964) have got evidences which do not support Herzberg's theory.

Dunnette is perhaps the most severe critic of the two factor theory. Criticising this theory, Dunnette (1965) remarks "………the two factor notion of job satisfaction is an oversimplified representation of the motivational milieu of the world of work."

METHODS USED TO IMPROVE JOB SATISFACTION

As the previous discussion indicates, a number of factors contribute to the development of job satisfaction of the workers in industrial organisations.

It is already an established fact that because of job satisfaction the level of morale improves, attitude towards management as a whole becomes favourable and a healthy and congenial atmosphere prevails in the company. There is no sign of conflict and unrest. The rate of absenteeism and labour turnover goes down. Above all, production in most cases improves. Thus, keeping these scientifically established facts in view, every management and organisation should take active steps to improve the level of the job satisfaction of its employees.

By improving the factors which contribute to it, job satisfaction can be improved. These factors already discussed earlier are : (1) Individual variables, (2) Factors related to job, and (3) Factors controlled by the management.

Though it may not be possible on the part of the management to improve the personality variables of the workers influencing job satisfaction the management should create proper atmosphere and opportunity for the fulfilment of the personality factors conducive to job satisfaction. Also, by following proper and judicious selection procedures, it can be ascertained whether a particular person will get satisfaction in the job for which he is selected.

As far as improving the second factor is concerned, the management should provide the opportunity for suitable working space, facilities to achieve one's status and prestige in job etc.

The factors of job satisfaction controlled by the management can be improved, by the organisation without any difficulty. Since security is the most urgent factor influencing job satisfaction, the management has to take special steps to improve the feeling of security of the workers on the job. A judicious promotion policy should also be followed by the company. Promotion should not be based on bias, prejudice and partiality. It should be based purely on competency, ability and efficiency.

Besides, by improving the Labour-Management relation and bridging the gap in communication between the employee and the employer job satisfaction can be increased.

However, before taking steps to improve the job satisfaction of the workers, the management has to measure their level of job satisfaction, morale and nature of attitude. If the management is convinced that the percentage of dissatisfaction is significant, steps should be taken to improve it by improving the factors contributing to job satisfaction.

QUESTIONS

1. What is meant by job satisfaction ? How does it differ from attitude and morale ?
2. Discuss the main characteristics of job satisfaction and point out the implications of studying job satisfaction of industrial employees.
3. Make a brief review of the recent studies conducted on job satisfaction. Justify the importance of job satisfaction research for improving the efficiency of the workers.
4. Is production related to job satisfaction ? Justify your answer with experimental findings.
5. Compare the factors contributing to the job satisfaction of Indian and Western employees on the basis of experimental findings.
6. Discuss the relative importance of the factors influencing job satisfaction.
7. How can job satisfaction be measured ? Discuss the steps taken by the management to improve job satisfaction.
8. Give a brief outline of the recent studies conducted on job satisfaction in industrial organisations.

REFERENCES

Ash, Philip. Job satisfaction difference among women of different ethnic groups, *Jn. of Vocational Behr.*, 1972, (October).

Blood, Milton R. Work values and job satisfaction, *Jn. of Applied Psy.*, 1969, 53 (6), pp. 456-459.

Blum, M.L. and Naylor, J.C. *Industrial Psychology*: *Its Theoretical and Social Foundations*, Harper and Row Publishers.

Blum, Peter. Cultural and situational determinants of job satisfaction among managers in South Africa: A Research note, *Jn. of Management Studies*, 1973, Vol. 10 (2), pp. 133-140.

Carrel, Michael and Elbert Norbert F. Some personal and organisational determinants of job satisfaction of postal clerks, *Academy of Management Journal*, 1974 (June), Vol. 17 (2), pp. 368-372.

Dunnette, Campbell and Hokel. Factors contribution to job satisfaction and job dissatisfaction in six occupation groups, *Organisational Behaviour and Human Performance*, 1967, 2, pp. 143-174.

Fisher, V.E. and Hanna, J.V. *The Dissatisfied Worker*, Macmilan, New York, 1931.

Fossum, John A. Urban and rural differences in job satisfaction, *Industrial and Labour Relations Review*, 1974, Vol. 27 (3), pp. 465-409.

Ganguli, H.C. *Industrial Production and Motivation-A Psychological Analysis*, Bomaby, Asia Publishing House, 1961.

Gilmer, V.B.H. *Industrial and Organisational Psychology*, Kousaka Publications, 1971.

Herzberg, F.B., Mausner, Peterson R.O. and Capwell, D.F. Job attitudes, review of research and opinion. *Psychol. Service of Pittsburgh*, 1957.

Hoppock, R. *Job Satisfaction*, Harper and Row, New York, 1935.

Hoppock, R.A. Twenty-seven years follow up on job satisfaction of employed adults, *Personnel Guidance Journal,* 1960, 38, pp. 489-498.

I.C.S.S.R. New Delhi, *Survey of Research in Psychology*, Popular Parkashan, Bombay, 1971.

Kunungo, R. Work alientation and quality of work life; A cross cultural perspective, *Indian Psychologist*, April 1982, Vol. 1, No.1.

Kunungo, R. Misra, S. and Dayal, I. Relationship of job involvement to perceived importance and satisfaction of employee needs, *Int. Rev. App. Psychol.* (1975), Vol. 24, No. 1.

Katz, D. and Hyman, H. Morale industry, in T. Newcomb and E. Hartley (eds.), *Readings in Social Psychology,* New York, Holt, 1947.

Kahn, R.L. Productivity and job satisfaction, *Personnel Psychology*, 1960, 13, pp. 272-287.

Maier, N.R.F. *Industrial Psychology*. Oxford and IBH Publishing Co., New Delhi, 1970.

Misra, S., Kanungo, R., Rosenstiel, L. Kunungo and Stuhler, E. The motivational Formulation of Job and Work Involvement : A Cross National Study, Human Relations, volume 38, No. 6, 1985.

Mohanty, Girishbala. Level of aspiration as a functioin of sex, S.E.S. and class performance, Ph.D. thesis, Utkal Univ., 1973.

Mohanty, Girishbala. A comparative study of job satisfaction variables of a group of female L.D. assistants and female college teachers of Orissa, 1981

Morse, N.C. *Satisfaction in the White Collar Job*, University of Michigan Press, Ann Arbor, 1953.

Prvbil, Lawrence D. Job satisfaction in relation to job performance and occupational level, *Personnel Journal* (1973), Vol. 52 (2), pp. 94-100.

Misra, S. Job involvement and alienation progress, issues and prospects, *Indian Jn. of Industrial Relations*, Vol. 14, No. 4. 1979.

Misra, S. and Kalro, A Job involvement of intrinsically and Extrinsically motivated Indian managers, *Human Relations*, Vol. 34, No. 5, 1981.

Sarveswar, Rao, G.V. and Ganapathi Rao, V. A study of factors contributing to satisfaction and importance of industrial personnel. A test of the two factor theory, *Indian Jn. of Industrial Relations*, 1973 (October), Vol. 9 (2), pp. 233-262.

Sarveswar Rao, G.V. and Ganguli, T. A study of perceived need satisfaction and importance of highly skilled and skilled personnel, *Indian Jn. of Industrial Relations*, 1971 (January), Vol. 63, pp. 277, 287.

Sarveswar Rao, G.V. Determinants of job satisfaction of Indian engineers, A test of two factor theory, *Indian Jn. of Industrial Relations*, 1973, April, Vol. 8 (4), pp. 605-19.

Stagner, R. Flebbe, D.R. and Wood, E.V. Working on the rail road. Study of job satisfaction, *Personnel Psychol.* 5, 1952, pp. 243~306.

Schneider, Benjamin and Snyder, Robert A. Some relationship between job satisfaction and organisational climate, *Jn. of Applied Psychology*, 1975, Vol. 60, No. 3.

Spillance Robert. Intrinsic and extrinsic job satisfaction and labour turnover. A questionnaire study of Australian managers, *Occupational Psy.*, 1973, Vol. 47 (1-3), pp. 71-74.

Sinha, D. *Studies in Industrial Psychology*, Sri Ram Mehra and Co., Publishers, Agra, 1973.

Srivastava, A.K. and Sinha, M.M. Employee's Job anxiety as a resultant of their level of job involvement. *Indian Psychologist,* June 1983, Vol. 2, No. 1.

Stogdill, R.M. *Individual behaviour and Group Achievement,* Oxfort Fair Lawn, N.J., 1959.

Tiffin J. and McCormick, E.J. *Industrial Psychology*, 5th ed., Prentice-Hall of India Private Limited, New Delhi, 1971.

Vroom, V.H. *Work and Motivation*, Wiley, New York, 1964.

Vroom, V.H. Organisational choice. A study of pre and post decision processes, *Org. Beh. and Human Performance,* 1966, pp. 212-225.

Watson, G. Work Satisfaction, in G.W. Hartman and J. New-combleds, *Industrial Conflict*, Corden Co., New York, 1939.

Watson, G. and Seidman, M. Dissatisfaction in work, *Jn. of Soc. Psychology*, 1941, 13, 183-186.

Weitz, J. A neglected concept in the study of job satisfaction, *Personnel Psychology*, 1952, 5, 201-205.

Williamson, T.R and Karras, Edward J. Variables among female clerical workers, *Jn. of Applied Psychology*, 1970, 54 (4), pp. 343-346.

Wickert, F.R. Turnover and employees, feeling of ego involvement in the day to day operations of a company, *Personnel Psychology*, 1951, 4, pp. 185-197.

17
Industrial Conflict

INTRODUCTION

Frustration and conflict are inevitable aspects of human life. Ottorank says that birth is the greatest frustration in human life. The underlying psychological implication of this view is that the frustration of the human life starts on the delivery table from the moment of birth.

Conflict is related to frustration and it is undoubtedly an undesirable aspect of human life. The stresses and strains of life, the varied problems one has to face during ones life time on and off the job and the inability to choose between two equally attractive goals lead to conflict. The tragedy is that in spite of everything, conflicts arise and can never be totally avoided.

Conflict has a number of undesirable effects upon the human personality. Conflict leads to tension, unnecessary wastage of energy leading to early onset of fatigue, anxiety, depression and finally, inefficiency in work. Due to conflict an employee is not able to maintain a proper balance in the psychological plane. Conflicts have also a few advantages.

Referring to the desirable aspects of conflict, Tiffin and McCormick (1971) state that "History and experience lead one to the conclusion, however, that conflict has undoubtedly brought about improvement in working conditions for employees". But they also hold that when conflict goes out of hand its destructive effect is evident. It has been suggested that good conflicts help creative and useful work. The management should therefore try to avoid tad conflict which the employees face on and off the job.

TYPES OF INDUSTRIAL CONFLICT

The industrial organisation is such that it carries with it built-in sources of strong and powerful conflict between different individuals and groups. Industrial conflict in general may be of two types.

Individuals may differ in their opinions about organisational policies or procedures.

Individuals may be mutually opposed to each other in terms of personality differences. Organisational units having different types of functions such as production, administration, quality control, sales, maintenance, financial control, and distribution may find themselves in conflict with each other due to their respective functions. However, probably the most powerful conflict arises from differences between management and employee groups regarding such matters as wage, factory environment, hours of work, overtime, shift duties, behaviour of the supervisors and other related matters.

CAUSES OF INDUSTRIAL CONFLICT

Conflict arises due to a difference of opinion, between two parties, the employee and the employer, the worker and the management.

Whatever may be the specific nature of conflict it arises primarily from motivational factors or simultaneous arousal of opposing impulses. Stagner expresses this view when he mentions that the phenomenon of industrial conflict (and its industrial cooperation) grows out of the needs of individual human beings. Stagner further says that motivation is distinctly an individual phenomenon, and there is no group mind. Groups cannot feel, see, desire, fear and hate any object. Individuals however can be influenced by group pressures, group influences and their motivation can thus be changed in group situations. These changes are generally in the direction of conformity to the group norms. A group of individuals with acceptable and meaningful common motivation can of course be in conflict with, say, another group having opposite or contradictory goals. For instance, workers demanding promotions on the basis of seniority may have conflicts, with workers who demand promotion on the basis of merit and qualification.

Related to motivation, perception also plays a role in the development of conflict. As held by Tiffin and McCormick, "human behaviour is predicted more on the perceptions of the people than on the basis of objective facts. The perception of people more often than not is distorted, the distortion generally being in the direction of conformity with one's own frame of reference". Selective perception is related to this phenomenon and refers to the tendency towards perceiving only those aspects of a situation that are compatible with one's frame of reference. Thus, if an employee group, interprets a supervisor's suspension or dismissal of a fellow employee as an act for disintegrating the group unity and damaging its morale, the members of the group tend to react as though these were the supervisor's motives even though this might not be the case. Therefore, it would be quite erroneous to say that for industrial conflict either the management alone or the worker alone is solely responsible.

Demand of the Worker

The needs of a person are diverse and unlimited. The worker as well as the manager of a factory has got a need though these needs differ from person to person. The needs may be for food, shelter, sex, power, prestige, security, recognition, dominance and social approval and self-actualisation etc. When the worker finds that the boss or the immediate supervisor is satisfying his own needs in most possible ways while he (the worker) is not able to satisfy most of his basic needs, dispute and conflict arise.

Therefore, the job of the management is to satisfy the needs of the workers as far as it is possible and practicable through his job and the working environment. Those tensions aroused by the job situation should be specifically satisfied in the job situation itself.

As previously indicated, industrial conflict may arise either caused by technology or by unsuitable interpersonal relationships in job or by both.

Many of the important needs of the worker such as the need for self-expression and self-actualisation, the need for power and creation may not be satisfied when the machine does all the work and man becomes only a puppet in the hand of machine.

According to Merton, "division of labour and mechanical work etc., are some aspects which block the need of the employee." When a worker who has acquired a lot of skill through much difficulty suddenly finds the machine doing all his work, he is faced with a great problem, a possible dilemma. He also develops an inferiority complex, due to the inability to put his skills into practice.

Interpersonal Relations and Disputes

The relationship between the worker and the management is not direct. Thus an order or news passes through many sources. Much of it is coloured and fabricated so that it creates misunderstanding between the two parties. Had the source been direct there would have been less chances of misunderstanding and disputes would not have been so much as they are. Without looking to the workers' needs and demands, without giving a chance to the workers to express their difficulties before the management and without giving them a patient hearing, the authority's main principle seems to be to get more production. Lack of decent human treatment and disregard of feelings and sentiments leads to a gap in interpersonal relationships. In this connection H.J. Ruttenberg says : "I live in a district where the workers live, and spend all my time with them and they are emotionally dissatisfied ... because of having to respond to technical changes which they do not originate, and in contrast to workers who increase production when they are consulted on technical changes .... One of the most fundamental impulses in a man, is self expression. If he is denied that in determining his wages, he feels much dissatisfied. If he is permited expression in the production set up, then he feels that he has made a contribution to the whole".

Conflicts and Disputes Caused by Frustration

In this complicated society of today where the needs, demands, and luxuries are varied, many of such needs and demands are not satisfied. This ultimately leads to frustration. This frustration is again transformed to the job indirectly, the outcome of which is tension, conflict and all kinds of disputes. both external and internal. Mohanty and Mishra (1980) conducted a preliminary study on the frustration of skilled and semiskilled industrial employees working in two well-established plants in Orissa.

The study was conducted on 250 employees of Kalinga Tubes Limited and 150 employees of the Orissa Textile Mills Limited, Chowdwar. All the workers were male, belonged to the lower socio-economic status getting emolument of Rs. 250-500 per month and were within the age group of 25-35 years.

The test to measure the level of frustration was administered on the sample in the factory premises. On the basis of the scores obtained; the respondents were classified into saturated and highly frustrated, average and least frustrated groups. The results indicated that out of 250 workers of the Kalinga Tubes Limited 68 belonged to the highly frustrated group and 43 to the least frustrated group. It is indeed surprising to note that no employee belonged to the clean group.

Similarly, out of the 150 workers of the Orissa Textile Mills Limited 12 belonged to the highly frustrated group and 37 to the least frustrated group. From the 37 least frustrated employees, 20 belonged to the clean group.

A comparison of the findings suggests that while in the Kalinga Tubes Limited, not a single case of the sample belonged to the clean group, in the Orissa Textile Mills Limited 20 of the 37 least frustrated employees belonged to the clean group. This suggests that the level of frustration is relatively less among the low socio-economic status employees of the Orissa Textile Mills Limited, in comparison to the Kalinga Tubes Limited. Therefore these findings need careful attention of the managements of both the plants. The management of the Kalinga Tubes Limited especially should be more concerned to reduce the level of frustration of the low paid workers.

After conducting special interviews with 10 highly frustrated workers selected at random from the sample and making careful analysis of the conditions of the frustrated workers, the following measures have been suggested by the investigators to reduce the level of frustration of the employees.

1. Revision of pay structure.
2. Suitable accommodation, transport and recreation facilities.
3. Revision is promotion policy.
4. Security in job.
5. Facilities for advancement and promotion.
6. Good employee-employer relationship.
7. Personal attention given to social and personal problems of individual workers.
8. Understanding, sympathy and cooperation.
9. Psychological counselling for highly frustrated workers.

It is also viewed that a wage rate should be psychologically adequate to prevent frustration and conflict. By psychologically adequate is meant the varying of wage rate according to the varied rates of the market and the varied needs of the individual.

The following underlying causes of dissatisfaction, conflict and dispute of an individual have been found out from various studies by French, Kornhauser and Marrow (1946).

They are :

(*a*) Factors in the Individual. Ability, age, health, temperament, desires and expectations, neurotic tendencies and unconscious conflicts.

(*b*) Factors in Life away from work. Home conditions, recreation, Consumer problems, labour union activities, social, economic and political conditions.

(*c*) Factors in Employment Relations. Wages or earings, steadiness, of employment, transfer, lay-off and hiring procedure, supervision, training, conditions of work social relationship on the job, recognition of merit, understanding and respect by the employer.

Factors responsible for dissatisfaction on the job are not only to be considered for reduction of conflict and disputes. As pointed out by Watson (1930), a person's dissatisfaction refers to both dissatisfaction inside the job and outside the job. Some dissatisfaction studies have been done by Hull and Kolstad (1942) from which they drew some important conclusions.

According to them, what is important is the psychological satisfaction that the worker gets from the job like recognition and getting respect for his personality.

Secondly, the attitude and morale of the worker is also determined by the supervision he gets from the foreman, manager and other higher officers coming in direct contact with the work.

In 1946, the British Institute of Public Opinion asked this question to the British people: "Apart form wages and security, what do you need most in a job for making you feel contented at work" ? Forty per cent of the answers came as "cooperation between the employee and management, appreciation of the employer, etc".

Keeping these facts in view, the conclusion that can be drawn in that many tensions and disputes are created by in plant causes, either directly or indirectly. Many needs and demands are frustrated in thus process.

According to Kornhauser (1965), conditions of work are generally more frustrating for the worker than for the management, and frustration increases when one is in a lower status in a job.

Thus, when most of the important needs of a person are dissatisfied, reactions to such frustrations occur. Some of these reactions are constructive and others are destructive. When there is a barrier between the worker and his goal and if the individual tries to meet the barrier intelligently without using regression and aggression, it becomes a healthy reaction to frustration. Compensation, substitution and adjustment etc., are also some of the more successful reactions to frustration on the job.

The reactions to frustration may be unsuccessful in the case of workers who have not been able to adjust successfully from the very beginning, and are greater sufferers of disputes and conflicts. Labour unions may be one of the many sources to get substituted satisfaction for one's frustrated desires, since the labour union to some extent, can suitably satisfy one's social and psychological needs.

Labour unions provide the individual worker with a sense of satisfaction an opportunity to express himself with speed and action and with much more freedom from fear of punishment on the job. It also provides an opportunity to the worker to achieve positions of leadership and authority, opportunities that are denied to him in the job. The worker gets a chance to take part in the various discussions. If a worker becomes a labour leader, he has got a better chance for promotion and can even become a member of the Assembly or Parliament. He may also earn a better position in society.

Though much of the tensions and disputes are reduced by the labour unions, when the labour union becomes very strong, 'in groups' and 'out groups' may be formed. This leads to further industrial conflicts. Industrial disputes may increase because of more strikes organised by lobour unions. Illogical aggressions against the management are very often created by the labour unions. Strike is one of the familiar patterns of aggression expressed by the worker on the management.

Conflicts and disputes would never have occurred in industry if the management has checked the needs and demands of the workers.

Personal frustration can also be reflected in the job even if the job gives full satisfaction to the workers. But industrial disputes may also be created without personal frustrations. For example, many workers join a strike or turnover only because they are forced to do so and without having any voluntary wish to join it. Some of the workers may indulge in industrial disputes because of threat of punishment, social pressure or because of a mere desire to adjust with the circumstances.

By and large, it can be opined that an industrial dispute may be a combined result of personal frustration, threats and dissatisfaction, or may be due to any of these specific factors mentioned.

Anxieties and uncertainties caused out of certain political situations, unpredictable markets and government regulations, dangerous and insecure future etc., may create disputes and tensions in the minds of the workers working in industry.

REDUCTION OF INDUSTRIAL CONFLICT

Industrial conflict of some type is inevitable but since its nature and intensity are to some degree the function of the situation, it can be reduced. Situational variables, no doubt influence conflict, so it is possible to modify the situation which can reduce conflict. Certain positive actions and programmes can be undertaken to function in the direction of conflict reduction.

According to Fellet, the only satisfactory method of dealing with a conflict is integration. The word integration here is used in the sense of readjustment of the individual. For this, an analysis of the whole situation is required. Readjustment and understanding must be made in accordance with the needs, demands and necessities of the workers.

Regarding the settlement of disputes, Fellet says that if we want settlement which means progress, greater success for business, we should try to include the values of both the employees and the employers. He further says that "our outlook is narrowed, our chances or success are largely diminished, when our thinking is constrained within the limits of an either/or situation. We shall never allow ourselves to be bullied by an either/or. Any human association can be effective and most fruitful when employers and employees are willing to sit down together, to try to solve their problems rather than to bargain on the basis of who possesses the greater economic power of the moment". In fact, mutual discussion and flexible attitude can solve many day-to-day labour management disputes.

Integration is a complex problem in the industrial organisations. It is an achievement which requires skill and effort. It is easier to give orders, to command, to impose one's power than to bring about a command understanding. Orderliness and control are essential in the individual's mind and in complex modern factories. Integration combines orderliness and control with freedom.

Besides these factors, economic, political and psychological factors are to be considered in taking suitable measures to reduce industrial conflict.

Psychological Programme

Under this programme, the frustration and the motivation of the workers are considered. The worker should be consulted whenever any new plan or programme is taken up by the company or management. Any technological change should be made after consulting the workers and their unions and the views of the workers should be given sufficient importance. When displaced workers are allowed to join in another job, they must be given sufficient time to do so.

Reduction of Tension Caused by Interpersonal Relationship

As already discussed, one of the major factors of industrial disputes in the relationship between the worker and the management. The contact between the two parties must be direct and intimate rather than indirect and superficial. For a better relationship, the personality of the supervisor and his capacity to deal with people, his technological knowledge, experience and training etc., should be considerd.

A suitable leadership training programme should also be given to the supervisors. The attitude of the supervisors should be changed in the friendly direction by the help of such training.

The discussion method and the role playing technique should be especially followed for the training of the supervisor.

Marrow and French (1948) did a study on the foremen of Harwood Manufacturing Corporation to find out the way for preparing supervisors for policy changes in industry. The common belief in any industry was that women over the age of thirty were not suitable for skilled jobs and so the supervisors hesitated to recruit older women. But during the war years when labourers were very much in demand, a psychologist tried to convince the supervisors of this plant to recruit older women. A research on women over thirty indicated that they could as well and with equal time, learn new skills. They had a better attendance record and lower turnover period. With these facts in hand, they tried to convince the supervisors, who strongly believed that older women were definitely inferior to younger women. Having failed to convince the supervisors a group education method was followed. The findings of this study were presented to a group of leaders and sub-leaders. Meetings and discussions were held about the result obtained and gradually the original belief and bias began to lessen. At last a decision was taken up by the group to verify the fact experimentally, by giving training to older women. On the basis of the experimental results they changed their views regarding the appointment of older women in skilled jobs.

It is generally held that supervisors who are selected according to their skill in leadership and have got adequate leadership training can suitably reduce disputes and dissatisfaction caused among the workers in industry. Secondly, personal contact between the workers and the management is very much required for reduction and prevention of disputes. This can be done by proper supervisory training.

Reduction of Disputes Caused by Inadequate Wages

If the wages are not sufficient to meet the demands and needs of the worker, the worker should get suitable compensations from the higher authority.

The wage must be psychologically adequate. But this is not usually done by the management.

If equal wage for equal work is given, it may decrease dissatisfaction to some extent. Besides free educations, giving mid-day meals to school-going children, old-age pensions, provident funds, insurance facilities, medical facilities, maternity aids, laundry, canteen, card and shopping facilities provided by the management or the government may also satisfy some of the needs of the workers. Frustration due to inadequate wage incentive plan can be reduced if the management makes necessary arrangements and considers the needs of the workers reasonably and sympathetically.

Reduction of Conflict Caused by Factors Outside the Job Situation

Industrial conflict may in some cases be the result of the personal frustrations of the workers and the management. To reduce conflict caused by such factors, it is desirable to take care of the mental and psychological health of the worker by the help of personnel counsellors and therapists. Any type of conflict either social, political or industrial is readily caused when the personality of the worker is sick or maladjusted.

Increase of mutual understanding may also reduce industrial disputes. Steps may be taken to bridge the gap in communication between the employees and the employer by mutual discussion between both the parties. The management should also try to keep the public free from getting all sorts of wrong views and rumours regarding labour management and disputes. Imagined grievances should also be reduced.

Katz (1962) has set forth three basic categories for dealing with conflict. They are :

1. Making the system work.
2. Setting up machinery for handing conflict.
3. Changing the organisational structure.

Making the System Work

It puts emphasis on human relation skills in the improvement of interpersonal relations. Relevant to this effort are the development of effective leadership participation and effective two-way communication including feedback to employees. The use of sensitivity training and group dynamics techniques can sometimes, bring about some modification of attitudes, since attitudes lie behind all conflicts.

Setting Up Machinery for Handling Conflict

This contributes to the control of conflict rather than reduction of conflict. It tries to reduce the likelihood of spreading conflict. Provisions are made for the resolution of differences at the points where they occur. If such conflicts and tensions cannot be resolved at that point, they may be carried a step higher.

Change in the Structure of the Organisation

In some circumstances, changes in the structure of the organisation or some segment of it can contribute to conflict reduction by creating conditions in which such conflict is likely to develop. In this connection, Katz (1962) offers some suggestions such as reducing process specialisation, decentralisation, restructuring to remove obvious differences in status symbols between hierarchical interest groups, development of meaningful cycles of work with opportunity for employees to complete tasks, and sharing in organisational rewards. Besides, job enlargement, reorganisation to facilitate communication and providing an opportunity for informal groups to develop and exist without fear of possible counteraction or punishment are also helpful in reducing conflict.

However, whatever the strategies adopted, they should be based upon an understanding of human behaviour including the role that motivation and preception play in human behaviour in conflict situations.

QUESTIONS

1. What is meant by industrial conflict ?
2. Discuss the various steps taken by industry to reduces conflict.

REFERENCES

Katz, D. *Approaches to Managing Conflict in Conflict Management in Organisations*, Ann Arbor, Michigan, *Foundations for Research on Human Behaviour*, 1961.

Kerr, W.A., Koppelmeier. G.J. and Sullivan, J.J. Absenteeism, turnover and morale in a metal factory, *Occupational Psy.*, 25, 1951, pp. 50-55.

McMurray, R.N. *Handling Personality Adjustment in Industry*, Harper Brothers, New York, 1944.

Mohanty, G.B. and Mishra, S.P. A comparative study of the level of frustration of skilled and semiskilled employees of two plants at Chowdwar, *Orissa, Proceedings of Indian Sc. Congress*, 1982.

Stagner, K. *Industrial Conflict*, New York, John Wiley and Sons, Inc., 1956.

Tiffin, J. and McCormick, E.J. *Industrial Psychology*, Prentice Hall of India Private Limited, New Delhi, 1971.

18

Industrial Absenteeism

INTRODUCTION

The phenomenon of absenteeism leads to one of the most common and important forms of wastage in industry. It is an established fact that absenteeism and labour turnover affect almost every type of organised set up. Its importance is realised and recognised from a government office to an educational institution and from a commercial house to a factory. But the seriousness of the problem is realised more in modern Industry than in any other concern. The absence of a foreman or supervisor leads to dislocation of work and indiscipline hands lead to a great loss in. The absence of trained production as well as to breakage in machines and this has its repercussions on many other workers and sections of the factory.

Not only do absenteeism and turnover, lead to wastage or breakage, the cost of breakage and time spent are also important factors.

Analysing the psychological tensions caused by absenteeism, Sinha (1973) writes "absenteeism in an industry is the indication of the lowered efficiency and often reflects an attitude of dissatisfaction, unrest, lack of interest in the job, real and imagined grievances". Absenteeism is considered by many industrial psychologists including, Tiffin, as an index of job dissafaction.

Absenteeism and labour turnover are related phenomena and most often, they go side by side. Usually a person who remains absent in most of the cases though not always leaves the job. Absenteeism and labour turnover being related, the factors related to them are the same.

MEANING AND DEFINITION

Absenteeism lacks a uniform definition and is generally understood differently by different persons. Thus, as pointed out in the Labour Investigation Committee Report (1940) the figures available are not always comparable.

Ordinarily, a layman defines absenteeism as remaining absent from work. It means leaving one's work-place without permission. According to the U.S.A. Department of Labour, absenteeism is the absence of a worker during a full shift that he is scheduled to work. J.D. Hackett (1929) regards it as a "temporary cessation of work for not less than one whole working day, on the initiative of the worker when his presence is expected".

P.S. Florence (1950) calls it "an absence ..... a failure to attend" while Ankalikar (1945) considers it as unauthorised absence of the worker from his job. These definitions are vague and too broad to give any specific connotation.

In the industrial field, absenteeism needs a more restricted connotation. It is thus the total number of workers absent expressed as a percentage of the total number of workers employed. Absenteeism in more technical jorgon may be defined "as the ratio of the number of production man-days or shifts lost, to the total number of production man-days or shifts scheduled to work" (Oakley 1945).

The Labour Department of the Government of India, in a circular issued to the provincial Governments, has given a more precise and comprehensive definition of absenteeism. The absenteeism rate is defined as the total man-shift lost because of absence as a percentage of total manshifts scheduled.

For calculating the rate of absenteeism, the number of persons scheduled to work and the number actually present is required. A worker who reports for any part of the shift is to be considered as present. An employee is to be considered scheduled to work when he has worked available, is aware of it, and when the employer has no reason to expect, well in advance, that the employee will not be available for work at the specified time.

Regularly scheduled vacations and holidays, ordered lay-offs, strikes and absence after dismissal have to be excluded from the calculation of absenteeism. The scheduled national holidays and strikes are not to be taken into account while computing the percentage of absenteeism.

STUDIES ON ABSENTEEISM

Before the Second World War, the problem of absenteeism was little known. But due to national exigencies and the need for extra production, when many unsuitable and unwilling people were employed in war industries, the problem of staying off from work became unavoidable and acute.

Raphael (1942), surveying war time attendance, found that the total time lost due to absenteeism was nine per cent even before the occurrence of air raids. More time was spent in night shifts and women showed a higher record of absenteeism than men. Married women showed a still higher percentage of absenteeism.

V.S. Gosden (1942) observed a similar phenomenon in amunition factory and recorded sickness as the most outsanding cause, though age was not found as a causative factor. However, he noted that older people remain absent because of illness and younger employees because of instability. Wells (1943) found that a higher age did not appear to affect absenteeism significantly.

Wyatt (1944) found that married women workers had an absence of 45.2 and 28.2 per cent as compared with 38.9 and 19.3 per cent of unmarried women.

Making a further survey of the sickness absence of about 20,000 women employed in 5 munition factories during the last six months of 1942, Wyatt found that frequent causes of long absences were diseases of the respiratory and digestive processes, and 21.2 per cent were due to causes diagnosed as nervous fatigue or general debility.

Scheduledt's study made an analysis of absence with reference to the individual and the collective effects of age, sex and length of service.

It was also quite interesting to note that women had three times the total and twice the sickness absenteeism of men. Last but not least, there was a slight tendency for the older employees to be absent more often.

Beatty and Beatty (1975) studied absenteeism for over a period of two years on 20 females working in an insurance company.

The results indicated that initial absenteeism was predicted by organisational factors, immediate work environment and personal factors, while longitudinal absenteeism was predicted by the immediate work environment and job content.

An analysis of the various studies on absenteeism indicate that the absenteeism and turnover have led to two important and problematic questions being asked in the field of industry.

1. Why do employees remain absent?
2. Why do they quit the job ?

While visiting the Harwood plant in 1944, Kurt Lewin expressed the view that most of the turnover might be caused by a feeling of failure on the part of the employees who quit the organisation. The conflict between the level of aspiration and attainment, *i.e.*, between increased desire to reach the standard and increased difficulty to reach the standard seemed to be responsible for this sort of feeling of failure.

It is needless to say that absenteeism is a common form of wastage of human material and requires scientific study and control. As far as practicable the causes of absenteeism should be found out, so that the rate of absenteeism can be controlled and held down to the lowest possible level.

A low absenteeism rate not only reduces wastage of man-power and national property, but is also an indicator of good employer employee relations, high morale and job satisfaction.

The loss due to absenteeism is two-fold. Firstly, there is a distinct loss to the workers because the irregularity in attendance reduces their income when "no work, no pay" is the general rule. Secondly, because of absenteeism both discipline and efficiency suffer. Besides, suitable substitutes are not always available to replace the absenteeism temporarily and they are often presented by worker's organisations as was observed in some textile mills around Nagpur some years back.

From this standpoint it is not only important but also essential to find out the causes of absenteeism. Absenteeism can not be completely eliminated. But the management should recognise its responsibility in controlling the rate if it crosses the limit.

CAUSES OF ABSENTEEISM

The causes of absenteeism may broadly be divided into : (1) Inplant causes, (2) Community causes, and (3) Personal causes.

Inplant Causes

The inplant causes responsible for absenteeism and turnover inside the factory are the following :

***(i)* Ineffective and Inadequate Selection and Placement Procedure.** Ineffective and inadequate selection and placement procedure encourage round pegs in square holes. As a result, there is unnecessary wastage of human power and energy and dissatisfaction in job.

Obviously, absenteeism and turnover may be reduced in industry by careful selection and by shifting men to work on jobs to which they may be better fitted.

***(ii)* Excessive Industrial Fatigue**. During the war years, it was noticed that overwork leading to excessive fatigue increased the rate of accidents.

Heavy pressure of work leads to frequent illness and hence the employee searches for a new job. Hours of work should, therefore, be reduced in the factories and frequent optimum rest pauses should be given as and when necessary.

***(iii)* Unsatisfactory Working Conditions**. Poor illumination, ventilation, lack of housing, canteen, refreshment and shopping facilities not only create unpleasantness in the social climate of the factory but also accelerate poor attitude and low morale among the employees. Dissatisfaction thus leads to dislike of work, and absenteeism and turnover become obvious consequences.

Thus, any improvement in the physical conditions of the factory will not only reduce absenteeism, but also the turnover.

***(iv)* Poor Supervision**. The studies conducted in the Western Electric Company, famous as the Hawthorne studies (1927), have already reflected what an important role the supervisor plays in the factory with its tremendous impact upon the attitude and morale of the employees. Poor and bossy supervisors very often lead to discontentment, unrest, conflict and tension, and hence absenteeism and turnover. It has been indicated in Hawthorne studies that absenteeism was reduced from 15 per cent to 3 per cent due to good supervisory relationship and judicious dealings.

Supervisory training, hence, is a necessary remedy to reduce absenteeism and labour turnover.

Among the other inplant causes, over-staffing irregular flow of production, ineffective use of skills, inadequate training programmes, inadequate incentive systems, ineffective grievance procedures, real or imagined grievances, low morale, lack of job satisfaction and poor employee-employer relations are important determining factors of absenteeism.

A study conducted by Giesen and Ruter (1949) indicates that the average morale index of the workers had a statistically significant correlation with absences of –0.47. In other words the departments with many absentees tended to have low morale and *vice versa.*

Community and Social Causes

War experiences have shown that : *(i)* inadequate housing and transport facilities keep the workers away from work.

So the workers should be provided with suitable conveyance facilities to reduce the rate of absenteeism and turnover.

(ii) Lack of suitable marketing and shopping facilities : Sometimes the workers remain absent periodically due to lack of marketing and shopping facilities. Also lack of laundry, banking,

childcare, education and other facilities lead to frequent absence from work. Therefore proper welfare measures like various shopping centres nearest to the employees colony, schools, childcare centre, laundry and banking facilities should be provided by the company or plant. In many modern organisations such facilities are being provided.

(*iii*) Lack of hospital facilities for treatment also leads to absenteeism. Hospital facilities should be provided by the management to reduce absenteeism.

(*iv*) Seasonal causes, *e.g.*, the cultivation season, the marriage season, amusements and religious festivals also lead to absenteeism especially in the case of Indian factory workers. Rao (1950) found that religous festivals and social functions are one of the important causes of absenteeism in India. There is no remedy for these seasonal causes of absenteeism except that a constant record of absenteeism may enable the management to reserve extra hands during seasonal periods so that there will not be much loss to the management.

Personal Causes

Recently, industrial psychologists interested in the study of absenteeism, have found that personal and psychological factors of personality, individual maladjustment, job dissatisfaction, age, sex and marital status etc., are of vital importance in influencing absenteeism and turnover in industry.

Henry Beaumont (1946) concludes in this connection : "the factors responsible for absenteeism are based on characteristics of personality and attitude which are in a way related to individual skill and efficiency".

He further adds "whatever the apparent causes of absenteeism may be, in specific case, it presents evidences of lack of occupational adjustment.

Lack of occupational adjustment thus lies at the core of personal factors.

Nervousness and Fatigue. According to Wyatt, 21.2 per cent of all absence due to sickness of women was due to causes attributed as nervousness and fatigue.

Jackson (1949) noted that the worker with a high absence rate is usually maladjusted and that a small percentage of the employees accounted for a large share of the total time lost.

Bashford did a survey on office workers. The result revealed that 10 per cent of the sickness absence among the post office workers was originally due to nervous illness. In another study on a large group of American industrial workers. Gafafer found that 4 per cent of the absence due to sickness were due to neurasthenia and nervous diseases.

Russell Fraser's (1947) famous study on 8,000 male and female workers indicated that more than 10 per cent (9.1 per cent of them were men and 1.30 per cent were women) of the workers suffered from definite and disabling neurotic illness and a further 20 per cent (19.2 per cent men and 23.0 per cent women) from minor forms of neurosis during die course of six months. Neurotic illnees was also the cause of 25 to 33 per cent of the absence due to illness, Neurosis was responsible for the loss of 1.09 per cent of men's possible working days and 2.04 per cent of women's a loss equivalent to an annual absence of three working days by every man studied, and of six days by every women.

Fraser concludes "clearly neurotic illness was an important cause of industrial disability among these workers".

Among other important findings, it was noted that absence from work was more frequent than average among married women with full or partial home duties, those with considerable abnormal responsibilities, those working over 75 hours per week, those usually receiving low wages, and those on very light and sedentary work.

Absence form work was less frequent among those who liked their work.

Certain Indian psychologists have also made definite attempts to find out die other personal factors of absenteeism.

In a Lantin factory, Sinha and associates (1954) found out the attendance record of workers and on that basis, divided, the employss into three groups :

1. Low absence group (2.04 days in a year),
2. Moderate absence group (8.2 days in a year),
3. High absence group (25.85 days in a year).

A neurotic inventory was administered to all die workers and the correlation between the neurotic score and percentage of absenteeism was + 0.63. This indicates that one of the important personal factors of absenteeism is neuroticism.

This finding supports die results of Fraser, Bashfold, Beaumont and Jackson and lends support to the contention of Wyatt and others who found neuroticism and fatigue as significant causes of absenteeism.

It is therefore clear that sickness, one of the commonest causes of absenteeism has its basis on the mental level. Thus Jackson and others have suggested that maladjustment among the workers happens to be one of the major causes of absenteeism. One of the indices of maladjustment is therefore absenteeism, *i.e.*, maladjusted worker is more often than not an absentee in the factory/industry. Finally, it can be held that if a worker is frequently absent he is either maladjusted with his job, his family life or a combination of both.

Other personal factors of absenteeism are :

(*i*) Illness of self or family;
(*ii*) Accident of self or family;
(*iii*) Household duties;
(*iv*) Seeking and searching other employment;
(*v*) Child care, recreation; and
(*vi*) Use of alcohol.

Age, tenure of service, pay, sex, marital status and experience, etc., add to the other personal factors of absenteeism.

Age and Experience. The United Bureau of Labour Statistics (1948) reveals that as the age and experience of the worker increases, absenteeism decreases. Murthy found workers with longer experience had a better record of presence. Sinha found less experienced workers to be more absent. He further found the highest record of absenteeism among workers of 18-34 years age group. Perhaps workers with long service are adjusted with the job and have greater satisfaction.

Sex. From the findings of a careful survey on the factory workers Schenet (1945) found that absenteeism was three times greater in women than in men. Studies by Sinha (1954) indicate that women have more absenteeism than men. But attributing such absences due to low morale and job dissatisfaction would be erroneous. Absenteeism in the case of women, and especially married women, can be due to many other factors such as home responsibilities, child care, care of sick husband and in-laws etc. Moreover working wives have to work long hours at home, in comparison with their male counterparts because of the existing social system. As a consequence, they remain absent from work.

Long Hours of Work. Because of the onset of fatigue due to overwork, workers working for longer hours are more frequently absent than workers working for shorter hours. Fleming's study (1964) supports this view.

Marital Status. Though Sinha (1954) did not find the role of marriage in absenteeism, other observations, for instance, by Girard (1958), show that married people overburdened with family responsibilities remain more absent as compared to unmarried ones.

However, this rule may not always hold good. But Murthy (1953) in his study proved that widows tended to remain absent more. Further, workers with their home in that area were less absent than workers coming from distant places.

Job Satisfaction. Mann and Baumgartiel (1952) conducted a study to find out the relationship between absenteeism and job satisfaction. The results of the study indicated that job satisfaction is negatively correlated with absenteeism.

In a steel plant Sinha (1961) found a significant negative association between the rate of absenteeism and job satisfaction among the workers.

Sinha and Nair (1965) conducted a study in a light engineering plant in South India. They noted a close relationship between the index of job satisfaction and absenteeism. The study revealed that low absentee workers are significantly more satisfied with their job. This investigation brings out sufficient evidence to show that job satisfaction is an important factor governing absenteeism.

Hrebiniak and Lawrence (1973) conducted a study to find out the relationship between need satisfaction and absenteeism among managerial personnel. Data indicated a positive relationship between dissatisfaction and absenteeism.

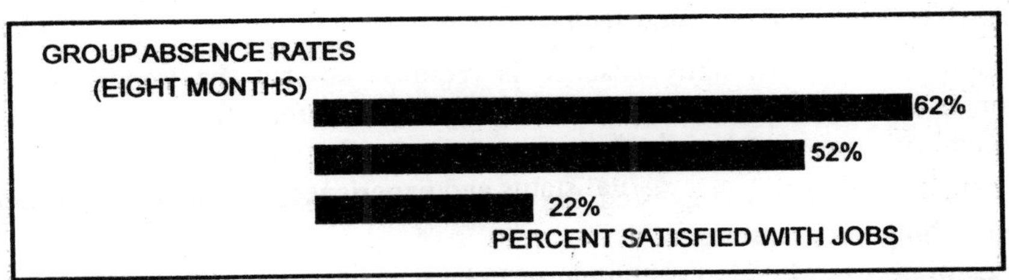

Fig. 18.1. Relationship between overall satisfaction with company and job and absence rate of employees. Based on the data of Mann and Baumgartiel (1952).

Nature of Pay. Many studies, including the study by Sinha (1954), indicate that workers with high pay are more regular. The high record of absence in low paid workers may be due to the fact that they may be on the lookout for other avenues of income which would enable them to lead a minimum standard of life. The Rege Committee reports that the level of absenteeism is comparatively high immediately after the pay day when the workers either feel like having a good time, or in some cases, return to their villages to make purchases and to meet the family. The Rege Committee has further remarked "probably the most predominant cause of absenteeism however is the frequent urge of the rural exodus".

INDIAN STUDIES ON ABSENTEEISM

Some more studies have been conducted in India which throw light on other causes of absenteeism.

V.R. Rao (1950) found that the rate of absenteeism is higher in our country than in the other Western countries and that the rate was higher in Northern than in Southern India.

S.A.S. Murthy (1953) found that workers from other states had more absence that those belonging to the provinces in which the factory was located. Persons staying further from the factory had more absences than those staying near it. Workers whose families were more susceptible to illness were more absent than other workers. Lastly, the more religious among the workers had higher rate of absence.

Sinha (1961) found that the place of residence is a factor governing the relationship between the distance from the factory and absenteeism, the relationship being + 0.43. Villagers had a higher record of absence than those from the town itself, possibly because the employees coming from rural areas usually go to meet their families· staying in the villages.

CONTROL OF INDUSTRIAL ABSENTEEISM

Absenteeism refers to the failure of workers to report on the job when they are scheduled to work. It is a broad term which is applied to the time lost because sickness or accident prevents a worker from being on the job, as well as to unauthorised time spent away from the job for other reasons. Workers who quit without notice are also counted as absentees until they are officially removed from the pay role.

After recognising the real causes of absenteeism and sorting out the false and alleged ones, one should try to control the rate of absenteeism whenever it is excessive.

A proper record of absenteeism should be maintained. In many factories workers remain absent, but nobody knows why. So every worker should be accounted for when he remains absent and the personnel officer's task is to ask each worker the causes of his absence on that day. This procedure has been adopted in some factories.

A careful record of monthly absence is required so that the trends of absenteeism in different months can be found out and if there is a regular trend for different works, the management can take necessary steps to reduce it. Substitutes can than be arranged in place of the absentees.

Elton Mayo (1933) has suggested the reduction of absenteeism by reducing neuroticism through counselling programmes.

Besides, proper conditions of work in the factory, adequate wages, protection from accident and sickness and facilities for obtaining leave for rest and other important engagements involve the most important and effective means of reducing absenteeism. The Rege Committee also suggests provision of holidays with or even without pay and permission for workers to attend to their private affairs occasionally, thus regularising absenteeism instead of merely taking disciplinary action for it. Provision for suitable housing in industrial towns is also necessary to control absenteeism.

Summing up the discussion on the control of industrial absenteeism Sinha (1973) says, "Other measures for controlling absenteeism would constitute adequate training, placement and selection programmes, proper supervisory training and practices, incentive and check on hours of work, accident, health hazards, fatigue factors and general improvement of employee-employer relationship in the organisation"

QUESTIONS

1. What is meant by industrial absenteeism ? State the causes of absenteeism in industry.
2. Make a brief analysis of the findings of studies conducted on absenteeism in industry.
3. Compare the main findings of the studies conducted on absenteeism in the West and in India and state briefly the similarities and differences in the causes of absenteeism in these two countries.
4. Why is it necessary to reduce absenteeism in industry ? Describe in detail how industrial absenteeism can be controlled.

REFERENCES

I.C.S.S.R. New Delhi. *A Survey of Research in Psychology*, Popular Prakashan, 1972, Bombay.

Bashford, as quoted by Fraser, R. in *The Incidence of Neuroses, Among Factory Workers*, H. M. Stationary Office, London.

Beatty, Richard W. and Beatty, James R. Longitudinal study of absenteeism of hardcore unemployed, *Psychology Reports*, 1975, (April), Vol. 36 (2), pp. 395-406.

Fleming, T.J. The World of Women at Work, This Week, February 9, 1964, 2, pp. 4-5.

Fraser, R. The incidence of neuroses among factory workers, *I.H.R.B. Report*. No. 90, 1947.

Giese, W.J. and Ruter, W.H. An objective analysis morale, *Jn. of Applied Psychology*, 33, pp. 421-427.

Gosden,V.S. *Journal of Occupational Psychology*, Vol. 16, No. 2.

Jakson, Joseph J. Factors involved in absenteeism as quoted by Gray, J.S., *Psychology in Industry*. McGraw Hill Book Co. Ltd., N.Y., 1952.

Mann, F. and Baumgartiel, H. Absence and. employee attitude in an Electric Power Company, Survey Research Centre, University of Michigan, 1952.

Murthy, S.A.S. *Absenteeism in Industry,* Bureau of Research Publications, Tata Institute of Social Sciences, Andheri, Bombay.

Oakley, C.A. *Men at Work*, Hodder and Stoughlen Ltd., London.

Patchen, M. Absence and employee feeling about fair treatment, *Personnel Psychol.,* 1960, 13, pp 349-360.

Rao, P.M. A study of absenteeism ill Modern Printing Press.

Sinha, D. Personal factors in absenteeism, Published in Studies on *Industrial Psychology*, Sri Ram Mehera and Co. Publishers, Hospital Road, Agra, 1973.

Tiffin, J. and McCormick, E.J. *Industrial Psychology*, Prentice Hall of India Ltd., New Delhi, 1971.

19

Labour Turnover

PROBLEM OF LABOUR TURNOVER

Accidents, absenteeism and high rate of labour turnover have been the disorganising factors in work and constitute the three common forces of labour wastage.

Labour turnover is a costly problem in industry. If even a single worker leaves the job, his replacement is recruited by advertisement. Tests are conducted and training imparted, and for all this a lot of money is spent as the cost of training is very expensive. New workers are not as good as the old ones. Hence, breakage takes place and production suffers. Thus, according to the report of the personnel Bulletin, Vol. 6, 1930, every name added to the pay rate costs the company $ 35. The Demison Manufacturing Company reports a cost of $ 80 before any new man is ready for average production. Some data of the United States showed that labour turnover increased very much at the end of the war. In a study in U.S.A. the labour turnover figure in 1939 was 80 per cent, after the war it was raised by 4.3 per cent. This indicates that 43 workers among 1000 leave the job every month.

Meaning

What is labour turnover ? When the workers quit the job on their own initiative it is called 'turnover'. Statistical analysis shows that an average plant with 1000 employees hires 42 men each month to replace those who have been laid off and discharged.

CAUSES OF LABOUR TURNOVER

Some of the labour turnover is inevitable. Some can be avoided. A knowledge of the important causes of avoidable labour turnover may lead to a reduction in the rate of turnover which ultimately can reduce the hiring and training costs. Moreover, new employees are more liable to accidents, cause more breakage and commit more errors than experienced workers.

Thirdly, labour turnover reflects conditions in the plant. A company with high labour turnover is regarded unfavourable by the employees and by the society.

Therefore, by analysing the causes of labour turnover, some of the faulty practices leading to labour turnover can be determined and avoided.

When the worker leaves the job, it is necessary to ask him why he is leaving it. The causes of leaving should be recorded for each worker who leaves the job. In fact, when the worker leaves the job he opens his heart more freely than ever before about the grievances towards the management. The reports of such people throw considerable light upon the causes of turnover.

Unavoidable Circumstances

Unavoidable forms of turnover are constant factors and influence all form of work. The causes of separation under this category are death, permanent disability, retirement, marriage and change of residence, etc.

According to Maier (1970), turnover caused by lay offs and seasonal conditions may depend upon factors beyond the employee's control, but he can influence these to a considerable degree. By carefully planning of work, it is possible to work out a uniform production schedule so that permanent staff is employed throughout the year.

When the employees are incompetent and inefficient a number of discharges and labour turnover are obvious. This can be reduced by a more careful selection and by shifting men into work for which they are better fitted. It is said that poor selection paves the way for inefficiency, wastage, loss of time, complaints and ultimate discharge.

Inadequate Information about the Job

Inadequate information about the job is also responsible for labour turnover. Often workers join a work without knowing its demands and requirements. It is also to be taken into consideration to what extent the job was accurately described when the employee was appointed. Along with finding out whether the employee is suitable for the job it should also be considered whether and how much the employee is also satisfied with the job and the company. It should be kept in mind that if he is to continue in the job, he needs job satisfaction.

Job Dissatisfaction

Usually overqualified and underqualified persons selected for the job are dissatisfied with the work and hence leave the job whenever they get a better job opportunity.

Kerr (1948) noticed a significant correlation of .25 for a sample of 98 workers between their job satisfaction scores and self reported tenure. Self reported tenure implies the number of years in a labour market divided by number of employers.

Though job dissatisfaction is a major cause of labour turnover along with resignation, there are also other reasons for leaving the job which should not be overlooked. Some people do not themselves know which job would suit them best and hence they move from job to job until they eventually find one which may be satisfying to some extent. In such case vocational selection and guidance is extremely essential. Proper and judicious selection methods would eliminate a good deal of the hiring of the misfits. Further skilled interviewing would help in better placement of dissatisfied employees.

Moreover, a better technique to detect unstable workers would be to get the information from the applicant about the number of previous jobs he has held, the length of time employed and the reasons for leaving the previous jobs.

There are some workers who leave their job voluntarily. In such cases, it is desirable to distinguish between the resignation of efficient and inefficient employees. If inferior and inefficient workers leave the job it is desirable for the company, but if competent, cooperative and efficient employees resign, it is a tremendous loss to the management.

Besides these general causes of labour turnover, there are also some specific factors related to labour turnover.

Low Morale

Giese and Ruter (1949) in a study on correlation between morale scores and turnover criterion found a negative correlation of— 42 for 25 departments, which in turn suggests a positive correlation between morale and tenure of service.

Length of Service

Scott and Clothier (1923) while analysing the labour turnover of a public service corporation, found turnover rate was 1026 per cent among the employees who were employed for less than a month. In sharp contrast to this, the rate was reduced to 226 per cent in the case of employees who were in the service from one to three months. Further observation indicates that in this company the turnover rate continued to fall with length of service. For example, after continuing in service for more than two years the turnover rate dropped to 11 per cent.

Another study of Scott, Clothier and Spriegel (1961) indicates that only a minority of employees usually leave the job and move from one job to another while the majority of them are stable and continue with the job.

The relationship between labour turnover and length of service therefore suggests that senior people should be more rewarded for their service to the company, because if senior and experienced people leave the job the organisations have to spend a lot of time and money in selection and training, etc. The production rate will also decrease in the case of new hands. Fluctuation from one job to another can be reduced by proper selection procedures, skilled and unbiased interview techniques and vocational guidance.

Age

It is generally held that young men show higher labour turnover than older men. An analysis of a study by Scott, Clothier and Mathewson (1941) on labour turnover in relation to age indicates that the desire to find suitable employment is very strong in young workers. This, in turn, is responsible for their quitting the job. Besides the desire for suitable employment, young people usually have fewer responsibilities and higher aspiration. So they may express their dissatisfaction with a job by quitting it. Sometimes one takes a job waiting for college or some other aspired job as a stop gap. Sometimes the job fills the gap between school or college and permanent service.

Lack of Responsibility

The importance of lack of responsibility as a cause of labour turnover also increases among workers who are more than 35 years of age. Another high point is at about 45 years. It is argued that the high point in turnover comes at an age when family responsibilities begin to decline because of the children having grown up and reached working age themselves. At this stage, the dissatisfied worker takes the opportunity of reduced responsibility to improve his working condition by joining a job according to his choice and satisfaction. A number of observations in the field of industry show that there is a tendency in the young workers below 20-22 years of age to move from job to job in spite of the facilities offered to them. One of the causes of this may be lack of family responsibility.

C.S. Yoakum gives statistics which show that there is a 400 per cent turnover between the age of 16-30 years as against a turnover of 40 per cent above 20 years of age.

After the age of 45 years people hardly quit their jobs, because after this age it becomes difficult for men to obtain new employment, so they more often than not remain with old job whether they like it or not.

Lack of Opportunity for Promotion and Advancement

This is also one of the causes of labour turnover. Many people leave a job because there is no security and future in the job. People with high achievement motivation and higher aspiration quit a job due to lack of opportunity for advancement and promotion.

Inadequate Supervision

The actions and behaviour of the supervisor play an important role in determining job satisfaction which ultimately influences labour turnover. If the supervisor in unsympathetic and callous, does not understand the problems and difficulties of the employees and misbehaves with them, the workers ultimately quit the job.

Besides these, unsound wage classification, unsatisfactory working conditions, inadequate grievances procedures, etc. also contribute to labour turnover.

Marital Status

The findings of several studies and general observations show that marital status is one of the causes which influence the turnover rate, married people quitting the job less frequently than the unmarried ones. It is viewed that probably marriages make for both stability and responsibility, which reduce the turnover rate under normal conditions of employment. But there is also the probability that job instability and avoidance of marriage may be caused by the same personality trait.

Intelligence

Maier (1970) opines that less intelligence may be expected to influence dissatisfaction and hence labour turnover in two ways. In the first place, a job which is too difficult will be a constant strain for the individual with insufficient intelligence. He is frequently scolded and blamed for inferior work, tends to worry over responsibility and feels insecure. Thus, he quits the job, if he is not discharged. On the other hand, an intelligent worker may find many occupations mechanical, repetitive and boring. So he may leave the job to seek occupations elsewhere which are more challenging, and need the exercise of brains and intelligence.

Labour Turnover among Men and Women

Sex. A study by Scott-Clothier (1923), conducted to find out the relationship between marital alertness and turnover rate in a group of male and female clerks, showed a difference in the trend of turnover caused by sex differences.

The findings suggest that superior men showed little desire to leave whereas superior women were among the most likely to leave. Inadequate promotion of superior women and discrimination on the basis of sex are probably responsible for such differences in turnover.

RELATION BETWEEN TURNOVER AND JOB COMPLEXITY

People of high and low intelligence are expected to show different degrees of satisfaction or dissatisfaction for the same job. This view has been supported by a study made on clerical workers by Bills (1923).

Findings of the study indicated that turnover increases with job complexity among individuals below average in mental alertness. On the other hand, turnover rate declines in individuals with high intelligence as the complexity of job increases. This type of labour turnover can be reduced by carefully placing the applicants in job suited to their levels of mental capacity.

Besides the factors just mentioned, seasonal causes like marriages, festivals and in plant causes like lack of proper medical facilities, child care, marketing, etc. are responsible for causing turnover.

Turnover due to seasonal causes can be met by storing products which are non-perishable.

Maintenance of a permanent staff may reduce the percentage of turnover and the cost incurred by that.

A company which permits security, retirement allowances and insurance benefit finds less labour turnover.

By and large, it can be said that any condition which improves morale and which is conclusive to better human relations can reduce turnover.

The importance of making a job fit the personal needs of the individual should not be overlooked if one wants to reduce the turnover etc.

By proving security and permanent occupation, fitting employees to jobs, reducing experiences of failure, by fulfilling the ambition of employees as far as practicable and by dealing with their personalised needs the turnover rate can be reduced.

RELATION BETWEEN TURNOVER AND ABSENTEEISM

According to Kilbridge (1961) both turnover and absenteeism have been shown to have different relationships with such factors as the industry or firm studied, the type of work being done and the sex of the worker, etc. In comparing repetitive with nonrepetitive jobs in two similar manufacturing firms in the same geographical area, the turnover rate in general was found to be higher in repetitive jobs.

An analysis of the data in terms of sex revealed that in both firm the turnover rate was higher for males than for females while the rate of absenteeism was higher for females than for males.

As pointed out by Gaudet (1963), job satisfaction was inversely related to both absenteeism and turnover rates, but the relationship was significant for absenteeism.

Maier (1970) finally comments, "Because both turnover and absenteeism are influenced by different patterns of variable, generalisations regarding their relationship to job satisfaction and employee needs must be made with caution".

INDIAN STUDIES ON LABOUR TURNOVER

There have not been many studies on labour turnover in India, though in certain industries like coal mines and on certain grades of staff the problem seems to be very acute. Only one extensive study has been conducted by Naidu (1963) over a period of three years on permanent employees in 45 textile mills around Coimbatore. Emphasis was given to the turnover among the technical and supervisory staff. The average turnover among the supervisory staff was 6 per cent compared to 2.8 for clerical employees and 2.9 for men workers. Variation in the turnover between mills, particularly as regards the supervisory staff was also very high. The analysis revealed that the most frequent cause of turnover was resignation following discharge, dismissal and retiremen The incidence was negligible in small units having fewer supervisory staff which were starte during the post war period. Two thirds of such units reported no turnover and were situated i small towns and rural areas. The absence of turnover in these mills was attributed to factors lik more personal contact, feeling of enhanced status, less opportunities for alternate employment i the neighbourhood and lower cost of living. Analysing the causes for employee turnover, it was observed that people left at all levels in the management hierarchy.

Also comparatively low salary was one of the major factors of turnover. It was also found to be high along those who held technical qualification. Moreover, approximately one half o those who changed their jobs belonged to the 20-30 age group and another one third to 30-40 age group. Various organisational and individual causes for turnover were studies.

QUESTIONS

1. What is meant by labour turnover ? How does it differ from absenteeism ?
2. Briefly describe the causes of labour turnover. Is there any overlapping of the causes of absenteeism and labour turnover ?
3. Discuss the importance of selection in reducing the rate of labour turnover in industry.

REFERENCES

I.C.S.S.R. New Delhi. *A Survey of Research in Psychology*, Popular Prakashan, 1972.

Kerr, W A. On the validity and reliability of the job satisfaction, Tear Ballot, *Jn. of Applied Psychology*. 32. 1948.

Maier, N.R.F. *Psychology in Industry*. Oxford and IBH Publishing Co., New Delhi. 1970.

Scott, W.D. and Clothier. R.C. *Personal Management*, New York. A. W. Shaw and Co., 1923.

Scott, W.D., Clothier, R.C. Mathewson, S.D. and Spriegel. W.R. *Personnel Management*, 3rd e New York. McGraw Hill. 1941.

Scott, W.D., Clothier, R.C. and Spriegel, W.R. *Personal Management*. 6th ed., New York, McG Hill, 1961.

20

Industrial Fatigue

INTRODUCTION

The problem of fatigue needs special study in industrial psychology for the reason that decline in the curve of production is often attributed to the fatigue of the employees. It not only reduces production but also creates a feeling of tiredness. Fatigue also increases the rate of accident. By eliminating fatigue the workers can be effectively motivated to work. Thus, in Blum's view (1956) "Industrial fatigue in spite of its illusive nature has been the subject of many investigations from both physiological and psychological point of view."

MEANING AND DEFINITION

Fatigue refers to reduction in the ability to do work because of the previous work. The general terms used for fatigue are tiredness, exhaustion, a feeling of being spent out, strain, etc.

As seen by Viteles (1932), Fatigue may be described as a diminishing of one's working capacity. Ordinarily the term fatigue is used to describe a general state of the individual, a state resulting from continuous activity or work. It is conceived as a reduction in the power to perform or to react. Long periods of activity, lack of opportunity for rest, strenuous or heavy work, etc. are considered as being conducive to the onset of fatigue.

Thus fatigue can be measured from the output or performance. If the output falls down, the occurrence of fatigue is indicated, keeping other factors constant. According to Maier (1970), fatigue is caused by length or intensity of some activity in a gainful occupation.

In an intensive study called "Fatigue and hours of service of interstate truck drivers" (1941) the term fatigue is defined as an altered psychological and physiological state in relation to the states of recovery or normal capacity.

According to Dill (1933) fatigue is not an entity but merely a convenient word to describe a variety of phenomena.

Muscio (1921) defines fatigue as "a condition caused by activity in which output produced by that activity tends to be relatively poor and the degree of fatigue tends to vary directly with the poorness of output". Muscio, however, is not satisfied with this definition because fatigue cannot be directly measured and because diminished output may also be cause of distraction. The most accepted definition of fatigue is "reduction in the ability to do work caused by changes in the chemical and psychological level".

Analysing the nature of fatigue, three different meanings have been attributed to the term fatigue.

1. Reduction in working capacity.
2. Fall in production.
3. Feeling of tiredness.

According to Viteles (1932) tension, speed, subjection to specialisation of work and a decrease in the enjoyment of work leads to fatigue.

Gilbreth (1911) holds the view that due to unsatisfactory and unsuitable working conditions, fatigue is caused and hence there is a daily loss of 20 cents per worker due to decrease in production. Adverse effect is also found in the individual and on the welfare of society.

NATURE OF FATIGUE

Blum (1956) opines that "Fatigue from short bursts of activity whether by the whole body or by isolated muscular groups, is characterised by increase in lactic acid and temporary inability to continue."

In fact, any type of muscular work will result in fatigue if the work of the muscles and the resulting expenditure of energy are at a faster rate than recovery. But one of the primary difficulties in understanding the true nature of fatigue is, that many factors in addition to muscle use do contribute to the onset of fatigue. Some of these factors are the length of the work period, the speed of work, the extent of muscles involved and the tensions accompanying the task. Since industrial fatigue rarely concerns a single muscle, but rather the individual as a whole, the problem of fatigue becomes more complicated. However, according to Blum (1968), "Depending on the strength, stamina and preparation of the individual, fatigue is manifested at different rates in different people". Being a general state of the individual, fatigue should show its effects in all aspects of behaviour and in all manifestations. It should be of the same order.

Various studies have been conducted to understand the nature of fatigue. Angelo Mosso (1915) developed an instrument called ergograph to record and measure the work done by the muscle inflexing a finger. By attaching a weight to the string tied to finger and strapping the hand so that only this finger was allowed to move, it was possible to obtain a fatigue curve using this technique. Mosso demonstrated the ratio and the extent of work that could be done by a single finger lifting a specific weight. He also demonstrated from this study that when a fatigued muscle is forced to work, the period of recovery is prolonged. In other words, if two minutes are required for recovery after a 12 minutes work period, for an 18 minute work period recovery may require more than three minutes, which is in fact more than one and half times the time required after a 12 minute work period. The ergograph studies the relation between fatigue and work in a relatively isolated part of the body.

Though Mosso's ergograph studies fatigue and even though it is a classic study, certain criticisms are advanced against it. Firstly, this study is done under extremely unnatural and artificial conditions. Secondly, it is argued that no job in the industry is likely to require the movement of only one finger. However, by this apparatus Mosso could measure fatigue without complicating it with psychological effects such as monotony and boredom which are likely to accompany longer periods of work.

Vernon (1924) developed a variation of the dynamometer which enables one to study the effects of work when the larger muscles of the body are involved. This apparatus requires the subject to pull with both hands on a handle attached to a spring balance. The pull on the balance is recorded by a pointer on the revolving drum. Vernon was able to show with this apparatus that tile strength of the pull varies with the height of the handle. He also found that the introduction of rest pauses increases the capacity for work and a change in posture during the rest pauses helps recovery to a greater extent than merely stopping work. Vernon's study has a more direct bearing on the various industrial jobs, and on the basis of the findings, rest pauses have been legitimately introduced during the work period. Change in posture during the work period has also encouraged as it helps in quick recovery.

Many more studies of similar nature have been conducted in the laboratory but the disadvantage of each of these studies is that it is conducted in artificial situations and while the study is being conducted, the subject is not actually working on a job. Therefore Blum (1956) has remarked, "Inferences drawn from the laboratory studies may not apply to industry because differences in work, speed, pace and continuity may exist".

As previously defined, fatigue is the reduction in the capacity to do work because of the previous work. Reduction in energy and chemical changes can be observed in the part of the body which is engaged in continuous work. But the feeling of fatigue is experienced as a whole. It is also possible that the effects of the fatigue can be specific in nature, *i.e.*, as a result of continuous activity there is just not one effect but many effects which may or may not be related. Some psychologists argue that if fatigue is a general state of the individual and there is a transfer of fatigue in all situations, then there should be an invariable concomitant in decrease in output, psychological condition and feeling of tiredeness. But it has been observed that when a reduction in output occurs, it is not necessarily accompanied either by an accumulation of the chemical byproducts of activity in the muscles, nerves, or by an increase in feeling of tiredness. Sometimes changes in work output have been a function of the degree of motivation and physical conditions like illumination and ventilation. A reduction in output may therefore occur from one of these factors rather than from continuous work and in such cases, would not be accompanied by an accumulation of physiological products of fatigue.

Further evidence that fatigue is not a general state of the individual, comes from studies of transfer of fatigue effects. If fatigue were a general state, the capacity of a person to perform other tasks would be equally diminished. Evidences show that decrease or reduction in performance is highly specific. The extent of transfer of fatigue effects from one task to another varies with the nature of the particular task being studied. The greater the similarity between the tasks, the greater is the transfer of fatigue effects from the one to the other.

To demonstrate fatigue as reduction in the capacity to do work, an experiment was conducted on six drivers for 120 days. In the alternative days the drivers were asked to drive 300 miles and on non-driving days they were given rest. On the driving and non-driving days they were given various tests such as postural steadiness, eye-hand coordination, visual efficiency tests, colour naming, mental addition, etc. The results of the experiment indicated significant and interesting differences between the driving and non-driving days. On the non-driving days there have been definite signs of decrement in performance.

Though fatigue usually occurs due to reduction in ability to do work, individual differences are also observed with regard to the onset of fatigue. In fact, some people get fatigued earlier and take more time to recover from fatigue than others.

INDUSTRIAL STUDIES ON FATIGUE

According to Blum and Naylor, Crowden (1932) classifies muscular work in industry into three general types.

1. Heavy muscular work, *i.e.*, too strenuous for a steady, continuous rate of work to be maintained, for example, loading trucks, constructing buildings and roads, and work in coal mines.
2. Moderately heavy work, *i.e.*, continuous work in which the rate of expenditure of efforts is much lower than in the first type and is somewhat balanced by the rate of recovery. For example, machine tending and many other kinds of factory works.
3. Light speed work which involves a relatively small expenditure of energy but which often requires a postural strain that causes unnecessary fatigue. Office work is a typical example of this type. Crowden found that in a 50 yard barrow run the worker spends approximately eight per cent of his energy in raising the handles, 22 per cent in attaining a wheeling speed and in stopping and the remaining 70 per cent in the run itself. This study shows the tremendous inefficiencies that would result from interfering with the run once it is started.

While studying the energy cost of moderately heavy work, Bedale (1924) found that carrying a load with a yoke as a milk-maid does is the most economical method from the point of view of expenditure of bodily energy. Any method of carrying weights which requires postural strain and displacement of the body when walking is more costly.

Crowden holds the view that light speed work involves little expenditure of energy, but that there may be considerable fatigue because of the cramped or uncomfortable position maintained by the worker. Blunt and Naylor (1968) opine that measurement of the actual expenditure of energy does not give a measure of fatigue with Crowden's method because he measures basically the oxygen consumption in excess of normal.

The United States Public Health Service (1941) conducted a very important and valuable investigation on the relationship between fatigue and hours of work of 880 interstate truck drivers in three cities. The aims of this study were :

1. To determine if various periods of truck driving would produce demonstrable and significant psychological changes.
2. To investigate the nature of these changes.

3. To discover whether a characteristic pattern of psycho physiological response occurs after long hours of driving known as the "driver's fatigue" syndrome.

The 16 factors which were considered as contributing to fatigue in truck drivers were the following :

1. Performance of skilled operation requiring a high degree of alertness and attention.
2. Nervous strain due to driving under adverse conditions.
3. Muscular exertion in loading and unloading, in the repair and maintenance of vehicles.
4. General irregularity of habits as a result of long distance drivers.
5. Failure to obtain satisfactory rest or sleep during rest periods or when off duty.
6. Physical condition.
7. Constant use of the eye, frequently under unfavourably conditions, such as glare, etc.
8. Social factors in the environment or occupational tradition, possibly promoted by enforced absence from home.
9. Monotony inducing drowsiness.
10. The consumption of coffee and alcohol.
11. Exposure to all types of weather conditions.
12. Exposure to toxic fumes and gases.
13. Economic insecurity, *i.e.*, fear of losing one's job, especially in the case of older men.
14. Noises.
15. Vibration.
16. Sedentary occupation.

The truck drivers were given a comparative battery of tests. Both simple and complex performance tests were used and non-performance tests were also included in this battery.

From the main findings of this study the investigators comment "It appears that a reasonable limitation of hours of service of interstate truck drivers will reduce the number of drivers on the road with loco functional efficiency. This, it might reasonably be inferred, would act in the interest of high way safety".

Results indicated that the men who were not engaged in driving prior to being tested had the highest average efficiency, those who had driven less than 10 hours had the next highest average efficiency, and those who had driven over ten hours had the lowest average efficiency in the following seven tests :

1. Speed of tapping.
2. Reaction coordination time.
3. Simple reaction time.
4. Manual steadiness.
5. Body sway.
6. Driving vigilance.
7. Ability to distinguish flicker.

According to Blum (1956) the men who had been driving prior to being tested performed less efficiently on the average than those who had not driven on tests of the following functions :

1. Aiming.
2. Resistance to glare.
3. Speed of eye movement.

The data on these tests, however, do not differentiate consistently between drivers who worked from one to ten hours and those who worked over ten hours. In items 1-7 this difference does occur. The heart rate decreased slightly with hours of driving. The average white cell count was higher in men who had driven since sleeping than in men who had not driven since sleeping.

No relationship was found between hours of driving and ability to estimate the size of known objects, differentiate white cell counts, hemoglobin content of the blood, acidity of the urine, specific gravity of urine, visual acuity and the total base and potassium concentration of blood serum.

Rayon (1947) admits in his book, "These chapters on the fundamental problems of efficiency (as he sees them) have raised more questions than they have answered".

LOCALISATION OF FATIGUE

Though fatigue is generalised in nature and experienced as a whole, experimental studies indicate that fatigue is also localised in certain organs of the body.

Muscle. If a piece of muscle is removed from the body and electric shock applied to it, it will contract. But as stimulation is made for a long time, gradually the contraction will diminish and at last a stage would arise when the muscle would no longer contract. This indicates how the function of tile muscle is reduced due to excessive work. But if again the muscle is washed in saline water, the accumulation of waste products and lactic acid is washed away and oxygen is supplied, the muscle contracts once more.

When due to heavy work glycogen decreases in the muscles, contraction also diminishes. The above experiment indicates the localisation of fatigue in the muscle.

Nerve. The muscle attached with a nerve is removed from an animal. Electric shock is applied to the nerve and so the muscle contracts. After sometime contraction diminishes, but when only the muscle is stimulated, it again starts contracting. This indicates that the capacity was reduced in the nerve, but not in the muscle. So only the nerve is fatigued and not the muscle.

Blood. When the blood of a fatigued organism is injected into a fresh organism, the latter becomes fatigued though the person has not done any manual or mental work. This proves the localisation of fatigue in the blood of the organism.

MEASUREMENT OF FATIGUE

Though fatigue can be measured by the amount of output, there are also certain scientific tests by which fatigue can be measured.

Thus besides production, there are physical, chemical, physiological, psychophysical and mental tests of fatigue.

Physical Test. Fatigue can be measured by a hand dynamometer. This is a finger ergograph originally devised and used by Mosso (1915). When the finger used in work in this apparatus gets tired, the 'S' is unable to move the apparatus. As a result, the graph becomes flat and a time comes when the 'S' is not able to move his finger at all which indicates the complete onset of fatigue.

Chemical Test. Various techniques devised for the analysis of blood, urine saliva and the corresponding changes in work indicates the occurrence of fatigue. Those by analysing the blood, urine and saliva of an individual it can be concluded whether he is fatigued or not.

Psychological Test. The amount of oxygen intake, examination of pulse rate and blood pressure, etc. can also indicate the onset of fatigue.

Mental Test. This can be applied for muscular and mental work. Tests of sensory discrimination, attention, memory, imagination and measurement of other higher mental processes of an individual also suggest whether the individual is fatigued or not. However, generally in industry these scientific methods are not used for the measurement of fatigue. Of course, the ergographic test of Mosso has been able to measure fatigue in a specific part of the body.

Besides production and scientific tests there are also some indirect ways of measuring fatigue. They are as follows :

Accident. During the First World War it was observed that when hours of work increased, the rate of accident also increased. This suggests that workers get tired because of long hours of work, become inattentive and commit more accidents. Muscio and Vernon's study (1921) supports this view. Because of this, perhaps women who are usually more fatigued than men commit more accidents as indicated in earlier findings by Vernon (1936) and Schenet (1945).

Absenteeism and Turnover. Rise in the rate of absenteeism and turnover indicates the onset of fatigue. An increase in hours of work per week more often than not leads to increase in absenteeism.

PRODUCTION CURVE

The graph indicating the reduction in the amount of production with the increase in working hours refers to the 'production curve'. According to Maier (1970), "When the amount of production is left largly to the individual and is not placed by the speed of the production line or of a machine, hourly production gradually falls off during both the morning and afternoon work period". Because of the onset of fatigue due to continuous physical work there is a progressive falling off of production. Such trend in production curve is observed when the work is not very much influenced by the effects of monotony.

Figure 20.1 represents a production curve. The broken line in the figure indicates production during the five hours of the morning and the solid line indicates production during the five afternoon hours. The warming up characteristics are not present in the afternoon period. However, the fatigue effects are more visible in the morning period.

As shown in the curve, the production curve can be divided into two parts.

1. Morning curve.
2. Afternoon curve.

Morning Curve

In the morning curve there is less rise in production during the first hour. This is due to the warming up period.

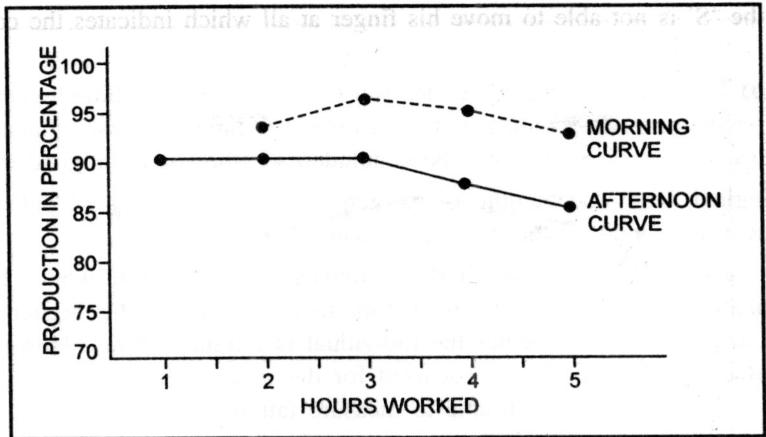

Fig. 20.1. Production curve showing warming up period and fatigue effect.

The warming up phenomenon is largely a matter of attitude, mental alertness and attention. So it takes some time for the subject to become absorbed in his task and disengage his mind from other matters.

This warming up phenomenon differs from individual to individual as it requires some physiological adjustments, such as change in blood pressure and circulation in accordance with the work space. The exact duration of the warming up period differs from individual to individual. But generally it is less than one hour and in some cases it may be a few minutes only. For the warming up period, certain psychological adjustments are necessary. Due to this production is slightly less during the warming up period in comparison to the duration between the second and third hour. After the warming up period, during the first two to three hours usually the level of production reaches its maximum and then falls. This continuous decrease indicates the onset of fatigue.

Afternoon Curve

In the afternoon production curve there is no indication of the warming up period and even if it is present, it is for a shorter duration. The afternoon production curve is definitely lower than the morning curve though it begins at a higher point than what was obtained at the end of the morning shift. Thus, after lunch, the curve beings at a higher level, but after sometime the curve falls more rapidly than the morning production curve. Towards the last part of the work, the lowest production of the day is observed mostly due to the onset of fatigue, though it may be partly due to the tendency to leave the job early.

End Spurt

A rise in production towards the end of the work period is called the 'end spurt'. The goal or motivation is nearly reached towards the end of the day and so there may be a temporary rise in the production level. This may be attributed to the motivation of approaching a goal. But the end spurt may appear in some cases only. It is not a regular characteristic of a production curve because usually the effects of end spurt are mingled with fatigue effects. But when production

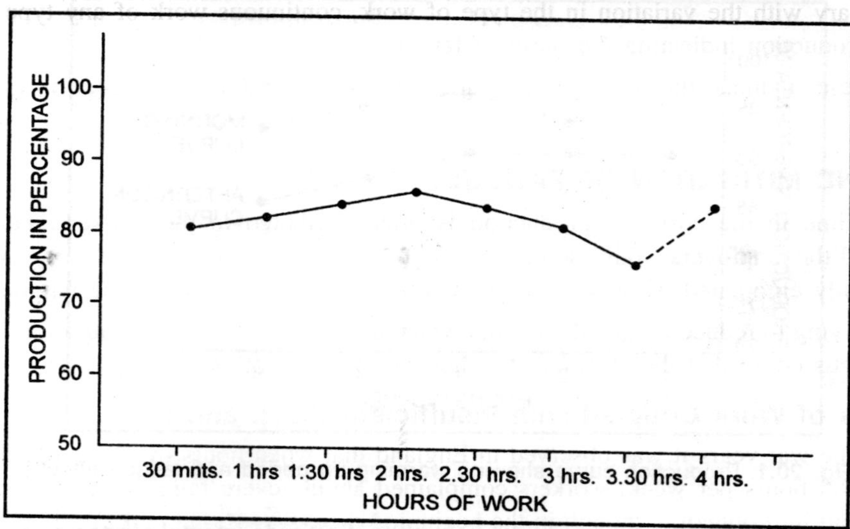

Fig. 20.2. Afternoon production curve. Dotted lines indicate end spurt.

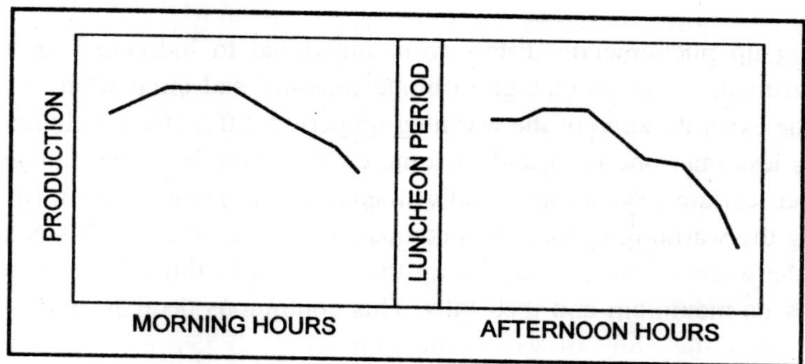

Fig. 20.3. Typical daily production curve.

is measured in a 15 or 23 minute period, end spurt may be visible. Figure 20.2 shows an afternoon production curve with end spurt.

The production curve may vary with the type of work done. When the work involves muscular exertion, there may be rapid and early rise in the work curve to a maximum, followed by a fall during the end of the forenoon. Figure 20.3 shows a typical daily production curve.

Similarly the end spurt is commonly found in those jobs which do not require much manual labour and physical exertion. Rise in production due to the end spurt takes place only for a few minutes after which there may be again a fall in production.

According to Maier (1970); The production curve thus reveals three characteristic features—the warming up period, the end spurt and the fatigue effects".

CHARACTERISTICS OF PRODUCTION CURVE IN LIGHT AND SPEEDY WORK

From a data cited by Muscio (1920), it is concluded that irrespective of the nature of work (light, medium or heavy; rapid or Slow) fatigue is a general outcome of work. Though the nature of fatigue may vary with the variation in the type of work, continuous work of any type leads to decrease in production indicating the onset of fatigue.

From these findings, the importance of attending to the problem of fatigue in industry is evident.

CAUSES AND MITIGATION OF FATIGUE

Since the decline in the curve of production is often attributed to the worker's fatigue, the employees and the employers would definitely like to eliminate fatigue. Fatigue is inevitable and cannot be totally eliminated. However, programmes can be taken up to reduce fatigue.

Before trying to reduce fatigue the factors which are responsible for the causation of fatigue should be discussed so that the relevant remedies can be brought about.

Long Hours of Work Coupled with Insufficient Sleep and Rest

During the war years it was observed in England that when hours of work were increased from 56 to 69.5 hours per week, workers complained about severe fatigue and there was also considerable fall in production, though in the beginning there was 10 per cent rise in production. The rate of accident also increased. After three to four months, production decreased by 12 per cent. On the contrary, in an ammunition factory, where working hours were reduced from 58.2 to 50.6 hours per week, output increased By 39 per cent. This indicates that long hours of work is one of the major causes of fatigue. In a study it was found that with eight hours of work per day, production was 94 per cent, and it was 90.3 per cent with 10 hours of work per day. Studies by Muscio and Vernon (1921) and Vernon (1936) support these findings. The British Medical Research Council concluded that the long work week is one of the important causes of fatigue. Thus in most of the countries, hours of work have been regulated by law. Eight hours of work per day seem to be the optimum with half holidays on Saturdays.

Inadequate Rest Pause

Rest periods delay the onset of work reduction. There are different types of rest pauses, such as long, medium and short. By and large, experimental findings suggest that frequent short rest intervals seem to be more effective than a few longer ones. Too long a rest period may create disturbance in different types of work as the person loses the continuity of the work or gets out of the mood for it. Industrial studies by Vernon (1921) show 10 to 20 per cent increase in production due to the introduction of rest pauses.

Different types of rest pauses are introduced in between working hours, depending upon the nature of the worker. For example, work requiring the use of muscles and other physical work should be given longer rest pauses. But for light physical work, short rest pauses may be given. Similarly, if the worker is physically weak and needs longer rest pause, he may be given the same. According to Shepherd (1928), heavy physical work needs at least 16.6 per cent of the time to be spent in resting if greatest efficiency is to be attained. Bills (1931) found that speed and accuracy are reduced when the work period continues. It is said that more output can be achieved by applying oneself more steadily, for a short period followed by rest than by applying oneself less steadily and having no rest pauses. Vernon and Bedford (1924) indicate that a ten minutes rest pause in the morning for girls engaged in labelling resulted in a 20 per cent increase in production.

In a study conducted in an ammunition factory, Vernon (1921) found that men engaged in active work took eight minutes voluntary rest, while workers engaged in passive work took 3.7 minutes rest for each hour of work. In another study, Farmer and Bevington (1922) found that the shape of production curve was entirely changed due to the introduction of rest pauses of seven minutes. Hence to reduce fatigue, sufficient and optimum rest pauses should be introduced, keeping in view the nature of work and the need of the workers.

Unsatisfactory Environmental Conditions

Unsatisfactory illumination, noise, ventilation, humidity and temperature, etc. during work are responsible for the onset of fatigue.

Low illumination may lead to headache, eye strain and irritability. If the distribution of light is not adequate and if illumination reflects glare, it may be undesirable for the workers. For instance, in a work like distinguishing black thread from black cloth, illumination of high intensity is required.

But with very low illumination, fatigue occurs early due to eye strain and efficiency is ultimately hampered.

Similarly, very high or very low temperature is undesirable for work.

Vernon, Bedford and Cowner conducted a study on atmospheric conditions in coal mines. They found that with satisfactory atmospheric conditions, a seven minutes rest per hour was required instead of 24.4 minutes rest per hour.

The remedy is, therefore, to reach the comfort zone. To avoid or eliminate fatigue temperature must be of the optimum level.

Bad Design of Machines

When man is fitted to machine rather than *vice versa,* it leads to all sorts of unnecessary work and extra expenditure of energy. Thus machines have to be designed according to the average make up of man. The different parts of the machine should be constructed in such a way that workers would feel comfortable while doing work.

Lots of unnecessary fatigue can be removed by improving the design of machines. This takes the help of human engineering. A lot of fatigue in industry occurs due to useless and unnecessary movements, faulty postures, jerky movements which are not rhythmic, etc.

Following the procedures of the time and motion study, one best method of doing work should be followed and wrong, unnecessary and useless movements should be avoided. Automatic machines and moving belts should be used to reduce fatigue and improve production.

Neuroticism

Under similar circumstances some people may experience more fatigue than others because of neuroticism. This happens because of individual differences.

Therefore, neurotic workers should be selected for jobs which are less repetitive, less monotonous and which provide rest periods in between work.

Neurotic workers may be segregated from normal workers by means of proper selection before appointing workers for different types of jobs.

Mental Health of the Employee

The mental health of the employee can be responsible for the causation of fatigue. Emotional disturbances on and off the work situation, domestic troubles, lack of adjustment with the work sphere, etc. may consume a lot of energy. Unnecessary energy consumption due to emotional disturbances and mental conflicts thus leads to the early onset of fatigue.

Under such circumstances the workers should be given proper counselling and guidance for a healthy and tension free mental life.

Neurotic Conflict

Neurotic conflict which has no apparent cause and which is free floating, reduces a lot of energy and hence fatigue is originated.

Under such circumstance, while selecting workers for different jobs, those scoring high in the neurotic inventory should be given jobs which are less repetitive. Secondly psychological counselling should be provided to the neurotic workers to reduce their conflict and anxiety which is mostly free floating in nature.

General Health of the Worker

A person having less energy gets tired very soon. Hence, in the case of a physically weak person there is quick onset of fatigue compared to healthy person.

Thus, workers should be provided with free medical facilities and should be trained to develop a consciousness to take all steps to improve the general standard of their health.

Eye Strain

Defective lighting leads to eye strain and unnecessary fatigue. Artificial lighting instead of daylight causes more eye strain. Lack of use of suitable spectacles while doing fine work causes severe eye strain.

Weston and Adams have shown that the feeling of fatigue can be greatly reduced and production can be increased by providing special glasses to the workers.

Two studies designed and conducted by Bartley (1942) indicate the rapid onset of fatigue due to eye strain caused by defective lighting arrangements.

Besides the factors mentioned, heavy traffic, speedy driving, the long distance trip from residence to office, transport difficulties and parking problems increase fatigue and strain to a considerable extent. So much so, that when the employee reaches the work place from his residence he is already fatigued.

These problems, in this age of speed and machine, need deep thinking for their solution. It is usually found that such outside causes of fatigue are totally neglected as a result of which the mitigation of employees fatigue becomes a complicated job.

The findings of empirical studies and day to day observations indicate that fatigue affects the health of the worker and reduces output. Moreover, it has also immediate and adverse effect on timing and integrative functions. The effect of fatigue is most significant on jobs which require high grade performance, concentration and sustained attention. This view is supported by the findings of the studies by Fraser at Cambridge on pilot errors (edited by Fleishman, 1961). These studies showed that there was a disorganisation of the receptor effector processes, as a result of which performance on a vigilance test showed variability more after flying than before, more after flights in jet aircrafts than in piston engine aircraft and finally more at night than in the day time.

In this connection Maier (1970) remarks, "Rise in variance will influence how well an air craft can be held on its course and although it might not affect the flying time, it could result in landing accidents".

Realising the seriousness of such accidents, steps should be taken to cover up the effect of fatigue by creating motivation and interest in the job.

QUESTIONS

1. Define fatigue. Examine the nature and characteristics of fatigue.
2. What are the causes of fatigue ? How can fatigue be reduced ?
3. Critically examine the localisation of fatigue.
4. Can fatigue be measured ? If so, discuss the techniques used for measuring fatigue.
5. Industrial fatigue is the outcome of continuous physical work. Examine the above statement in the light of experimental studies.
6. Write notes on :
   (*a*) Production curve.
   (*b*) Symptoms of fatigue.
   (*c*) Effect of rest pause on fatigue.
   (*d*) Warming up phenomenon.

REFERENCES

Bartley, S.H. A factor in visual fatigue, *Psychosom.* 1942, 4, pp. 275-396.

Blum, M.L. and Naylor, J.C. *Industrial Psychology: Its Theoretical and Social Foundations,* Harper and Row Publishers, 1968.

Dill, C.A. The nature of fatigue, *Personnel,* 1933, 9, pp. 113-116.

Fatigue and hours of service of interstate truck drivers, *Public Health Bulletin* No. 265, Government Printing Office, Washington, D.C., 1941.

Fraser, D.C. *Recent Experimental Work in the Study of Fatigue in E.A.*, Fleishman, (Ed.), *Studies in Personnel Industrial Psychol.*, New York, Dorsay, 1961, pp. 473- 478.

Hours of work and production, *Labour Information Bulletin*, 1944, 2, pp. 4-7.

Hours of work and output, Bulletin No. 917, U.S., Deptt. of Labour, Government Printing Office, Washington D.C., 1947.

Maier, N.R.F. *Psychology in Industry*, Oxford and IBH Publishing Co., New Delhi, 1970.

Mosso, A. Fatigue, Putnam, New York 1915.

Muscio, B. Is a fatigue test possible, *British Jn. of Psychology*, 1921, 12; pp. 31- 46.

Muscio, B. and Vernon, H.M. *Industrial Fatigue and Efficiency,* London, Routledge, 1921.

Rayon, T.A. *Industrial Psychology*, New York, Dorsay. 1961, pp. 473-478.

Shepherd, G. Effects of rest pause on production, *Personnel Journal*, 1928, 7, pp. 86-202.

Vernon, A.M. The influence of rest pauses on changes in posture on the capacity of muscular work, *Industrial Fatigue Research Board Report,* No. 29, 1924.

Viteles, M.S. *Industrial Psychology, Norton*, 1932.

21

Monotony and Boredom

INTRODUCTION

It has been often said that monotony is the curse of modern civilisation. Due to the advancement in the fields of science and technology people have become mere puppets of machines.

According to Maier (1970), "It is claimed that repetitive work makes robots of men and that it destroys such human values as pride in workmanship and individuality". It is the common belief that boredom and dissatisfaction are very common in our present method of production. But to what extent a state of boredom really affects production needs careful consideration.

MEANING AND DEFINITION

Monotony or boredom is commonly referred to as mental fatigue or psychological fatigue which leads to work decrement. Monotony is an important aspect of industrial unrest and work decrement. It may be responsible for the increase of nervous disorders in modern life. Boredom is usually associated with work that is basically uninteresting to the individual performing it. Boredom is often associated with jobs that are repetitive or relatively simple. Monotony and boredom refer to the undersirable effects or repetitive work. This is actually a state of mind caused by repetitive work. According to Maier, monotony and boredom are influenced by the way a person views his task from time to time causing the output to fluctuate rather than to fall off progressively. With low motivation in a particular task the effect of mental fatigue becomes apparent very early. But when the motivation and interest in job is high there may not be a quick onset of monotony and boredom.

The motivation theory of fatigue advanced by Maier (1970) suggests that motivation increases the will and desire to work. The amount of energy necessary for doing work is released according to the strength of motivation. This theory advocates that high motivation makes more energy available and low motivation releases less energy for the performance of the task.

Maier further states. "Motivation reduces fatigue by increasing the allocated energy supply whereas such factors as rest periods and speed of work reduce fatigue by causing the energy to be spent efficiently regardless of the amount allotted".

Wright (1906) conducted an experiment to measure the ability of subject to do physical work under different conditions of motivation. The findings of this study support the contention that with expectations defined, higher motivation occurred and increased the amount of energy made available for work.

Hence with low motivation in a particular type of work, the effect of mental fatigue becomes apparent very early. But when the motivation and interest in the job are high there may not be a quick onset of mental fatigue until physical exertion overshadows mental fatigue.

Maier (1970) states that monotony and boredom are produced by similar conditions and that boredom is a more pronounced state of monotony. Division of labour has divided the work into different parts. One part of it is done by one individual always and hence the repetition of the same work leads to monotony. Mono means one and tonus means tone. One thing being repeated so many time over and over again creates "monotony".

The exigencies of scientific management break work into very small units and these units are to be performed by an individual in an entirely repetitive manner. Concentration on a particular minute unit for a repeated number of times makes the work meaningless and mechanical for the worker. Monotony is especially associated with automatic and semi-automatic type of work. But it is more the individual's reaction and attitude towards work that creates a feeling of boredom than the nature of the job itself.

Usually monotony is confused with fatigue, as both of them have a direct impact on output. But monotony is psychologically different from fatigue. Fatigue occurs due to continuous physical work, while monotony usually occurs due to the repetitive nature of work, lack of interest and motivation. Objectively speaking, studies conducted on behalf of the Industrial Health Research Board (1937) indicate that on the psychological plane different feelings underlie boredom and fatigue.

CHARACTERISTICS OF MONOTONY

1. Pleasure of work is denied due to monotony.
2. Work being entirely repetitive becomes meaningless.
3. Monotony lacks feeling of satisfaction.
4. Job satisfaction is missed by the average worker experiencing monotony.
5. Various industrial studies indicate that the mental state during the experience of monotony is associated with definite fluctuations in the rate of working and with a fall in production.

EXPERIMENTAL STUDIES ON MONOTONY

The characteristics of monotony can be further understood by analysing the laboratory experiments conducted in this area.

Wyatt, Langdon and Stock (1937) studied the effect of fatigue on work and found that the monotony curve was the inverse of the typical fatigue curve.

Wyatt and Frasner (1937) made a study on 68 workers who were classified in different groups such as A, B, C and D on the basis of their production curve. The first one was a regular fatigue curve and the other three curves were monotony curves.

The extent of monotony in different groups as found by Wyatt and Frasner was A = 0.9, B = 1.70, C = 2.80, and D = 3.60

Wyatt and Frasner gave these curves to some judges to judge whether they were fatigue or monotony curves, and noted that out of 68 cases, identification was correct with 51 cases. Thus, there was substantial agreement on the amount of monotony experienced. Hence, Wyatt, Langdon and Stock view that monotony is objectively a distinct kind of phenomenon and it should not be confused with fatigue.

One of the most enlightening studies on monotony was conducted by Kurt Lewin (1935) on the college students of Germany University, The subjects were asked to draw continuously vertical lines on sheets of paper and to follow a certain pattern, such as alternatively grouping the lines in twos and threes. The subjects were not allowed to stop at all. It was observed that gradually the quality of performance decreased and after about four hours the period of complete satiation came in, which indicated that the subjects could not proceed any further. Similar results were obtained when persons were instructed to read the same poem over and over again. Gradually, the quality of performance decreased and finally the stage of inability to talk was reached. This complete withdrawal from work indicated the onset of the period of satiation, Maier (1970) views that the stages of variability, reduction in quality, difficulty in continuing to make the necessary movements and complete inability to go on with the work characterise the course of satiation.

After the period of satiation Lewin changed the drawing altogether. Thus output and efficiency suggested that the period of satiation is not due to fatiguing of the musculature involved, but due to the psychological feeling of fatigue. The period of satiation is hence purely a psychological phenomenon.

MONOTONY CURVE

Wyatt and Frasner and Wyatt, Frasner and Stock separately did two studies on boredom and industrial repetitive work. From these studies the following conclusions were drawn about the characteristics of the monotony curve.

1. There is a great fluctuation in output.
2. The effects of monotony are more pronounced in the middle of work period and hence in a monotonous work curve output is very low in the middle spell of the curve.
3. Production is low and variable during periods when boredom was experienced.
4. The production of individuals who feel very bored is lower and more variable than that of the individuals who did not feel bored.

In another study, 355 workers were classified by Wyatt, Stock and Frasner on a five point scale of boredom.

Wyatt, Frasner and Stock, after finding the degrees of boredom, found that in these cases output was very low and had declined. The study further suggested that large number of the workers suffer from various degrees of boredom and that it is a universal problem.

In order to examine the theory of mental fatigue Arai (1912) engaged herself in doing the task of mental multiplication of four place numbers. After practising to develop skill, she worked on such problems continuously for 12 hours on four successive days. The average time taken per problem was 9.5 minutes on the first day and 7.5 minutes on the last, indicating that there was no detrimental carry over from one day to the next. The improvement can be attributed to practice.

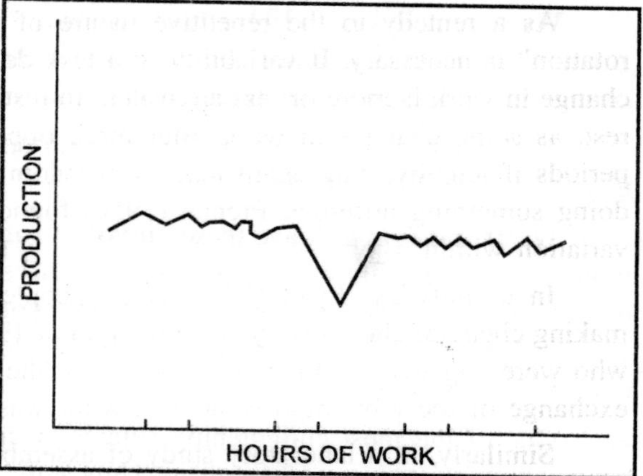

Fig. 21.1. Typical monotony curve.

According to Maier (1970), "The striking feature of this experiment is that the reduction of efficiency is so small that one cannot assume that similar cases of endurance will occur in industry because a high degree of motivation is not attained when a person must perform his duties, day after day in order to earn his living".

Painter (1916) who wished to test ability of the brain to continue activity, began work on mental multiplication problems at 11 p.m. Within four hours, *i.e.*, by 3 a.m. he was so fatigued that he required the assistance of his wife in getting to bed. His problem solving time increased 5 times during the four hours he was able to do work.

Maier (1970) conducted an experiment on himself after a hard day's work in his office so that the two test situations would be different. The findings of his experiment indicated that mental fatigue may reach a certain stage at which mental work and concentration are entirely impossible, This eventually indicates the onset of the period of satiation.

It is obvious from the following facts that a significant percentage of the loss in production of repetitive work is due to specific conditions of boredom rather than due to fatigue.

1. Afternoon monotony effects do not exceed those of the morning as might be expected from accumulated fatigue.
2. The anticipation of the end of the work period tends to abolish signs of monotony.
3. The intelligent workers are more subject to monotony effects than the less intelligent ones.

CAUSES AND MITIGATION OF MONOTONY

As evident from various studies conducted on monotony and boredom, boredom is not a product of one's imagination and it has a considerable adverse effect on efficiency and production. Thus, employees and psychologists showed definite concern over the matter and tried to find out the apparent causes of monotony, so that suitable steps could be taken to eliminate it. Mitigation of monotony is a serious challenge to modern industrial organisations. As success or failure of modern management depends upon this, steps should be taken to reduce monotony and boredom.

Repetitive Nature of Work

It is true that monotony is associated with repetitive work. This is especially so when the work becomes automatic and semi-automatic. Obviously when the work becomes machine like and requires no brain work and concentration, attention fluctuates to something else and the worker appears to be bored.

As a remedy to the repetitive nature of work, exchange of jobs otherwise called "job rotation" is necessary. If variability in a task delays the onset of satiation, it can be said that a change in work is more or less equivalent to rest. In some cases, even change may be better than rest, as some changes in work offer more opportunities for variability than rest periods. Rest periods if lengthy, may again lead to boredom. Change in work gives a person experience in doing something different. French (1950) found that there was improvement in morale due to variation within a job.

In a study by Wyatt (1929) some people were engaged in cutting cigarette papers and making cigarette alternatively, at an interval of 1½ hours. Their performance was better than those who were engaged in either of the tasks for the whole day. Maier (1970) found that because of exchange of the jobs improvement in work was noticed.

Similarly, in a laboratory study of assembling bicycle chains, Wyatt (1929) observed that output increased from 2.4 to 5 due to change in work. Wyatt and Frasner concluded that reduction in output is constantly noted, especially where there is constant complaint of boredom. Thus, variability in the same job should be permitted as far as possible.

To measure the effect of job rotation on performance, the present author (1979) conducted a study on herself. The study consisted of two types of work performed under two different sessions. In the first session the author kept herself engaged in her research room in the writing of a textbook from 11 a.m. to 4.30 p.m. for 15 days without any formal rest period or change of work except a break of 3 minutes at 3 p.m. for tea.

In the second session she took the help of job rotation by exchanging jobs. She wrote a chapter for the above textbook for an hour and then for another half an hour engaged herself in the knitting of a complicated design. This continued alternatively from 11 a.m. to 4.30 p.m. for another 15 days with only a break of 3 minutes for tea at 3 p.m. After each hour of work the investigator recorded her feelings of boredom through a five point scale such as very fresh, fresh, neither fresh nor bored, bored and extremely bored. The scale values given were 1,2,3,4, and 5 respectively.

TABLE 21.1
Showing the Average Performance During Repetitive Work and Job Rotations

Session	*Nature of task*	*Average Performance per hour*	*Scale value*	*Feeling of boredom*
(*i*)	Writing text-book only	4 pages per hour	4,50	Strong feeling of boredom and onset of period of satiation.
(*ii*)	Writing text-book and knitting alternatively	5.50 pages per hour	2,00	Feeling of freshness throughout the test and no onset of period of satiation.

Findings

The above findings suggest that performance was better both qualitatively and quantatively in the second session when there was job rotation. In addition to the improved output, she further did not experience feeling of boredom which is an usual experience in repetitive work. On the contrary, in the first session the performance was relatively less and strong feeling of boredom was experienced by the investigator due to her engagement in a single repetitive job. Moreover, the quality of writing suffered as the investigator could not be able to concentrate in her creative work due to want of 'change' in job. There was also regular onset of period of satiation usually between 3 p.m. and 4.30 p.m., when the investigator could not proceed in the writing work in spite of repeated efforts. These results strongly indicate the favourable effect of job rotation in reducing monotony and improving production.

Intelligence

It has been found that intelligent and highly intelligent workers are great sufferers of monotony. For example, a worker with low intelligence may be satisfied with the job of plate washing or stitching buttons, as such jobs do not require much intelligence.

But under such situations an intelligent worker will not find any interest and job satisfaction. There will obviously be fluctuation of attention and the onset of boredom. Evidences show that low intelligent workers are better adapted to repetitive work. But data on this is not clear-cut.

Bills (1931) studied the turnover rate of clerical workers and found that the labourer turnover was the highest in the intelligent group, because clerical work was considered monotonous by them. Similarly, the findings of a study by Kornhauser on office workers having high I.Q., showed the highest turnover. Viteles (1932) found positive correlation between the highest intelligence group and turnover. The more intelligent workers were more steady in their work pace and more satisfied with their work. However, interestingly, the production of the more intelligent workers exceeded that of the less intelligent ones in spite of their dislike for the work and variation in work rate.

Wyatt, Frasner and Stock (1929) studied the I.Q. of various workers in different factories. A questionnaire revealed the extent of the boredom experienced. However, the data obtained neither gave reliable results nor was there much significant relationship between I.Q. and boredom.

The present author (1967) conducted a study entitled "Sex and intelligence and monotony in continuous mental work" on a group of male and female college undergraduates. In this study, the author made an attempt to find out whether (*a*) intelligence helps in the quick onset of monotony and whether, (b) sex has any effect on the number of trials required to experience monotony. 35 male and 25 female under graduate students of Ravenshaw College, Cuttack (Orissa) were selected at random for the study. Their age ranged from 15 to 21 years (mean age of males = 18 years, mean age of females = 17 years 7 months).

The experiment was conducted individually in a quiet testing room. The testing was divided into two sessions. In the first session progressive matrices (adult form) were administered individually. After a time gap of two hours, each subject was asked to do multiplication work following a certain specific procedure till the 's' expressed strong feeling to fatigue. After each trial, which continued for 5 minutes the report of the 's' about feeling of fatigue was measured by a 5 point scale. Performance was measured through the amount of multiplication-work done during the test period and the errors committed.

The results of the study are presented in Table 21.2.

Results

As seen in Table 8 there was no statistically significant difference between male and female subjects in the number of trials required to experience monotony.

The product moment coefficient of correlation between scores on the progressive matrices test and the number of trials required to experience strong feeling of monotony was—0.72. This suggests that more intelligent students experienced monotony quickly in comparison with the less intelligent students.

TABLE 21.2

Table Showing Mean Trials Required to Experience Monotony and Correlation Between Scores on Progressive Matrices Test and Number of Trials Required to Experience Monotony

	Male	*Female*
N	35	25
Mean	6.22	7.68
S.D.	2.41	2.33
S.E.	0.46	0.45

between scores on progressive matrices test = – 0.72
(C.R. = 0.21 not significant.)

Therefore, on the basis of these findings it may be concluded that, by and large, intelligence is positively associated with monotony and boredom.

Rest Periods

By and large, frequent rest periods seem to be more effective than a few longer ones. A too long rest usually creates disturbances in different types of mental work because the person loses the continuity of work and gets out of the mood for it.

Though the amount of rest pause varies with the nature of work, generally rest pauses of about 5 minutes in length seem to be beneficial.

It is, however, true that the actual percentage of rest required for any mental work is less than that for manual work.

Feeling of Experience of Progress

As studies indicate, the absence of experience of a goal or an end toward which one moves may appear quite different to subjects with different backgrounds. The same person on two different occasions may view the same task differently. If a change in the view and outlook regarding the task can be possible, monotony can be reduced. This has been demonstrated in Lewin's study (1935) conducted on a group of unemployed college students. In this study it was also noted that the pleasantness and unpleasantness of the task had no important effect on the rate of satiation. So experience of progress is to be introduced in work to avoid monotony.

Neuroticism

Various studies indicate that neuroticism is related to monotony. The attention of neurotic workers fluctuates more rapidly than normal ones. So they lose interest in the job and get bored very quickly.

There can be two remedies to reduce monotony. Firstly, neurotic workers should not be employed in jobs which are repetitive and monotonous. Secondly, psychological guidance and counselling should be given to neurotic workers.

By Relating the Job to a Larger Picture

Monotony can be reduced by relating the job to a larger picture. Whether progress is experienced or not depends on the way the individual views the job. If a boy who is washing dishes in a hotel experiences each dish as just another dish, washing a large stock of them will not probably give him an experience of progress. But for another boy who loves to wash dishes and considers each dish as a separate one, the experience of progress would be rapid and work interesting.

Thus, by teaching employees the meaning of their work, how it fits into the total picture and how tile records are arranged, etc., monotony can be avoided. Secondly, by giving employees, responsibility and opportunities for judgement, a more effective result is obtained.

Use of Sub Goals

Distant goals are usually less effective and practically non-existent. Hence, it is necessary to introduce sub goals. Rest pauses can serve a dual function by decreasing boredom and also other forms of fatigue. Sub goals can also be introduced by grouping the production into larger units. Instead of making many more parts, if the work is divided into larger units, the sub goal is introduced which makes work more interesting.

Group decision can be used to reduce boredom. According to Maier, if a specified amount of production is set, then a given number of units function as final goals. When production is made a part of the sub goals, it serves to increase the importance of these goals and makes progress towards them more meaningful and apparent.

As suggested by Maier (1970), "The practice of breaking up tasks by introducing rest periods and by grouping the production units is an important method of reducing boredom. Since some form of this procedure can be applied to many types of work, it should be given serious consideration".

Music

The introduction of music has become a common phenomenon in most of the industrial organisations today with the purpose of reducing monotony and improving output. Research work on the effect of music on the production and on the mental state of the employees has been quite encouraging.

To start with, Wyatt, Langdon and Stock's study (1937) indicates that production increased by 6 per cent due to the introduction of music during work. While conducting a study on a radio tube assembly factory Humes (1941) investigated the effectiveness of fast, mixed and slow music on performance. Result showed that with either fast or slow music the scrap page rate was less than when there was no music or when fast and slow music programmes were alternated. It was further noticed that music improved the morale of the employees.

A study by Kerr (1945) suggested that music not only improved production, it also improved the attitude of the workers and had a favourable effect on their mental state.

Smith (1947) reported a finding which revealed that there was an average increase of 7 per cent in the day shift and 17 per cent in the night shift with the introduction of music. However, McGehee and Gardner (1949) did not find any improvement in production due to the introduction of music.

An overall analysis of the research findings do suggest that music helps in reducing monotony, improving the mental state of the workers and raising the level of production.

Use of Pacing Method and Automatic Work Habits

According to Maier (1970), "Our analysis has shown that repetitive work creates mental satiation and perhaps boredom as well not because the activity is repetitive, but because it creates the experience of marking time. If one can change the experience but leave the activity, the same boredom will partly disappear".

Keeping Maier's view in mind, if repetitive work is made entirely automatic or semi-automatic the feeling of monotony can be reduced to a considerable extent. For example, knitting a simple mechanical pattern for long periods will not appear monotonous if the mind is kept engaged in some other task. Walking from residence to college daily will not appear monotonous either.

Experience of Completion

Incomplete tasks create monotony because of a sense of dissatisfaction. In every management the tasks should be divided into different sub parts. When a part is completed the employee experiences a feeling of completion. When the interest of the worker is not sustained in the job, or the job appears to be monotonous it should be divided into parts, to create a sense of motivation after the completion of each part.

Work in the telephone industry, training shops, clerical jobs, etc. have been made interesting by increasing the experience of completion. However, if the job is interesting or short, the experience of completion will arise automatically and the work need not be divided.

According to Maier (1970), "Task completion represents a form of motivation inherent in the nature of job and therefore is one of the most practical ways for creating job interest".

QUESTIONS

1. Define monotony and discuss its characteristics.
2. Is psychological change a cause of monotony ? If not, give the causes of monotony bring out its remedies.
3. Compare the physical fatigue curve with the mental fatigue curve. How can boredom be eliminated by job rotation ?
4. Describe the effect of monotony on industrial work. Does monotony affect industrial efficiency ?
5. What are the causes of boredom ? Supplement your answer with experimental findings.
6. Write notes on the following :
   (*a*) Job rotation
   (*b*) Experience of progress.
   (*c*) Monotony and boredom.
   (*d*) Neuroticism and monotony.
   (*e*) Effect of music on repetitive work.
   (*f*) Fatigue and monotony.

REFERENCES

Bills, A.G. *General Experimental Psychology*, New York, Longmans, Green, 1931.

Kerr, W.A. Effects of music on factory production, *Appl. Psychol.* Monogr, 1945.

Maier, N.R.F. *Psychology in Industry*, Oxford and IBH Publishing Co., New Delhi, 1970.

McGehee, W. and Gardner, J.E. Music in a complex industrial job, *Personnel Psychol.*, 1949, 2, pp. 405-417.

Mohanty, Girishbala. *Monotony and Job Rotation*, 1979.

Mohanty, Girishbala. Sex and intelligence and monotony in continuous mental work, *Indian Jn. of Applied Psychology,* 1967, 5, No. 2, pp. 90-91.

Smith, H.C. Music in relation to employee attitude piecework production and industrial accident, *Appl. Psychol. Monogr,* 1947, pp. 14.

Wyatt, S., Frasner, J.A. and Stock, F.G.L. The effects of monotony in work, *industrial Fat. Board*, 1929, Ref. No. 56.

Wyatt, S., Langdon, J.N. and Stock, F.G.L. Fatigue and boredom in repetitive work, *Indust. Health Res. Bd.*, 1937, Rep. No. 77.

Viteles, M.S. *Psychology in Industry*, Norton, 1932.

22

Working Environment

INTRODUCTION

The classic findings of the Hawthorne studies indicate that physical environment has nothing to do with the level of production. In other words, the increment and decrement in production does not necessarily depend upon the level, of illumination. But it cannot be denied that the consideration of physical environment in industrial psychology is necessary for the very fact that environmental factors affect and influence the worker's behaviour.

NEED OF SUITABLE WORKING ENVIRONMENT

Because of the limitations of human sense organs one cannot work in darkness. Low illumination is associated with eye strain, headache, fatigue, low quality of work, increased number of accidents, low output and ultimately, low morale among the employees.

Besides, a change in the physical environment will bring a change in the social climate of the factory. With the improvement in physical environment the workers feel that something is being done for them. This feeling gives them psychological satisfaction and a sense of importance.

The consideration of working environment in industry is therefore necessary.

ILLUMINATION

Several studies conducted on illumination suggest that since human organs are very adjustable, sometimes the results become very unreliable, *i.e.,* they are not treated as scientific. It is also a fact that minimum lighting for each and every type of work cannot be fixed and predetermined.

However, because of the limited capacity of our sense organs, optimum illumination is essential and desirable for efficient production. Until 1937, proper care was not taken for suitable illumination. In 1937, the Factory Act was approved and only since then have regulations been made for optimum illumination.

Experiments on Illumination

In 1933, out of 476 factories in England only six per cent had proper lighting arrangements. This report indicates how proper lighting was neglected in factories. It has been found that the quality of output can be increased by improving the quality and quantity of illumination. The Electric Lamp Manufacturer's Association in 1943 gave sufficient evidence to support this statement. A study conducted by the National Industrial Fatigue Research Board (1929) indicated that there is decrement in efficiency due to inadequate illumination. Optimum illumination is, therefore, required for better efficiency and comfort. The quality of work improved because of optimum illumination, as properly distributed lights enabled the eye to see things quickly and smoothly.

In a type-setting work, when the lighting was less than two-foot candles, printers made two and a half times as many mistakes but at seven-foot candles, the efficiency increased to a great extent.

Industrial surveys further indicate that production continues to rise as illumination is raised from 6-20-foot candles and that at 20-foot candles the rise in production follows a sharper upward trend than does the increase in the cost of lighting. Studies show that with increased illumination, depending upon the nature of work, production increases from eight per cent to 27 per cent. Roughly 20 per cent of the factory accidents in U.S.A. are due to inadequate lighting or defective eye sight or a combination of both. Evidences indicate that because of optimum illumination the physical and mental health of the workers improve.

In a tile-pressing factory, Adams found that when illumination was increased from 1.7-4.7-foot candles output increased by six per cent. Adams thus views that this improvement in production is largely due to the tonic effect of increased illumination. Since adequate light helps in the accuracy of work waste products are reduced. Lastly, when there is good lighting workers can do less mischief and if they do, can be easily detected.

Problems of Illumination

Illumination has got certain problems which need consideration for improving the efficiency of industrial employees.

Distribution of Light. The Illumination Research Committee in 1933 suggested that it was more desirable to consider the lighting of the total visual field rather than the field of observation only. Thus, a lot of trouble in industry can be eliminated by proper distribution of light. However, uniform distribution of light is not desirable as in such cases the figure ground phenomenon does not operate. For the sake of brightness and constant variation in lighting, unequal distribution of illumination is necessary. Thus, the whole field may be more or less uniformly distributed while the working surface may have some additional light. But this variation should not be sudden or else it would cause eye strain. Walls which have poor reflecting qualities reduce the illumination of the outer parts of the visual field, and so even though a large amount of light is used in the room, total field is not uniformly lighted.

Moreover, with the rapid and sudden change of illumination it becomes difficult for the eyes to adjust as a result of which fatigue and eye strain are caused.

Intensity of Light. Intensity of light varies from job to job and individual to individual. It also depends upon the type of job the worker is engaged in. Studies indicate that intensity of light up to particular limit is followed by increased production and reduced number of accidents. Moss and his associates, on the basis of the findings of some studies, concluded that increment of illumination should be up to a particular limit, otherwise it would cause various inconveniences with several after-effects. This led the government to pass various Factory Acts. In a study at an Ahemdabad textile mill, production increased from seven to 11 per cent because of increased lighting.

Moss and Luckiesh (1937) have presented the data given in Table 22.1, on the basis of a study conducted by them on the effect of the intensity of illumination on output, which suggests that is there improvement in output due to increased illumination.

TABLE 22.1

Type of work	*Previous illumination*	*New illumination*	*Increment in output*
1. General Efficiency	6.0 F.C.	16 F.C.	9%
2. Word making	2.5.F.C.	14 F.C	9%
3. Weaving	13.3 F.C.	29 F.C.	25%
4. Fine engineering (Leather products)	4 to 8 F.C	12 to 20 F.C.	15%

Though intensity of illumination varies from job to job, on the basis of several findings, the average degree of illumination can be fixed for different types of work. For example, for office work and fine leather work, the estimated illumination ranged from 3-20-foot candles. But for fine work, such as distinguishing black thread from black cloth, the intensity of 400-foot candles has been recommended by Luckiesh and Moss (1937). It has also been suggested that fine work requiring discrimination, precision and accuracy needs the light of 50-foot candles. Though work of a gross style may be done in the light of 6-10-foot candles, good lighting always facilitates work without giving extra trouble to the workers.

Keeping in view these facts and findings it can be suggested that for different types of work, the optimum intensity of illumination is to be found out, depending upon the size, duration and brightness of the object, in contrast to the background and shadow of light, etc. For example, certain works require critical observation of minute details. Such tasks can be performed only in high intensity of light. But it should not be forgotten that increase in intensity may affect the eye if the light is not distributed properly. As found from the study of Ferree and Rand (1918) high intensity of illumination with direct lighting may be very disturbing.

Duration. Experimental results indicate that when the workers get more time to look at the objects, they see much smaller objects in comparatively low intensity of light. Therefore, light should be provided for sufficient duration to facilitate work and efficiency.

Brightness. Brighter is the object, more light is reflected by it. Spencer and his associates found that there was rapid increment in visual acuity with increase in brightness from .01 to 1.00 mm. But excessive light is undesirable as it gives rise to the problem of glare.

Object in Contrast to the Background. If the object to be seen is lost in the background more intense light is required. On the contrary, when the object is brighter or darker than the background it creates a contrast effect. In such a case, less intense light can also do.

Visual Acuity of the Worker. For every plant or organisation, work and the work situation may be important, but the condition of the worker has also to be considered. If the visual acuity of the employee is high, very intense light may not be necessary.

Problem of Shadow. Apart from intensity there is the problem of shadow. It has been found that benches, desks, tables and machines cast shadows in the factory. These shadows cut across the work situation and thereby adversely influence the workers. Shadows on the walls, patches on the floor and roof give a dismal appearance to the factory. In such a dark and dismal situation workers have been found reacting emotionally. On the other hand, a bright surrounding makes the mind bright and cheerful.

When supplementary lights are put on the roof, shadows are avoided and the situation improves. Supplementary adjustable local lights on the tables are also advisable as they provide additional light and at the same time dispal shadows. Shadows can be removed by providing light at the working tables. When the indirect system of lighting is used shadows are eliminated to a great extent. But of course, it should be kept in view that sometimes soft and well illuminated shadows are helpful in discriminating details, and at the same time, are soothing to the eyes.

Problem of Glare. Glare is caused due to excessive reflection of light. Because of glare when eyes are overflooded with light, eye strain, fatigue, annoyance and injuries to the delicate cells of the eyes are caused.

In an ammunition factory production was lowered due to the undesirable effects of glare. So glare it to be avoided as it not only lowers production but also creates an unfavourable attitude among the workers.

Glare is of two types : (1) Successive glare; and (2) Simultaneous glare.

Successive glare : Successive glare is experienced when our eyes are overflooded with excessive light all of a sudden. For example, when we come across a car in the road, our eyes are overflooded with successive glare.

Simultaneous glare : Simultaneous glare results from a highly bright and localised source of light in the field of vision, which is more or less continuous but not sudden. This may be direct or indirect. It is direct when the light comes directly from the light source to the eye. For example, when a bulb of high C.P. is localised in front of an individual, direct glare is caused. Indirect glare is found when light is reflected by a polished object in the field.

The problems of glare have to be avoided because they not only lower production but develop undesirable attitude among the workers. They can be controlled to a great extent through proper distribution of light and by die indirect lighting system.

Problem of Colour of Light. Difficulties arise when employees react differently to different colours of light. Thus, from the efficiency point of view, this problem needs consideration. As colours do possess feeling tones being associated with the past experience and association of the individual, individuals obviously react differently to different colours.

Social norms are also fixed for different colours of light. For example, white signifies purity, red festivity, black misfortune and blue, romanticism. For such reasons, possibly it has been suggested, that in the selection of the colour of light, these personal and social factors should not be ignored.

Besides, the reflection of light also depends on the colour of light as well as on the colour of the surface. Ruffer (1928) in a study tested visual acuity, speed of vision and eye-hand-coordination under green, yellow, red and blue lights. Results showed that there was no relation between the colour of general illumination and production. However, with regard to illumination of work space, yellow was found to be the most advantageous colour. Green, red and blue were the other colours in order of preference. Many other investigators obtained similar results.

Maier quotes an experiment by Fernberger and associates (1934), on inspecting white flannel cloth for defects under three sources of light. It was found that visual acuity was greatest under the day light lamp and least under mercury vapour lamp.

According to Maier (1970), the economical operation of vapour lamps makes it desirable to know the relative effectiveness of coloured lights for vision. From a study by Ferry and Rand (1931) it was noted that in nearly all cases, the order of superiority was found to be yellow, yellow-green, green, red, blue and green-blue. The light from the Mazda lamp was superior to any of the coloured lights. So the extensive use of coloured lights was not advised.

It is suggested that in selecting the colour of illumination the following facts should be considered.

(*a*) The colour of light should be such that the objects can be seen in their true colour.

(*b*) The amount of reflected light should be such that the objects can be seen in their original colour.

(*c*) Lastly, the reflection of light should neither be too little nor too much to cause discomfort to the workers. It must be optimum.

For there reasons, yellow is considered to be the best colour as white gets dirty very soon and so looks clumsy. Also yellow as a colour is preferably natural and does not involve any feeling tone.

For proper reflection of light, cream white ceiling, cream white upper walls and grayish green colour walls are usually preferred.

It has been calculated that in order to look after and solve the problem of illumination, the cost of improvement in terms of production is less than five per cent. But the net gain in production is much more than the cost of improvement. Hence, proper lighting arrangements in factories should not be neglected at any cost. Good lighting is cheerful and stimulating. It creates a favourable attitude and high morale by creating pleasent surroundings.

NOISE

Problem of Noise. According to Dr. May Smith a 'golden age' is frequently described as one in which noise was unknown. The importance of noise is well understood from this remark of Dr. May Smith. It is an accepted fact that every individual in the modern age is daily exposed to some noise in one form or the other. It is only the exceptional person who is free from such noise sources as the automobile, traffic, radio, children at play, aircraft and a host of common noises in varied fields to which persons are normally exposed.

Adverse Effects of Noise. Specifically, modern industries are characterised by noise as gigantic machines working all the time produce sounds together with intermittent shouts of the people around. It is commonly held that noise has got a very disturbing effect and hence it is a highly undersirable element in industry. Apart from the general public, medical men have also risen against noise as their contention is that noise affects our health adversely. In a noisy atmosphere a task demands more attention and more energy. This induces nervous disorder in the workers.

It is held that noise produces four adverse effects.

1. It distracts the attention of the workers. More distraction leads to extra expenditure of energy.
2. Health is affected adversely.
3. Efficiency is lowered.
4. A tinge of unpleasantness and a feeling of discomfort is attached to noise.

Thus, noise has become one of the problems of modern industry and it can be easily held that noise is disagreeable to most of us.

Before tackling the problem of noise, it becomes necessary that noise should be measured. Only then can remedies to the problem be brought about.

If noise is within a certain limit the problem can be neglected or overlooked. But when its intensity exceeds a particular limit one may be anxious about it. Oakley (1945) remarks that care has to be taken when noise exceeds 85 decibels. However, normally noise rarely exceeds this limit.

There are individual differences with regard to susceptibility to noise, in that a sound which appears to be noisy to one may not be a noise to another. Also the effect of noise depends upon the situation, the work one is doing, and lastly, on habit. For example, music may appear to be a noise when one is working out a complex and difficult problem of mathematics, while it may not have the same disturbing effect when one is doing a simple or mechanical job like knitting a sweater. Similarly, the noise experienced in tile railway station is not noise for those, who live nearby. This is because of habituation or negative adoptation. But this habituation is easier in the case of continuous noise and difficult in the case of intermittent or discontinuous noise.

The phenomenon of noise is therefore a subjective affair. It defies all the objective measurements when it is subjective, as the experience depends upon the feelings of the individual at different times. All these make noise a complex phenominon.

Meaning and Definition of Noise

There are wide and varied disputes as far as the meaning of noise is concerned, as it has got different meanings for different people and different meaning for the same person at different times. Thus a noise to one may be music to another. The same music may be a noise to 'x' when he works out sums, while it may not be so when he is talking with a friend.

However, the most common and acceptable definition of noise is, "Any loud, meaningless, disagreeable and discontent sound is referred to noise."

There are two kinds of noises.

1. Periodic or continuous noise.
2. Non-periodic or discontinuous noise.

Adjustment is easier in the case of continuous noise. But it becomes difficult to adjust in the case of discontinuous noise. Observation and other evidences indicate that unless noise is sudden, unusual and loud, the factory and office workers pay little attention to it.

Experimental Studies on Noise

Noise being one of the important problems in industry, its effects have been studied both in laboratories and in industries under artificial and natural situations, respectively.

Pollock and Bartlett (1932) conducted a study on students who were asked to do all kinds of tasks from manual to mental work under noisy and quiet situations. The results indicated that to begin with, noise produced slight deficiency in the beginning of test. But there was quick habitation and adjustment after sometime and hence their efficiency did not decrease.

Especially with regard to mental work, it was noted that speed decreased due to noise. It was further found that continuous noise had no such adverse effects as discontinuous noise, which created headache, irritability and strain.

Bartlett further found the differential effects of meaningful noise on different people; *i.e.*, some were disturbed by noise, others were not. In this connection, Maier views that noises which are generally unpleasant may be a factor in social relations even when they do not markedly influence the individual performers.

In a study, Allport and Cantril observed that music has not got any marked disturbing effect upon efficiency.

One of the earliest studies was done by Morgan (1916). The subjects in this study were required to translate letters into numbers and numbers into letters. The difficulty to the task varied in different parts of the experiment. Production was measured both qualitatively and quantitatively. Moreover, energy expenditure was measured by noting changes in the character of breathing and the amount of pressure exerted upon the keys used in recording the translation. In the experiment, quiet and noisy situations were provided alternatively. It was found that to begin with, subjects took more time in translation, but it was followed by rapid rise in the speed of work with the result that six out of eight subjects showed greater output during the noisy period and particularly in the beginning of the experiment. The experimenter concluded that noise has got an energising effect in spurring the organism to increase activity. Analysing Morgan's findings Blum and Naylor have commented that noise does not necessarily interfere with efficiency as measured by production, it results in inefficiency as measured by energy cost.

The results of this experiment, therefore, mostly go in favour of noise, indicating that noise creates motivation to do a particular work. Ford (1929) has obtained similar findings. Besides, he has also noted that a person who has adjusted himself to a noisy work situation can be distracted by a sudden silence.

Lairde conducted an experiment on four typists under noisy and quiet situations. It was noted that during the noisy phase the average expenditure of energy was 71 per cent higher during the typing period than in the resting period. But output was 51 per cent more during the noisy situation. This increased effort is responsible for higher production during noisy phase.

Park and Payne (1963) found that the performance of the average worker was not affected by intense noise, but the variability of performance became much greater when the task was quite easy and boring. For highly difficult tasks no noise effect was observed.

Adams (1932) has studied the effect of noise on the output of 11 women weavers in a weaving factory. The weavers were provided with ear defenders on every alternative week. It was found that the use of ear defenders increased production by one per cent on the average during these weeks when they used ear defenders. Moreover, those who used ear defenders wanted to use them in future for the sake of restfulness which they experienced with it. The benefits of reduced noise were more marked in the morning than in the afternoon. Culbert and Posner (1960) made an attempt to examine the degree to which individuals can successfully adjust to noise. The results indicated that after a period of several weeks, individuals could adapt to a noise which was tense as a jet aircraft. No change in performance was observed due to this adaptation.

McCartney (1941) also found that the work of assembling temperature regulators increased more than 37 per cent both qualitatively and quantitatively in a quiet situation than in a noisy situation. Errors also decreased by 13 per cent when the workshop was removed from a noisy section to a quiet one. The noise reduction also decreased turnover rate by 47 per cent and absenteeism by 37.5 per cent. This study strongly emphasises the adverse effects of noise.

Kornhauser (1927) made a study on four typists and found no significant difference when errors, the amount typed and the number of discarded letters were considered.

As regards the feeling of fatigue, no significant difference was found between the two conditions.

By and large, Kornhauser did not find any marked advantage of one condition over the other. He suggests the important psychological element to be considered in accounting for the present result by saying that the work studied was highly automatic and stereotyped. It is probable that noise decreases efficiency more in activities which are less stereotyped, or in which greater thought and concentration of attention are involved.

This study on typists does not show any adverse effect of noise on production.

In a film processing plant in England, a study on the effect of noise in the work situation was conducted by Broadbent and Little (1960). Results showed that the rate of work was not improved by noise reduction but the errors were significantly less frequent when the noise level was less. Evidences are also present to show that in the case of certain types of tasks, continuous work over a period of hours under a high degree of noise, may affect work performance. This may particularly hold good for paced tasks that need extreme speed in responding to the stimuli. The work involved in the operation of machines and inspection of items on a conveyor-belt may be cited as examples of jobs requiring high speed in responding to the stimuli. Broussard's study (1953), in which attempts were made to measure choice reaction time under conditions of 90 decibels noise and 45 decibels noise for two hours, supports the view mentioned earlier about the adverse effects of noise.

The results graphically presented in Figure 22.1 indicate that reaction time to a faint visual signal, under noise, increased gradually during the two hours period.

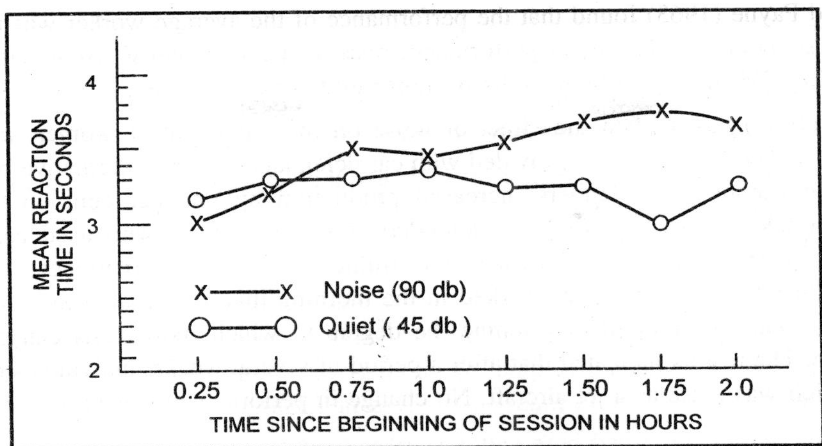

Fig. 22.1. Reaction time to faint visual signals under noise (90 decibels) and quiet (45 decibels). Based on data from Broussard (1953).

Murray (1972) has pointed out the present position of noise and the law in the United Kingdom. According to him the Robens Committee on the Safety and Health at Work has recommended that in addition to a code of practice there should be legislation and a special inspectorate to deal with noise. The question of prescribing occupational deafness as an occupational disease giving entitlement to compensation has been under consideration for sometime and a decision is expected in the near future.

In another study conducted on the effects of noise on the hearing of air crew personnel, Tobias (1972) noted that flight inspectors showed a moderate average hearing loss, flight instructors and commercial pilots showed mild to moderate average loss and agriculture pilots showed uniform hearing losses.

Chatterjee and Krishna Murthy (1972) investigated the effects of noise on performance with regard to the interaction of environmental stress and stimulation. Twenty professional typists typed for 10 minutes from predetermined materials and their performance was measured. Findings indicated that in psychomotor activity, performance is a function of skill, intermittent noise acts as an environmental stress affecting performance more than continuous noise, and lastly, for highly skilled subjects continuous noise of optimum intensity may act as an arouser of performance.

While studying the psychological consequences of aircraft noise, Stockbridge and Lee (1973) noted the complaints and social disamenity caused by aircraft noise. In this study, the investigators have discussed the effects of aircraft noise and have concluded that technologists can and will decrease engine noise levels if social pressure is applied.

The present author (1980) has conducted a study on the effect of periodic and non-periodic noise on the multiplication work of a group of students. The subjects of the study were 10 college undergraduates and 18 school students studying in tenth grade, all male. While the subjects were engaged in multiplication work, for a session of 45 minutes, periodic and non-periodic noises were introduced by the help of a tape recorder on alternative days. In the third condition they were allowed to multiply under quiet situation. Errors along with the subjective feeling of fatigue of the sample were recorded.

The above results suggests that out of 28 subjects 21 showed decrement in performance during non-periodic noise. However four college students and three high school students showed little decrement in performance during this period though initially they took more time to complete a trial. This extra time was probably required to adjust with the noisy situation.

The introspective report of the subjects indicated that 95 per cent of the sample experienced a feeling of extreme unpleasantness and irritation during the introduction of non-periodic noise in comparison to periodic noise.

Findings

However, an overall analysis of finding justifies the view that though periodic noise is less disturbing than non-periodic noise, quiet situation is the most preferable, for mental work in particular, to produce better performance and pleasant feeling.

All these studies described here and a number of other studies lead one to conclude that in some cases a noisy situation is favourable while in some other cases a quiet situation is favourable. Looking at the findings, it is very difficult to give a generalised conclusion on the effect of noise.

The effects of noise will thus depend upon the nature of the task, the type of the worker and the character of the noise. All these factors would contribute to the effect of noise.

TABLE 22.2

Mean Performance Scores in Multiplication Work During Periodic and Non-periodic Noise

Nature of noise	*Nature of test*	*N*	*Increase or decrease in performance*	*Introspective report*
Periodic	Multiplication work	28	in 70/28 Sc performance decreased	in 90/28 Ss unpleasant and irritative experience reported.
Non-periodic	Multiplication work	28	in 21/28 Ss performance decreased	in 27/28 Ss unpleasant and irritative experience reported.
Quiet situation	Multiplication work	28	in 01/28 Ss performance decreased	27/28 Ss reported pleasant feeling and no disturbance.

One of the limitations of the investigations conducted in the area of noise is that the experiments conducted in the laboratory are artificial and they may not correspond to the results of factory investigations. Hence, the laborotory results cannot be directly applied to the plant situation. Besides, it has been usually found that motivation is greater in laboratory work. Hence, more studies are required to be conducted in plants and organisations under natural situations in order to arrive at a general stand. In spite of the confusing experimental findings, however, it cannot be denied that, by and large, noise has got, some adverse effect upon production, It is widely agreed that loud noise of a high pitch produces a startled reaction and this disturbs sleep, thus having a bad effect on health. Irritation caused due to disturbance also affects mental health.

On the basis of several experimental findings. Viteles views that except certain meaningful noises, there is wide agreement that noise is a disagreeable and uncomfortable accompaniment of work. It not only affects physical and mental health but also has an adverse effect on the morale of the employees due to its unpleasant nature.

Noise and Individual Differences

Why are some people susceptible to noise while others are not ? Is it related to the personality of the individual ?

In this connection Cuplin and May Smith have suggested the relationship between susceptibility to noise and nervous temperament. According to Fraser, in ten per cent of the workers disturbed by noise, the reaction was due to neuroticism. Cuplin and May Smith have interviewed 49 girls, 19 students and 155 workers and found that individuals who were more neurotic were more disturbed by noise. Thus, on the basis of the findings of Fraser, it can be held that neurotic individuals are undoubtedly hypersensitive to noise.

Oakley (1945) makes an interesting remark in this connection, "Noise does not make normal people neurotic; what it does do, is make some neurotic people more neurotic".

Control of Noise

According to Oakley (1945), there are two general approaches to noise abatement.

1. Making of noise may be stopped.
2. Noise may be prevented from reaching the people.

Since it is an agreed fact that loud noise has got some disturbing effects, steps should be taken to control noise in various industries and organisations. Elimination of noise is neither possible nor necessary. But noise should be reduced to reasonable levels in accordance with the type of work and the nature of workers.

1. Machines should be designed in such a way that they are capable of absorbing sounds.
2. Neurotic workers may be selected for jobs providing less noise.
3. Workers should be instructed to use ear devices such as ear plugs and ear muffs whenever they feel its necessity. But the difficulty is that very few workers use ear defenders, probably because they consider this to be an insult to their ability and efficiency.
4. Departments containing noisy machines may be segregated from the walls and floors by means of rubber, cork, etc. In this connection it may be mentioned that the department of Scientific and Industrial Research, England, has formed a committee to find out the methods of reducing the transmission of noise in buildings.

Soundless machines should be designed and manufactured. Defects in machines caused by unpleasant noise should be avoided, such as noises coming from the driving, belt of the rotating fan etc. Such noises should be rectified while designing new machines. For example, now-a-days soundless refrigerators and generators are being manufactured, while there are some refrigerators which make periodic sounds. Noiseless typewriters electric motors, vehicles and machines should be designed more and more to prevent noise.

Oakley (1945) says, "To sum up this discussion on noise abatement we would say that if greater attention were given to the elimination of industrial noises, the consequences would be beneficial both to the employees and the employers".

Conclusion

Noise not only affects the morale of the workers by creating irritable conditions but also creates unfavourable attitude towards the management. Discontinuous noise is more subjectively disturbing than continuous noise. Meaningful noise may be less disturbing than unmeaningful noise as it is interesting and familiar. Correction of unpleasant noise therefore leads to better morale and favourable attitude. In fact, even if noise does not influence production markedly, it does influence the feelings of the workers. Hence, noise as a disturbing factor of factory environment should be carefully attended to by the management.

ATMOSPHERIC CONDITIONS

Ventilation

Importance of Suitable Ventilation. We live in air as fish do in water. Air is very important for any life to exist and continue. Pure air consists of 20.93 per cent of oxygen, 79.04 per cent nitrogen and .03 per cent of carbon dioxide.

When several individuals work together they exhale poisonous gas and the air is bound to get polluted and unhealthy for the workers. It also raises the temperature and the moisture content. As a result, there is a rise in humidity and temperature. When carbon dioxide exceeds a certain limit in the air, care should be taken to check it. But in a factory carbon dioxide rarely goes above .03 per cent and oxygen rarely goes below 19 per cent. Though in factories the air rarely goes below this limit, under certain cases the temperature is influenced, thus creating problems. As atmospheric temperature influences our body temperature, it is important to keep it at a certain level.

Experimental Studies on Ventilation. One of the earliest studies on ventilation was done by Vernon on tinplate factory workers for six years. Vernon found that temperature was inversely related to output. In the month of August temperature was the highest and production was the lowest. But in January, temperature being the lowest, the highest production was recorded. Production was ten per cent less in August than in January which shows that they are inversely related.

The research findings of Vernon, Bedford and Warner (1927) indicate that manual work was greatly affected by temperature, either high or low, as also the rate of accidents.

This is also the view of the New York State Ventilation Commission (1923). The degree of temperature for different works varies. But optimum temperature depends upon the nature of work and the worker, habit and automatisation. Still Vernon, Bedford and Warner (1927), have found 64° F and 68° F as the most comfortable zone and 67° F as the most desired temperature. But this comfort zone may not be applicable to other tropical countries with different climates like India. Moreover, the comfort zone also depends upon habit. Accidents, according to Vernon *et al.*, also increased alarmingly when the temperature went below 52° F and above 67° F.

The Factory Acts have recommended the maintaining of ideal temperature for the sake of workers and their efficiency. Vernon, Bedford and Warner (1927) have found different zones for different types of work.

For average secondary work, they found the zone to be 67° to 69° F, for light active work, 62° to 65° F, and for heavy active work the zone was 55° to 60° F. For very heavy manual work the zone was 50° F with air movement.

Vernon, Bedford and Warner have also conducted a study on mine workers. Studying temperature and air velocities in various pits they found that time lost from sickness were greatly influenced by temperature. Miners working in higher temperatures experienced 65 per cent more sickness than those working at lower temperatures.

Meckworth (1950) holds that a skill, whether manual or mental, goes on decreasing with 80° F. He holds 85° F to be the critical point where there is a sharp drop. This range is different for more efficient workers. He found that the accident rate also rose alarmingly when temperatures went below 52° F and above 67° F.

The New York State Commission on Ventilation (1923) has made several investigations, the findings of which show that physical work is definitely impaired by high temperatures.

In one experiment by the Ventilation Commissions, men were required to lift a 5 pound dumb bell through a distance of two and half feet. They were tested under temperatures of 68° F and 75° F, with the air either fresh or stagnant (Table 22.3).

TABLE 22.3

Temp.	*Air*	*Unit of work*	*Fall due to stagnation*	*Fall due to low temp.*
68° F	Fresh	100.00	8.90	14.80
68° F	Stagnant	91.00	8.90	14.80
75° F	Fresh	84.80	—	—
75° F	Stagnant	76.20	8.60	14.50

Analysis of the table indicates that stagnant air caused production to fall approximately by 9 per cent. Increased temperature caused 15 per cent reduction of production under the most favourable condition.

All these lead one to conclude that temperature does influence the well-being of the workers and their efficiency. Physical work, in particular, is definitely influenced by atmospheric conditions because it interferes with the maintenance of a constant body temperature.

Edholm and Adam (1962) found in the course of a study, that when the subjects had to lift 50 pound loads under high and low temperatures, there was increase in the pulse rate as well as in the body temperature.

A study was conducted in an industrial situation by Grieve (1960) to obtain the physiological measures of the worker's energy expenditure. In areas where there was minimum air movement and highest temperature, the thermal loads was found to be the greatest. Also the workers made complaints about discomfort due to heat.

In order to improve the attitude and morale of the workers, comfort should be given to both manual and mental workers. However, the need and comfort of the manual workers should be looked into first, in view of the adverse effects of temperature on manual workers.

Humidity

Associated with the problem of temperature is the problem of humidity or the moisture content of the air. Humidity is responsible for interfering with the process of maintaining constant body temperature. When the atmosphere temperature is low and the air humid, one feels cooler.

Since humidity interferes with body temperature it requires more attention and consideration.

Experimental Studies

Vernon, Bedford and others did a study on coal miners under varying conditions of temperature and humidity. The results suggest the workers took seven minutes rest per hour under the most favourable conditions. But when the conditions were the most unfavourable they took 22-40 minutes rest every hour. Moreover, when conditions were more unfavourable, they took more time to feel the cold, were involved in accidents very frequently and lost more time due to sickness.

Another experiment conducted by the New York Ventilation Commission on office workers indicates that mental work may be performed as effectively under humid and hot (moisture content being 80 per cent and temperature being 86°F.) stagnant air conditions as under optimal conditions. Efficiency of brain workers is not much affected by these factors, but it was found that under unfavourable conditions manual workers tended to take more rest pauses. Mental workers were also affected to some extent.

Ashebean, Saily and others did a study on military men. These military men were asked to march for 4 hours at the rate of 3 miles with a 20 lb. pack on their backs.

The results showed that it is hard to work if the air is hot and humid. On the other hand when the air is dry one can tolerate even high temperature.

Conclusion

High temperature and increased humidity may be desirable in some textile industries. Even is such industries temperature and humidity are to be kept within the optimum and desired limit. It has been observed that in iron, steel, tinplate and glass factories the output is the highest when temperature is low, *i.e.*, in winter.

Hence it can be reasonably concluded that the problem of moisture content requires consideration. Although it does not affect mental work, it shows its effect indirectly by influencing the mood and attitude of the workers.

Attention therefore should be given to both types of workers. On the basis of these studies and research findings it can be held that manual workers definitely require more attention than mental workers as they are more affected by atmospheric conditions.

Movement of Air

When there is no movement in air most of the troubles of ventilation arise. The movement of air prevents the formation of packets of warm and moist air and also prevents stagnant air from accumulating about the body or around the machinery. Any undesirable property of such air is removed by its mixture with other air in the room. It has been found out in factories which do not have forced circulation there may be a great deal of variation in the cooling properties of the air in various parts of the same room, although the temperature difference may be very small.

Experimental Studies

Wyatt, Fraser and Stock (1926) carried out an experiment on weavers. The experiment continued for a period of six weeks and fans were operated every alternative week. The results indicated that the hourly output was much higher on days on which fans were used. The beneficial effect of fans was greater in the afternoon than in the morning.

Sayers and Horington conducted a study on mine workers. In metal mines they found the adverse effects of high temperature and humidity. Physiological and psychological changes under these conditions included a rapid pulse rate, a marked loss of weight accompanied by physical weakness and exhaustion. They also felt difficulty in carrying out mental work, but when movement in air was made, these troubles disappeared. This indicates that movement in air increases efficiency of the workers and has a cooling effect. Heat emitted by the body should always be removed by air. This is not done when air is stagnant.

This is the reason why, when the air is stagnant, the temperature becomes more uncomfortable. The adverse effect of high temperature and humidity was also observed on the workers. Physiological and psychological changes were noticed such as rapid increase in pulse rate, heart beat, loss of weight and physical weakness, etc. But these symptoms gradually disappeared with the movement in air. Due to proper ventilation the attitude of the employees also improved.

The findings of the study by the New York Ventilation Commission (quoted in Viteles-1932) showed that fall in output was 9 per cent when air was stagnant. But it was 24 per cent when temperature was high and air was stagnant. It is, however, important to note that natural ventilation is always preferable to artificial devices. Moreover the ventilating system should be of such a nature that it can filter the air also. It should remove dust, etc. from the air. This controls the temperature and humidity.

In a further study by the New York Ventilation Commission workers were instructed to enter into a room provided with foul air by the help of a pipe. In another condition workers were surrounded with fresh air but were breathing foul air. Results indicated that the first group reported illnesses such as headache and other physical troubles, while the second group did not report anything of poor ventilation though actually this group was breathing foul air.

In another study by the New York Ventilation Commission, workers were asked to work in a building without any window, though excellent ventilating devices were provided without the knowledge of the workers.

It was found that workers constantly complained about poor ventilation and also demonstrated the after-effects of unsuitable ventilation. However, after a time when they were told about the ventilating devices all these symptoms disappeared.

From these findings, it is clear that proper ventilation has got a tonic effect which also gives psychological satisfaction. Hence, not only should the air which we breathe be fresh but the air which surrounds us should also be fresh. In other words, these studies indicate that not only is the composition of inhaled air important but the composition of the air surrounding the body and the attitude of the individuals concerned are also important.

Studies on the effect of Ventilation on Mental Work

The New York Ventilation Commission conducted some experimental studies, the results of which showed that mental work can be performed as effectively under humid, hot and stagnant air conditions as under optimal conditions. Though frequent rest pauses may be necessary under adverse atmospheric conditions, it was really strange to note that even under the most unfavourable conditions mental work was very little affected.

Multiplication work under hot and comfortable conditions also indicated no difference in another study by Givoni and Rim (1962). Most likely the high motivation present in experimental tests counteracted the unfavourable effect of discomfort.

In spite of these findings the possibility of mental workers being affected by unsuitable ventilation cannot be ruled out. Continuous and unfavourable ventilating conditions may influence mental performance. Though the interest of the manual workers should be looked into first, mental workers should also be given some comfort. In many countries including India however, comfort for the physical workers is usually denied. This is highly undesirable because mental workers are not as directly affected by poor ventilation as tile manual workers.

Since suitable ventilation and optimum temperature of the work place has stimulating and favourable effect on attitudes and job satisfaction, the management should take advantage of it by keeping the temperature at the optimum level and by making ventilation suitable.

Maier (l970) has suggested that supplying the workers with salt tablets would relieve some of the weakness and time losses caused by excessive perspiration in the summer. Working near doors which are frequently closed and opened in the winter affects efficiency and leads to accidents and sickness. Change of temperature from hour to hour should also be avoided.

The workers should be advised to dress themselves according to the condition of ventilation so that they can get maximum comfort from it.

Indian Studies

A few studies on temperature and humidity have also been conducted in India.

Rao (1947) analysed Some of the physiological problems in tropical life. He also conducted an experiment in 1952 on the comfort zone in tropical Calcutta. The optimum level was observed to be 78.5° F. Since the climatic conditions in Delhi are different, summer being very dry and hot, and winter being much colder than what is experienced in Calcutta, Mukherjee and Sharma (1953) found that the corresponding comfort range in Delhi was 70° F to 80° F in summer, and 60°F to 65° F in winter.

Keeping in view the various research findings on atmospheric conditions, it can be concluded that atmospheric condition is one of the important aspects of the physical environment. Adverse atmosphere is not only injurious to health, but it also has got undesirable effects. It gives rise to subjective feelings of headache, drowsiness, and a general feeling of discomfort. The objective effects are decreased output, increased sickness, absenteeism, turnover and accidents. Lastly, it influences the workers' attitude and has got far reaching consequences on all types of workers.

HOURS OF WORK

Introduction

A largely held conception is that greater hours of work lead to larger out put and that production can be increased by increasing the working hours. Hence, during the First World War, workers had to work 90 hours and sometimes even 100 hours per week. Production increased for some time but afterwards it decreased. That rate of absenteeism and accidents also increased. Contrary to popular belief, several research findings also indicated that production did not increase with the increase in hours of work. Thus, there was widespread confusion regarding the relationship between production and hours of work.

Studies on Hours of Work

Vernon conducted some studies in ammunition factories and found that when the working hours were reduced from 66 hours per week to 48 ½ hours, production increased by 15 per cent. Vernon concluded that workers possess a limited capacity to work and with long hours of work this capacity decreases. So 8 hours work per day may be more beneficial than 10 hours work per day. On the basis of their investigations several committees recommended that hours of work should be reduced and 48 hours of work per week was suggested to be the ceiling.

The same procedure of increasing hours of work to 70 to 75 hours per week was repeated during the Second World War. Initially production increased but decreased after a brief period. When hours of work were decreased, production increased 10 to 12 per cent. The accident rate also decreased. Several experimental studies have also been conducted on this problem. The U.S. Department of Labour (1944) made a study in 12 metal working plants and found that the 40 hours a week and the 8 hours a day brought the highest production for each hour worked. This survey also indicated that six days work in a week is more economical than seven days work per week.

Observations and evidences indicated that though working hours may be increased, actual hours of work are not increased. Workers take voluntary and illegal rests, they adjust themselves to longer working hours by slowing down, taking rest pauses, remaining absent and changing work pace. The U.S. Health Public Service found that 8 hours work per day increased performance more than 10 hours work per day.

Maier (1970) conducted an investigation on apple packers and noted similar results. In a study Angels (1930) found that production increased considerably when working hours were reduced.

In a munition plant reduction of working hours from 58.2 hours per week to 50.6 hour per week was followed by an increase in the hourly output by 39 per cent. The total output increased by 21 per cent. Maier found that when working hours were reduced from 66 hours to 48 ½ hours per week production increased by 16 per cent.

All these studies point out without any reservation that lesser working hours are always desirable from the point of view of efficiency, production and also from the humanitarian angle.

In the studies discussed, the following adverse effects of long working hours have been observed.

Adverse Effects of Long Working Hours

1. Excessive Fatigue. The feeling of fatigue increases due to long working hours and whatever benefit is obtained from more working hours is neutralised by decrement in efficiency due to the onset of fatigue.

2. Intentional Restriction of Output. When the worker finds that he has to work for longer hours he adjusts himself to the long working hours by consciously or unconsciously restricting output. The interest of the workers also decreases. Vernon's findings have supported these points.

3. Unauthorised Rest Periods. Due to unreasonably long working hours workers usually take rest to which they are not legally entitled and hence production finally decreases.

The present author (1976) observed a large number of skilled, semiskilled and unskilled workers engaged in the construction of a building for about three years, to determine the relationship between long hours of work and productivity. It was noted that when the author (owner of the building) was present on the work spot and supervising their work, they could not take illegal rest as a result of which they had to work for comparatively longer hours, that is, from 8 a.m. to 1 p.m., and from 3 p.m. to 6 p.m. Interestingly, however it was found, that this out put was not higher than when they worked for about 6½ to 7 hours per day in the absence of the author.

Further, when the workers had to do overtime work (with extra wages) their performance showed a qualitative and quantitative decrement in proportion to the hours of work. The author observed that when asked to work for long hours they took illegal rest, slowed down the speed of work, voluntarily restricted output and engaged in talk and gossip at the slightest opportunity. The output on the whole, was slightly more when the working hours were 6 to 7 hours instead of 8 to 9 hours per day.

Length of Working Hours

Keeping in view the adverse effects of long working hours, the question arises as to what should be the duration of the working day and working week. This requires a careful study of working hours. Lee has pointed out that opinions differ greatly and one is treading on dangerous grounds if one attempts to predict an optimal work hour without an analysis of the work itself.

When work largely depends upon the operation of machines, working hours should not be reduced.· But reduction of hours of work is essential when the work is done manually by the employees. It also depends upon the type of work. If the work needs strenuous physical labour or mental work of a serious nature shorter working hours are desirable. Maier (1970) states that if the working week is reduced below five days and the working day is reduced below six hours, even hourly output does not increase because it creates suspicion in the workers minds. Hence they lengthen the work.

Lippman suggests that there can be no single length of working day optimal for all industries; all departments and all workers. The problem is tremendously complicated by the use of leisure time by the workers, the relationship between the length of working period and the satisfying nature of work, etc.

Studying diverse industries Lippman found that the optimal working day varies between 6½ and 10 hours and the optimal working week from 33 to 48 hours. The optimal working day was found to differ in different industries. It lies between 5.8 and 6.1 hours in the glass industry with a median of 5 to 5.9 hours, between 7.2 and 7.7 hours with a median of 7.4 hours in the tool making industry and between 10.5 and 13.6 hours with a median of 11.9 hours in the textile industry.

According to Blum (1956), "Keeping in view the research findings, observations and in view of the current trend in determining the ultimate work week it seems safe to say that we are on the brink of a 30 hours work week. In manufacturing and retail organisations such a work week brings maximum production and satisfaction".

A comparison of the workers in the field also showed that the optimal time is longest for workers between 30 and 35 years.

Rest Pauses

Rest pauses are extremely essential to raise production and efficiency. This view has been supported several research findings. But the question arises as to what should be the duration of the rest pause. The management should give regular rest pauses to the workers. Otherwise, the workers will take it some how or other anyway.

It has been found that workers do take illegal and unofficial rest pauses by slackening work and adjusting the speed to the working spell. Sometimes, they also get rest due to various exigencies of machines and technicalities. The unauthorised rest pauses should be replaced by official and authorised rest pauses. Authorised rest pauses are preferable due to several reasons. Viteles (1932) is of the opinion that the authorised rest pause is five times better than the unauthorised rest pause. The reason according to him is two-fold.

1. Unauthorised rest pauses are very little planned, so they happen at odd months when production shows an increasing tendency.
2. When unauthorised rest pauses occur due to external reasons such as stoppage of machines, delay in getting material, failure of current, etc., workers feel irritated instead of feeling easy and comfortable. Moreover, this type of rest creates guilt and suspicion in the workers' minds.

On the other hand, authorised rest pauses have a favourable effect. Workers take these rest pauses as their own and relax to their satisfaction. Moreover, such rest pauses are planned and fixed according to the need. In addition to this, workers look forward to them and therefore, they also have incentive value.

Investigations allowing rest pauses to workers have shown improvement in production. This may be explained by the fact that due to rest pauses the decline in the output as a result of accumulated fatigue is checked. After the rest period, workers start at a higher level.

The curve in Figure 22.2, is, a, visual presentation of higher production after a rest period. Wyatt suggests that the rest pauses should be introduced at about the time when production reaches its maximum and production curve tends to fall. At this stage working activity is about to decrease and hence the beneficial effect of the rest pause will retard the onset of factors responsible for decreasing output. It also tends to maintain working activity at a higher level

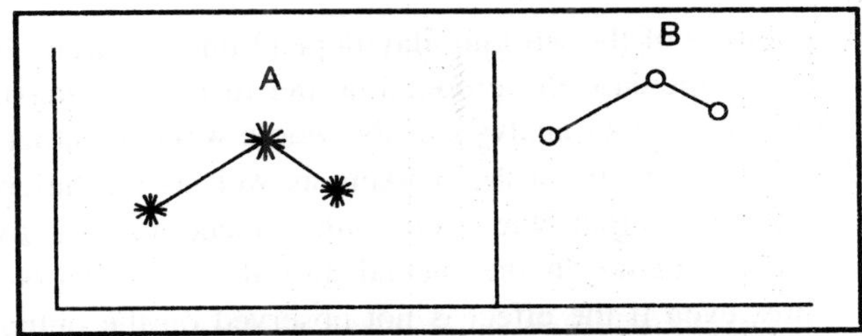

Fig. 22.2. Production A = Before rest, Production B = After rest.

during the remainder of the spell. If it is introduced earlier, it will check the incitement. Again, a rest pause should not be given at the end because a longer rest pause is needed to remove the accumulated fatigue and it would check the end spurt also. So rest pauses should be introduced after maximum production.

When work is repetitive and mechanical the work curve is irregular. Under such circumstances it is advisable to give rest pauses more frequently.

Length of Rest Pauses

Now the question arises about the duration of the rest pause. It has been suggested after a number of observations and empirical studies that the rest pause should not be too long to kill the effect of incitement nor too short to be insufficient to remove the fatigue and monotony effects. When a too long rest pause is introduced the warming effect' is spoiled.

Studies on Rest Pauses

The findings of a number of investigations suggest that the length and position of the optimal rest pauses depends upon the nature of work, length of working day, nature and necessity of workers and allied factors which influence production and fatigue. The optimum rest pause is one which preserves all the benefits of incitement and at the same time eliminates fatigue as much as possible.

Graft introduced rest for half a minute, 2 minutes and 5 minutes duration in a 4 minute period of mental addition, and discovered that the 2 minutes rest was the most beneficial. When the work expanded for 80 minutes, a 5 minute rest pause was most desirable. Amberg found that whereas a rest pause of 5 minutes should have a favourable influence on production, a pause of 15 minutes introduced half way in a work period of 1 hour had an unfavourable effect on production.

It has been generally found that in light work, a 15 minutes rest in the middle of the working spell in the morning and after-noon is good. If the work is heavy, a longer rest period may be recommended.

After studying rest pauses, Ritcher points out that the productive value of a rest pause depends upon : (*a*) the kind of work, (*b*) the type of worker, (*c*) the location or rest pause, (*d*) the length of rest pause, (*e*) the day of the week, and (*f*) the shape of the work curve. Thus, the effects of the rest pause depend upon varied factors.

In a study on the effect or varying rest on mental work, Mohanty (1981) found that in a 9 minute duration of multiplication work, 2 minutes rest period was the most effective.

Conclusion

The duration and condition of the working day depend upon rest and no hard and fast rule can be prescribed. In order to increase the production and to provide maximum satisfaction to the workers, it is essential that a proper analysis of the whole working situation should be made. Otherwise there will be adverse effects on the workers as well as on the community. The most important influence in increasing output when hours are reduced and rest pauses are introduced is not relief from fatigue, but change in the mental attitude of the workers particularly with respect to supervision. Thus, even if the effect is not observed on the output, the morale of the workers is raised and the goodwill of the plant is increased.

MUSIC

Following the research findings during 1940-50 on music in industry many plants and organisations have provided music for their employees, with the purpose of increasing morale and improving performance.

Experimental Studies on Music

To verify this belief several researches have been conducted on the effect of music on work. Analysing the review work of Uhrbrock (1961) on the effect of music on work, Tiffin and McCormick (1971) have commented as follows. "It is apparent from Uhrbrock's summary that music has not proved to be a universal boon to industry and it should not be viewed as a panacea for all of the production ills of an organisation. Perhaps the most relevant considerations in contemplating a music programme would be the reaction of the employees to it and the type of work in question. Music probably can be of greater value as a morale booster in the case of employee on simple routine tasks than on more complex tasks."

Kerr (1954) has conducted some brilliant as well as stimulating studies on the effect of music on production. The first experiment of Kerr shows that with the introduction of music there is a slight increase in production, but there is also an increase in wastage. In the second experiment. Kerr found the facilitating effect of music on production. In the third study Kerr found that there is no definite relationship between the order of preference as to the type of music and production. His study further indicated that music of an unpopular variety does not affect production at all.

A study by Hume indicated that music reduced wastage in industry. This partly goes against the findings of the first study by Kerr.

As indicated by Smith (1947) music has an extremely favourable effect upon production, especially in repetitive work. In this connection Smith remarks, "Music probably produces its major direct effect when the individual's capacity for attention is not absorbed by this work, in this circumstance, music appears to direct unused attention from brooding, talking or off the job activities."

Contrary to the findings of Kerr and Smith, McGehee and Gardner (1949) found that music had neither a favourable nor an unfavourable effect on production, though a questionnaire survey indicated that workers believed that they produced more with the introduction of music. The results further indicate that music does not increase production when the job is complex.

Blum and Naylor (1968) hold the view that "Possibly music influences production to the maximum extent when its rhythm is compatible with the employee's rhythm of work, or when it tends to pace him".

Fax and Embrey (1972) employed a total of 27 inspectors in four experiments to investigate the relationship between the playing of background music during the performance of repetitive work and task efficiency. The findings strongly supported the view that economic benefits can accrue from the use of music in industry. Music increased efficiency even when it competed with the unfavourable conditions produced by the noise of machines.

The present author (1981) conducted a study on the effects of music on three different types to tasks.

TABLE 22.4
Table Showing the Effect of Light Music on Performance in Three Different Types of Tasks

Sl. No.	*Nature of condition*	*Nature of task*	*Time per trial*	*Average performance*	*Average error*	*Introspective report*
1.	Experimental	Light repetitive manual work (cutting potato chips).	1 hour with light music	1 kg potato per hour	—	Report of pleasant feeling
2.	Controlled	-do-	1 hour without any music	750 gms potato	—	Report of pleasant feeling
3.	Experimental	Light mental work (cancellation of letters)	1 hour work with light music	12.30 columns	15	Report of pleasant feeling
4.	Controlled	-do-	1 hour work without any music	13.10 columns	11	Report of feeling of boredom
5.	Experimental	Heavy mental work (multiplication of digits following a principle)	1 hour work with light music	6.50 columns	32	Report of disturbance due to music but pleasant feeling was experienced
6.	Controlled	-do-	1 hour work without any music		18	Report of strong feeling of boredom.

Four male college adults, two female college teachers and four female school teachers had to perform three different types of tasks such as light repetitive manual work, light repetitive mental work (cancellation of letters) and heavy repetitive mental work (multiplication of digits) when light music was played from a tape recorder. Care was taken not to repeat the same music again and again. The experiment continued for six days with one trial a day and two trials for each type of tasks.

Result

Analysis of the findings of the study indicates that in all the subjects except one college student music had a favourable effect on the performance of repetitive manual work in comparison to the performance in the controlled condition where music or any other relaxation was not provided. Introspective report of the subjects further suggested the fact that music also created a pleasant feeling among the subjects while doing light repetitive manual work and light repetitive mental work. Further analysis of the effect of music on the second and third types of work indicates that while in all subjects except one music had no effect on the performance of light mental work, it had adverse effects on the performance of mental work of the serious types such as in this study, multiplication of digits following a certain principle. In addition to this, all these subjects held that music disturbed their thought process, distracted their attention and created unpleasant noise while they were engaged in the multiplication work. However, while doing repetitive and light manual work, music introduced a pleasant feeling, reduced boredome and elevated the motivation and desire for work.

All subjects except one reported that music had no distracting or facilitating effect while engaged in light mental work. However, in the case of one adult college male music facilitated work and brought a pleasant feeling in all the three types of work. The introspective report of this subject indicated that he was highly interested in music and music as such brought concentration in work; whether manual or mental, heavy or light. Possibly, such a result may be attributed to the personality, interest and aptitude of the subject.

Though no clear-cut conclusion can be drawn on the basis of these findings on the effect of music on work, due to the small sample and some other uncontrolled variables like age, sex and interest of the subjects, yet this study no doubt encourages additional research in this area.

Effect of Music on Performance

An overall review of the various findings do suggest that with the introduction of music on job production may increase to some extent, but there is also the possibility of wastage when music diverts attention and disturbs concentration. Usually music introduced for a short period is more effective than when it is introduced for a long period. Though it is difficult to decide whether production is partly a function of music, the facilitating effect of soothing music on the attitude of the worker cannot be denied. However, the effect of music on production depends upon nature of the worker and the type of music being played, etc.

Additional research on the effect of different types of music on different types of work, on the attitude of the workers and the relationship of the effect of music with personality variables would be extremely helpful in facilitating a generalised and clear-cut view on the effect of music on performance.

QUESTIONS

1. What do you understand by 'work environment' ? Analyse the importance of illumination in improving the efficiency of workers.
2. Examine the importance of illumination in increasing industrial efficiency. Justify your answer with experimental findings.
3. Discuss the problem of distribution of light, indirect light, intensity of light, coloured light and their adverse effects.
4. What are the environmental factors necessary for industrial efficiency ? Discuss the various problems of the environment in the light of experimental studies.
5. What is understood by atmospheric conditions ? Examine the importance of temperature on industrial efficiency.
6. Discuss the influence of humidity and temperature on the efficiency of employees.
7. Describe some experiments conducted on ventilation. Analyse the effect of ventilation on manual and mental work.
8. What is the importance of hours of work on industrial output ? How can optimal working hours be determined for work ?

9. What is the relationship between hours of work and the rest period ? Does the efficiency of the worker depend on the duration and localisation of rest period ? Justify your answer with experimental findings.
10. Why is a golden age frequently described as one where noise is unknown ? Does noise hamper efficiency ? Support your answer with recent experimental findings.
11. Describe some experiments on noise. How can noise be abated ?

REFERENCES

Blum, H.L. and Naylor, J.C. *Industrial Psychology : Its Theoretical and Social Foundations*, Harper and Row, Publishers, New York, 1968.

Boaz, M.Z. *Papers on Industrial Psychology*, Harper and Row, Publishers, 1968.

Broussard *et al.* *The Influence of Noise on Visual contrast Threshold,* Army Medical Research Laboratory Report, 101, November 6, 1953.

Chatterjee, Amitava and Krishna Murthy, V. Differential effect on noise as an environmental stress, *Behaviouristic,* 1972, vol. 2 (1), p. 8.

Fernberger, S.W., Viteles, M.S. and Carlon, W.R. The effect of changes in quality of illumination upon visual perception. *Jn. Appl. Psychol.*, 1934, 18.

Ferree, C.E. and Rand, G. Lighting in relation of the eye, Proc. *Amers Phil. Soc.* 1918, 57. pp. 440-478.

Kerr, W.A. Experiments on the effect of music on factory production, *Applied Psychol.* Monograph. No. 5, 1945.

Kornhauser, A.N. The effect of noise on office output, Industrial *Psychology*, 1927, 2, pp. 621-622.

Luckiesh, M. and Moss, F.K. *The Science of Seeing,* Princeton N.J Van Nostrand, 1937.

Maier, N.R.F. and McCartney J.N. *Psychology in Industry*, Oxford and IBH Publishers, New Delhi, 1970.

Noise Drives Crazy, Reprinted by the National Apartment Councel, New York, 1941.

Mayo, E. *The Human Problems of an Industrial Civilisation,* New York, 1933.

Mohanty, Girishbala. *Effect of Periodic and Non-periodic Noise on Performance*, 1980.

Mohanty, Girishbala. Relationship between working hours and productivity, 1976.

Mohanty, Girishbala. *Effect of Light Music on Three Different Types of Tasks*, 1980.

Mohanty, Girishbala. Effect of varying rest on mental work, 1981.

Murray, R.M. Medico-legal aspects of noise in industry, *Applied Ergonomics*, 1972, December, vol. 3 (4), pp. 216-218.

Oakley, C.A. *Men at Work*, Hodder and Stoughton Ltd., University of London Press Limited, 1945.

Pollock, K.G. and Bartlett, F.C. *Two Studies ill the Psychological Effects of Noise*. Industrial Health Res. Board, Rep. No. 65, London, 1932.

Proffenberger, A.T. *Principles of Applied Psychology*, New York, Appleton, 1942.

Smith, May. *An Introduction to Industrial Psychology*, London, 1952.

Smith, H.C. Music in relation to employee attitudes, Piece work production and industrial accidents, *Applied Psychol.* Monographs, No. 14, 1947.

Stockbridge, H.C. and Lee, Marry. Behaviouristic. 1972, vol. 12, (1).

Tiffin, J. and McCormick, E.J. *Industrial Psychology*, 5th ed. Prentice Hall of India Private Ltd., 1971.

Tobias, J.V. *Auditory Effects of Noise on Aircraft Personnel*, F.A.A. Office of Aviation Medicine Report, 1972, November, No. 72, p. 7.

Vernon, H.M. and Warner, C.G. Objective and subjective test for noise, *Personnel Journal*, 1932, 11, pp. 141-149.

Viteles, M.S. *Industrial Psychology,* Norton, 1932.

23
Industrial Accident

PROBLEM OF ACCIDENT

With the growth of mechanisation the number of fatal accidents both in locomotion and in factories have increased in an alarming way. Consequently, the rate of death due to accidents has also increased. As records show, in 1953 in U.S.A. about 95,000 people were killed and innumerable people were seriously injured. Traffic was the main cause of such injuries and death. Death in factories is also pretty alarming. In another estimate it has been noted that roughly two million people are disabled each year. The cost of this is over two billion dollars. During the year 1963 there were about 2,000,000 disabling injuries in industry including about 80,000 cases of permanent impairment. The National Safety Council estimated an economic loss of about $ 5,3000,000,000. Industrial accidents are in the rise with the rise in the number of factories and industries.

On the basis of the analysis of accident data, Vernon estimated that the loss in potential production amounted to $ 643 million in 1932 in U.S.A. But it was $ 5 billion in 1962. The indirect cost of industrial accidents is many times as great as the direct cost which includes time lost because of accident, breakage, the hiring and training of men to replace the injured, work stoppages and welfare costs.

Thus, accidents are not costly to the economy of the industries and do not only create a tremendous financial problem, they also lead to anguish, pain, injury and death to the unfortunate persons who are involved. They also lower the morale of the workers and decrease the rate of production. Therefore, accident is a problem which needs careful consideration.

MEANING AND DEFINITION OF ACCIDENT

There is a general belief that accident is something unexpected and that it occurs without any definite cause. Thus, accident popularly implies that it is an unexpected event without any apparent cause, a mishap which occurs by chance, perhaps due to ill luck. It is commonly held that "accidents are accidental." They occur by chance without any apparent cause.

But the findings of several studies indicate that accidents are not accidental and they have definite causes. Accidents do not just happen. In fact, they can be considered as being brought about by certain preceding circumstances and events, some of which may be associated with the individual themselves and others with situational and mechanical factors. There would have been little scope and justification for action if accidents happened purely by chance. Expert believe that 98 per cent of these causes may be controlled or eliminated.

Depending upon the circumstances or purpose, accidents have been defined in various ways.

Heinrich (1959) defines an accident as an unplanned and uncontrolled event in which the action or reaction of an object, substance, person results in personal injury or the probability thereof.

CAUSES OF ACCIDENT

Accidents are not accidental, but they have got definite causes. Sometimes the causes of accident are attributed to physical factors and sometimes they are related to human causes. It is to be kept in mind that accidents are caused, they do not just happen.

TABLE 23.1

Primary causes of accident in order of preference	*Per cent*
1. Faulty attitude	14
2. Faulty judgement of speed and distance	12
3. Failure to recognise potential hazard	12
4. Impulsiveness	10
5. Failure of keep attention constant	8
6. Irresponsibility	8
7. Nervousness and fear	6
8. Defective vision	4
9. Certain organic disease	4
10. Slow reaction	4
11. High blood pressure	2
12. Senility	2
13. Worry and depression	2
14. Fatiguability	2
15. Improper distribution of attention	2
16. Inexperience	2
17. Miscellaneous	6

Keeping in view the loss caused by accident, the management should take special interest in tracing the causes of accidents, so that necessary preventive measures can be taken. According to Gilmer (1971), unsafe acts and unsafe conditions may interact in such a way that an accident may be caused by both. Also these two factors may be separately responsible for accidents.

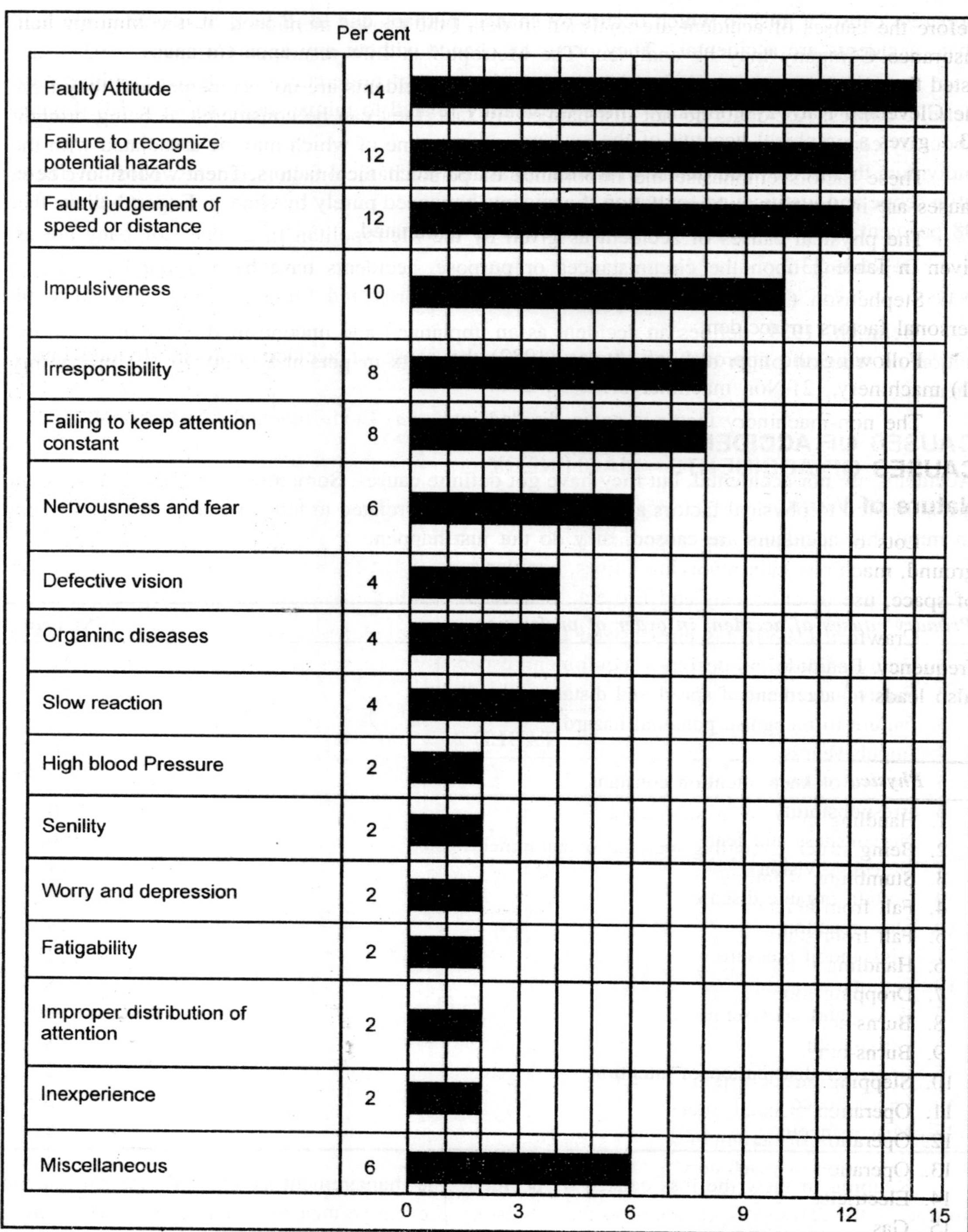

Fig. 23.1. Primary causes of accident according to a survey among 50 motor men of the Cleveland Railway Company.

Before the causes of accident are analysed in detail the causes mentioned by the Metropolitan Insurance Company may be analysed. The Metropolitan Life insurance Company (1931) has listed the primary causes of industrial accident, in order of preference, among the employees of the Cleveland Railway company. These are mainly related to human factors (Table 13). Figure 23.1 gives a graphical account of the survey.

These factors emphasise the importance of personal factors in accidents. Most of these causes are in the person himself.

The physical causes of accident as given by the Metropolitan Insurance Company are as given in Table 23.2.

Stephenson (1927) analysed certain accident records and found out the importance of personal factors in accident.

Following the approach of Viteles (1932) the cause of accident may be divided into : (1) machinery, (2) Non machinery.

The non-machinery factor is again divided into : (*a*) Environmental, (*b*) Personal.

CAUSES OF ACCIDENTS—MACHINERY

Nature of Work

Lots of accidents are accountable to the nature of work. Work being done on slippery ground, machines with revolving knives, circular saws, tins etc., lead to accidents. The necessity of space, use of chemicals and fire etc., also lead to some amount of accident.

Crawford (1960) has emphasized the importance of the job itself in relation to accident frequency. Besides, had design of equipment, especially the physical condition of the equipment also leads to accidents.

TABLE 23.2

Physical causes	*Per cent*
1. Handling material of equipment	27.90
2. Being struck by falling material of equipment	11.90
3. Stumbling of falling	9.80
4. Fall from heights	3.60
5. Fall from stairs	0.60
6. Handling tools	3.20
7. Dropping tools	0.80
8. Burns-acid	1.10
9. Burns-others	3.80
10. Stepping on, or striking objects	8.20
11. Operation of hand trucks	2.30
12. Operation of automobiles	2.40
13. Operation of machinery	9.60
14. Electricity	4.00
15. Gas	1.70
16. Foreign bodies in eye	4.60
17. Miscellaneous	4.50

Faulty Design of Machines

Faulty design of machines such as faulty controls may lead to accidents and are quite unsafe.

Lack of Use of Safety Devices

To ensure maximum safety there are definite provisions or safeguards to guard the machines. For example, safety devices are to be fitted to the machine. These devices become a part of the work and need utilization. But all the safety devices cannot be fitted to machines such as goggles, glasses, particular clothes, gloves, rubber soles etc. These are to be put on by the employees who operate the machine so that accidents can be prevented.

While making a survey of accidents, Stephenson (1927) came to the conclusion that many of the safety devices to be worn by the workers are actually not used by them, perhaps because of resistance or because they consider this to be an insult to their intelligence and efficiency. This resistance is psychological and based on pride in ones skill, workmanship etc. There are ample evidences which indicate that sometimes work becomes comfortable due to the use of safety devices. Resistance to the use of safety devices is therefore partly due to negligence and partly due to ignorance on the part of the workers. Hence Stephenson suggests that throughout the training period workers ought to use the safety devices so that a habit can be formed. Greater vigilance on the part of the supervisory staff is advised by Stephenson. Supervisors should help the workers to put on the safety devices whenever necessary.

Infact, a large number of accidents can be prevented by discouraging the worker to work without putting on guards. By putting psychological and social pressure on the workers they can be coaxed to use safety devices.

CAUSES OF ACCIDENT—NON MACHINERY

Environmental

1. Physical Conditions of Work. ***Temperature.*** Excessive heat or cold makes people clumsy and uncomfortable and there is disturbance in skill which leads to accidents.

In a boot and shoe factory a relationship was noted between temperature and accident (Hambly and Bedrord 1921). The accident rate was highest over 69° F and lowest between 55° F and 59° F. Between 59° and 69° F the accident rate was moderate.

A study on about 10,000 coal miners showed the relationship between temperature and accidents of varying severity. Observation of relationship of temperature to accidents in coal mines indicated that high temperature over 70° F was a much more serious cause of accidents in older men than in younger miners. Osborne (1922) showed that minor accident frequency is very large when the temperature is eigher very high or very low.

When there is moderate temperature the rate of accident is low. Temperature has also an effect on the accident rate of both men and women in munition factories, the effect of high temperature being more clearly visible in the case of men, perhaps because of the nature of their work, which is different from that of women.

According to Vernon (1921) impairment of skill occurs because of the undesirable atmospheric temperature, humidity and movement in air. Vernon (1936), in a further study, found that the rate

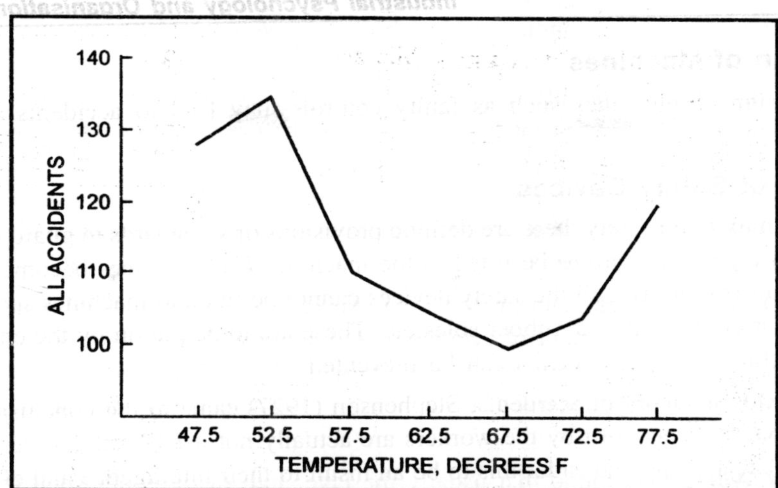

Fig. 23.2. Relation between accident frequency and temperature.

of accident reduced when the temperature is near about 70° F. But when it is below 65° F or above 75° F the rate of accident is much higher. The graph in Figure 23.2 demonstrates the relationship between accident, frequency and temperature.

Light. There are some instances in industry where accidents have occurred because of insufficient light, the reason being that eyes cannot work under low illumination. A survey conducted by an insurance company indicated that 25 per cent of all industrial accidents are due to poor lighting. Stanley's (1966) study indicated that 25 per cent of the accidents is due to artificial lighting.

Fall accidents in 80,000 American factories were more frequent in the winter months. But though December was the darkest month, maximum accident occurred in the month of January, the coldest month. Cold and insufficient light taken together probably had something to do with the increase in accident rates. During the war years in England factories used artificial light and 25 per cent more accidents occurred.

Lack of illumination is responsible for three types of accidents.

1. Contact with machinery—27 per cent
2. Object dropping on a person—15 per cent
3. Persons falling—12 per cent.

Artificial light also causes accidents. Insufficient light causes eye injury because workers bring objects very close when they have difficulty in seeing which causes eye injury. Vernon and Osborne (1922) have also conducted some studies in industries which show the influence of bad light on the accident rate. Excessive glare causes eye strain and it becomes one of the frequent causes of accident. This is the view of DeSilva (1942). Therefore, to control industrial accidents light should be proper and optimum.

2. Speed of Work. An analysis of accident rates hour wise indicates that there is a definite rise in the frequency of accidents with the rise in the speed of work.

In three extensive surveys conducted by Osborne and Vernon (1922), the speed of work has been found to be related to accident frequency during day time, though a similar relationship was not found in the night shift. This difference may possibly be explained by the fact that on a night shift, workers ordinarily have been up for several hours before going to work whereas workers have been awake a much shorter time before beginning work on the day shift. Excessive speed also introduces early fatigue which may lead to accident. Many automobile accidents occur due to the high speed of driving. Accidents due to high driving speed can be checked by constructing rumblers on the road to arrest speed.

3. Long Hours of Work. During the First World War it was noticed that increment in working hours resulted in increment of accidents. Reduction of hours of work reduced accident by about two and a half times. Thus hours of work and the accident rate are positively related. So far as hours of work are concerned, eight hours of work per day may be fixed to prevent accidents.

4. Time of Work. It is found that usually the latter half of the work spell leads to higher frequency of accidents, most probably due to the onset of fatigue.

5. Fatigue. Fatigue occurs either due to the speed of work or long hours of work without rest. Fatigue makes the work unpleasant and the individual loses attention and concentration in work which subsequently leads to accidents.

Various studies in the United States, England and Germany support fatigue to be a very important factor in accident. As previously mentioned, accidents increased two and a half times when working hours increased. Muscio (1922) found that there is a constant increase in accidents as hours pass, both in the morning and evening spells; but they are higher in the morning than in the end hours. He further found that the maximum number of accidents occurred at 11 a.m. and again between 5 and 6 p.m.

Osborne and Vernon (1922) have found out that with the reduction in hours of work there has been a reduction of accidents.

Besides these factors, Kerr (1950) noticed that accidents occurred more frequently in the departments, where there was high noise, low promotion facility etc. Similar investigations indicate handling of heavy materials, unfavourable living conditions, dirt and perspiration etc., to be responsible for accident.

Personal

If for people in the same work situation there are consistent differences in accident frequency among the individuals, it is to be assumed that same personal factors are operating. The personal factors will vary from job to job.

1. Age and Experience. Vernon (1945) has found that there is a significant relationship between young age and less experience and the accident rate. Approximately 50 per cent of the employees had accidents in their first six months, and only 5 per cent had accidents after they had two and a half years of experience. Van Zelst (1954) also suggests that accident rates tend to be higher among young persons.

The Metropolitan Insurance Company suggests, on the basis of age, that the younger people are the greatest sufferers. In a textile mill it was found that among the younger group, for every

100 workers 80 were involved in accidents, whereas the number of accidents was 12 in the 30-35 years age group.

During the first few months on the job, the injury frequency for newly employed workers is higher than it is in the succeeding months and years. The same has been observed in the case of street car motor men and motor coach operators in a large metal plant.

By and large, both these studies indicate that workers have a greater accident frequency rate in the first few months on the job than during later periods.

Therefore, the need arises for efficient training of longer duration concentrated on developing safety habits. This has been supported by the evidence obtained from the study conducted in metal plants.

Newbold (1926) suggests that accidents seems to decrease with age, but not with experience. When age is kept constant, the relationship between increased accident rate and increased length of service vanishes. On the contrary, when the length of service remains constant, the relation between decreased accident and increased age remains constant.

Thus, by and large, it can be viewed that the accident rate decreases steadily with age. The rate of accidents compared with age is shown in Table 23.3 for both men and women.

TABLE 23.3

Age group	*Male rate Per hundred*	*Female rate per hundred*
17-21	172	41
21-28	75	36
28-35	65	17
35-45	50	26
45-60	42	37
60+	35	0

From this table it is evident that accidents decrease steadily with age for men, but no clear correlation between accidents and age for women is observed.

In the case of women, the rate of accident is lower, perhaps because of the safer jobs they were doing such as clerical and administrative jobs.

Table 23.4 also indicates the accident rates for the various age groups, for fatal as well as non-fatal accidents.

An analysis of the table suggests that the accident rate is highest under the age of 20 when the trend for accident is combined and then it drops until the age of 3.5 years.

For fatal accidents the two youngest age groups and the two oldest age groups have rates which exceed the total average of 56. Between 30 and 65 years no age trend is visible.

These differences in the trend for fatal and combined accident rates indicate that the causes of different types of accidents differ.

2. Health. A record of the number of visits to the hospital because of sickness indicates that accidents are significantly associated with the number of visits to hospital because of sickness.

TABLE 23.4

Automobile Accidents According to Age

Age group	*Fatal accidents per 100,000 drivers*	*All accidents per 100 drivers*
All drivers	56	21
Under 20 years	90	30
20-24	90	30
25-29	57	23
30-34	48	18
35-39	43	19
40-44	46	17
45-49	46	17
50-54	42	16
55-59	41	18
60-64	46	15
65-69	55	23
70-74	68	11
75 and over	86	14

Source : National Safety Council—1964, Chicago.

In an automobile plant, this relationship was observed for 352 male metal workers. Similar but slightly less positive results were obtained for five other groups of male and six groups of female workers. As suggested by Newbold (1926), poor health and low vitality lead to accident as monor sickness is correlated with accident (+ .3).

Dispensary visits are not a measure of general health, but they are a mark of instability of personality in wanting to avoid work. This instability makes one susceptible to accidents.

3. Sex. Data from the transport department shows that in general women seem to have more accidents than men. Women engaged as taxi drivers had three times more accident than men.

In 1945, in England at a time when labour was short, women were engaged as taxi drivers and the rate of accidents increased. Other data also support the thesis that women are more prone to accidents, considering the degree of exposure to risk. So until more data becomes available, it is not possible to compare the safe driving abilities of men and women. However, it is found that females under 26 years are safer drivers; have fewer accidents than males of this age group.

4. Alcohol. During an alcoholic state a person's limbs are not under full control, *i.e.*, the sensory motor coordination is disturbed. In industry, drinking is not permitted. So there is no data about it. But transport cases supply lots of such data. The examination of the urine of drivers committing accidents indicates whether alcohol has been taken by the driver or not.

Drunkenness as a contributory factor in accidents has been supported by the studies of Srinivasan, *et al.* (1970). The results of their studies indicated that approximately 28 per cent of the drivers in Delhi were under the influence of alcohol while driving. The same result was obtained in Tamil Nadu, though it was declared as a dry state by the government during 1970.

Alcoholism may be due to maladjustment in family and society, lack of congenial relationship with co-workers, conflicts and tensions on the job, and frustration etc. It is a problem of the society and needs social guidance.

5. Absenteeism. The absence records of a company over a period of four years showed a direct relationship between accidents and absenteeism. In a sample of 289 employees, 200 employees who had no accidents averaged 15 absences, while the remaining 89 who had accidents, averaged 24 absences (Hill, 1955).

Similarly, in a group of Steel Company employees, a survey conducted in 1953 indicated that the absence rate for employees with accidents is higher than for the accident-free individuals.

6. Vision. In many types of jobs, vision is found to be associated with accident frequency. Results from several plants show that employees whose vision is adequate for their jobs have fewer accidents than employees with less adequate vision (Kephart and Tiffin, 1950). The results of several studies clearly show the relationship between vision and accident experience on some types of jobs. It is viewed by Tiffin and McCromick (1971) that "if all plant employees had been required to pass the critical vision test, the lost time accident rate among the employees would have been markedly decreased."

But one should not, however, conclude that faulty vision is the only cause of industrial accidents. It is, however, one of the factors related to accidents in some cases.

The prevention would, therefore, be to select employees after examining their visual acuity for jobs requiring acute vision.

7. Carelessness. Though it is purely personal and does not mean much, it is a prime condition of accident Carelessness can be removed by constant reminders to be careful.

8. Emotional Factors. In specific work situations, general emotional maturity and emotional condition at the time of accident are found to be related to accident. The analysis made by the Metropolitan Insurance Company on 50 motor men shows that emotional conditions such as faulty attitudes, impulsivesness, nervousness and fear, worry and depression account together for 32 per cent of the accidents among the group studied.

Individuals differ in their emotional condition between high and low states. The relationship between high and low emotional cycles and the frequency of accidents has been shown in an investigation by Hersey (1929). He found that the average worker is emotionally low about 20 per cent of the time and more than half of the 400 minor accidents occurred during their low periods. This suggests the importance of emotional depression on accident causation. In a further study Hersey (1936) emphasised that production of individual workers is about 10 per cent higher during periods when the man is elated, happy, hopeful and cooperative than when he is suspicious, peevish, angry, disgusted, pessimistic, apprehensive, and worried. Other emotional disturbances like moodiness, irritability, lack of coordination are responsible for accidents.

The relationship between certain aspects of emotionality and accident frequency was observed by Farmer and Chambers (1920) and Snow (1926).

In a study on emotional stress and driving performance McMurray (1970) attempted to measure the effect of divorce. For this purpose, he analysed the driving records of 410 persons involved in divorce proceedings. It was noted, that during the stress period, the types of violations found more often are speeding, failure to yield, prohibited turns, following too closely and trying to overtake.

Hence for safety and prevention of accidents a favourable emotional condition of the employee is desirable. Workers should also be selected on the basis of emotional stability scores. Such an individual should be dealt with clinically to bring to the surface the cause of his unsatisfactory emotional· life. If the emotional problems of an employee cannot be solved this way, he should be placed in the hands of a professionally trained person such as a clinical psychologist or a psychiatrist who by means of interview and counselling should release the repressed emotions.

Lastly, if all attempts fail, he. should be kept off the job which has the chance of being affected by his unsatisfactory emotional state.

9. Perceptual Motor Coordination. The importance of perceptual motor coordination has been realised especially with relation to accident-proneness. Drake (1940) conducted a study and found that accident-prone persons tended to have motor test scores that were relatively higher than their scores on the perception tests. It was noted that the accident-free individuals had motor tests scores that were lower than their scores on the perception test. Studies by Farmer and Chambers (1929) and Drake (1940) indicate that there is a definite relationship between poor sensory motor coordination and accidents (Chambers 1929, Drake 1940). Since sensor motor coordination is associated with accidents it is reasonable to suppose that clumsiness, inadequate skill, slowness of response and definite sensory organs contribute to accidents. Drake's statement suggests that "individuals whose level of muscular action is above their level of perception are prone to more frequent and more severe accidents than those individuals whose muscular actions are below their perception level. In other words, the person who reacts quicker than he can perceive is more likely to have accidents than is the person who can perceive quicker than he can react."

While explaining the influence of accident-proneness, Drake (1940) has viewed that "where that perception level is equal to or higher than the motor level, the employee is a relatively safe worker. But when the perception level is lower than the motor level, the employee is accident-prone and his accident proneness becomes greater as this difference increases."

Thus, to prevent accidents, employees should be selected with proper perceptual motor coordination, especially for jobs which require this ability.

10. Mental Ability. Snow (1926) found that in some circumstances mental ability is found to be related to accident frequency. For some jobs a minimum mental ability is required to escape the dangers that occur on the job. Chambers (1939) found that very few accident-prone individuals were above average in intelligence and learning ability, dependability and industry. Accidents happened to individuals who were relatively low in the traits associated with mental ability. However, other studies have revealed no correlation between the degree of mental ability and accident frequency.

While some studies show no significant correlation between I.Q. scores and accident frequency, other studies indicate a greater incidence of accidents among workers who were below average in traits connected with mental ability than among those who were average in these traits. These contradictory findings lead to very confusing problems. Intelligence may be an important factor in some kinds of work, but not in all. Most likely for all occupations, a minimum amount of mental ability is necessary to show accident-free behaviour. Therefore, while selecting workers for various jobs, important mental ability requirements should be taken into consideration.

11. Neuroticism. Psychologists are of the opinion that neuroticism is positively related with the rate of accident. Farmer and Chambers found a positive correlation between minor illness and accident. Minor illness is also related to accident as indicated from the records of hospital visits of the workers. Since minor illness is related with neuroticism, neurotic workers commit more accidents. Dispensary visits are a mark of the instability of personality, of wanting to avoid work and this instability is important in susceptibility to accidents.

12. Frustration. The frustration aggression hypotheses advanced by Miller and Doob (1961) clearly indicates that frustration causes a person to be accident-prone, especially when he shows aggressive, regressive or fixative actions as a reaction to frustration. Aggression and hostility make the normal individual temporarily unbalanced, and consequently the person may be engaged in breakage and throwing things around, and generally going against safety behaviour.

Regressive behaviour, according to Maier (1970), reduces fine sensory and motor skills, stimulates indecision and stifles resourcefulness. Finally, the symptoms of fixation interferes with learning and adaptation, and makes a person rigid and resistant to changes.

13. Personality Characteristics. A number of studies have been conducted to determine the relationship existing between susceptibility to accident and personality characteristics.

Besides other studies, in a valuable work on personality dynamics and accident susceptibility, Crawford (1960) administered a sentence completion test to a high incidence of accident group and no accident group persons. A comparison of results indicated the high accident employees were significantly low in the socially desirable personality dispositions like optimism, socio-centricity and trust.

In another illuminating study, Balkan (1963) obtained a relationship between scores on an introversion-extroversion test and performance on an auditory vigilance task. In this task, the subjects were instructed to detect a numerical relationship while they listened to a tape recording of spoken digits. Results indicated introverts showing superior performance than extroverts. This is most probably so, as introverts are more alert and vigilant in a situation demanding sustained attention. Hence introverts may be safe workers in jobs requiring high attention.

Anderson, Nilsson and Hernriksson (1970) made a study of personality differences between accident loaded and accident free young car drivers. The study consisted of two groups of car drivers, one group of twenty two, 20-27 years old male car drivers with a high record of traffic damages, and the second group of twenty-two accident free control subjects, to study personality as a factor in accident causation. The groups were similar in a number of background variables. Compared with the control group, the accident loaded group was more often found to be hyposensitive to intraceptive perception. This is an attribute which indicates the individual's nature of extreme dependence on external factors (environment). This ultimately suggests weak inner control or delay of action.

14. Risk Acceptance. Risk acceptance as a basic human factor of accident has got recognition recently. It is defined by Gilmer (1971) as the behaviourial trait of an individual to engage in an activity where there is some specific probability of failure. Rockwell's (1962) study on risk differences revealed that the high risk group had committed more accidents and were less skillful, possessed greater variability in task performance than the low risk group. All these traits do not go with the activities necessary for safe behaviour.

Recently, Cervantes Sorondo, Emilio of the Provincial Institute of Applied Psychology and Psycho technology, Logrono, Spain, have made a review of the various causes of accident. The review work indicates that during this century, the search for the cause of accidents has been accelerated with emphasis changing from mechanical and environmental factors to include human factors. Studies have examined alcoholism, vision, intellectual ability, attention, motor abilities, reaction time, emotional stability, motivation, personality and 'accident proneness'.

From this review the importance of personal factors in accident is cleary evident.

In a study conducted by the Camden Works of the Radio Corporation of America by Kerr (1950), it was noticed that accidents occurred more frequently in those departments with low promotion facilities, low intra company transfer and high noise. Greater accident severity was found in departments having more male workers, low suggestion records etc.

An analysis of all the mechanical, environmental and personal causes of accidents reveals that so many factors come to operate in the causation of accident that it would be unwise to study a single factor in isolation.

A more recent approach to the study of the causes of accident is the "global approach."

ROAD ACCIDENT AND SAFE AND UNSAFE BEHAVIOUR OF DRIVERS

Following the illuminating study of DeSilva (1942) on "why we have automobile accidents," various performance and non-performance tests have been used for the evaluation of safe-unsafe drivers. Such tests include measures of attention, attitude and personality, aptitude etc. Moreover, tests like reaction time, eye hand coordination, visual acuity, and glare-recovery have been used. But as Bhalla (1977) points out, only the attitude and adjustment measures have indicated significant relationship with accident experience whereas psychophysical tests have not shown sufficient evidences. To explain this, two reasons may be advanced. Firstly, more often than not, the tests employed were basically designed for other purposes of application in the field of industrial psychology and were not properly modified to suit the specificity of the situation under reference. Secondly, validation studies carried out for these tests also suffered from a lack of reliable criterion.

The main purpose of administering the psychological tests on the drivers is to select the safe driver and reject the unsafe ones in order to reduce road accidents. But the predictive validity of the tests available at present are so poor, that its purpose to predict future behaviour of drivers has failed miserably. Under these circumstances the problem of screening and selection of drivers has not been solved so far. Thus, a study group of OESD (1970) have commented on the basis of a review that "Although psychological selection methods have an edge over conventional methods; the final solution to this problem in driver psychology has not yet been found."

In spite of the limitations of the psychological and psychophysical tests, it would be sheer injustice not to recognise the fact that at least these texts have made significant contributions towards the screening if not the selection of drivers.

Many psychologists as well as the Centrol Road Research Institute, New Delhi have taken the initiative to conduct several tests on the screening of the safe and unsafe behaviour of the drivers.

The findings of such studies indicated that attitude and personality factors explain, to some extent, the safe-unsafe behaviour of driver. However, performance on intelligence tests is at the lowest ebb so far as screening of drivers is concerned (Goldstein, 1962).

Brodly's study (1966) indicates that accident repeaters as compared with the non-accident group "show a high level of excitability or tension, less ability to telerate or sustain this tension and hence a tendency to act out these emotions or tensions." Plenty of previous studies indicate that accident repeaters are psychologically sick and accident involvement is a function of this sickness. Broadly made a further excellent observation by stating "safe and unsafe behaviours are not discreet things but belongs to the same continuum."

However, more controlled and scientific experiments with more refined tests need to be carried out before establishing a relationship between attitude, personality factor and accident.

STUDIES CONDUCTED IN INDIA

The behaviourial problems in safe-unsafe behaviour relating to road accidents have been very much neglected in India. In fact, work done in India in this area is of a preliminary nature. Most of the studies in this area have been conducted at the Central Road Research Institute, New Delhi, Madras and Bangalore, using selected psychophysical and psychological tests. Bhalla, *et al.* (1968), and Bhalla (1970) have conducted most of the studies. The main purpose of these studies was to establish screening measures for drivers, their understanding capabilities and limitations and to suggest the need for initiating remedial measures for better training facilities.

An analysis of these results indicated that Indian drivers are slow to react, and poor in visual acuity, depth perception, night vision and glare recovery. They are not well acquainted with the driving rules. The results also indicated that the safe and unsafe drivers differ significantly on reaction time, distance judgement, field of vision, night vision and driving know-how.

The study of Srinivas *et al.* (1970), on the effect of alcoholism on accident indicates that 28 per cent of the drivers in Delhi and Madras were under the influence of alcohol while driving.

Srinivasan *et al.* (1971) made a further study on the impact of alcoholic intoxication on driving functions. The results indicated that alcohol impairs mental functions like simple reasoning and judgement. Besides, loss of sensory motor coordination and impaired field of vision was also due to the adverse effects of alcohol.

ROAD ACCIDENT IN ORISSA

A survey report (1985) indicates that about 1 lakh 61 thousand vehicles are moving on the roads of Orissa. Findings of surveys on road accidents in Orissa reveal that in comparison to all other States of India though lowest number of vehicles move on the roads of Orissa, unfortunately Orissa secures second position in road accident next to Madhya Pradesh.

Reports indicate that in 1983, 5076 road accidents occurred in Orissa in which 719 people died and 4224 were injured. In 1984 in 5231 road accidents 826 people died and 4565 people were injured. In the Cuttack Bhubaneswar Road (Bhubaneswar is the Capital of Orissa) alone in

1983 there were 83 road accidents in which 83 people died and 70 people were injured. In 1984 on the same road 105 accidents occurred, 23 people expired and 93 were wounded. The alarming increase in the rate of death due to Scooter accidents on the Cuttack Bhubaneswar Road for the last five years has been a matter of great concern. That is why use of helmets by the Scooter riders has been made compulsory in Orissa.

In 1969 a high power Committee was constituted by the Orissa Government to investigate into the causes of road accidents in Orissa. The Committe indicated that along with other causes, careless and speedy driving of the vehicle, drunken state of the drivers, lack of proper scrutiny of the drivers before issuing driving license, sale of wine in the 'Dhabas' located on the main road and national high ways, lack of awareness of the public about rules and laws of traffic are the main causes of road accidents in Orissa.

Thus it has been suggested by the high power committee that road accidents can be reduced by issuing driving license only after careful and specific test on the applicants, to make them vigilant and careful by introducing driver's refreshers course, construction of Check Posts, construction of humps to check speed, fine and punishment for speedy and careless driving, use of helmets by the scooter drivers, stopping the sale of wine and liquor on the road side dhabas and by developing a consciousness among the drivers to drive slowly and carefully. This can be done by making compulsory completion of a refresher's course for 30 days or more for all applicants aspiring for driving license. Use of Posters and Placads indicating the plight and consequences of accidents on the road side, *audio visuals* indicating the negative consequences of speedy driving through radio, T.V. etc. have also been suggested.

All these would definitely help to develop a consciousness to be cautious and careful while driving on the road.

ACCIDENT-PRONENESS

Several researches in the field of accidents and safe-unsafe behaviour have been carried out with the persistent and firm belief that keeping some other factors constant, some individuals are more prone to accidents than others. It is also believed that most of the accidents happen due to the personal characteristics leading to unsafe behaviour of this small percentage of people.

This idea has led to the concept of accident-proneness. According to this concept, the factors which make a person liable to accidents will vary from person to person. Infact, there does not appear to be certain specific traits to call a person accident-prone. A person who is accident-prone in one specific situation may not be so in another.

However, Harrell (1964) has defined accident-proneness as "Accident-proneness is the continuing tendency of a person to have accidents as a result of his stable and persisting characteristics."

It has been suggested by some investigators that there are certain personal characteristics which make people liable to commit more accidents than others in whatever situation they may be. Thus the liability for accident is unequally distributed according to this group.

In the opinion of Blum and Naylor (1968) the statement that "accidents do not distribute themselves by chance, but happen frequently to some men and infrequently to others as a logical result of combination of circumstances" has become a generalisation. This statement explains the principle of accident-proneness.

Blum and Naylor (1968) comment that "Mintz and Blum found a considerable amount of careless reporting, illogical reasoning and unfamiliarity with the statistical theory underlying accident proneness. Their analysis shows that 60 to 80 per cent of accidents reported appear to be attributable to unpredictable factors and the remaining 20 to 40 per cent to the component of accident-liability, which includes both personal characteristics and environmental conditions attributing to accident records. Thus accident-proneness does not seem to be the major factor in understanding or attacking the problem of accidents."

The view that a small percentage of the workers were responsible for rather a large proportion of accidents does not by itself substantiate accident-proneness.

In this connection Blum and Naylor state "statements to the effect that 10 per cent of the population have 30 per cent of the accidents, or that 25 per cent have 75 per cent of them must be regarded as inconclusive unless the total population and the total number of accidents are known. Only when these figures are obtained it can be established the extent to which the distribution of accident is due to chance expectancy and the extent to which other factors such as accident-proneness enter."

Greenwood and Wood (1919) studied the susceptibility for accident on 648 workers in a steel factory. Accidents were analysed into a number of groups.

1. Persons having no accident.
2. Persons having one accident.
3. Persons having multiple accidents.

If the principle of accident-proneness is to be upheld, more people should have no accidents than would be predicted by chance. In three of the five groups this holds true being 6, 3, and 10 per cent, but in the other two it does not. These percentages are to be attributed to accident-proneness in certain people, but there may be other causative factors like length of employment, job hazard, training, design of machines etc.

Greenwood and Wood's study does establish the principle of accident-proneness, but it does not suggest the degree to which it is responsible for accidents. Further research in this area also indicates that the extent of accident-proneness has been over rated.

APPROACHES TO ACCIDENT-PRONENESS

Sensory Motor Coordination Approach

The first approach is called sensory motor coordination approach advanced by Farmer and Chambers (1929). People commit accidents if there is disturbance in the sensory motor function. This approach is more specific. Farmer and Chambers analysed 681 subjects of different trades and gave them three groups of tests.

1. Sensory Motor Coordination Tests. Under sensory motor coordination tests, dotting test, reaction time, and pursuit meter tests are notable. Most of these tests have one symbol, either auditory or visual, and other things are done by the appropriate motor action.

2. Emotional Stability Tests. Tests of muscular balance, tests of emotional stability, tests of tremor, psychogalavanic reflex tests etc., come under the emotional stability tests.

3. Intelligence Tests. Scores on various intelligence tests divided workers into superior and inferior groups. It was found that those worker who were doing better on these tests, had an average of 48 per cent less accidents than the workers of the inferior group. Scores on these tests are correlated to a considerable extent with the accident score. Temperamental tests also showed indications of such relationship.

However, it can be concluded that accident-proneness cannot be predicted from sensory motor coordination, though the general clumsiness of the workers may lead to accidents.

DeSilva and Fletcher (1942) approached automobile accidents in a similar way. They used a group of tests on drivers such as reaction time, coordination in driving testing apparatus, test of special visual characteristics, test on judgement of speed and distance, peripheral and central acuity, tests of sensitivity and glare, distractability, reaction in an emergency situation and lastly intelligence tests.

The results of such tests confirmed Farmer and Chamber's finding, that on all tests the poor drivers had a longer reaction time than the good drivers. The error score of poor drivers were greater than that of the good drivers.

Sensitivity to glare was also tested. Here it was observed, that poor drivers had an abnormally high sensitivity to glare. The average score for good drivers was 3.5, while for the poor ones it was 2.4.

Poor drivers scored very low in visual acuity. Thus, Fletcher and DeSilva concluded that the poor drivers had inferiority in scoring on tests of reaction time, coordination and perceptual discrimination. Intelligence scores however did not very much.

Farmer and Chambers thus concluded that accident-proneness results out of defective aestheto-kinetic coordination. DeSilva, moreover, found that the perceptual and visual acuity of accident-prone drivers were inferior.

Psychoanalytic Approach

Dunbar (1948) has advanced the psychoanalytic approach, towards the causation of accidents. According to this approach, accident-proneness is not so much an isolated functioning as it is a syndrome of nonspecific or general factors present in the personality of the person itself. In other words the clinical or psychoanalytic approach emphasises the generality of accident-proneness.

Dunbar (1948) applied a more refined technique of using the Rorschach test on two groups of patients and tried to prove that the causation of accidents is related to certain ill-defined aspects of personality. She viewed that accidents which happen due to faulty attitude or absent-mindedness or failure to coordinate are because of personality characteristics. This composite personality pattern can be derived from the analysis of the case studies of two groups of patients.

In the group committing more accidents, it was found from their early case history, that there is greater frequency of minor neurotic traits such as lying, stealing, sleep walking etc.

Secondly, an analysis of emotion showed that the accident group was emotionally impulsive. Moreover, there is a tendency to escape from authority. Thus, the accident-prone group has emotion as a distinct feature.

To study the emotional stability of the drivers of the Yellow Cab Company of Chicago, Snow (1926) developed a test coupled with sensory motor and intelligence tests. There drivers had an average rate of accident of two per person for a period. But the unselected group had one accident per man.

He found that the nature of accident-proneness lies in disturbed sensory motor coordination.

Snow further found that where the perceptual level was lower than the motor level employees were more accident-prone.

Harris (1950) studied two groups of workers who were equated except for the number of accidents, using items from the Bernreuter, personality inventory, the Rosenzweig picture frustration test and the multiple choice research. He, however, found no personality differences in the two groups.

CRITICAL EVALUATION OF ACCIDENT-PRONENESS

In recent times, accident-proneness has been criticised by Mintz and Blum. Mintz and Blum (1949) conclude that most of the researches have been ill conceived and are wrong from the point of view of methodology. There is considerable amount of careless reporting about accidents and statistical flaw in thinking that chances for accidents are equal for everybody if circumstances are equal. But conditions differ for the same department. So no equation can be made here.

From further analysis Mintz and Blum concluded that 60 per cent to 80 Per cent of accidents were attributed to unpredictable factors whereas the remaining 20 per cent to 40 per cent could be attributed to accident liability, personality characteristics and environmental conditions causing accidents.

Using some figures Mintz and Blum concluded that though there is unequal distribution of accidents, yet the factor of accident-proneness is grossly exaggerated by psychologists.

The arbitrary classification of people, who have more than the average number of accidents as accident-prone, is also erroneous. It has already been mentioned that some people may have two or three accidents entirely on the basis of chance expectancy. This view towards accident-proneness is partly supported by Cobb 1940 and Johnson (1946). Arbous and Kerrich (1951) in this connection view that "Accident-proneness percy is a figment of the imagination resulting from wishful thinking." This points to a view of accident prevention since it means that an individual's ability or proneness to accidents in one set of circumstances will give little indication of proneness to accidents in another. Thus Arbous and Kerrich remark "This does not mean that accident-proneness does not exist, but that so far we have not succeeded in defining it, assessing its dimensions and constituent elements, nor evolved a technique for putting it to practical use." Besides the factors already mentioned, other personal factors found in some situations are motor performance, personality and temperamental factors. Kerr (1952) for instance, found that workers who were most liked by fellow workers tended to be accident-free while most of the high accident rates were found among the men most disliked by their fellow workers.

Conclusion

Analysing these research findings and views advanced by different psychologists, it would be justifiable to hold that at present there is no definite or clearcut evidence regarding the presence of any consistent characteristics which could be said to be contributing to accidents in a major way.

According to Bhalla (1977) whatever studies have been conducted suffer from a lack of coherence and validity. According to Snow (1971) the characteristics (leading to accident-proneness) that have been observed are too diverse and varied and different studies have arrived at different findings in this regard. Thus finally Bhalla (1977) concludes, "at present this or that or every thing constitutes accident-proneness."

REDUCTION AND PREVENTION OF ACCIDENTS

Accidents have multiple causes. Realising the fact there are many elements which contribute to an accident, a person who is accident-prone can reduce his accident record by dealing with the other factors which contribute to his accidents. This is because accident-proneness accounts only for about 20 per cent of the accidents and the rest of 80 per cent accidents can be explained by other factors discussed earlier.

Hence, besides the specific remedies for the specific causes, by and large, certain general remedies and preventive measures may be taken up.

1. Awareness. Studies and investigations show that accidents are more at the construction phase or pre production stage than at the post production stage. This may be due to lack of awareness to prevention of accident. Lack of awareness undoubtedly is a major factor of accident.

Though industrialization is progressing in a rapid speed, lack of awareness regarding accident susceptibility in different types of jobs, lack of knowledge regarding various safety devices and mind set not to use the safety devices are major causes of accidents. It is amply seen that people take the helmet with them, but do not use it while driving a scooter, refuse to use seat belts while driving a car or riding it. This is probably because of their peculiar mindset. Once I asked a few persons why they are not using helmet while riding a scooter, promptly a few replied that they feel uncomfortable while using it. But they never thought of head injury when there is an accident. Lack of seriousness in adopting safety devices are found even in many skilled workers. But the industry or the traffic control department should enforce strict rules and heavy fines for the defaulters who do not use safety devices.

The worker unions should have adequate representations in the safety committees for the assessment of the safety conditions available for their members. In several participatory programmes, the management and workers should come together to discuss and make every one aware of the need of preventing accidents and injuries through the use of safety devices and by becoming careful while dealing with risky jobs. Wide spread campaigns and awareness weeks should also be implemented in true spirit. If an orientation programmes for awareness is taken up with sincere efforts through awareness generation activities mishaps can be reduced. An institute or training centre on safety management should also be established in each state.

2. Uses of Safety Devices. The use of safety devices is very essential and has been previously discussed. Not only physical safety devices alone but also psychological safety devices are essential. In some cases rewards may be provided for committing less number of accidents as it leads to psychological competition to commit less accidents. Some modern industries and business organisations in India have used this technique with successful results.

3. Safety Campaigns. Safety campaign and poster stimulate safe behaviour. Accident prevention week should be observed with slogans, posters etc., to bring social consciousness.

There should be social pressure about these positive messages, like "Every worker won't like me" (the one causing accident). But posters, conveying general messages specially in negative terms, are less effective than specific messages in positive terms. Negative messages may create resentment, fear and sometimes anger. Infact, posters should carry simple, reasonable and constructive messages in positive terms such as "wear hard hats here"; "better late than never"; "Deposit cigarette butts in the container"; "Use glasses before entering inside"; "It is better to be Mr. late than late Mr." etc. Posters should be used in such a way to attract maximum attention. They must be unique. To make posters effective, the location, size and colour of posters should be considered. If the posters and placards dealing with accident prevention tell the new employees, in particular, what to do and not to do, it may help in the prevention of accidents.

4. Safety Consciousness. If the management becomes safety conscious, the rate of accident frequency is lowered. It has also been noted that accident frequency is less when classes in accident prevention are conducted by the company, and attended and participated by top officials and executives.

5. Safety Habits. Safety habits should be developed during the period of training so that it becomes an integral part of the total skill.

6. Careful Training Programmes. Careful training programmes should be adopted to train workers to develop a consciousness to be very careful about not committing accidents as far as practicable. Training programmes should be developed for new employees before they begin their job, in order to familiarise them with possible hazards and with those practices and methods that will minimise likelihood of their having accidents. It would also lead to the development of a proper attitude towards safety practices.

Walker and Potter (1954) have emphasised the importance of worker participation in safety training.

Emphasising the importance of training on prevention of accidents, Ravens (1958) comments, "The larger establishments which can accord trained safety engineers and which conduct intensive safety programmes generally have the lowest rates. Usually the medium sized plants have the highest rates and the smallest establishments show rates some how below the medium sized plants but above the average for the industry."

Goldstien (1975) presents guidelines that related to learning principles which may be employed in the design of the training environment, and which are relevant to the general training programme construction and to the special application of safety training to reduce accidents.

Grether (1975) has discussed the psychological concepts and principles bearing on industrial safety.

7. Education Measures. Certain educational measures can also be used through audio visual education, such as T.V., motion pictures and the radio etc., to educate the workers on the importance of not taking risks while driving or operating a machine.

8. Better Selection. Farmer and Chambers (1929) have suggested the use of better selection procedure or screening of workers by the use of tests. This has been discussed earlier under selection.

9. Good Housekeeping. Longmerir states that accidents can be prevented by good housekeeping. Orderly housekeeping is essential for accident-free behaviour. Lack of adequate space to store equipment and tools may lead to unsafe behaviour. Further, to maintain a safe work atmosphere housekeeping details must be attended to. Poor housekeeping like slippery, greasy, wet or dirty floors, misplacement and bad arrangement of material and machines lead to accidents. Hence research on equipment design in necessary to prevent accidents.

10. Conferences and Discussions. It is held by Tiffin and McCormick (1871) that a systematic and comprehensive series of conferences and discussions covering this specific information is a much more effective means of informing the employees, than the chance or casual learning obtained from posters or from observations that the employees may make. Once the information has been given to the employees, still further education is necessary to make sure that they believe as well as known that certain practices are unsafe.

Laner and Sell (1960) have made an investigation on the effect of using safety posters. According to them, when safety posters were used, safer behaviour was observed during a six week test period at seven British plants. In 17 out of 13 shops safe behaviour increased by more than 20 per cent.

Various kinds of personal protection devices are used to minimise the possibility of injury. Such devices include safety goggles, safety shoes, safety belts, harnesses, special clothing, helmets etc.

Of course it is found quite often that workers resist the use of such safety devices.

For instance, in spite of repeated and frequent deaths due to scooter accidents in India many do not like to use helmet while driving a scooter. They often resist.

But through training and other methods of communication such as posters, radio, television etc., it is possible to reduce the resistance and develop a consciousness to avoid accidents as far as possible.

Besides the preventive measures already mentioned various techniques should be used to motivate safety. The participation of the employees in the determination of various safety devices would lead to better results. Then only the workers will not think that safety devices are useless and imposed upon them by the management. Protective devices should be fitted to machines.

Gilmer (1971) rightly points out that employee participation is necessary for motivating safe behaviour. It will provide a basis for constant retraining and reminding, wearing of safety shoes, glasses, gloves and helmets. During discussions the safety engineer should not make any comment but should only stimulate the discussion when necessary. A need for better discipline in the wearing and design of protective clothing seems to be imperative.

Glimer (1971) also suggests that to prevent accidents a personal record of accident for each worker should be maintained by the company for future reference.

Since prevention is better than cure, major emphasis should be given on the preventive measures of accident.

Blum and Naylor (1968) have developed two approaches to the problem of accident reduction as related to human factors : Actuarial method and Educational campaign.

Actuarial Method

"In brief the actuarial method involves studying accident statistics to determine based upon statistical data those things which seem to be related to accident frequency," (Blum and Naylor 1968).

According to Blum and Naylor, McFarland and Moseley's (1954) study "clearly indicates that accident repeaters committed many more violations than did accident-free drivers. The number of violations of accident repeaters is much greater than proportional expectations. McFarland is inclined to believe that a man drives as he lives."

Speed in private driving and violations which reflect attitude towards authority seem to be characteristic of repeaters.

On the other hand Forbes (1939) holds the view that accident repeaters account for only a small portion of the total traffic accident problem. From the sample of 29351 drivers, he found that less than 4 per cent of the accidents in a three year period involved repeaters from the prior three year period. Thus, contrary to the view of McFarland, involvement in accidents does not appear to be a highly stable characteristics of individual drivers.

California (1964) has studied on automobile accidents. It was found that about 85 per cent of the driving population is accident-free over three year period and about 60 per cent of the driving population is conviction free over the same period.

The actuarial method thus emphasises finding the causes of accident based on actual data and developing reduction of conducted accident programmes from that angle.

11. Safety Education Programme. Accidents of accident-prone employees can also be reduced by safety education programmes arranged by the management and employee groups. Meetings conducted by foreman can be helpful in reducing accidents. More and more safety committees should be formed to reduce accidents. In some coal mines of England, an experimental group was compared with a control group. The situation was identical except that an accident prevention programme was carried on with the experimental group. In nine months the experimental group had reduced its accident record to 54 per cent below the other group.

The United States Department of Labour (1947) has issued a Guide to Industrial Accident Prevention, through a joint labour management safety committee, which suggests an eight point programme for a safety committee.

1. Make immediate and detailed investigation of accident reports.
2. Develop accident data to indicate accident scores and injury rates.
3. Develop or revise safe practices and rules to comply with plant needs.
4. Inspect the plant to detect hazardous physical condition or unsafe work method.
5. Makes changes or additions to protect equipment and devices to eliminate hazards.
6. Protect safety and first aid training for committee members and workers.
7. Participate in advertising safety and in selling the safety programmes to workers.
8. Conduct regular schedule meetings.

Today both management and union officials realise the importance of safety committees and are striving for improvements through joining safety committees.

The committee of Highway Safety Research of the National Academy of Science (1952) has done very useful research in the area of accident prevention.

The committee's data can be summarised as follows :

1. Seventy-five to ninety per cent of automobile accidents are due wholly or in part to human errors and lapses.
2. The accident records kept have value as a general index but are of the questionable value as a criterion for research on accident causes.
3. Many drivers having multiple accidents in one period are accident-free in a later period.
4. Factory leading to accidents are largely correctable or may be compensated for by greater caution.
5. Drivers between 18 and 25 years of age have far more than their appropriate share of accidents.
6. The effect of intensive safety education and enforcement campaign has been shown to be immediate but temporary.
7. Psychophysical driver tests are probably of more value as educational rather than as selection devices.
8. Clinics for accident-repeaters have been shown to have value. Whether this is due to increased knowledge, attitude change or motivation is not known.

12. Psychological Tests. Accident rates can also be reduced by proper selection through psychological tests.

It has already been discussed that accidents occur due to several personal factors such as age, experience, neuroticism, visit to hospitals for minor sickness, visual acuity, reaction, time, perceptual motor coordination, mental ability, environmental conditions of work and bad housekeeping etc.

Hence at the time of selecting workers for different jobs, various psychological tests should be applied and they should be selected on the basis of scores obtained in these tests. These tests include intelligence test choice reaction time test, sensory motor test, coordination test, dotting and pursuit meter test, test of vision, various tests of personality including psychometric tests and projective techniques.

By using the Otis self administering test of mental ability, the Bennett test of mechanical comprehension, the Kuder vocational interest test, the Bernreuter personality inventory and the Minnesota multiphasic personality inventory a group of long distance drivers were studied for a relationship between accidents and characteristics measured by these paper pencil tests. The authors concluded that accident rates were determined on the basis of miles driven per accident, but continued to follow the normal distribution when distance was held constant.

A motor man selection test was found effective in reducing accident rate. This is a work sample test in which the subject learns to operate controls in response to sounds and lights and to resist distracting noises. Only 0.6 per cent of the men selected by the test had to be discharged for accidents, in contrast to 14.1 per cent of operators who had not been selected by the motor man test. It was calculated that the use of the text saved $ 60,000 in a year's time.

Operators working for the Boston Elevated Railway who had frequent accidents scored worse on a series of psychological tests than did operators whose records were better. Tests for speed, accuracy, oscillation, perseverance and tapping were applied.

A comparison of test results with accident records is shown in the following table.

TABLE 23.5

Grade	*Test scores of elevated high accident group*	*Test scores of low accident group*
A (Good)	16	20
B (Medium)	19	21
C (Poor)	18	02

It has been specially noted that psychological test for picking safe employees have had some success in the transportation industry.

FUTURE RESEARCH ON ACCIDENT PREVENTION

Researches and scientific investigations are extremely necessary to reduce and prevent accidents. Regular and coordinated efforts should be made to modify the existing texts, make them more refined, reliable and valid. New tests should also be constructed to further enrich the data already obtained.

The establishment of accident prevention clinics in large numbers is a must to diagnose particular causes of accidents.

More and more research work should be taken up on the design of equipment. Equipments should be designed keeping in view the physical and psychological capacities and limitations of individual workers.

McFarland and Moore (1963) conclude "accidents, now out rank diseases as a leading cause of death from age 1 to age 34. Industry is now increasing its attention to off-the-job accidents as a major step in preserving the working effectiveness of its employees.

Major strategies of accident prevention include the control of exposure to risk, the reduction of accidents during risk, the prevention of injury when accidents occur and minimising the residuals of injury."

QUESTIONS

1. Accidents are not accidental. Do you agree ? Give reasons for your answer.
2. Discuss along with experimental findings the mechanical and non mechanical causes of accident.
3. What are the remedies of the environmental causes of accident ?
4. What do you understand by the personal factors of accident ? Discuss the importance of psychological tests in preventing the personal causes of accident.
5. What is meant by an accident-prone personality ? How can the personal causes of accident-proneness be prevented ?
6. Elaborate some studies on accident-proneness and critically examine the concept of accident-proneness.
7. Critically examine the different hypotheses advanced to explain the cause of accident.
8. Give a critical analysis of road accidents and safe-unsafe behaviour of drivers.
9. Write notes on the following :
   (*a*) Unequal liability hypotheses.

(*b*) Causes of accident given by the Metropolitan Insurance Company.

(*c*) Safety measures used for prevention of accident.

(*d*) Sensory motor coordination approach.

REFERENCES

Anderson, Alf L., Nilsson, Alf and Henriksson, Nils, G. Personality differences between accident loaded and accident free young car drivers, *British Jn. of Psy.*, 1970, 61(3), pp. 409- 421.

Bhalla, S.K. *Issues in Psychology of Traffic Safety and Strategies for Their Resolution,* Paper presented in the Indian Science Congress, 44th session, 1977.

Blum, M.L. and Naylor, J.C. *Industrial Psychology and Its Social Foundations,* Harper and Row, 1968.

Chambers, E.G. A preliminary inquiry into the part played by character and temperament in accident causation, *Jn. of Mental Science*, 85, 1939, pp. 115-218.

DeSilva, H.R. *Why We Have Automobile Accidents.* New York, Wiley, 1942, pp. 18-21.

Drake, C.A. *Accident-proneness-A Hypothesis, Character and Person*, 1940, 8, pp. 335-341.

Farmer, E. and Chambers, E.G. A psychological study of individual differences in accident rates, *Industrial Fatigue Research Board*, 1926, Rep. No. 38.

Farmer, E. and Chambers, E.G. A study of personal qualities in accident-proneness and proficiency, *Industrial Fatigue Research Board Report,* No. 55, 1929.

Gilmer, V.B.H. *Industrial and Organisational Psychology,* McGraw Hill, Kausaka Publications, 1971.

Hambly, W.D. and Bedford, T. Preliminary notes on atmospheric conditions in boot and shoe factories *Industrial Fatigue Research Board Report,* No. 11, 1921.

Harrell, T.W. Industrial Psychology, New York, Rinchart, 1958.

McMurray, Lucille. Emotional stress and driving performance, The effect of divorce. *Behavioural Research and Highway Safety*, 1970, Vol. 1, (2), pp. 100-114.

Mintz, A. and Blum, M. *Accident-proneness is Overrated*, Paper read before the Eastern Psychological Association.

Newbold, E.M. A contribution to the study of human factor in the causation of accidents, *Industrial Fatigue Research Board,* 1926, Rep. No. 34.

Snow, A.J. Tests for *chauffeurs, Industrial Psychology*. 1926, pp. 30-45.

Maier, N.R.F. *Psychology in industry*, Oxford and IBH Publishing Co., 1970.

McFarland, R.A. and Musely, A.L. *Human Factors in Highway Transport Safety*, Harvard School of Public Health, Boston, 1954.

Osborne, E.E and Vernon, H.M. The influence of temperature and other conditions on the frequency of industrial accidents. *Ind. Fatigue Res. Board, Report* No. 19, 1922.

Tiffin, J. and McCormick, E.J. *Industrial Psychology*, 5th ed., Prentice Hall of India Private Limited, 1971.

Vernon, H.M. Accident and their prevention, *Industrial Fatigue Research Board Report* No. 11, 1921.

Viteles, M.S. *Industrial Psychology*, Norton, 1932.

24

Human Engineering

INTRODUCTION

Since the second world war one of the areas in which rapid expansion has taken place is the area of human engineering, popularly known as engineering psychology. It is also called applied psycho-physics, system research and the man-machine system. The large volume of research done in this area has given engineering psychology an independent status. Historically, this branch as a field of specialisation came into prominence after the Second World War. Before the war also, some studies had been conducted, but they were not so clearcut and prominent as to give engineering psychology recognition and special status.

Engineering psychology owes its existence to a type of cooperative research where experts from different fields like engineers, psychologists, statisticians, medical men, physicists and physiologists have made their significant contributions.

IMPORTANCE OF HUMAN ENGINEERING IN INDUSTRY

A machine, no matter how automatic, requires a man to handle it. He operates the machine, controls its speed according to the necessity and requirements. He gives signals whenever the situation demands. Thus, for the perfect operation of a machine, a capable and competent operator is required. But when the engineer designs a machine for more output in a shorter period, he is not usually concerned with the human being whose cooperation is necessary for operating the machine. He quite often forgets the man who has to operate the machine. In this process, sometimes he overlooks the limited capacity of a human being, to operate a very complicated machine. Machines are designed first and it is usually taken for granted that the man will adjust himself to the machine. This outlook created a lot of problem not only for the operators and employees who deal with the machines, but for the management also. The dream of an engineer thus often turned to be a nightmare for the operator. This particularly happened when many complicated machines were designed and manufactured during the war years.

The system of human engineering developed as a solution to such problems. When engineers realised that man unlike the machine cannot be redesigned, they started with the man and designed the machine around the man to suit his abilities and capacities, keeping in view the various limitations of the human operators.

The increased mechanisation of work thus developed a feeling that man and machine must work in relation to each other. In engineering, the machine is designed first and there is no consideration whatsoever for the human being who usually operates the machine. But in human engineering the purpose is to design the machine in accordance with the human needs, abilities and limitations.

Thus Blum (1956) remarks "Human engineering is that endeavour which seeks to match human beings with modern machines so that their combined output will be comfortable, safe and more efficient." In these lines Blum has indicated the need for the co-operative endeavour of psychologist and engineers to successfully match human beings with modern machines. In fact, psychologists and engineers have joined hands and worked in collaboration with each other to develop this new system.

It was further recognised that as long as man operates a machine, one must design the machine in relation to and around the man. For this purpose the knowledge and skill of psychologists are utilised by the engineers.

A human engineering psychologist is mostly interested in knowing and studying the characteristics of machines and it is his job to determine how well a person can work with the machines, what are the difficulties he might face, etc. Hence, while the design of a machine is an engineer's job, perfect and easy operation of the machine is the human engineer's prime responsibility. A human engineer is therefore mostly interested in the psychological aspects of the man-machine system, while an engineer is concerned with the physical aspects of the machine.

DEVELOPMENT OF HUMAN ENGINEERING

The historical analysis of human engineering indicates a three-line development.

1. Time and Motion Engineering

Human engineering is said to be the extension of the time and motion study. The time study movement inaugurated by Taylor indicated that the time relations and sequence of motions are utilised to find out the one best way of doing work.

Mr. Gilbreth, an engineer, and Mrs Gilbreth, a psychologist, together contributed to this branch besides Taylor. They were able to show how a man can operate a machine in the best possible way by using minimum motion and minimum time. In this way, the best way of doing a work can be found out. Time and motion engineers were also interested in job simplification. In most cases time and motion engineers designed the machines in such a way that a lot of time could be saved, workers were also less fatigued and worked comfortably.

Thus the time and motion study contributed to the first phase of human engineering.

2. Personnel Selection

This constitutes another line of development of human engineering. This is based on the realisation of human variability and recognition of the concept of individual differences. Thus only the best fitted person for a job is selected.

In personnel selection, while emphasis is given to the concept of human variability in selecting the most suitable person for a job, in engineering psychology the emphasis is slightly different.

The engineering psychologist is more interested in designing a machine in such a way that the average man can handle the machine most efficiently. Here the emphasis is not given on the best man selected for a job.

According to an engineering psychologist a task should not be beyond the capacity of an individual having the average capacity, ability and skill. For this purpose machines must be designed in such a way that individuals of average capacity and skill can handle it without difficulty.

Personnel selection is possible when from a large number of applicants are to be chosen. Otherwise, people of superior ability needed for certain types of jobs, cannot be available. However, where complex machines are to be handled, workers with superior abilities are required. In such cases, personnel selection is absolutely essential.

3. Designing Machines Keeping in View the Limitations of Human Organism

In designing a machine, the limitations of human capacity and ability should not be overlooked. With the development of human engineering there was this realisation that the design of machines is not so important as the fact whether such machines can be operated and handled by the worker without difficulty. This is the most significant job of an engineering psychologist. Hence tasks required to operate the machine should not be beyond the capacity of the individual. This problem came into light specially during the war years when many complicated machines were designed and operators were not able to handle them perfectly. The military authorities found that certain complicated machines were designed which were rather inferior from the efficiency point of view. So the engineers realised that machines whose handling was beyond the ability of human beings should not be manufactured and jobs beyond the reach of the workers should not be designed. At this stage engineering psychology came into full operation.

A brief analysis of the three-line development of human engineering indicates that the primary object of a human engineer is to develop a science to deal adequately with the design of machines for human use. The aim of an engineering psychologist is, therefore, to see how efficiently and economically a person can deal with the machines.

PROBLEMS OF HUMAN ENGINEERING

It has been said that human engineering problem seems to arise whenever man is confronted with technical achievements.

It has also been viewed that until the machine age was well advanced in the nineteenth century, no body worried about the fact that man was actually the weak sister in mechanised production. But in the early decade of the twentieth century both engineers and psychologists began to attempt to adopt human beings to the demands of a technological society. The growing tendency was felt by every one that before a machine could guarantee better performance it must take into consideration the physiological and psychological limitations of human beings related to visual acuity, reaction time, sensory motor and perceptual motor coordination, strength and capacity, intelligence and ability etc. Undoubtedly, machines run much faster. But man cannot operate the machines with the same speed. Various electronic and radio communication systems and aircrafts etc., cannot be operated by the human beings most efficiently and speedily because of the physiological and psychological limitations. This is one of the major problems that the human engineer has to face.

The second limitation of complicated designed machines is that untrained people employed in certain complicated and mechanical jobs take a long period to reach the standard. It should be accepted beyond dispute that electronics and other communication systems require a particular potentiality of a worker which may not be found in all workers.

Therefore, while designing the various complicated machines and electronic devices, care should be taken to consider the physiological and mental limitations of the person dealing with such machines.

Keeping in view the various difficulties that the engineer faces while desinging a machine on job, Morgan and his associates have classified the problems of human engineering under five specific heads.

1. Appraising New Equipment. This refers to testing the design of a new equipment and fixing its price. For improvement in the system of human engineering, new designs may be experimented with the already existing ones by logical analysis of the characteristics of the new design. Accordingly, changes in the old or new designs can be brought about to ensure efficiency.

2. Optimal Method of Work. Keeping in mind the limitations of human beings, the engineering psychologist should find out the best way of operating the machine so that the individual will feel safe and comfortable. He can perform efficiently and finish the work in less time. The human engineers should therefore find out the best method of doing work following the principles of scientific management.

3. Design of Instruments. New instruments should be designed and old instruments should be redesigned to suit human ability, capacity and limitations. The dials, sounds, breaks and controls, signals etc., should be designed in such a way that the worker can handle them with minimum effort. The average reaction time of human organisms, perceptual motor and sensory motor coordination capacities, strength, balance and visual acquity etc., should also be taken into consideration by the technocrats while planning a new machines or a new task.

4. Design of Tasks. All the tasks should be classified and analysed under different heads to make the performance of the job more systematic and economical. The different tasks, if necessary, can be modified for developing and implementing one best method of doing work.

5. Design of Systems. This is otherwise known as the system research.

System research is divided into

1. Equipment display, and
2. Equipment control.

The various studies in the field of human engineering have led to various principles related to the design of displays and controls.

Equipment Display

Equipment display is concerned with the display or arrangement of scales, meters, dials and graphs in the work place. The problem of equipment display thus refers to the design of the instrument for conveying information from the machine to the man.

When the equipment is applied to the man-machine system it refers to display. Display is a means of providing information which an operator may not be able to get directly through his senses. This information is given to the operator through various cues such as visual cues, auditory cues, tactile cues etc. This information is necessary to run the machine effectively. Further, various informations should be provided to the operator as quickly as possible, for the effective operation of the machine and the avoidance of hazards. Many difficulties are faced when the psychological characteristics of the operator is ignored in the design of displays.

Researches on design of displays have brought into light the effectiveness of certain types of displays and controls. For instance, it been found, as pointed out by Blum and Naylor (1968), that a fixed dial with a moving pointer is better than a moving dial with a fixed pointer. Finer markings are more helpful for speed in dial or counter reading. Research has also shown that all dials showing increasing magnitude should rotate in the same direction preferably upward or clockwise. Displays should be at eye height whenever and whenever possible. Spacing between markings on dials should be consistent and the distance should be about one half an inch. Shapes, sizes and colours of controls should be designed to reduce or eliminate confusion errors.

Visual displays are found to be more important compared to all other displays, as the operator has to read the dial, meter, graph and the scale etc. A large number of studies have been conducted to determine the relative importance of different displays. In the operation of an aircraft engine it has been found that out of displays which one has use in taking off the plane, 53 were operated in response to some sort of visual cues. Studies also show similar results in industrial situations.

Experimental Studies

Study conducted by Dashevesky (1964) indicated that dial reading can be vastly improved by system research. Following the Gestalt view of figural continuity, Dashevesky hypothesized that "Since prior research had shown that pointer alignment aided dial reading, extending the line formed by the pointers across the entire display should be even more effective." He developed six different types of displays as demonstrated in Figure 24.1 for the examination of his hypothesis.

The results of his study indicated that in comparison to open displays the use of extended displays brought about 85 per cent more efficient dial reading performance.

Jenkins (1947) found 11 knob shapes that can be readily identified by touch even when gloves are used. Blum and Naylor state " Even though this research was related to aircraft it is entirely possible that such designs of knobs would be appropriate for automobile dashboards and other types of machines."

Smith and Thomas (1964) made an attempt to compare the relative effectiveness of colour coding displays and shape coding displays in an information processing task. They found that colour coding was the most effective technique to reduce the number of errors committed by a person.

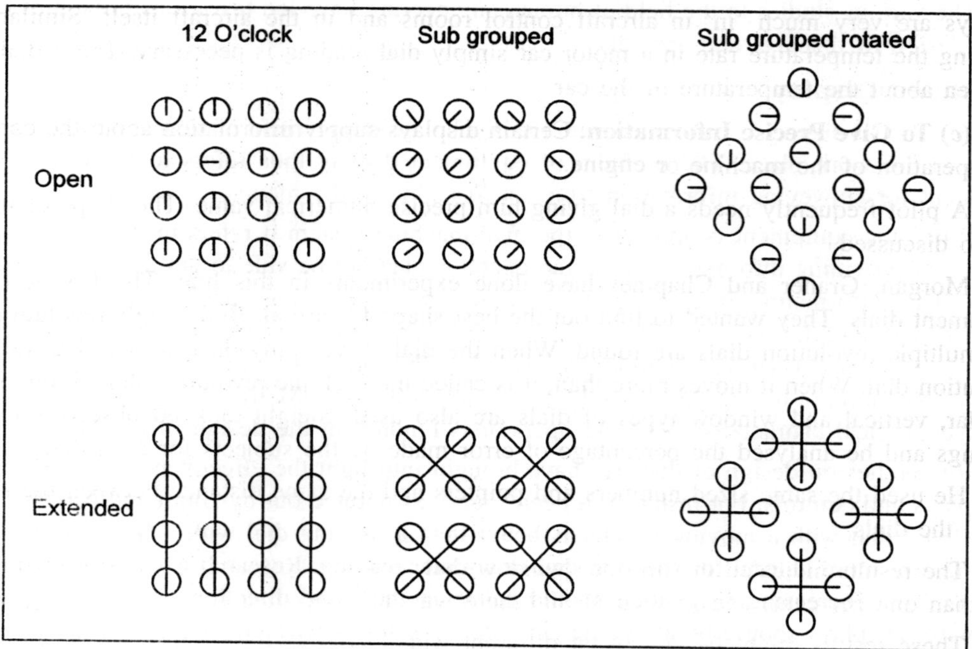

Fig. 24.1. Dial Display

McFarland (1953 a, 1953 b) has conducted a number of investigations on the problem of the man-machine system in relation to automobiles and other kinds of vehicular equipments. In one study attempts were made to evaluate the cabs of 12 vehicles. Its main purpose was to determine the suitable arrangement of controls, displays, seating and window areas for efficient, comfortable and safe operation of vehicles.

McFarland *et al.* found plenty of defects in the design of truck cabs. In such cases recommendations were made to design the machine to conform to human needs.

FUNCTION OF DISPLAYS

Functions of visual displays can be classified under three headings.

(*a*) To Show Whether Something is Working. This may be characterised as check reading. The motor car with directional signals is an example of the working purpose. For example, when a left hand turn is to be taken at a particular spot, a light blinks at the rear and simultaneously a light starts blinking in the dashboard. Two directions are working here, with the blinker remaining there as long as the turn is completed. In this case, direction indication is working and usually such instruments do not require any dials.

Instruments bringing this function of an indicator are said to fulfil the check reading.

(*b*) To Give Warning. Warning displays give a qualitative indication regarding an instrument. If, suddenly, something goes wrong in the instrument, there is a warning. Like for instance, the red light in the switch board indicates that somewhere there is any trouble and so on. By looking at this warning the control room operator can know what is happening where. Thus looking at the visual displays one can say whether things are going on well or not. Warning through visual displays are very much 'in' in aircraft control rooms and in the aircraft itself. Similarly for knowing the temperature rate in a motor car simply dial reading is necessary. These dials give the idea about the temperature of the car.

(*c*) To Give Precise Information. Certain displays supply information about the condition and operation of the machine or engine.

A pilot frequently needs a dial giving him precise numerical value. The shape of the dial is also discussed.

Morgan, Graner and Chapines have done experiments in this line. The first test is on instrument dials. They wanted to find out the best shape for a dial. Both single revolution dials and multiple revolution dials are found. When the dial moves only once it is called the single revolution dial. When it moves more than, it is called the multiple revolution dial. Semi-circular, circular, vertical and window types of dials are also used. Sleight took 60 observers to make readings and he analysed the percentage of error made by the subjects for each dial.

He used the same sized numbers and pointers and the same distance between the number on all the dials.

The results indicated that in open window dial there was practically no error (errors were less than one per cent) and in vertical dial there was the maximum error.

These results might be somewhat different with longer reading times and if readings of several different dials had to be done rapidly.

There has also been a controversy as to whether there should be dials or counters.

A few studies indicate that counters worked better than any dials. This does not necessarily imply that all the dials can be changed to counters. In the first place, engineers may not be able to build instruments with counters only. Secondly, counters are more difficult to read than dials, specially when the numbers change more rapidly. Actually, in the case of altimeters, the engineers combine the two. They set a counter in the middle of a dial.

DIAL SCALES

Dial scale deal with the questions, "How many marks should there be in a dial ? How far apart should they be ? How many marks should be numbered ?" These are all inter-related questions concerning dial scales.

The specific factors that make the dials more legible are still not fully known. However, on the basis of information gathered during the war years, Graner and Morgan etc., have reached the following general conclusion about the dial scales.

1. A dial of about 2.75″ or 3″ in diameter is probably the best all round size if one is going to read it at a distance of 30″ or less.
2. Marks should be located at the 0, 5, 10, 15, 20, 25, 30 positions, with an interval of 5 between each mark. The marks at the 0, 10, 20 and other positions should be longer than those at 5, 15, 25 and other positions. Only the marks at 0, 10, 20 should be numbered.
3. The distance between the numbered marks should be half an inch as measured around the circumference of the dial.

4. The separation behaviour scale markers should be the same all through the dial.
5. There should be a gap between the beginning and the end of the scale.
6. Values on the scale should increase in a clockwise direction.

Equipment Control

The problem of equipment control deals with the design of controls that human operators must use. A control is something attached to a panel or a machine. A worker operates the machine through its controls. A number of problems are found relating to the placement of controls, shape of controls, size, direction and movement of controls. An engineer sometimes designs the control of a machine so that no one but a genius with ample time to spare can run it accurately. Further, he blames the operator or the maintenance man when something goes wrong.

Psychologists and other experts in this area tried to find out the types of mistakes committed in using controls. Little scientific and clear information is available on this subject. Much of the information concerns aeroplane pilots since the effects of controls in this type of work have been most obvious. It is found that confusion of controls is the most common error made by aeroplane pilots which means that the operator mistakes one type of control for another. Other sources of errors among the pilots are pushing control in the wrong direction say, to the right instead of left, clockwise instead of anti-clockwise, and forgetting to use particular control etc.

Thus, the question arises, how can controls be designed for the best human skill ? The first step is to find out what kind of control is best for a particular task. In fact, engineers may have constructed too complicated controls for the use of the operators. Often the operator may need a control to go on or off the machine. In such cases, contact control may be provided, that is, one that merely turns things on and off with simple effort and less motion.

Sometimes the operator needs selector controls which allow selection of one of the several positions. Sometimes one needs adjustment controls which enable him to make any desired setting. In many cases, before timing the control, the first job is to determine what the operator actually has to do.

PRINCIPLES INVOLVED IN THE DESIGN OF CONTROLS

There are some principles which can help the engineer in designing effective and useful controls.

Controls Should be Preferably Used by Organs other than the Hands

It is suggested that the hands should be freed or relieved of all actions that can be performed by the legs and the feet.

Now one has to find out what are the operations that can be performed by hands or feet ? Physiological and psychological studies of movement are to be referred to solve this problem. Careful experimentation is necessary to find out the operations to be done by the hands and feet. For example, to find out what kind of flying controls can be adequately operated by the pilot's feet, several careful experimental studies are necessary. In thus case, a group of psychologists found that anus control were consistently more accurate than foot controls. Any time precise adjustment in needed, the anus control should be used. The same group of psychologists found that controls operated by one hand were as accurate as controls operated by both hands.

Controls Should be Realistic

Research investigations also indicate that control should be realistic. The more realistic and natural the controls, the more easily they can be handled. For example, if one wants to make a clockwise turn, the control should go clockwise. If a movement is to be produced to the left, the control should move to the left. If we want to use the right hand, the control should be on the right side and not on the left. If a downward movement is necessary, provisions should be made for pushing down the control.

However, it is unfortunate to note that this commonsense principle is sometimes forgotten. Sometimes it is not obvious which is the most natural and realistic way for control to operate. In such cases simple experiments can bring about a lot of information and clarification. The control can be presented to a group of operators and without any specific instruction they can be asked to use the controls in a manner which they think would achieve a particular result.

Controls should be Distinguishable

The more distinguishable the controls, the more easily they can be used. In this case every little bit helps. Another important point to note is that what is easy for trained operators may be very difficult for the untrained operator. Thus it is desirable to make different controls which must have the quality of being differentiated from each other. By using different colours, sizes and shapes for different controls, they can be easily distinguished.

SYSTEM ORDER

It is generally viewed that the higher the system control order, the more complicated is the task of the operator.

Blum and Naylor (1968) have described three orders of control.

1. Zero Order Control. A zero order control system is otherwise known as positional control. In this type of control the person has only to make a response that is proportional to the desired system output.

In other words, the control system asks the operator to make responses proportional to the input signal.

2. First Order Control. It is often referred to as a rate or velocity control system. This order of control gives the operator control over the rate or velocity of movement of the system output. The operator here controls the rate of change of system position rather than its position. Blum and Naylor (1968) have explained the first order control through the following example. According to them, when the control device is linked to a motor so that a position movement by the operator changes the speed of the motor which in turn is hooked up to the gear box, it is called the first order control.

3. Second Order Control. According to Blum and Naylor (1968), when the operator has control over the rate of system change, it is called the second order control, Thus, a positional response by the operator results in a change of acceleration on the part of the system output.

QUESTIONS

1. Human engineering is that endeavour which seeks to match human beings with modern machines so that 'their combined output will be comfortable, safe and more efficient." Explain the man-machine system with reference to the above statement.

2. Examine the factors responsible for the development of human engineering as an independent system.
3. Discuss the various problems of human engineering. How can such problems be solved ?
4. What is meant by system research ? Explain the concept of equipment display and its importance in the design of machines citing some experimental studies.
5. Discuss in detail the functions of equipment display.
6. What is equipment control ? Analyse the principle involved in the design of controls.
7. Make a critical evolution of the importance of human engineering in industry.
8. Write notes on :
   (*a*) Visual displays
   (*b*) Dial scales
   (*c*) Colour coding displays and shape coding displays
   (*d*) Shape of dials.

REFERENCES

Blum. M.L. *Industrial Psychology and Its Social Foundations*, Harper and Row, 1956.

Blum, M.L. and Naylor, J.C. *Industrial Psychology* : *Its Theoretical and Social Foundations*, Harper and Row Publishers, New York, 1968.

Birmingham, H.P. and Taylor, F.V. A human engineering approach to the design of man operated continuous control system.

Dashevesky, S.G. Check-reading accuracy as a function of pointer alignment, patterning and viewing angle, *Journal of Applied Psychology*, 1964, 48, pp. 344-347.

Fleishman, E.A. and Ellison, G.D. A factor analysis of fine manipulative tests, *Journal of Applied Psychology*, 1972, 46, pp. 96-105.

Gilbreth, F.B. and Gilbreth, L.M. *Applied Motion Study*, Macmillan, New York, 1917.

Jenkins, W.O. *Tactual Discrimination of Shapes for Coding Aircraft Type Controls*. In P.M. Fitts *Psychological Research on Equipment Design*, Government Printing Press, Washington D.C., 1947.

McFarland, R.A. *et al. Human Body Size and Capabilities in the Design and Operation of Vehicular Equipment*, Harvard School of Public Health, Boston, 1953.

Smith, S.L. Farquhar, Barbara and Thomas, D.W. Colour coding in formatted displays, *Journal of Applied Psychology*, 1955, 49, pp. 373-398.

Taylor, F.W. *Principles of Scientific Management*, Harper and Row, New York, 1947.

25

Effect of Frustration and Anxiety on the Goal Striving Behaviour of Industrial Employees of Orissa*

About six decades back, industrialists and managements considered it their duty to be mainly concerned with the plans and decisions regarding finances, with the supervision of production and by and large with higher production with minimum cost and minimum expenditure of energy. Regarding the psychological variables in question, the management was interested in the selection of most judicious and apt individuals in devising payment plans and work methods which would provide optimum motivation. To add to this, leadership seemed mostly to involve giving clear directions about what was to be done.

Today however the situation has changed. Social psychologists and psychopathologists have explored many areas of the industrial problems and have made genuine advances towards understanding the situation, the problem of the employees, their frustrations and shortcomings. They have shown tremendous interest in understanding the problems connected with the working group, the worker as an individual, his psychological and motivational drawbacks and so on and so forth.

The manner in which an employee sets his goal in the industry relative to his abilities and past experiences has considerable effect on his level of production. Two employees may possess

* The author is grateful to Education and Youth Services Deptt., Govt. of Orissa for granting study leave for completing this research project. She is also thankful to C.A.S., Deptt. of Psychology, Utkal University for providing facilities for research.

the same abilities. Yet one may set his goal very high while the other may be satisfied to aspire for nothing higher than what he is producing at present which is not helpful for the management. Similarly understanding and over rating one's performance may be possible due to several factors. This is also not conducive to higher production. Again when one aspires beyond his capacity and fails to meet his aspiration, experiences severe frustration.

Although in the modern competitive organisations goal directed behaviour and the factors influencing the setting of goals are of great importance, research in the area began about six decades back by Hoppe (1930), Dembo (1931), Frank (1935), Gardner (1940), Rotten (1942) and Lewin (1944). The goal setting behaviour represents as accurate as possible an estimate of a person's urge or drive to achieve goals or ends as he sees them. The factors which affect and influence goal setting behaviour of an individual in spite of its general nature are varied like success and failure, scholastic achievement, S.E.S. Culture, frame of reference, age, IQ and educational level. Among the psychodynamic and personal factors anxiety and frustration also do influence the goal setting behaviour of industrial workers, independent of their ability and capacity.

Gardner and many others have found experimental support to this fact. Frustration has therefore been described as one of the major factors in influencing goal setting behaviour of employees. The effect of frustration on L.O.A., varies with the employee's capacity to tolerate frustration. A worker who has fewer frustrations in life is less erratic and more realistic oriented and hence sets his level of achievement nearest to his performance. A frustrated worker with successive failures in life and job tries to set lower goals and there may be wide gap between his aspiration and achievement. Interruption of goal setting behaviour causes serious problems among the industrial; organisational workers. Due to severe frustration their L.O.A. is pushed down, achievement motivation becomes low and ultimately efficiency goes down.

One of the major symptoms of frustration being regression and withdrawal behaviour, a frustrated employee may indicate very low erratic .goal setting behaviour by withdrawing from the situation' in spite of having the capacity and ability to produce more. Lower achievement motivation, a production of low aspiration leads to a state of mind which may be described as one of 'giving up'. This low aspiration is expected to influence his level of production adversely. In industry such a resigned individual develops an inferiority feeling and looses hope for bettering his conditions. The frustration arising out of dissatisfaction of needs, demands and luxuries is transformed to the job indirectly, the outcome of which is tension, conflict and all kinds of disputes internal and external.

In view of these, the most important function of a psychologist in an industry is to deal with the frustration, conflict, stresses and strains of life of the employees. The industrial psychologist helps the workers as well as executives to bring to the surface many of their repressed and suppressed feelings helping them to see their own problems and solve them judiciously.

CAUSES OF FRUSTRATION AND DISPUTES

The following underlying causes of dissatisfaction, frustration and conflict of an individual have been found out from various studies by French, Kornhauser, Marrow (1946).

***(a)* Factors in the individual**. Ability, age, health, temperament, desires and expectations, neurotic tendencies and unconscious conflicts.

(*b*) Factors in life away from work. Home conditions, recreation consumer problems, labour union activities, socio-economic and political conditions.

(*c*) Factors in employment relations. Wages earnings, steadiness of employment, transfer, layoff and hiring procedure, supervision, training, conditions of work, social relationship on the job, recognition of merit, understanding and respect by the employer.

Factors responsible for dissatisfaction on the job are not only to be considered for reduction of conflict or disputes. Watson (1930) points out that a person's dissatisfaction refers to dissatisfaction inside and outside the job. Hull and Kolstand (1942) have conducted some studies in this area and have obtained the following conclusion.

1. Psychological satisfaction that the worker gets from the job like recognition and getting respect for his personality.
2. Attitude and morale is influenced by the behaviour that one receives from the foreman, manager and higher officers. In support of this view the British Institute of Public Opinion (1946) found that apart from wages and security, cooperation between the employee and management, appreciation of the employees etc. were important factors attributed by 40 per cent of the answers.

Thus, it would not be erroneous to conclude that many tensions and disputes are caused by in plant causes either directly or indirectly. Many needs and demands are frustrated in this process.

According to Kornhauser (1965) conditions of the work are generally more frustrating for the worker than for the management and frustration increases when one is in the lower status in the job.

When most of the important needs of a person are frustrated reactions to such frustrations occur. Some of these reactions are constructive and others are destructive when there is a barrier between the worker and his goal and if the individual tries to face the barrier intelligently without using regression or aggression, it becomes a healthy reaction to frustration. Compensation, substitution and adjustment etc. are also some of the more successful reactions to frustration on the job.

The reactions to frustration may be successful in case of workers who have not been able to adjust successfully from the very begining and are greater sufferers of disputes and conflicts.

Labour unions may be one of the many sources to get substituted satisfaction to one's frustrated desires since the labour unions to some extent can suitably satisfy one's social and psychological needs. Labour unions provide individual workers with a sense of satisfaction, with an opportunity to express himself with speed and action and with much more freedom from fear of punishment in the job.

Though much of the tensions and disputes are reduced by labour unions, when the labour union becomes very strong, in groups and out groups may be formed. This further leads to industrial conflicts. Industrial disputes may increase because of more strikes organised by labour unions. Illogical aggression against the management are very often created by the labour unions. Strike is one of the familiar patterns of aggression expressed by the workers on management.

Conflicts and disputes would hardly occur in industries and organisations if the management would care to check the needs and demands of the workers.

Over and above, anxieties and uncertainties caused out of certain political situations, unpredictable markets and government regulations, dangerous and insecure future etc. may create frustration, anxiety and conflict among the employees.

EFFECT OF ANXIETY ON THE GOAL STRIVING BEHAVIOUR OF INDUSTRIAL WORKERS

Anxiety is a state of mental distress with respect to some anticipated frustration causing a feeling of uneasiness, apprehension and fear. Besides, psychological disturbances like profuse sweating, rapid heart beat and trembling are normal accompaniments. Anxiety has its origin in the birth trauma and it more arises out of loss of love than lack of love.

Moderate degrees of anxiety serve adoptive purpose, elevating general arousal to a state where the person is more alert, sensitive and better prepared to meet the dangers of life.

Research findings of Martin (1961) indicates that anxiety improves performance only up to a point. But after reaching a certain intensity it has adverse effects. It disrupts efficient operation of the ego, interferes with perceptual and thinking processes. Extreme degree of anxiety produces neurotic symptoms and immobilises the individual in totto. Constructive activity comes to zero point when there is extreme experience of anxiety.

Anxieties and frustrations have become common experiences for the employees of modern industries and organisations. It has therefore become imperative to study the effect of anxiety in addition to frustration on the goal striving behaviour of industrial employees.

History of organisational psychology reveals that practically no research has been conducted in this area. It has therefore remained a much neglected area. Probably this is the first attempt by the investigator in India to study the effect of anxiety on the goal striving behaviour of industrial employees.

Very high and very low anxiety have adverse effects upon the employees aspiration level. While extreme degree of anxiety interferes with perceptual and thinking processes, and disrupts efficient operation of the ego, very low level of anxiety makes the individual lethargic and the motivation to aspire, learn and perform becomes very slim. If the goal or aspiration is set at a lower level, even if one has the ability to produce more, he automatically strives to produce less. Hence ability without proper aspiration and goal setting is useless and a wastage of man power.

Thus, in the present investigation (Mohanty 1985) attempts have been made to examine the effect of frustration and anxiety of employees working in heavy, medium and light industries of Orissa. By reducing the level of anxiety, the achievement motivation and level of production of the employees can be increased.

The present research is also undertaken to advise the management to keep the goals of the employees close to their level of production. The goal should be clear and properly adjusted to ability. According to Mace, performance could be more effective when the goal setting is adjusted according to the level of ability and skill of the workers. This can be possible by reducing the level of frustration and extreme anxiety among the workers.

If the L.O.A. is properly set, it regulates the ego from frustration. It also keeps the goal above his achievement. In case, the L.O.A. of the employee is set low due to feeling of frustration and if he underestimates his abilities and performances, he would not be motivated to proceed ahead.

According to Maier (1970) the aspiration level should always be set above the performance level for higher efficiency. In developing countries like India especially, the L.O.A. of industrial employees should always be set a little above their performance for better production.

Mohanty (1977) found that workers employed permanently in different organisations indicated lower G.D.S., had more typical shifts and were less rigid in their L.O.A. probably because of greater economic security, lower frustration and anxiety. In contrast, the unemployed graduates scored significantly higher G.D. score, had less typical, and more atypical shifts and more rigidity. Such significant differences in the primary and secondary measures of L.O.A. clearly suggest that employment gives security and has a less frustrating and more satisfying effect. The feeling of the satisfaction, acts as a positive reinforcement to motivate the workers to keep their aspiration reasonably ahead of their performance.

The purpose of present research was (1) To investigate the difference in the average aspiration and goal discrepancy score of highly frustrated and least frustrated, highly anxious and least anxious semiskilled and unskilled workers. (2) To compare the differences in the highly frustrated and least frustrated, highly anxious and least groups in secondary measures of aspiration such as shifts and rigidity.

RESEARCH HYPOTHESIS

The following hypotheses were framed.

1. Highly frustrated workers in general would set erratic L.O.A. and high positive and negative G.D.S.
2. Highly Frustrated workers would score more atypical shifts and show greater rigidity in their L.O.A. behaviour than the least frustrated group.
3. Significant differences would be observed in the aspiration scores of highly frustrated and least frustrated workers.
4. The goal striving behaviour of the extreme anxiety group would be more erratic with high positive and negative G.D.S. than the low anxiety group.
5. Moderate anxiety group would show greater aspiration than the extreme and low anxiety group.
6. Significant differences would be observed in the Secondary measures of L.O.A. of high and low anxious groups. A pilot study was conducted to determine the suitability of the test materials and to select the sample.

On the basis of the scores obtained in the frustration and anxiety tests, 60 highly frustrated (semiskilled and unskilled) and 60 least frustrated semiskilled and unskilled, 60 highly anxious, 60 moderately anxious and 60 least anxious (30 from each category) employees were selected for the final study. Rotter's level of Aspiration Board was administered on the sample and various primary and secondary measures of L.O.A. were calculated.

Thus, data was collected from 300 semiskilled and unskilled workers of the following industries of Orissa.

1. Steel Plant, Rourkela.
2. Orissa Cement Ltd., Rajgangpur.

3. FACOR, Bhadrak.
4. Orissa Textile Mill, Chowdwar.
5. Kalinga Tubes, Chowdwar.
6. Spinning Mill, Baripada.
7. Glass Factory, Barang.
8. Prawn Factory, Brahmagiri..
9. Prawn Factory, Paradeep.
10. Bear Factory, Paradeep.

All the workers were male, belonged to lower socio-economic status getting an emolument of Rs. 255-600 per month.

Result and Interpretation

In support of hypothesis I, highly frustrated workers in the present investigation have scored either high positive and or high negative G.D.S. In short, there is a wide gap between their aspiration and performance level. This is mostly due to the feeling of insecurity, lack of confidence in self and absence of fixed goals. The underlying causes of dissatisfaction, conflict, dispute and frustration are varied and wide-spread, but can be mainly categorised into factors in the individual, factors in life away from work and factors in employment relation.

Frustration mostly arises out of disstisfaction. A person's dissatisfaction includes dissatisfaction inside and outside the job. In the opinion of Hull and Kolstad (1942) what is important is that the worker gets from the job recognition and gelling respect for his personality. Lack of cooperation between the employee and the management, lack of appreciation of the employer etc. also lead to frustration. Failure experience being the major causes of frustration is associated with high negative and high positive goal discrepancy scores. This is supported by Rotter (1943), Himmelweit (1949), Worell (1959), Byers (1962) and Muthayya (1968).

The erratic gap between the aspiration and achievement is an outcome of frustration arising out of feeling of insecurity, inferiority and lack of confidence, and dehumanised working conditions. Frustrated and insecured persons try to withdraw from the situation and hence show erratic L.O.A. as observed in the present investigation. High Positive Negative G.D.S. is therefore less conducive to production and efficiency and is a dangerous psychological tendency for developing countries like India.

As hypothesised, highly frustrated employees have shown greater rigidity in their goal striving behaviour and have scored greater atypical shifts in comparison to their least frustrated counterparts. But there is only obtained difference and it is not significant either at .05 or .01 level.

Thirdly, a brief comparison of the aspiration scores of HF and LF groups indicates significant difference, the H.F. group showing relatively lower aspiration than the L.F. group. This has a very simple explanation. H.F. group is highly insecured, has less self confidence with continuous and habitual failures in life. A H.R. person losses hope and confidence in self and hence sets his aspiration at a lower level. This underestimation of self reduces his performance and achievement levels also.

The high anxiety group in the present study has shown (sign at .01 level) high positive G.D.S. than the low anxiety group. Although, for learning and better motivation a moderate amount of anxiety is essential, extreme anxiety creates severe personality and adjustment problems and hence is less conducive for a balance between aspiration and performance.

As Symonds has indicated, anxiety which grows out of many frustrating situations, serves as a driving force for a large number of subsequent adjustments. Moderate degrees of anxiety serve adoptive purpose elevating general arousal to a state where the person is more alert, sensitive and better prepared to meet the demands and dangers of life.

But as Martin (1961) points out, anxiety improves performance up to a point beyond which it has several adverse effects, both on aspiration level and actual performance. In extreme cases, it produces neurotic symptoms and immobilises the individual as a whole.

In comparison to the aspiration of the high and low anxiety group, the aspiration of moderate anxiety group is higher. This is self explanatory. Moderate anxiety groups are therefore predicted to have better performance than H & L anxiety groups. Finally, as anticipated H and L anxiety groups have shown greater number of atypical shifts than the moderate anxiety group. A correlational analysis also indicates high positive correlation between the measures of L.O.A. of Highly Frustrated (H.F.) and High Anxiety (H.A.) groups.

All these observations lead to a straight and precisely clear conclusion. The H.F. and H.A. employees of the present investigation have shown by and large general similarity in G.D.S., average aspiration scores and atypical shifts.

The frustration and anxieties of the employees originating out of varied situational and personal factors in life should be reduced as far as possible since these are not conducive to improved production and efficiency. Anxietes and uncertainties, conflicts and disputes between employees and management should be reduced by mutual discussion, by increasing pay packets and by providing better financial benefits to workers, by looking towards their personal difficulties with patience and understanding, by encouraging their inner abilities to flourish, by recognising their merit, by providing scope to encourage their inner potentialities, by allowing them to have a say in matters of mutual interest. In brief, a congenial employee-employer relationship can undoubtedly reduce frustration, anxiety and raise the aspiration level of the employees. A patient, understanding, sympathetic and tolerant supervisor/manager can be more conducive to less frustration, greater security and self esteem, and a moderate degree of anxiety among the employees is necessary for motivating one to perform.

The author had a series of discussions with the personnel officer/managers of several industrial organisations of Orissa, while she was attempting to locate the major problems of the industrial employees of Orissa.

She also had a "on the spot" discussion with several men and women factories, industry workers particularly working at Steel Plant at Rourkela, Cement Factory at Rajgangpur, Glass Factory at Barang, Spinning Mill at Baripada, Prawn factories at Paradeep and Brahmagiri, Bear factory at Paradeep, etc. which include heavy, medium and light industries.

A comparison of the views of the employees and management of these factories, indicates a common agreement regarding the necessity of improving the financial incentives. In addition to the financial benefits which ought to be improved, most of the employees interviewed were also of the view that working hours should also be reduced a bit and they should be provided with housing, transport, medical and educational facilities for their children. Women employees working in large numbers in Prawn factories and Spinning Mills gave good supervisors preference next to high wage. Less working hours got the third preference.

The author was told by some managements that revised scales of pay, D.A. incentive, bonus and reward scheme, gratuity scheme, E.P.F., Festival Advance, L.T.C., H.R. Allowance and other benefits linked with pay are given to certain categories of employees including executives.

The author was also assured that steps are being taken continuously to promote and maintain the highest possible degree of good industrial and personal relations at all levels to maintain discipline, improve efficiency, achieve maximum productivity and eliminate all wasteful practices particularly in respect of the following areas :

1. Efficient handling of raw material and reducing waste.
2. Improvement in yields.
3. Improvement in housekeeping.
4. Improvement in techno-economic parameters.
5. Reducing unauthorised absenteeism.

Orissa which has undoubtedly progressed in the industrial sphere during the last decade is still in the process of development. Much remains to be done to reduce the frustration and anxieties of the H.F. and H.A. employees as these are responsible for lower aspiration and erratic G.D.S. which is never-the-less dangerous for a developing state like Orissa.

Although wages and pay scales of employees have been revised from time to time in the best interest of the State, employees should be provided with better financial benefits since the present pay packets are not optimum. They should be provided with the money to meet the basic and minimum requirements of life, and cost of living etc.

Steps should also be taken to improve their literacy standard, to understand them, their ego and difficulties. Personal and emotional problems arising due to situational and personal factors should also be carefully analysed and uprooted. A joint effort by the managements and employee unions taking into consideration the above factors can help reducing frustration and anxieties which are basically responsible for lower aspiration and hence lower motivation.

QUESTIONS

1. Discuss the impact of frustration on goal striving behaviour of employees.
2. How frustration and anxiety affect productivity ?

REFERENCES

Mohanty, G.B. Role of frustration and anxiety on the goal striving behaviour of industrial.

Mohanty, G.B. Employees of Orissa. Post Doctoral Research Project Level of Aspiration as Function of Sex Socio Economic status and class performance. Ph.D. thesis in Utkal Univ. 1973.

26

Decision Making

In our normal day to day work, every one of us has to take a decision, either at home or in the office, market or in an organisation. What is meant by decision making ? It means deciding to choose one of several alternatives. You have gone to buy a dress worth Rs. 1,000. There are several dresses and you have to decide on one. This is in simple terms decision making. While making such a decision one has to consider the colour, quality, texture, design, durability and above all whether it is the "in" thing in the current society. When the budget is fixed the scope of decision making is narrowed down. Sometimes one has to make a compromise in decision making. In other words, one may not be very much satisfied with his decision, but he has to make it due to other limitations.

Decision making involves complicated judgements. If not delivered carefully and without due reasoning the conclusions sometimes become hasty. When there is a crisis of self confidence or when things are done hastily, bad decisions are taken. But there are some who repeatedly make bad decisions and repent afterwards. Analysis of the cycle of their personal history reveals that they can not take right decisions and depend upon others for help. If they are asked to make their own decision, they commit mistakes and are criticised. This further devaluates their self confidence and a fear psychosis develops when they think of taking decision. Thus they withdraw from taking a decision. Such people because of lack of self confidence and some other maladjustment fail to take decision correctly or can not take a decision at all.

When the alternatives are only two or three it is easy to give a decision. But when there are more alternatives and all more or less look alike the process of decision making becomes very complex due to confusion and the job becomes very tough. In such a situation it will be wise to eliminate some alternatives as soon as possible and then select between the limited alternatives on the basis of various factors and characteristics. Effective occupational adjustment involves correct and timely decision making. Also decision making is an important managerial requirement. An executive, supervisor or head of the office must have decision making quality. Indecisive heads are useless as they can not give proper direction and guidance to the subordinates and lower level employees leading to total mess in administration and management. For upward mobility in any job decision making process is of vital importance. The person sitting in the chair of decision making should not be influenced by fear and favour. The decision should be reasoned and transparent after careful examination and analysis of all advantages, disadvantages, rules and regulations. An employer or a manager who wants to manage things properly has to take practical decisions. The decisions which can not be implemented in reality arc useless and do not serve any purpose. Rather they induce confusions and frustrations. Usually flexible and dynamic personalities are good decision makers, of course keeping other factors constant.

DECISION MAKING PROCESS

Understanding of the problem which has created the need for a decision, can give an idea of decision making process. Unless the problem is adequately understood or defined, decision making becomes difficult. Larson states four different types of decision problems.

(*i*) When definition of the objective and indentification of alternative courses of action are complete the job is to decide which course of action is best.

(*ii*) When the objective is defined but the courses of action which will tend to achieve this objective arc not known, the job is to undertake the determination of possible alternatives and selection of the most effective and desirable alternative.

(*iii*) When the objective is not formulated, the job is to make a comprehensive choice concerning the alternatives.

(*iv*) When the identified situation is considered as currently or potentially undesirable in future, the job is to devise actions which will eliminate or alleviate these undesirable conditions.

Decision making involves a matter of taking responsibility *i.e.* he must be ready to assume responsibility for any future consequences. Daily the executives, supervisors and other decision making authorities, bureaucrats, and administrators take certain decisions on diverse matters and they have to explain, defend and justify their actions in future if necessary. A company executive is making certain promotions and transfers on certain grounds. He is accepting certain tenders and refusing others. Decision making becomes particularly difficult when there is no specific guideline and one has to attribute his own reasons for taking such a decision. Though decision making is not a pleasant task and sometimes involves risk, it is a necessity to run any organisation and industry effectively.

STEPS OF DECISION MAKING PROCESS

Calkins (1959) holds that an administrator has to follow the following five steps for an appropriate decision making.

1. Identification and understanding of the problem.
2. Defining and clarifying goals.
3. Alternative goals.

4. Analysing the anticipated consequences of each alternative.
5. Selecting a course of action.

The most desirable and effective alternative leading to the goal is to be selected in the fmal step of decision making process. But in order to make the decision making effective and goal oriented one has to follow 1 to 4 analytical stages bit by bit and then follow the last step. However, there may be flexibility in following the steps depending upon the need of the hour and conditions of the circumstances.

According to Schmidt (1958) each and every decision involves framing of a hypothesis about the future on the part of the decision maker *i.e.,* what is being expected in the future say whether the value of a particular share will rise in the coming three months or not. This tenacity or rejection of the hypothesis will depend upon the actual market· performance of the stock in future. After the hypothesis is formulated a decision is to be made by the executive about the future course of action. Schmidt has given four different kinds of executive decision situations and their consequences such as Delays, stays, delight and fright. After correctly guessing the future occurences when the executive decides not to take any action, he only delays the decision by mentioning. "please wait" Discuss' put up after 15 days' etc. Such a decision leads to unnecessary delay.

(*ii*) When the executive has wrongly guessed what is going to happen in future and stays the operation of the decision his hypothesis becomes false. It he would have acted on the hypothesis, he would have been wrong.

Mager (1964) has suggested a second Pchemetical model for the decision process. Here there are various alternative courses of action just like the branches of a tree. There may also be only two alternatives from which the executive has to choose one. In such a situation all other factors influencing the decision like role of the competitors in the market, share price etc. are to be examined in great length before taking a decision. Mager holds that for making sound decisions all possible outcomes of different factors are to be considered before taking a final decision.

INDIVIDUAL AND DECISION MAKING

As already discussed under introduction, there is person to person difference in decision making. Since personalities differ, there is individual difference is decision making capacity. Certain decisions involve special risk and responsibility and as we know from day to day experience some people are tremendously adverse to risk taking. But there are others who get excessive pleasure in taking a risk and making a decision. Such people have more self confidence also. According to Atkinson (1957) one category of people have greater motivation to achieve success than to avoid failure. The second category of people have greater motivation to avoid failure than to achieve success. They do not like to take a chance and gamble but loose.

Shubik (1958) an economist has opined that a decision maker must be very rational in his approach while making a decision. He should take the decision in terms of economic value system. He should try to take such a decision to get maximum return. Simen (1957) is of view that the correct decision maker should be a satisfying man. He chooses such a decision which atleast gives certain minimum gains but is satisfactory. The third category of decision makers has been suggested by Boulding (1958). It is a decision strategy which helps in taking bold decisions.

In real life situations such decisions sometimes help although the risk factor is there. Original life situation experiences reveal that "man does not tend to behave the way in which an optional decision strategy would dictate that he should behave." (quoted from Blum and Naylor). Instead he opts for a probability matching strategy, where the person would like to spread his predictions in such a manner that his probability of prediction would match the actual probability than adopting a strategy of always making the most likely right decision. This is known as the probability matching strategy.

There are also two types of decision making such as rational and non rational as advanced by Simen (1959).

The first category refers to the quantification of the decision making process in terms of the utility value of various outcomes, the probability of occurrence of the various outcomes etc. After this is done, a formal mathematical system is to be developed for optional decision making choices. Simen views that these models can be used as idealized standards against which man's performance can be compared.

The second category *i.e.* the nonrational decision making models are also called the organionic approach. These models insist on making decision making as a joint or group process in an organisation. Thus such decisions makings are obviously influenced by group size, organisational structure and motivation of the members of the organisations. The motivational variables like needs, rewards, punishments and penalties, attitude of the group towards the management, job satisfaction, financial and nonfinancial incentives play their respective roles in such decision making.

There are also other modes of decision making such as normative models of individual decision making which include Brunswik Lens Model, Bayes Model of Decision making etc. Friedman (1960) has summarized the rules to follow in a competitive decision making situation.

1. Determine the underlying rules of the game and the extent of the restrictions upon all the competitors.
2. Describe in as much detail as possible the particular situation in which competitive decisions are to be made by the competitors.
3. List all the alternative courses of action which are available to the competitors.
4. Calculate or estimate a final utility to each of the competitions as a result of the selection of the various alternatives.
5. Study individual competitors and their past behaviour to determine possible strategies they might use in arriving at their decisions in the particular situation being studied.
6. Estimate a priori probabilities that the competitor used and given strategy and a posteriori probabilities that the observed events would have occurred with the given strategies.
7. Calculate the final relative probabilities for the various hypothesis concerning competitive strategies.
8. Estimate the probabilities of a competitors use of his alternative courses of action in the situation being studied.
9. Given the estimated probabilities of the competitors use of his alternative courses of action, choose the alternative course of action which maximizes expected utility. (Quoted from Blum and Naylor)

DECISION MAKING IN ORGANISATIONS

Psychologists currently have paid due attention to the problem of organisational decision making as it has become the pivort variable in modern organisational administration. Proper decision making as a process not only helps in able management and administration, it also improves the over all level of productivity. Leavilt and Bass (1964) have indicated three important factors which appear to be the basis of organisational decision making problem. They are feasibility issue, normative-descriptive issue and the algorythmic heuristic issue. The feasibility issue refers to the usual reluctance on the part of the decision making authorities to take a final decision as per the formal decision making models. In other words, the formal decision making models lack feasibility. The normative descriptive approach deals with the fact as to whether optional decision making strategies be developed to implement directly or serve as a standard or norm to make some one aspire to make a decision. The third approach refers to the application of a standardized and guaranteed decision making routine. The algorythmic heuristic approach is most helpful when the decision problem is simple. In complex decisions this method may not be successfully applied as experience shows.

In the present circumstances, decision making process both in industries and organisations however small or big plays a paramount role in influencing both work and workers, output and employees. Currently it has become one of the main thrust of research undertakings relating to interaction of man with his environment. It is needless to mention here that a great deal of the effectiveness a manager off at any level or an executive of an organisation depends upon his decision making capacity.

QUESTIONS

1. What is decision making ? Is decision making essential ?
2. Give a brief idea on the decision making process.
3. Discuss the role of individual in decision making.
4. Cite same significant experiments and investigation on decision making in industrial context.
5. Discuss in detail the significance of decision making process in industrial and organisational set ups.
6. Give an idea on different types of decision making.
7. Critically examine decision making process in organisations.
8. Write brief notes on the following.
   (*a*) Models of Decision making.
   (*b*) Role of individual difference in decision making.
   (*c*) Decision making and personality factor.
   (*d*) Effect of decision making on organisational climate.

REFERENCES

Atkinson J.W. *Motivational Determinants of Risk Taking Behaviour,* Psychol. Review 1957, 64.

Edwards, W. *Behavioural decision theory—Annual Review of Psychol.* 1961, 12.

Blum, M.L. and Naylor, James, C. *Industrial Psychology,* Theoritical and Social Foundations, Harper International Edition, 1968.

Friedman, L. *Decision making in Competitive situations,* Management Technology, 1960.

Leavitt H.J. and Bass, B.M. *Organisational Psychology—Annual Review of Psychology,* I964, 15, 371-378

Simon, H.A. *Models of man —Social and rational,* Wiley, New York 1957.

27

Consumer and Advertising Psychology

CONSUMER PSYCHOLOGY

With the rapid progress in civilized and developing as well as under developing countries in all spheres of life the needs and aspirations of people have been raised immensely. Due to the increasing needs of people at all levels of the society, manufacture of various goods and commodities for the consumers and their marketing have occupied central position. People engaged in manufacturing, advertising and marketing business have foreseen vast development is these areas. To manage these works more effectively and profitably research in areas like consumer psychology-cum-consumer behaviour, market survey and market research, advertisement etc. are being conducted worldwide keeping in view needs and demands of national and international consumers.

It is therefore imperative to study consumer psychology and consumer behaviours. Inspite of the diversities existing among people, there are also certain common qualities which can be generalized to form consumer behaviour and consumer psychology. Once the psychology of different types of consumers is traced, marketers can design marketing strategies that influence consumers having some similar characteristics. Secondly, by studying consumer psychology manufactures and marketers can understand and predict consumer behaviour specially with reference to purchase, maintenance and disposal of goods. Further the well spread adoption of the marketing concept by American business provides the impetus for the study of consumer behaviour.

Consumer psychology-cum-behaviour is defined as that behaviour which consumers display in searching for purchasing, using, evaluating of products, services and ideas that they expect will satisfy their needs. Various consumer researches are conducted at every stage of the consumption process, *i.e.* before, during and after the purchase. Consumer behaviour is quite vast and interdisciplinary. It is dealt by psychologists, sociologists, social psychologists, cultural anthropologists and economists.

Several questions perplexing the manufactures and marketers relating to the 'why' of consumer behaviour have been answered by consumer research. Currently consumer research has drawn active attention of many industrial and organisational concerns for their increased contribution to explore the 'why' of buyer and consumer behaviour. It is considered as an useful tool for marketers who desire to know the actual causes of consumer behaviour, consumer research not only helps identifying consumer needs, demands and habits and locate appropriate target markets but also to gain insight into the why of consumer behaviour compared to what the conventional marketing research technique conveyed. Recent and compelling evidences indicate that the unconscious and subconscious area of the mind may determine the causes of a large number of purchases and consumptions of a particular human being. The new science of semiotics is concerned with the subconscious meanings of nonverbal symbols to consumers. Motivational research helps in identifying both the felt and unfelt needs. It also helps the marketers to learn and perceive the products from the consumers view point, their attitude before and after advertisements and promotional campaigns. Why and how a consumer makes his purchases and consumption decision are to be kept in mind by the marketers.

PERSONAL CONSUMER AND ORGANISATIONAL CONSUMER

There are two types of consumers, personal and organisational. Personal consumers buy goods for their own use while organisational consumers buy for profit in business. Govt. agencies and institutions buy products for the use of their organisations and institutions.

PERSONALITY FACTORS OF CONSUMERS

Motivational research in the area of consumer behaviour also brings insight into the development of new ideas and concepts for promotional needs that can get into the consumer's conscious awareness by appealing to unconscious needs. Consumer research also throws light on the various avenues of advertisement techniques to penetrate into the psychology of the consumers. Inspite of certain drawbacks motivational research has proved to be of great value to marketers concerned with new ideas and novel samples to appeal the consumer's mind. Marketers also make efforts to trap the consumers by analysing their personality. Different personalities have different types of choices to buy and use goods. What consumers purchase, why they purchase and when and how they consume are likely to be influenced by personality factors. In view of the deep relationship between personality pattern and various types of consumer behaviour efforts have been made to analyse different aspects of consumer behaviour through motivational and consumer research. Different types of personality traits like innovativeness, dogmatism, social character, optimum stimulation level and desire to seek variety and novelty help in the promotion of new products. But lacking these qualities with a rigid personality and fondness for old products do not help in promotion of new goods. How receptive consumers are to new products and innovative materials, new services and practices are of immense importance to marketers.

1. Consumer Innovativeness

Consumer innovativeness being one of the major asserts of promotion and sale of new products steps are taken by marketers to measure the level of consumer innovativeness area wise.

This provides an insight into the fact as to what degree the consumers are willing to innovate and accordingly new products are manufactured. Open minded persons with low degree of dogmatism prefer new and modified products more than the old and traditional goods such people always look for a change and usually do not prefer to use old fasioned, traditional and conventional goods. Conversely, closed minded persons who are highly dogmatic persons prefer already established than new products. They do not like to take a risk by experimenting with new products. That is why important person like experts, celebrities and reputed personalities are used to make advertisement and change the attitude of dogmatic and closed mind persons. Modern research also shows that low dogmatic consumers are relatively more receptive to messages that emphasise factual differences and product benefits.

2. Social Character

Social character as a trait of personality immensely influences consumer's behaviour. It ranges from a continuum from inner directed to other directed observations and evidences which indicates that persons directed by innerself *i.e.* one's own reasoning and conscience tend to depend more on their inner values and norms in evaluating new products and are more likely to be consumers innovators. Conversely other directed consumers usually look to others for direction on what is right and what is wrong. They are ordinarily not guided by their own self for making purchasing decisions. For example such people always take with them some of their friends and relatives while going for major shopping. This is because they lack self confidence and decision making capacity so far shopping is concerned. In view of personality difference the two cetagories are influenced differently by different types of promotional message. It is viewed by Sachiffman and Kanuk (1995) that inner directed people prefer more advertisements which emphasise product features and personal benefits and other directed consumers prefer advertisements that signify a social environment or social acceptance. In other words, they have no own choice. They prefer what others prefer. If two or three persons say that this suit length is excellent they buy it immediately. These persons are said to think in terms of a likely social approval of a potential purchase.

Persons who are susceptible to other people's influence in purchase and consumptions or are responsive to the influence of others are said to be suggestive persons. In order to pinpoint them recently a 12 point scale has been developed to measure consumers susceptibility to interpersonal influence. The main purpose of this scale is to study how social influence operates to encourage or discourage the acceptance of new products and services.

3. Need for Cognition

It is another personality quality found in consumers who are more attracted to advertisements rich in product related informations and descriptions. Further they are less responsive to the contextual or peripheral aspects of the ad like the presence of a celebrity or reputed person in ad (international cricket players, film and T. V. Stars, famous models, political persons, poets and writers). Conversely consumers low in N.C. are more likely to be attracted to the background or peripheral aspects of the ad like an attractive model or cinema star.

4. Ethnoecentrism

Consumers with a disposition to accept or reject foreign made materials are identified through a consumer ethnoecentrism scale. Ethnocentric consumer feel that it is inappropriate to purchase foreign made goods because of its unfavourable impact on domestic and inland economy. On the contrary, the non ethnocentric consumers evaluate foreign made products more objectively for their extrinsic charateristics. Accordingly, the inland and foreign marketers can take advantage of this quality of the consumers and design their advertisements to suit this intrinsic quality of the consumers.

SELF IMAGE AND MULTIPLE SELF

Available research data indicate that people buy products which tally with their own images and idea of things. Secondly, they also prefer to help retailers with images and personalities similar to their own. They make purchases consistence with their relevant self image only and avoid those who are not consistent. The social role of a normal individual changes with changing circumstances and situations. This is called multiple self. Thus keeping in mind the multiple self of the normal consumers tile marketers should target their products and services. This refers to the idea of situation segmentation.

Certain other psychological factors of the consumers personality should also be noted by the marketers and manufacturers for making their business a success. They should have knowledge of the consumers need, value and past experience, age, intelligence, socio-economic status to develop advertisements having good scope of being perceived and produce goods which they would like to buy. Recent research shows that marketers and manufacturers use Weber's law in the products to determine JND. The concept of selectivity in perception and the factors that determine selectively also operate while selecting goods for consumption. Besides the factors operating from the external environment, personal predispositions like learning and motivation based on past experience also influence consums psychology. Figure and ground phenomena has a tremendous role to play in advertisements. Consumer psychologists have stressed that the object or stimulus that needs to be seen must be seen as figure and not ground. The background of an ad must not detract from the product being advertised. The phenomena of grouping being intrinsic can also be used by marketers to their advantage. The tendency to fill up the gap, perceptual defence and blocking should also be kept in mind while making advertisements for various products.

Service quality like good environment, the pleasantness and social attractiveness of the receptionist and the professionalism of the hotel manager one very important to influence the consumers as every consumer is genuinely attracted by such considerations. Similarly in a bank, the services rendered to the client must be very quick. A favourable service environment creates the perception among the consumers that the service itself better satisfies their needs. A pleasant shopping experience, good and polite behaviour of the salesman attract more buyers. Incomplete ads can be shown to the consumers to involve them. The consumers would indirectly involve themselves with ad and be influenced by it. Consumers usually judge the quality of a product according to a variety of informations like colour, size, flavour, aroma, price, brand image and service environment etc. which are intrinsic and extrinsic to the product. Every buyer must have the knowledge about his role as a consumer *i.e.*, how to buy and where to buy, what to buy and the appropriate criteria of selecting a good, maintaining and disposing them. Existing attitude of consumer towards a particular campany or brand determines one's purchasing behaviour. It is essential to know how consumers attitudes arc formed and how they are changed, so that consumer behaviour can be controlled and directed in the desired direction. Attending to an ad depends upon this attitude. Attitude towards different goods and commodities are influenced by friends, relatives and near and dear ones. Salesmen, mass media and advertising agencies also form, influence and change attitude towards various goods, purchasing and consuming habits. Through personal and mass media communications, feed back is provided. It helps to know how well the message has been received. Emotional appeals and audience participation are also considered effective communication strategies to influence consumers and internalized, or "sallow in" the advertising messages. In the process of socialisation and social interaction family, friendship groups, formal and informal social groups, shopping groups, consumer action groups and work groups influence the consumption behaviour of people. Consumer reference groups like film stars, models, players, political figures renowned industrialists and experts in the area also influence consumer psychology. Various advertising agencies use the reference group appeal and prestige suggestion for promoting their production. This increases brand awareness and reduces perceived risk among prospective consumers.

The purchasing style of a family and its consumption behaviour is decided by his socio economic status and standard of living, life style, spending capacity, perceived risk and time constraints. A family not having enough time to make daily purchases may purchase goods for a fortnight or for the entire month. Some house wives can not remain in peace unless they have food stuff atleast for one month ahead. Through the process of socialisation the family imparts consumer relevant knowledge, altitudes and skills to the consumer. Further education, occupation, income, quality of neighbour, number of members in the family etc. determine the style of consumption of particular persons. Due to constant-tendency of people for upward social mobility marketers and manufacturers incorporate the symbols of higher class people in advertisements meant for lower class consumers. Cosmetic surgery which was a distant dream for the middle class people some decades back has now drawn the attention of middle class consumers particularly in the rich and developing countries. As the average household income increases the goods once considered luxurious becomes a necessity and the motivation to purchase these commodities increases. T.V., Fridge, telephones and scooters which were a luxury for the lower middle class people have now become a necessity.

Marketers usually divide their markets on the basis of social class. They use social classification as an effective way to identify and segment target markets. Of late, a few marketers have used the geodemographic clustering as a substitute of social class typology. It is a technique which makes a synthesis of geographic and socio-economic factors to identify concentration of consumers with particular characteristics and consumer habits. Social class differences are basically reflected in clothing habits, home decoration, leisure activities, saving, spending and credit habits. Keeping in view the psychology of the consumers belonging to different social classes, marketers should make specific products and generate promotional strategies for each social class.

ROLE OF CULTURE ON CONSUMER PSYCHOLOGY

It is well established that culture influences one's psychology and determines behaviour. The various learned beliefs, values and customs serve to regulate the consumer's behaviour. Beliefs and values influenced by mass media also determine consumer's behaviour. Products and product concepts are also promoted by mass media. Advertisements communicate symbolically with the consumers.

Various values like activity, work and efficiency, practicability, achievement and success, progress, material comfort, freedom humanitarian fitness and health, etc. which vary culture to culture determine consumer behaviour. Food habits, traditions, customs, rituals festivals etc. are determined by the socio cultural traditions. They in turn determine the purchasing needs of individuals in their respective cultures. In Hindu culture taking beef is prohibited. Hence in areas where most of the people are Hindu, beef and beef products do not have any market. But in cosmopolitan cities of India beef products may have a good market.

By touching the humanitarianism many manufacturers try to appeal to consumers. They express their concern for environmental and social issues by donating a lot of money for charity purposes. By helping common causes they also gain public support for their goods. In cultures where over weight and obesity are very much deplored, and people like to remain young through out their life, lots of advertisements are directed to create further sense of urgency to retain one's youth and remain fit.

Since culture has a profound influence on all consumer behaviour, those behaviour which are considered as a taboo are avoided. Thus on the basis of homogeneity of culture marketers try to segmentize larger societies and cultures in to smaller subgroups. Each subculture showing homogeneity in relation to certain customs and ways of behaving provide important marketing opporunities for deciding marketing strategies. Nationality, religion, geographic society, marriage, sex and working status determine the psychology of consumers. Consumer psychology and behaviour vary from culture to culture and society to society since geographical and regional differences along with socioeconomic status bring variation in consumer behaviour. In Orissa in some regions people prefer tea while in other regions coffee. In urban areas prople wear more western dresses while in rural areas national dresses are preferred.

Various studies in U.S.A. indicate that elderly consumers use credit cards less frequently, go for more shopping, get more health exercises, drive out frequently and meet socially. Modern working women and mothers spend less time in shopping than nonworking women. They also make purchases during evening hours and on week ends. Marketers therefore should try to find out how specific subcultural membership interact to influence the consumers purchase decisions.

Cross Cultural Consumer Analysis

To what degree the consumers of two or more nations are similar or different in consumer habits is determined by cross cultural consumer analysis. By this analysis marketers tend to make an idea of the psychological, social and cultural characteristics of the foreign consumers they wish to bring to their fold and make effective marketing strategies for each national market involved. Evaluation of potential markets in foreign countries is nevertheless desirable for making business a success. It is said that human beings are deeply the same and yet different. The marketing strategies must be prepared according to the psychological, social, cultural and functional needs of the individuals in foreign countries. Cultural differences playa vital role in marketing. What Indians prefer to buy and consume, American may not like. What the tribals like to consume the non-tribals may not like. Hence different needs and satisfactions are to be identified in different cultures for studying consumer psychology.

CONSUMER'S DECISION MAKING PROGRESS

A decision is a selection of action from two or more alternative choices. If there is no alternative, the question of decision does not arise.

How consumers make decisions ? It is said that currently about seventy five to eighty per cent of all buying decisions are influenced by direct or indirect recommendations. Social interactions influence a lot of purchasing decisions besides advertisement through various mass medias. Friends, acquaintances, coworkers, relatives and neighbours, even children in the family put a lot of pressure in the individuals style of consumption behaviour by participating in product related conversations; consumer researches are also attempting to identify the role of opinion readership on consumption behaviour through self designing, sociometric, key informant and objective methods. Imposing and self assertive opinion leaders having self confidence, expertise, sociability, social attractiveness, desire to talk are more successful in influencing consumer behaviour. Recent researches show that persons scoring high on the public individuation scale are more likely to be better opinion leaders as they have their own identity and personal opinion and individualism. Consumers also involve experts in the area for decision making process because of their high knowledge in the specific field. More people would like to be influenced by the views of a textile engineer when they arc going to make purchases of cotton materials than by a lay man.

When more than one alternatives are available and one has to choose one from them he has to take a decision. Various models of man like the cognitive man, the economic man, the passive man and the emotional man influence the decision making process differently. Hence purchasing decisions vary from person to person.

1. Cognitive Model

A cognitive man is a consumer who is receptive to products and services that fullfil their needs and brings enjoyment. Here consumers are taken as information processing systems relating to preferences and purchasing intentions. By and large, a congnitive man develops short out decision rules to make the decision making process easy and economical. They also use decision rules to adjust with information overload. The cognitive man is a well educated and involved person who seeks information to make satisfactory purchasing decisions.

2. Economic Model

A economic man makes rational decision in terms of economic considerations in a competive market before buying a material. But the economic man has been rejected by may on the grounds of unrealistic idea, lack of adequate and accurate information on the all available product alternates and their ranks, advantages and disadvantages, the lack of sufficient motivation to take a correct decision on economic ground. Thus it is said that the economic model is too idealistic and simple. It is practically impossible to operate in the decision making process.

3. Passive Model

In passive model the consumer has a submissive role in the decision making process. He depends a lot on the suggestion of the salesman and advertisers who dominate in the process. He can be easily allured and manipulated by the marketers according to this model. But nevertheless the consumer can not be taken for grated as an object of manipulation. The consumer therefore plays equal if not dominant role in many buying situations.

4. Emotional Model

While making a purchase various emotions play greater or smaller roles. Many purchases a customer makes not because they are necessary, for him, but because the purchaser loves them to poosess. These purchases are made on impulse without being carefully examined on different considerations. Buying such products gives an emotional satisfaction. Here rationality, utility and financial consideration do not just work.

In view of the tinge of emotion in various purchases, advertisers and marketers emphasize more on emotional and feeling oriented advertising. For instance the Cadbury chocolate with the line "For Some One You Love" contributes to the emotional tone and people are impressed and encouraged to buy it and present to some one they love, like and respect.

Besides emotions, moods of the consumers also play important role while making up mind to buy a commodity. Modern research reveals that the image or atmosphere of the shopping complex or store can affect the mood of the shopper and ultimately the shopper's mood can influence the duration of his stay in the store. Some people do not like stores crowded all the while as less attention being paid to them. Some dislike delay. Consumers with positive mood call for more informations about a product compared to those in a negative mood.

By giving personalised service to the consumers, making them feel special, by sending them gifts, calendars, diaries on special occasions, long term bonds can be established between the customers and the marketers. A jewellery shop used to send sweets to his customers on every Diwali festival Similarly another marketer used to send birthday gifts to each of his regular customers to maintain an emotional bond. Marketers and salespersons with social attractiveness, charming smile generate interest among the shoppers and thereby compel them psychologically to visit the shop again.

An ideal decision making model which binds together the psychological, social and cultural concepts into an easily understood framework for consumer decision making can be obtained from a combination of the cognitive and emotional model. This model can synthesize and coordinate the relevant into a significant whole. The socio cultural environment of the consumer, his psychological field like attitude, mental set, perceived risk etc. are taken into consideration in this model. This further includes the consumers recongnition of a need, prepurchase search for information and evaluation of alternates while making a decision to purchase and consume a commodity or class of commodities. Finally feed back is provided into the consumers psychological field through actual purchase and post purchase decisions. This in turn influences the consumers future decision making process.

Though consumer researches have made fabulous contributions to one's knowledge and understanding of consumer behaviour, some areas still lag behind. Further, to remove inadequacies, weaknesses and loopholes in the advertising programmes and market research, studies should be designed to explore, identify and document various areas of consumer psychology through coordinated and interdisciplinary research. More and more studies in depth research should also be encouraged on consumer behaviour in the Indian socio, cultural and economic contexts.

ADVERTISING PSYCHOLOGY

Most of the consumers are influenced either directly or indirectly through advertising and selling. Currently with the rapid expansion of electronic media scope of advertisement for tile sale and promotion of different goods has increased immensely. In Indian television net work owned by the Govt., it is not only surprising but agonising to find 30 advertisements in a serial of 30 minutes. 30 advertisements on the average take 20 minutes and only the rest 10 minutes are spent on the serial for which the viewers wait so anxiously. From this example one can very well imagine the scope of advertisement and its burden on the viewers and consumers. It is a fact that people react in varying ways to the different advertisements in radios and TVs and try to avoid particularly boring, exaggerated and extremely colourful advertisements made without the use of brain and intellect. Some however like to view the advertisements with strong visuals when they are novel and prepared to touch both the brain and the heart, the intellect and the emotion.

This being the position of advertisement today, it has been a novel branch particularly to influence consumer's psychology. Advertising is ordinarily defined as any paid form of nonpersonal presentation and proniotion of ideas, goods as services by some identified sponsor. The media of advertising includes news papers, magazines, catalogues, billboards, various programmes in between theatres and movies, placards, pamphlets, radio and television etc. Similarly sign boards, bill boards, neon signs, loud speakers propagate messages which can be named as advertisement. The purpose of advertisement is to influence people in their decision to purchase consumer goods. In any advertisement the advantages of a particular material is highlighted in comparison to another. The advertisement is usually designed in a careful way to influence the decision of people in a competitive market. Obviously, when there is no competition for a particular product, there may not be any need for advertisement only when several brands of a particular goods are available in the market, and the buyer is indecisive on which brand to buy, in such a situation advertisement may help to some extent. The advertiser hence has to have a creative mind.

Advertisements as a means to influence the psychology of consumers have gained high place in the wes.ern world compared to India. The advertisement should be such that it must have the knack for picking one's brains without his knowing it. Advertising should also be done in a scientific, systematic and creative manner so that it can touch the emotion of the consumers in a favourable direction. Experts tend to believe that inspite of the accumulation of knowledge and the tremendous power for new technology, great creative advertisements currently are found less than before in tile U.S. and India.

Many people consider advertisement as a type of propaganda and give it a negative touch. Some hold that the public is being mainpulated and misguided by advertisements. Vance Packard in his best selling of the 1950s complained that the advertisers use the expertise from psychiatry and the social sciences to channel our habits, our purchasing decisions and our thought processes. Psychologists have been able to tell the manufacturers, why people buy or do not buy a particular product. Kenleth Galbraith in his much celebrated title "The Affulent Society" has opined that advertising induces people to buy products that they do not need and perhaps can not afford. It is a fact that many advertisements use so strong· visuals, alluring irresistible and eye catching advertisements that people tend to be frustrated when they are unable to buy such goods because of their sky reaching prices.

ADVANTAGES OF ADVERTISEMENT

However, the advantages of advertisements have also been highlighted by the various advertisement ağencies and advertisement men. Advertising agencies believe that in the 21st century the power and potency of advertisement will influence the consumers of the entire world. They are very hopeful and optimistic about the remarkable influence of advertisement on people. Some of the advantages of advertisement are given below :

1. Advertisement keeps media independence alive. News papers, magazines, radio, television and other types of mass media get enough money from advertisement agencies to manage and sustain themselves independent to Govt. control. Without this money tile media would obviously depend on government or on other vested interest parties for its survival thus lossing their freedom.
2. Advertisement helps in economic development by improving sale of various goods. It also creates new jobs and opens avenue for maintenance of already created jobs in the advertising agencies, market research and promotion of goods through exhibition etc.
3. Advertisements are also made by Govt. organisation for promotion of the economic standard, living conditions and health habits of people, their educational status, literacy etc. Unfavourable attitude towards child marriage, dowry, oppression of women, bad house keeping, tax evasion etc. are developed among the people through various advertisements and propaganda. People are recruited to various jobs through advertisement.
4. Advertising gives the public the opportunity to choose from different brands of the same goods, the goods having the lowest price or highest quality. It is argued that without advertisement the consumer may be at the mercy of a few high priced or low quality brands.

According to R.K. Swamy, a famous and experienced adman of India, advertising helped America become the world economic power. High consumption is the final stage of the five stages of economic growth because of proper advertisement. America reached the high consumption stage in 1920 while Europe reached only after 1945. It is said that America reached the final stage of economic growth because advertising and attention to the consumer created the mass markets needed for high consumption. To make the advertisement more effective persons with dignity and reputation in the society and social attractiveness are used in the advertisement of goods. Famous movie stars, sprotsmen, cricket and chess players and beauty queens, and persons who have earned prestige, name and fame are utilised in advertisement of various goods. Inspite of the tricks used to catch the attention of the consumers more than fifty per cent of the persons have the power to ignore advertisements. They are strong willed unsuggestive persons without being influenced by advertisements. Their decision to buy a particular good is not usually influenced by advertisements as they are strong willed, rational and less suggestive.

Unless a particular habit is changed through some techniques of advertisement, a person will continue to buy the old brands. Advertising tries to control and determine the ways in which one changes his behaviour through learning. Through market research at the outset, the personal habits of different consumers are identified. The manufacturers also try to understand why people buy a particular brand and why not the other brand or product. Why they prefer a particular type of detergent or food product. The house wives are interviewed and contacted over and over again through survey method. Even small defects in consumer goods, mean a lot to change the purchasing habit of such goods, like difficulty in opening the packet, reclosing, space required to store, very small opening space, materials being spoiled quickly etc. Old habits some times work as a tremendous reinforcer, to continue it, inspite of various oppositive forces working against it. Sometimes people also do not want to take a risk by buying new goods. They say "old is gold". In such cases it becomes very hard and tough for the admen to change the old habits. The success of a new product depends a lot on whether consumers can be induced to change from the former ones to new brands. Secondly for the continuance and success of an already established brand depends on the capacity to strengthen existing habits through repeated advertisements. For the promotion of sale besides advertisement the attitude of the sales man towards the customer, his social attractiveness are also important. The sales man should try to understand the behaviour of the customer and take small cues from it to allure the buyer. The success and failure in selling depends a lot on the personality of the salesman. If the salesman does not behave properly, does not show proper interest in displaying goods to the buyers the consumer leaves the store in disgust never to enter it again. When a lady is in conflict as to which colour she should select, sometimes the salesman comes to her rescue by helping her to select a particular colour. "See Mam this saree matches brilliantly with your skin colour", etc. they are often heard saying. The advertiser or the salesman on the whole taps the psychology of the consumer and helps him in justifying his behaviour. Purchasing behaviour of the consumer is influenced by the current psychological and sociological factors. The why of purchasing behaviour is to be traced to make it more effective. This needs active and indepth research in motivation and personality differences. Beliefs and financial condition to a great extent influence the purchasing behaviour of the consumers. If somebody has a strong belief that beef is bad for health, how much one tries to change this attitude, he may not be successful. Equally important is the paying capacity of the consumers in a particular town or locality. In an area with people of poor socio-economic status, it is meaningless to advertise stuffs of high value. Not only they will not be able to purchase it, further they will experience frustration and conflict for not being able to buy these costly goods.

Advertisements are also used for promoting social causes like "cigarette smoking is injurious to health", "Better late than never" "Not every one who drives drunk dies", "Prevention is better than cure". etc. Advertisements also help in reducing dowry deaths, population explosion, women's misery, misconceptions and superstitions relating to family planning, child birth and breast feeding etc.

ADVERTISEMENT AND PROPAGANDA

Though propaganda uses advertisement as technique to change the belief and attitude of people, propaganda and advertisement are not same as considered by some. Propaganda is a very broad and wide concept while advertisement is a narrow one. Some say that there is no line of demarcation between propaganda and advertisement particularly when it comes to the shape of institutional advertisement. The institutional advertisements found in news papers and other electronic media try to secure the good will of the consumers and control the market through it. In fact, the institutional advertisement regularly enters into the domain of propaganda proper to impress upon the audience favourably the merits of a given product and drive competing item. Both propaganda and advertisement can not tolerate any competition. Both play deliberately with the psychology of the consumers and try to explore their impatience, irrationality, ingnorance and make them suggestible. Advertisement refers to a limited commercial context. It grows out of restricted monetary motives. It is mainly concerned with controlling of the market and commonly regulated by some informal code of ethics to avoid confusion and encourage conformity. However, propaganda by and large is free from these commercial ethics, propaganda is made to generate confusion and by this take advantage of it. Propaganda has a more political, etiological and social conflict involved in it.

The purpose of advertisement is definite and selective to get the patronage and support by a large number of consumers. While propaganda monopolises the vigour loyalties and supporting conduct of a huge population, advertisement helps in propaganda of any kind as the propagandist tries to exercise their power more extensively from advertisements. It thus appears that the difference between propaganda and advertisement are minor and subtle. Both help in influencing the psychology of people.

ADVERTISING IN U.S.A.

In U.S.A. advertising has come a long way since the 18th century when most advertisements were made in news papers, in the shape of informations and announcements. George Rowell (1871) in his most publicized title "Forty years in the advertising Business" has given his advice on advertisements "come right down with the facts, boldly, firmly, unflichingly, say directly what it is, what it will do. Leave out all its, say flatly, the best or nothing. Donot refer to rivals, ignore every person, place or thing except yourself, your address or your article. If these advices are followed, advertisement will not be looked upon negatively as it is being done".

Advertising in America expanded rapidly after the civil war. It was extended to various consumer goods, telephone, different brands of automobiles, radio, electric light bulbs, camera etc. During the 19th century magazine advertising came into being and by the turn of the century advertisement flourished in U.S.A. through various bodies and advertising agencies and associations. It is estimated that the total amount spent on advertising world wide in 1996 is abouts 377 billion which includes abouts 174. 1 billion only in the U.S. This data indicate the importance being put on advertisement in U.S.A. to influence the American consumers.

ADVERTISING IN INDIA

During 1995 it is estimated that advertisers in India spent a total of more than Rs. 30 billion on advertising. According to Ayer "Advertising in India reflects the social, political, economic and cultural environments in which the advertisements were created". Satellite T.V. has influenced advertisements in India emphasising more on the emotional and visual appeal of the consumers. The main purpose of the current advertisers in India is to catch the psychology and attention of the audience' and viewers. The purpose is to reach the consumers at any cost. Different Indian products face neck to neck competition with the inland and foreign products particularly after economic liberalization between 1991-1996. Many experts opine that advertisement should not be looked upon negatively and with malice since it helps in communication and assists people to select the best, to be guided by society acceptable values. Many advertising agencies in India are found to be influenced by their western counterparts. They should however be selective in adapting from the American experience. They should keep in mind their own culture, tradition and more so, the psychology of the consumers of India, to make advertisement more successful. Mistry has rightly opined that Indian admen should adopt the technology of the west and the soul of India. He further remarks, "The American sophistication in tools and techniques is instructive but we must remember that in the Indian context life styles have changed but not the values". The good things of American advertising are attention to details, professional integrity and a strong balance between the concept and execusion, and time managements says Mistry. The Indian advertising agencies may keep in mind these advises of Mr Saurav Mistry president and C.E.O. of Mcconn Erikson which is said to be the world's biggest agency. Thus advertisement in India should be a blend of the east and the west and not of the imitation of the west only.

The main purpose of advertising agencies is to explore the weaknesses of the consumer goods used earlier and highlight the advantages of the goods for which advertisement is done currently. By this procedure the psychology of consumer is controlled and directed to tile best advantage of the advertising agencies. This is kept in mind by tile advertising agencies of the world irrespective of society or culture and advertising strategies arc planned accordingly.

QUESTIONS

1. What is understood by consumer psychology ? How consumer behaviour is influenced ?
2. Discuss the importance of study of consumer psychology for the economic development of the country.
3. How consumer psychology is related to consumer behaviour ?
4. Can marketing effort change consumer's need ?
5. "Marketers can not create needs. Need preexist among the consumers" Critically examine the above statement.
6. Indicate the role of motivation and motivational research in determining consumer psychology.
7. Critically examine the specific personality factors determining the style of consumer behaviour.
8. Elaborate the role of various models in the consumers decision making process. Which model do you consider most suitable and an ideal ?
9. Discuss the role of socialisation and cultural factors in shaping consumer behaviour.
10. What do you understand by advertisement ? Is it different from propaganda ? Answer with suitable examples.
11. Examine and elaborate the role of advertisement in shaping consumer behaviour.
12. What are the needs and advantages of advertisement ?
13. Compare the present advertising system in India and U.S.A.
14. Write brief notes on the following:
    (*a*) Motivation and consumer behaviour.
    (*b*) Influence of family and friends on the psychology of consumer.
    (*c*) Socio economic status and consumer behaviour.
    (*d*) Market survey.
    (*e*) Advertisement in India.
    (*f*) Purpose and aim of advertisement.
    (*g*) Advantages and disadvantages of advertisement.
    (*h*) Social attractiveness of the marketers and consumer psychology.

REFERENCES

B.Lise, P. (Ed) *Marketing and the Behavioural Sciences.* Beston Ally and Bacon 1963 Applied Psychology.

Gilmer, B.V.M. *Problems in Living and work.* McGraw. Hill Inc. 1967.

Herbert Krusgman. *The impact of Television Advertising.* Learning without involvement. Public opinion quarterly, 29 Fall, 1965.

Ivey, P.W. *Successful salesmanship Engelwood Cliffs.* N.J. Prentice Hall, 1947.

Lawrence Solay & Gary Kurbard. *Sex in Advertising* "A comparison of 1964 and 1984". Magazine Ads Jnt of advertising **15**(3), 1986.

Madhu S.R. Parsuaders—*An overview of advertising India and the U.S. Span,* Vol. XXXVII. No. 4. June/July 1996,

Ray Aroda. *Consumer involvement and Advertising Strategy.* International Journal of Advertising, 1985.

Ronald, J. Faber, and Thomas C.G. *A clinical screenes for compulsive Buying.* Jn of consumer Res. 19 Dec. 1992.

Ruth, Ann Smith. *The effects of visual and verbal advertising information on consumers Inferences-* Jn. of advertising as Dec., 1991.

Schiffman, L.G. *Consumer Behaviour,* 5th edition.

Kanuk, L.G. Prentice Hall of India Pvt. Ltd. New Delhi, 1995.

T. Wedt, D.W. *Consumer Psychology Annual Rev.* Psychology, 1965.

28

Stress in Organisations and Its Effect on Performanace

INTRODUCTION

Stress is a very commonly used and widely experienced concept in modern civilized society and in every sphere of life. Inspite of the amenities of modern civilization wishes are many but sources are few. Problems are ample, but time and scope are less for solution. Human wants are unlimited and desires are countless but the scope and time to fulfill such desires are limited. Problems are more, so pressures are more. Besides the experience of stress because of common day to day problems like various sad occurrences in life, major life changes, uncertainty, racial and sexual discrimination, loss of jobs, financial disaster, lack of social support, criticism produce various adjustment problems and contribute to the experience of anxiety and stress. Similarly physical and mental health problems, daily hassles and demands, working deadlines, lead to growing tension. In various organisations, pressure from the work place, and more demands on a person from the environment reduces his performance ability, he connot cope with the situation and hence experiences stress. Various findings show that besides common stress, work stress reduces efficiency and productivity even in most efficient, experienced and qualified persons. When I work in the kitchen normally I take one and half to two hours to complete the entire work. But when I am under stress because of some unhappy occurrences last night or in the early morning, I not only take more time to finish cooking, but also the quality of cooking deteriorates.

Therefore discussion on the causes of stress and how they can be managed should be given prime attention in different organizations. By only managing the work place stress the problem cannot be solved fully. The employee carries the anxiety and stress caused at home to the work place. Hence this has to be also taken care of Stress should be managed and controlled properly as it strengthens one for the next failure and next frustration. We all know that failure is to the pillar to success. So some amount of stress and anxiety seem to be essential to make the person more active, effective courageous and encounter the future situation. Some amount of stress improves learning and that is its positive value, stress is infact an opportunity when it offers potential gain.

Concept, Meaning, Nature and Symptoms of Stress

When an incident or occurrence distresses a person to such an extend that his state of health or his physiological and psychological well being or physical and mental wellness is affected, he is called to be in a state of stress. It is an individual's reaction to a disturbing factor in the environment. Pollution, noise, crowding, unemployment discrimination, religious, social and sexual harassment, loneliness, failure in life, inability to cope with the existing environmental conditions at home and work place, organizational rules and structures, pressure from the employer to speed up work and production level, work culture, all lead a kind of uneasiness, anxiety and psycho physiological discomfort. Thus stress is experienced on and off the work place due to the above factors and it is an integral part of modern employee's life. Obstacles of the environment and organizational set up put adjustive demands on the person interfering his well being. Thus in simple terms stress is a demand on the person arising out of obstacles and it is highly related to frustration and anxiety. Stress and anxiety have a negative impact on the psychological and mental health of the person. But constructivity and creativity is not possible without some stress and some anxiety. Success and good performance may be delayed without some degree of stress. However, excessive stress is undesirable. In fact stress acts as a motivator or energies and increases efficiency. Stress improves ones adoptive system and those who do not experience any stress in their life have a poor adoptive mechanism. Positive stress leads to positive experience and energises the person with positive feeling. Positive stress does not affect the mental and physical health. But more stress is undesirable and unhealthy. Infact, to rise to the occasion and give more positive performance many use stress as a reinforcer.

Definition.

Stress can be shortly described as a group of responses an organism makes to a stimulus disturbs the physical and mental health of a person. The term stress means to an engineer any external force directed at some physical object. The results of the force is a kind of strain which refers to a change of in the structure of an object. Stress is thus considers as an external event or stimulus which affects work moderate well being. Strain caused by stress are the anxiety and distress. Stress may be defined as a dynamic condition in which the individual is confronted with an opportunity, demand or resource related to the individual desires and for which the outcome is perceived to be both uncertain and important.

So what exactly stress means different people based an their individual experiences can define stress in various ways. In the oxford dictionary stress is defined as a state of affair involving demand on physical or mental energy. It is a condition which is not always adverse or negative. It is a demand on the mind and body balance when one tries to cope or adjust with stress condition appears to be relative in nature. As already discussed extreme stress condition deteriorates human physical and mental health, but moderate degree of stress is normal and in many cases proves useful. Usually when we speak of stress it is understood that it as negative influence on human being.

Stress produces ones body's physical, mental and chemical reaction to circumstances that frighten confuse, endanger or irritate a person when stress is handled poorly it becomes harmful to body, raises blood pressure producer, ulcer, asthma and overactive thyroid. (Stress can lead to negative emotions and emotional unhappiness, strained relationship with other people etc.

Stress can also be defined as an adoptive response to an external situation that results in physical psychological and behavioural deviations to organizational participants.

Ivancevict and Matterson defines stress as follows. "Stress is an adoptive response mediated by individual differences and/or psycological processes that is a consequence of any extend (environmental) action, situation or event that places excessive psychological and physical demands upon a person."

Job or work place stress is a type of condition which arises from the interaction of the people and their jobs and characterised by changes within the person which forces him to deviate from their normal functioning.

Stress is normally defined in terms of adjustment, when a person is not able to adjust to the demands which exceeds his adjustment or coping capacity, he experiences physical and psychological changes and shows behaviour problem. So Hans Selye (1956) has conceptualized stress as a "*general adaptation syndrome*".

Bittle (1986) hords that stress is a physiological and emotional reaction to time pressure frustration, conflict, disobedience and ill treatment of subordinates and various other factors found in the work environment as well as personal, private life. One can cope with normal stress, but excessive stress turns to distress that can lead to physical problems and behavioural symptoms. If the job environment creates a threat to the individual because of excessive demand on him, he experiences stress and discomfort. Stress is caused by real or imagined fear because of the inability to cope. This produces fatigue, tension and high blood pressure. The tension caused by stress lead to the inability to adjust with the present or the future changing conditions. Changing conditions intensify stress than static conditions. In simple terms it can be said that stress is a load—physical or mental that causes a deflection between what a person can easily handle and what he cannot. When a stress becomes intolerable it causes temporary intellectual deficiency in behaviour. They show symptoms of sudden irritation, anger and get upset in small matters. These behaviour though appears abnormal to others are normal for the person for the time being. If the stress does not reduce, they show physical illness and may take recourse to drugs or show other dysfunctions including adjustment dysfunction. In worst circumstances they may collapse mentally and experience break-down.

NATURE, PROCESS AND SYMPTOMS OF STRESS

As discussed earlier stress has both positive and negative effects. Stress up to a limit helps in efficiency and performance. Stress in fact is not negative or bad in itself. But when it is caused by undesirable out comes it turns to **distress** which is not good for the person. When stress is an outcome of desirable and successful effects it is called Eustress. Eustress is said to be a positive, healthy and progressive stress response. Here we will basically discuss about causes and management of the stress which turns to **distress**. Distress type to stress requires careful examination and steps taken to manage need to be discussed.

Stress normally occurs when is more demand on the person or has high constraints. In other words, his constraints or limitation (physical or mental) prevent him from coping with a situation. When a person could not see a long waited movie because of his examination next day, and so feel distresses, it is because of the demand on him. But when a person cannot view a movie because of want of money and hence experiences stress, it is a case of stress caused by constraint. Demands and constraints may lead to potential stress. A potential stress becomes an actual stress when the person is uncertain about the out come of the stress and the out come is significant for him. For example, a person has appeared in the interview for the Civil Services Examination. He is uncertain about the result and this result is very significant for him as it may turn the course of his life. So he experiences anxiety and stress till the result is out. Any out come or result which is significant for a person but there is no uncertainly, he will not experience stress. For instance, if one is certain that he will get the I.A.S. Job which is very significant for him. he will not experience stress. Similarly if there is uncertainty, but getting a job is not important for him, he will also not experience stress.

Stress and anxiety are not same, though a stress may include anxiety. While an anxiety is emotional and psychological, a stress creates both physiological and psychological problems.

Process of Stress

Stress is a process the arousal of which depends on what events or occurence a person notices, how he notices and how it is appraised or comprehended. There is individual difference in the existence of stress and response or reaction even to a similar situation. The response to a stressful situation is a function of individuals personality, his past experiences and above all capacity to tolerate frustration. The interpretation of a stressful situation varies from person to person. A situation which is stressful to one may not be so to another because of the personality differences like capacity to tolerate frustration, positive out look towards occurences producing anxiety and stress, optimism and also the resources and time available at the disposal of the person. An unhealthy, moody and already aggrieved person will be more distressed than a healthy, relaxed and happy person.

The process of stress starts with the stressors and their dimensions, intention, duration and predictability. Stressors influence and affect the physiological, psychological and cultural characteristics of a person. Moreover, how one reacts to a stress or copes with it, depends upon his past experience of dealing with such a situation, his personality pattern his perception of the stressful situation, his frustration and stress tolerance capacity. A person who controls the stressful situation in a positive way or considers it a day to day affair experiences less stress than another person who perceives the stressful situation as uncontrollable, traumatic, and is scared with such experience.

Thus, it is the attitude and temperament towards the stresser and towards the self that determine ones reaction to stressful situation. A person who is confident, secured and considers himself healthy psychologically and physically to deal with the crises situation and feels that he would get social and family support to meet it, experiences less stress compared to his counterpart who has no such advantages. If a person has managed to handle similar stressful situations in the past most successfully, he will not experience the severity of stress.

Thus stress passes to the individual through a systematic process and it includes environmental and personal events which threaten the security, well being and happiness of the person. To meet the stress, psychological counselling, medical care, personal skills, adjustment style, social support and professional help etc. are necessary.

Typical Symptoms of Stress

Chronic worry, nervousness and tension, inability to relax, high blood pressure, digestive problem, emotional instability, feelings of inability to cope, uncooperative attitude, sleeplessness and other problems with sleep, use of drugs, tension headache, reduction of performance in quality and quantity, irritation, restlessness, feeling or uneasiness, conflict with family members, coworkers and customers, bad interpersonal relationship, easily provoked, feeling burnt out and exhausted, complaining attitude. The above systems of excessive stress are observed when the stress is long term or experienced for quite a long period. But temporary stress and setting realistic goals, short term tensions may reduce stress to a great degree. Increased stress leads to absenteeism even, turnover and accident proneness.

Levels of Stress

Stress is mostly individualistic in nature, some people have high tolerance for stress and adjust well in the face of normal stressors in the environment. Stress may occur at a biological or psychological level. Pneumonia viruses produce stress on a biological level and the adjustive demand involves the biological defences of the body. Guilt produces psychological stress where basically ego defences are involved. Stress also may occur at individual and group levels. For example wars as well as economic depressions put stress on groups as well as individuals. It is seen that some people have very low level of tolerance for stress and they become paralysed when they have to interact with everyday routined activities.

At psychological level arousal plays a major role in stress related reactions. Hypothalamus initiates action in two pathways. The first pathway involves release of large amount of catecholamine from adrenal glands in to the blood stream. The second path way involves the pituitary gland which secrets the corticosteroid which provides energy. Stress can be classified in to high level, medium level and low level. The reaction to different levels of stress is also different. While optimum stress helps in high performance and good health, high and low stress produce negative effects and lower performance. Optimum level of stress is different for different individuals. However, an acceptable level of stress may be worked out through research.

The emotional reactions to stress include fear, anger and sadness. The behavioural and cognitive responses try to master, reduce or tolerate the demands created by the stress. Recent research shows that stress may lead to susceptibility to upper respiratory illnesses, poor immunity, increase in blood sugar level, job dissatisfaction, lack of involvement in job are the most direct and obvious symptoms of stress.

Stressors

Stressors are said to be activators who activate the stress. A stresser is an event or situation in one's environment which causes stress. It may be external or environmental, psychological or social. Environmental stressors refer to noise, air pollution and excessive heat. Psychological stressors are conflict, frustration, guilt feeling, too much pressure, sudden shock due to death of near and dear ones. Social stresser may be break of relationship with intimate friend, lack of friendship with neighbours, loneliness etc. The stressers create reactions of various types such as physiological, emotional, cognitive and behavioural. In short stressors, are stimulus situations that lead to stress.

Kaplan and Sadock (stressors) have given a list of various events leading to creation of stress of different degrees. They are brake up with boy friend or girl friend, change of school, expelled from school, birth of sibling, divorce of parents, unwanted pregnancy, arrest, sexual and physical abuse, death of one or both parents, overcrowded living quarters, family arguments, chronic disabling illness in parent/parents, chronic parental discord, harsh, rejecting and unaffectionate parents, chronic life threatening illness in parents, multiple, foster home placements, recurrent sexual or physical abuse, etc.

Regarding Psychological Stressors the following areas may be considered :

1. **Conjugal** such as engagement, marriage discord, separation, death of spouse.
2. **Parenting** like becoming a parent, friction with the child, illness of the child.
3. **Interpersonal.** Problems with ones friends, neighbours, associates, co-workers or nonconjugal family member like illness of best friends, discordant relationship with boss.
4. **Occupational** work, unemployment, retirement, the school college, office problems.
5. **Living Circumstances.** Change of residence, threat to personal safety, immigration.
6. **Financial.** Inadequate finances, change in financial status.
7. **Legal**. Arrest, imprisonment, law suit or trial.
8. **Development.** Phases of life cycle *i.e.,* puberty, transition to adult status, menopose becoming 50.
9. **Physical Illness or injury** such as illness, accident, surgery, abortion.

Other psychological stressers like natural or man made disaster like Drought, Cyclone, Tsunami, Flood etc., persecution, unwanted pregnancy, child to unwed mother.

Miscellaneous Stressors. Cold, hostile, intrusive, abusive, conflictual or confusing inconsistent relationship between parents or towards child, physical or mental illness in a family member, lack a parental guidance, or excessively harsh or inconsistent parental control, insufficient, excessive or confusing social or cognitive stimulation, anomalous family situation *e.g.,* complex or in consistent parental custody foster family, Institutional rearing, loss of nuclear family members.

One or more negative stressors can produce adjustment disorders. The severity of the stresser however is not always predictive of the severity of the adjustment disorder. The severity of a stressor is a complex function of degree, quantity, duration, reversibility, environment and personal context. For example the loss of a mother is quite different for a 10 year old and a 45 year old and hence the degree of stress is different.

Various psychoanalytic researchers have analysed the capacity of the same stress to produce different range of responses in different normal human beings. Freud was consistently interested to trace why the stresses of ordinary life produced illness in some persons and not in others. He concluded that constitutional factors interact with a person's life experiences to produce fixation. Psychoanalytic research has also emphasized the role of the mother and the rearing environment in a persons later capacity to respond to stress. Winnicott's concept of the "good enough mother" who adopts to the infant's needs and provides enough support to enable the growing child to tolerate frustrations of life explains the above stand point.

An adjustment disorder is caused by a stressor but may or may not be immediately. If the stressor ceases, it may cease, but if it continues the adjustment disorder may continue for life long.

As mentioned earlier, the reaction to stressors may be physiological, behavioural, emotional and cognitive. Stress is associated with demands and resources. Demand refer to responsibilities, pleasures, obligations and even uncertainties that the individuals face in the work place. Rsources refer to things within an individual's control that can be used to resolve the demands. This demand-resource model has received increasing support as data show (2003). When demands and resources match stressful nature of demand is reduced. Some stressors can be good and some can be bad.

Types of Stressors-Negative and Positive Stressors

Stressors are usually negative in character which has been discussed earlier. Although we normally think that stress arises from negative situations in our life, there are certain positive events which are called positive stressors and they do not produce any negative effect on adjustment or produce adjustment disorder. Those stressors which produce positive effects on the day to day functioning of the personality are called positive stressors. Here some amount of stress motivates a person to struggle, for existence and survival. Some degree of force or stress is necessary to make learning, or performance effective. For time bound work stress has a very positive role to play. Example of positive events (stress) which lead to constructive behaviour has been given earlier.

Challenge stressors are positive and associated with work load, dead line or pressure to complete a task within a time frame. Hindrance stressors are negative and they keep one away from reaching the goals. Evidences and research show that challenge stressors are less harmful than hindrance stressors (2007).

Examples of positive stressors which make a person extremely happy and produce stress are getting married, receiving a scholarship, pursuing higher studies in a foreign university, or an unexpected promotion. I myself have experienced this positive stress when I was awarded Ph.D degree in Psychology in 1973. I became highly emotional and tears rolled down from my eyes when I got this news. I was reminded of my late father who inspired me till his death to pursue a carrier inspite of my marriage. With two small children on my lap, with the responsibilities of a family and work out-side I was not sure if I could achieve this. Hence a positive stressor also produces stress. One person being excessively elated died from heart attack when his long lost son was standing near him.

Characteristics of Stressors

1. Stresses are so intense that they produce a state of **overload** *i.e.,* they become so strong and of high degree that one can no longer adopt to them like death of a spouse or only son.
2. Stressors evoke incompatible tendencies in the organism who face it like tendencies to both approach and avoid some object or activity. Suppose you saw a thief coming to steal things from your house. Immediately you are panicked but you feel the tendency to encounter him. But then you are scared of your life and so feel like avoiding him. You are in a conflicting situation and can't decide what to do.
3. Stressors are uncontrollable *i.e.,* beyond one's power to control. Examples of such stressors are death of a spouse or intimate friend.

When individuals can predict, control and terminate a situation, they consider it to be less dangerous and less stressful than when they feel that it is beyond their control.

Effect of Stress on health, Performance and Physiological responses to Stressors

Studies show stress has inverted relationship with performance. Low to moderate stress increase the ability to react are often perform better. Psychosomatic disorders like hypertension, heart problems, asthma, diabetis, ulcers, migrane headaches, czema, low back pain and other related health problems are influenced by stress. Similarly many students are found suffering from various health problems like fever, stomach problems, coughs and cold, etc. as examination becomes nearer. It is also seen that those persons who know how to adjust or cope with their stresses successfully are happy people and enjoy life. They fall sick less than those who are unhappy in their personal lives. Since there is a close connection between the mind and the body when the stress continues for a longer period it not only affects the physical health of a person but also disorganizes the psychological functions.

Psycho physiological disorders may be the outcome of the individual's primary reaction tendencies to stress and the primary reaction tendency vary in every infant. Wolff (1950) has suggested that people can be classified to stomach reactors, pulse reactors, nose reactors depending on what kind of physical changes that stress characteristically trigger in them. For example, a person who reacts to emotional stress with high blood pressure will be susceptible to hypertension. On the other hand one who reacts to stress with excessive secretion of stomach acids will be more likely to develop peptic ulcer.

Alexander (1950) has hypothesized that each kind of psychological disorders connected to a particular type of stress. Peptic ulcers for instance are associated with the stress caused by the need for love and protection. But this view could not receive wide support from subsequent researchers. It can however be assumed that a wide range of stress situations can lead to a given type of disorder and a wide range of disorders can result from a given type of stress.

When the stress becomes long standing and chronic, it impairs ones ability to think and perform efficiently in day to day activities. I have found that the day when I face some sort of stress or pressure, I take a longer time to finish my day to day work. Not only the duration becomes longer, also the quality of work deteriorates compared to non-stress days. When I am under stress even I forget if I have put salt in the curry and I feel totally disturbed. The entire day's works become disorganised. I feel very irritable and respond to others in an irritable manner without obvious reasons. Similarly, when I have to work hard than my usual routined work, for example on certain festival days or when some guests arrive, I feel highly pressurized and tensed. I feel helpless and my back pains, I've sometimes headache under these pressures till my work is completed. Once the work is completed, I fell relaxed. Due to excessive pressure of work I feel physically and psychological exhausted at the end of the day. This is technically called "burnt out" due to continuous work related stress. In the same manner when my maid servant goes on leave or the part time maid stays away without notice I also experience work related stress. When one has to look after ill or old age family members for a long time single handedly or when a working woman has to balance between the home and office experience of stresses at the physical and psychological level become inevitable.

Similarly tragic life events like sudden death of spouse or parents, severe illness of near one, separation, divorce, natural disasters, unemployment, failure in examination, suspension and termination of jobs etc. produce all kinds of physio-psychological diseases, mental disorders. Particularly when people have to live under stressful situations for a continuous period (like an uncertain, threatening and unpleasant situation) there is physical and mental disorder, in some cases of mild type, in some cases of severe type. Some also try to manage the stress by various coping procedures.

Why this type of reaction to stressful situation happens ? **Hans Selye** tried to answer this question by proposing **General Adaptation Syndrome** (GAS). This syndrome explains the physical or bodily consequences of stress. GAS is a three step profile of physiological reaction to stress. It is a flight to flight syndrome controlled through the sympathetic nervous system. Usually these responses are brief and soon normalcy is restored.

Stage-1. Alarm

It is an alarm reaction, a non specific mobilization phase that activates the sympathetic nervous system. It is the experience of a stressor or the presence of a stress arousal stimulus in the environment say, sudden accident of a young son or only child. In such a situation the adrenal activity and the cardiovascular and respiratory functions (Sympathetic Nervous System) are heightened as the body makes its preparations to face the situation arising out of the accident of the son or only child. The stress hormones like cortisol, epinephrine and no-repinephrine are released in high amounts.

Stage-2. Resistance

During the stage two, arousal is lower than stage one. In this stage, the body reserves are ready to deal with the stressor and cope with the situation in a constructive manner, like telephoning the doctor, running to the spot of accident and carrying the son to the hospital etc. During this stage the person makes constant resistance to the stressor and a relative decrease in the response to other stimuli present in the environment. In resistance the body maintains a moderate level of physiological árousal and the individual has increased his ability to tolerate the original stressor which brought the alarm reaction. The body continues at an above normal rate to cope effectively with the stressor. The resistance stage begins if the stress is prolonged.

Stage-3. Exhaustion

Exhaustion occurs when the organism fails to overcome the threat because all the reserves of the body are exhausted due to continuous exposure to the stressor. When after trying here and there for blood, the father does not get it from any where, he is exhausted and leaves the hope of saving his son. At this stage the person is no longer able to resist the stressor. He gives up all hope and resigns to his fate. This exhaustion stage may lead to various physical illnesses like high blood pressure, cardiac arrest or paralysis or death. The degree of illness varies from situation to situation. If the stress is severe the illness is acute and mild if the stress is mild.

Suppose you are going on the road and at once you find that three people with big knives and pistols have come to attack you. At once you are panicked and feel the alarm bell ringing. Your blood pressure goes up, heart beat rises. These prepare you to defend yourself. So you start running away with all your energy. Thereafter you start resisting them by the help of your pant belt when they came nearer you. You may try other means of attack also.

But when you found that you are exhausted and they have overpowered you by giving a heavy blow or your back, you have no other option but to lie down on the floor. In dangerous situations the secretion of the endocrine grands increases to face the danger physically and psychologically. But if the stress is prolonged, if every day you find somebody is ready to attack you, you brake down. All your bodily energies are consumed day by day and efficiency of different systems of your body is gradually reduced. Evidences also show that negative emotions like grief and depression for a continuous period affect and suppress the body's immunity and resistance capacity and ultimately the organism becomes susceptible to various diseases. Various researches are now being undertaken to substantiate the relation between stress and illness.

As mentioned earlier the functioning of the general adaptation syndrome depends upon how the organism perceives the stressor. Unless and until he perceives it as a threat to him, he would not experience stress. Uncontrollable stressors put more adverse, effects on the immune system than controllable stressor. If the organism feels that he can control the stressor, he will not be affected by the stressor and will be able to cope with in situation successfully. A depressed or frustrated person is more susceptible to be affected by a stressor. Social and emotional support also help in coping with the stressor successfully. Optimistic, detached and relaxed persons, persons with 'B' type personality are less affected by stressors.

Selye's GAS provides two important conclusion (*a*) providing a frame work of understanding our physiological responses to stressful events. (*b*) Suggests a reasonable explanation for the relation between stress and illness. Chronic stress can lead to a lowered resistence to disease.

Limitations of GAS

Selye's model fails to consider the importance of cognitive processes in determining whether we interpret a specific event as stressful.

Nobody would deny that this difference (Baron-2004) is because of the cognitive appraisals that under similar situations some person experience stress where as others do not. Suppose the grandson has not returned from school in time. The grand mother experiences severe stress anticipating some problem like abducation, but the grand father remains calm and says don't worry he will come within half and hour. The child returns home after 15 minutes. The cause of delay was—the Rickshaw was punctured.

Hence stress occurs only to the extent that the persons involved perceive :

(*a*) that the situation is some how threatening to their important goals (Primary appraisal)

(*b*) that they will be unable to cope with these dangers or demands (Secondary appraisal)—Croyle, 1992, Lazarus and Folk man 1984.

The amount of stress one experiences therefore depends upon one's cognitive appraisals of the event *i.e.,* the extent to which one perceives it as threatening and hence he will be unable to cope with it. Thus cognitive and social processes influence one's responses to stress. If the coping mechanisms are through to be inadequate stress is experienced. Otherwise no stress is experienced.

TYPES OF STRESS

On the basis of varied type of stressful experiences, stress may be categorised into three major types, environmental, psychological and social. However all types of stresses are interrelated and overlap with each other.

1. Environmental Stresses like earth quakes, Tsunami, Super Cyclone and flood are sudden and they have powerful influence. These are called disasters. These events affect the health and mental life of a large number of people and they take long time to cope with it. Take the case of Super Cyclon in Orissa in 1999 and Tsunami in Asia like Indonesia, Sri Lanka, India etc. Environmental pollution, noise and crowding etc. may be second category of environmental stresses whose effects are mild.

2. Psychological stress. Psychological stresses are personal and unique to the persons who faces it. Psychological stresses are said to be internal sources of stress like frustration, conflict, tension and pressure etc.

3. Social Stress. When social events and situations lead to stress it is called Social Stress like severe illness or death in the family, divorce, separation, quarrel with a best friend, unwed mothership, bad neighbour etc. If small quarrels continue daily it cannot be avoided, so stress is experienced.

4. Work Place Stress. Stress caused by poor work environment, bossism of the employer or supervisor, bad behaviour, conflict with coworkers, excessive pressure to more production, dislikeness for job and immediate supervised isolation from group etc. relate to work place stress.

COMMON SOURCES/CAUSES OF STRESS

Nobody can avoid stress. It is a reality in everyday life. Sources or causes of stress refer to the factors contributing to stress. The sources of stress may be trival, may be external/situational, may be physical. Very simple incidents may also cause stress in persons, who perceive it differently, like delay of a plane, safe arrival of a train, quarrel with a friend, loss or theft of money and property, ups and downs in the share market, stress due to heavy income tax etc., not getting a telephone call from the girl friend and son at U.S.A. and so on. The degree of stress varies with brief upsets and quick recovery depending upon the causes of stress. A stressful life style resulting from day to day problems of finance, family relationship, excessive work, insecurity and to possess more and more may lead to stress. Low self confidence and low self esteem may produce higher stress. Jobs that provide a low level of variety, significance autonomy, feedback and identity to incumbants create stress and reduce satisfaction and involvement in job.

The sources of stress are classified as follows :

Stressful life events coming from the physical environment. This has been described earlier under stressors. In the study of Holmes and Rahe (1967) on stressful life events, it was found that greater values were assigned to death, divorce, marital separation etc. and amaller values to minor quarrels, transfer from job, change of school and residence etc. My tenant has given me a notice that he will leave my house next month which he took on rent. I'm for that reason experiencing mild stress as I have to choose a new tenant and how he will deal with us, whether he would pay the rent regularly or not etc., all these bother me.

Their study further revealed that the greater was the number of 'stress points' for different people, the higher was the chance of becoming seriously ill. This thus suggests a high positive correlation between stress and illness. In a study it was found that subjects who reported chronic stressors (longer than a month) were more likely to develop cold. This suggested that chronic stressors may lead to illness than short term stressful events.

Frustration arising out of physical, Social, and Internal Stressors. Frustration is a great source of external/situational, social and internal stress. Frustration arising out of interference of goal oriented behaviour may be physical, social and internal. If the frustration is minor, the stress is less and if major the stress is high. If the frustration prolongs for a long period the stress becomes chronic and causes serious illness. **Physical/external Frustrations** coming from the environment lead to a varieties of stress. Fire, injury, flood, accident, war cyclones are examples of physical source of frustration. Obstacles from the physical environment provide the most commonly experience stress through frustration. The checks, value system such as restriction on intercast or inter-religion marriage, rapid social change, competition and rivalry, general social uncertainty and religious intolerance put a great deal of stress and produce feelings of inadequacy, discomfort, isolation, insecurity, anguish and pain. These are called **Social frustrations** and come under external sources of frustration.

Internal frustration arises out of any sort of personal limitations or personal factors like physical deformity, lack if intelligence, ugliness, struggle for power, prestige and recognition or any other personal reason earlier discussed. Unrealistically high standards of life, high level of aspiration without basic capacity also become the sources or causes of stress.

3. Threat. Many stress situations do not carry a major threat to our biological or psychological needs in our day to day life. Cold, hot, noise, and mild work place threats are not serious enough to produce stress of high degree. But certain stress situations which we perceive in our cognitive field as damaging or threatening to our survival produce stress of high order. Diagnosis of cancer, fear of AIDS, brain tumour, loss of social status due to the inter-religion marriage of the daughter in a conservative society carry a high degree of threat. Certain situations which the individual perceives beyond his capacity to cope, or which threaten the worth of self produce stress. An insecured person constantly experiences threat to his personality in various situations while a secured person does not perceive so. Low self concept and inadequate image of self, inferiority complex lead to severe stress. Threat arouses anxiety which has serious implications on physical and mental health and adjustive behaviour.

Stress caused by disloyality of a friend is greater than loss of a gold ring for one person while it may be the reverse in case of another. Thus individual difference exists in the perception of a situation. A stressful situation will be difficult to bear or withstand when one is ill, unhappy, or angry. When one is already in a condition of stress any additional stress will work like the last load on the camel's back and disintegrate his total personality.

4. Minor hassles of everyday. Our daily life is filled with innumerable, minor irritations which are literally called hassles. The minor hassles have relatively lower intensity but have higher frequency. In other words they are frequently experienced in our day to day life, but they are low in degree or intensity, like common quarrel at home, problems relating to the education or home work of son, shopping, having too many things to do in a less time or at once. Simultaneously, financial difficulties, poor result of children in school, decoration of home, buying a new car or house etc. difference of opinion with wife, familial quarrel, scolding by wife for coming home drunk etc. etc. act as sources of stress.

Though these minor hassles of day to day life appear to be mild and minor in their face value, daily occurrence of such hassles are an important cause of stress as suggested by the findings of Belongis, Folkman and Lazarus 1988, Kanner *et al.*, 1981, Lararus *et al.*, 1985. A hassle scale was developed by these investigators on which people indicate upto what extent they have been hassled by such common events during the past month. Strong positive correlation is seen between minor hassles of day to day life and disorganised psychological symptoms. The more one experiences such hassles everyday the more is the psychological disorder. Stressful events at home and outside may be carried to work place.

5. Work Related Stress. In this competitive age importance given to work culture. Many people spend more time at work than in any other single activity. People to-day are more career conscious and the influence of American work culture on the youths and adults of the world, need of money to lead luxurions life, also the need to work and get job satisfaction and many other related factors have motivated the modern men and women to work hard and work for a longer duration than their physiological limit. Under these circumstances jobs and careers have become the major sources of stress. Many other factors produce stress in work place besides long hours of work. They are sexual harassment, gender discrimination, bias and prejudice towards lower class people, too much competition with coworkers to get a promotion, bad behaviour of employer or immediate supervisor, low salary but more work, discrimination on the ground of race and caste, honesty and merit not being rewarded and so many other factors.

Sometime back it came out in the media that a computer engineer in India committed suicide because of over load of work. A Scientist working in a famous institute at Bombay committed suicide because he was superseded. Many high level executives, engineers and administrators leave their job by resigning and join else where because of work place stress. Misbehaviour of the management with the employees day in and day out produce work place stress which slowly kills the man physically and psychologically. Instances are many to substantiate this point.

Similarly underload or being asked to do little work also can cause stress. It produces strong feelings of boredom and becomes very stressful. When some body who is quite efficient is asked to do less work, he feels neglected and perceives this as an insult to his ability and intelligence. Less work is equally harmful like overwork. Everything should therefore be balanced in work place to work in a relaxed and hassle free way. Too much bossism and autocratic attitude also produces stress.

Other work related stress are **role conflict** which means the employee becomes the target of conflicting demands from different groups of people. Newly recruited executives or C.E.Os or managers of a particular company or organization are pressurized by their subordinates (who are old employees) to take immediate action on their various grievances. The various labour unions and associations put tremendous pressure to improve their physical environment, work assignment, salary, fringe benefits, while the employer or the boss wants and expects the manager to do just the opposite. This type of conflict due to incompatibility leads to pressure and stress. The poor manager is in between "Do and Don't do", and it produces a stressful situation for him.

Performance appraisal is another factor which may cause stress in some people. It means procedures and methods used to evaluate an employee's performance. Now a days we find many banks use this technique by taking the view of the customers. A questionnaire is handed over to you to rate the performance of the employees to whom you have come to get your work done on that day and from that the performance of the officer is rated. Similarly other techniques are also used like appraisal by the branch manager or boss. Now a days performance of the teachers in the class room are appraised by students in many colleges and universities. This causes stress in many teachers. Thus if the employee perceives it fair, there is no stress, but if he perceives it unfair the stress becomes very high. The procedure of assessing the performance of employees and officers through Annual Character Record (ACR) or confidential character record (CCR) has been criticized for some employees as they are subjected to grudge and bias particularly by many and hence in many institutions now open performance appraisal systems are being introduced. Even self appraisal systems are in vogue in some organisations.

When a worker feels that a particular technique of performance appraisal like annual confidential record is, arbitrary, biased, subjective and is sometimes maintained to harras an exployee who is not in good terms with his boss, he experiences terrible stress. By this he feels his promotion, increment and bonuses are held up in an unjust manner and so experiences stress.

Besides the above factors uncertainty and ambiguity about duties and responsibilities, by not allowing the worker to participate in decision making and responsible works, unpleasant and unhealthy work environment, conflict with boss and coworkers, lack of support from them, long distance between the office and residence etc. may also cause work related stress.

The work place stress can be reduced by proper selection of job and worker according to the abilities of the worker, and nature of job, through social support, properly planned work habits, etc. Lastly, the unfavourable effects of work place stress can be reduced by tackling the internal personality factors of the employee, through various intervention and counseling programmes. These interventions will help him to adjust successfully with the work place stress and give up unhealthy practices. The worker or employee must match with the job to avoid work place stress.

Internal Sources or Stress

Internal sources of stress arise out of inner pressure, personality variables, personality type, and conflict.

(*a*) **Inner Pressure.** Pressure may be external or internal. External pressures come from the physical and social environment which have been discussed earlier. Inner pressures involve pressure from one's self, ideal or conscience which produces guilt feeling and hence stress. Inner pressure also comes from one's level of aspiration, unrealistically high standrard of level of aspiration (which does not match with one's ability and achievement) courage and social responsibility. In a highly competitive society determination to reach the top or to be the best can lead to continuous and severe pressure and a significant degree of discomfort. Inner pressure may produce severe guilt feeling when the ego desires fail to maintain a balance between the Id desires and commands from the super ego.

(*b*) **Personality Variables-traits and types.** It has been discussed earlier how personality characteristics of a person make him more susceptible to stress.

INTROVERSION AND EXTROVERSION

Introverts are more susceptible to be influenced by a stressor. On the contrary extroverts who are happy go lucky persons take this events of life as normal and routined. In short, they do not take the stressors seriously, but try to cope with them successfully, resist them whole heartedly instead of being carried away by them 'X' fails in the examination and commits suicide because of sevior stress, while 'Y' who also fails in the examination without loosing heart prepares for the next examination. 'X' is an introvert and pessimistic while 'Y' is an extrovert and optimistic.

Individuals differ in their resistance to stress because of difference in tolerance capacity.

Some other people who are prone to illness and fall ill regularly, they are called disease prone, and suffer even from mild stressors. Others who have the capacity to face challenges and hardships in life are less affected by stressful stimulants. Some call themselves healer and they behave very effectively even in the face of great mishaps and big failures.

All these happen because of the optimistic and pessimistic dimensions. Optimistic people perceive the bucket as half full while pessimistics perceive the bucket as half empty. Optimistic people have a positive approach towards all events and situations in life, while pessimistic people analyse the world with a negative approach. Studies show that optimistic people are more stress and frustration resistant than pessimistics. Findings of studies also show that optimism is positively correlated with better mood, high number of helper T. Cells involved to immune reactions to infections and higher natural killer cell actively (Barron-2005). Results of studies further show that optimists and pessimists appear to adopt different techniques or tactices to adjust with stress. While optimists seek social support, the advice and help of others, and make specific goal oriented plans to face the stressors bravely, the pessimists try to withdraw from the stress provoking situation or giving up the goal with which stress is interfering or through denial behaviour that there is no stress. Flexible strategies are more successful in coping and managing with stress than rigid strategies. Thus, stress can be best accomplished by using a large varieties of coping techniques.

According to Baron while optimists use stratergies like problem focused coping, suppressing competing activities, seeking social support, pessimists use denial or distancing, disengaging from goal or focusing on the expression of feeling.

Both biologically and psychologically people vary in their susceptibility to certain kinds of stress. Some can tolerate their stress and frustration while others are not. It is earlier discussed how variation in the perception of the situation decides individual variation in the experience to threat. Many factors like biological, social and environmental interact with each other to develop the capacity of stress tolerance.

Personality Types

Earlier, under the chapter three personality types have been discussed *i.e.,* type A, type B and type C.

Type A. personality works under pressure for high achievements. High powered, ambitious, competitive, workaholics belong to A type personality. They are prone to stress since they want to complete more work in less time, are highly ambitious and always work under pressure. They are never relaxed. Because of high achievement motivation they want to compete with others aggressively and experience stress. These persons are therefore more prone to cardiac diseases.

Type B. Persons are the opposite of type A and hence are less prone to stress. They have the capacity for stress tolerance. They can successfully cope with the stressful environment and manage their stress as a normal occurrence of life. They take life easily and see things positively.

Type-C. Morris has named a "Type C" personality as cancer prone. A type C person is cooperative, unassertive and patient. He or she suppresses his or her negative emotions like anger, hostility and rage etc. The blocking of emotions raises certain neuro peptides in the brain as a result of which his homeostatic mechanism is disrupted and the capacity of the body becomes weak and less resistant to defend itself from cancer cells, particularly lung cancer. However, further research should be carried out on this view if Type 'C' personality is prone to cancer.

Studies indicate that no sex differences are found in Type A and B personalities. However, the higher the job status the incidence is greater for Type A personality. This is why it is seen that high profile persons and V.I.Ps suffer more from heart attacks and cardiac diseases.

Besides conflict for power, adverse decisions made by the management which affects the interest of the workers unhealthy and excessive competition, lots of pressure in work front, instability in organisational structure, frequent transfers, misbehaviour from the management and colleagues, unhealthy personal relationship with coworkers, frequent quarrels and backbiting, sexual harassment of female worker, odd schedules of work alloted to female workers, increased mechanisation of work, boredom and monotony, are some of the worthy causes of stress in work situation. Further massive changes in social structure, continuing technological growth, inflation and generation gap among the youngs and olds, the tendency to revolt against the management due to misunderstanding and gap in communication, change of work, excessive desire for power, prestige and recognition, desire for self esteem and status, lack of job feed back, and job security, economic problems, failure to reach the target, unrealistically high level of aspiration and personal problems, divorce and no children, and allied factors produce pressure and stress among employees. Change in life style also causes stress. When the life style of employees become complex or frequently change, anxiety and stress are the consequences.

When conditions of professional work generate moderate to high degree of stress, employees develop various symptoms of anxiety which become harmful to job performance. Also absolutely no stress or zero stress lowers performance because of want or motivation. Although reasonable stress is necessary to meet the challenges and requirements of work situation, excessive stress interferes with performance. The employee looses the capacity to cope, lacks decisiveness or makes erratic decisions.

He becomes nervous, irritable and develops chronic worry, looses patience and initiative. Absenteeism increases due to stress as employees take long leave to withdraw from the stressful situation. To avoid depression and stress, he may take recourse to drug and alcohol. Others suffer form repeated illness which are basically psychosomatic in nature. In extreme cases if the job situation appears to be unbearable, he quits the job or avoids work. A popular person has usually less stress than an unpopular person who faces problems everyday without being able to solve them amicably. Mostly negative, culturally undesirable life events increase stress.

People having better social support however develop the capacity of stress tolerance. Studies show that the effect of negative life events may be felt less when one has strong social support. Hence social support system should be better to cope with stressful life events. When the internal body system is unable to tolerate too much stress and decreases coping capacity, he may develop various physical dysfunctions; hysterical symptoms and psychosomatic disorders. Some western studies have been conducted by Cooper and Payne (1978) on the association of stress with psychological symptoms like conflict, ambiguity and overload relating to the predominant role and task characteristics. Panda (1983) has observed that a major factor of stress in an organisation is "mental overload".

Perception of the stress situation and attitude towards it also determines causation of stress. Tolerance and healthy resolve of stress is extremely desirable to make the employees physically and mentally healthy and hence fit for work. Lack or concentration is one of the major causes of excessive stress.

Some recent researchers like Mishra and Bhattacharya (1984). Dogra and Mishra (1988) Mishra (1989) conducted studies on executives and non-executives of public and private sector industries and organisations of Orissa. Findings of these investigations suggest the need to conduct more research in this area and evaluate the functional relationship between work environment, work culture and psychological well being.

Among on the job conditions and job related factors, working environment like poor illumination, bad house keeping, excessive noise coming from gigantic machines all the time, transfer, over work, dismissal and suspension, warning and censor, in decisiveness, inadequate capacity to fulfil one's responsibility, high achieving boss, inferiority complex, frustration due to improper inter personal relationship with coworkers and subordinates, improper communication, meaningless work, lack of job satisfaction, interpersonal conflict etc., play major role in the onset of stress. Off the job conditions relate to familial problems like material discord, divorce, separation, problems related to children's health condition and employment, property problems, isolation and loneliness etc. However, during work, working relations mostly cause stress.

Some jobs are dangerous and conflict with the moral standard of the employee like manufacturer of bombs and explosives. This may be a constant and continuous source of high degree of stress and anguish to the person. Lack of security in the job and constant threat of turn-over or lay-off may lead to stress. Due to want of autonomy and independence in work and undue interference potential stress may be caused. Inter-dependence between various tasks further aggravates the stress factor. **Overload** also increases stress particularly when a person has more work to do than he can handle in a smaller period. Similarly under work also causes boredom, anxiety and tension leading to stress.

Too much pressure on the employee because of his specific role say manager or house-keeper or immediate supervisor may lead to stress. This is called stress caused by the specific role because of role conflict. What is a role conflict ? It arises when different persons differ in their expectations of a particular employee, and contradictory demands are placed upon an employee simultaneously. Similarly, when one person is asked to remain in different charges which oppose each and play other different roles simultaneously, he experiences role conflict. A maid servant misbehaves with you terribly for years togather but you cannot throw her out because your son and daughter in law want her to continue. This creates stress in you, because you cannot manage with her nor throw her out.

Ambiguous jobs also cause stress. When a newly solved worker is not clear about what he has to do and what is expected from him will cause stress because of high degree of role ambiguity.

When a person is compelled to work with seniors, coworkers and subordinates with whom he cannot get along or cope because of ill relationship causes severe stress. If this type of ill interpersonal relationship continues the person either remains absent from job frequently or searches for new jobs. One of my relations, a talented youth left an outstanding job because of the above factors.

Individual differences lead to difference in stress tolerance. Many stresses occur due to wrong perception.

Leadership style also sometimes creates tension. The typical style of working of some managers and leaders may produce tension, fear and anxiety in the subordinate workers. They are highly automatic, give utmost importance on punctuality, like to have tight control on workers, are very very strict and rigid. These are sufficient factors to produce stress. When certain organizations become sick employees also feel stress. Lack of group cohesiveness can also produce stress. Hawthorne experiments have proved this. Lack of social support, organisational climate, experiences of continuous conflicts also lead to stress. Robbins *et al.* (2009) have described three major sources of stress, (1) Environmental, (2) Organisational and (3) Personal.

1. Environmental. Uncertainty and sudden changes in work and work related factors is a major cause of organisational stress. Environmental uncertainty is again devided to (*a*) economic, (*b*) political and (*c*) technological. Job insecurity due to recession and other factors, reduction in salary and perks, involve economic uncertainties. Unstable political system also causes stress. Technological changes like new innovations may produce threat to the workers security and in skills and intelligence.

2. Organisational. Pressure to complete work in limited time, work boss, uncooperative coworkers, etc., may cause stress. The organisational factors are, thus, divided into task, role and interpersonal demands.

3. Personal. Problems at home like economic need, mental discard, illness of self and relations, divorce, separation, education of child produce stress.

Reactions to Stress

The reactions to stress can be categorized as (*i*) Physiological, (*ii*) Behavioral, (*iii*) Psychological.

(*i*) Physiological. Undue fatigue, headache, sweating various types of psycho physiological dependent like migrain, headache, insomnia, alcoholism, peptic ulcer, high blood pressure, asthma, coronary diseases, rapid breathing and heart beat, tensed muscles, skin problems, muscular twitchess, baldness come under the physical reactions to stress.

(*ii*) Behavioural. Behavioural disorders produced by stress are usually quarrelsomeness, lack of efficiency, and competency, low quality of over eating and under eating, absenteeism and turn over, in efficiency, low productivity, low performance, lack of concentration, absenteeism, irregularity, lack of job satisfaction and frequent change in job. Smoking and drinking persons who are very sincere and perfect and get their only satisfaction in life from job and work show major break down when confronted with stress and anxiety. Thus dissatisfaction with one's work and on the job conditions is found to be stressful to many people.

(*iii*) Psychological. Dissatisfaction breeds discontentment. (lack or confidence, poorself esteem, lack or concentration). So the employees prefer to withdraw and avoid their job. They avoid work through many pretentions like being irregular, remaining absent frequently, doing work without any interest, dedication and motivation etc. Job dissatisfaction also produces conflict, frustration, anguish, and frequent irritability.

The above physical, behavioural and psychological reactions to stress adversely affect the physical and mental health of the workers.

Effects of Stress on Health and Performance

This has been discussed earlier under different areas of stress. However here we will discuss in brief the effect of stress of health and performance. Stress can influence our physical and psychological health, our performance in many tasks and even our career.

Effect of Stress on health

Many psycho-physiological disorders are caused partly or wholly by stress. Ulcer is the best example of a disease caused by stress. The stomach wall erodes so that open sores develop. Similarly migrane headache, Eczema, hypertension, asthma, colitis are caused by severe stress. Headaches upset stomach and skin allergies and irruptions may be the outcome of stress and tension. When working under pressure many people develop tension headache. When one is worried or experiences strong anger he has severe headache. Initially though stress may not cause health problems, continuous and chronic stress leads to severe health problems and minor and major illness. Various cardiac problems, high blood pressure, paralysis etc. are caused by severe stress. Examination stress also leads to fever, stomach trouble and cold etc. Low back pain etc. are even due to stress. If everyday hassles continue daily it also leads to illness. Since mind and body are related any adverse effect on the mental condition influences the body. By draining ones energy and resources and creating psychological and physiological imbalances stress upsets the body chemistry of a person. It may interfere with the operation of the individual's immune system. Prolonged and continuous exposure to stress disrupts the immunity of a person. Optimism and regular exercise, yoga and tolerance, and control of stressful situations can lead to reduced suppression of immune system. Complex and high life style should be changed to simple style of living. Stress produces hypertension. As a result, heart problems, ulcers, asthma and other psydiosomatic disorders occur. Also blood pressure and stress are highly and positively correlated. To-day diabetes which is a very common disease is highly related to stress. High stress increases the level of blood sugar giving rise to diabetes.

Effects of Stress on Performance

Findings of several studies show that stress reduces performance. Tests performed under anxiety and stress show poor results compared to tests performed under normal mental conditions. Stress affects the attention, organising capacity and efficiency of the person by negatively affecting his mental condition. For coping with stress the person has to spend a lot of energy and attention. Since the energy is reduced and mind is distracted performance is less under stressful situation. This is also a common day to day experience. When we are experiencing stress we even perform our daily routined activities with less efficiency. The quality and quantity of performance also suffers. When there is stress, performance deteriorates. This has been experienced hundred per cent in our day to day life.

Though earlier psychologists believed that stress improves performance on a variety of tasks because that arouses, energizes or drives a person to the goal or work. But beyond certain points or limit stress becomes distracting and performance is reduced. Further research in this area suggests that though this may be correct under certain conditions, even low or moderate levels of stress can interfere with performance. More research in this area is required as different research give controversial views regarding the effect of low to moderate stress.

In the modern complex work situation, people experience more stress than during earlier years when the work situation was simple. Hence, even the levels of stress are low, they also interfere with performance. Moderate levels of stress never the less interfere with many types of performance. But keeping in view the concept of individual difference stress does not always and in all people affect performance. It has been earlier discussed how individual difference plays a major role in reaction to stress. Moreover performance in many situations depends upon many factors besides stress. So no one should not generalize the effect of stress on performance.

Effects of Stress on Mental Health

From the psychological stand point this is an age of stress and hypertension. Now a days people, particularly adolescents, adults and middle aged persons are running to clinical psychologists and psychiatrists for treatment of mental illness arising out of different types of stress. Most important stress induced ailments in this age are depression, anxiety, panic attacks, insomnia or sleeplessness, Obsessive Compulsive Disorder (OCD) and various other similar types of disorders.

STRESS MANAGEMENT

It refers to effective way of handle stress. Low and moderate levels of stress if are continuous and sustained for a long period may have bad effect and so should be managed. Stress is a very common experience in modern life. Work load, pressure, doing more work in less time, high aspiration, greed for money, power and prestige, various failures in life and competition are common stressors and influence the physical and mental health of the person. Since stress is a part of every one's life it is difficult to avoid it completely. Though low to moderate level of stress experienced by the employees may not be a cause of concern to the management, high stress is definitely detrimental from every angle since stress has various impacts on the behaviour, physiological and psychological health of the organism disturbing the peace and happiness of an organism, it is essential that steps should be taken to reduce stress on human life. Stress also disrupts normal day to day activities as well works of complex nature. This is why to-day psychologists, psychiatrists and clinical psychologists are trying hard to device various means to reduce the effect of stress on human beings. The problem of control and management of stress has received active attention even in the area of Yoga.

Since stress is produced by several factors, the management and control of stress or coping with the stress also require a number of measures. Keeping in view the above factors, the individual and organisational strategies towards managing stress may be discussed. Since there is individual difference in stress tolerance and coping with stress, one should not however generalize. For management of stress, prevention is also important.

1. Style of Living. The style of life of modern man particularly middle and higher class people is such that they do less physical work. Modern gadgets and various techniques of doing work through mechanical devices like Calculator, Computer, Laptop, Teaching machines, Washing Machine, Grinder, Fridge, Oven, Cleaning Machine, Car, Scooter have reduced physical work and made people physically lazy. Mental exercise for relaxation are also not up to the mark. Thus, both mind and body are vulnerable to the various types of stressors. This is why to-day psychologists and health specialists advice to do physical and mental exercise like Yoga and meditation which will be discussed later on. By changing one's life style one can check a lot of stress and also can cope with stress. Instead of using all gadgets to simplify work and complete it is less time people should do work manually as far as practicable. I use mostly manual techniques of doing work and inspite of heavy pressure of work I enjoy my work mostly feel relaxed and cope with stress successfully.

Food habits should be changed. Habit of taking fast foods should also be changed. Simple type of food should be taken to keep the body fit and free from small and big illnesses. A life style which includes balanced food and low fat, low spices diet, taking food at regular times, exercise and continued physical activity is less vulnerable to stresses.

2. By having Optimistic and positive outlook towards life. Optimistic attitude and a general tendency to have a positive out look towards everything can reduce a lot of stress. It has been earlier discussed how optimistic people are less affected by stress because they know how to manage and control it. Instead of taking a stressful event too seriously, if it is taken lightly and rationalized as a normal occurrence of life and every body is subjected to it, the depth of the stress will definitely reduce. Optimistic persons emphasize positive aspects of any stressful events. A thief took away property and money worth one lakh. The owner said "Thank God he has not killed me. I'm saved. I'm not sorry for property. I'm happy my life was saved." This is a positive attitude to a negative stressor which helps in reducing or managing stress.

3. By using various successful defence mechanisms. To cope with a stressful situation people use various defence mechanisms like rationalization, sublimitation, withdrawal, regression, reaction formation, projection, etc. some of which are successful and others are unsuccessful. However one should only use successful defence mechanisms like sublimation and rationalization to cope with the stressful situation. But too much use of rationalization and sublimation is also not desirable.

4. By maintaining balance between ability, aspiration and achievement. Too much or too little aspiration leaves the person no where because too less aspiration makes the person in-active and too much aspiration produces frustration and stress, as the person is not able to reach the goal set for him. A balance between ability, aspiration and achievement can make the person balanced, self sufficient, reality oriented with very few frustrations in life. It frustrations are less obviously the effect of stress is less experienced. An actualized person has full satisfaction in life as he progresses keeping in view his abilities and aptitudes. A person has better stress tolerance capacity if his goal discrepancy score (G.D.S) is very small in various areas of work.

Time management is extremely necessary to prevent stress. Daily a priority list should be prepared about the works to be done keeping important ones on the top. By managing time properly and proper planning one can do a lot a work in a small period.

5. Hardiness. It is a personality character which reduces the adverse impact of stress. Hardiness is a personality trait characterized by commitment, challenge and control. These qualities resist stress strongly. It is also found that individuals having high degree of hardiness are less susceptible to various illnesses.

6. Detachment. Detachment means not outcome oriented. Detached persons do not show interest in property, wealth, name, fame, power prestige and recognition. Saints and Sadhus are detached persons and they experience less stress. It is said that wealth brings unhappiness. The more wealth you have, the more you are worried about their maintenance, investment etc. Detached persons do their work but donot wait for the outcome. So when they do not get a reward for which they were nominated, they don't feel unhappy or experience stress. This view is supported by studies which show that people who are less out come oriented experience less stress, less physical and mental strains. A detached wife goes to sleep immediately after going to bed, but it is not same with an aspirant husband having high goals and aspirations in life.

7. By reducing anxiety and tension. If the individual tries to have an anxiety free tension free life by planning his day to day work, finances and activities in a constructive and organized manner, he will experience less anxiety and less tension keeping other factors constant. Therefore the environment or field in which one lives must be planned accordingly so that he has to face few stressors and without anxiety and tension he can cope with the stressors in a constructive way.

8. By improving stress tolerance capacity. Everyone does not have stress tolerance capacity. Some react to stress negatively without coping with it, or tolerating it. The stress tolerance capacity is to be developed from the early childhood. Instead of immediate fulfillment of all wishes and desires, it may be delayed for a reasonable time so that the child can learn to wait or tolerate the frustration arising out of it. Through the process of socialization frustration tolerance is also developed. He may wait patiently for a delayed meal in the hotel or he may wait patiently in his car when there is traffic zam. He does not get upset if his play in interfered by his little brother. He is not very upset if he misses a bus, or having a promise broken, his girl friend not telephoning at the promised time or having to wait in a queue for a long time, if he has developed the capacity to tolerate stress. This develops gradually and by the time he reaches adulthood he has very little problem with minor or moderate stressors. In case of more serious stresses he is disturbed but he can still control himself. He does not withdraw, does not show tantrums of anger and rage or does not use unsuccessful defence mechanisms to cope with the stress. Inspite of the death of his wife he is able to carry on with his life. Though in this case his emotional reaction will be intense, he will nonetheless carry on his everyday activities and duties. He will not loose his sense of direction or his touch with reality which are the symptoms of mental disorganisation.

9. Ability to handle stress bravely (Fortitude). A well adjusted person bravely faces the stressful situation and also handles it in a normal manner. In order to cope with or manage the stress every person is required to endure it bravely and then to make plans to handle it effectively. Fortitude and courage are essential to overcome a stress.

On the otherhand a coward, fearful and over dependant person is not appreciated by anybody. He also may lack real power to face the challenge in times of stress.

10. Use of a substitute goal. When a person faces a stressful situation he has to examine it and find out what can be the possible solutions. Suppose a person got a notice from the income tax department on some problems about his tax payment. Instead of being panicked he must first try to consult his lawyer calmly. But instead of doing that if he is very scared thinking about what will happen to him, how much more he has to pay, whether he will be sent to police custody and so on and does not take any positive step, he cannot cope with the situation.

The person has to think of alternate goals, if one goal does not solve the problem. If he perceives that nothing can be done, then he may give up. Change of goal is therefore essential is case the original goal cannot be achieved. A person met an accident and his leg was amputed. But he tried to adopt himself for different types of work using a wooden leg. He was not disheartened but faced the crises bravely with an alternate goal. A well adjusted person should endure frustration bravely and make plans to handle it as effectively as possible.

11. Preparation for Stress. During bad periods when the possibility of disappointment is strong, one should prepare himself in advance to cope with the stressful situation, find alternate means to face it or accept it as the case may be. Such preparations make it easier to manage the stressful situation. If a stressful situation comes all of a sudden, the shock is more than when some one is aware of it and makes advance preparation as how to face it.

12. Familial and Social Support. When a person facing a stressful situation receives the support, sympathy and help of his family members, neighbours and society he successfully manages to cope with it without being reacting negatively which may produce bad impact on his health and psychological make up. Family members and society should come foreward to console a person whose wife or husband has died so that he can face the calamity bravely without generation of stress.

Similarly, during natural calamity like earth quake, super cyclone or Tsunami people from other places, countries and government should come foreward to help the affected persons by providing means of rehabilitation, food, shelter, medical help and psychological counselling. Man is a social organism. Hence he needs social support to meet the demands of any stressful situation.

13. By taking recourse to recreation, hobbies and relaxations. Stress can not be reduced by sitting at home and brooding. Mind can be diverted from stress by being engaged in various recreations like viewing the T.V., listening to music, attending various cultural programmes in which the person has interest, visiting places of interest and being engaged in relaxations. When a person is engaged in various hobbies like embroidery, knitting, writing, cooking and trying new recipes, reading story books, joining a club, his mind is relaxed and he is able to cope with the stress. Diversion is a very important technique of adequately coping with the stressful situation.

14. By laughing and being humourous. To-day man is more miserable than he was fifty years back. Despite being more prosperous or having better personal success, better standard of living man is not happy to-day. His life is backed by anxiety, tension and stress. Because of stress man sometimes overeats and becomes obese. Man laughs less to-day than he did four-five decades back. According to the evidence presented in the International Congress of Humour in Switzerland the average man laughs for 18 minute a day in 1950. But in the 1990's we laugh for only six minutes a day despite huge rise in standard of living. "We seem to have created to-day a society which puts such a high premium on performance and success that when people fail to reach these levels, they are possessed with a sense of shame and depression" said Dr. Michael Tritz, a German psychotherapist. He further said "People think, they have no reason to laugh, even at themselves during adversity". We are deeply dissatisfied despite being richer. The way we live rather than our genes induces in our bodies low levels of serotonin, the brain chemical for happiness. Money provides only superficial satisfaction and hence those who value money are less satisfied and have poor mental health.

The statistic on laughing time indirectly suggests how depressed and unhappy we are because of stressful situations around the world due to war, threat of war, natural calamities, economic depression, social disorganisation, violence, sexual and mental harassment etc. Every one probably does not know that laugh is a great medicine to relieve tension and anxiety and reduce stress from mind. So one should create environment and situations for himself as well as others for laughing which does not cost a paise.

15. By becoming assertive and confident. If more work is given to him, he should protest mildly instead of loosing his temper.

16. Level of adjustment. By improving one's level of adjustment stress can be controlled. One's level of adjustment depends upon the interaction between the severity of stress and the adjustive resources of the person. Low stress tolerance, immaturity, a distorted frame of reference, lack of competencies lowers the individual resources for dealing with stress and make him susceptible to stress. But sometimes a mature, stable personality may also be vulnerable to stress. When the stress appears to be too great for the adjustive capacity of the person, mental disorder occurs.

The individual is continuously faced with adjustive demands from the environment which place him under stress, and he persistently attempts to cope with stress. One should readjust his goal if he fails to reach the fixed goal. The person ofter readjustment must be sure about his ability and resources to reach the goal.

Besides the above effective measures of handling stress, below are discussed some stress management techniques.

Proper planning of day to day work in advance is very essential to complete work in time and avoid stress.

SOME STRESS MANAGEMENT TECHNIQUES

Evidences are there that stress has some influence on 50 to 70 per cent of the total physical illness like blood pressure, cardiac disease, ulcers, diabetes, migrane and tension headaches are highly related to stress. Besides for control of stress at individual levels and by simple methods some techniques of stress management have been developed.

1. Cognitive-Behavioural technique

Cognitive-behavioural techniques usually have three stages such as education, training and practice.

Education. In this stage the participants are made aware of the nature and effects of stress, recognizing their own stresses by knowing the symptoms of stress.

Training. Training provided to the participants enable them to learn time management, social skills, use of relaxation techniques, setting realistic goals. Positive self-talks are rewarding when the goal is achieved (reinforcement).

Practice. In the practice stage the participants relearn and reherse the skills learned through real life situations and training.

Sri Sri Ravisankar Jee, the internationally famous yoga specialist and spiritual Guru of millions of people around the world has started giving "The Art of Living" training to reduce stress. Art of Living technique is a great stress reducer as many people who have practiced it say. It provides good and simple procedures to reduce stress by controlling diet, style of living, and by performing regular exercises including breathing exercises.

Sudarshan Kriya

Experience and research show that Sudarshan Kriya is a very successful technique of managing stress. **Sudarshan Kriya** discovered by Spiritual Guru Sri Sri Ravi Shankar Jee helps control both physical and mental stress. This reduces the chances of high blood pressure, hypertension, diabetes, migrane headache, back pain, ulcer etc. according to objective study conducted by All India Institute of Medical Sciences (AIIMS). New Delhi and National Institute of Mental Health and Neuro Sciences (NIMHANS) Bangalore. This has been reported to the PTI by chief of the institute's rotary cancer hospital at AIIMS Dr. Vinod Kochupillai as per the report in New Indian Express dated 2.9.2004. Many people who have performed the Kriya have also told me that they have got immense benefit at the physical and psychological level.

To asses scientifically the effect of Sudarshan Kriya on people who work under stressful conditions a team of the institute studied two groups of policemen as they experience a lot of physical and mental stress while discharging their duties. One group (experimental group) was asked to perform the Kriya for six months while the other group (Control group) was asked not to follow breathing exercises. After six months both the groups were tasted for stress levels. It was noticed that stress level went down significantly in the group which performed Sudarshan Kriya while no change was observed in the control group which did not perform the Kriya.

Kochupillia thus held "The study suggests connections between body and the mind and implies that emotional state and thought processes affect brain, endocrine system and also the immune system." Besides, surveillance, cells of immune system that destroy tumour cells also increased significantly in the Kriya practitioners.

An EEG test administered on the people who practiced the Kriya for over six months to measure the activities of their brains indicated that they were more active than others even when relaxing reported Dr. Kochupillai.

Working women particularly Indian working women always work under stressful conditions as they have to manage office work as well as domestic work including child rearing and family care. Indian culture is such that even if a woman works outside, he has to take care of everything at home. While males just sit and relax after office work, a woman has to start working immediately after she returns from work or outside. In meeting both the ends she has to experience stress all the time. In my opinion working women should perform Sudarshan Kriya to cope with the stressful condition of the body and mind due to over work, hypertension and anxiety.

Biofeed back. Biofeed back is a procedure by which an external censor is used to provide a person with an indication of the state of a specific bodily process such as heart rate, blood pressure etc. These physiological aspects of stress are monitered and controlled through the process of bio feed back in collaboration with some learned methods like hypnosis, yoga and transdental meditation. By providing feedback or information about the biological functioning of the body, a person is trained to recognise and control it. We must think of the actions of the glands and internal organs concealed inside the body in the same way as we think of the actions of the muscles producing easily observable movement. Miller found that 75 per cent of the persons with muscle tension headaches and migrane headaches benefited from biofeed back technique.

The skill to control possible blood pressure and dangerous cardiac problems is an extremely valuable contribution of biofeed back technique.

Relaxation Techniques

Stress can be reduced to a considerable extent by relaxation as state of relaxation is opposed to stress. By reducing or minimizing muscle tension the feelings of anxiety and stress can be reduced. While writing this book I sit for six-eight hours daily. So I feel tension in the muscles of my arm, body and neck and experience stress because of pressure of continuous work. Thus I stop writing at 6 P.M. every day and then relax by lying down, viewing T.V. or reading magazines. I sleep at 11 P.M. and next morning when I get up I feel very relaxed and stress free. If I would not have relaxed and continued to write for another 3-4 hours in the evening I must have experienced severe stress with headache, anxiety, muscle pain etc.

In the relaxation technique usually relaxation starts from the lower part of the body and progresses up to the facial muscles as a result the whole body is relaxed and the person's stress is reduced. He is able to do his normal work without pressure and anxiety.

Exercise. Various exercises are emphasized to-day to reduce stress, anxiety and depression. Swimming, brisk walking, aerobic, performing various asanas, pranayam, cycling, skipping, dancing, going up and down the stairs, engaging mind in various types of work without sitting lazy, all help in reducing stress.

Even physical work at home help in reducing stress as one is engaged. Exercise and Dhyana (Meditation) should be done regularly to improve concentration, flexibility of mind and body, cardio-vascular fitness and above all **Stress tolerance.**

Laughter. Laughter is said to be the best stress reliever. Doctors say that regular laughter lead to good physical and mental health. In the to-day's world very few people get the opportunity to laugh and relax through it. According to the University of Nebraska website "laughter acts as a very powerful medicine to lower stress and dissolve anger." It is a great instrument which can manage and dissolve anger. Just like the saying one apple a day, keeps the doctor away", a hearty laugh everyday contributes to reducing the distressing process of the individual. Laughter not only is an expression of happiness and indicates the relaxing state of mind, it also exercises facial, throat and chest muscles, doctors claim.

According to medical men, the principle of Jacobsons Progressive Muscular Relaxation (JPMR) method can be applied to the process of laughter.

In the process of laughter muscles are artificially tightened and then relaxed to remove tension. In the method of relaxation psychiatrists and clinical psychologist use laughter to induce relaxation in the client. Now a days in many cities laughter clubs are opened to laugh and reduce anxiety and stress. When muscles are used to laugh anxiety is reduced in a retroactive manner (backward or reverse manner). In other words, the positive impulses travel in the reverse direction from the muscles to the brain, in contrast to the genuine laughter when the relaxation process starts in the brain itself.

Normal adults particularly old and ageds, senior citizens taxed by the existing life style and communication gap very often experience anxiety and stress. Laughter is a very good method to reduce these strains of life and bring relaxation. Therefore every individual should try to laugh regularly or produce circumstances where they along with others ought to laugh. Many people prefer to see humourous witty films to laugh generously. Pictures of Lauren and Hardy or Mehmood and Jony Walkar are examples. Others like to read witty and humourous books and magazines to laugh heartily. It is observed now a days there is increase in the purchase of such books and magazines.

Organisational Coping Techniques

Besides the above factors, people working in organizations, should also use specific coping strategies to cope with stress. They are discussed below :

1. By Proper Selection and Posting of Employees. Each person is physically and psychologically unique in character. So keeping in mind this individual difference proper tests and interviewed should be conducted for selecting employees for various jobs. Some people with 'A' type personality are usually more susceptible to stress and anxiety. So stressful jobs should not be allotted to such persons keeping in view the personality and attitudinal differences workers should be selected and placed. People having proneness to high stress should be placed in jobs producing low stress and the *vice versa*, so that production and work climate will not be affected.

2. By Redesigning jobs keeping in mind Human Engineering. The job should be redesigned, the materials and instruments should also be redesigned, keeping in view the limitations in the ability and capacities of employees. Instead of fitting the man to the job, the job should be fitted to man. Jobs should also be redesigned and planned in such a way that the work would be meaningful, interesting relaxing to the worker's and also they get more responsibility, more feed back and more independence. Through job redesigning and change of curriculum, more motivation can be provided to the workers. This would reduce stress and improve the quality as well as quantity of output.

3. By building group morale and team spirit. The employer should develop a work environment and organisational culture so that the employees would get pleasure in doing a work in group. Team work can also increase morale, better interpersonal relationship and reduce interpersonal conflict. They should give social support to each other instead of developing criticising and fault finding attitude. They should work as a member of the same family.

4. By having a balanced goal. The goal setting behaviour of each worker should be fixed as per his ability and achievement. It one fails in reaching the goal it may be refixed. If it is observed that the goal set is lower than ones capacity, it should also be refixed. Over estimation or under estimation of self and level of aspiration should be discouraged by the management. By setting proper goal production can be improved, motivation can be enhanced and there will be reduction in the frustration and stress of employees.

5. By improving communication between employees and employers. Gap in communication breeds misunderstanding, anxiety, and stress. Employees due to improper communication are totally confused about what they have to do and how they have to progress. So proper communication is to be improved to prevent stress.

6. Sharing the decision making process. Each employee even if he is a at low level, should be involved in the decision making process. By allowing them to participate in various decision making processes of the organization uncertainty of their goals is minimized, they feel great and their motivation is enhanced.

7. By improving physical fitness and mental health. Stress can be prevented by encouraging the workers to keep themselves physically and mentally fit. The management should allow and support them to take up various health measures. Play grounds, Swimming pools and gyms should be provided to improve their wellness. Orientation programmes, seminars and work shops should be conducted to create health awareness among the employees, so that stress can be reduced and the workers can cope with challenging situations. By developing various techniques of human resource managements also wellness of the employees can be ensured.

All the above discussed stress management programmes and strategies can be applied either individually or in combination with various of these techniques either to prevent or reduce stress.

Dynamics of Organisational Stress on terms of the Buffering Hypotheses

Several researches during the past 40 years have indicated a positive relationship between major negative or culturally undesirable life events and stress. Persons who experience such life events show psychological symptoms which are indication of stress. (Coates *et al.*, 1969, Brown 1970, Myers 1971, 1972, 1774, Dohrenwend and Dohrenwend-1974, Gensten *et al.*, 1974, Muller and associates 1977, Thoits 1981.) However desirable life events increase stress slightly. It is also seen that the relationship between number of life events and subsequent feeling of anxiety and distress is only moderate. It is further found that some people who experience many life events do not necessarily become distressed, while some others who experience few life events become highly distressed. Thus there may not be a high positive relationship between number of life events and amount to stress. This is determined by personality type and personality factors. From these facts follows the **Buffering Hypotheses.**

Buffering Hypotheses

Buffer means "moderate". Various investigators on the basic of their findings have hypothesized that the social system may help moderate or buffer the effects of life events upon his or her psychological state (Antonovsky-1974). This is called the Buffering Hypotheses. According to this hypotheses individuals with a strong social support system are better able to adjust with various important life changes and crisis and people with little or no social support may be more susceptible to show negative reactions and distress to life changes. Thus the buffering hypotheses emphasizes the tremendous impact of social support system on the behaviour of the individual by reducing or preventing the onset of stress behaviour. Social support simply refers to the encouragement and support that one gets from the members of the society like neighbourhood, friends, peers etc. in his various activities, sufferings etc. The support may be social, emotional, economic and religious. A person who wants to marry in a different religion unless gets support from persons in his social net work upon whom he relies, will not be able to cope with the situation and would experience stress.

It has been observed that the life events that occur in the presence of social support produces less stress than when the life events occur in the absence of social support.

The Buffer hypothesis thus puts special importance to the social support system on the prevention or management of stress. However, further research on this hypothesis should be carried out to reach at an acceptable conclusion.

Sabbaticals. Some sabbatical leaves encourage personal education and stress relief. By providing unpaid leave, L.T.C., earn leave and partially paid leaves, study leaves, the stress of the employees are reduced. On return from leave most of them are seen fresh, emotionally sound and feel their gratitude and gratefulness towards the management. The side of cross training on the colleagues during workshops and orientation course add to organisational flexibility, competancy and self-esteemed.

INEFFECTIVE WAYS OF HANDLING STRESS

While some people handle stress in a positive and effective manner other's make ineffective responses to stress.

1. Ineffective responses

Ineffective responses to stress lead to physical and mental illnesses which have been discussed earlier in this chapter as and when required. Many people fail to make appropriate responses to stressful stimulus due to their personality factors like introversion, lack of emotional intelligence, pessimism, inability to handle a situation tactfully etc.

Some of these ineffective responses are discussed below

***(a)* Ignoring the problem.** Some people think that they can face the stressful situation and overcome the stress by ignoring the problem which is not the correct procedure of handling a stressful situation.

***(b)* Giving up or withdrawing from the stressful situation** is another ineffective way of coping with the stressful experience. Some people with-draw without even trying to face it. A successful person gives up or withdraws only after trying all alternatives and when the goal seems unattainable he faces the situation boldly. But a timid, ineffective person with low self confidence withdraws and gives up without trying. Withdrawal behaviour never helps in reducing stress as stress relapses again and again.

***(c)* Expression of anger, hostility aggression and regression instead of confronting the problems.** Reacting to stress with anger, hostility and aggression never reduces it. These are all unsuccessful attempts to handle the stress. People having less emotional quiotient (EQ) handle stress in this manner. Such reactions instead of reducing stress aggravate it. A person who fails in the examination cries and cries for several days and does not take his food, is not engaged in any normal work, shows regressive behaviour. Instead of confronting the situation by preparing for the next examination he remains in side his room and broods and broods. This is a very ineffective behaviour to handle the stress arising out of failure in examination. This instead of helping to reduce stress aggravates it.

***(d)* Use of unsuccessful defence mechanisms.** When unsuccessful defence mechanisms like regression, aggression reaction formation, projection, introjection repression etc. are used to cope with the stress they do more harm than good. Successful defence mechanisms like rationalization and sublimation may be used sparingly as and when extremely required. Use of too much defence mechanisms make the ego weak and unstable.

(*e*) Handling the stressful situation without determination and courage, makes it more complicated. The person who feels weak and insecured without strength of mind to tackle a stressful situation proves to be ineffective to cope with it.

Finally it can be concluded that the ineffective ways of handlings stress are the opposite of effective ways of handling stress which have been discussed earlier.

Prolonged stress affects a person physically and psychologically.

Many day to day stresses arise out of pressure. Every person should therefore try to prevent the stressors as far as practicable through proper planning and tactful behaviour. However, those stresses which occur beyond one's control like sudden death of a close family member, accident, natural calamity, financial crises like loosing in the stock market should be faced and countered bravely with fortitude and courage. Instead of being panicked one should deal with all minor or major stresses of life with determination, courage and confidence that he can solve it.

He should realize that every one is subjected to stress in his life and therefore it is a common experience of life, which is sometimes inevitable. Therefore one should take it lightly in a relaxed manner without being very much concerned about it.

Some of the ineffective and problem centred coping behaviour of stress are summarized below :

1. Hiding poor examination performance from parents and relatives.
2. Finding fault with the teachers or a tution master for doing poorly in the examination and hence blaming them.
3. Eating a lot during examination.
4. Trying to escape or withdraw.
5. Using ego defensive mechanisms.
6. Rigidity and lack of compromise in behaviour.
7. Pessimistic and negative attitude.
8. Trying to meet daily hassles through negative behaviour and uncompromising attitude.
9. Lack of planning and preparation.
10. Erratic reaction to stress etc.

CONCLUSION

Besides the various techniques of stress management discussed earlier, discussed below some additional ways of coping with stress which can be extremely helpful for the common man. It is proved that though the negative impact of stress is slow, it never the less makes progressive damage to one's cardiovascular system as well as day to day life. The coronary arteries are gradually damaged due to a continuous life style leading to regular stress. Anger and intolerance are the best enemies of a person. Anger is like a fire that burns the person more than it burns others. By being tolerant and controlling one's anger one can cope positively with any stressful situation. It is always wiser to expect ungratefulness in people's behaviour and be ready to accept it without nursing a grievance. Stress is just like an explosive which should be diffused in time. Some common reactions to stress are expressed in increasing number of mistakes in work.

Frequent colds and infection, tension headaches, restlessness, anxiety, feeling of tiredness and lack of energy, sleep disturbance depression, loss of appetite, irritation, high blood pressure, and lack of interest in life are symptoms of stress. Therefore, it is high time that one should take care of his stress instead of taking it lightly.

Some people are by nature perfectionists and they cannot stand if anything goes wrong or if not done according to their instructions. So they get upset and irritated early. By this the biochemical equilibrium is affected. Due to stress and anger secretion from a number of hormones increases one's cholesterol and raises blood pressure. So one should not get upset on trival matters. He should overlook them considering the dangerous impact of anger and stress on health.

The environment of every person should be joyful. All people, young and old should do things that really bring them pleasure. New hobbies and interests should be created to keep one away from stress. Always something different should be done to make life valuable and meaningful. Hence depression should be avoided through various engagements like going to clubs, making now friendship, playing indoor and outdoor games. Particularly, those who have a fixed and rigid life everyday without any change get easily bored. Avoidance of dull life-style is essential to combat stress. This can be possible by inducting novelty to one's lifestyle.

One should also develop the habit to smile, laugh and enjoy every minute of his life without brooding over the past or anticipating future hazards in life. Attitude towards life should be positive and optimistic so that one can be protected from diseases as well as bring improvement in his quality of life. One should travel places, visit friends and relations, join picaics, parties, visit religious places like temples, mosques and churches to avoid stress.

Past events and errors, ingratitude of a friend or relation, criticism, insult etc. should not be taken seriously, but should be overlooked or taken lightly. It is no use to brood over matters and incidents which do more harm than good. Constructive attitude towards life can be developed by forgetting unpleasant incidents and forgiving people for their misdeeds. It is said that cropping over the split milk serves no useful purpose. To err is man and hence errors committed by oneself or others should not be taken seriously. Grumbling over trival matters should be avoided. Thank God for what you possess and don't have a longing for what you don't have or what you connot achieve. These are two simple ways of coping with stress.

Today. **counselling** also helps a lot in managing heavy stress. Trained counsellors may counsel employees. Friends, relatives and company physicians may also provide counselling to manage one's stress.

QUESTIONS

1. What is stress ? How is it related to mental and physical illness ?
2. Discuss about the nature, characteristics and process of stress.
3. Define stress and discuss its process.
4. Discuss in detail the causes of stress.
5. What is a stressor ? Discuss the various characteristics of stressors.
6. Discuss the various types of stress.
7. Examine the various sources of stress.

8. How stress affects physical and mental wellbeing and performance ?
9. What is stress management? How stress management is possible ?
10. Discuss the various techniques used to handle stress effectively.
11. Analyse the various organisational coping techniques of stress management.
12. Examine the dynamics of organisational stress in terms of the Buffering hypotheses.
13. Critically analyse the unsuccessful ways of handling stress. How this should be avoided ?

REFERENCES

Carneigie, D. How to stop worrying and start living Orient Paper Back. Delhi 1972.

Gupta, S. and Josi, R. Organisational Behaviour, Kalyani Publishers New Delhi.

Mayers, G.C. Managing Crisis, Unwin Paper Backs 2008.

Mishra, P.K. and Pattanayak, B. Organisational Behaviour in corporate sector psychological perspective and centre for good living, Cuttack 1995.

Mohanty, G.B. Text book of abnormal psychology, Business 1987. London, Kalyani Publishers, New Delhi, 2006.

Mohanty, G.B. Text book of Industrial psychology and organizational behaviour, Kalyani Publishers, New Delhi, 2006.

Warshal, J. Managing stress, Addison Wesley Publishing Company I.N.C., New York 1985.

29

Mental Health of Organisational Employees

INTRODUCTION

The classic Hawthorne experiments conducted in the Western Electric Company by Prof. Elton Mayo between 1924-27 indicate the importance of good interpersonal relationship and sound mental health of the workers. To be more particular, the specific study on 'personnel counselling' brought the idea of interpersonal relationship between the employees and the employers to light. It revealed that the mental health of the workers plays a prominent role in personal adjustment, adjustment with the work and management. The purpose of discussing mental health is to make the management aware of the importance of good mental health. Since mental health prevention is better than cure the employer should make cautious efforts to keep the mental health of the workers sound.

DEFINITION

Mental health refers to sound personality. Health normally refers to both physical health and mental health. Both go together and are dependable upon each other. Without good physical health, mental health cannot be sound and without sound mental health physical health cannot he good. So both are to be kept at the optimum level by taking care of both. By and large, mental health refers to the psychosocial well being of a person. Mental health can be defined as a state of emotional and psychological well being where a person is able to use all his psychological functionss like cognitive, emotional, learning, sensation, perceptual and remembering capabilities effectively in the society to meet the demands of day to day life.

Employees with good and judicious mental health have the capacity to cope and adapt to the stresses and strains arising from the environment where they live. They not only adjust well to the day to day life events, but also are willing to improve their own workability and conditions of the society. They can work effectively and productively with others in groups as well as individually. Their relationship with the coworkers and management, with the people coming in contact with them is by and large cordial and smooth. Persons with good mental health are a boon to the society. Because of their will to adjust and good socialization they get social support from their family, working groups, subordinates superiors and on the whole from all sections of the society. People with poor mental health experience anxiety, tension, identity crisis, ego centred thoughts, defiance, show disobedience, violent reactions, depression and day dream.

In short, mental health is an ability to adjust satisfactorily with the present and in all probability with the future. Therefore for the benefit of the organization or business enterprise the basic objective should be to select and recruit persons with sound mental health. Findings of various studies show that the mental health of the worker plays a paramount role in personal adjustment, adjustment with the work, work environment and management. During the Hawthorne experiments it was noticed for the first time that freedom from anxiety, stress and other psycho-neurotic symptoms, less emotion and more understanding etc. on the part of the first line supervisors who come with immediate contact of the employees and the workers are necessary for better employee-employer relationship and higher output. It was also suggested that mental health of the workers can be improved through personnel counselling programmes. That was the observation 85 years back. To-day when the mankind has already entered the twenty first century, at this cross road one finds organisational stress and mental illness, anxiety, conflict and worry of employees put undue pressure on the socio-psychological climate. Competition from various sources, also pollute the mental health of the industrial and organization employees and employers as well. There is experience of frequent anxiety and tension indicating poor mental health due to unhealthy competition.

Since any organization and industry, small or big employs men for managing it, every person so employed either as an executive or as a low level worker should have sound personality and proper mental health for smooth and effective management of the work allotted to him. Hence every applicant before selection and recruitment should go through proper psychological and personality tests so that persons with sound mental health can be selected and posted in various positions in organisations. This applies to all levels of employees, starting from the lowest to the highest level.

Sound mental health depends upon sound personality. When all the psychological processes of the individual like attention, perception, learning, remembering, thinking, reasoning, creativity and emotional intelligence etc. function in a normal manner he is able to adjust and cope with his environment. He meets the various demands of his life on his own quite successfully, and is said to have sound mental health. Such a person experiences reasonably less tension, less anxiety, less worry, less conflict, less stress and hence is able to resolve the emotional problems in a reasonable and balanced way. In short a person with sound mental health solves the various problems of life successfully. But a person who on the contrary fails to do so, is said to have an unsound personality and is affected frequently by stress, hypertension high blood pressure, depression and in worst cases various psycho somatic disorders. On the other hand discipline in work habit punctuality, dedication and adjustment are signs of good mental health.

At the time of initial recruitment one may pass successfully in mental health tests or may have a healthy personality, but subsequently due to lack of job satisfaction, continuous and constant familial problems, lack of job safety and job security, fear of termination, constant and continuous ill treatment and discrimination by others in work situation etc. may affect his mental health. Conditions of job, socio-environmental and psychological factors may also contribute significantly to the detorioration of mental health leading to high degree of stress and anxiety.

In view of the findings of various researches indicating that lack of sound mental health leads to more organisational stress and decrement in performance, the management should not only prevent the entry of candidates with unsound mental health but also it should try to improve the conditions of the work place including maintenance and continuance of the same. Because of the positive relationship between mental health and performance more and more researches are being conducted in this area to prevent organizational stress and lower production. It has been found from studies that job dissatisfaction breeds discontentment. So the employees prefer to withdraw and avoid their job. They avoid work through many pretentious like being irregular, remaining absent frequently without any genuine reason, coming late to work, loose interest in work (so the quality and quantity of out put suffer) fail to show dedication and motivations etc. Job dissatisfaction also produces conflict, frustration, anguish and frequent irritability. Such physical, behavioural and psychological symptoms due to poor mental health adversely affect the well being of the worker and reduce workability and out put level.

In modern industries and organisations, due to repetitive nature and specialization of work, work has become very monotonous. Since most part of the work is being done by machines and computers, the individual gets very little scope to utilize his brain and initiative. Application of mind is absent. In low level workers lowest level of skill is utilized. Their special qualities and creativeness their intrinsic interest, tact and initiative etc. are not utilized. Thus, sense of vacuum is created in them and they feel alienated from the job. Work to many appears as meaningless dull and unchallenging because of poor organisational culture. Particularly people with average or higher intelligence are unable to adjust with such type of work. A sense of boredom further creates in them unpleasant feeling and stress. They lead a poorly adjusted mental life showing undue anxiety, tension, hostility contempt, irritability and aggressiveness etc. which coworkers and people in the society do not appreciate. In any work situation, the work must be interesting, motivating and meaningful requiring tact, initiative intelligence and creatively, so that the person can have self actualization required for good mental health. The adverse mental health of such persons affect their relationship with family members, peers, close associates and friends. Similarly middle level and high level managers and executives also suffer from poor mental health and lack of decisiveness due to the above factors along with some other factors like competition and strong dedication to job. Those who like their job too much, are highly competitive, time bound, punctual, duty bound, result and action oriented and have by and large good mental health.

The foregoing discussions on mental health lead to one basic conclusion *i.e.,* lack of adjustment on the part of the low level, middle level and high level employees leads to the onset of poor mental health. Along with the work and job condition the personal, cultural and social values, traditions and morals, nature of work, the organisational climate, the supervisory role also play their part in the onset of poor mental health.

Since the Indian social conditions value system, culture, child rearing practices are different from that of the western countries one has to approach the causes of poor mental health from a slightly different angle as such factors also interfere their behaviour in organisations and industries. Adequate research in this area should be conducted in Indian organisations in stead of basing one's view on the findings of the western organisations alone.

CAUSES OF POOR MENTAL HEALTH

1. Poor quality of working life. Observations and suggestions of many researches indicate significant positive relationship between good quality of work life and good mental health. Suttle has observed that the poor quality of working life leads to poor mental health among workers. He suggests that by improving the quality of working life the mental health of the workers can be improved.

Improved quality of work life leads to more healthier, more satisfied and more productive employees. Consequently, production level and quality of out put in the organisation is improved and it is categorised under "Profit making organisation."

What is meant by quality of working life ? It briefly refers to objective of work, situational and environmental conditions in the organization where the person works, plus the objective experience of the worker related to such work. Obviously the mental health conditions under the quality of working life vary among the under developed, developing and developed countries. The quality of work should be such that it should be able to satisfy major personal needs of the worker through the job.

2. Work Alienation. While work alienation through the job leads to poor mental health, work involvement because of good quality of work leads to good mental health. Good work experience satisfies the important needs of the individual and hence works as a positive motivator or reinforces to work better. Kanungo (1979, 1981, 1982) has viewed the concept of work involvement and work alienation as opposite poles of the same phenomena.

3. Stress. Many western and Indian researchers have noted the relationship between stress, psychological symptoms and poor mental health. The psychological symptoms are by and large conflict, overload and ambiguity (Cooper Payne-1978). Panda conducted a study on Indian organization and noticed that mental overload works as a prominent factor in producing stress among industrial and organisational workers. By reducing stress mental health can be improved.

4. Lack of satisfaction of needs of the worker. The job with which one is engaged should fulfil his needs for better mental health. On the contrary, if it does not, poor mental health increases. The fundamental point to be noted by every employer and management is that with satisfaction of needs the degree of poor mental health due to on the job conditions is reduced. The work allotted to a person should be considered as pleasurable and interesting and not a burden. Once it is considered as a burden, there is internal as well as external resistance for doing the work and the mental health deteriorates which ultimately affects the quality and quantity or work. A child who loves to go the school, a worker who loves to do his work because of the satisfaction of his respective needs shows better mental health and better performance keeping other factors constant.

By selecting the right person for the right job and taking care of his work related needs, mental health can be improved.

5. Separation from the Group. Man is a social animal and is gregarious by nature. He loves to remain in groups and work in groups this a can be called a basic social need. But if the management some how feels that by segregating each worker from the other and his work separately production can be raised it is a false notion.

It is seen that quite a number of employers segregate their workers and ask them to work alone, thinking that they may gossip with each other and work would suffer. But this notion is wrong. It is seen an individual is able to perform better in a group than when alone because of the sense of competition, "we" feeling and togetherness.

6. Loneliness, Introversion and Day dreaming. These factors may aggravate poor mental health. When a person is lonely, many negative thoughts come to his mind. He broods over his past failures and faults, his under achievements and frustrations. He day dreams about his future with a feeling of inferiority and desperation. All these lead to mental stress and ultimately mental unhealthiness.

7. Stress. Stress is a major cause of mental distress and mental malfunction. Stress leads to depression, irritation, negative thoughts, alienation from environment. This has been discussed in detail under 'Stress' chapter earlier.

General physical health. Beside, the above causes general physical health or well being and whether a person is physically well or not influences mental health. When a person suffers from various illnesses minor or major, he reaches a state where inspite of everything like wealth, money, social and familial support, he feels very miserable. It is a fact that inspite of everything no body can take away his pain and discomfort. Physical illness has a very depressing effect on mental health. To cite one case, a person was well to do financially and had a good family support. But he was suffering from several diseases from an early age. The illness was continuous and pain was severe. He also had a guilty feeling for he thought that he was bothering his family members for his ill health. Thus, he went through a stage of severe depression and guilty feeling. One day he committed suicide. This is an example of mental disturbance due to ill health. Every student of psychology knows clearly that physical and mental health are highly correlated and interdependent. The wellness of one depends upon the wellness of the other.

8. Stress at work. As we know a person cannot live happily without some sort of work, whether it domestic work or office work, social work or work in the factory or organisation, every one needs to work. The work may be paid employment or unpaid employment, but there must be some kind of work to do as nobody can sit idle or else he will loose his balance and go mad. So work is very urgent for sound mental health. Work provides the worker a sense of purpose. It is a medium through which ambitions, aspirations, goals and interests are fulfilled. The self actualization motive of a person is only fulfilled through work and achievement.

But the next question is if the work is not interesting and meaningful to the worker, if the work environment is unsuitable, if the job is not up to the expectation of the employee, if there is over work and extra burden, if there is no recreation and relaxation there will be stress in the job. Stress is manifested physically, behaviourally and psychologically which is dangerous for sound mental balance of the employees.

During the working career of every individual if interpersonal relationship and relationship with coworkers is not congenial it causes stress which affects mental health. Similarly if there is no job satisfaction also mental health is affected.

9. Nature of Work. Nature of work is also a cause of poor mental health. To day because of specialization in work and need for mass production, so many machines are used to simplify the work and raise production level. So the work becomes repetitive and mechanical requiring low level of skill. The worker has not to use his potentiality. There is little opportunity to use ones genuineness and skill. Thus the work becomes dull and monotonous, without any intrinsic value. Because of specialization, a particular portion of the work is done by a group of workers. The final product is not seen by many of them. As a result they don't get the pleasure of manufacturing or seeing a finished product. Money or salary is the only motivation here and the work appears to be meaningless and this may have negative effect on mental health.

A study conducted in U.S.A which compared the mental health of car assembly workers with white collar workers found that the car assembly workers were much more poorly adjusted in their anxiery, tension, self esteem, hostility and morale compared to the white collar workers. The difference in the mental health of the two groups of workers was attributed to the significant difference in their nature of work. For the automobile workers, their work (only assembling the parts of the automobiles) was meaningless, boring and these factors deteriorated the mental health of the employees. Interestingly these effects on the mental health of the workers did spread to personal and family life also.

10. Low status in work. It has been observed that employees engaged in low status occupations suffer from poor mental health because of the job conditions. They do not get all the facility of higher status workers.

Resistance to change. Employees put strong resistance to change. Most of the change of any sort disturb the work equilibrium of the environment where people work, produces psychological disturbances and fear of something unknown and nonfamiliar.

Mental over load. In many people mental overload produces various mental disturbances.

11. Type of personality. It is found that high status employees like executives who have 'A' type personality, are highly motivated, very competitive, and strongly committed to their is job. They are result oriented, serious minded aggressive personalities who always feel the pressure to meet the dead line and also try their utmost to maintain the dead line. Such people are anxious type and are prone to poor mental health than an average person.

12. Physiological cause of poor Mental Health. Neuro science, a very recent development has helped in the area of neuro psychology. Neuro scientists have claimed that neuro developmental experiences received from one's environment and genetic programming jointly lead the brain to choose which connections to continue and which connections to destroy. If this is done accurately, the individual's physical and mental health grow normally without any problem or dysfunction and he reaches adulthood with all normal psycho-social functions. His personality becomes balanced and he is able to cope with the society like any other normal human being.

But due to faulty selection of neuro connection contrary to this happens and the person develops neuro developmental disorders like schizophrenia, becomes maladoptive and disorganised and cannot cope normally with happenings of day to day life thus indicating the signs of poor mental health. Early childhood experiences (favourable or unfavourable) influence the wiring of the brain and the connection in his nervous system. It the child gets loving, supportive and caring parents and caretakers, the synapses of the brain grow properly and the existing connection of the brain becomes stranger. But if the early stimulations are very few or negative in nature, the synapses will not grow properly and hence the brain will make fewer connections. Thus the neuro psychologists argue that there exists a close positive connection between early attachment and biogenic amine systems. It is also viewed that severe attachment problems with the caregiver shows negative impact on the mental life of the person. To name a few, he cannot manage his emotions, becomes hyper sensitive, may show schizophrenic symptoms and may also show other signs of poor mental health. Early stimulation determines how children will learn and interact with others in the society through out life. Thus, the positive and negative experiences of childhood influence the neuro transmitter of the brain and determines mental health. Recent research findings indicate that stressful experiences during childhood shape and influence negatively the development of brain by secreting hormone cortisol. High secretion of cortisol leads to the death of brain cells and reduces the connection between the cells in certain areas of the brain. On the contrary babies with strong positive emotional experiences and relationship with parents secret lower level cortisol in their brains which help in development of good mental health. So a negative, and unstimulating childhood environment plays a powerful negative role in the growth of mental health. Under these circumstances early childhood experience should be favourable for the development of good mental health during adulthood.

IMPROVEMENT OF MENTAL HEALTH

Because of poor mental health all the psychological functions of a person are affected. Inspite of sufficient intelligence, ability, skill and other acquired qualities a person with poor mental health cannot cope with the situation and adjust with the environment. So not only production hampers the person suffers from various adjustment and anxiety problems. He tries to avoid the job, withdraw from the work situation and hence remains absent from job as far as possible. In worst circumstances he goes on long leave or finally leaves the job. It is observed in a many situations people change from one job to another frequently because of these factors. They dislike their job, their colleges, their work environment and even their superiors.

Further, the workers engaged in various organisations and industries can not leave their personal problems with the security in the gate and enter in to the work place with a relaxed and free mind. The truth is that the employee goes there as a total person with all his personal, familial and socio cultural problems. Socio cultural background, academic qualification, training and post experience, attitude and temperament all taken together influence him while doing his job. It is impossible to segregate the effect of these factors on the employee.

Thus by promoting personal and social satisfaction of the employees, by proper planning, coordination and organisation of work, by preparing a priority list and time table for each day of work, by motivating employees to do better through various economical methods and time and motion study techniques workers can have better mental health and performance can improve.

Given below some suggestions to improve mental health of employees

1. Job Satisfaction. With job satisfaction there is less frustration and less unwanted antisocial, asocial or erratic behaviour. Production increases in quality and quantity. The workers like to continue in their job for a long period and frequent change of job is restricted. Absenteeism and turnover is also reduced. Observations further show that workers doing the same job for long long period without any change in the nature of work, are susceptible to mental breakdown because of monotony and boredom. Job dissatisfaction is very stressful to most of the employees since the job does not fulfil their needs, motives and interests. They in fact donot get pleasure from the work they do. On the contrary, a job of one's choice gives tremendous psychological satisfaction, pleasure and satisfaction in job keeps the mental health of a worker in balance keeping other factors constant. Hence all possible steps should be taken to ensure job satisfaction of the workers. The employees should not only be given proper pay and other financial benefits, but also steps should be taken to provide all social and psychological incentives. Involvement in job should be encouraged to provide sound mental health.

2. Reduction of overload of stress, anxiety and depression. Due to over work, under payment and stress caused by several personal, environment and on the job factors the mental health of workers deteriorates. Stress is a major cause of poor mental health. Particularly, work place stress is very harmful and produce various disturbances and disorganisations in the psychological functioning of the person. So over work, over load of stress, anxiety and depression should be minimised by providing, better facilities, better working conditions and better financial and nonfinancial incentives.

Besides regular paid job, one has to keep himself engaged in other self actualized work for relaxation and self satisfaction. The special and gifted qualities of a person are to be unfolded. He must be kept engaged in physical exercise, games and sports, painting, reading, singing, playing musical instrument, gardenings, fine arts, knitting and embroidery, and stitching etc,. By developing certain hobbies one can get enough relaxation which is extremely necessary to reduce monotony and boredom and improve one's mental health.

3. Involvement in group activities. The worker must make efforts to involve himself in group activities and joint performance as separation from a group leads to loneliness, introversion and day-dreaming which are ultimately not conducive for sound mental health. By engaging one self in group activities like worships, festivals, picnics, excursions, study tours, eating out with others, one can remove his loneliness, get chance for self satisfaction and ease his mental problems. Remaining in isolation and loneliness should be avoided and discouraged. As much as practicable, communication with others should be encouraged.

4. Interesting Jobs. The employees should be allowed to do such jobs which give them pleasure and happiness. They must be ego involved in the job if it is interesting to them. It an employee is pressurized to do certain jobs to which he is allergic, it would aggravate his mental problems. Slowly and gradually steps may be taken to condition him to such a work rather than putting sudden pressure on him to take up the work. A teacher who strongly dislikes to teach a particular branch of psychology or business administration or any other particular subject should not be pressurized or forced to teach the same without giving him time, and scope to adjust or change his attitude. He may also be provided counselling to remove the dislikeness towards a job which may be due to personal or social reasons and improve his mental health. Otherwise, his mental condition may deteriorate.

5. Updation of Knowledge and skill through orientation and training programmes. To adjust successfully with the changing circumstances inside and outside the work environment and change in the content or technique of doing work, the workers should be given enough scope to update his knowledge and skill. For this purpose regular special training and orientation programmes should be imparted to the needy workers so that they will not feel deficient develop inferiority complex and insecurity feeling. Provision for a good library with proper sitting arrangements, illumination and ventilation should be made so that the employees can update their knowledge and skill.

6. No overwork and enough scope for relaxation. The employees and various members in the organisation at all levels should not be overworked. Enough time should be provided for relaxation and fulfilment of hobbies. Inside the organisation as far as possible there should be club, swimming pool, small shoping complex, play ground and provision for indoor and outdoor games, so that they can utilize their rest periods in fulfilling their hobbies. By and large worker oriented attitude than work oriented attitude should be preferred to provide sound mental health to the workers.

7. Provision for Crecz and Baby sitting inside the work complex. Now a days even in India many married women are going for work outside. But they experience severe mental stress when they don't find any one with whom they can leave their babies and small children and work peacefully. Therefore, every organisation should provide as far possible creczs and baby sitters near the work place so that working women can leave their children there work peacefully in their respective organisations.

8. Patient listening of the problems of the employees. To reduce organisational and familial stress and provide sound mental health the boss or the first line supervisor should be a patient listener than a big talker. He should have deep insight in to the personal problems of all his employees, should know all personally well even by name and face. Face to face contact and direct interaction between the worker and the management is necessary to chanalize tension and anxiety in a healthy and adoptive manner.

9. Good Interpersonal relationship. Findings of the famous Howthorne studies interestingly indicated that good interpersonal relationship is condusive to good mental and physical health and high production. The interpersonal relationship among the workers, the first line supervisors and the management or top boss should always be cordial and healthy based on common motivation, trust, confidence and faith. Both the parties should interact with each other informally and regularly and share each other difficulties, problems handicaps. Each one should try to cooperate and sympathize with the other to solve various problems. In such circumstances, a worker oriented attitude and a democratic work culture can influence maximum production and also provide sound mental health and happiness to its workers.

10. Provision for Counsellor. Every organisation should have an employee counsellor who will not only study systematically the prominent stresses prevalent in the organisation but also would try to improve the mental health of the employees. The counsellor can help the mentally unhealthy employees to reduce stress by making them develop insight into their own problems. He can show the mirror on which the mentally unsound workers can reflect their emotional and personal problems. The counsellor can also help in the communication between the employee and the employer. By listening patiently and sympathetically to the problems of the workers, particularly of emotional and psychological nature, the counsellor can help them automatically solve many of their problems and cope better with the working conditions and work environment. By exchange of ideas things can improve a lot. The duty of the counsellor is also to advice the management to be more considerate, sympathetic and patient with the workers and their problems. Thus, the main objective of the counselling programme is to improve the mental health of the employees which ensures the growth of self confidence, understanding, cooperation and ability to give the best to the organisation.

11. Provision for Yoga, Meditation Pranayam, health clubs and other spiritual methods. Many current psychologists and proponents of Yoga, Pranayam, Meditation and other physical exercises suggest the same for reducing stress, anxiety, hypertension and improving mental health. Observations show that these health techniques have helped in elevating sound mental health.

Spiritual discourses generate a feeling of wellness influencing their value system and judgement. They change from egocentrism to socio centrism and their identity problems are also solved.

Spirituality not only generates discipline it also makes them selfishless, and cooperative. They learn to care for others as well as share others views and sacrifice for them. They develop a sense of commitment to others and make meaningful adjustments in life.

Therefore all types of physical exercises and spiritual thoughts improve mental health and psychosocial well being of the person. Now a days all organisations are aware of this and are taking steps to improve the mental health of their employees through Yoga, Pranayam, Health clubs and spiritual discourses like 'Prabachan'.

12. Sleep. For good mental health sound sleep is necessary. Seven to eight hours sleep is a must. One should go to bed early and rise early. He or she should not sleep in the day. Bath before sleep is required for sound sleep. Before going to bed one should relax and keep mind free from tension.

13. Stress Management Programmes. Various stress management programmes earlier discussed under the chapter stress and stress management should be under taken to improve mental health. Stress and mental health care negatively correlated. So to improve mental health and psycho-social physical well being stress management programmes should be introduced regularly, on or off the job conditions. Peace of mind and happiness in life being the crux of sound mental health, every possible steps should be taken by the employers and workers themselves to ensure their psycho-social physical well being.

Now a days it is found that in various business organisations and even in management campuses employees and students become acutely depressed for various reasons such as over work, over ambition, not being selected for various jobs in campus selections or in interviews, higher aspiration with lower performance etc. Business schools and various organisations are so busy with higher performance and higher standard of academic excellence that emotional health of their employees and students is completely neglected. They are so allured by the high-phi of their organisations that they rarely expect any ups and downs or plateau in their lives. They have to remember that the world outside does not always guarantee hope and success. Take the case of global economic slow down and recession. Many executives and employees of the corporate sector have committed suicide, attempted suicide or gone under depression due to this world wide. Many farmers in India committed suicide because of failure in production. So every one should be prepared for the worst. Everybody should remember that along with hope and success there is disappointment and failure. Otherwise they will breakdown showing poor mental balance. Every employee should be prepared for criticism along with praise. As this is not usually done they suffer from anxiety, depression and poor mental health. Now a days it is seen that there are many managers in their early 30-40's suffering from low self esteem, high anxiety, milder forms of depression and many other symptoms of poor mental health. All these conditions and traumas can be entirely avoided with good child care during childhood, congenial interpersonal relationship and concern of the management for the good mental health of its employees both at top, medium and lower levels.

Currently it is seen that every people working in organisations everyday come a cross the threat of pay cut and retrenchment due to global recession. But some are coming under severe stress and committing suicide while others having good mental health are able to adjust with the situation or coming under mild depression. How these traumas can be avoided ? It is viewed that if only business schools and organisations can allot 25-30 hours on emotional literacy and emotional intelligence, this can be avoided and mental health can be improved.

Business and management schools all teach theory on cognitive dissonance, hierarchy of needs, field theory, emotional intelligence, physiological, social and psychological needs. But they do not practically use it for their students and employees. At behavioural scientist must see that only theoretical knowledge will not improve sound mental health. They must know how to implement it in their real life. Academically excellent people may not always succeed in their emotional and social life. Their emotional health is far from satisfactory. Some institutes have now decided to introduce a 24 hour capsule on emotional intelligence. The curriculum includes knowledge of one's emotions, managing emotions, sympathy, social behaviour and the art of dealing with people and its application while dealing with them. They learn how to handle the various positive and negative emotions in themselves and also in others. They are taught many life skills like managing by heart, emotional integrity, patience and goodwill. They learn that life consists of ups and downs, success and failure and one has to live with it. They also learn that life is about making choices and accepting the consequences of those choices.

The cost of emotional illiteracy is vast and it has dangerous repercussions on the mental health of a person. Emotional illiteracy produces depression, loneliness, eating disorders, anxiety, drug abuse etc. Meditation, Yoga, practice of art of living are necessary to improve the mental health of people before and after they join work. Though development of sound mental health is a life long process, it is most important during childhood. So the various business organisations, management schools, industries and business schools should all be aware of this and also take steps to generate awareness among parents, teachers, the person himself and the society at large. It is to be kept in mind that however brilliant a person may be, however academically excellent he may be, but what is most important is his **emotional health**. Hence all possible steps should be taken right from the moment of birth till death to keep intact the psychological health of a person. Sound mental health is most essential for every person and it overrides all other personality factors of an individual. Hence managements should ensure sound mental health of each and every member of their organisation and take necessary steps to ensure this at all levels.

QUESTIONS

1. Indicate the relationship between mental health and productivity.
2. What is meant by mental health with special reference to organisational employees ? How mental health affects general well being of a person in the industrial context ?
3. Indicate the steps used to improve the mental health of the workers.
4. Write brief notes on the following :
   (*a*) Situational and genetic factors of poor mental health.
   (*b*) Relationship between frustrations and mental health.
   (*c*) Quality of work and mental health.
   (*d*) Job satisfaction and mental health.

REFERENCES

Gupta, S.K. and Joshi, R. Organisational Behaviour, Kalyani Publishers, New Delhi 2008.

Mishra, P.K. and Pattanayak, B. Organisation Behaviour in Corporate Sector Psychological perspectives centre for good living, Cuttack 1995.

Mohanty, G.B. Text Book of Industrial Psychology and Organisation Behaviour, Kalyani Publishers, New Delhi 2006.

Mohanty, G.B. Text Book of Abnormal Psychology, Kalyani Publishers, New Delhi 2006.

Mohanty, G.B. Health Psychology and well being of a person, U.G.C. Chief Guest lecture at K.K Women's College Balasore Orissa, Sept., 2007.

30

Career Planning and Career Counselling

MEANING AND INTRODUCTION

The word career derived from the French word "Carriere" literally means the 'road ahead'. In other words, the road through which an individual proceeds in his life's journey in relation to job and employment refers to career planning. But from the linguistic point of view a career refers to the confidence and competence that emerge out of socialization of one's personality when individuals assume new roles in the society. **Van Manner** and **Schein** brought in to lime light the concept of external and internal careers. According to them while internal career is a persons self concept, the external career reflects one's perception of the organisation. These two types of careers are essential to be developed. Career management practices have moved from an external perspective to an internal one. Internal career development is an organizational need for overall success of a person in his life. Idea of internal career is also necessary to plan career management.

CAREER ANCHOR

Career anchor is a concept developed by **Schein.** He coined the concept for assessing career orientation of individual. It is a break through in career research as it shifts the focus from external to internal careers of individuals. In simple terms, career anchor is a self belief of the a person about his talents and potentialities that have led to success in different types of work settings, with different needs and motives. It also refers to the attitudes and values that a person develops on the basis of his encounters with the work situation. Those employees who have established a career anchor in themselves will not compromise with their needs, values and motives. Different people develop different types of career anchors based on their experiences and encounters in life.

Different Types Career Anchors

1. Technical. People developing a technical or functional career anchoring give full attention to their craft and their main concern is to pay full attention to their work and special abilities. They give full attention to the area of their specialization that to generalized work.

2. Managerial. People with managerial anchoring try to go up and up the ladder without break and with zeal and interest. Their basic aim is to integrate the efforts of others, be accountable in all situations and in all responsibilities given to them along with the interest to coordinate the functions of different sections in an organisation. Such people prove very successful in managerial career. They prove to be good in management psychology.

3. Autonomous. People with autonomous career anchoring are independent minded and they do not normally compromise with their freedom and independence. They cannot work successfully in a career where they have to depend on others for intimation. They prove successful when they get a career at the top post where they can work without anybody's interference and take independent decisions. They usually work to free themselves from organizational rules and restrictions and develop a career in which they decide what, when and how to work.

4. Secure or stable. Individuals with a desire to stabilize their career through promotions and security are said to have developed a secure, and stable career anchoring. For this kind of people promotions are reinforcing and they are highly motivated by promotions and security in jobs. Their major concern is to stabilize their careers and so they hanker after jobs which have promotional facilities as well as security. They don't like temporary and unstable jobs even though they are highly rewarding financially. Some people it is seen while selecting a career have special preference for a government job with promotion facilities even though they are less paying than a job which gives high salary but is insecure and has less promotional facilities.

5. Entrepreneurial. People with this type of anchoring like to choose a career where there is scope for innovation even though there is risk. They like to start new ventures, and take up challenging jobs though there may be a risk. So they want to start new products and new services and like to join a career where such chances are available.

6. Dedicated. People who are dedicated, like to join a career which requires great social service and dedication to a cause. Their ideology is to work to help others in their life, to grow and prosper. People with this type of anchoring prove successful as social activities and social workers. They succeed in a career having scope for social work and work for the benefit of others in the society.

7 Challenge loving type. It is observed that a category of people are there who always like challenges. They welcome problems and get satisfaction in solving them. In this way they try to win their tough opponents. They like to face challenges and win. So they become successful when they take up a career where there is scope for challenges.

8. Status and prestige oriented with a strong desire for ego identity. Though every person loves to prove his own identity through power, prestige and recognition there are some individuals who are very status and prestige conscious. They have a higher ego. The identity oriented professionals through out their career are too much status and prestige conscious and give over weight to it. So when their status or prestige is affected they are likely to leave that career. Such people should they choose a career where self respect, prestige and dignity of the person are highly protected. It they get such a career they sustain there, otherwise they leave it.

Now a days, various career management organisations particularly various I.T. organisation and Business Schools are recognizing the importance of a proper career planning and selection from various specific angles.

(*i*) The traditional organizational or external career development system and the emerging internal or individual career development programme.

(*ii*) Keeping in view the various organizational realities faced in day to day work life currently, career development systems are becoming more flexible more pluralistic and more supportive of individuality *i.e* supporting the human resource development (HRD) factors along with less rigidity. Currently the various management training institutes in India and abroad are more keen to give training on career development keeping in view the **individual factors** than giving only generalized training.

(*iii*) To-day various new and innovative career planning programmes are being developed and imparted in various business and management institutes and organisations. But that is not sufficient. There is a greater need to explore various other novel career management practices to fulfil the diverse internal career anchors or internal qualities developed for a career building of employees of all categories in an organisation. Particularly the Indian Information Technology Organisations should be more careful to design the career management practices keeping an eye to cater to pluralistic career orientations of trainees and students. So far, the use of career anchors for career management practices has been very less in Indian I.T organisations. But that they are exploring this concept to plan and design innovative career management practices in their organisations is a good sign.

The **occupational self concept** of a person technically called **"career anchor"** should be used to understood the specific career needs of a particular I.T. professional; so that career planning for him can be most successful, employees can be retained in a job, production will be more and turnover will be less. A correct career anchor based on the needs, motives, aptitudes and ability plus experience of a person can enhance the psychological contact between a professional and his organisation and help adequately in their job satisfaction and obviously retention. The internal career which is different for different employees is perhaps more important to-day for proper career planning and hence should be given special attention.

Individual Differences in Career Planning

Taking in to consideration the concept of individual difference in ability, capacity and interests, special abilities, personality traits and internal and external career anchors, different individuals become suitable for different jobs and careers. Because of this each and every person cannot fit to each and every job. Only round pegs can fit to round holes and not to square holes. If a round peg is some how pushed in to a square hole a lot of human resources and man power etc. are lost everyday as there is neither the proper aptitude nor any job satisfaction for that type of job. The employee cannot perform efficiently and put his best inspite of his best efforts because he lacks the basic abilities or interest or both for performing that job.

It is to be noted that each individual has a unique personality with unique personality traits and each job has also some basic components which are different from other jobs. So all persons do not fit to all jobs. While making a career planning for any body for any job basic thing are required.

Steps Required for Career Planning

1. Proper job analysis. Each job has some basic components. So it is always desirable to work out components of various jobs through job analysis techniques. For selection of any type of career say teaching, medicine, engineering, clerical, administrative, social work, public relations, advertisement, computer science, scientist, research work, pilot, driving, tailoring, office management, hospitability, hospital administration, receptionist, travel agent, tourism, guide, counsellor, clinical psychologist, fashion technology, guide, vocational counsellor, manager, house management, nursing, home management, telephone operator, call centre, masion, skilled, semiskilled and unskilled operator, work in infrastructure sector, advertisement, Insurance sector, Banking sector, Public relations sector line man etc, job analysis is required.

2. Analysis of the personality of the individual for fitting in to a job. After working out the components of a particular job, the personality qualities of the applicants necessary for the job should also be found out through the application of various tests, physical and psychological and interviews. Vocational career planning and guidance demands that the selector or the psychologist engaged in career guidance must know about the qualities of the person and ingredients of the job and then relate each other before taking a decision on career guidance or selection. As already mentioned every job is unique and every person is also unique though people and jobs have similarities between themselves. People differ in their abilities, interests, level of aspiration, ambition, accountability, honesty, sincerity managerial, acting and administrative qualities, writing, singings temperament, and obviously mental health. So each person cannot be fitted to each and every job irrespective of his qualities. Hence administration of tests are essential to know career anchor and give proper planning and guidance for a career.

A person who proves very successful in one job may prove useless for another job because of these factors. A few years back I went to Rajasthan. While visiting a place of historical importance we had to engage a professional guide. But the guide while showing us the places was speaking so fast and without any clarity that we could not understand most of what he said. He narrated the incidents in such a manner that half of the words were inside his mouth. That day I felt that he is most unfit for the job of a guide. But if he would have faced proper career planning tests interviews and selection techniques including communication skill, probably he would not have got the license of a guide. First of all requirements of a job should be analysed and listed and persons should be fitted according to these requirements. Those who do not fit for a particular career should be completely eliminated and those who can fit after training and orientation should be advised to undertake career development programmes before joining a career. Planning and guidance of a career should not be made just looking at certificates or asking a few unrelated questions. It is understood that in western countries, particularly I know about U.S.A. where even masions and other skilled workers get license on the basis of scientific tests and interviews. Even Baby Seaters rampantly found in U.S.A. are selected for this career on the basis of their special aptitude like patience, understanding, anxiety free personality loving nature, caring attitude etc. These Baby Seaters are only given license after careful testing of the qualities of the person and requirements of the job of a baby seater. Others are rejected. In another case, a professional nurse was appointed to take care of an oldman aged 80 years, who was a paralytic. After she joined the assignment it was found that she was very harsh to the old man and even refused to give him bed pan for urinating and eliminating. One day when the old man urinated on the bed, she also refused to change the bed cover. The nurse was a divorcee and away from her only child who was with her ex-husband. She had a lot of frustration and was going under mild depression. She did not have good mental health also. Such a lady should not be appointed as a nurse because a nurse should be very patient, sympathetic, lovabable, soft spoken and dedicated having an aptitude for social service, caring and nursing. Such people cannot be retrained for a long time if they choose such a career as they are most unfit for nursing career without having the basic minimum qualities of a suitable nurse. Even in various nursing-homes and hospitals it is regularly alleged that nurses and doctors misbehave with the patients without obvious reason. Particularly the allegation is more about nurses. So the personality characteristics of the person intending to choose a career of nursing should properly match with the job content and requirements of nursing profession so that there will be no problem afterwards. Similarly, take the career of a politician. Every body cannot match to this profession. Those who cannot match are failures. The politicians should have proper communication nac, aptitude for social service, leadership, quick decision making power, honesty, dedication etc. so that they can retain this career for a long long period with success and satisfaction.

Similarly persons with eye for minute details, patience and artistic temperament do very well when they opt for a career of stitching, embroidery and cooking because these are fine arts. Cooking is also a fine arts as it requires a lot of artistic ability and patience to be a good cook.

Thus, before planning and giving advice for a career, the career counsellor should first work out the job components, then take the biodata of the applicant, and then administer general ability test, various individual and group tests required for job, various medical tests of vision, hearing, blood, urine, heart etc. (as per the requirement of the job). For example, jobs requiring fine coordination requires good vision and a person with defective eye sight cannot manage in such a career. A maid servant or an unskilled labourer who has severe leg or hand problem cannot do physical work. They both become unfit for such jobs and so should be discouraged to take up such jobs.

For some one wishing to go for a driving career, first the job components of driving are analysed which are basically visual acuity, balanced sensory motor coordination, judicious reaction time, no accident proneness, no movement sickness and good aptitude for travel and tour. If the person scores above the qualifying marks in these traits he is advised to take up the career of a driver. Particularly people with low visual acuity, very high or very low reaction time, proneness to accidents and imperfect sensory motor coordination are discouraged to take up the job a driver. Here in India, it is very easy to get a driving license compared to U.S.A. In many cases even it is found that driving license is issued without proper tests and investigations as a result the driver not only commits accidents but also may prove a failure as a driver. A person with travel sickness may suffer from sickness after driving a few kilometers and so may take leave.

Fortunately now a days, special aptitude tests are constructed to use in different jobs while choosing a career. In addition to tests like intelligence, personality, ability and attitude, special ability tests like clerical aptitude test, linguistic aptitude test, engineering aptitude test, english as a foreign language test, music and fine arts test, trade test, balance test, sensory motor coordination test, reaction time and many more tests are conducted before selection of a career. Similarly, youths lacking in abstract intelligence who score low in mechanical or mathematical aptitude test are not advised to join various branches of engineering. A college student wanted to be an architect. He went to U.S.A. to study architect, spent a lot of money for 2 years but could not complete the course as he failed miserably. He thus gave up his dream to be an architect which he and his parents nurtured and leaving that career joined english language class. The man power, human resources, time and money spent in studying architecture was wasted because of improper career selection. The person who failed in architecture was very bad in drawing, geometry and had no clear idea of space, form and figures. A lady who wants to be a dancer should score high in fine muscular coordination, symbolic gesture and interest for music and dance. Every person cannot be a good musician or a renowned dancer inspite of training and only those environment facilities who have these special qualities can succeed in the career of a dancer.

Selection for a career should be made on the basic of objective data or scores. There should not be any bias, subjectivism, erratic selection or favouritism of the career planner. But this guidance for the choice of a career should start from the secondary school stage. Late career planning does not help. Much wastage of man power, time and frustration can be avoided through proper planning, and cognizanee of career anchor. Decisions about choosing a career should not only be taken up early, it should also be based on aptitude (ability plus interest) and job prospects.

An incident comes to mind in this connection. A student wanted to opt for arts stream after his secondary education. But his father insisted him on joining the science stream as he wanted his son to be a doctor. Under parental pressure he joined the science stream, but some how managed to get a third division in plus two examination though he got first division in his school certificate examination. Then he could not get in either to medicine or engineering. So ultimately he joined arts stream to the utter displeasure of his parents. He topped the list in Psychology Hons examination in first class, did his post graduation and Ph.D. in psychology, joined as a lecturer and finally was elevated to the post of professor. This example shows ample evidence of how improper career choice leads to failure and frustration and how proper career choice leads to success, stabilization in profession, name and fame.

When a person does not fit in to a job because of lack of proper career choice he is dissatisfied from various angles and ultimately changes from one job to another in the shortest possible time. Because of lack of job satisfaction he looses confidence in self and his assertiveness, ego identity and self esteem etc. are lowered. There is identity crisis, failure in adjustment to work situation. Since he cannot cope with the job conditions or perform efficiently either be cause of lack of specific abilities required for the job or because of lack or interest, he gets disappointed. While selecting any career what is most importantly required is careful planning on the basis of tests of personality and abilities and right decision making. Suppose a man has got offer for three jobs at a time with more or less equal salary and similar fringe benefits. Now which job he has to choose for a career ? Here comes a psychologist in assisting him objectively to choose one of these three jobs. Keeping other factors constant, the job for which the person has best ability, interest and aptitude should be advised to accept. As a first step of advice to choose a career, the psychologist or vocational counsellor should ask the candidate for details of his biodata in an information sheet including his marks and grades in different subjects, his success and failure, his interest and hobbies, his likes and dislikes etc. A test of his mental health is also made. Through job analysis the qualities required for the jobs are ensured. Then various tests are administered on the candidate to trace whether the qualities required for these jobs are present in the candidate and if present to which degree on the basis of scoring. After the scoring is completed, the candidate is interviewed by a psychologist or a group of psychologist to acertain his interest and preference, his career anchor etc. After compiling and integrating the various scores obtained in tests, and interviews. the candidate is finally advised which job is most suitable for him to join in order of preference and why.

INGREDIENTS OF CAREER PLANNING

1. Utilization of holidays for career planning. Children in schools get ample holidays particularly Christian holidays and summer holidays. Most of the parents do not often plan how their children would spend these holidays. Now a days most of the parents leave their children to see T.V. or play at home or do some home work. But they rarely think of utilizing these long vacations for preparing the career of their children.

But some wise parents do utilize these holidays for career planning. Summer and winter holidays are probation periods for practicing for a career ahead. Preparation for entrance examinations, attending coaching classes, summer camps, computer training, orientation courses and even advance classes for forth coming public examinations, mental health programmes like attending Yoga, art of living and pranayam classes, playing games and joining athletics etc. help in career planning. They plan the entire holiday where their wards not only get relaxation and enjoyment, but also prepare them selves for a future career directly or indirectly.

Now a days it is observed that even without any major competitive event most of the parents want their children to do something useful for their future career. But when some parents due to some reason or other do not send their wards for any of these summer or winter programmes, they are not appreciated by others in the neighbourhood who send their children to these camps. Now a days many summer camps on different areas of career are rampant in big cities of India without any obvious planning and proper objective. They forget that the objectives should match to the needs of the students and should also be linked to one's life's skill or career growth. When parents put their wards in various institutes during vacation not out of concern for their career building but to get rid of them, it is also dangerous for the child's mental health. The parents have to spend sometime with their children during holidays and show love and affection to them which help in sound mental growth along with career development.

Secondly, parents should carefully scrutinize the institutes and orientation centres before sending their wards there because as it is seen to day many commercial minded people open fake institutes or institutes without proper infrastructure or staff just to grab money from parents. This makes more harm to them than gain. It is also to be examined whether the summer course is relevant for the child's personality development or career building. Parents should not out source their parental responsibility by getting their children admitted to summer schools merely as a status symbol or to get rid of them.

Parental concern for their children's career is well understood. But over reaction and excessive concern is unadvisable as it produces anxiety in them and certainly parental anxiety is dangerous for sound mental health of a child as it in may ruin their as well as their children's happiness and mental functioning. It will pull down the confidence and identity level of both of them. As a consequence, negative communication between parents and their children starts harming both. Parents start blaming and ridiculing the child for his slightest mistakes because of their anxiety and stress. Their good for nothing angry reactions towards the child only reflect their own poor mental state. Further unhealthy comparison of the child with his class mates or siblings because of poor performance or the like poses dangers for the child's mental health.

If we do that, the child will also start comparing the parents with one another like "Mama is better than Papa" or such and such neighbours next door or relatives are better than his papa. How will the parents feel then ? Won't they get angry ? Won't they feel bad ? An ward may be excellent in studies and has good academic career, but if his mental health is not sound and if he cannot cope with his working conditions or senior officers it is of no use. I know several cases where brilliant students fail to build a good career and survive in a job because of these negative factors. They shift from job to job and finally sit at home without a career and became a burden on the family and ultimately society. The need to be fit, strong and flexible, to survive is well understood, but that is not all. Along with it psychological and physical well being is essential.

2. Role of Parents. The children should also be taught various health well being techniques like art of living and Yoga etc., to negate the effect of unsound conditions on the personality of the child. Children should not be spoon fed regarding their career. They should also be allowed to choose what career they want, but the final selection of a career for them should be based on the scores of tests, questionnaires and interviews. Parents and teachers should therefore respect their choices. If a boy is saying that he would like to go for computer engineering, let for the parents also consider his views objectively. By that his self confidence would increase. Instead of limiting their choices students should be given the confidence that they can achieve in whatever field they go. Thus the parental **mind set** is very important in the career building of the student. Information is very essential for career provided enough scope is provided to get all types of information to widen his knowledge and broaden his out look. **Information provides Knowledge** and **knowledge is power.** So Internet and books are very useful sources of information regarding career search. Networking with professionals also do help in this regard.

Always parents and teachers should be a positive role model to the child. The best method to make one's child successful in his career is to be a powerful role model in his profession with sound ethics, personality success and style. The child imitates the parents most. So they should first introspect themselves before imposing on the child their views and aspirations about a child's career. My father wanted me to be a doctor and so I offered mathematics optional in matriculation on his advice. But I did not want to go for medical career. So I gave up mathematic optional after test examination and took another optional, subject of course without the knowledge of my father. When my mark sheet came he know this and got terribly angry, but there was no way out. Then he asked me to go for science stream. But I was able to impress him that I can do better in arts and he agreed. When I passed my B.A. Hons. examination in first class topping the list in the university, he suggested me to go for civil service. But I liked the teaching line and joined as a teacher. I liked my job, and I also proved very successful. When by chance I become an educational administer in various top level posts for long 13 years. I also liked administration as it was very very challenging. My name was recommended for I.A.S. of course I did not get it and that is another issue. The purpose of citing this example is two fold. Let the readers know that a person can be successful in more than one career if there is dedication, commitment, honesty and sincerity. Hard work with aptitude for a career pays best. Secondly, parents should honour the view of their children regarding choice of career just as my father did.

3. Information on career planning from different sources. It has already been mentioned earlier that information provides knowledge which is essential for choosing a career. Besides getting information from internet, books, journals and news papers one should also obtain detailed information regarding a career from different institutes providing training on career building and also from institute of vocational guidance and counselling which operates in many states of India and abroad. More specifically, arranging an interview with some one in the industry or institute dealing with career planning is also an effective method of getting information. This interview will help one to explore various careers and clarify various questions regarding different careers as well as can give the most up to date career information.

4. Experience. During vacations a person can join some institutes or organisation for a few days or months in a part time basis to gain first hand experience. It may be paid or unpaid, does not matter. In western countries this method of gaining first hand experience before choosing a career is rampantly observed. Particularly in jobs where you are interested you can choose to work temporarily to get an experience of the real work life nature of the job and the specific skills required in the job. Candidates should also join career fairs, group discussions and workshops on career development.

5. Career fairs and group discussions. Now a days various organisation are arranging career fairs in big cities in every state. They also conduct talks on career trends. Even in various coaching institutes currently, lectures and discussions on various careers like M.B.A, Medicine, Hospitality, Travel and tourism, Hotel management etc. are arranged on nominal fees. Students and career seekers should visit such places so that they can get an insight into career opportunities. Even various career clubs are coming up in different urban areas where talks and group discussions are arranged for career youths for career search. Eminent and experienced career planners, vocational guidance experts and management gurus come to address the participants and answer their queries.

6. Creation of career goals. With the slightest opportunities scope should be generated for career goals. We usually start thinking of a career after we pass high school certificate examination. But no one should think of a career much early. He should plan from the middle school standard. By knowledge of one's own abilities and interests plus understanding of the career options *i.e.,* different types of career he can go for, will enable one to pinpoint and fix at the careers that are most suited to one's aptitudes, interests and personality types. Initially a student should decide whether he would go for arts, science or commerce stream. Then after passing the plus two examination, he may decide which career, he has to opt of course on the basic of his abilities and interests. Further those who want to study medicine, para medicine and genetics they may opt for biology. Those who want to go far engineering, electronics, tele-communication, I.T. etc., they may opt for math and physics. Those who wish to opt for Chartered Accountancy, business management and business administration, banking and insurance sector, or business should go for commerce. Besides students opting for journalism as a career may consider doing graduation in Mass communication. Then later on if one wishes, he can change from print media to television.

7. Academic achievement. To go for a good and much sought after career having many many future prospects one has to do well in examination although it is not the primary factor in determining the aspirant's success. Your examination grade or score is a basic factor considered by the organisation or institute where you want to pursue your career. It is one of the (though not the only one now a days) objective indications of a student's ability to learn and perform effectively. Hence good performance at the under graduation, graduation and post graduation level is essential. The academic performances along with other performance helps one to enter in to a career.

Different Types of Careers Most Sought After to Day

With the outstanding development in science and technology and globalization phenomenon various types of careers are coming to focus to-day. Fifty years back there was limited scope for opting for varieties of careers. But now the picture is very very different. To-day so many career options are coming up that one is confused to select a particular carrier.

Described below some of the most sought after careers having better future prospects.

Besides the earlier described ones a few important areas of modern career are : Genetic engineering, Biotechnology, Information technology, Computer application, Mass communication, Architecture, Space science, Oceason graphy, Marine engineering, Hospitality administration, Hotel management, Travel and Tourism, Accountancy, Insurance and Banking, Journalism, Human Resource Development, Marketing Event Management, Design, Company Secretaryship, Law, Legal advisor, Clinical psychology, Psychiatry, Neuro Psychology, Organizational behaviour, Fashion Technology Manager and Supervisor, Finance, Civil service, Software engineering administration, Consultancy, Leadership, Infrastructure sector, Builder, Contractor, Politics, Policing and Law and Order managers, Media Advertising.

Languages. We will discuss here the last three careers in detail as they are recently developed and very much in demand.

Media. Freelance journalism, be it feature writing or news reporting is a very lucrative career for who have flair for writing and keen interest in current affairs. Content development opportunities exist in online media. News papers are also in demand in electronic medias like television and radio.

Even without a background in Mass Communication one can do diploma in journalism offered through in full time, part time and distant learning training and that can serve the purpose of preparing one for freelance journalism. Also short term training programmes are periodically offered by Indian Institute of Mass Communication New Delhi and various other institutes of Mass Communication. The Bharatiya Vidya Bhavan offers a part time diploma for one year in journalism in several big cities of India. Reputed Distant Learning Programmes include those offered by Symbiosis Institute of Mass Communication and Journalism, Pune and IGNOU, New Delhi.

Television and film are challenging areas of work that offer several diverse job openings. There are several television and film institutes in India which offer training on pre producer and producer, researchers in film production, script writers, Directors, Set designers, make up artists, costume designers, dubbing artists etc.

ADVERTISING AND EVENT MANAGEMENT

This is quite a recent area which youths now a days are giving priority as a career. Those with academic backgrounds in Mass communication, graphic design, English literature and journalism can choose a career of running small or moderate advertising services for local business. Basically such a career would include design, printing and distribution of advertising, advertisement campaigns for clients. There are various advertising clubs in India which periodically conduct part time training programmes.

Freelance event managers are very much in demand today. Birth day parties, wedding receptions, marriage anniversary parties, launching of new books, fashion shows and various other function of this type are planned and organized by event managers for individual and corporate clients.

Languages. A career in languages is now very much in demand. Earlier a language graduate or post-graduate was only teaching in a school or college. But due to globalization the scope of language as various careers is increasing day by day. From translation to online journalism a variety of alluring careers are available for those with language degree. These include

1. Foreign language teaching at language institutes/schools or for various clients like film stars, cricket players and corporate clients.
2. English language teaching for students, corporate clients or any other person who wants to go abroad and needs specialized knowledge in language.
3. Career in other languages like French, German, Russian, are also in demand to-day.
4. Designing educational materials such as books and educational CDs for language teaching.
5. General technical and library translation and interpreters in various language for embassies. With the increase in foreign tourists more and more interpreters and freelance language teachers are in demand either part time or full time.

Factors Helping in the Choice of a Career

What are the requirements of a job ? How the right job or right career is selected ? These questions perturb many who want to extract the best from every student or employee who chooses a career. Along with performance they are also interested to keep themselves happy and joyful with lots of job satisfaction. Interest in a job is sustained if the qualities of a person match with the job components. This can be possible through the application of various standardized tests and inventories on the person applying for a job. Mere written tests and interviews or both including academic career do not always select the best worker. Use of various ability and aptitude tests standardized in the country where the test is administered helps in right choice of a career in life. Psychological identification with work and job involvement lead to stability in job. Job involvement is related to personal characteristics, situational characteristics and work out comes. The situational variables appear to have greater effect on the attitudes of the low job involved persons than of high job involved persons. Psychologists view that the tentative profile of a job involved person is that he is a believer of work ethics, has internal locus of control has strong growth needs, has a stimulating job which provided high autonomy, decision making power, variety and feed back, etc. He participates in decisions affecting him, has a history of success, is satisfied with the job, and because of all these factors, he is less likely to leave the organisation. To achieve all these proper career planning and proper selection by a psychologist is essential.

Certain jobs require more than average practical intelligence. Some other jobs require more of emotional intelligence where one has to handle the public daily like jobs in banks, post offices advertising agencies. Sales assistants, people working in life insurance agents, receptionist, call centre employees, telephone operators and many more such jobs also require better emotional intelligence.

Similarly, concentration is essential for the job of a pilot or even a driver on the road. Frequent fluctuation of attention of a person will not wake him suitable for such jobs. Suitable people can be selected through the application of tests designed to assess different necessary qualities.

Various paper pencil tests, advertisement and aptitude tests, performance tests, speed and power tests, tests of proficiency, comprehension, temperament and character, personality, interest and creativity are applied before the choice of a career. All these tests are conducted by a trained psychologist starting from construction, standardization, administration and evaluation test of results and finally on providing counselling on the basis of test scores. The role of a psychologist is therefore of utmost importance in the choice of a career. Half hazard application of tests, and wrong observation by the untrained psychologists lead to many biases and errors in selection for which there is tremendous loss of human resources and national wealth. In addition to these, mental health problems like frustration, anxiety, stress and hypertension produce many adjustment problems leading the work place to be most unsatisfactory for the employees. For right choice of a career, the candidates have to take the help of psychological counsellors. In school also there should be a career or vocational counsellor for a group of schools or group of colleges in a particular locality or area. The counsellor gives right guidance to the students both in choosing the subjects of their study and career.

Requirement of a field or a job

Before guiding a person to choose a career the requirements of a particular job is to be analysed point by point. For instance to choose the career of a doctor one has to pass Plus Two with biology then pass MBBS and then do house surgeonship. While studying MBBS one has to discest dead bodies or postmortem them, give injections and assist in various operations in practical classes. While studying M.B.B.S one has to remember a lot of names and contents. Since the course is very heavy and quite lengthy one has to have patience and he also he has to take a lot of strain. Many students jump at the idea of pursuing a career as a doctor. But those who are scared of dead bodies, blood injection and cannot stand the right of broken legs, human suffering crying and operation should not join this career. The strain of doing an operation is very high. Heart and neurosurgery operations take long hours.

Though about 4-5 decades back no body was aware of various tests for selection of a career, now every one is aware of it. Unless tests are conducted one cannot know his hidden qualities and potentialities. Potentialities are to be brought to the lime light by tests and developed by suitable facilities provided by the environment. Today guardians have become more conscious and application of tests for the selection of a career has become most indispensable. Those parents who are ignorant or such tests do not use this opportunity. Unfortunately in many states of India no such facilities are available. The directorate of school and college education should take steps to provide such opportunities. In western and some Asian countries appointment of school psychologists and vocational counsellors is compulsory. We in India should at least have one vocational-cum-career counsellor in one locality or district to guide the students in the proper choice of a career so that a lot of wastage, mental torture, inefficiency and stress can be eliminated.

Job Analysis

It is always desirable to work out components of various jobs particularly of jobs which are commonly selected like teaching, engineering, medicine, clerical, administrative, social work, public relations, advertisement, computer science, research work, pilots, driving, tailoring, office management, hospitability, receptionist and guided, hotel management, human resource management, first line, second line and third line supervisors, managers Chief Executives of companies, space scientists etc. Similarly there are various branches under engineering like electrical, mechanical civil, electronics, computer application, construction, marine, automobile, textile, architecture, etc, which require specific skills, qualities and abilities. Each of these jobs should also be specifically analysed and job components worked out. Thus requirements of each type of job should be listed and persons should be matched according to the requirement. Those who do not match to a particular job should be eliminated.

Matching Individuals with jobs

After finalizing the components of each job which is called job analysis individuals who match to the components of a job are selected for that job. While through job analysis job characteristics can be known, through application of psychological tests, the characteristics of the person is traced. Then the two are matched. If matching is hundred per cent which is rarely observed in real field the person is best suited for the job. In order to avoid square pegs is round holes job analysis is essential. Job analysis can be regarded as the foundation upon which a system of efficiency is built. Job analysis also gives information about personnel, administration work design and administrative control etc. Before applying tests and questionnaires on the candidate, job analysis is essential. Mere application of psychological tests without job analysis will lead to failure. Through observation and interview the observer or psychologist collects data on job description right on the job. Also through questionnaire, work dairies, moving pictures etc. components of job can be collected. Through job psycho-group job components are collected (see job analysis chapter).

Scientific Ways to Choose a Career

Even to-day inspite of so much talk about the option to select one's own career, most of the parents impose their wish on their wards in choosing a career. Besides the candidate at this stage is going through a transitional period. He has not that self confidence to take a decision on his career. So he also depends upon others like parents and teachers or well wishers. Under these circumstances, without the use of proper career assessment techniques, he is sometimes fitted in a wrong place. Sometimes it is seen that the father could not be a doctor, so he wants his son to be a doctor. So sometimes parents want their children to become, what they could not be came. They try to realize their dreams through their children.

But for choosing a career same body's advice or emotional desire is not enough. The career choosen by any one should be based on one's personality, academic achievement, background, childhood interests, likes, and dislikes aptitude, skill, special abilities and strengths. Not only strength, but also weaknesses and dislikes stand on the way of a particular career even if one is able to manage it effectively.

For the above, many tools have been developed which help one in choosing the right career. Each person has a unique personality and no two personalities are ever equal. So career assessment tests help one to identify personal traits that match up with skills and competancy for various areas of work. One's talents, abilities, skills, values, likes and dislikes, emotional life, experiences are all measured to limit the choices to a career that fits with one's life style, interest and personality make up. For example a person with 'A' type personality who likes to work and has hypertension when he is under worked cannot survive happily in a job which offers less work and less facilities to take a decision. Results of assessment tests work as a feedback and provide in- put which give one an opportunity to explore a career that one will enjoy and find highly motivating and personally reinforcing.

Career Assessment Tools

Various career assessment tools are constructed to determine the suitability of an aspirant for a particular career. These tools consist of a series of questions which are asked to the candidate.

On the basis of his answers the career assessment psychologists help one to

(*i*) Clarify one's interests and aptitudes.

(*ii*) To match one's skills and competency to a couple on specific fields.

(*iii*) To identify one's strong points, weaknesses and work style.

(*iv*) To determine whether one likes public contact jobs, analytical jobs, or hand on jobs, etc.

(*v*) To indicate jobs which can lower or higher one's stress.

(*vi*) To select a job that his education can help to perform.

(*vii*) Besides, various personality, intelligence, aptitude, special ability, physical and psychological tests should also be conducted depending upon the need of a job.

After the career assessment tests are conducted and a particular or a couple of careers are identified for the person concerned, one can explore and investigate jobs in each field. Instead of giving generalize conclusions about choosing certain careers one can select same specific jobs which can give job satisfaction. One's career search should include the following :

(*a*) Job descriptions to learn required skills.

(*b*) Identifying education paths.

(*c*) Talking with experts and taking their advice after certain fields or careers are selected.

(*d*) Learning about related jobs.

(*e*) Reviewing compensation, challenges and opportunities.

(*f*) Learning about the plus and minus points, positive and negative aspects of the career or jobs selected.

(*g*) Analysing whether the job qualities match with your interest, aptitude and skill.

What are the advantages of assessment test ? By taking the assessment test not only time is saved, one can also focus at specific points required for the career. The findings of the career assessment tests and one's subsequent investigation about job opportunities about a selected career well help in performing the job better. When one's personality qualities, skills and interests match with what the employer wants you become successful, there is stability and satisfaction in the job. Thus, testing is a very sensible part of one's personal career development plan.

Other determinants of choice of a Career

To-day the youth is confused and illusioned by so many jobs and careers present in his environment and is baffled as to which one he has to select. Is it true that choices they make to-day will have a major impact on their future career. Every child or adolescence should begin a career planning when he enters the high school standard and each student must familiarize himself with the process of career planning as early as possible latest by class X.

Late career planning is not fruitful. The students should be made aware of different types of carrer options available to them or their qualification. Students should be encouraged to develop their self concept and self confidence in proper perspective. They should know their abilities and develop aspirations to match their abilities. Too much ambition without ability leads to frustration. A boy of class X who always secures C grade in school examination if aspires for a career in Indian civil service, he will experience frustration and misery because he may not be able to make it. Hence every one must introspect and try to analyse his qualities scientifically without basis and prejudice. In order to know one's qualities accurately, one has to take the help of a vocational guidance officer or a psychologist who can give correct information on him after conduction of appropriate tests and help him to see what he actually has. He can only show the mirror to the student to explore himself. His trend of performance in the class also helps him to have an idea about his knowledge, power and talents.

Career Counselling

One's career choice can make or break one's future. Therefore instead of choosing a career hastily, one should spend enough time choosing the right career that matches one's skills and interests.

It is well evident that our careers are central to our life and determine our success or failure in life. To some choosing a career and joining it indicates a complete change in life style as they leave home, home land and even the country to pursue a career.

Choice of a career should be used for one's own advantage. When you take up a new career in a new place leaving your home, you have to make some new arrangements and adjustments in yours style of life. Try to learn more and more about the organisation (you have joined recently) its policies, employees and socio-cultural differences. Try to develop interest in work, mix with coworkers. If you keep your interest alive half of the problem is solved. Different jobs require different levels of expertise, competency and challenges. Try to achieve all these to make your employee and yourself happy in the job.

Always keeping in mind about your goal. By giving yourself a goal you make a permanent commitment to yourself. Through ups and downs, encouragements and failures whatever may be, the situation, always try to achieve your final goal.

To achieve success in a career one has to be hardworking, sincere, effective, efficient, sociable determined, competent, and above all honest. Nothing should come between duty and achievement because achievement is the final goal. One has to interact with like minded people with positive attitude who will encourage as well as challenge you. Healthy competition is a stimulation one needs to proceed to wards goal. Be honest, and work for the best of the organisation where you are working and you will get best in return, you will also be appreciated. Your efforts will be rewarded materially and non-materially. Be punctual and make maximum use of your time. The time that passes will never come back. Keep a happy balance between your work and your life. Your work should not clash with your personal life under any circumstances. Get some relaxation from work. Don't overwork and get stress. Plan your work in such a way that you enjoy the work and don't have pressure and anxiety. It you follow these counsellings, you can make best use of a permanent and happy career.

Career counselling is used at 2-3 stages of one's career. During high school stage the first counselling made and then at a plus two stage which seems to be transitional stage where a student selects whether he has to opt for arts or science or commerce or whether he has to go for technical or professional education. Accordingly, he has to choose his subjects so that the basic foundation of a specific career is built in the initial state.

After passing out from the higher secondary class he again has to seek the advice of a psychologist or career counsellor for specific guidance. For instance after passing plus two science, a student has four options to choose a career. He many continue in the general science education stream by studying B.Sc., he may appear in the common entrance examinations for admission in to medical or engineering college or he may change the stream and go for arts or commerce. At this stage the career psychologist also shows him the way after making enough verifications of his grades, achievements, likes and dislikes conducting necessary tests on him, and advises him which career he should join. A poor student passing in the first division wants to apply for a clerical post and chooses a clerical career because of his poverty. He can not continue further studies due to financial constraints. Now he has to go to a psychologist or ask a career counsellor to find out if he is suitable for a clerical job. First clerical aptitude test is administered on him and his scores obtained in the test are calculated. Then the candidate is interviewed to acertain his interests, likes and dislikes for the job. Then only he is advised whether to proceed for the job or not. If he scores very less in clerical aptitude test he should be advised not to apply for a clerical post or join it if he gets through the examination.

Similarly for administrative or judicial posts one should have the ability and talent for the same and this can only be detected by a career counsellor after fulfilling various formalities as discussed above. Under no circumstances, the counsellor should allow himself to play foul by misinterpreting the qualities and special abilities of a candidate coming for advice. He should not also misinform or misguide him. The advise given to him should be based on facts and findings. Even now a days students and career aspirants are taking counselling from experts through post and internet. Many news papers and T.V. channels are also providing career counselling and giving various informations on different types of careers, their pay scales, job prospects and basic qualification required to give a preliminary idea to the candidates.

A career counsellor must be well trained and well versed in the area, and he or she must have genuine interest in counselling. Suppose the counsellor is biased towards a teaching post.

That does not mean that the client or candidate will not be allowed to take up this career, if he has abilities, capacities and aptitude for it. Even with average ability but great deal of interest one can show efficiency in that career with perseverance, hard work and dedication. On the contrary, a person may be talented and fits to a job but if some how he does not have interest in the job for intrinsic or extrinsic factors he becomes a misfit for that job. Therefore interest for a job should be given equal priority along with job qualities.

It is estimated that due to rapid advancement in technology a person who is 20 years old now may have five to six careers during his life time as he has the scope now for changing from one career to a better one. Hence the student or career seeker must have foresight and his plannings and decisions should be future oriented. Before choosing a career all advantages and disadvantages should be carefully analysed. At this juncture the career counsellor who should basically be a psychologist comes to the rescue of the career seekers. Right and judicious decisions solve the problem in the right direction where as wrong erratic and hasty decisions based on bias, prejudice and unscientific data cause problems in the future. Misguidance is more dangerous than guidance, this every career aspirant and career counsellor should keep in mind. A counsellor must we well trained and should cautiously and carefully examine all aspects of the job and all aspects of the candidate and then reach at a decision regarding choice of a career. Sometimes it is seen that if the father or mother is a doctor he a she wants that his son should also be a doctor to manage his clinic/nurshing home or profession. Similarly it is also observed quite often lawyer parents want their ward to join legal career so that not only he would learn from them and help them but also utilize their library. But they never try to know if he is fit for this career. In the same way family politics is very rampant in India. Instances are many where the great grand parents, grand parents, parents and even children of a politician join and practice, active politics without even knowing if every one in the family tree joining polities is suitable for it or has the ability and interest for it. There are examples of cases where without proper and scientific investigation one joins a career because it is like a family business. A cloth merchant or jeweller merchant asks his ward to come to the shop in the evening after study hours and assist him without even knowing or ascertaining if he is capable of this career or interested in it. If he is not interested in the family business, he just becomes a misfit for this career and leaves it after 10 years of training. These are examples of wastage of human resources and man power. Sometimes even if he is not interested in such a career he may just drag on or some how manage it in the fear of being scolded by his father or when he has crossed the age to join a new career, he somehow continues there of course without interest. May be this person would have been a great success in some other job.

Before choosing any career the candidate should be well informed about the job. He must be aware about the past, present and future prospects of the job, the scope the job provides for promotion, job satisfaction, expression of special abilities, autonomy in work and decision making etc. besides salary, fringe benefits and other financial incentives.

In the orissa Staff Selection Commission. I worked for about 5 years and interviewed thousands of candidates for different jobs. Surprisingly, in several cases it was found that the candidates did not know anything about the job, and job prospects. Even they did not know about the nature of work of various jobs, what to talk about other prospects like promotion, fringe benefits, whether the job is transferable or not, etc. When asked how has he come to the interview without these basic informations one candidate promptly replied. "I have to do same job since I am unemployed for the last 10 years. So, where is the question of selecting a job ?" But even if one is in need of a job badly, he should atleast try to gather the information on the above aspects of the job before coming to the interview or latest before joining it. The source of information may be electronic and print media, books and magazines, internet and even the organisation which has advertised the post.

It is universally seen that one person may like a job while another may not. Some people prefer non-mobile or desk jobs while some other touring jobs. There are others who like both the types. Thus, every person has some amount of choice in every work including choosing a career or joining a job. Many people join a job and leave it after some time because they do not pull on well with the job or the boss or both. Some people may not like the work atmosphere or the evaluation method. Rigid work schedules also may not be liked by many. To avoid all these complications one has to gather all informations from various reliable sources and through spot visit of the organisation where he has to work prior to joining. Many want autonomy in work and decision making. Business connections, advertisements in media and employment news also provide informations about job opportunities.

Fitting the worker to the job represents the first and foremost steps in promoting individual efficiency and adjustment in organisations and industries. It is said that getting a job is not necessarily so important as getting the right job. Similarly getting a man is not so important as getting a right man. Improper and careless selection of careers lead to tremendous wastage of human power and national wealth. If the person does not fit to a job, he is not interested in it. He may not appreciate his coworkers. Besides constant irritation, carelessness in work, lack of desire to specialize in the job and inattentiveness due to boredom lead to further loss both to the employee and to the management. Failure as an effective and efficient worker leads to inferiority complex and frustration leading to maladjustment both in professional and personal life. Therefore right choice of a career is essential and for this one has to take the help of career counsellor and counseling.

Career Options for Women

Four/five decades back women were interested in two three specific careers like teaching, medicine and house work. All other careers were considered unsuitable for them keeping in view their social status, physical make up and mind set of the society. The common opinion of the public even of women was that women should go for soft jobs. But to-day things have changed rapidly and attitude of people towards women choosing a career has also changed. People to-day appreciate and respect women who go for tough jobs like policing, Air force, navy, army and other tough and courageous posts. To-days women can choose from several vocational avenues that are flexible enough to provide a satisfying and rewarding career to them. Earlier woman never thought of joining police, army, air force, defence, civil service, administration, driving, pilot, sells and advertisement, Media and event management, judiciary, and fashion technology. But to-day the picture is completely different with more and more women coming out of their four walls to join various job discussed above. The scopes and prospects for varied career selection have increased. Now women are not untouchable for any profession. Since through out the world child rearing and house work were considered the basic career for women in earlier days, no one not even women themselves dreamt of any other career. Since women still continue

The selection procedure for the job of a Police is very tough. It involves written, physical and psychological tests and interviews. Hence a lot of preparation and home work is necessary for taking up the career of policing.

QUESTIONS

1. What is career planning? Why it is necessary ?
2. Explain the concept of career anchor and indicate different types of career anchors.
3. Explain the importance of individual differences in the choice of a career.
4. How career planning requires to take in to account individual differences ?
5. Explain how application of psychological principles and tests help in the choice of a career ?
6. What do you understand by matching round pegs in square holes ? Indicate its adverse affects on career.
7. Critically examine the ingredients of career planning.
8. What are the adverse effects of wrong choice of career ? Explain with suitable example.
9. Discuss with example the role of parents and teachers in career planning.
10. What are the most sought after careers to-day ? Describe with examples.
11. Analyse the different factors helping in the choice of a career.
12. Examine the various scientific ways to choose a career including the various career assessment tools.
13. What is career counselling ? Indicate how counselling helps in career planning.
14. Discuss the various stages of career counselling.
15. Critically examine counselling the various career options for women and challenges faced by them with special reference to Indian socio-cultural conditions.

REFERENCES

Mohanty, G.B. Text Book of Psychology Part II. Kalyani Publishers, New Delhi 2009.

Mohanty, G.B. Industrial Psychology and Organisational Behaviours, Kalyani Publishers, New Delhi 2006.

Articles Published in New Indian Express at different times.

31

Effective Communication and Organisational Success

INTRODUCTION

Various ideas experiences, feelings, emotions, sentiment and finally knowledge is transmitted from one person to another through language. Hence language is the chief mode of communication from one person to another. Good communication involves a very important ingredient of good management. Everything is determined in an organisation through communication, without communication one cannot live or work together in an industrial set up even at home in an organized way. Effective communication enables one to understand others as well as make himself understood to others. In democracy communication is the main force influencing the opinion of people. Social organisation is not possible without communication. It is always seen that keeping other factors constant, good managers are good communicators and poor managers are poor communicators.

MEANING AND DEFINITION

The term communication has been derived from the Latin word "communis" which means "common". Thus communication means sharing of ideas in common. When one communicates he attempts to establish sharing of common ideas or information. Communication is bilateral and cannot be one sided or unilaterally. Suppose a friend is talking with another person regarding ensuing election. They share common ideas, common views and common attitudes and common feelings and emotions. A communication cannot last longer if the ideas and attitudes are not of common interest. If I am not interested in politics or election for that matter the exchange of ideas and knowledge about election between me and my friend will end in a few minutes or in a few seconds. So when the receiver and the sender join together for a particular information or message with a common intention or interest the communication continues successfully. Communication may take place between two or more persons. It is a means of transmission of information from one person to another. For the purpose of transmission of information the following five components are necessary, (1) Source (2) Transmitter (3) Channel (4) Receiver (5) Destination.

In a democratic country communication is the main force of influencing the opinion of people. Social organisation and any kind of group activity or knowledge is not possible without communication.

A teacher communicates with the students in the class room when he teaches or gives a lecture. Through his language (spoken and written) he informs the students about various things. Even the students ask questions to the teacher. But when the students are not able to understand what the teacher says the communication system fails or there is no communication. In addition to language spoken and written, communication is also possible through gestures, symbolic movement of lips and various other physical postures and gestures like movement of hand and head etc. Suppose you want to tell some one "don't come here". You can just move your head or wave your hand to instruct him not to come. In an organisation or industry various views, ideas orders, appeals, instructions, suggestions and observations or information of any type are exchanged among the managerial personnels like top order, middle order and low order employees. Communication is necessary for coordination, planning improvement in employee-employer relationship, for imparting innovating ideas for good personal relationship, better management and high production, etc. Even the regular orientation courses conducted by the management and weekly meetings with the staff also communicate various day to day matters including what the employer wants from the employees and *vice versa*. If there is a gap in communication between various levels of management even in a family it negatively affects production, and performance creates misunderstanding and lowers morale and group cohesiveness. Gap in communication also produces discontentment and anxiety. Hence the importance of communication is extremely high in any organisation.

DEFINITIONS

Below are given a few standard and working definitions of communication to explain the concept in organisations.

1. Communication is a systematic and continuous act or process of telling, listening and understanding of ideas and informations from one person to another. It is sharing views between two persons or imparting information and knowledge of importance to another person.
2. Communication which is fundamental to all human beings is the process of passing information and understanding from one person to another. It is a human interchange of ideas and opinions through language and gestures and it must be understand by the person to whom the information is passed.
3. Communication is a process of conveying message which includes facts, ideas opinions, attitudes, stereotypes and even prejudices from one source to another.

4. The term communication has been defined by Willam Scott as a process which involves the transmission and accurate replication of ideas ensured by feed back for the purpose of eliciting actions which will accomplish organizational goals.

All these definitions of communication suggest that communication is not merely sending and receiving information or ideas, it is also proper understanding of the information or message. Some communications may be accepted and some may not be accepted. But by and large, the purpose of transmitting a message is to accept and implement it, if the communication so instructs, particularly in industries and organisations.

General Characteristics of Communication System

From the above described definitions and meaning of communication some general characteristics are noticed.

(*a*) **It involves at least two or more persons** the sender and the receiver who are expected to exchange ideas and informations.

(*b*) **The message or contents of communication** is the most important characteristics of communication.

(*c*) Communication may be **positive or negative** oral or visual written or gestural.

(*d*) It involves waving of hands, movement of eye and movement of the lip. Communication must be understood by both the parties *i.e.,*who communicate and to whom communication is made. So it is a two way process.

(*e*) **Understanding** the information or message is the end result of communication, but it may be acceptable or unacceptable.

(*f*) The basic aim of communication is to **motivate or direct** a person to some action or influence human behaviour. In propaganda communication is the most important ingredient through which any type of propaganda is made, be it for education, for election, for health and family planning for literacy and empowerment of women.

A good drafting of message with lively, reality oriented informations can influence the receiver to accept and implement the message if it so demands.

(*g*) **Communication should be relevant to the situation** so that it should not appear useless, meaningless or irrelevant to the situation. The receiver of the message must not consider the message theoratical or meaningless.

Process of Communication

The process of communication are as follows :

(*i*) Formulation of a clear idea and view about facts, opinions and informations that the communicator desires to communicate.

(*ii*) Encoding of the message or information through translation of ideas in to words, symbols or gestures, which the receiver must understand.

(*iii*) Selection of suitable media for onward transmission of the message, telephone, telegraph, T.V., Radio, Internet or news paper. During general election 2009, many candidates made propaganda to vote them through these mediums.

(*iv*) The message is received by the communicatee and he tries to understand it.

(*v*) Action is taken by the communicates on the information recieved.

(*vi*) As a last step in the process of communication the effectiveness of communication is measured through feed back or response. If the communication brings some positive changes in the behaviour of the communicatee like agreeing to give vote or giving vote in favour of the communicator or accepting what the management instructs through the massage, the communication said to be successful. On the contrary if there is no change in behaviour or there is undesirable or negative change then the communication is said to unsuccessful.

Need or Purpose of a Communication system

The purpose of sending a message to some one through communication system is to bring effective changes in his behaviour. Sometimes a communication is also made not to make a positive response, like a political agent of a candidate may request his friend or relation not to vote in favour of the opponent candidate.

Communication is a social behaviour and man is a social animal. So a person who rarely communicates with other members of the society or group is called a social isolate. Without proper communication allround development of the personality is affected. Due to lack of proper communication he can neither contribute nor receive anything from others in the society. He can neither understand others nor make others understand him without proper communication. Without communication one cannot live in the society in an organized way. Further those who communicate very little are considered un-popular in the society. You go to a relations place to exchange views. But the person only say 'Yes or No' and rarely talks with you. So what idea you would make about the person. You say he is unsociable or proud. Communication is a system that binds people together in the family, in the neighbourhood or in the organisation. It helps in the allround development of one's personality.

Communication in organisation basically helps the management to plan and coordinate all actions effectively and also control its members effectively. Unless members of an organisation do not communicate their difficulties, problems and suggestion, it becomes difficult for the management to know their problems and act effectively. Communication should extend to others social groups also as it is an important key to social structure.

According to **Clover J.G.** the important purposes of communication are as follows :

1. Communication keeps the employees and members informed about necessary facts, orders and instructions in connection with their duties and responsibilities.
2. Through communication employees also give their view that may help management in day to day functioning.
3. Through communication the management expresses his pleasure and happiness towards a worker if he functions effectively and the *vice versa*.
4. Communication helps in the development of interpersonal and intrapersonal relationship. So labour turnover and absenteeism are reduced.

Types/patterns/Category of Communication

Formal. In a **formal communication** the highest boss in the organisation say the C.E.O. or chief executive officer would not directly communicate with the subordinate employees. But the communication will flow in a descendant manner, *i.e.*, the CEO will communicate the message to the Heads of the Deptts and Heads of the Deptt. to the Manager and the Manager to the Deputy Manager and so on downwards. For instance in formal communication a minister will write to the secrotary of the Deptt, the secretary will pass on the messege to the H.O.D and the H.O.D to Additional Director and so on and finally the file containing the message will go to the section assistant. So formal communication follows the formal channel in the organizational structure.

Informal. But informal communication flows from informal channels which are not provided in an organizational structure, like the message is sent by the minister directly to the H.O.D and not through the secretary. When the M.D. of the company transits the message to the Dy Manager or immediate supervisor it is a case of informal communication. Informal communication develops among members out of personal contact or when something urgent is necessary to be done immediately as otherwise the process may take time. Now a days single window systems have become very effective and economical. In providing quick action and implementation it is a vital part of the process of exchange. Informal communication is implicit, multidimensional, spontaneous and various. It operates with much greater speed than formal communication. It goes in between informal groups with common interest. To strengthen the formal channel an organisation can make use of informal format of communication.

Communication flows up and down. As indicated above communication can flow downward from the highest boss or C.E.O. of the organisation to the most subordinate officer and upward from the subordinate officer to the superior officer or head of the organisation (through the in between officer). So it can go in an adscendant or descendant order as the requirement may demand.

Horizontal, Lateral or sideward communication. The transmission of information between people on the same level of organisational hierarchy is called horizontal communication. It can also flow side to side *i.e.,* between two or more persons operating at the same level of power and authority, like two assistant directors or two section officers having same authority. Thus communication can be sideward or horizontal or lateral.

Usually sideward communication refers to inter departmental communication; say the communication beween two officers of the same status or level in two departments or among subordinates working under one C.E.O. This type of horizental communication speeds up information or message and encourages mutual understanding. It enables the officers of the same level to work in a planned and coordinated manner without referring all matters to the higher authorities. To-day single window delivery system is found in many organisations to speed up work. The horizontal communication is usually informal in character. One departmental head can contact another departmental head directly either orally or in writing.

Complex. In a group of only two persons thc patterns of communication is of the simplest type. But when the number increases, it becomes difficult to understand the pattern of communication as it becomes like a complex net pattern. Thus the pattern of communication tends to be complex with the increase in number of members in a group.

Intense and Free Communication Channels

The intensity of the communication pattern also depends upon traffic density. Some communication nets are extremely busy and they are frequently used. Here there is traffic density.

Now a days mobile phones and e-mails are very much used as communication channels. Conversely if an existing channel is not used frequently for the purpose of communication, it can be deleted from the communication net. By analyzing traffic density one can find the bottle necks and blockings in group communication which ultimately decrease the morale and efficiency of the group.

The pattern of communication changes as the group communicates and interacts with others. A group continues to communicate until a uniform pattern is attained, once this uniform pattern is attained there is no longer any need to communicate. Again when some new item of information is introduced there is fresh interaction and the pattern of communication may be further complicated.

Diagonal Communication

Diagonal communication refers to the transfer of information between people who are neither in the same department or section nor on the same level of organisational hierarchy. For example when a deputy director in the planning and coordination section communicates with the section officer of non government collage section directly relating to some of their demands it is a case of diagonal communication. This type of communication increases the organizational efficiency by speeding up information and avoiding delay and departmental barriers. A single window system is followed now a days in many organisations to avoid delay and dissatisfaction.

Written, Oral or Non-verbal Communication

This is a classification of communication types based on Media or Expression. It refers to the medium used in the transmission of message. The communication through language and words may be written or oral.

Written communication refers to transfer of message in pen and paper. It includes diagrams, graphs, pictures, file noting, written information and orders. Reports, policies financial matters, legal issues, rules and orders, important instructions and agreements are transmitted in writing to maintain accountability and for efficient management of the organisation. Written communication emphasizes that every one concerned must get the same information. It provides a permanent and written record of communication for all future purposes. When someone is paid arrear or salary or some urgent instruction is issued by the legal authorities written informations are transmitted in pen and paper. In all government semi-government and public sector undertakings and organisations every information is recorded in black and white and then transmitted to all concerned. The written communication should be clear, precise, comprehensive and correct to be effective while written communications are very very authentic though they kill time, are expensive and formal.

Oral Communication. Conveying and transmitting messages through spoken words or orally through. Intercom, telephones or public speech personally is called oral communication. It is a type of face to face communications between individuals. A lot of oral communication is used daily in every organisation and it is preferred to written ones because of its speedy nature. It is more personal and informal, and takes less time than written communication. It should however be used only in times of emergency and when the message is not very very important needing accountability and having future purposes.

But oral communication is less reliable, has less accountability and it may be influenced by personal interest, bias and prejudices. The information may be distorted and it may be affected by language problems.

Gestural or Non-verbal Communication. Expression through body parts is called gestural communication. Through movement of lips, wink of eyes or wave of hands one way convey a message and make it more meaningful and effective. Dance is a kind of gestural communication where various dancers communicate messages through their physical gestures. It is sometimes used as a supplementary method of communication.

Written communication may be preferred in lengthy messages and when a large number of persons scattered over distant places and where the information needs accountability, authenticity and for future record. It is used in case of important messages which needs to be repeated and recorded. **Elements of communication** include a communicator, a communicatee, a message of communication, a channel communication and response and feed back of the communicatee.

As already indicated the agents of communication are slogans, lectures, public meetings news papers and magazines, pamplets, radio, motion picture and T.V., computer, internet and laptop, etc.

BARRIERS OR OBSTACLES TO COMMUNICATION

Introduction

To-day the problem of communication has been a headache to all the organisations. Good communication is necessary for the smooth operation of the organisation. People in organisations usually spend over seventy five per cent of their time in an interpersonal situation. Thus the crux of a large number of problems in an organisation is poor communication. The management has to maintain an effective flow of communication in all direction. It is essential to discuss barriers of communication first so that the factors of effective communication can be discussed next. All messages are not effectively transmitted or received. Several obstructions, and blockades, hurdles, bottlenecks put obstacles on the way of effective communication and distort the messages. Consequently communication becomes in effective and useless. They produce misunderstanding and conflict among people in the society, in the organisations, in the family and even among people world around who may be stranger. Take the example of various communal riots. A slight carelessness on the part of the media regarding transmission of information about the riot or telecast/broadcast/printing of false and exaggerated information may prove very very dangerous for the nation. Thousands of managerial and interpersonal problems, poor employee-employer relationship is due to ineffective and faulty communication. Working in the same organisation, living in the same family people do not talk and communicate with each other for days and even months. Then what type of good personal relationship one can expect. Will it not lead to misunderstanding, conflict and depression ? Communication is complicated by the complex and conflicting relationships that exist in work. It is essential to know first the barriers of communication so that by removing the barriers effective communication can be ensured.

Barriers

1. Physical barriers. Distance between the sender and the message, noise and environmental pollution and other problematic work environments, faulty pronounciation, stuttering, stammering etc. block communications.

2. Personal barriers. Biased attitude, prejudice, stereotypes, faulty social values and faulty judgement, inferiority complex, vested interest, misunderstanding, wrong perception, less time, in ability to communicate properly due to speedy and unclear pronounciation produce gap in communicate and increase the psychological distance between the sender and receiver of the message. Inconsistency between what one says and what one does also produces a barrier.

3. Resistance to change which is a psychological barrier. When people get some information which are novel and different from the old and traditional, it is a common tendency not to accept it. They like to stick to the old used and traditional patterns of life. So they resist change and it is an usual phenomena observed almost in all persons. Such new ideas introduced are likely to be overlooked or not attended or even rejected and opposed. This resistance to change creates a major barrier in communication.

4. Superior-subordinate status barrier. It is seen that status in the hierarchy of any organisation stands as a major barrier which obstructs the free and independent flow of messages. To maintain status difference the boss or superior officer may not give all the informations to the subordinates, but only a few that is required. Similarly, subordinate employees usually give only those informations to the superior officer which they think he will like and appreciate. This type of selective communication creates distortion of information in downward and upward communication. The gap in status many a times create mistrust and thus the original information is not communicated.

5. Barrier caused by unsound organisational structure. Sound organizational structure helps in effective communication. If the organizational structure is complex and complicated there is distortion in the communication of original messages. Suppose there are several positions through which a file has to pass and go to the highest authority in an organisation. It is the common tendency to distort some fact at every stage and that happens. It is seen that communication gets distorted as it goes up in the hierarchy.

6. Barrier caused by bias and prejudice. Because of prejudgement and bias some people have the tendency to form a judgement before listening to the full message. This is called premature evaluation and it distorts the original information. Prejudies and biases help in adding or substracting as per one's needs and beliefs. This process may be conscious, subconscious or even unconscious.

7. Barrier due to lack of trust and common interest. If the information transmitted is of common interest to both the receiver and the sender then it is okay. Otherwise lack of trust and common interest may make the communication ineffective.

8. Existing beliefs and emotional attitudes may put a barrier to effective communication. It is observed often that emotion and strong beliefs of both the sender and the receiver of the message influence effective communication negatively. They stand on the may of free flow of information as well as proper understanding of the message.

Poor Memory stands as a barrier in the reuse, of communicated informations in the future. Failure to retain and retrieve becomes a major barrier when the information is required to be used in future.

Since in can organisation people with varied experience, different age, different educational status, qualification, and different positions work, it is difficult to eliminate the barriers fully. But steps can be taken to remove the barriers as far as practicable.

Steps of effective Communication

Effective communication is an essential component of organizational success at all levels whether it is at the interpersonal, intergroup, intragroup, organisational or external levels. For the success of an organisation, effective communication is very essential. What is ineffective communication ? It is one which is accepted by the receiver of the message and accepted well or taken care of by the receiver. It is a bilateral or two way process.

Effective communication can be possible if all the barriers of communication discussed above are taken care of, solved or overcomed.

1. Language barrier is to be overcomed by use of proper language. As the choice of works in which a sender encodes a message influences the quality of communication, careful use of language should be done. The language should be clear and not confused. In confused language different people can add different meanings to the same word depending upon their needs and values. Language should be such that there should be no scope for different interpretations. The language should be brief, clear and simple. The message should be complete in all respects. It is important to note that language of communication should be such that it would not provide any scope for confusion and wrong interpretation. To avoid semantic barrier the message should be communicated in simple, brief and clear language.

2. Selective hearing and ignoring non-verbal cues stand on the way of effective communication so steps should be taken to rectify this barrier.

3. Clarity and completeness of the Message. First of all one has to know the audience or viewer for whom the message is being transmitted. For example, for an illiterate mass, the language should be different from that of highly qualified intellectuals. The receiver must understand rightly what the message means. The communication should be complete to indicate its exact meaning and purpose, so that communication can have correct impact on the receiver.

4. Accurate and appropriate organisational structure. In order to make the communication effective in an organisation, the organizational structure must be appropriate to the needs of the organisation.

5. Orientation course and proper interpersonal relationship. This will help the employees to know and understand each other, minimize conflicts and reduce distortion of messages. Biases, prejudies and stereotyped thoughts should be removed through orientation course, education and training. The members should be trained to understand the objectives, goals, rules, regulations, policies of the organisation so that they can better understand a communication from their point of view.

6. Good and Patient Listener. One should patiently listen to the whole of the message so that proper meaning of it can be understood and interpreted. This can also avoid premature evaluation of communication. The higher officers should develop the habit of patient listening and avoid premature evaluation of communication received from their subordinate employees. They should not add anything or substract anything to suit their interest.

Need of motivation and mutual confidence

The message should be designed in such a way that the receiver of the message will be motivated and his response will progress in desired direction. Thus the purpose of the communication can be served.

Information channels should be effective

Formal channels of communication must supplement with informal channels so that there can be a coordination between both and that would make the communication more effective. Use of appropriate media is essential.

Feed back

The sender of the message must know or get the feed back from the receiver of the communication. The effectiveness of the communication can be judged from the feedback. Hence feedback must be encouraged and analysed to make communication effective.

Avoidance of inconsistent attitude of the management

The management must ensure that they have followed in letter and spirit what they have communicated. This can produce trust among the employees and make any communication effective.

Avoidance of emotional out brust and preconceived notions

To make a communication most effective personal and emotional factors should be kept away. Neither the sender nor the receiver should try to colour any communication with emotional tinge and preconceived notions. The message should be understood and interpreted in a cool mind.

Gestures, voice and good behaviour

Various gestures and modulation of tone are essential. One should have appropriate facial expression, soit and impressive voice, smiling face inorder to make a message effective. Moods, emotions and sentiments should also be controlled in the positive direction, so that it can influence positively the receiver of the communication. The behaviour of the sender of the message particularly in case of face to face or auditory messages should be congenial. Good behaviour helps a lot in making communication effective.

There should also be integrity and consistency in communication. The communication should be based on truth so that nobody can doubt its integrity and consistency.

The principle of flexibility and use of informal communication can further make a message effective.

The American Management Association has given the following factors of good communication.

1. Seek to clarify your idea before communicating.
2. Examine the purpose of each communication.
3. Consider the total physical setting whenever you communicate.
4. Consult with others where appropriate in planning communication.
5. Be mindful while you communicate of the overtones as well as basic content of your message.
6. Take the opportunity when it arises to convey something of help or value to the receiver.
7. Follow up your communication.
8. Be sure your actions support your communications.
9. Seek not only to be understood but understand.

Video conference for Effective Communication

Video conferencing allows face to face communication over almost any distance. People in a video conference can see each other, speak to each other, show graphic images. Modern technology has made communication system easy and trust worthy through personal computers, e-mails and video conferencing and even through fax.

Such systems are a substitute for travelling to different sites for meetings. Even mobile phones are used to transmit messages once they are recorded. Now a days desk top video conferencing is also used for communication purposes.

Today multimedia personal computers are also used in the field of communication. Business presentations along with colour graphics, photographs, video images and background sound etc. are now made, with the help of computers, laptops and videos. Such visual presentations have very very dramatic effect on the audience. Projectors are also used to communicate ideas, thoughts and messages in an effective manner, because visual and graphic presentations have always greater impact than auditory ones in communication of ideas and messages.

Importance of Effective Communication

Effective communication to-day is very essential to get into a job. The management carefully observes how you are presenting yourself in a group discussion and in interviews. Sometimes the interviewer asks you to tell them about yourself so that from this talk they can make an assessment on your communication skill. Various presentations and communications are used as a formal, method for bringing people together to plan, monitor or review any kind of progress. An employees effective presentation skill reflects his personality. It enhances his image as a manager or supervisor or a public relation officer or Marketing manager. Particularly officers dealing with public should have the capacity for effective communication. Effective communication quality is a human resource. It is an opportunity to build trust in one's leadership ability and decision making functions. The management or senior officers are impressed when one has the skill and ability to communicate effectively. It also speaks the mind and personality of the presenter.

Effective communication is necessary for making a good presentation. What is important in communication is how effectively the message is received. A communication becomes a failure if the receivers are not persuaded of its merits and advantages for them or for the organisation. The objective of the communication should be to make it simple, lucid, understandable and remembered.

However, the mode of communication is to be adjusted depending upon the type of person/ persons for whom the message is made. Since the average human being has a very short attention span, the message should not be very lengthy. It should be shortcut, direct and comprehensive. The aim of effective communication should therefore be to hold the attention long enough to make the communication effective.

In verbal communications the audiences are restricted to the order of the presenter which should be kept in mind. The sender of the message should try to get sustained attention. Lengthy, complicated and confused messages should be avoided.

QUESTIONS

1. What is meant by communication in organisations ? How effective communication helps in organizational success ?
2. Discuss the various characteristics of communication system.
3. Describe the need of a communication system in an organisation or industry.
4. Describe the various types or categories of communication.
5. Explain the barriers of communication.
6. Explain the various steps of effective communication.
7. What steps one would take to improve the communication system in an industry ?
8. Highlight the importance of effective communication with the use of modern devices.
9. Differentiate between verbal and non-verbal communication and indicate their advantages and disadvantages.
10. Write brief notes on the following :
    (*a*) Diagonal communication.
    (*b*) Oral communication.
    (*c*) Gestural communication.
    (*d*) Barriers of communication.

REFERENCES

Gupta, S.K. Joshi, R. Organizational Behaviour—Kalyani Publishers New Delhi 2008.

Mohanty, G.B. Text book of Social Psychology, Kalyani Publishers, New Delhi 2008.

Articles Published in New Indian Express from time to time.

32

Recent Indian Studies on Industrial Psychology and Organisational Behaviour

Ahmad, Sameena, James, Jesssy and Ahmad, Safia. (Xavier Inst of Management, Bhubaneswar) in a study on "Organisational role stress : A psychological study of middle managers". (1991)—examined the relationship between organizational role stress (ORS), as measured by a scale developed by U. Pareek (1981), and job satisfaction and personality dimensions of neuroticism-stability and extraversion-introversion, as indicated by the Maudsley Personality Inventory. Ss were 50 middle managers. Results indicated that ORS was significantly but negatively correlated with all factors of job satisfaction (nature of job, management, personal adjustment, and social relations). The neuroticism-stability dimension of personality was significantly and positively related to 6 dimensions of ORS, including role amibiguity. Only 1 dimension of ORS (role expectation conflict) had a significantly negative relationship with extraverstion introverstion.

Ahmad, Sameena and Varghese, Asha, R. (Xavier Inst of Management, Bhubaneswar) in a study. Learning styles of Indian managers : Some explorations. (1991)—attempted to validate aspects to D.A Kolb's (1974) experimental learning theory in Indian context, and examine the relationship between learning style mismatch and job satisfaction. 103 management students and 68 practising managers were given the Learning Styles Inventory and a short form of the Minnesota Satisfaction Questionnaire. Indian managers were more oriented toward the concrete and active ends of the concrete/abstract and the active/reflective dimensions as compared with Kolb's sample of their Western counterparts. The functional areas within the field of management were dominated by the people with the particular style profile demanded by the area. A significant relationship emerged between a match of learning style with the work area and job satisfaction.

Alva, H.R. (HMT Ltd, Bangalore) in managing the change process. (1991)-discussed change in the corporate world, particularly in India, which reflect increased international influences, an orientation toward products rather than functions, and the supremacy of competence. The importance of learning to change and adapt is discussed. Action research and organizational development research are compared. The various dimensions of organizational development are discussed in terms of the nature of the intervention and the structure and process.

Barnes, B.L. (SNDT Women's U, Bombay) made a study on "Stress in aviation personnel". 1992 - 25 aircraft captains, 16 flight engineers, and 11 cabin crew members from Air India (all adult males aged 20-50 yrs) were tested in different stress indices to evaluate their health status and adjustments to occupational stressors. The group on the whole showed heightened state and trait anxiety as a characteristic feature of the sample. However, the pilots had significantly higher trait anxiety, attributable to high responsibility and accountability expected by the nature of their job specifications. Cabin attendants had significantly higher scores on health problems, work overload, and stress-prone diet than did pilots. The cabin attendants also exhibited low self-esteem and high frustration.

Barnes, B.L. (SNDT Women's U, Bombay) in a study "Stress in transport workers." 1992, evaluated varied stress factors of transport workers using 3 groups of personnel from aviation (n = 52), railways (n = 46), and roadways (n = 45). Tools used were Health Adjustment Inventory, modified Girdano's Stress Profile Questionnaire, and State and Trait Anxiety Inventory. The aviation workers experienced high state anxiety as well as frustration, boredom and noise pollution. Trait anxiety was manifested in both aviation and railways but not in roadways personnel. Roadways workers manifested poorer health status. Frustration and boredom were commonly present among all employees. The roadways personnel manifested stress on indices like adaptation, diet, self-perception and were of Type A personality make-up. Both roadways and railways personnel showed anxious reactive personality, work overload and fatigue.

Beena, C. and Poduval, P. R. (Cochin U of Science and Technology) in "Gender differences in work stress of executives" (1991)—studied gender differences in relation to the work stress of 80 first-level executives with age as another independent variable. Ss completed a 25-item Work Stress related Scale adopted from C.A. Iliggins (1991). Results indicated that stress experience increased with increasing age. Sex was found to be a major facter affecting stress condition.

Bhadury, Bikash. (IIT, Kharagpur) made a study on "Work culture : An exposition in the Indian context." 1991—examined the influence of work culture on organizational effectiveness and on motivating individual employees. Cultural and social factors relevant to work culture in Japan and India are compared. Work ethos differs from work ethics in that the former is the prevalent disposition toward work, while the latter are the attitudes deemed appropriate for achieving the organizational goals; while ethos implies what is, ethics imply what ought to be. The creation of a new organizational culture must focus on the creation of loyalty and discipline at all levels of hierarchy, promotion of cooperative effort, and motivation to improve the activation levels of all employees. The importance of leadership, motivation through innovation, and organizational structure in determining work culture is discussed.

Bharati, T.; Nagarathnamma, B. and Reddy, S. Viswanatha. (Sri Venkateswara U, Tirupati) studied the "Effect of occupational stress on job satisfaction." (1991) They investigated whether occupational stress had any relationship with job satisfaction among 90 clerical employees of 3 different organizations in India. Ss completed the Occupational Stress Index and R.N. Kanungo's (1982) Job Satisfaction Scale. Occupational stress was significantly related to job satisfaction, such that the greater the stress, lower the satisfaction.

Bhargava, Shivganesh and Sinha, Beena. (IIT, Bombay) studied Prediction of organizational effectiveness as a function of type of organizational structure. (1992) They investigated the organizational characteristics of effectiveness in a hierarchical and heterarchical structure. 20 final-year university engineering students (mean age 21 yrs) and 20 engineers (mean age 23.5 yrs) working in a large public enterprise participated in the study. Comparative analysis showed a significant improvement in organizational effectiveness under a heterarchical structure. Results are discussed within the structural perspective of the organizations.

Bhatia, P.; Shipra and Muhar, I. S. (Maharshi Dayanand U, Rohtak) studied the effect of low and high intensity noise on work efficiency. (1991)-100 students (50 with high and 50 with low noise sensitivity) were randomly assigned to 5 high and 5 low noise sensitivity groups, each having 10 Ss. A multigroup design investigated the effects of the low and high intensity noises of continuous and unperiodic nature on a multiplication subtraction task. Quantitative, qualitative, and physiological energy expenditure, inferred from the drop of forearm skin resistance, was measured. The significance of the difference among various group means was tested by employing Duncan's Range Test and Students t-test. Findings indicate that due to adaptation, efficiency was not much affected even under high intensity noise in the case of low noise sensitivity Ss, but adaptation was not effective and efficiency was adversely affected in the case of high noise sensitivity Ss under both high and low intensity of noises.

Biswas, S.N. (U Allahabad, U.P.) in a study on "A comparative study of attitudes of bank managers across three states in India". (1992)—studied the role of culture and economic development in explaining the similarities and differences in Indian managerial attitudes. 127 bank managers from 3 states participated as Ss. An examination of the economic profiles of the 3 states suggested that states with highly contrasting economic profiles also had a higher contrast on managers attitudinal variables.

Chatterjee, Amitava and Roy Debdulal Dutta. (Psychological Consultancy Centre, Calcutta) in a study on "Awareness of external environment, environmental satisfaction and mental health". (1991)—studied the relationship between 2 predictors—awareness of external environment (AEA) and environment satisfaction (ES)—and the criterion variable of mental health (MH). 200 Ss from each of the 2 heavy engineering organisations were interviewed with a structured questionnaire. Results revealed that ES compared to AEA gives better prediction of mental health. EA alone failed to predict MH when ES was regressed from EA standardized partial regression analysis.

Ghosh, Anjali. (Indian Statistical Inst., Calcutta) in "Self Description Inventory as a predictor of managerial success". (1991)—investigated whether different facets of managerial talent can be used as predictors of managerial success in a group of 74 managers (mean age 35 yrs) working in public and private sector organizations. Managerial talent was assessed by responses to the Self-Description Inventory (E.E. Ghiselli, 1954). Indices of managerial success were career progression, salary progression, and salary gain. Multiple regression analysis showed that managerial success in terms of rate of progression cannot be effectively predicted on the basis of different facets of managerial talent. Age was the only factor that significantly correlated with rate of progression.

Kaur, Parvinder and Sinha, Arvind K. (Management Development Inst., Haryana) studied the "Dimensions of Guna in organizational setting". (1992) It presents an empirical analysis of the Indian concept of guna on the assumption that this construct·would be of interest from the organizational behaviour perspective. 310 male executives in 3 cities answered the 37-item guna questionnaire of S. K. Chakraborty (1985). The construct of guna was operationalized, and was assessed using factor analysis. Four factors emerged from the analysis : tamas (inactivity) guna, rajas (activity), positive guna, sattwa (inactivity) guna, and rajas negative guna.

Kunhumoidee, U.A. and Karuness, S. (IIT, New Delhi) in a problem named" Adequate compensation" and "care for employees' safety" as dimensions of organisational climate : "Perceptions of management experts". (1991)—interviewed management experts to determine their perceptions about the impact of adequate compensation and care for employees' safety on organizational climate. 34 senior personnel executives from 29 industries and 32 academic professors/consultants from 19 institutions responded to a questionnaire. Data were analyzed to obtain averages and variances and the means were compared. The difference in perception between the 2 groups was significant. Both groups agreed about the positive relationship of both compensation and safety to organizational climate.

Mathew, M.K. (U. Calicut) in "Managerial satisfaction in relation to on-the-job activities" (1992)—analysed variations in managerial satisfaction in relation to the reality of managerial activities. 170 middle level managers from 51 orgnisations completed the Managerial Activity Scale (Mathew, 1989) and Job Descriptive Index (Smith, Kendell, and Hulin, 1969). Findings indicate that manager's satisfaction with the job is determined by what managers really do at their job. Manager's actual work and the frequency of performance of various activities are important in determining the effect of various factors on different aspects of satisfaction. Findings are discussed in relation to their practical implication.

Mehra, Gita and Mishra, P.C. in "Mental health as a moderator variable of intrinsic job satisfaction and occupational stress". (1991)—explored the relationship between perceived occupational stress (OS) and job satisfaction (JS), as well as the moderating effect of employees' mental health on the relationship between the 2 factors. 250 industrial workers completed a Mental Health Inventory (Jagdish and A.K. Srivastava, 1983), the Occupational Stress Index (Srivastava and A.P. Singh, 1981), and the S.D. Employees Inventory (D.M. Pestonjee, 1973). Regression analysis suggested that mental health has a moderating effect on the relationship of intrinsic JS and OS.

Mishra, P.C. (U Lucknow, U.P) in "Powerlessness stressor as a moderator variable of the job involvement job satisfaction relationship". (1991)—explored the potential moderating effect of the powerlessness stressor on the relationship of job satisfaction and job involvement. 400 first-line industrial supervisors (mean age 45 yrs) completed the Occupational Stress Index (A.K. Srivastava and A.P. Singh, 1981), the S.D Employees Inventory, and the Job Involvement Scale (R. Kapoor and A.P. Singh, 1978). Moderated regression analysis and subgroup analysis indicated that the powerlessness stressor docs not represent a moderating effect upon the job involvement-job satisfaction relationship.

Mishra, R.K. and Nandagopal, R. (Osmania U. Campus, Inst of Public Enterprise, Hyderabad) in "Efficiency through organisational innovativeness in passenger road transport". (1991)—studied the working of Road Transport Corporations in Tamil Nadu which have been lauded by the World Bank and others as efficient transport organisations in the public sector. The paper brings out clearly the inter-relationship between organisational innovativeness and efficiency in the State Transport Undertakings in Tamil Nadu which will help the policy makers with an alternative model to tone up the working of the Road Transport Corporations in other states.

Mishra, Sarita. (Utkal U. Bhubaneswar) in "TISCO : A psychological study of its organizational life. (1991)—explored the relationships among work-related values, perceived organizational support, organizational effectiveness, and coping in 45 executives and 45 non-executives representing different departments of the Tata Iron and Steel Company (TISCO). No significant relationship was found among all the variables for executives. For both groups, the relationship between coping and organizational effectiveness was significant. The coping styles of non-executives were contingent on their perception of physical well-being.

Misra, G. (Barkatullah U, Bhopal) in "The process and techniques of personnel selection : An overview." (1991)—presents a process and technique of personnel selection in terms of its major stages. The 1st stage usually involves identification and specification of the need for personnel, followed by recruitment. After identification of the potential applicants, the next step consists of choosing for employment a subset of applicants available for hire. Selection techniques and the interview are discussed. Recent developments in selection techniques include computer interactive performance tests, life history data, physical ability testing, and job-related medical standards.

Mukthamath, G. C.; Gaonkar, V. and Khadi, Pushpa B. (U. of Agricultural Sciences, Coll., Dharwar) studied on "Factors influencing job involvement and job satisfaction among women teachers." (1991) They investigated job involvement and job satisfaction of 176 married female teachers from colleges in India, Ss completed questionnaires assessing job involvement, altitude toward teaching, family responsibility, and income. Results show that family responsibility and attitude toward teaching were the most influential factors for job involvement and satisfaction. Family responsibilities and job involvement were inversely related.

Pandey, Anirudh (Western Railway, Bombay) in "Employee occupation and age as moderators of the relation between the absence of job alternatives and job satisfaction". (1992)—explored whether employee occupation and age influence the relationship between perceived absence of job alternatives and job satisfaction. Linear Discriminant Function (LDF) analysis was carried out using the survey responses of 12 Assistant Station Masters (ASMs) and 43 Research Assistants working in Indian Railways. Analysis revealed that perceived absence of job alternatives, employee occupation, and employee age interaction significantly predicted job satisfaction. Educational level of the employees had no significant association with job satisfaction. Promotion, organizational tenure, and education predicted job satisfaction of the research personnel and the ASMs differently.

Pandey, Ashok K. in "A study on employees' role conflict, role ambiguity and their anxiety". (1991)—examined the relationship between role conflict and anxiety, and between role ambiguity and anxiety. 100 employees of a chemical plant completed the Role Conflict Scale (A.K. Pandey, 1987), the Role Ambiguity Scale (Pandey, 1987), and the Anxiety Scale (A.K. Sinha and L.N. Sinha, 1973). The role conflict and role ambiguity were both high having a low correlation with anxiety.

Pestonjee, D.M. (Indian Inst of Management, Ahmedabad) made a study on "Top management stresses : Suggested HRD interventions." (1991) and investigated organizational stress among 221 top managers (aged 33-57 yrs) with the help of the Organization Role Stress Scale. Leading stressors identified were role erosion, role expectation, conflict, role isolation, and interrole distance. Suggested human resources development (HRD) interventions include, respectively, improving the executive's integration in the organization, undertaking role clarity exercises so that roles are clearly defined, role playing and communication exercises, and helping the individual to fulfil the demands of different roles.

Pestonjee, D.M. and Muncherji, Nina (Indian Inst of Management, Ahmedabad) in "Executive health : An oft-neglected aspect of HRD". (1991)—suggests that human resource development (HRD) interventions can help in promoting the physical, mental, and social well-being of the executive. They have described the physiological basis of the capacity of human beings to cope with stress. Major psychological, psychosomatic, and physiological ailments suffered by executives are described, and various techniques for coping with stress are evaluated, including relaxation techniques and exercise. Finally, suggestions are made for integrating concern for health with HRD processes in organizations.

Prakash, Anand. (U. Delhi) in "Organizational socialization and values in Indian context". (1991)—outlines structuralistic, developmental and individualistic perspectives on organizational socialization and proposes a comprehensive view of organizational socialization that includes anticipatory socialization, personal values, background factors, and organizational factors. It is pointed out that the interaction of personal factors and organizational factors decide the status of organizational socialization, which in turn influences outcome factors.

Prakash G.P. (B.K. Coll, Jhansi, U.P.) made a study on "Stress : Discrepancy model of perceived demand and perceived capability". (1991) He tested a model of stress that describes the importance of perception in the experience of stress, using 50 university teachers classified in either a high- or low-stress group. According to the model the disparity between perceived demand and perceived capability produces a feeling of stress. Responses to the Occupational Stress Inventory indicated a negative relationship between perceived capability and perceived demand, The difference between the 2 stress groups was significant on the basis of perceived capability and perceived demand.

Ramachandran, P.V. (IIT, Kharagpur conducted a study on "Prophylaxis meant for improved organisational health in public sector : A clinical perspective". He discusses the concept of codetermination in the context of determining organizational health in the public sector organizations. Codetermination refers to participative management and is assumed to enhance morale, group cohesion, and commitment among workers. Both the commitment of workers and the leadership of managers must be considered while assessing organizational health. Clinically, organizational maladies can be diagnosed at the level of individual deficiencies. Intervension techniques include quality circles, Gestalt techniques, and sensitivity training.

Reddy, V. Srikanth and& Ramamurti, P. V. (Sri Venkateswara U, Tirupati) in an investigation the relation between stress experience on the job-age, personality and general ability. (1991)—examined the effect of age, personality, and general intellectual ability on stress in 200 male executives in 4 age groups (21-30, 31-40, 41-50, and 51-60 yrs). Ss took the Standard Progressive Matrices, the Sixteen Personality Factor Questionnaire (16PF), and a measure of stress and coping. Results of a stepwise multiple regression analysis show there were age differences in the sources of stress. The influences of personality and general ability on stress experience were limited but significant. It is suggested that stress experience may be better conceived as an interplay of the factors studied and other situational and organizational factors.

Roy D. Dutta. (Indian Stat Inst., Calcutta) made a study on "A model of change in organizational health to improve quality of life." (1991). He studied the relationship between organizational health and quality of work life by administering a scale developed to measure 11 attributes of organizational health to 82 managers, 131 supervisors, and 186 rank-and-file workers of 2 heavy engineering organizations in the private and public sectors. Each organizational health attribute was positively related with self-reported general health. Involvement, Environment Awareness, Creativity, and Physical Health accounted for maximum variances of general health. Involvement, Environmental Awareness, Creativity, and Physical Health accounted for maximum variances of general health. Recommedations for improving employee quality of life are suggested.

Shankar, Arti, Ansari, Mahfooz A. and Saxena, Seema. (IIT, Kanpur) made a study on "Ingratiation in organisations : A bystander's perspective. " (1992) They examined the effects of goal of the influence attempt and tactics of ingratiation on the bystander's evaluation of the ingratiator, bystander's prediction of compliance by the target to the ingratiatory attempt, and the acceptance of such behaviour by the bystander. 60 Male engineering undergraduates participated in role playing situation and were assigned the role of bystanders to an interaction between an ingratiator and his or her immediate superior. Major findings were: (1) the main effect of the goals of the influence attempt on bystander's rationality was found to be significant; (2) the tactics of the ingratiation used strongly affected the evaluation by a bystander; (3) evaluation was a function of the interaction between goals of the influence attempt.

Sharma, Prabhavati. (Ravishankar U. Raipur) conducted a study on "Need motivations as a function of age, educational status and cognitive style of managers and workers." (1991) They Investigated the effects of age, educational status, and cognitive style on the need for affiliation, power, achievement, and approval in 90 managers and 90 workers at steel plant. When educational status and cognitive style interact with each other, they show a highly significant result on need for achievement of managers. The significant main effect of age on need for approval can be attributed to the consequences of advancement in age. Superior educational background helps managers develop a different pattern of cognitive style that helps them display significantly greater power motivation than the workers. Findings indicate psychlogical processes of managers and workers that emerge from their structures and functions in the organization and determine their power, position, roles, and status.

Sharma, Sagar and Acharya, Tilak. (Himachal Pradesh U. Shimla) in a study entitled "Strategies and job anxiety." (1991)—investigated the dominant coping strategies used by 150 male electrical engineers (aged 30-44 yrs) working in a state electricity board to deal with their job hierarchy and job anxiety. Ss completed U. Pareek's (1983) Organizational Role Pics and A. K. Srivastava's (1978) Job Anxiety Scale. Job hierarchy did not significantly determine the nature of the dominant mode of coping. Irrespective of job hierarchy, Ss with higher job anxiety exhibited a greater proportion of avoidance-coping relative to total coping efforts. It is aruged that the causal relation between coping and job anxiety appears to be bidirectional.

Sharma, Subhash. (Inst of Rural Management, Anand) in "Managerial discretion and organizational slack : A commentary". (1991)—discusses important theoretical frameworks (*e.g.*, the neoclassical and the behavioral theories of the firm) for understanding the phenomenon of managerial discretionary behaviour (DB). It is suggested that the political-economy framework is useful in gaining insights into the modalities of managerial DB. Frameworks are proposed for identifying situations in which DB leads to the creation of organizational slack. The implications of managerial discretion for explaining organizational slack arc interpreted.

Singh, Satvir. (Guru Nanak Dev U. Amritsar) in an investigation named "Psycho-social factors associated with small-scale industrial growth". (1991)—determined psychological factors associated with differential rates of small-scale industrial growth (IG) in 448 metalworking entrepreneurs (aged 25-57 yrs). Ss were given a battery of tests, including the Sixteen Personality Factor Questionnaire (l6PF) and the Survey of Work Values (H. Singh, unpublished manuscript). Factors associated with fast rate of IG were entrepreneurial competence, approach-avoidance motive, emotional stability, and high esteem. The inhibitors of a fast rate of IG were low achievement and resistance to change. Fast-progressing Ss were upwardly striving, punctual, and competitive and had a better education; slow-progressing Ss were tense, emotionally unstable, and conservative concerning IG.

Singh, Satvir. (Guru Nanak Dev U. Amritsar) studied "Second order values and personality factors associated with small-scale industrial growth". (1991). He investigated values, life styles and personality characteristics associated with industrial growth. 224 small-scale industrial entrepreneurs of Punjab comprised the sample. Results indicated that self-assurance, emotional maturity, potential for change, competitiveness, punctuality, tolerance and vigorous action were associated with progressive entrepreneurial behaviour. Tough mindedness, high risk-taking and resistance to change were associated with static or declining entrepreneurial success.

Srivastava, A.K. (Banaras Hindu U. Varanasi) in a study on "Moderating effect of mode of coping on the relationship between occupational stress and performance". (1991)—examined the effect of approach and avoidance modes of coping on the relationships of occupational stress and job performance. Performance was measured on the basis of time saved out of standard time allowed. 352 employees operating in a locomotive workshop completed the Occupational Stress Index and a semi-projective measure of copying style. A significant inverse relationship was obtained between perceived occupational stress and performance. An approach mode of coping attenuated and an avoidance mode of coping intensified the inverse relationship between occupational stress and job performance.

Singh, Shailendra. (SRC for Industrial Relations and Human Resources, Delhi) made an interesting investigation on "Executives under stress : Search for some preventive measure" (1991). He Outlined some personal and organizational attributes that can prevent stress. 250 junior and middle-level male executives (aged 23-57yrs) from 7 private and 3 public sector manufacturing organizations of North India provided personal data on 10 dimensions of organizational stress, namely, lack of group cohesiveness, role conflict, experience of inequity, role ambiguity, role overload, lack of leadership support, constraints of change, job difficulty ,job requirement-capacity mismatch, and inadequacy of role authority. Findings suggest that organizational stress could be prevented by attracting highly qualified people and retaining them on equitable compensation. People with a highly expressive work ethic might also resist stress.

Srivastava, A.K. (Banaras Hindu U. Varanasi) in "A study of role stress-mental health relationship as moderated by adopted coping strategies." (1991) examined the effects of avoidance and approach modes of coping in relation to organizational stress and mental health. 300 supervisory personnel (aged 38-51 yrs) took the Organizational Role Stress (RS) Scale (U. Pareek, 1981), the Mental Health Questionnaire (MHQ), and the Projective Instrument for Coping Strategies. RS was positively related to mental illness. Stress from role ambiguity and role stagnation correlated most intensively with mental illness. General RS correlated with somatic concomitants of anxiety. The approach group experienced more RS than did the avoidance group, but scored lower on the MHQ than did the avoidance group. The findings suggest that approach coping contributes to immediate perceived stress, but in the long run reduces tension and anxiety. Avoidance strategies, however, may reduce immediate stress, but in the long run contribute to greater tension and anxiety.

Srivastava, A.K. and Krishna, A. (Banaras Hindu U. Varanasi) in a study entitled "A test of inverted "U" —hypothesis of stress- performance relationship in the industrial context". (1991)—analyzed the relationship of different degrees of occupational stress and job performance by administering the Occupational Stress Index to 352 technical workers in a locomotive industry. Ss who experienced a moderate level of stress performed their job most efficiently. Low occupational stress correlated positively and high stress correlated negatively with job performance. A moderate degree of stress correlated positively, but not highly, with performance. Results confirm the inverted V-shaped hypothesis of stress and performance in the industrial context.

Suar, Damodar. (Xavier Institute of Social Service, Ranchi) in a problem entitled "Work values of managers and workers." (1992)—analyses the importance of work values and difference between managers and workers. The Work Values Inventory (WVI) of Super (1968) was filled by 30 managers and 30 workers of Kalinga Iron Works, Orissa. Results revealed that managers put more emphasis on work values of self-actualisation, social concern, and self-expression while workers care more for materialistic values than for other values in work. However, employees from lower as well as higher levels seek equal satisfaction with socio-psychological values of achievement and human relations at work. Results help develop a conceptual framework for value orientation of employees. The implications of the findings are also discussed for organizational development.

Tandon, Kanika; Ansari, Mahfooz A. and Kapoor, Alka. (II, Kanpur) In "Attributing upward influence attempts in organisations." (1991)—investigated the attributional processes involved in the success and failure experiences of upward influence tactics in a survey of 260 male low and middle managers from 4 manufacturing firms. It was hypothesized that the success or failure of tactics that affect the self esteem and self-perception of the subordinate should be attributed to an ego-defensive bias. A stepwise multiple regression analysis indicated that the success or failure of reasoning as a tactic was due to a defensiveness bias, success of personalized help and ingratiation and a more factual attribution. Results for the tactics of definance and for conditional coorperation and confrontation, however, show attributional dynamics only for failure. In general, subordinates tended to attribute success to the self and failure to external factors such as lower job status.

Tiwari, A.K. (K.S. Saket Postgraduate Coll, Faizabad) in "A study of control of unions in textile organisations". (1992)—compared the amount of control of worker unions with the control of different hierarchical groups of organisations, and investigated the nature of relation between union's control and some measure of organisational effectiveness. The control curve technique developed by Tannenbaum and his associates was used. Distribution of control among top managers, middle managers and supervisors was in accordance with their hierarchical positions, but the amount of control of workers was higher than their supervisors. The control of unions was found to be very high, though it was not related in any way with organisational effectiveness.

Tiwari, N.K. and Srivastava, S.K. (Gurukul Kangri U. Hardwar) in "Effect of insufficient housing accommodation, medical facilities and industrial morale upon organisational effectiveness : A case study". (1991)–examined the effect of insufficient housing accommodation, medical facilities, and industrial morale on organizational effectiveness among 325 employees of 9 different categories of workers at a manufacturing plant. Ss completed questionnaires indicating their level of satisfaction with the 3 variables. The different level of satisfaction influenced the choice of forms of strike and organizational effectiveness differently in case of different categories of employees.

Vijayakumar, C. (SITRA, Human Relations Dvn, Coimbatore) in a study called "Entrepreneurial knowledge and performance." (1992)—attempted to relate the knowledge awareness of the entrepreneurs with their success. 160 entrepreneurs – 80 each in successful and not – successful groups – were studied. It was observed that successful entrepreneurs possessed knowledge awareness than the not-successful entrepreneurs.